Readings in Urban Economics

BLACKWELL READINGS FOR CONTEMPORARY ECONOMICS

This new series dovetails with a variety of existing economics courses at the advanced undergraduate, graduate, and MBA levels. Readings consist of classic and contemporary journal articles, news clippings, and excerpts from popular books.

Published
Wassmer: *Readings in Urban Economics: Issues and Public Policy*
Cabral: *Readings in Industrial Organization*

In preparation
Kuenne: *Readings in Applied Microeconomic Theory: Market Forces and Solutions*
Kuenne: *Readings in Social Welfare: Theory and Policy*
Rasmusen: *Readings in Games and Information*

Readings in Urban Economics

Issues and Public Policy

Edited by

Robert W. Wassmer
California State University, Sacramento

To my parents, Bob and Sandra Wassmer

Copyright © Blackwell Publishers Ltd 2000
editorial matter and organization copyright © Robert W. Wassmer 2000

First published 2000

2 4 6 8 10 9 7 5 3 1

Blackwell Publishers Inc.
350 Main Street
Malden, Massachusetts 02148
USA

Blackwell Publishers Ltd
108 Cowley Road
Oxford OX4 1JF
UK

Library of Congress Cataloging-in-Publication Data

Readings in urban economics: issues and public policy / edited by
    Robert W. Wassmer.
        p. cm. — (Blackwell readings for contemporary economics)
    Includes bibliographical references and index.
    ISBN 0–631–21587–5 (hb. : alk. paper). —ISBN 0–631–21588–3
(pb.: alk. paper)
    1. Urban economics. 2. Regional economics. 3. Regional planning
—Economic aspects. 4. Economic policy. I. Wassmer, Robert W.
II. Series.
HT321.R42 2000
330.9173'2—dc21   99–39728
                                                                CIP

British Library Cataloguing in Publication Data
A CIP catalogue record for this book is available from the British Library.

Typeset in Ehrhardt 10 on 11.5pt
by Kolam Information Services Private Ltd., Pondicherry, India

Printed in Great Britain by MPG Books, Bodmin, Cornwall
This book is printed on acid-free paper.

Contents

Notes on Editor and Authors

About the Editor

Rob Wassmer holds a B.S. in economics from Oakland University in Rochester, Michigan (1983); an M.A. in Economics from the State University of New York at Binghamton (1985); and a Ph.D. in Economics from Michigan State University (1989). Professor Wassmer held the position of assistant professor in the Department of Economics and research associate with the College of Urban, Labor, and Metropolitan Affairs at Wayne State University in Detroit. He is now an associate professor in the Graduate Program in Public Policy and Administration at California State University, Sacramento. Professor Wassmer also holds the position of director of the system-wide California State University Faculty Fellows Applied Research Program that is managed by the Center for California Studies at Sacramento State. His research on topics relating to urban economic development and state/local public finance has appeared in *Government and Policy*, *Journal of Housing Economics*, *Journal of Urban Economics*, *Land Economics*, *National Tax Journal*, *Public Budgeting and Finance*, *Public Choice*, *Public Finance Review*, *Regional Science and Urban Economics*, and *Urban Studies*. Professor Wassmer has a book, co-authored with John Anderson, *Bidding for Business: The Efficacy of Local Economic Development Incentives in a Metropolitan Area*, published by the Upjohn Institute for Employment Research.

He maintains a web site at http://www.csus.edu/indiv/w/wassmerr

Alex Anas
Department of Economics, University of Buffalo

Professor Anas received his Ph.D. in economics from the University of Pennsylvania in 1975. He has held prior academic appointments at Northwestern University, University of Illinois at Urbana-Champaign, and Stanford University. Currently, he is the Goodyear Professor of Economics at the State University of New York at Buffalo. Alex Anas has published broadly in urban and regional economics. He has contributed to the theory of urban structure, urban growth and urban spatial self-organization, housing market dynamics, the regulation of housing markets and the structure of housing prices, transportation and its relationship to land use and residential location, environmental economics and private infrastructure investment in developing countries. His contributions have been theoretical, empirical, and policy oriented. Among his books is *Modeling in Urban and Regional Economics* (1987), which is volume 26 in *Fundamentals of Pure and Applied Economics*.

Visit his web site at: http://www.acsu.buffalo.edu/~alexanas

David C. Anderson
Author

David Anderson is a 25-year crime reporter, first for the *Wall Street Journal* and more recently for the *New York Times*. He has also served on the *New York Times* editorial board. Mr. Anderson is the author of *Crime and the Politics of Hysteria: How the Willie Horton Case Changed American Justice* (1995). This book provides a behind-the-scenes look at the Willie Horton Case and its political, penal, and judicial implications for the American criminal justice system. More recently, he completed a book on *Sensitive Justice: Alternatives to Prison* (1998). In this book, he looks at "alternative sanctions": probation-based supervision and rehabilitation programs involving no time in prison. Anderson cautions that these type of sanctions demand thoughtful planning, "adequate funding and human resources, and . . . the support of public officials who believe in the need for them."

Richard Arnott
Department of Economics, Boston College

Dr. Arnott received his Ph.D. in economics from Yale University in 1975. Before coming to Boston College in 1988, he taught at Wesleyan University and Queen's University. Professor Arnott's research interests are in urban economics, public finance, uncertainty, incentives, contract theory, and transaction costs. Professor Arnott has published over 40 major refereed articles. Recent samples of his research can be found in the *Journal of Public Economics, Regional Science and Urban Economics*, and the *Journal of Urban Economics*. He has also published a book on *Rent Control and Options for Decontrol in Ontario* (1981).

Visit his web site at: http://fmwww.bc.edu/EC-V/Arnott.fac.html

Roy Bahl
School of Policy Studies, Georgia State University

Roy Bahl earned his doctorate in economics from the University of Kentucky in 1965. He is now Dean of the School of Policy Studies and Professor of Economics and Public Administration at Georgia State University. Previously he held positions at West Virginia University, Syracuse University, and the International Monetary Fund. He is the author of numerous books, monographs, and scholarly papers, and has served on the editorial boards of several journals. He is principal economic advisor to IBM's

Worldwide Tax group, a member of the Board of Directors of the Land Reform Training Institute in Taiwan, and former Chairman of the International Tax Advisory Board of KPMG-Peat Marwick. He has served widely as an advisor on fiscal matters to governments all over the world. In addition to his many previous journal articles and books, he has recently published a co-authored book on *The Guatemalan Tax Reform* (1996).

Visit his web site at: http://www.gsu.edu/~prprwb/homepage.html

Timothy J. Bartik
W.E. Upjohn Institute

Dr. Bartik received his Ph.D. in economics from the University of Wisconsin-Madison in 1982 and was an assistant professor of economics at Vanderbilt University prior to joining the Upjohn Institute in 1989. At Upjohn, he conducts research on state and local economic development and local labor markets. He is currently researching alternative policies for increasing labor demand for the urban poor. Recent publications include "Can Economic Development Programs Be Evaluated?" (with Richard Bingham) in *Dilemmas of Urban Economic Development: Issues in Theory and Practice* (1997); "Economic Development Strategies" in *Management Policies in Local Government Finance* (1996, 4th edition); "The Effects of Metropolitan Job Growth on the Size Distribution of Family Income" in *Journal of Regional Science*; and "The Estimation of Demand Parameters in Hedonic Price Models" in the *Journal of Political Economy*. In the field of local economic development, he is best known for his widely read book on *Who Benefits from State and Local Economic Development Incentives* (1991).

Visit his web site at: http://www.upjohninst.org/staff/bartik.html

Jim Blair
Freelance Journalist

Marlon G. Boarnet
Department of Urban and Regional Planning, University of California, Irvine

Professor Boarnet graduated in 1992 from Princeton University with a Ph.D. in economics. Since then he has held the position of assistant professor of social ecology and economics at the University of California, Irvine. His research interests include transportation policy, local economic development, and intrametropolitan population and employment settlement patterns. Among other places, his research has appeared in the *Journal of Urban Economics, Regional Science, Journal of the American Planning Association*, and *Urban Studies*. With Randall Crane, he has recently published a book on *Travel by Design: Urban Design and the New Transportation Planning* (1999).

Visit his web site at: http://www.seweb.uci.edu/faculty/boarnet.html

Christopher Cornwell
Department of Economics, University of Georgia

Chris Cornwell earned his doctorate in economics from Michigan State University in 1985. From 1985 to 1988, he was an assistant professor of economics at West Virginia State University. Currently, he is an associate professor of economics at the University of Georgia. His research interests include the econometrics of panel data and productivity analysis. Professor Cornwell's research outlets have included the *Review of Economics and Statistics*, *Journal of Econometrics*, and the *International Economic Review*. Recently he produced a co-authored book on *Pensions and Productivity* (1998).

Visit his web site at: http://blaze.cba.uga.edu/economics/facpages/cornwelv.html

Anthony Downs
Economic Studies, Brookings Institution

Dr. Downs earned his doctorate in economics from Stanford University in 1956. He is a former chairman of the board for the Real Estate Research Corporation, former senior analyst for the RAND Corporation, and former faculty member at University of Chicago. Anthony Downs is widely respected among urban scholars and policymakers for his research expertise in democratic theory, demographics, housing, real estate, real estate finance, and urban policy. Along with numerous journal articles, Dr. Downs is known for the books he has written on urban policy and economics. These include: *New Visions for Metropolitan America* (1994), *Stuck in Traffic: Coping with Peak-Hour Traffic Congestion* (1992), *The Revolution in Real Estate Finance* (1985), *Urban Decline and the Future of American Cities* – with Katharine L. Bradbury and Kenneth A. Small – (1982), and *Neighborhoods and Urban Development* (1981). He is currently working on a book titled *The Costs of Sprawl, Revisited.*

Visit his web site at: http://www.brook.edu/scholars/ADOWNS.HTM

William Duncombe
Department of Public Administration, Syracuse University

Professor Duncombe completed his Ph.D. in public administration at Syracuse University in 1989. He was an assistant professor of political science at the University of Georgia until 1991. At that time, he returned to Syracuse University where he is now an associate professor of public administration and a senior research associate at the Center for Policy Research. His current research interests are in education costs and finance, elderly migration, state and local fiscal health, and public sector production. In 1991, he published a book on *Economic Growth and Fiscal Planning: New York in the 1990s* (with Roy Bahl). His research has also appeared in the *Review and Economic Statistics, Journal of Public Economics*, and *Economics of Education Review*.

Visit his web site at: http://cpr.maxwell.syr.edu/vitae/wddvita.htm

Timothy Egan
Pacific Northwest Correspondent, New York Times

Timothy Egan is a third generation westerner who writes for the *New York Times*. He often writes on urban and social issues, but has covered almost everything else in his newspaper stories. Mr. Egan is also the author of books titled *Portrait of Seattle* (1989), *The Good Rain: Across Time and Terrain in the Pacific Northwest* (1991), *Breaking Blue* (1996), and *Lasso the Wind: Away to the West* (1998). In *Lasso the Wind*, Egan examines the myths and realities of the Old West and the New West in 14 essays; each set in one of the 11 states west of the one-hundredth meridian.

William A. Fischel
Department of Economics, Dartmouth College

Dr. Fischel completed his Ph.D. in economics at Princeton in 1973. He holds the position of professor at Dartmouth College. Between 1984 and 1990 he was an adjunct professor at Vermont Law School. His research interests are primarily in local government, land use controls, and school finance. Professor Fischel wrote *Regulatory Takings: Law, Economics, and Politics* (1995) and is also the author of recent articles in the *National Tax Journal*, *Vanderbilt Law Review*, and the *Encyclopedia of Law and Economics*. His book, *The Economics of Zoning Laws: A Property Rights Approach to American Land Use Controls* (1987) is widely cited.

    Visit his web site at: http://www.dartmouth.edu/artsci/economics

Ronald C. Fisher
Department of Economics and Honors College, Michigan State University

Professor Fisher received his doctorate in economics from Brown University in 1976. Since then, he has held an academic appointment at Michigan State University, but between 1983 and 1985 he was Deputy State Treasurer for the State Of Michigan. Currently, he is Director of Michigan State University's Honor's College. His current research interests are in local government structure in metropolitan areas, inter-jurisdictional competition, and economic education. His research has recently appeared in the *National Tax Journal, Public Finance Review, Public Budgeting and Finance and the Journal of Urban Economics*. In 1997, he edited a collection of articles on *Intergovernmental Fiscal Relations*. Perhaps Professor Fisher is best known for his popular textbook: *State and Local Public Finance: Institutions, Theory, Policy* (1995).

    Visit his web site at: http://www.econ.msu.edu

Louis Freedberg
Journalist, San Francisco Chronicle

Dorian Friedman
Journalist, U.S. News and World Report

Stuart A. Gabriel
Department of Finance and Business Economics, University of Southern California

Professor Gabriel received his Ph.D. in economics from the University of California, Berkeley in 1985. Before coming to the University of Southern California in 1990, he was an economist with the Board of Governors of the Federal Reserve System, Washington, D.C. At USC, he is a professor of finance and is co-director of the USC Minority Program in Real Estate Finance and Development. Dr. Gabriel is a specialist in real estate economics and finance, housing and mortgage markets, forecasts of housing market activity, interregional migration and regional economic development, and racial discrimination in housing and mortgage markets. His current research pertains to risk and returns in local real estate markets, population mobility and urban quality of life, and microfoundations of mortgage default and prepayment. In recent years, he has also been a visiting scholar at the Federal Reserve Bank of San Francisco. His research has appeared in the *Journal of Urban Economics*, *Review of Economics and Statistics*, *Journal of Housing Economics*, and the *Southern Economic Journal*.
  Visit his web site at: http://www.marshall.usc.edu/FBE/index.html

Peter Gordon
School of Policy, Planning, and Development; University of Southern California

Dr. Gordon obtained his Ph.D. in regional science from the University of Pennsylvania in 1971. He is currently a professor at the University of Southern California and has held several administrative positions there. He is also the director of the Master of Real Estate Development Program. Professor Gordon has written widely on the problems of the New Urbanism. He is also the co-editor (with David Beito) of a book on *Voluntary Cities* (forthcoming) and currently at work on a book on the sprawl debate (with Harry W. Richardson). He co-edits *Planning and Markets*, an all electronic refereed journal. Gordon and his colleagues at USC have developed the Southern California Planning Model. They are now using this model to calculate the economic costs of major earthquakes and other natural disasters. Peter Gordon has published in most of the major urban planning, urban transportation and urban economics journals. He has consulted for local, state and federal agencies, the World Bank, the United Nations and many private groups.
  Visit his web site at: http://www.usc.edu/dept/sppd/faculty/gordon.html

S.C. Gwynne
News Correspondent, Time Magazine

Mr. Gwynne is a long-time news correspondent for *Time Magazine* who writes primarily on business and economics. He has been awarded numerous journalism awards. In 1986, he published a book on *Selling Money* with Jonathon Beaty. In 1993, they again published a book on *The Outlaw Bank: A Wild Ride into the Secret Heart of BCCI*. This book provides a behind-the-scenes look at the BCCI scandal, describing a complex web of intrigue, kickbacks, corruption, cover-up, and their cloak-and-dagger investigation into the case. *Business Week* magazine named this one of the best business books of 1993.

Thomas L. Hungerford
U.S. General Accounting Office and American University

In 1989, Dr. Hungerford received his doctorate in economics from the University of Michigan. He is now a senior economist with the U.S. General Accounting Office in Washington D.C. His research interests are in labor and housing policy. He has taught at Wayne State University and is now an adjunct professor at American University. His research has appeared in the *Review of Economics and Statistics, Journal of International Economics, Economics of Education Review, Review of Income and Wealth*, and the *Journal of Human Resources*.

Keith R. Ihlanfeldt
School of Policy Studies, Georgia State University

Keith Ihlanfeldt received his Ph.D. in economics from Washington University in St. Louis in 1978. He is currently professor of economics and senior research associate in the Policy Research Center within the School of Policy Studies at Georgia State University. His research has focused on a wide range of urban problems, including discrimination in the housing and labor markets, urban poverty, neighborhood decline, housing affordability, and economic development incentives. He has published widely and has received grants from numerous organizations, both public and private. Currently, he serves on the editorial boards of four urban and regional economics journals. Besides his many journal articles, he has written a book on *Job Accessibility and the Employment and School Enrollment of Teenagers* (1992).
    Visit his web site at: http://www.gsu.edu/~ecokri/homepage.html

Leon Lazaroff
Freelance Journalist

From his New York home, Mr. Lazaroff primarily writes on urban related issues for the *Christian Science Monitor*. His work has also appeared in *City Limits* (New York's Urban Affairs Magazine) and the *Empire State Report*.

Arthur Levine
Teacher's College, Columbia University

Dr. Arthur Levine serves as President of Teachers College at Columbia University. He is also a professor of education. Previously, he held an academic appointment at the Harvard Graduate School of Education. His research interests include college students and multiculturalism, college and university leadership, curriculum development, and the history of higher education. In 1998, he co-authored a book-length study on *When Hope and Fear Collide: A Portrait of Today's Student*. In addition to other books and journal articles, he also respectively co-authored and edited *Beating the Odds: How the Poor Get to College* (1996) and *Higher Learning in America 1980–2000* (1994). Professor Levine is also a senior fellow at the Carnegie Foundation for the Advancement of Teaching.

Luan' Sende Lubuele
Department of Economics, Northwestern University

Dr. Lubuele earned his doctorate in economics in 1978 from Universite de Kinshasa in Zaire. He has been a lecturer at the Universite de Kinshasa and an officer in the United Nations' Development Program in Zaire. Recently, he taught economics at Northwestern University. His research interests are in urban economics, financial intermediation, and general equilibrium real-business cycles. In addition to his publications in the *Journal of Economic Literature* and *Journal of Urban Economics*, his research has appeared in the *Journal of Real Estate Finance and Economics*.

John Machacek
New York Congressional Correspondent, Gannett News Service

Mr. Machacek writes about the U.S. Congress and the state of New York for the Gannett News Service. His newspaper articles have appeared in papers across the country. In 1972, when he was a reporter for the *Rochester Times-Union* newspaper, he and Richard Cooper won the Pulitzer Prize for Local General Spot News Reporting for their coverage of the Attica, New York prison riot.

Laura Meckler
Correspondent, Associate Press

Debra Meyers
Citizen Editorialist

Edwin S. Mills
Department of Finance, Northwestern University

Professor Mills earned his doctorate from the University of Birmingham in England in 1956. He has held academic positions at the University College of North Staffordshire, Massachusetts Institute of Technology, Johns Hopkins University, Princeton University, and the University of Colorado at Boulder. At Northwestern University, he currently is a professor of real estate and finance and director of the Guthrie Center for Real Estate Research. His research interests are in real estate economics, urban economics, environmental and waste management, and traffic and transportation. With Bruce Hamilton, in 1993, he published a fifth edition of their widely used *Urban Economics* textbook. Professor Mills has served on the editorial board and published in most of the academic outlets available to urban economists.

Visit his web site at: http://www.kellogg.nwu.edu/faculty/bio/mills.htm

Roger G. Noll
Department of Economics, Stanford University

Professor Noll received his Ph.D. from Harvard University in 1967. Between 1970 and 1973, he was a senior fellow at the Brookings Institution. From 1974 to 1984, he was a professor of economics at the California Institute of Technology. Since 1984, he has been as a professor of economics and director of the Public Policy Program at Stanford University. Professor Noll is also a nonresident senior fellow at the Brookings Institution. He lists his research interests as regulatory policy and economic models of politics. His research has found journal outlets in the *American Economic Review*, *Rand Journal*, and the *Journal of Risk and Uncertainty*. Dr. Noll is also the author of numerous books, including the *Government and the Sports Business* (1974), and has edited (with Andrew Zimbalist) *Sports, Jobs, and Taxes* (1997). He was also a consultant for the nine-part Ken Burn's documentary on baseball in America.

Visit his web site at: http://www-econ.stanford.edu/faculty/nol/htm

Janet Rothenburg Pack
Wharton School, University of Pennsylvania

In 1965, Professor Pack received her doctorate in economics from the University of California at Berkeley. From 1970 on, she has been at the University of Pennsylvania and served as the chairperson of the Public Policy and Management Department between 1992 and 1997. Her previous appointments include Yale University, Southern Connecticut State College, The New School for Social Research, and the Brookings Institution. Dr. Pack's areas of research include fiscal federalism and intergovernmental relations, political economy of economic policy, urban and regional economic development, foreign aid, and privatization. Janet Rothenburg Pack served as the associate editor and editor of the *Journal of Policy Analysis and Management* between 1984 and 1999. In addition to her numerous journal publications, she has co-edited a book on *The Political Economy of Privatization and Deregulation* (1995) with Elizabeth Bailey.

Visit her web site at: http://www.wharton.upenn.edu/faculty/packj.html

Neil R. Peirce
Washington Post Writer's Group

Mr. Peirce is a well-known and respected writer and columnist for the *Washington Post* newspaper. His columns on politics, regions, urban issues, and economic development are often included and cited in other newspapers throughout the United States. Neil Peirce is also the author or editor of books which include *Breakthroughs: Re-Creating the American City* (1993), *The Electoral College Primer* (1996), and *Citistates: How Urban America Can Prosper in a Competitive World* (1994). *Citystates* illuminates the major urban challenge of the day: the necessity of metropolitan-wide solutions in a governmental system still divided between urban, suburban and ex-urban freedoms.

Lawrence O. Picus
School of Education, University of Southern California

Professor Picus earned a Ph.D. in Public Policy Analysis from the Rand Graduate School in 1988. He has a strong background in research design, statistics and econometrics, and is an expert in the application of microcomputers to research. Dr. Lawrence Picus is an associate professor in the School of Education at the University of Southern California. He serves as the director of the Center for Research in Education Finance. His research focuses on issues of school finance and productivity. Professor Picus maintains close contact with the superintendents and chief business officers of school districts throughout California and the nation, and is a member of a number of professional organizations dedicated to improving school district management. In addition to authoring numerous journal articles, Dr. Picus is the co-author of *School Finance: A Policy Perspective* (1992) with Allan Odden, and of *Principles of School Business Administration* (1995) with R. Craig Wood, David Thompson and Don I. Tharpe. In addition, he is the senior editor of the 1995 yearbook of the American Education Finance Association, *Where Does the Money Go?: Resource Allocation in Elementary and Secondary Schools* (1995).

Visit the web site at:http://www-bcf.usc.edu/~lpicus/index.html

John M. Quigley
Department of Economics and Goldman School of Public Policy, University of California, Berkeley

Professor Quigley received his doctorate in economics from Harvard University in 1972. Currently, he is Chancellor's Professor of economics and public policy at the University of California at Berkeley. He also serves as editor of *Regional Science and Urban Economics*. From 1997 to 1998, he was president of the American Real Estate and Urban Economics Association. John Quigley's current research interests are in the municipal bond market, option pricing of mortgages, low wage labor markets, and the integration of housing and financial markets. Besides producing numerous other journal articles and books, he has recently edited collections on *Modern Public Finance* (1994), *The Economics of Housing and Housing Markets* (1997), and *Government for the Future: Unification, Fragmentation, and Regionalism* (1997).

Visit his web site at: http://emlab.berkeley.edu/users/quigley/index.html

Harry W. Richardson
School of Policy, Planning, and Development; University of Southern California

Dr. Richardson is currently a professor of economics and planning at the University of Southern California. He has written a book on *Economic Prospects for the Northeast* (1984) and recently edited a book on *Analytical Urban Economics* (1996). Professor Richardson also co-edits *Planning and Markets*, an all electronic refereed journal. Richardson and his USC colleagues have developed the Southern California Planning Model. They are now using this model to calculate the economic costs of major earthquakes and other natural disasters. In addition to his books, Dr. Richardson has published in *Urban Studies, Regional Studies, Annals of Regional Science*, and the *Journal of Urban Economics*.

Susan Rosenblum
Researcher, National League of Cities

Ms. Rosenblum examines issues regarding workforce development and poverty reduction for the National League of Cities. She works with local officials and other key leaders in up to five cities on strategies to help local residents move out of poverty through improved workforce development strategies. Activities include project meetings and on-site consultations with teams in each city on how to improve the effectiveness of local systems that enable people to qualify for, obtain, and maintain living wage employment.

Visit her web site at: http://www.nlc.org/Urbpov.htm

Kenneth A. Small
Department of Economics, University of California, Irvine

Professor Small earned his doctorate in economics in 1976 from the University of California at Berkeley. Currently, he is a professor of economics at the University of California, Irvine, but he has also taught at Princeton University. At Irvine, Dr. Small has held the position of Associate Dean for Graduate Studies and Economics Chairperson. Ken Small has served on the editorial boards of numerous urban and transportation journals and was the North American co-editor for *Urban Studies* between 1992 and 1997. His research interests are in urban economics, transportation economics, discrete-choice econometrics, and environmental economics. A representative sample of the journals he has published in include the *Review of Economics and Statistics, Journal of Urban Economics, Econometrica, Journal of Political Economy*, and the *American Economic*

Review. In 1989, the Brookings Institution published his book on *Road Work: A New Highway Pricing and Investment Policy*.

Visit his web site at: http://aris.ss.uci.edu/econ/personnel/small/small.html

William N. Trumbull
Department of Economics, West Virginia University

Professor Trumbull received his Ph.D. in economics from the University of North Carolina in 1985. Currently, he is an associate professor of economics and department chairperson at West Virginia University. He is also a faculty research associate at West Virginia University's Regional Research Institute. Dr. Trumbull's research interests include public finance, economic evaluation and cost–benefit analysis, economics of crime, law and economics, and comparative economic systems. In addition to the *Review of Economics and Statistics*, his research has found outlets in *Public Choice*, *Economic Journal*, and the *International Regional Science Review*.

Visit his web site at: http://www.be.wvu.edu/divecon/econ/trumbull

Richard A. Voith
Federal Reserve Bank of Philadelphia

Dr. Voith received his doctorate in economics from the University of Pennsylvania in 1986. Currently, he is employed as an economic advisor for the Federal Reserve Bank located in Philadelphia. Richard Voith's research interests are in housing, transportation, and city-suburban relationships. In addition to his extensive publication record in the Federal Reserve's publication *Business Review*, his research has appeared in *Urban Studies*, *Journal of Urban Economics*, *Journal of Regional Science*, and *Regional Science and Urban Economics*.

Visit his web site at: http://www.phil.frb.org/econ/br/brnd96in.html

George F. Will
Columnist and Author

Dr. Will received his doctorate in politics from Princeton University. Prior to entering journalism, Will taught political philosophy at Michigan State University and the University of Toronto. Until becoming a columnist for the *Washington Post* and *Newsweek*, Will was Washington editor of the *National Review*. In 1976, he won a Pulitzer Prize for commentary. In 1981, he joined ABC's Sunday news program *This Week with David Brinkley*, and is a regular on the program to this day. His book titled *Restoration: Congress, Term Limits and the Recovery of Deliberative Democracy* (1992) argued for the need to limit politicians' time in office. The sixth book collection of his work is *The Woven Figure: Conservatism and America's Fabric, 1994–1997* (1997). George Will's latest book on baseball in America is *Bunts: Curt Flood, Camden Yards, Pete Rose, and Other Reflections on Baseball* (1998).

Visit his web site at: http://www.washingtonpost.com/wp-srv/politics/opinions/will.htm

Ann Dryden Witte
Department of Economics, Florida International University

Dr. Witte received her doctorate in economics from North Carolina State University in 1971. She is currently a professor of economics at Florida International University. Prior to this, Anne Dryden Witte held academic positions at Wellesley College and the University of North Carolina at Chapel Hill. Her research interests are in law and economics, applied microeconomics and econometrics, and urban economics. A representative sampling of her research can be found in the *American Economic Review, Review of Economics and Statistics, Journal of Econometrics*, and the *International Economic Review*.

Visit her web site at: http://www.fiu.edu/~wittea

Jamie Woodwell
Research Manager, National League of Cities

Jamie Woodwell currently works as a research manager for the National League of Cities. Previously she worked for the Metropolitan Washington Council of Governments. She has served on the Federal Geographic Data Committee put together by the Department of the Interior. She is also coordinates the National League of Cities annual survey of fiscal conditions in America's cities.

John Yinger
Department of Economics, Syracuse University

Professor Yinger received his doctorate in economics from Princeton University in 1974. He has served as a senior staff economist for the Council of Economic Advisors and as a professor at Harvard University and the University of Michigan. Currently he is a professor of economics and public administration, and associate director for the Metropolitan Studies Program at the Maxwell School of Citizenship and Public Affairs at Syracuse University. From 1998 to the present, he has been the forum editor at the *National Tax Journal*. John Yinger's current research interests are in housing discrimination, racial and ethnic integration, education costs, state education aid to support performance standards, and school district efficiency. In addition to journal article in places like the *National Tax Journal, Journal of Urban Economics, American Economic Review*, and the *Journal of Political Economy*, he has published books on *Closed Doors, Opportunities Lost: The Continuing Costs of Housing Discrimination* (1995), *America's Ailing Cities: Fiscal Health and the Design of Urban Policy* (1991), and *Property Taxes and House Values: The Theory and Estimation of Intrajurisdictional Property Tax Capitalization* (1988).

Visit his web site at: http://www-cpr.maxwell.syr.edu/~jyinger

Andrew Zimbalist
Department of Economics, Smith College

Dr. Zimbalist received his Ph.D. from Harvard University in 1974. Since then, he has been in the economics department at Smith College. He is the Robert A. Woods Professor of Economics at Smith College and a member of the Five College Graduate Faculty. He has consulted for various sports players' associations, cities in sport facilities matters, and law firms in numerous sports litigations. Professor Zimbalist also testified before the U.S. Congress on several occasions concerning trade and sports legislation. Dr. Zimbalist has published eleven books and several dozen articles primarily in the areas of comparative economic systems, economic development, and sports economics. In 1992, he published *Baseball and Billions: A Probing Look Inside the Big Business of Our National Pastime*. *Business Week* listed *Baseball and Billions* as one of the top eight business books of 1992. Dr. Zimbalist's articles and essays have also appeared in *The New York Times, The Wall Street Journal, The New Republic, The Brookings Review, Washington Post, US News and World Report*, and *USA Today*. His latest book, *Unpaid Professionals: Commercialism and Conflict in Big-Time College Sports* is due in 1999.

Visit his web site at: http://www.smith.edu/economics/Faculty/azimbali.html

Acknowledgments

Al Bruckner, Executive Editor at Blackwell, was the first to see the need for this book and encouraged me to produce it. Six outside reviewers, who have remained anonymous, read the initial prospectus and offered comments that shaped the book's final form. Katie Byrne, Development Editor at Blackwell, energized me to completion and smoothed out all of the technical details on the way. Jenny Lawson of First Class Publishing truly did a "first class" job of turning my ideas and others' previously published articles into this collection.

I am most grateful to the scholars that introduced me to the subject of applied and policy-orientated urban economics and continue to keep me interested in it today. These include: John Anderson, Tim Bartik, Tom Bogart, Ralph Braid, Jan Brueckner, Jeff Chapman, Michael Dardia, Ron Fisher, Allen Goodman, Al Gutowsky, Bill Herrin, Harry Holzer, Larry Ledebur, Joyce Mann, Terri Sexton, Steve Sheffrin, Ken Small, Dave Sjoquist, Jon Sonstelie, and Bob Waste.

Thanks are also due to the many publishers who gave permission for articles and extracts to be reproduced in this volume:

Anas, Alex., Arnott, Richard and Small, Kenneth A. (1998) "Urban Spatial Structure," *Journal of Economic Literature*, 36, September, 1426–64. Reprinted by permission of American Economic Association.

Anderson, David C. (1997) "The Mystery of the Falling Crime Rate," *The San Diego Union-Tribune*, 4.6.97. © 1997.

Arnott, Richard (1995) "Time for Revisionism on Rent Control," *Journal of Economic Perspectives*, 9(1), Winter, 99–120. Reprinted by permission of American Economic Association.

Bahl, Roy (1994) "Metropolitan Fiscal Disparities," *Cityscape: A Journal of Policy Development and Research*, 1, 293–306.

Bartik, Timothy, J. (1994) "Jobs, Productivity, and Local Economic Development: What Implications Does Economic Research Have for the Role of Government?" *National Tax Journal*, XLVI.

Bates, Timothy (1995) "Political Economy of Urban Poverty in the 21st Century: How Progress and Public Policy Generate Rising Poverty," *Review of Black Political*

Economy. Reprinted by permission of Transaction Publishers. © 1995 Transaction Publishers. All rights reserved.

Boarnet, Marlon G. and Bogart, William T. (1996) "Enterprise Zones and Employment: Evidence from New Jersey," *Journal of Urban Economics*, 40, 198–215. © 1996 Academic Press, Inc. All rights of reproduction in any form reserved.

Boarnet, Marlon G. (1997) "Infrastructure Services and the Productivity of Public Capital: The Case of Streets and Highways," *National Tax Journal*, 50(1), 39–57.

Brueckner, Jan K. (1996) "Default Rates and Mortgage Discrimination: A View of the Controversy," *Cityscape: A Journal of Policy Development and Research*, 2(1), February, 65.

Case, Karl E. and Mayer, Christopher J. (1996) "Housing Price Dynamics Within a Metropolitan Area." *Regional Science and Urban Economics*, 26, 387–407. © 1996 Elsevier Science. Reprinted with permission from Elsevier Science.

Cornwell, Christopher and Trumbull, William N. (1994) "Estimating the Economic Model of Crime with Panel Data," *Review of Economics and Statistics*, 76.

Crihfield, John B. and Panggabean, Martin P. H. (1995) "Is Public Infrastructure Productive? A Metropolitan Perspective Using New Capital Stock Estimates," *Regional Science and Urban Economics*, 25, 607–30. © 1995 Elsevier Science. Reprinted with permission from Elsevier Science.

Downs, Anthony (1998) "How America's Cities are Growing. The Big Picture," *The Brookings Review*, Fall. Brookings Institution Press, Washington DC.

Duncombe, William and Yinger, John (1997) "Why is it So Hard to Help Central City Schools?" *Journal of Policy Analysis and Management*, 16(1), 85–113. © 1997 Association for Public Policy Analysis and Management. Reprinted by permission of John Wiley & Sons Inc. New York.

Egan, Timothy (1998) "Dreams of Fields: The New Politics of Urban Sprawl." *The New York Times*, 15.11.98. copyright © 1998 by the New York Times Company. © 1999 Dow Jones & Company, Inc. All rights reserved.

Fischel, William A. (1997) "Comment on Carl Abbott's The Portland Region: Where Cities and Suburbs Talk to Each Other and Often Agree," *Housing Policy Debate*, 8(1). © 1997 Fannie Mae Foundation. The copyrighted material is used with the permission of the Fannie Mae Foundation.

Fisher, Ronald C. and Wassmer, Robert W. (1998) "Economic Influences on the Structure of Local Government in US Metropolitan Areas," *Journal of Urban Economics*, 43, 444–71. © 1998 Academic Press.

Fitzgerald, John M. (1995) "Local Labor Markets and Local Area Effects on Welfare Duration," *Journal of Policy Analysis and Management*, 14(1), 43–67. © 1995 Association for Public Policy Analysis and Management. Reprinted by permission of John Wiley & Sons Inc. New York.

Freedberg, Louis (1998) "Race Panel Divided Over Poverty: Experts Disagree on Causes, Cures of Urban Problems," *San Francisco Chronicle*, 12.2.98. © 1998 The San Francisco Chronicle. Reprinted with permission.

Freeman, Richard B. (1996) "Why do so Many Young American Men Commit Crimes and what Might We Do About It?" *Journal of Economic Perspectives*, 10(1), Winter, 25–42. Reprinted by permission of American Economic Association.

Freeman, Scott, Grogger, Jeffrey and Sonstelie, Jon (1996) "The Spatial Concentration of Crime," *Journal of Urban Economics*, 40, 216–31. © 1996 Academic Press, Inc. All rights of reproduction in any form reserved.

Friedman, Dorian (1998) "The Draw of Downtown: Big Growth Predicted for Many U.S. Cities" *U.S. News & World Report*, © October 5, 1998. Visit us at our Web site at www.usnews.com for additional information.

Gabriel, Stuart A. (1996) "Urban Housing Policy in the 1990s," *Housing Policy Debate*, 7(4), 673–93. © 1996 Fannie Mae Foundation. The copyrighted material is used with the permission of the Fannie Mae Foundation.

Giuliano, Genevieve and Small, Kenneth A. (1993) "Is the Journey to Work Explained by Urban Structure," *Urban Studies*, 30(9), 1485–1500. Taylor & Francis Ltd.

Giuliano, Genevieve and Small, Kenneth A. (1991) "Subcenters in the Los Angeles Region." *Regional Science and Urban Economics*, 21, 1485–500, © 1991 Elsevier Science. Reprinted with permission from Elsevier Science.

Glaeser, Edward (1998) "Are Cities Dying?" *Journal of Economic Perspectives*, 12(2), Spring, 139–60. Reprinted by permission of American Economic Association.

Glaeser, Edward (1994) "Cities, Information and Economic Growth," *Cityscape: A Journal of Policy Development and Research*, 1, August.

Gordon, Peter and Richardson, Harry W. (1998) "Prove It: The Costs and Benefits of Sprawl," *The Brookings Review*, Fall. Brookings Institution Press, Washington DC.

Gottlieb, Paul D. (1994) "Amenities as an Economic Development Tool: Is There Enough Evidence?" *Economic Development Quarterly*, 8(3), August, 270–85. © 1994 Sage Publications Inc. Reprinted by permission of Sage Publications Inc.

Gramlich, Edward, Laren, Deborah and Sealand, Naomi (1992) "Moving Into and Out of Poor Urban Areas," *Journal of Policy Analysis and Management*, 11(2), 273–87. © 1992 Association for Public Policy Analysis and Management. Reprinted by permission of John Wiley & Sons Inc. New York.

Grogger, Jeff (1992) "Arrests, Persistent Youth Joblessness, and Black/White Employment Differentials," *Review of Economics and Statistics*, 74, 100.

Gwynne, S. C. (1998) "Miracle in New Orleans: What do a Bunch of College Professors Know about Fixing Public-housing Projects? A Lot, it Turns out." *Time Magazine*, 9.3.98. © 1998 Time Inc. Reprinted by permission. © 1999 Dow Jones & Co., Inc. All rights reserved.

Hanushek, Eric (1998) "School Resources and Student Performance," from Gary Burtless (ed.) *Does Money Matter?* Brookings Institution Press, Washington DC, p. 43.

Heikkila, Eric (1996) "Are Municipalities Tieboutian Clubs?" *Regional Science and Urban Economics*, 26, 203–26. © 1996 Elsevier Science. Reprinted with permission from Elsevier Science.

Henderson, Vernon, Kuncoro, Ari and Turner, Matt (1995) "Industrial Development in Cities," *Journal of Political Economy*, 103(5). © 1995 The University of Chicago Press. All rights reserved.

Holzer, Henry J. (1994) "Black Employment Problems: New Evidence: Old Questions," *Journal of Policy Analysis and Management*, 13(4), 699–722. Association for Public

Policy Analysis and Management. Reprinted by permission of John Wiley & Sons Inc. New York.

Hungerford, Thomas L. (1996) "The Dynamics of Housing Assistance Spells," *Journal of Urban Economics*, 39, 193–208. © 1996 Academic Press, Inc.

Ihlanfeldt, Keith R. (1997) "Information on the Spatial Distribution of Job Opportunities within Metropolitan Areas," *Journal of Urban Economics*, 41, 218–42. © 1997 Academic Press. All rights of reproduction in any form reserved.

Jensen, Mark J. and Leven, Charles L. (1997) "Quality of Life in Central Cities and Suburbs," *Annals of Regional Science*, Springer-Verlag, Heidelberg.

Johnson, James H. Jr., Jones, Cloyzelle K., Farrell, Jr., Walter C. and Oliver, Melvin L. (1992) "The Los Angeles Rebellion: A Retrospective View," *Economic Development Quarterly 6(4), November, 356–72.* © 1992 Sage Publications Inc. Reprinted by permission of Sage Publications Inc.

Jordan, Stacy, Ross, John P. and Usowski, Kurt, G. (1998) "U.S. Suburbanization in the 1980s." *Regional Science and Urban Economics*, 28, 611–27. © 1998 Elsevier Science. Reprinted with permission from Elsevier Science.

Kriesel, Warren, Centner, Terence J. and Keeler, Andrew G. (1996) "Neighborhood Exposure to Toxic Releases: Are There Racial Inequities?" *Growth and Change*, 27, Fall, 479–99. © 1996 Center for Business and Economic Research, University of Kentucky. Published by Blackwells Publishers.

Krugman, Paul (1998) "Space: The Final Frontier," *Journal of Economic Perspectives*, 12(2), Spring 1998, 161–74. Reprinted by permission of American Economic Association.

Ladd, Helen (1994) "Fiscal Impacts of Local Population Growth: A Conceptual and Empirical Analysis." *Regional Science and Urban Economics*, 24(6), 661–86. © 1994 Elsevier Science. Reprinted with permission from Elsevier Science.

Lazaroff, Leon and Blair, Jim (1998) "Bright Lights, Big City and Safe Streets: Urban Dwellers Bask in Greater Sense of Security, as Crime Rates Drop Even Further" *Christian Science Monitor*, 5.1.98. © 1999 Dow Jones & Company, Inc. All rights reserved.

Leete, Laura and Bania, Neil (1999) "The Impact of Welfare Reform on Local Labor Markets," *Journal of Policy Analysis and Management*, 18(1), 509–76. © 1998 Association for Public Policy Analysis and Management. Reprinted by permission of John Wiley & Sons Inc. New York.

Levine, Arthur (1998) "Why I'm Reluctantly Backing Vouchers" *The Wall Street Journal* 15.6.98. Reprinted with permission of *The Wall Street Journal*. (c) 1998 Dow Jones & Company, Inc. All rights reserved.

Ludwig, Jens (1999) "Information and Inner City Educational Attainment," *Economics of Education Review*, 18, 17–30. © 1998 Elsevier Science. Reprinted with permission from Elsevier Science.

Machacek, John (1998) "U.S. Cities Coming Back from Decades of Decline," Gannett News Service. © 1998.

Man, Joyce Y. and Rosentraub, Mark S. (1998) "Tax Increment Financing: Municipal Adoption and Effects on Property Value Growth," *Public Finance Review*, 26(6), November, 523–547. © 1998 Sage Publications Inc. Reprinted by permission of Sage Publications Inc.

Martinez–Vazquez, Jorge, Rider, Mark and Walker, Mary Beth (1997) "Race and the Structure of School Districts in the United States," *Journal of Urban Economics*, 41(2), March, 281–300. © 1997 Academic Press.

Meckler, Laura (1999) "Big U.S. Cities Carry Welfare Burden: Deep Poverty, Isolation from Suburbs Keep Many from Independence," *The Detroit News*, 19.2.99

Meyers, Debra (1997) "Why I Love The Suburbs," *Buffalo News*, 3.8.97. © 1999 Dow Jones & Company, Inc. All rights reserved.

Mieszkowski, Peter and Mills, Edwin S. (1993) "The Causes of Metropolitan Suburbanization," *Journal of Economic Perspectives*, 7(3), Summer, 135–47. Reprinted by permission of American Economic Association.

Mieszkowski, Peter and Smith, Barton (1991) "Analyzing Urban Decentralization: The Case of Houston." *Regional Science and Urban Economics*, 21, 183–99. © 1991 Elsevier Science. Reprinted with permission from Elsevier Science.

Mills, Edwin S. and Lubuele, Luan' Sende (1995) "Projecting Growth of Metropolitan Areas," *Journal of Urban Economics*, 37, 344–60. © 1995 Academic Press Inc. All rights of reproduction in any form reserved.

Mills, Edwin S. and Lubuele, Luan' Sende (1997) "Inner Cities," *Journal of Economic Literature*, 35, June, 727–56. Reprinted by permission of American Economic Association.

Noll, Roger G., and Zimbalist, Andrew (1997) "Sports, Jobs, and Taxes: Are New Stadiums Worth the Cost?" *The Brookings Review*, Summer. Brookings Institution Press, Washington DC, 1998.

Papke, Leslie (1994) "Tax Policy and Urban Development: Evidence from the Indiana Enterprise Zone Program," *Journal of Public Economics*, 54(1), 37–49. © 1994 with permission from Elsevier Science.

Peirce, Neal R. (1997) "Ohio Looks Hard at What's Lost Through Business Subsidies," *The Sacramento Bee*, 5.6.97.

Picus, Lawrence O. (1996) "Current Issues in Public Urban Education," *Housing Policy Debate*, 7(4). © 1996 Fannie Mae Foundation. The copyrighted material is used with the permission of the Fannie Mae Foundation.

Porter, Michael E. (1997) "New Strategies for Inner-City Economic Development," *Economic Development Quarterly*, 11, February. © 1997 Sage Publications Inc. Reprinted by permission of Sage Publications Inc.

Quigley, John M. (1998) "Urban Diversity and Economic Growth," *Journal of Economic Perspectives*, 12(2), Spring, 127–38. Reprinted by permission of American Economic Association.

Rauch, James E. (1993) "Productivity Gains from Geographic Concentrations of Human Capital Evidence from the Cities." *Journal of Urban Economics*, 34, 380–400. © 1993 Academic Press, Inc. All rights of reproduction in any form reserved.

Rothenburg Pack, Janet (1997) "You Ride, I'll Pay: Social Benefits and Transit Subsidies." *The Brookings Review*, Summer. Brookings Institution Press, Washington DC, 1998.

Roychoudhury, Canopy and Goodman, Allen C. (1996) "Evidence of Racial Discrimination in Different Dimensions of Owner-Occupied Housing Search," *Real Estate Economics*, 24(2), 161–78.

Small, Kenneth (1993) "Urban Traffic Congestion: A New Approach to the Gordian Knot," *The Brookings Review*, Spring, 6–11. Brookings Institution Press, Washington DC, 1998.

Small, Kenneth A. (1992) "Wasteful Commuting: A Resolution," *Journal of Political Economy*, 100(4). © 1992 The University of Chicago Press.

The Economist (1998) "The State of the Cities: Downtown is Up," *The Economist*, 22.8.98. © 1998 the Economist Newspaper Ltd. All rights reserved. © 1999 Dow Jones & Co. Inc. All rights reserved.

The Economist (1998) "Or, Why Motorists Always Outsmart Planners, Economists and Traffic Engineers: The Unbridgeable Gap," *The Economist*, 5.9.98. © The Economist Newspaper Ltd. All rights reserved.

Voith, Richard A. (1998) "Do Suburbs Need Cities?" *Journal of Regional Science*, 38(3), 445–64. © 1998 Blackwell Publishers.

Voith, Richard A. (1997) "Fares, Service Levels, and Demographics: What Determines Commuter Rail Ridership in the Long Run?" *Journal of Urban Economics*, 41, 176–97. © 1997 Academic Press. All rights of reproduction in any form reserved.

Wassmer, Robert W. (1994) "Can Local Incentives Alter a Metropolitan City's Economic Development?" *Urban Studies*, 31(8), 1251–78. Taylor & Francis Ltd.

Will, George, F. "Al Gore Has A New Worry: Smart Growth to Cure Suburban Sprawl is the Newest Rationale for Government Growth," *Newsweek*, 15.2.99

Witte, Ann Dryden (1996) "Urban Crime: Issues and Policies," *Housing Policy Debate*, 7(4), 731–48. © 1996 Fannie Mae Foundation. The copyrighted material is used with the permission of the Fannie Mae Foundation.

Woodwell, James and Rosenblum, Susan (1998) "No Easy Way Out: Study Finds Urban Poverty Digs Heels in," *Nation's Cities Weekly*, 17.8.98. Reprinted by permission of National League of Cities, Washington DC.

U.S. cities coming back from decades of decline
JOHN MACHACEK

WASHINGTON – America's cities are rebounding from decades of decline thanks to a booming economy, but still have miles to go until they are truly healthy. **Urban crime** rates are down, especially in New York City, once derided as the "crime capital of the world." Billions are being spent on rejuvenating downtowns and downtrodden neighborhoods. Federal tax breaks and other incentives generate big-bucks private investment that is fueling the comeback in bigger cities such as Detroit and Philadelphia, and smaller ones such as Rochester, N.Y., and Camden, N.J.

"New York City is a different place than it was four years ago," New York Mayor Rudolph Giuliani, bragged in welcoming delegates at the New York state Republican convention last week. "We were once the crime capital of the world; now we're leading the country in the reduction of the crime. We have 1,000 fewer people on welfare than three years ago. From a city of dependency we have literally and figuratively become a city of opportunity."

But urban experts say safer streets, new sports stadiums and gleaming skyscrapers, are only masking fundamental problems: school systems that aren't producing an adequately trained work force, lack of decent housing and jobs for the poorest of the poor, and increasing suburban sprawl that saps people and jobs from cities. Those conditions, unless addressed soon, threaten to block the urban recovery, regardless of whether the economy goes into a tailspin, urban leaders said here Monday at a "State of the Cities" forum sponsored by the Brookings Institution, a liberal think-tank. "If we can't do something about the quality of the work force, the potential of rethinking cities as places to create wealth is diminished," said Jeremy Nowak, executive director of the Delaware Valley Community Reinvestment Fund in Philadelphia. Nowak said high school graduates in the Philadelphia area are graduating with eighth-grade math skills while 10th-grade skills are needed for "advanced manufacturing" which uses computer-aided machinery.

An investors' group, led by Chase Manhattan Bank, is trying to reverse urban decay in Harlem, the symbolic capital of black America in upper Manhattan by building a $65 million retail and entertainment center. New York City leaders are counting on the center to reverse the flow of money from Harlem and provide the jobs that reduce a 19 percent unemployment and 35 percent poverty rate. About 70 percent of Harlem's $6 billion in disposable income now goes elsewhere – lower Manhattan or New Jersey – because of a lack of retail stores. But Harlem's rebirth cannot be sustained unless schools, housing and the appearance of neighborhoods are improved, said Deborah Wright, president of the Upper Manhattan Empowerment Zone, a federal-state-city initiative that is adding $11 million in loans to the project. "Our shabby infrastructure gives you the perception of crime," she told the conference. "We have to invest in physical rehabilitation, as well as in marketing. And we are still struggling with all of the other liabilities."

Although the urban rejuvenation is creating new housing and jobs for low-income persons and the middle class, it is bypassing the poorest of the poor, said Barack Obaman, an Illinois state senator representing some of the poorest areas of Chicago. "There is better housing in areas that have hubs like a university or United Center," a sports and convention facility a few miles west of downtown Chicago, he said. "But at some point we have to deal with the problem of getting poor people to entry level jobs in the suburbs and allow them to exercise housing options."

Evan Dobelle, president of Trinity College in Hartford, Conn., said urban colleges and universities could help their cities by investing some of their bulging endowments in neighborhood renewal. Trinity already has given Hartford $6 million and plans to add $4 million. Trinity has an eye on its future, but the investment also is the "right thing to do," Dobelle said. "How can we call on our students to lead, if we as an institution behave irresponsibly?"

Congress is helping subsidize child care and transportation to the suburbs for workers coming off welfare under new workfare laws. Now, city officials need to make sure that money, which is funneled through the states, "shows up at the local level," Wright said.

But Milwaukee Mayor John Norquist said cities should rely less on federal government, and work with state government and the private sector to improve housing, create jobs and reform schools. "You can't build a city by begging and you can't do it on pity," he said. Under Norquist, Milwaukee has developed a school voucher program that gives parents a choice of schools for their kids for kindergarten through 12th grade. "Even (with cities) in an improved state, many people don't want their kids to go to school in cities," he said.

With people and jobs still fleeing center cities, urban officials must push the federal government to change policies that subsidize "suburban sprawl" – uncontrolled growth in the outer suburbs at the expense of cities and older suburbs, the Brookings Forum concluded. "Cities aren't really cities anymore; They are metropolitan regions," said Camille Barnett, chief management officer of Washington D.C. "We are trying to create a sustainable city-state."

CHAPTER ONE

Introduction

ROBERT W. WASSMER

I chose the Gannett News Service story by Machacek (1998) to open this book of readings because it accurately summarizes the popular and professional perceptions of the condition of large US cities and urban areas as they enter the twenty-first century. Under a nationwide economic expansion that began over eight years ago, large US cities and urban areas are, by some indicators, doing better at the end of the 1990s than at the beginning. However, as Machacek points out, behind the veneer of economic prosperity are critical urban issues that refuse to go away. Since most of these issues have at least part of their causal roots in economic relationships, it is appropriate to use economics to better understand these issues and to try to derive suitable public policy responses. This book's purpose is to further this cause by offering a collection of recent literature in applied and policy-orientated urban economics.

My motivation to put together a volume of articles on urban issues from an economic and policy perspective sprang from my own recent experience at developing and teaching a graduate level course titled "Urban Problems, Economics, and Public Policy" at California State University, Sacramento. This course is offered as an elective to Master's level students in public policy and in economics. The catalog description summarizes its contents well:

> Historical development, economics, and possible policy solutions relating to the most pressing problems facing central cities and urban areas. Problems discussed include poverty, crime, urban abandonment, suburban sprawl, edge cities, deteriorating infrastructure, and fiscal stress.

Many textbooks on urban economics already exist. These texts do a good job at covering urban economic theory, important issues faced by urban areas and central cities, and possible policy solutions. A graduate student, and even an upper-level undergraduate student, though, benefits immensely from exposure to direct and recent writings on a topic. Such exposure allows for a more in-depth and current analysis of issues covered in the standard textbook. Just the knowledge that these outside sources exist, and what some of them are, is also important.

To my dismay, I discovered that a recent book of readings on applied urban economics did not previously exist. In talking with urban economists, I found that such volumes have existed in the past, but they knew of no recent compilations that would be accessible to upper-level undergraduate students and Master's level graduate students. Thus the beginnings of what turned out to be the volume that you now hold in your hand.

The background necessary to follow the articles chosen for this volume is not much more than an understanding of the material taught in an intermediate undergraduate course in microeconomics and a course in applied regression analysis. As mentioned above, the book's intended audience range from upper-level undergraduate to Master's students taking courses in urban economics, urban policy, urban studies, or urban planning. The book is also appropriate as a reader for doctoral students in urban policy, urban studies, or urban planning courses. Though the policy nature of the articles chosen for this book may not make it wholly appropriate for use in a doctoral course in urban economics that emphasizes economic theory, it could be used as a recent look at urban issues that still need the further attention of economic theory. As a current summary of recent academic work on their craft, this collection of readings should also appeal to urban academics, practitioners, and policymakers.

In choosing the articles for this collection, I first divided the topic of applied urban economics into the nine categories that represent the remaining eight parts of this book: urban growth; land use; economic development; race, employment, and poverty; public education; housing; crime; transportation; and local government. I am certain that many will quibble with this division, suggesting one or two topics that should be deleted or added. I went through the quibbling process myself. In the end, I decided upon nine broad categories because they are what I think are the most interesting and the most relevant. The chosen topics also parallel many of the chapters already included in textbooks on urban economics.

There is also a method to the articles chosen within each of the remaining nine parts of this book. First, each part begins with at least one popular press article on the subject. These are taken from major US newspapers and weekly newsmagazines. This approach, though nontraditional for a reader of this sort, is intended to frame the issue in a popular and current framework. Instructors who use this book of readings may want to consider sharing similar articles with their students that are more recent, or from a local newspaper. Even doctoral students can benefit from this real-world foundation. Second, each of the remaining nine parts contains at least one review of the applied economics literature on the issue under consideration. These are written by prominent urban economists and, in most cases, offer their perspective on economic theory, empirical analysis, and public policy regarding a specific urban issue. Also, each of the remaining nine parts of this volume contains at least one regression-based empirical study. These empirical studies were purposefully chosen for their public policy content. Their interpretation requires little more than an introductory exposure to statistical regression methods.

To insure that this book of readings is current and likely to remain so for awhile, I have as much as possible restricted my choice of articles to ones published after the mid-1990s. This book is not intended to be a collection of *classic* articles on urban economics. Instead, it is a current review of policy related work in the area. With the exception of verbal summaries contained in some of the literature reviews, there are no articles in this reader that are purely theoretical in their approach to analyzing an urban issue. This was a conscious choice on my part and based on the multi-discipline accessibility that I desired for this volume.

The applied and policy related urban issues that are important in one country or one region of the world are similar to what is important in other countries or regions of the world. However, to some extent, they are also different. Thus an editor of a volume of this nature must choose a particular country or region as their focus before deciding upon the topics and articles to be included. My choice is the USA in particular and North America in general. The reader will find much overlap of the urban issues discussed here and those that are important in other areas of the world. Though if your focus is not the USA or Canada, you will likely need to supplement the readings contained here with ones more focused on the urban institutions and issues particular to the country or region of the world in which you are interested.

After completing my review of the recent literature in applied urban economics, I found more quality articles than could be possibly contained in a book of this sort. To share some of these findings, each of the remaining parts of this book closes with an annotated list of further readings. The annotation consists of the abstract from the article or a few paragraphs taken from it. A reader interested in the wider economic literature available on any of the topics included in this volume should begin by consulting this list of readings, and the references given at the end of these articles and the full articles contained here.

To assist in the understanding and evaluation of the articles, at the conclusion of the remaining nine parts I also include a set of discussion questions based on the readings. The individual can use these to review their own comprehension of what they just read. An instructor could assign them as student exercises and the basis for classroom discussion. Finally, at the end of the volume, there is an appendix that lists the major academic journals in urban economics and policy, their web address, and a brief description of each. This list of journals is provided to assist the reader wishing further academic articles on a particular urban subject. As noted in the appendix, many of the journal's web sites have search engines that allow key word searches on previous contents and even the ability to download abstracts.

This introduction continues with a brief review of some numbers relating to urban issues in the USA. To keep these numbers contemporary, I focus on their values in the early and late 1990s. After the review of these numbers I offer a summary, done by each of the remaining parts, of all the articles contained in this volume. This provides an overview of all material in the book and should assist the reader interested in only a select reading of it.

Some Trends in the Numbers Relating to Urban Issues in the 1990s

As Machacek (1998) describes in the newswire article that opened this chapter, there are reasons to believe that US cities, during the 1990s, made some progress towards reversing decades of decline; but, as he also points out, there are other indicators that suggest little improvement in many of the issues troubling large cities and metropolitan regions. To shed further light on this, I offer next a very abbreviated statistical profile of central cities and metropolitan areas in the USA during the 1990s. All of the numbers cited in this section are taken from the 1998 *Statistical Abstract of the United States* (US Department of Commerce, Bureau of Census). A more complete review of the appropriate numbers from

US metropolitan areas is later provided in Edwin Mills and Luan' Sende Lubuele's (1997) article on *Inner Cities* contained in this volume.

The 1990s began with 79.7 percent of the US population living in metropolitan areas. By 1996, this figure had risen only slightly to 79.8 percent, but, in the four most populated states – California, New York, Texas, and Florida – the percentages of the state's population living in metropolitan areas in 1996 were respectively 96.6, 91.8, 84.2, and 92.9. An examination of the ten most populated cities in the USA in 1996 – New York, Los Angeles, Chicago, Houston, Philadelphia, San Diego, Phoenix, San Antonio, Dallas, and Detroit – reveals that 8.8 percent of the country's total population lived in these cities in 1990, while 8.4 percent of the population lived there in 1996. This decrease in overall large-city living in the USA occurred even though only three of these cities – Chicago, Philadelphia, and Detroit – experienced a decline in population between 1990 and 1996.

To illustrate the concentration of racial and ethnic minorities in large US cities, note that 12.6 percent of the total US population was African American in 1996 and 10.3 percent was Latino. In the same year, six of the ten most populated US cities had more than twice the US percentage of African Americans and Latinos living in their boundaries. At the extremes, in 1996 Detroit was 75.7 percent African American and San Antonio was 55.6 percent Latino.

Moving beyond simple demographics, 10.7 percent of the US population lived below the poverty line in 1990. By 1996, even after five years of economic recovery, the percentage of the US population in poverty climbed slightly to 11.0. Behind this slight increase in total poverty, African American poverty rates fell from 29.3 percent to 26.1, while the rate of Latino poverty rose from 25.0 percent to 26.4 percent, and the poverty rate of Whites rose from 8.1 to 8.6 percent. This slight increase in US poverty could not be due to an increase in the percentage of US high school students that drop out. The drop-out rate in the US between 1990 and 1996 fell from 10.1 percent to 9.4 percent, but, at the same time, the rate of African Americans dropping out of high schools rose from 10.9 to 11.0 percent.

The violent crime rate for the entire USA – murders, rapes, robberies, and assaults per 100,000 population – was 732 in 1990. As Machacek emphasizes, by 1996, the violent crime rate in the USA had fallen to 634. The number of murders in the US fell from 20,273 in 1990 to 15,848 in 1996. Though the rate of violent crime has recently fallen in the USA, there still are significant differences in the rate of violent crime between US metropolitan and rural areas. In 1996, the violent crime rate in metropolitan areas was 715 per 100,000 population; in rural areas, it was only 222.

Finally, during the 1990s, there appeared to be no reduction in the love of private automobiles in the USA. In 1990, 82.2 percent of all dollars spent on private and for-hire transportation were on privately owned automobiles. By 1996, this figure had risen slightly to 83.0 percent.

Part I: Urban Growth

What are the determinants of urban growth? As recognized by Edwin Mills and Luan' Sende Lubuele (1995), the answer to this question is important to both scholars and practitioners. For practical reasons, business and individuals like to know what the prospect for growth is before investing in a city or region, or deciding to leave or stay. For fiscal policy purposes, state and local governments also require an accurate forecast of growth. Part I of this volume offers a perspective on urban growth through two popular press descriptions of projections for continued growth in many of the USA's central cities, an academic review of how diversity encourages urban growth, and an empirical analysis of the determinants of US metropolitan growth.

The *U.S. News and World Report* article by Dorian Friedman (1998), that opens part I, briefly describes the conclusion of a Fannie Mae and Brookings' Institution Conference that many central city populations and particular downtown neighborhoods will continue to grow into the new millennium. *The Economist* (1998) article that follows offers a similar assessment by focusing on specifics that have occurred in one area of Chicago's central business district. *The Economist* piece concludes that it was not just a strong economy that revived Chicago's State Street in the 1990s, but the use of a redevelopment tool called Tax Increment Financing. The background necessary to begin to evaluate this conclusion is provided later in part III: "Local Economic Development Initiatives."

The review article by John Quigley (1998), "Urban Diversity and Economic Growth," stresses the role that diverse business enterprises play as a determinant of urban economic growth. Quigley describes four periods in which economists have intensely and uniquely studies cities. We are now in the fourth period and "bursts of understanding" are flowing from this period's recognition of the agglomerative benefits of size and diversity in cities. Quigley also provides a review of the theoretical benefits of heterogeneity and empirical evidence in support of these theoretical benefits.

Mills and Lubuele (1995) conclude my choice of applied economic articles on urban growth with an empirical examination of what determines metropolitan growth. Using a simultaneous equation regression model and a data set drawn from 320 US metropolitan statistical areas from 1970, 1980, and 1990, they find that jobs follow people more than people follow jobs and that high wages in a metropolitan area attract people. Forecasts for the year 2000 are given for population, employment, and wage for all US metropolitan areas included in their sample.

Part II: Location, Land Use, and Urban Sprawl

Framed in popular terms like "urban sprawl" and "edge cities," the debate at the local and regional level on land use in a metropolitan area is stronger than ever. With presidential candidate, Al Gore, leading the charge, this debate has even made the leap to the national political arena.

In its colloquial use, sprawl usually refers to unlimited outward extension of development in a leap-frog fashion, low-density new settlements, fragmentation of land use powers, transport dominated by private automobiles, widespread "strip mall" development, the reliance of trickle-down for low-income housing, and fiscal disparities among localities (Downs, 1998). Much of the blame for urban traffic congestion, air pollution, loss of open space, labor shortages in suburban areas; and concentrated poverty, crime, and poor public schools in central cities and inner-ring suburbs, has been placed on urban development that has been allowed to proceed in a sprawling fashion. Though others point to the benefits that unregulated land use decisions generate for citizens in metropolitan areas. These benefits include the preferred low-density lifestyle, broad choices of where to live and work, shorter suburb-to-suburb commutes, and the ability of higher socioeconomic groups to separate themselves from the problems associated with lower ones. Location and land use in US metropolitan areas in the late twentieth century are truly issues that encompasses all the other urban issues included in this book. It is for this reason that part II is the longest in the volume.

Part II opens with Timothy's Egan's (1998) article from the *New York Times* that describes the increased political saliency of urban sprawl. Nationwide, in the fall of 1998, voters approved nearly 200 state and local ballot initiatives designed in some ways to curb sprawl. Egan also describes the attempt by Vice President Gore to make sprawl a key issue in the upcoming presidential campaign. George Will's (1999) column from *Newsweek* is offered as an alternative take on Gore's support for a national public policy concerning sprawl. Not surprisingly, Will is of the opinion that "smart growth" to cure suburban sprawl is just the newest rationale for government growth. In this column, he drives home the point that 75 percent more US families choose to live in sprawling suburbs rather than in compact central cities.

A summary of some of the previous academic literature on location and land use in urban areas is contained in a review of theoretical and empirical studies on "Urban Spatial Structure" by Alex Anas, Richard Arnott, and Kenneth Small (1998). Their review opens with a history and description of urban spatial structure in the USA and continues with background information on the various theoretical models adopted by economists to describe it (monocentric, polycentric, and agglomeration). Anas, Arnot, and Small conclude their review with a policy-centered discussion on the efficiency of sub-center formation, traffic congestion and decentralization, land use controls, and the role of government. This piece is a must read for those interested in a positive look at an issue that is more often discussed in a normative framework.

The review of academic thought on location and land use in urban areas continues with summary pieces from three prominent urban economists on opposite sides of the sprawl debate. In "Prove It: The Costs and Benefits of Sprawl," Peter Gordon and Harry Richardson (1998) make the case that sprawl is the preferred life-style of Americans and that critics of it vastly overestimate its social costs. Anthony Downs (1998) recognizes that sprawl provides benefits to individuals, but in "How America's Cities Grow: The Big Picture," he chooses to emphasize the negative social effects of sprawl. To Downs, the most egregious is the concentration of poverty in US central cities and their inner-ring suburbs. He suggests that managed growth strategies be pursued in the USA after citizens are convinced of his belief that the social costs of sprawl are greater than its private benefits.

In part II, I violate a standard upheld in other parts of this volume. The applied study by William Fischel (1997) is not regression or data based. Fischel describes his analysis of Portland's use of an urban growth boundary to contain sprawl in its metropolitan region as a parable that employs simple economic principles. In the form of a story based in logic, he illustrates the new costs created by a public policy solution designed to reduce the social costs of sprawl. From his parable, Fischel derives policy alternatives, that he prefers to an urban growth boundary, to reduce metropolitan sprawl.

The regression study included in part II is by Richard Voith (1998). His study provides some of the empirical evidence necessary to settle the continuing debate on what to do about location and land use decisions that generate sprawl. As Downs points out, the argument for adopting public policies designed to redirect housing and economic activities back to central cities is stronger if these policies also generate suburban benefits. Voith looks for the possibility of this benefit by empirically measuring the simultaneous relationships between central city and suburban growth in the USA between 1960 and 1990. Over this period, he finds that greater income growth in large US central cities resulted in higher income growth, house value appreciation, and, to a lesser extent, population growth in the suburban areas that surround them. This suggests the possibility that both cities and suburbs could improve their welfare through cooperative actions that reduced central city decline.

Part III: Local Economic Development Incentives

An urban economics issue that has direct policy overtones is the use of local economic development incentives to try to sway the business location decisions of private firms. This issue naturally follows the previous discussion of land use and the generation of sprawl in urban areas because some have suggested that the appropriate use of incentives could help to steer metropolitan economic activity back to its core. Though as the articles included in part III indicate, it is not certain that such a strategy would even work and whether the large dollar cost of such a strategy would be justified with equal or greater social benefits.

The first article in part III is from a newspaper column by *Washington Post* writer Neal Peirce (1997). In this column, he applauds Ohio State Senator Horn's attempts to truly assess the benefits of local subsidies to business relative to their cost. For instance, when a community provides a tax subsidy to a manufacturing plant, do taxpayers win or lose? Peirce laments that such a question has not been appropriately answered because of the economic and political forces that steer policymakers away from an honest answer. As is shown in the remainder of part III, policymakers may just want to ignore the answers that have already been provided by economists.

Some of these answers have been clearly provided by Timothy Bartik (1994). An example is his review of current economic thinking in regards to the relationship between local jobs, local productivity, and local economic development incentives. His review is designed to offer guidance to policymakers regarding the appropriate role of the local, state, and federal governments in offering and regulating the use of economic development incentives. Bartik concludes that the traditional financial and tax subsidies offered by local government in an attempt to buy local growth extort a high price per new job created. Reiterating some of the material presented in part II, he argues that benefits large enough to justify such high costs are more likely to be found when incentives are successfully used in the distressed core of most metropolitan areas. Readers interested in specific policy prescriptions regarding local incentives do not want to miss the two hypothetical memos that Bartik writes to a Mayor of Jurisdiction X and to the President of the USA.

Public subsidies to privately owned professional sports teams is taken up next by Roger Noll and Andrew Zimbalist in an article that summarizes a 1997 book they edited on *Sports, Jobs, and Taxes*. Experts estimate that between 1997 and 2006, more than $7 billion of public revenues will be devoted to the construction of professional sport's facilities. Though this is less than $50 billion in total expenditure on all economic development incentives over this period that was earlier suggested in Peirce's column, it is still a significant chunk of change. Noll and Zimbalist describe the economic and political reasons why cities subsidize professional sports, the role of monopoly leagues, and what could conceivable be done to reduce these public subsidies. They are in favor of such a reduction because of the widely supported finding that a new sports facility has an extremely small or even negative effect on overall economic activity in a city or its metropolitan area.

Finally, in part III, I include an article that describes my own statistical attempt at determining if local incentives exert any significant influences on various measures of local economic development. Proponents of the use of local incentives to encourage local economic development (like property tax abatements, tax increment financing, downtown development authorities, or industrial development bonds) suggest that they exert an *additive* effect. Such an effect can be defined as pulling a community above its long-term trend in local economic activity. In 25 percent of the cases of different forms of local incentive use in the Detroit Metropolitan Area, examined through an appropriate regression procedure, I find no significant additive or negative effect, which means the incentive offer did nothing. Indeed, in 44 percent of the cases, the offering of a particular local incentive is significantly correlated with the community falling below its long-term trend in economic development after the incentive is offered. In only 31 percent of the cases is the usual presumption of a local incentive generating an additive effect justified. Also, certain types of incentives exhibit the desired additive effect in only communities where local characteristics thought to repel business are the largest. Results from regressions of the type presented in this article could be used by policymakers to decide which incentives are the most effective in a city, which incentives a city should not use, and even which incentives should be abandoned by all cities.

Part IV: Race, Employment, and Poverty in Urban Areas

In part IV, I have gathered three popular press articles, a review article written by two prominent urban economists, and a survey-based regression study that cover the important interrelated issues of race, employment, and poverty in urban areas. As documented in Edwin Mills and Luan' Sende Lubuele's review article on *Inner Cities*, minorities (especially African Americans and in some places Latinos) are disproportionately located in the central cities of the USA. This fact, and the fact that the majority of metropolitan growth in the last half of this century has occurred in the suburbs, has motivated economists to look specifically at the issue which is the subject of this chapter.

The "spatial mismatch" hypothesis states that suburban growth and racial/economic housing segregation have combined to create a surplus of low-skill minority workers in central cities and a shortage of low-skilled workers in the surrounding suburbs. If true, this occurrence contributes to the higher unemployment and poverty rates observed among some minorities in the USA. The obvious policy solution is to do something to correct this mismatch.

Part IV opens with an associated press article by Laura Meckler (1999) that describes the influence of spatial mismatch on recent efforts to reform the welfare system in the USA. Using Detroit as an example, Meckler points out that the largest cities in the USA are home to an increasingly larger percentage of welfare cases. It is difficult for former welfare recipients without automobiles to get where the job openings are. The *San Francisco Chronicle* article by Louis Freedberg (1998) raises the questions of why African Americans and other minorities disproportionately live in central cities, why are they disproportionately poor, and does racism have something to do with both. The last popular press article in part IV, by Jamie Woodwell and Susan Rosenblum (1998), offers the more optimistic fact that, according to a recent US Census Bureau study, poverty is only a chronic condition for about five percent of the US population. Chronic is defined as living below the poverty line for two or more consecutive years. Howbeit, the Woodwell and Rosenblum article also lays out other facts from the Census study that support the spatial mismatch hypothesis.

The review article by Mills and Lubuele (1997) describes and interprets data and previous economic studies relating to the social and economic conditions found in the inner or central cities of US metropolitan areas. This article does an excellent job of documenting the degree to which US cities contain higher concentrations of racial and ethnic minorities, low-income people, and chronic social problems. Mills and Lubuele specify, in a manner accessible to most with a basic economics background, how this spatial concentration came about and the interrelationships among it and how employment suburbanization is caused by and causes inner city problems. Their exposition on the "Flight from Blight" theory should not be missed.

For those interested in international comparisons, Mills and Lubuele also compare the USA with 22 other OECD countries regarding 13 social indicators like GDP per capita, life expectancy, pupil-to-teacher ratios, infant mortality, etc. As a whole, the USA does poorly in this comparison. Only when social indicators for Whites are compared to the totals for OECD countries, the US ranking greatly improves. They conclude that inner city/suburban gaps in social indicators are large and have increased by most measures during the last 30 years.

The empirical piece chosen for part IV is an investigation of the knowledge that people in a metropolitan area have of the spatial distribution of jobs in the area. Keith Ihlanfeldt (1997) examines the results of a large survey conducted of Atlanta residents regarding the best areas within the region to look for a job. Individual responses are compared with what office managers of employment agencies thought are the best places to look, and actual employment and job vacancy data from the Atlanta employment commission. Findings in the paper come from a comparison of descriptive statistics and a regression analysis. Ihlanfeldt concludes that the tendency of African Americans to reside in the central city of Atlanta (6.5 times greater than Whites) accounts for most of their disadvantage in not knowing the true availability of low-skilled jobs among different regions in the metropolitan area. However, regardless of race or labor force status, people looking for low-skilled jobs possess poor information on where openings exist. This suggests that information dissemination could reduce the unemployment and poverty caused by the presence of spatial mismatch on some US metropolitan areas.

Part V: Urban Public Education

Part V begins the second half of this volume and a focus on more specific topics. The first topic is public education in US urban areas. It is included in this volume because the dissatisfaction that many express over public schools is usually not directed at the entire system of K-12 public education in the USA, but instead at the minority of public school districts that are performing below what is socially optimal. As described by the authors included in Part V, a large majority of these low performing public schools are located at the urban core.

As Lawrence Picus (1996) points out in his summary, about one-fourth of the nation's public elementary and secondary students attend the largest 100 districts in the USA. With some exceptions, these 100 districts encompass the 100 largest cities in the USA and can essentially be considered urban districts. No surprise after reading the Mills and Lubuele (1997) summary of inner-city characteristics in part IV, these 100 districts serve large numbers of low-income families, racial and ethnic minorities, and students who speak limited English at home. Most, if not all, aggregate indicators of student perform-ance are significantly lower in these urban districts and hence the desire to do something about it. Policy reforms ranging from more money, administrative accountability, charter schools, and vouchers have been suggested and tried. An economic perspective on all of this is contained in part V.

An editorial column by Arthur Levine (1998), President of Teachers College at Columbia University, is the popular press article I chose for this section. No matter the policy reform that one currently prefers for urban public schools, Levine's opinion piece will stimulate thought. It is from a respected academic in the education establishment who has gone from opposing vouchers for public schools to supporting them for urban public schools. He suggests a national program of vouchers for those attending the bottom 10 percent of public schools in urban areas. Levine believes that this would offer low-income children a way out of poor-performing schools (something the non-poor already have), a chance for urban public school systems to shut down inferior school buildings and concentrate their limited resources on others, and encourage better public and private urban schools through competition.

The Picus (1996) article is an excellent summary of issues facing urban public schools and the policy reforms that have been suggested for them. His summary begins with a comparison of the characteristics of student spending patterns, and revenue patterns in urban school districts to all US schools. Picus next provides a review of policy reforms designed to improve the performance of urban public schools. The reforms he sees as promising are working within the current public school system to improve site-based management and compensation reforms designed to reward newly hired and high-performing teachers. He sees less promise in just throwing more money at the problem, charter school establishment, school choice within the public system, and vouchers for private schools.

The issue of throwing money at the problem of poorly performing urban public schools is addressed in the empirical study on *Why Is It So Hard to Help Central City Schools?* In this article, William Duncombe and John Yinger (1997) ask why existing school-aid formulae fail to provide the resources needed by central-city school districts to bring their educational outcomes up to an acceptable level. The answers they investigate are the failure of state aid programs to recognize the higher cost of providing comparable education services in central cities and that outside aid may actually reduce the efficiency of educational production in a large district. Duncombe and Yinger lay out a design for a new system of state aid that accounts for cost differences between urban and non-urban districts. However, using a data set from New York State, regression analysis, and well-crafted simulations, they show that feasible aid programs (i.e., ones that do not require new state or local revenue) do little to help central cities. By their calculations, there are aid programs that would dramatically boost educational outcomes in urban schools. The lack of political support for such programs is what makes it truly difficult to help poorly performing urban schools.

Part VI: Urban Public Housing

Part VI deals with housing issues that are particularly prevalent in urban areas. These include the shortage of affordable rental units, mortgage finance-related constraints on homeownership, housing assistance to the poor, and equal opportunity for housing finance. Economists have something to say about these issues because many are tied to private market failures and may call for public intervention. The economic examination of the nexus between government and shelter in urban areas is the subject of this part. The three authors included in part VI explore the housing situation in US urban areas and offer their assessment of government attempts to improve it. Particular attention is paid to recent changes in Federal Housing Administration (FHA), the US Department of Housing and Urban Development (HUD), and the system of public housing in the USA.

S.C. Gwynne's (1998) article, that appeared in *Time* magazine, is a popular description of one result of reforms adopted by the US Department of Housing and Urban Development during the 1990s. By the mid-1990s, public housing in New Orleans was some of the worst in the country. Since 10 percent of the city's total population lives in such housing, the issue raised serious concerns. In 1996, HUD turned the complete operation of the Housing Authority of New Orleans over to Tulane University. The relative success of this radical experiment is described in Gwynne's article.

A portrait of *Urban Housing Policy in the 1990s* is contained in the review article written by Stuart Gabriel (1996). Gabriel's article begins with an overview of recent changes in housing conditions and homeownership opportunities in the USA. Regarding homeownership opportunities, he describes trends that have made the situation worse in many US urban areas (house price run ups, decrease in homeownership rates for African Americans and Latinos, etc.) and offers his appraisal of policy efforts under way to try to reverse these trends. Citing the fact that one-fourth of the nation's renters are low income and receive some form of government assistance, Gabriel goes on to describe the US housing programs that are in place and the sad state of many of them. Reform efforts, such as the one described in Gwynne's article, are described and evaluated. A short background on discrimination in housing and mortgage markets is also provided. Gabriel concludes that the budgetary and political environment surrounding housing policy in the USA has evolved immensely since 1994. The environment of the late 1990s seeks to diminish the role of the federal government and emphasize enhanced flexibility in funding and administrative responsibility at the local level.

Thomas Hungerford (1996) provides an informative examination of the duration of public housing assistance spells in the USA. He argues that knowing the characteristics of people who receive public housing assistance for short periods of time has important policy implications for the long-term composition of public housing residents and for the targeting of scarce HUD funds to increase self-sufficiency. Using a hazard regression model and individual data from the Survey of Income and Program Participation, Hungerford finds that individuals who are more job ready, non-disabled, under age 65, and less tied to other welfare programs are more likely to live in public housing for a short period of time.

Part VII: Urban Crime

The crime rate in US central cities and urban areas has always been greater than in rural areas. This differential is often given as a reason why individuals and businesses leave central cities for suburban and rural locations. However, in the second half of the 1990s, there has been a dramatic drop in overall crime in the USA. Has crime fallen in central cities and urban areas in the 1990s to the extent that it has fallen throughout the country? If so, what types of urban crime have decreased the most? For the analysis of existing public policies in place and the development of new ones, it is also consequential to understand the factors responsible for the lower crime rate. These issues, in one way or another, are accounted for in the four articles included in part VII.

As pointed out by David Anderson (1997) in the *San Diego Union-Tribune*, the exact cause of the drop in US crime rates remains a mystery. Anderson offers evidence that stiffer penalties are now in place, but offers no convincing evidence that these are the primary cause of decreased crime. He points to New York City's falling crime rate, and its effort at increasing the number of police officers and mounting an increased effort to prosecute "quality of life" crimes, as a cause-and-effect case study that may offer one explanation for declining crime in the USA.

An article from the *Christian Science Monitor*, by Leon Lazaroff and Jim Blair (1998) also describes policy changes in New York City policing and the production of its lowest homicide rate in 30 years. Yet, as Lazaroff and Blair point out, in 1997, the homicide rate in Los Angeles was also at a 20-year low and throughout the 1990s Chicago, New Orleans, Dallas, Baltimore, and San Francisco experienced continuous declines in their murder rates. Perhaps the fall in crime is due, in at least part, to all of the above reasons plus the 1990s' continuing economic expansion, fewer young men between age 16 and 24, and waning crack epidemic. Applying a more academic approach, this is taken up in part VII by Ann Witte (1996) in her survey article on issues and policies relating to urban crime.

Witte provides a sweeping prospective of the social and criminal justice factors and public policies that are linked to urban crime. In doing so, she offers the background necessary to better understand recent trends in urban crime and whether they will continue. Witte begins her review by inventorying policy issues that are related to urban crime: drugs, domestic violence, property values, and economic activity in urban ghettos.

For each of these policy issues, she provides a summary of current thinking on its interrelationship with urban crime. Next, she reviews the local, state, and federal public policies that affect urban crime rate. On a sobering note, Witte concludes by pointing out that even though overall crime rates have fallen, and, in some cases, even central city crime rates have fallen, the rate of violent crime among young urban males continues to rise. To counter this disturbing trend, she suggests specific policies for at-risk youth.

The final article in part VII is an admirable example of the approach that economists have used to isolate the causal factors responsible for differences in crime rates across jurisdictions. It is included here to offer a specific data-based perspective on the possible causes of falling crime rates in the USA. Christopher Cornwell and William N. Trumbull (1994) use the standard economic model of criminal activity first proposed by Gary Becker, a data set drawn from North Carolina counties over time, and advanced panel data regression techniques to show that both labor market and criminal justice strategies exert significant influences on crime. Perhaps most important to the debate over the effectiveness of populist get-tough measures like "Three-Strikes" legislation, Cornwell and Trumbull provide empirical evidence that the influence of law enforcement incentives (such as arrest and conviction probabilities) on jurisdictional crime rates have been greatly exaggerated.

Part VIII: Urban Transportation

Stuck in traffic. Probably one of the least pleasant circumstances that someone experiences in an urban area. Unfortunately for those who reside in major metropolitan areas its occurrence seems on the rise. Actual and suggested policies to ease metropolitan traffic congestion and an examination of the link between traffic congestion and labor productivity/output in a region are the issues covered in part VIII. The chapter opens with a popular explanation of how economists think about traffic congestion and how motorists have a habit of counteracting their best-laid plans to reduce it. Next comes a more academic review of the approaches suggested by economists to reduce urban traffic congestion, and a second academic review of the social benefits of government subsidies to urban transit. Finally, there is a regression-based analysis of the effect of street and highway congestion on labor productivity and output.

The 1998 magazine article from *The Economist*, selected for part VIII, opens with the problem of whether to build another bridge to relieve congestion on one currently bringing people into a city. Would a new bridge serve that purpose or will it just the pave the way for more traffic? The article first addresses this issue through an accessible explanation of the microeconomic concept of a "negative externality" and estimates of the social costs of traffic congestion. The author concedes that traffic congestion represents a market failure but questionably concludes that "this failure is mostly of fairly minor economic importance" (*Economist*, 1998). Getting back to the question of another bridge, *The Economist* article correctly points out that building it may just attract drivers who previously took other routes or never came into the city. Even after bridge or highway construction, metropolitan traffic congestion may remain unaltered.

On a slightly different but related note, Janet Rothenburg Pack (1992) offers a cautionary tale regarding how to think about the benefits of government subsidies to local transit systems. Pack begins with the fact that for every dollar that US transit riders pay in fares, taxpayers throughout the USA match with two dollars of subsidy. Is there any justification for this high rate of subsidy? The answer she provides is that it is "worth every penny." Pack supports this conclusion by showing that not just transit riders, but society as a whole benefits from the existence of publicly provided transportation. The social benefits she calls attention to are reduced road congestion and accidents, reduced noise and air pollution, reduced congestion on alternate transit facilities, and the increased welfare of transit riders. All but the last benefit is distributed to all of society. For Philadelphia's commuter rail system in the 1980s, Pack puts a dollar value on these benefits and show that, in total, they are greater than the subsidy provided. In conclusion, she suggests that, to fund their service, transit authorities capture some of these benefits by taxing the local property value enhancement that occurs because of it.

Kenneth Small (1993) next offers his highly informed opinion on new approaches to untying the "Gordian Knot" of urban traffic congestion. Like *The Economist* article, Small also eschews increased capacity as the solution to congestion. Latent demand is sure to appear as soon as additional road space is added. Like most economists, the policy prescription he advocates is the use of fees to allocate scarce highway capacity or "congestion pricing." For it to work, he believes the fees structure must vary widely by day and "peak-load" fees must be high enough to seriously reduce single occupancy auto travel during peak times. The use of such fees would provide revenue for needed infrastructure and are easily collected using the high-tech toll mechanisms available today. The biggest obstacle to putting these fees in place is people's resistance to pay for something that has been viewed as a free good. Small suggests that this resistance be broken down by offering legislators or voters a specific plan that calls for fee revenue to be equally distributed: (1) to frequent user of affected transportation system, (2) to reduce other existing transportation taxes, and (3) to expand and improve transportation services for all.

Marlon Boarnet (1997) wrote the empirical article on urban transportation that is included in part VIII. Boarnet tries to tie increased highway congestion in California counties, holding all else constant, to a decrease in labor productivity and output in these counties. Regression techniques are used that allow a comparison between the labor benefits of an increased stock of highways in a county, versus reducing traffic congestion on existing highways. Using the appropriate statistical methods, Boarnet shows that a public policy of reducing traffic congestion through peak-load pricing would offer a greater "bang-for-the-buck" to labor than a policy of simple highway expansion.

Part IX: Local Government

Part IX concludes this volume of readings in applied and policy related urban economics with a examination of local government in urban areas. Beginning with the work of Charles Tiebout in 1956, economists have looked to a system of local governments in a metropolitan area as a way of introducing competition, and the benefits derived from it, into the public provision of local goods and services. Albeit, economists have also recognized that a system of independently operating local governments in a metropolitan area generates significant geographical spillovers and equity concerns. The study of local public finance is the attempt to consider all of these issues in a simultaneous fashion. Therefore, a reader on urban economics that focuses on applied and policy related issues would not be complete without a section on local government.

Part IX opens with a viewpoint newspaper column from Buffalo suburban dweller Debra Meyers (1997). Though not as formal as the theorizing of economists, Meyers does an admirable job of describing the reason why over three-quarters of US metropolitan dwellers choose to live in the "burbs" over the central city. Suburban living is preferred based on safety, schools, a sense of community, convenience, and local government that "seems to be more representative and accountable to its citizenry." As with much covered in this chapter, this column could just as appropriately been placed in part II: *Location, Land Use, and Urban Sprawl.*

In his review article on metropolitan fiscal disparities, Roy Bahl (1994) chooses instead to emphasize the geographical spillovers and equity concerns that arise from a system of fragmented local government in a metropolitan area. Bahl reinforces the point, given earlier in part IV: *Race, Employment, and Poverty in Urban Areas*, that median income is lower in US central cities than suburban areas and social problems are greater. In general, central city government and infrastructure are also more impoverished than their sub-urban counterparts. Writing in the early 1990s, he maintains that these conditions have not improved over the last 20 years. The extension that Bahl offers is that there is a connection between the problem of fiscal disparities and the suburbanization of metro-politan areas.

In the first half of his article, Bahl defines what he means by "fiscal stress" and shows that city–suburb fiscal disparities have existed for over 30 years in the USA. He documents that the early 1990s saw little reversal in this trend. In the second half of the article, he offers his informed opinion on the policy role that federal aid and state assistance can and should play in reducing these disparities. Bahl broaches the issues of metropolitan government and regional tax base sharing, but for reasons he provides, does not believe that they are likely to be adopted on a large scale in the USA and thus are not viable policy options. In the end, he believes that the states are the ones who can be expected to equalize revenue disparities within metropolitan areas, if it is done at all.

Ronald Fisher and I (1998) co-authored the empirical piece on local government in metropolitan areas that concludes this part of this volume. Though Tiebout's model of local government formation in an urban area – and the competitive benefits to be derived from it – is broadly accepted by economists and cited widely in applied and policy related analysis, there has been little formal testing of its major tenant, i.e. that the greater the inter-metropolitan variation in citizen demand for the services provided by local governments, holding all else constant, the greater should be the number of governments in a metropolitan area. We set out to test this theory through a 1982 data set containing observations on the number of municipalities and school districts, and relevant explan-atory variables from the 165 largest metropolitan areas in the country. Through multiple regression analysis, we find statistical evidence that greater variation in income and education in a metropolitan area yields a larger number of municipal and school governments.

Conclusion

This concludes my editor's introduction to this volume. The articles just described, additional readings, and discussion questions based upon the included articles follow. In the process of assembling this collection, I learned a lot about applied and policy related urban economics. My hope is that you can say the same after reading the volume.

PART I:
Urban Growth

Understanding how and why MSAs grow and/or shrink is perhaps the most important subject that urban scholars can study.

Edwin S. Mills and Luan' Sende Lubuele

CHAPTER TWO

The Draw of Downtown: Big Growth Predicted for Many U.S. Cities

DORIAN FRIEDMAN

Source: U.S. News & World Report, © October 5, 1998.

Could it be that America's formerly great cities are rising anew, phoenix-like, from the ashes of urban squalor? Not quite, but a new study has encouraging news about the future of the nation's downtowns. Among 21 big cities surveyed, all but one – Atlanta – expect their center-city populations to grow in the next dozen years. In some cases, especially where "downtown" is defined narrowly as a neighborhood, the projected increases are huge: 228 percent in Cleveland, 166 percent in Denver, and 121 percent in Seattle. Even places like Philadelphia that have hemorrhaged for decades expect double-digit growth. The findings – headlining a conference this week on America's cities sponsored by the Fannie Mae Foundation and the Brookings Institution – reflect a new trend, but one still dwarfed by the ongoing exodus to the suburbs. But thanks to an urban building boom, many formerly blighted areas are bustling today with new waterfront malls, gleaming sports arenas, and other attractions luring people downtown. The new report suggests that yuppies and "empty nesters" are settling downtown to soak up urban buzz and culture. "Cities are the nexus of civilization," notes biographer Robert A. Caro, the conference's main speaker. "For too long, we didn't understand that the qualities that made a city wonderful were not huge public works but ... the human values that come together there."

CHAPTER THREE

The State of the Cities: Downtown is Up

THE ECONOMIST

It was a typical story of urban woe. In 1983, Sears, Roebuck closed the doors of its State Street store in Chicago after 51 years in business. Two neighbouring retailers had gone bankrupt; pedestrians had all but abandoned the street. End of the story? No. Sears is coming back. The retailer has announced plans to open a five-storey, 237,000-square-foot store on State Street by the spring of 2000. In a revival matched by the downtown areas of many other American cities, Chicago's State Street is once again a place for doing business.

All Chicagoans can hum "State Street, that great street." Alas, they have not always meant it. State Street was the heart of Chicago's retail world in the early 1900s. The second half of the century was not so kind. Shoppers flocked to new suburban malls. Some Chicago retailers went bust; others migrated to trendier Michigan Avenue. Then, in 1979, the city made bad worse by converting State Street into a "transit mall". It was closed to all vehicles except public transport; the pavements were widened to make it feel like a suburban mall.

Far from attracting more shoppers, this repelled them. As the planners have since learned, some spaces can be too open. The wide, grey pavements were empty and uninviting. The increased bus traffic, belching exhaust, made things still bleaker. By the time State Street hit bottom, seven department stores with a total of 2.5m square feet of retail space had closed.

Nearly two decades later, the city has taken another crack at redeveloping State Street, and this time it has done a better job. To begin with, the transit mall was scrapped and traffic was re-introduced in 1996. The pavements were narrowed from 36 feet to 26 feet, providing "a pleasant sense of bustle". The street got a $25m facelift designed to recall its greatness in the early 1900s: old-fashioned subway entrances, landscaped flower beds, decorative newspaper kiosks. The designers even found the company that made the first street lamps in 1926, and ordered replicas. All this not only drew sightseers, it won the American Institute of Architects' honour award for urban design.

And business followed the award. The total available retail space in the State Street area increased by 8% between 1990 and 1997, and vacancy rates fell from 6.4% to 1.8%. The Palmer House Hilton, a smart hotel just off State Street, is enjoying its highest occupancy rate since it opened in 1924. The south end of the street has evolved into an "education corridor"; on one count, more than a dozen local universities and colleges have come to show off here, bringing 40,000 students with them.

It is a good time for downtowns in many parts of America. The demand for office space is growing; consumers are spending freely. And a more subtle and potentially longer-lasting force is at work: demographics. Young professionals are having children later and are therefore staying in cities longer. (Many would not leave at all, if the schools were better.) At the same time, "empty-nesters", couples whose children have left home, are moving back to the city because it is more practical than a big, empty house in the suburbs. Both groups have a taste for sports, culture and entertainment, all of which can be found in town centres.

Meanwhile, since the suburbs are now saturated with malls, retailers are rediscovering downtown. Chicago's central business district has the second-largest concentration of office space in North America. More than 15,000 workers walk by some downtown blocks every day. Many of them, with more money than time, do their shopping there. Toys "R" Us has a large new store on State Street; that is where your correspondent buys nappies.

But it is not just a strong economy that has revived State Street. The redevelopment programme has made aggressive use of a public-finance tool called tax increment financing (TIF), which allows the city to finance economic development by tapping into the future tax revenues it is expected to generate. The city identifies a specific area that is economic-ally stagnant and then issues bonds to pay for projects to give it a boost – anything from renovating historic buildings to subsidising private developers. The bonds are later paid off by using the new tax revenues generated by rising property values in the TIF district.

Chicago's mayor, Richard Daley, loves this device. The city has created 44 of its 54 TIF districts since he was elected in 1989. All told, they have earned $270m in incremental property taxes. The city boasts that each dollar of tax increment financing generates $6 of private investment.

Critics argue that TIF often puts money in developers' pockets for doing things they would have done anyway. They add that success stories like State Street draw tenants away from other parts of the city. The programme also puts the government in the position of parcelling out subsidies (Sears is asking for an undisclosed amount of TIF money to help its move back to State Street). Still, this is a way to raise money for economic development at a time when Chicago's ration of federal money for such projects has fallen by 56% since 1980.

The bigger problem is that the success of central business districts has not spread to the poorer parts of America's cities. Most cities will probably finish the decade more segreg-ated by race and class than they started it. Most are still losing middle-class residents. The bulk of America's job growth is still in the suburbs. It is too early to hold a parade to celebrate the rebirth of America's cities. Still, you can take a very pleasant stroll down State Street.

CHAPTER FOUR

Urban Diversity and Economic Growth*

JOHN M. QUIGLEY

Source: Journal of Economic Perspectives, 12(2), Spring 1998, 127–38.
Reprinted by permission of American Economic Association.

At the risk of some simplification, it is possible to identify four periods of intense study of cities by economists. Each of these has led to an increased understanding of the economics of urban areas and the unique role played by cities in the modern economy.

The first of these periods occurred in the decade after World War I – only about ten years after the truck revolutionized the transport of goods within urban areas. This period included the first systematic empirical analysis of the forces affecting the location of firms and households within cities. Robert Murray Haig (1926) and a number of other micro-economists at Columbia analyzed the spatial patterns of manufacturing activity in lower Manhattan and in the rest of New York City. Haig and his colleagues devoted consider-able attention to "where things 'belong' in an urban area" (p. 402), providing the first systematic economic analysis of urban spatial structure. For example, they analyzed the garment industry, concluding that it was destined "by nature" to disperse north of 14th Street, and predicting that it would follow the established spatial pattern of the cooperage (barrel-making) industry. Standardization in size and quality of barrels had meant that identical barrels could be made throughout the New York metropolitan area, even in New Jersey, and the introduction of the truck meant that they could be transported cheaply throughout the region and exported.

The second of these periods – though not in chronological order – began in the mid-1960s. It formalized many of the insights about location incentives within urban areas which had been uncovered a half century before, mixed them with the logic of von Thünen's (1826) ancient theories about agricultural crops and land values, and applied them to the household sector. The works of William Alonso (1964) and John Kain (1962) exemplified this new approach, which was thoroughly worked out and picked over during the 1960s and 1970s. According to these theories, in a world of identical households, all would be indifferent among residential locations within the city, since spatial variations in housing prices would equalize utilities. Differentiation in the population would lead to

* This paper benefited from the comments of J. Bradford De Long, Masahisa Fujita, J. Vernon Henderson, Eugene Smolensky, and Timothy Taylor. Research assistance was provided by Scott Susin, and financial support has been provided by the Fisher Center for Real Estate and Urban Economics of the University of California, Berkeley.

predictable differences in location patterns, as land and housing prices adjusted to the spatial differentiation of demand. In this framework, the widely observed pattern of decline in housing prices and a steeper decline in land prices with distance to the urban center arises from a residential equilibrium in which higher income households live further from downtown and commute longer distances, but consume more housing in less dense accommodations. The poor outbid the rich for central locations with higher housing and land prices because they consume only small quantities of housing services.

The third concentrated period of advancement in our understanding of cities also arose from intensive analysis of the nation's primary city, New York. In the late 1950s, the Regional Plan Association and a group of economists at Harvard combined in a three-year study of the New York Metropolitan Region – an area which contained 10 percent of the U.S. population at the time and which stretched from Monmouth County, New Jersey, to Fairfield County, Connecticut. The Regional Plan Association sought to project economic and demographic conditions three decades into the future, and this practical objective provided academic researchers with a golden opportunity for intensive study of the fundamental factors affecting the development of industry and the location of economic activity. This effort ultimately resulted in publication of nine books and several technical reports, including an honest-to-God projection of economic conditions.[1] The hallmark of the New York study is the use of the concept of "external economies of scale;" that is, the notion that some firms can achieve cost savings when they operate in the context of a larger local economy. The summary volume of the New York study by Raymond Vernon (1962) includes a chapter devoted to the "rise and spread of external economies" and to the impact of these externalities on firm location and the well-being of central cities.[2]

We are in the midst of the fourth of these bursts of advancement in understanding the economics of cities. This era was ushered in by a reconsideration in the 1980s of the nature of economic growth. It has drawn new attention to aggregate cross-section and time-series data on cities, using variation between cities as the vehicle for analyzing and evaluating the nature and causes of economic growth.

The parallelism between the first two sets of developments and the latter two is striking. Much of the work on residential location theory of the 1960s can be traced to the original New York study of the 1920s. Similarly, much of the current emphasis on externalities and the growth of urban areas can be traced to the influential New York study of the late 1950s. The first two sets of developments emphasized the intrametropolitan location patterns of households and firms. The latter two have emphasized the overall patterns of growth of cities and metropolitan regions.

For example, *Made in New York*, a compendium of descriptive case studies of manufacturing in New York, includes the following passage (Hall, 1959, pp. 12–13).

Rubbing elbows with others of their kind and with ancillary firms that exist to serve them, [firms] satisfy their variable wants by drawing upon common pools of space, labor, materials, and services. In more concise language, they can take advantage of external economies.

The economies are external in the sense that the firm obtains them from outsiders, and they are economies in the sense that the firm can satisfy its variable or part-time needs in this manner more cheaply than it could satisfy them from within. The outsider, in turn, can afford to cater to the firm's fractional needs because he also caters to many other firms. The external economy may derive from an electrician or a sewing machine repairman or a free-lance photographer, responding to the call of a firm which does not need him full-time. ... It may even grow out of a revolving supply of specialized labor, such as garment workers accustomed to seasonal cycles, printers, staff writers, editors, or electronic engineers. Such a supply enables a firm to pick up employees quickly and let them go with equal suddenness, and makes it unnecessary to maintain a stable force of workers for an unstable demand.

Thus, it is obvious that external economies reduce the cost of doing business just as labor and transport [savings] do. Indeed, there is no real line of demarcation.

This description seems surprisingly close to more recent formal models in which the production of individual firms is competitive with constant returns to scale, but there are socially increasing returns as aggregate production rises. In the world of these recent models, capital investment has external benefits not reaped by private investors. The private investors solve well-specified optimization problems, and the economy of the urban area is more productive due to the external effects of this investment. With the benefit of hindsight, of course, the theoretical model is obvious. It has been said that the essence of really good theorizing is results which convince us that, in retrospect, it is all clear and it has been clear all along.

The original applications of the modern endogenous growth models emphasized the stock of accumulated knowledge. Paul Romer (1994) refers to this as the stock of "results" in a paper in this journal. Lucas (1988) was more precise in specifying the embodiment of results in human capital. Ideas can clearly benefit others as much or even more than they benefit the inventor of the idea. Knowledge or human capital, take your pick, may be the most important example of the application of the theory of endogenous growth. Nevertheless, cities have other important attributes which affect the growth of the economy in analogous ways – most especially their internal heterogeneity and diversity.

Recall that in the 1920s, the standardization of barrel manufacturing was associated with its decentralization to outlying parts of the New York area. A central conclusion of the Hall (1959, p. 8) volume, published almost 40 years later, detailing trends in the apparel, publishing, and electronics industries, was the following:

> The chief common denominator in these manufacturing operations that were attracted more strongly to other places than to the [New York] region appears to be standardization. The rest of the country gained relative to New York in products whose specifications could be planned in advance with reasonable assurance. Large numbers of identical copies – house dresses, magazines, radio sets – could be poured out of the plants without making any changes in the design. ... But the fact remains that the manufacture of standardized products ... has shown pervasive tendencies ... to prefer locations far from New York.

Of course, those conclusions referred only to the New York City metropolitan region and only to a small number of industries studied intensely. But within these limits, the evidence showed that firms producing nonstandardized differentiated output were more strongly attracted to the urban core than those firms producing homogeneous products. Even more directly, Benjamin Chinitz (1961) speculated that an urban environment with many firms producing heterogeneous output is more conducive to economic growth than an environment dominated by a few large firms or a single industry. This argument was based upon the superior competitive conditions fostered in an environment with smaller firms, more entrepreneurial activity, and a more adaptable investment and banking infrastructure. Again, this speculation was based on a specific comparison of two cities, New York and Pittsburgh, during the postwar period. The general models came much later.

Implications of Agglomeration

How do diversity and large size affect the level of output and the level of well-being achievable in a city? Table 1 suggests that there are at least four ways, not even including the knowledge spillovers which have figured so prominently in the debate about the new growth theory. Many of the arguments here were first put forward in a recognizably modern form by Alfred Marshall in his *Principles of Economics* and *Industry and Trade* (David and Rosenbloom, 1990). However, the concepts have been sharpened and differentiated over time.

The first – scale economies or indivisibilities within the firm – are the historical rationale for the existence of cities in the first place. Indeed, it has been long understood that, without the existence of scale economies in production, economic activities would be dispersed to save on transportation costs. Without scale economies, there is no role for the city at all.[3] Just as many urban industrial activities display economies of scale over some range, exhibiting U-shaped average cost curves (Mills, 1967; Mirrlees, 1972), so too do many public facilities like sports stadiums, swimming pools, and so on. For many of the collective consumption goods provided to urban residents (for example, walking in the park), the average cost of enjoyment declines with additional residents over a broad range. At some point, however, the average cost turns up again with more residents, at the point where congestion in the park becomes important.[4] To the extent that heterogeneity or

Table 1 Agglomerative Implications of Size and Diversity in Cities

Factor	Example	Theoretical Argument
1. Scale Economies		
in production, within firms	larger plant size	Mills (1967), Dixit (1973)
in consumption	public goods: parks, sports stadiums	Arnott and Stiglitz (1979)
2. Shared Inputs		
in production	repair, accounting, legal, advertising	Krugman (1993)
in consumption	theater, restaurants, high/low culture	Rivera-Batiz (1988)
3. Transaction Costs		
in production	labor market saving	Helsley and Strange (1990)
in consumption	shopping districts	Acemoglu (1996), Artle (1959)
4. Statistical Economies	unemployment insurance	David and Rosenbloom (1990)
in production	resale market for assets	Helsley and Strange (1991)
in consumption	substitute goods	Mills and Hamilton (1984)

variety encourages larger-sized urban areas that can take better advantage of scale economies or indivisibilities, these basic factors will increase the output of larger cities and the
utility of their residents.

The second factor – shared inputs in production and consumption – encompasses the
"economies of localized industry" described by Alfred Marshall, as well as its consumption analogue. The production aspects of these shared inputs are aptly described in the
passage quoted above from Hall (1959), as well as in the more modern treatment by
Krugman (1993) explaining how the ready availability of workers (in a metropolitan area),
and of particularly specialized workers in accounting, law, advertising and other technical
fields, can reduce costs for businesses. Shared inputs in consumption include networks for
disseminating information about cultural activities, as well as the facilities for such
activities. The use of shared inputs to produce more differentiated consumption goods
in large cities is apparent in all manner of fashion, culture, and style – where seemingly
identical inputs of cloth (or acting talent) are rearranged to produce quite different
products, and where equivalent inputs of crayfish and rice can be transformed into
Cajun meals, Creole meals, or authentic Dublin Bay scampi.

A third possible reason why a metropolitan area may provide greater economic efficiency arises from reductions in transactions costs. On the production side, this factor
includes the possibility of better matching between worker skills and job requirements.
This reduces the search costs of workers with differentiated skills and employers with
differentiated demands for labor, as pointed out in the theoretical works by Helsley and
Strange (1990) and more recently by Acemoglu (1996). Of these two papers, the Helsley
and Strange model is more directly relevant to cities, and the authors take pains to
compare the effects of labor market search costs upon equilibrium city sizes. The
Acemoglu analysis focuses on investment in physical and human capital and the external
pecuniary effects of these decisions. It builds upon the observation that there are complementaries in production between physical and human capital. Thus, when a group of
workers increases its stock of human capital, firms that expect to employ them will choose
to invest more in physical capital. With heterogeneity, costly search, and imperfect
matching, however, some workers not in the group will end up working with more
physical capital, earning higher returns on their human capital. Thus, the return on the
human capital to a worker in a city rises as the stock of human capital in the city rises, and
the return on physical capital investment to an investor also increases with the stock of
capital in the city. Acemoglu demonstrates that this result can obtain even when all output
in the city is produced with constant returns to scale and with no technological externalities.

The reduced transactions costs in larger cities also include lower search costs for
consumers. Larger cities are better able to support agglomerations of similar shopping
outlets in particular districts. Examples range from the familiar side-by-side placement of
used car lots in smaller cities to the specialized consumer services of the diamond
exchange on New York's 47th Street; Artle (1959) offers extensive empirical evidence
on the co-location of various types of retail establishments.

Finally, there are a set of potential economies and cost savings that arise, in the
description of Mills and Hamilton (1984), from the application of the law of large numbers
to the fact of fluctuations in the economy. For example, to the extent that fluctuations in
purchases of inputs are imperfectly correlated across firms, employment can be stabilized,

since some firms are hiring while other firms are not. To the extent that fluctuations in sales of output are uncorrelated across buyers, firms need carry less inventory, since some consumers are buying while others are not. These represent real savings to business firms and to the larger economy.

Theoretical Models of Heterogeneity

The factors noted in Table 1 reflect implications of both the size and the heterogeneity of cities. As emphasized above, scale economies, by themselves, provide the historic rationale for cities. But economies from the shared inputs in production and consumption, from reduced transactions costs from matching, and from reductions in variability all increase with the diversity of economic activities. Interesting and powerful models of these implications of diversity have been around for less than a decade and are still under development. Many of these general equilibrium treatments are based upon the perspective of monopolistic competition and optimum product diversity introduced by Dixit and Stiglitz (1977). This influential work considered explicitly the trade-off between the output of goods and their variety.

When considering consumption, the general form of these models assumes that household utility depends on consumption of traded goods, space or housing, and a variety of local goods. The markets for traded goods and housing are competitive, while the differentiated local goods are sold in a monopolistically competitive market. If there is less differentiation among local goods, then variety loses its impact on utility; greater differentiation means that variety has a greater effect on utility. Under reasonable assumptions, the utility of a household in the city will be positively related to the aggregate quantity of local goods it consumes and the *number* of types of these goods which are available in the economy.[5]

On the production side of the economy, the importance of a variety of locally produced inputs can be represented in a parallel fashion. For example, suppose that the aggregate production function includes labor, space, and a set of specialized inputs. Again, the markets for labor and space can be taken as competitive, while the differentiated local inputs are purchased in a monopolistically competitive market. If there is less differentiation among inputs, then variety loses its impact on output; greater differentiation means that variety has a greater effect on output. For example, a general counsel may operate alone. However, she may be more productive if assisted by a general practice law firm, and even better served by firms specializing in contracts, regulation, and mergers. Again, under reasonable conditions, output in the city will be related to quantities of labor, space, and specialized inputs utilized and also to the number of different producer inputs available in that city.[6]

Theoretical models built along these lines can yield a remarkable conclusion: *Diversity and variety in consumer goods or in producer inputs can yield external scale economies, even though all individual competitors and firms earn normal profits.* The intuition behind this result works in this way. In these models, the size of the city and its labor force will determine the number of specialized local consumer goods and the number of specialized producer inputs, given the degree of substitutability among the specialized local goods in consumption and among specialized inputs in production. A larger city will have a greater variety of consumer products and producer inputs. Since the greater variety adds to utility and to output, in these models, larger cities are more productive, and the well-being of those living in cities increases with their size. This will hold true even though the competitive and monopolistically competitive firms in these models each earn a normal rate of profit.

Now, these advantages of size do not literally go on forever, even in the models that incorporate one or the other of these types of heterogeneity – at least not in the most recent models (Henderson, 1974; Henderson et al., 1995). Explicit recognition of the land market and the necessity of commuting suggests that, at some point, the increased costs of larger cities – higher rents arising from competition for space and higher commuting costs to more distant residences – will offset the production and consumption advantages of diversity. Other costs like air and noise pollution no doubt increase with size as well. Nevertheless, even when these costs are considered in a more general model, the optimal city size – if it exists – will be larger when the effects of diversity in production and consumption are properly reckoned. Urban output will be larger and productivity will be greater. The utility of residents will be higher. Larger cities contribute more than proportionately to national output.

Empirical Support

The theoretical models of the economic advantages of heterogenous products and inputs that have been developed over the past decade provide a compelling framework for synthesizing a broad range of empirical results.

During the 1970s, for example, a number of studies estimated production functions for specific industries, using metropolitan statistical area (MSA) aggregates as the units of observation. The general finding is a parallel shift outward in the production function for larger metropolitan areas. For example, Shefer (1973) analyzed a group of 20 industries across MSAs, concluding that doubling city size would increase productivity by 14 to 27 percent. Sveikauskas (1975) used more sophisticated methods but a smaller number of industries and found that a doubling of city size would increase output by 6 to 7 percent. Segal (1976) aggregated across industries but constructed careful measures of urban capital stocks and concluded that in "large" cities of about two million or more in population, productivity was about 8 percent higher than in smaller cities. In the 1980s, Nakamura (1985) conducted a similar analysis using data on Japanese prefectures. His work confirmed the importance of agglomeration and localization economies, and concluded that a doubling of the size of a prefecture was associated with roughly a 3 percent increase in productivity. Somewhat weaker results were found for Canadian municipalities (Soroka, 1984). Similar empirical studies were undertaken using U.S. data by Beeson (1987) and others, with broadly consistent results.

The 1990s have seen an outpouring of sophisticated empirical analyses relating city size, the concentration of certain economic activities or else the diversity of a city's industrial mix to the level of economic output, or its growth in output. Several of these investigate explicitly the link between the urban human capital stock and productivity. Rauch (1993) provided the first empirical test of the labor market matching and human capital externality theories discussed earlier. If these externalities are significant, then otherwise identical workers will be more productive and will earn higher wages in those cities in which the spillovers are larger – or to put it differently – skilled workers in human-capital-rich cities will earn more than those in human-capital-poor cities. Rauch provides convincing tests of these propositions, using 1990 data on individual workers living in over 200 U.S. metropolitan areas. He finds robust confirmation of these hypotheses – specifically a metropolitan area with an average educational level one-year higher than another would have about a 3 percent productivity advantage. Rauch's results are consistent with an external effect of education on productivity in cities that is almost 70 percent as large as the direct private effect. From the theoretical arguments summarized earlier, Rauch's results should underestimate the productivity advantages of large, human-capital-rich cities.

On the consumption side, workers should also be willing to work for lower wages to live in these more diverse environments. However, I am aware of only one study presenting any evidence on this point. Getz and Huang (1978) offer weak evidence that the availability of a broad range of publicly and privately provided consumer goods is reflected in local wage rates.

Analysts cannot directly observe "knowledge" as it spills out among buildings and the streets in cities, but some of this spillout does leave a paper trail. The geography of one paper trail has been mapped recently by Jaffe, Trajtenberg, and Henderson (1993). The authors compared the geographic location of patent grantees with the locations of the intellectual and/or commercial forebears of those innovations. These latter locations are determined by the geographic location of the owner of an existing patent cited in a subsequently successful application. Thanks to a careful experimental design and designation of controls, some of their results can be presented as straightforward cross-tabulations of patents and the patents they cite. The authors analyze cohorts of patents originating in 1975 and 1980, finding a clear localization in their pedigrees. The strength of the geographical associations is stronger in more recent data and the citations are more localized to the same state and the same metropolitan area than could be explained on the basis of pre-existing concentrations of activity. The patents cited as antecedents are five to ten times more likely to come from the same metropolitan statistical areas as are the patent citations of control groups. The evidence also suggests that the intrastate and intrametropolitan linkages are stronger for the patents held by private corporations than for those originating in universities.

Based upon more sophisticated statistical analyses, the authors estimated the decay in the localization of citations as the interval increases between the year of the approved patent and the approval of the patent it cites. The localization of patents erodes with this interval, but the erosion is far less for intrametropolitan geographical linkages than for other geographical linkages. These general findings were similar for patents in a variety of technical fields.

The geographical localization of patent citations within urban areas and the persistence of this localization over time are both quite striking. The local as well as the national role of universities in disseminating knowledge is also clearly documented in the results.

Much recent empirical work linking productivity and the urban economy has been focused on dynamic, or at least intertemporal, issues. This interest can be traced to the influential empirical analysis by Glaeser et al. (1992). By gathering a comparable body of data on city-industries at two points in time, the authors are able to investigate the effects of initial conditions (in 1956) on subsequent performance (in 1987). For a large sample of cities, the authors analyze the industries which were largest in 1956 and their subsequent performance. The analysis is rich and complex, but from my vantage point, the most striking finding is the importance of industrial diversity on subsequent economic perform- ance. This is consistent with the informal arguments of Jane Jacobs (1969) about the stimulation of "ideas" in heterogeneous surroundings and also with the view that diversity fosters specialization in inputs and outputs, yielding higher returns.

Subsequent work has confirmed this basic insight and elaborated on it. Henderson et al. (1995) consider a broadly representative body of cities and industries from 1970 to 1987. Their careful empirical analysis suggests that the extent of diversity in manufacturing industries at the start of the period was not very important in affecting employment outcomes and the subsequent performance of mature industries, but it did matter in attracting "new" or high tech industries (such as scientific instruments and electronic components) and in permitting those new industries to flourish.[7] In the same spirit, a recent historical analysis found that industrial diversity in 1880 had a substantial effect on output in 1890, using Census of Manufacturers data for 79 American cities (Bostic et al., 1997). Other recent research, related to states rather than to cities, reports analogous findings. For example, Garcia-Mila and McGuire (1993) find that the industrial mix of the state economy affects its level of economic growth over the period 1969–1985, even after controlling for the growth and variability of industries at the national level, the relative composition of fast and slow growth industries at the state level, and the relative mix of variable and stable industries by state. Ciccone and Hall (1996) also analyze productivity at the state level, relating gross state product to the concentration of economic activity as measured by the density of employment.

It is tempting to interpret these various empirical findings solely in terms of knowledge or education, so as to put them into the framework of modern growth theory. However, no matter how the results are described, it remains clear that the increased size of cities and their diversity are strongly associated with increased output, productivity, and growth. Large cities foster specialization in production and sustain a broader range of final products, increasing the returns of their firms and the well-being of their residents.

Conclusion

It is hardly surprising that economies of scale in production give rise to the higher density living and commuting arrangements that we call cities. It is only rather recently, however, that models of the variety available in cities have been developed to emphasize the independent role of diversity in enhancing economic efficiency. The logic underlying these models suggests that national growth is enhanced by the heterogeneous features of modern cities, and the empirical evidence suggests that these efficiency gains are not trivial.

However, traditional models of the optimal city size (Mills, 1967; Henderson, 1974) establish clearly that we would not be better off collectively living in Greater New York. Land and housing prices increase with city size and commuting costs do as well. These factors place efficiency limits on city sizes. More recent models emphasize the importance of unpriced congestion, pollution, and other externalities in further limiting the size of the efficient city. Some of the evidence presented in the accompanying paper by Edward Glaeser in this symposium also suggests that crime and victimization increases with urban scale, and some of my own work (O'Regan and Quigley, 1996a, b) suggests that the poverty concentrations arising from urban life have external effects upon employment outcomes.

The economic costs, even the external costs, of urban scale are undoubtedly large. However, the modern perspective on urban diversity surveyed here does remind us that large cities have been and will continue to be an important source of economic growth and improved living standards.

Notes

1 Dick Netzer (1992) has provided a provocative evaluation of these projections – comparing forecasts published in 1962 with outcomes in the 1970s, 1980s, and 1990s.

2 The study also paid careful attention to Scitovsky's (1954) distinction between "technological externalities" and "pecuniary externalities."

3 The economic inefficiency of cities, absent scale economies, is sometimes called the "Starrett theorem," after the work of Starrett (1978). One exception to this conclusion is the original von Thünen (1826) market village – a central node through which goods pass to be exported to world markets.

4 The development of club theory in local public finance is premised on significant scale economies in publicly provided consumption and on the congestion that arises ultimately when these facilities are rationed by average cost pricing through local taxation (Scotchmer, 1994).

5 For example, if the utility function of consumers is Cobb-Douglas in traded goods, housing, and local goods, and if there is a constant elasticity of substitution in utility among locally produced consumer goods, then the utility of consumers increases with the quantity of local goods and with the number of types of local goods available. For an introduction to these sorts of models, see Abdel-Rahman (1988), Fujita (1988), and Rivera-Batiz (1988). See Krugman (1993) for a later treatment.

6 The conditions closely parallel those mentioned in the previous footnote. For example, if the production function for goods is Cobb-Douglas in the three inputs and the specialized inputs have a constant elasticity of substitution in production so that they have a symmetric effect on production, then output increases with the quantity of specialized inputs and also with the number of types of input. See the references in the previous note for detailed expositions of models of this kind.

7 A potential criticism of all the work based on U.S. Census data is the aggregation of industries into "two-digit" Standard Industrial Classification (SIC) categories. Is this the best level for measuring diversity of output? Do larger or more diverse cities simply specialize in more productive subcommodities? Some empirical evidence is now available (Moomaw, 1998) suggesting that little is lost by the aggregation of industries for all these empirical analyses using SIC categories.

References

Abdel-Rahman, Hesham M. (1988) "Product Differentiation, Monopolistic Competition, and City Size," *Regional Science and Urban Economics*, 18(1), 69–87.

Abdel-Rahman, Hesham M. and Masahisa Fujita (1990) "Product Variety, Marshallian Externalities, and City Sizes," *Journal of Regional Science*, 30(2), 165–83.

Acemoglu, Daron (1996) "A Microfoundation for Social Increasing Returns in Human Capital Accumulation," *Quarterly Journal of Economics*, August, 111(3), 779–804.

Alonso, William (1964) *Location and Land Use*. Cambridge, MA: Harvard University Press.

Arnott, Richard and Joseph E. Stiglitz (1979) "Aggregate Land Rents, Expenditure on Public Goods, and Optimal City Size," *Quarterly Journal of Economics*, November 1979, 93(4), 471–500.

Artle, Roland (1959) "On Some Methods and Problems in the Study of Metropolitan Economies," *Papers and Proceedings of Regional Science Association*, 8, 71–87.

Beeson, Patricia (1987) "Total Factor Productivity Growth and Agglomeration Economies in Manufacturing," *Journal of Regional Science*, 27(2), 183–99.

Bostic, Raphael W., Joshua S. Gans and Scott Steins (1997) "Urban Productivity and Factor Growth in the Late 19th Century," *Journal of Urban Economics*, 4(1), 38–55.

Chinitz, Benjamin J. (1961) "Contrasts in Agglomeration: New York and Pittsburgh," *American Economic Review*, May, 51, 279–89.

Ciccone, Antonio and Robert E. Hall (1996) "Productivity and the Density of Economic Activity," *American Economic Review*, 86(1), 54–70.

David, Paul A. and Joshua L. Rosenbloom (1990) "Marshallian Factor market Externalities and the Dynamics of Industrial Location," *Journal of Urban Economics* 28(3), November 1990, 349–70.

Dixit, Avinash K. (1973) "The Optimum Factory Town," *The Bell Journal of Economics and Management Science*, 4(2), 647–54.

Dixit, Avinash K. and Joseph Stiglitz (1977) "Monopolistic Competition and Optimum Product Diversity," *American Economic Review*, 67(3), 297–308.

Fujita, Masahisa (1996) "On the Self-Organization and Evolution of Economic Geography," *Japanese Economic Review*, March, 47(1), 34–61.

Fujita, Masahisa (1988) "A Monopolistic Competition Model of Spatial Agglomeration: Differentiated Product Approach," *Regional Science and Urban Economics*, 18(1), 87–124.

Garcia-Mila, Theresa and Therese J. McGuire, (1993) "Industrial Mix as a Factor in the Growth and Variability of States' Economies," *Regional Science and Urban Economics*, 23(6), 731–48.

Getz, Malcolm and Yuh-Ching Huang (1978) "Consumer Revealed Preference for Environmental Goods," *Review of Economics and Statistics*, 60(3), 449–58.

Glaeser, Edward L., et al. (1992) "Growth in Cities," *Journal of Political Economy*, 100(6), 1126–52.

Glaeser, Edward L., Jose A. Scheinkman and Andrei Shleifer (1995) "Economic Growth in a Cross Section of Cities," *Journal of Monetary Economics*, 36(1), December, 117–43.

Haig, Robert Murray (1926) "Toward an Understanding of the Metropolis," *Quarterly Journal of Economics*, 40(1), 402–34.

Hall, Max, (ed.) (1959) *Made in New York*. Cambridge, MA: Harvard University Press.

Helsley, Robert W. and William C. Strange (1990) "Matching and Agglomeration Economies in a System of Cities," *Regional Science and Urban Economics*, 20(2), 189–212.

Helsley, Robert W. and William C. Strange (1991) "Agglomeration Economies and Urban Capital Markets," *Journal of Urban Economics*, January, 29(1), 96–112.

Henderson, Vernon J. (1974) "The Sizes and Types of Cities," *American Economic Review*, September, 64(4), 640–56.

Henderson, Vernon J., Ari Kuncoro and Matt Turner (1995) "Industrial Development in Cities," *Journal of Political Economy*, 103(5), 1067–90.

Hobson, Paul A. R. (1987) "Optimum Product Variety in Urban Areas," *Journal of Urban Economics*, 22(2), 190–97.

Jacobs, Jane (1969) *The Economies of Cities*. New York: Random House.

Jaffe, Adam B., Mannel Trajtenberg and Rebecca Henderson (1993) "Geographic Localization of Knowledge Spillovers as Evidenced by Patent Citations," *Quarterly Journal of Economics*, August, 108(3), 577–98.

Kain, John (1962) "The Journey-to-Work as a Determinant of Residential Location," Papers and Proceedings of Regional Science Association (9), 137–60.

Krugman, Paul (1993) "First Nature, Second Nature, and Metropolitan Location," *Journal of Regional Science*, 33(2), 129–44.

Lucas, Robert (1988) "On the Mechanics of Economic Development," *Journal of Monetary Economics*, July, 22(1), 3–42.

Mills, Edwin S. (1967) "An Aggregative Model of Resource Allocation in Metropolitan Areas," *American Economic Review*, May, 57, 197–210.

Mills, Edwin S. and Bruce W. Hamilton (1984) *Urban Economics*. Third edition, Glenview, IL: Scott, Foresman, and Co.

Mirrlees, James A. (1972) "The Optimum Town," *Swedish Journal of Economics*, 74(1), 114–35.

Moomaw, Ronald L. (1998) "Agglomeration Economies: Are They Exaggerated by Industrial Aggregation?" *Regional Science and Urban Economics* 28(2), 175–97.

Nakamura, Ryohei (1985) "Agglomeration Economies in Urban Manufacturing Industries: A Case of Japanese Cities," *Journal of Urban Economics*, 17(1), 108–24.

Netzer, Dick (1992) "The Economy of the New York Metropolitan Region, Then and Now," *Urban Studies*, 29(2), April, 251–8.

O'Regan, Katherine M. and John M. Quigley (1996a) "Teenage Employment and the Spatial Isolation of Minority and Poverty Households," *Journal of Human Resources*, 31(3), 692–702.

O'Regan, Katherine M. and John M. Quigley (1996b) "Spatial Effects on Employment Outcomes: The Case of New Jersey Teenagers," *New England Economic Review*, March/June, 41–58.

Rauch, James E. (1993) "Productivity Gains from Geographic Concentration of Human Capital: Evidence from the Cities," *Journal of Urban Economics*, 34(3), 380–400.

Rivera-Batiz, Francisco L. (1988) "Increasing Returns, Monopolistic Competition, and Agglomeration Economies in Consumption and Production," *Regional Science and Urban Economics*, 18(1), 125–54.

Romer, Paul M. (1994) "The Origins of Endogenous Growth," *Journal of Economic Perspectives*, 8(1), 3–22.

Scitovsky, Tibor (1954) "Two Concepts of External Economies," *Journal of Political Economy*, April, 62, 143–51.

Scotchmer, Suzanne (1994) "Public Goods and the Invisible Hand." In John Quigley and Eugene Smolensky, eds., *Modern Public Finance*. Harvard University Press, 93–125.

Segal, David (1976) "Are There Returns to Scale in City Size?," *Review of Economics and Statistics*, August, 58(3), 339–50.

Shefer, D. (1973) "Localization Economies in SMSAs: A Production Function Analysis," *Journal of Regional Science*, 13, 55–64.

Soroka, Lewis (1984) "Manufacturing Productivity and City Size in Canada, 1975 and 1985: Does Population Matter?" *Urban Studies*, 31(6), 895–911.

Starrett, David A. (1978) "Market Allocations of Location Choice in a Model with Free Mobility," *Journal of Economic Theory*, 17(1), 21–37.

Sveikauskas, Leo (1975) "The Productivity of Cities," *Quarterly Journal of Economics*, August, 89(3), 393–413.

Vernon, Raymond (1962) *Metropolis 1985*. Cambridge, MA: Harvard University Press.

von Thünen, Johannes Heinrich (1966 [1826]) *Der Isolierte Staat in Beziehung auf Landwirtschaft und Nationalekonomie*. Stuttgart: Gustave Fischer.

CHAPTER FIVE

Projecting Growth of Metropolitan Areas

Edwin S. Mills and Luan' Sende Lubuele

Source: Journal of Urban Economics, 37, 344–60.

1. Introduction

This paper is about the determinants of growth of metropolitan areas (MSAs). The subject needs little justification; it is important both for scholarly understanding of urban development and for practical use. Understanding why and how MSAs grow and / or shrink is perhaps the most important subject that urban scholars can study. Practically, businesses and households would like to know about growth prospects before making business and household location and investment decisions in MSAs. State and local governments want to know about prospects for MSA growth to forecast expenditure needs and tax revenue growth, and to formulate government policies to promote, or perhaps slow, MSA growth. Of course, to the extent that private or government behavior is influenced by initial forecasts, the prospects for growth are affected. Such applications require iterations between growth models and sectors that might respond to growth forecasts.

Several related literatures exist. Many books and papers have been written on the relationship between the growth of the urban sector and the growth and sectoral structure of the national economy. Some publications are historical, some are theoretical, and some are statistical. A second literature pertains to the determinants of the sizes of urban or metropolitan areas. Some of this literature is positive and some is normative. A third literature concerns the size distribution of MSAs. Most of this literature is empirical, although a handful of theoretical and normative papers have appeared. A fourth literature concerns migration to urban areas, from other urban areas, from rural areas, or from foreign countries.

Anas [1], Henderson [4], Henderson and Ioannides [5], Fujita [2], and Greenwood [3], are important recent references for the four kinds of related literature, and contain many references to earlier works.

The growth of individual MSAs relates to all four kinds of literature. Individual MSAs grow in the context of growth of the urban sector. However, the overall growth of the urban sector is a poor predictor of the growth of particular MSAs, especially in an economy such as the United States which is near the upper edge of percent urban among highly urbanized countries and whose percent urban increases only slowly. In addition, an individual MSA grows or shrinks as parameters that affect its size change.

However, no study has succeeded in relating empirical MSA growth to parameter changes of formal models of the determinants of MSA size.

The relationship of this study to the third type of literature requires a bit more comment. This size distribution of MSAs is remarkably stable over several decades. However, that does not imply that particular MSAs cannot grow much faster than average. Although the relative sizes of MSAs that occupy particular ranks change only slowly, different MSAs occupy particular ranks from one decade to the next. For example, from 1970 to 1990 the fastest growing U.S. MSA grew at a compound rate of 7.1% per year, more than four times as fast as the average MSA growth. In 1970 it had a population of 39,000, not even qualifying as an official MSA. By 1990, it had a population of 154,000, making it the 221st largest MSA (out of 320 MSAs in 1990). Nevertheless, it is important to keep in mind that the growth of individual MSAs occurs in the context of a remarkably stable MSA size distribution. Finally, there is an enormous migration literature. MSAs have been substantial net recipients of migrants since MSAs have been defined. Differences in net migration are a large fraction of the differences in total population growth of MSAs. Net migration depends on economic parameters in origin and destination locations and on MSA location. (For example, Albuquerque is more likely to be the destination location for Mexican immigrants than is Minneapolis.) The other component of MSA growth is natural growth. The natural population growth is the excess of births over deaths, both of which depend on the MSA age distribution, on MSA economic conditions, and on other factors.

There is a scattered literature on the determinants of growth of particular MSAs. Anas [1], Henderson and Ioannides [5], and other papers, especially those by Satterthwaite and O'Huallachain, in Mills and McDonald [6], are important recent contributions that contain references to earlier work.

Three characteristics distinguish the research reported in this paper from earlier studies. First, this is a study of the growth determinants of all MSAs. It employs census data for 1970, 1980, and 1990 for all 320 MSAs that were defined in 1990. Each MSA's growth enters the model and we present forecasts to the year 2000 for all 320 MSAs. Thus, this is a study of the growth determinants of all MSAs, not of particular MSAs or MSAs in particular states, regions, or size ranks. No scholarly literature exists on this subject, despite its importance. The U.S. Department of Commerce [7] has an MSA forecasting model, as have Woods and Poole [8] and several consulting firms. All but the U.S. government model are proprietary. A major goal of this paper is to begin scholarly analysis of such models. Second, this study employs a simultaneous equation model in which each MSA's population, employment, and wage rates interact with each other. As far as can be ascertained from published sources, no other model used to forecast growth of all MSAs employs a simultaneous equation system. Third, it employs a simple quasi-linear model which, however, captures whatever local and regional determinants persist for the 20-year sample period.

2. MSA Growth from 1970 to 1990[1]

From 1970 to 1990, the U.S. population grew about 1% per year, whereas the MSA population grew about 1.6% per year, 60% faster than the national growth rate. In 1970, the MSA population was 68.6% of the U.S. population; by 1990, it was 77.2%.

Table 1 presents summary MSA growth statistics for the periods 1970–1980 and 1980–1990. For each period, the table first shows decade growth rates by quartile of MSA

Table 1 Summary Statistics on MSA Growth

	Growth in the 1970s		
Quartiles	*Population growth*	*Employment growth*	*Wage growth*
Decile 1	0.0686	0.2249	0.1970
Quartile 1	0.1261	0.2794	0.1751
Quartile 2	0.1703	0.3025	0.1750
Quartile 3	0.1845	0.3408	0.2109
Quartile 4	0.1272	0.2579	0.2194
	Regional averages		
Region	*Population growth*	*Employment growth*	*Wage growth*
New England	0.0217	0.1925	0.1423
Mid-Atlantic	−0.0066	0.0877	0.1263
Midwest	0.0191	0.1344	0.1761
Plains	0.0729	0.2822	0.2497
South	0.2286	0.3587	0.1906
Southwest	0.2939	0.5739	0.3222
West	0.1866	0.4143	0.2885
Pacific	0.1937	0.3917	0.1703
All MSAs	0.1061	0.2565	0.1969
	Growth in the 1980s		
Quartiles	*Population growth*	*Employment growth*	*Wage growth*
Decile 1	0.1198	0.2576	0.1476
Quartile 1	0.1240	0.2693	0.1254
Quartile 2	0.1188	0.2408	0.0787
Quartile 3	0.1150	0.2457	0.0452
Quartile 4	0.0509	0.1633	0.0245
	Regional averages		
Region	*Population growth*	*Employment growth*	*Wage growth*
New England	0.0615	0.2227	0.2648
Mid-Atlantic	0.0465	0.2077	0.1556
Midwest	0.0127	0.1544	0.0394
Plains	0.0900	0.2304	0.0613
South	0.1620	0.3356	0.1151
Southwest	0.2197	0.2816	−0.0418
West	0.1386	0.2867	−0.0025
Pacific	0.2398	0.3204	0.0386
All MSAs	0.1163	0.2526	0.0752

population in 1990 and then growth rates for each of the eight census regions. Growth rates are presented for each of the three dependent variables of the model analyzed in subsequent sections: population, employment, and real wages.[2]

In the 1970s, the most rapid population and employment growth were in the third and fourth quartiles of the MSA size distribution. In the 1980s, the fastest MSA population and employment growth occurred in the top three quartiles of the size distribution. In the 1970s, rapid wage growth tended to be in the bottom two quartiles, whereas in the 1980s it tended to be in the top two quartiles.

Both the 1970s and the 1980s showed a strong tendency for population and employment growth to be concentrated in the bottom four of the eight regions as listed, i.e., those in the southern and western parts of the country. In the 1970s, rapid wage growth was concentrated in the southern and western regions, whereas in the 1980s, rapid wage growth was concentrated in the northeastern and midwestern regions.

The table also shows the well-known decrease in real wage growth in the 1980s, less than half as fast as that in the 1970s. The minimum and maximum wage growth figures suggest an enormous dispersion in real wage increases among MSAs in both decades. Finally, the table displays the extremely rapid growth of employment relative to the growth of population in both decades, with employment growth exceeding population growth by more than a factor of two.

The table confirms the well-known fact that employment and wages grew much more rapidly in the southern and western regions than in the northeastern and midwestern regions in the 1970s. However, the regional divergences of the 1970s were reduced or reversed in the 1980s. During the early 1990s, the eastern and western regions appear to have fared poorly, relative to other regions.

3. The Theoretical Model

This paper employs a relatively simple three-equation model to represent the interactions among population, employment, and wages in an MSA. The model is semistructural and is based on conventional relationships among the variables. The equations are written in linear form here, but Box–Cox estimation is employed to permit non-linear forms, as will be discussed in Section 4.

$$P_{it} = a_0 + \sum_{j=1}^{7} a_j R_j + a_8 W_{it} + a_9 E_{it} + a_{10} P_{it-1} + a_{11} P_{it-1}^2 + u_{Pit}$$

$$E_{it} = b_0 + \sum_{j=1}^{7} b_j R_j + b_8 W_{it} + b_9 P_{it} + b_{10} E_{it-1} + b_{11} E_{it-1}^2 + u_{Eit} \qquad (1)$$

$$W_{it} = c_0 + \sum_{j=1}^{7} c_j R_j + c_8 P_{it} + c_9 E_{it} + c_{10} W_{it-1} + u_{Wit} \,,$$

where P_{it} is the population of the ith MSA in year t, E_{it} is the employment of the ith MSA in year t, w_{it} is the earnings per worker in the ith MSA in year t, and R_j is a dummy variable that takes the value one if the ith MSA is in region j and is zero otherwise. Eight census regions are employed; New England is represented in the constant term, so there are seven dummy variables in the regressions. Lagged endogenous variables are included among the predetermined variables, and the squares of the lagged population and employment variables are also included in their respective equations. u_{Pit}, u_{Eit}, and u_{Wit} are error terms. The data are 1970, 1980, and 1990 census data for all 320 MSAs that were defined in 1990. Thus, some included MSAs did not qualify as MSA in 1970 and/or 1980. Local geographic, topological, social, and political conditions affect MSA size and growth. Persistent local conditions are captured by inclusion of the 1970 lagged dependent variables and estimating the model with 1980 and 1990 observations.

The basic conceptual notions behind the model are widely used and accepted in urban and regional analysis. An increase in population should stimulate employment and an increase in employment should stimulate population. These relationships are at the base of the jobs-follow-people vs people-follow-jobs controversy. Presumably, both relationships exist and our model permits estimation of the relative strengths of the two effects. High wages should deter employment. High wages should attract population as labor suppliers, but should repel population as consumers, since high wages make locally produced goods and services expensive. Thus, the net effect of wages on population is ambiguous. An increase in employment for a fixed population should increase wages, and an increase in population for fixed employment should depress wages, since the population increase increases labor supply. Population, employment, and wages should of course be increasing functions of their lagged values. The squares of the lagged endogenous variables are expected to have negative coefficients, since the positive effects of lagged population and employment on population and/or employment are expected to dissipate for MSAs with large population and/or employment.

There are of course no predictions as to the signs of the seven regional coefficients. However, it must be borne in mind that the model contains values from 1970 of the three dependent variables for each MSA as the initial conditions. Coefficients of lagged dependent variables are likely to represent regional as well as local effects.

4. Estimation

The simultaneous equation model was estimated by two-stage least-squares with corrections for autocorrelated residuals and for heteroskedasticity. We employed the Box–Cox transformation to estimate functional forms whose extremes are linear and log–linear equations. See the Appendix for more details. It is worth noting that population and employment vary by more than a factor of 100 within the sample, whereas real wages vary by only about a factor of 4.

In our estimation, we experimented with a variety of possible values of the λs. $\lambda = 0$ is the logarithmic specification and $\lambda = 1$ is the linear specification. There is no statistical rule to choose the λs in a simultaneous equation model. It is possible to permit the λs to vary among the three equations and to choose each so as to maximize R^2. That seems somewhat *ad hoc*. Perhaps more importantly, R^2s for this model are typically in excess of 0.95 for a variety of a λ values. Instead, we choose the estimates to be included here on the basis of the plausibility of the estimated coefficients and the forecasts.[3] Estimates and forecasts for λs in the vicinity of 0 or 1 are less plausible than those for λs near the middle of the permissible range. The estimates and forecasts reported here are for all λs = 0.75.

Estimates are given in Table 2. Most coefficients have anticipated signs. Population and employment attract each other, as anticipated. The larger and more significant coefficient

Table 2 Model Estimates for λ s = 0.75

Variables	Population	Estimate Wage	Employment
Constant	−7.152	0.3378	−9.515
	(−1.61)	(1.68)*	(−4.09)**
Pop	–	0.01238	0.3170
	–	(1.47)	(8.98)**
Wage	0.2061	–	0.3269
	(2.09)**	–	(3.93)**
Empl	0.06856	0.002657	–
	(1.94)*	(0.608)	–
I pop	0.9629	–	–
	(24.7)**	–	–
Lwage	–	1.073	–
	–	(40.9)**	–
Lempl	–	–	0.8193
	–	–	(21.7)**
SLpop	−2.589E-0.5	–	–
	(−0.313)	–	–
SLempl	–	–	0.0003205
	–	–	(7.77)**
Great Lakes	−14.24	−0.6513	−4.192
	(−3.24)**	(−5.45)**	(−2.01)**
Mid-Atlantic	−5.628	−0.4198	1.696
	(−1.35)	(−3.35)**	(0.831)
Mount	−11.51	−0.6043	3.296
	(−2.13)**	(−3.99)**	(1.38)
Pacific	−0.8778	−0.6785	1.113
	(−0.151)	(−5.41)**	(0.496)
Plains	−6.349	−0.4711	−1.058
	(−1.50)	(−3.73)**	(−0.507)
Southeast	−8.820	−0.3318	1.843
	(−2.14)	(−2.86)**	(0.952)
Southwest	−5.517	−0.7861	−11.71
	(−1.05)	(−6.46)**	(−4.63)**
R^2_i	0.9531	0.8730	0.9843
R^2_s	0.9566	0.9311	0.9908
DF	308.0	309.0	308.0
Durbin-W	0.7322	2.722	1.185
HeteroRsq	0.6161	0.6218	0.2660
HeteroFs	31.11	31.85	7.801

* Significance at the 10% level.
** Significance at the 5% level.

of population in the employment equation than of employment in the population equation supports the notion that jobs follow people more than vice versa. High wages attract people. The positive coefficient of wages on employment is contrary to anticipation. Undoubtedly, both wage coefficients basically reflect the fact that large MSAs have higher wages than small MSAs, since land values increase in MSA size. All three lagged dependent variable coefficients have large and highly significant coefficients. The squared lagged population coefficient is negative, as anticipated, but insignificant. The squared lagged employment coefficient is positive and highly significant, undoubtedly reflecting the general acceleration of employment growth in the 1980s.

The regional dummies are of varying signs, sizes, and significance levels. Since the initial values of the MSA dependent variables are included on the right-hand sides of the equations, their coefficients may capture not only regional but also local effects. R_i^2 is the R^2 corresponding to the second regression of the two-stage least-squares procedure. R_s^2 is the R^2 based on residuals obtained from the structural specification; it is not necessarily bounded between 0 and 1. Durbin-W is the Durbin–Watson statistic of the residuals of the first layer of regression. It indicates the extent of the original autocorrelation problem. HeteroRsq and HeteroFs are, respectively, the R^2 and the F-statistic of the regression of the logs of the squares of the residuals. They indicate the extent of the heteroskedasticity before its correction.

5. Forecasts to the Year 2000

Table 3 presents summaries of forecasts from the estimated model in Table 2. The last line presents the summary data for total forecast growth rates of all MSAs. The forecast

Table 3   Projected Growth Summarized by Quartile Rank in 1990 and by Region

| | Growth by groups of MSAs ranked by population in 1990 | | |
Quartile	Population growth	Employment growth	Wage growth
Decile 1	0.0888	0.3360	0.5628
Quartile 1	0.0796	0.2243	0.2586
Quartile 2	0.0491	0.1402	0.1384
Quartile 3	0.0310	0.0850	0.1129
Quartile 4	−0.0471	−0.0510	0.0789

| | Growth of MSAs grouped by regions | | |
Region	Population growth	Employment growth	Wage growth
New England	0.0647	0.2346	0.2780
Mid-Atlantic	0.0414	0.2814	0.2601
Midwest	−0.0128	0.1456	0.1177
Plains	0.0509	0.1672	0.1477
South	0.0813	0.2423	0.1993
Southwest	0.1215	0.1952	0.1891
West	0.0673	0.2421	0.1633
Pacific	0.1453	0.3719	0.2897
All MSA	0.0699	0.2469	0.1997

MSA population growth of nearly 7% is a bit more conservative than most such forecasts. The forecasted employment growth of nearly 25% is undoubtedly too high, reflecting the rapid employment growth of the 1980s and the fact that nothing in the model ties employment to demographic data at the national level. The nearly 20% forecast growth of real wages is a little faster than that reported in Table 1 for the 1970s and considerably faster than that for the 1980s.

The summary growth projections by quartile size in 1990 indicate a greater concentration of growth among large MSAs in the 1990s than shown in Table 1 for the 1970s and 1980s. The regional summary distribution in Table 3 is somewhat similar to the regional summaries in Table 1, especially for the 1980s.

The summary projections in Table 3 suggest strongly that the detailed projections for the year 2000 are by no means simply extrapolations of experience in the 1970s and 1980s.

Projections for each of the 320 MSAs are given in Table 4. It is easy to see that growth projections deviate from the experience of the 1970s and 1980s for many MSAs. Many relatively small MSAs that had modest or substantial growth in the 1970s and 1980s are projected to shrink in the 1990s. Some large MSAs are projected to grow considerably faster in the 1990s than in the previous 2 decades.

It is important to understand what can cause trend reversals in our model. If the only independent variables were lagged dependent variables and regional dummies, then virtually all projections would be simply historical trends. The only additional variables in the model are interactions among the dependent variables and the acceleration effect as captured by squared lagged variables. Thus, the interaction and acceleration effects are the primary bases of trend reversals in the predictions.

6. Conclusions

This paper has estimated a three-simultaneous-equation model of growth determinants of MSAs. The three dependent variables are MSA population, employment, and real wage rate per worker. The model was estimated from 1970, 1980, and 1990 data for all 320 MSAs that had been defined at the time of the 1990 census. Then projections were made of the three dependent variables for the year 2000. It is shown that the interaction effects among the dependent variables are strong enough to cause deviations from historical trends in the growth predictions for the year 2000.

The most important purpose of the paper is to stimulate research on MSA growth determinants. Scholars are blessed with superb data for U.S. MSAs. There is almost no end to the set of local, regional, national, and international influences that could plausibly be introduced in such models. Future research should gradually indicate what effects are important.

Table 4 Forecasts to 2000 for 320 MSAs

	Population in 000s	Population Growth is %	Employment in 000s	Employment Growth in %	Wages in 000$	Wages Growth
ABILENE, TX	117.7	−1.7	46.7	−31.7	8.9	6.8
AKRON, OH	642.1	−2.5	362.6	9.1	11.2	15.1
ALBANY, GA	102.8	−8.5	63.3	0.6	10.3	9.7
ALBANY-SCHENECTADY-TROY, NY	912.0	4.2	623.8	21.5	14.0	22.0
ALBUQUERQUE, NM	524.1	8.7	337.8	11.0	12.0	8.6
ALEXANDRIA, LA	117.1	−10.8	58.8	−3.5	7.6	11.6
ALLENTOWN-BETHLEHEM EASTON, PA-NJ	724.3	5.2	413.6	19.4	12.4	28.9
ALTOONA, PA	120.1	−7.9	64.8	−0.5	8.7	12.1
AMARILLO, TX	189.2	0.7	80.0	−18.6	8.9	8.0
ANAHEIM SANTA ANA, CA	2806.9	15.7	2062.9	37.5	19.6	49.9
ANCHORAGE, AK	268.0	18.6	191.3	26.3	18.7	16.6
ANDERSON, IN	108.3	−17.1	46.6	−23.2	9.2	−0.7
ANDERSON, SC	141.2	−3.0	70.7	3.8	7.8	14.6
ANN ARBOR, MI	286.1	0.8	224.0	7.0	17.3	6.1
ANNISTON, AL	102.6	−11.4	57.5	−4.6	8.9	9.6
APPLETON OSHKOSH-NEENAIL, WI	315.5	−0.2	189.1	4.1	11.3	7.7
ASHEVILLE, NC	175.5	0.1	118.0	10.5	10.6	10.3
ATHENS, GA	163.7	4.3	95.0	12.9	9.2	11.3
ATLANTA, GA	3376.2	18.4	2624.4	41.8	22.3	65.7
ATLANTIC CITY, NJ	351.2	9.6	274.6	23.3	14.4	5.6
AUGUSTA, GA-SC	425.3	6.9	277.1	21.5	12.1	13.2
AURORA-ELGIN, IL	367.6	2.6	197.3	8.6	10.4	11.0
AUSTIN, TX	961.6	22.1	601.6	27.5	12.6	21.4
BAKERSFIELD, CA	647.0	18.2	331.7	31.0	10.4	28.0
BALTIMORE, MD	2555.0	6.9	1824.5	28.7	18.0	52.7
BANGOR, ME	155.5	5.8	94.9	10.3	11.2	19.8
BATON ROUGE, LA	541.5	2.6	322.8	17.2	12.0	28.2
BATTLE CREEK, MI	116.6	−14.4	55.8	−18.6	10.6	2.7
BEAUMONT PORT ARTHUR, TX	345.5	−4.3	151.4	−9.9	10.5	14.8
BEAVER COUNTY, PA	165.5	−10.9	54.7	−11.4	8.6	43.3
BELLINGHAM, WA	142.6	10.6	81.9	16.1	8.2	8.2
BENTON HARBOR, MI	138.0	−14.6	69.4	−16.1	8.6	1.0
BERGEN PASSAIC, NJ	1292.3	1.2	957.1	19.4	18.0	21.7
BILLINGS, MT	104.1	−8.2	71.7	2.5	9.6	8.2
BILOXI GULFPORT, MS	196.0	0.7	115.5	9.0	9.0	12.8
BINGHAMTON, NY	261.7	−1.1	155.5	10.3	11.7	11.8
BIRMINGHAM, AL	925.9	1.8	585.0	18.8	13.1	29.9
BISMARCK, ND	79.1	−5.5	45.2	−10.0	9.6	8.8
BLOOMINGTON, IN	99.2	−9.3	54.1	−15.6	8.4	−3.7
BLOOMINGTON NORMAL, II	121.5	−6.6	74.5	−8.3	10.9	−2.2
BOISE CITY, ID	217.8	5.0	154.7	16.6	11.4	8.3
BOSTON-LAWR. SALEM-LOWELL-BROCKTON, MA	3977.6	5.1	3322.4	29.8	25.6	65.6
BOULDER-LONGMONT, CO	240.1	6.2	195.1	19.5	12.5	3.6
BRADENTON, FL	244.1	14.1	123.1	27.3	7.3	15.4
BRAZORIA, TX	198.3	3.2	65.5	−17.7	10.0	13.2
BREMERTON, WA	221.0	15.3	118.9	24.6	9.5	11.6
BRIDGEPORT STAM NORWALK DANBURY, CT	868.6	5.0	651.0	19.5	20.7	23.1
BROWNSVILLE HARLINGEN, TX	282.1	7.9	89.9	−6.8	4.9	6.8
BRYAN COLLEGE STATION, TX	132.0	8.0	51.5	−20.3	7.5	−3.9

Table 4 (*Cont.*)

	Population in 000s	Population Growth in %	Employment in 000s	Employment Growth in %	Wages in 000s	Wages Growth
BUFFALO, NY	949.0	−1.9	616.5	15.4	13.1	27.7
BURLINGTON, NC	104.9	−3.4	70.4	4.2	9.3	6.2
BURLINGTON, VT	154.3	12.1	117.0	17.6	15.4	13.1
CANTON, OH	369.4	−6.3	198.5	0.5	9.6	12.2
CASPER, WY	43.3	−28.7	30.2	−20.7	11.9	22.3
CEDAR RAPIDS, IA	165.0	−2.5	111.0	0.9	13.3	12.0
CHAMPAIGN-URBANA RANTOUL, Il.	159.9	−7.7	105.8	−6.5	9.8	−1.4
CHARLESTON, SC	553.4	8.7	358.7	24.0	11.3	21.7
CHARLESTON, WV	229.1	−8.4	135.5	1.8	11.7	19.4
CHARLOTTE GASTONIA ROCK HILL, NC-SC	1309.3	12.1	959.1	27.9	16.2	33.1
CHARLOTTESVILLE, VA	135.1	2.7	98.8	11.0	11.9	6.8
CHATTANOOGA, TN-GA	432.1	−0.4	277.4	13.9	11.4	18.1
CHEYENNE, WY	64.7	−11.6	44.9	−2.0	10.9	9.0
CHICAGO, IL	6185.4	1.8	4873.3	31.9	25.9	81.9
CHICO, CA	206.4	12.6	96.3	20.7	6.3	8.9
CINCINNATI, OH KY-IN	1494.7	2.7	1051.4	20.1	15.0	27.7
CLARKSVILLE HOPKINSVILLE, TN KY	171.5	0.8	93.6	8.1	8.3	16.1
CLEVELAND, OH	1800.8	−1.6	1251.5	14.6	16.6	32.8
COLORADO SPRINGS, CO	446.6	12.0	305.3	26.2	10.9	10.3
COLUMBIA, MO	114.6	1.7	78.2	2.4	10.5	6.6
COLUMBIA, SC	480.9	5.7	366.6	19.3	13.1	15.3
COLUMBUS, GA-AL	235.9	−2.9	149.4	8.5	9.9	12.3
COLUMBUS, OH	1474.2	6.6	1051.4	22.5	14.8	28.3
CORPUS CHRISTI, TX	358.7	2.4	164.6	−3.9	9.1	12.2
CUMBERLAND, MD-WV	90.5	−10.9	42.7	−5.2	8.0	11.2
DALLAS, TX	3021.8	17.6	2213.1	33.3	21.5	53.1
DANVILLE, VA	95.0	−12.2	50.2	−7.2	8.2	9.4
DAVENPORT ROCK ISLAND MOLINE, IA-IL	313.3	−10.6	186.6	−5.0	11.4	12.7
DAYTON SPRINGFIELD, OH	951.4	−0.1	607.2	13.3	13.2	19.7
DAYTONA BEACH, FL	438.1	17.0	221.2	33.8	7.3	24.9
DECATUR, AL	127.8	−3.0	65.4	5.5	8.4	11.7
DECATUR, Il	93.2	−20.3	51.0	−23.8	11.7	1.1
DENVER, CO	1771.3	8.9	1401.1	26.0	18.5	36.9
DES MOINES, IA	413.3	4.7	311.0	12.4	14.3	16.4
DETROIT, MI	4374.5	−0.3	2832.6	27.5	20.4	65.9
DOTHAN, AL	126.5	−3.5	76.2	5.1	9.6	8.9
DUBUQUE, IA	76.0	−12.1	45.5	−14.7	11.2	15.1
DULUTH, MN-WI	216.9	−9.5	120.8	−3.0	9.7	14.4
EAU CLAIRE, WI	124.0	−10.1	62.3	−15.4	7.7	−0.6
EL PASO, TX	662.0	11.2	295.3	14.0	8.0	19.4
ELKHART GOSHEN, IN	156.1	0.5	115.3	1.5	13.3	0.6
EL MIRA, NY	87.6	−8.1	48.2	−1.3	9.1	7.8
ENID, OK	45.1	−20.0	7.7	−74.9	8.0	6.4
ERIE, PA	268.6	−2.5	156.4	8.7	10.7	15.9
EUGENE SPRINGFIELD, OR	293.2	3.0	173.7	13.3	9.0	12.6
EVANSVILLE, IN-KY	264.7	−5.2	161.5	−1.3	10.9	7.7
FARGO MOORHEAD, ND MN	157.7	2.7	100.1	4.2	10.2	11.8
FAYETTEVILLE, NC	283.4	3.0	166.6	13.6	10.0	16.2
FAYETTEVILLE-SPRINGDALE, AR	112.7	−1.0	74.9	7.0	9.2	4.9
FLINT, MI	401.8	−6.7	199.0	1.4	12.8	13.8
FLORENCE, AL	117.5	−10.4	62.5	−2.1	8.5	14.9

Table 4 *(Cont.)*

	Population in 000s	Population Growth in %	Employment in 000s	Employment Growth in %	Wages in 000s	Wages Growth
FLORENCE, SC	107.6	−6.1	70.3	2.6	9.7	7.3
FORT COLLINS-LOVELAND. CO	197.9	5.8	127.2	19.4	8.8	4.6
FT LAUDER.-HOLLYWOOD POMPANO BEACH, FL	1427.3	12.9	888.1	34.4	12.7	41.1
FORT MYERS CAPE CORAL, FL	419.8	23.7	245.6	38.1	8.9	21.4
FORT PIERCE, FL	311.4	22.4	157.8	35.8	8.4	25.5
FORT SMITH, AR-OK	174.8	−0.9	110.4	9.9	9.3	12.1
FORT WALTON BEACH, FL	157.6	8.9	100.8	19.0	9.7	9.5
FORT WAYNE, IN	358.7	−1.7	249.0	6.1	12.9	7.1
FORT WORTH ARLINGTON, TX	1591.7	18.7	883.2	29.9	13.4	41.8
FRESNO, CA	783.7	16.6	429.6	28.5	10.4	10.9
GADSDEN, AL	86.6	−13.3	38.6	8.8	8.1	13.5
GAINESVILLE, FL	217.6	6.0	143.1	17.8	10.1	8.1
GALVESTON-TEXAS CITY, TX	222.8	2.3	78.8	−13.9	8.4	6.8
GARY-HAMMOND, IN	563.9	−6.7	289.5	2.5	11.5	20.5
GLENS FALLS, NY	118.4	−0.4	68.4	7.9	8.9	5.3
GRAND FORKS, ND	66.7	−5.6	37.1	−12.5	9.5	7.4
GRAND RAPIDS, MI	740.0	7.0	506.7	18.6	13.6	15.4
GREAT FALLS, MT	63.3	−18.5	40.0	−9.6	8.5	5.4
GREELEY, CO	122.8	−6.9	71.8	5.9	7.3	−0.2
GREEN BAY, WI	192.1	1.7	118.3	0.6	11.5	4.1
GREENSBORO-WINSTON SALEM-HIGH POINT, NC	1012.4	7.1	733.2	22.1	14.9	29.2
GREENVILLE-SPARTANBURO, SC	690.4	7.3	488.4	21.0	13.4	23.7
HAGERSTOWN, MD	121.9	0.1	71.0	9.0	10.2	9.8
HAMILTON MIDDLETOWN, OH	292.5	0.0	119.2	3.4	8.1	13.1
HARRISBURG-LEBANON CARLISLE, PA	616.3	4.6	434.2	17.7	14.2	19.7
HART.-NEW BRIT.-MIDDLETOWN-BRISTOL., CT	1210.4	7.6	934.5	21.9	21.4	30.2
HICKORY-MORGANTON, NC	227.6	2.4	168.1	11.9	11.8	10.9
HONOLULU, HI	905.3	7.9	654.3	20.2	15.4	19.2
HOUMA THIBODAUX, IA	172.4	−5.5	70.3	−2.7	8.5	37.0
HOUSTON, TX	3722.1	12.3	2445.5	29.4	21.4	73.2
HUNTINGTON-ASHLAND, WV-KY-OH	285.9	−8.4	142.6	4.8	9.1	20.6
HUNTSVILLE, AL	263.0	9.7	196.2	22.4	15.3	7.1
INDIANAPOLIS, IN	1309.1	4.4	911.6	18.9	14.9	26.8
JOWA CITY, IA	100.7	4.2	63.6	0.8	11.7	7.0
JACKSON, MI	131.0	−12.8	51.2	−20.0	8.5	5.7
JACKSON, MS	410.7	3.7	264.9	15.0	11.4	20.4
JACKSON, TN	71.7	−8.1	50.5	0.2	10.9	5.2
JACKSONVILLE, FL	1041.2	14.1	705.4	30.6	14.3	31.5
JACKSONVILLE, NC	164.8	9.3	91.0	15.3	8.6	13.0
JAMESTOWN-DUNKIRK, NY	131.7	−7.1	71.5	0.3	8.4	11.6
JANESVILLE BELOTT, WI	122.4	−12.4	58.4	−17.0	8.9	−0.4
JERSEY CITY, NJ	550.8	−0.3	333.1	15.2	13.7	16.2
JOHNSON CITY KINGSPORT BRISTOL, TN-VA	428.7	−1.7	252.9	12.8	9.6	18.9
JOHNSTOWN, PA	218.7	−9.2	104.1	2.2	7.8	19.5

Table 4 (*Cont.*)

	Population in 000s	Population Growth in %	Employment in 000s	Employment Growth in %	Wages in 000s	Wages Growth
JOLIET, Il.	390.6	−0.1	150.7	9.7	7.3	9.3
JOPLIN, MO	132.6	−2.0	80.5	0.8	8.2	5.6
KALAMAZOO, MI	215.9	−3.6	131.9	−0.3	12.7	4.5
KANKAKEE, IL	75.0	−22.1	29.8	−34.4	7.5	−3.6
KANSAS CITY, MO-KS	1685.6	7.3	1207.8	23.7	16.5	40.9
KENOSHA, WI	113.1	−12.1	35.3	−28.7	7.9	15.7
KILLEEN-TEMPLE, TX	276.1	7.6	124.8	−5.1	8.3	6.9
KNOXVILLE, TN	627.2	3.5	409.5	19.3	11.1	22.7
KOKOMO, IN	78.7	−18.7	41.2	−24.1	13.0	−0.3
LA CROSSE, WI	87.4	−11.0	50.9	−18.9	10.6	1.8
LAFAYETTE, LA	210.4	0.9	129.5	8.7	12.0	24.8
LAFAYETTE-WEST LAFAYETTE, IN	120.6	−7.9	67.3	−12.2	10.3	1.5
LAKE CHARLES, LA	157.6	−6.2	79.4	1.1	10.6	23.6
LAKE COUNTY, IL	555.4	7.0	346.5	18.4	12.4	7.5
LAKELAND WINTER HAVEN, FL	453.9	11.2	246.9	23.7	9.8	28.7
LANCASTER, PA	464.2	9.2	287.9	20.5	11.6	18.9
LANSING EAST LANSING, MI	427.6	−1.4	257.9	7.4	12.4	10.0
LAREDO, TX	146.0	8.7	37.8	−26.3	5.0	0.3
LAS CRUCES, NM	151.7	11.6	44.9	−20.2	5.7	1.3
LAS VEGAS, NV	949.8	25.6	604.4	40.6	14.5	30.4
LAWRENCE, KS	83.7	1.8	43.3	−4.9	8.1	8.3
LAWTON, OK	102.6	−7.9	36.6	−38.5	7.6	−3.2
LEWISTON AUBURN, ME	109.0	3.4	56.3	2.4	9.5	20.7
LEXINGTON FAYETTE, KY	366.6	4.7	280.2	16.8	12.8	14.8
LIMA, OH	137.8	−10.8	76.8	−12.4	10.2	3.7
LINCOLN, NE	224.4	4.6	160.1	8.5	12.1	10.2
LITTLE ROCK NORTH LITTLE ROCK, AR	535.8	4.2	364.3	17.5	12.4	21.9
LONGVIEW MARSHALL, TX	161.8	0.5	68.9	−21.6	9.3	6.9
LORAIN ELYRIA, OH	248.5	−8.4	101.4	−6.2	8.5	8.5
LOS ANGELES LONG BEACH, CA	9993.9	12.2	8132.4	49.7	34.1	141.2
LOUISVILLE, KY-IN	958.3	0.5	676.9	17.6	13.7	29.8
LUBBOCK, TX	223.9	0.3	110.6	−12.9	8.9	5.4
LYNCHBURG, VA	134.6	−5.3	93.8	3.9	12.0	10.1
MACON WARNER ROBINS, GA	284.6	1.1	184.4	14.7	11.3	11.1
MADISON, WI	385.3	4.5	284.4	9.4	13.2	9.0
MANCHESTER-NASHUA, NH	386.8	14.9	273.2	23.3	16.0	19.7
MANSFIELD, OH	106.9	−15.2	57.7	−18.8	10.2	1.0
MCALLEN EDINBURG MISSION, TX	440.3	14.0	150.4	11.0	4.7	11.9
MEDFORD, OR	155.4	5.4	79.7	11.3	7.3	8.2
MELBOURNE TITUSVILLE PALM BAY, FL	481.5	19.6	280.3	35.1	12.0	22.3
MEMPHIS, TN-AR-MS	1034.5	5.1	722.0	21.5	14.3	29.6
MERCED, CA	206.3	14.9	86.6	18.8	6.7	14.1
MIAMI-HIALEAH, FL	2129.3	9.3	1435.3	28.6	16.5	53.2
MIDDLESEX-SOMERSET HUNTERDON, NJ	1132.1	10.7	827.1	28.4	18.9	21.2
MIDLAND, TX	116.4	8.9	44.7	−26.5	12.3	17.6
MILWAUKEE, WI	1464.0	1.9	1006.1	16.0	15.4	31.1
MINNEAPOLIS-ST. PAUL., MN-WI	2748.8	11.0	2120.3	29.4	21.2	52.2
MOBILE, AL	490.1	2.5	264.2	17.3	9.3	26.6
MODESTO, CA	446.4	19.4	212.8	31.7	8.5	21.7

Table 4 *(Cont.)*

	Population in 000s	Population Growth in %	Employment in 000s	Employment Growth in %	Wages in 000s	Wages Growth
MONMOUTH OCEAN, NJ	1082.8	9.4	592.1	33.3	10.7	28.3
MONROE, LA	132.7	−6.6	70.4	1.8	8.8	13.6
MONTGOMERY, AL.	296.6	1.3	186.4	13.1	10.8	14.8
MUNCIE, IN	97.3	−18.6	46.8	−24.5	8.7	0.0
MUSKEGON, MI	141.8	−11.0	58.5	−16.4	8.5	6.3
NAPLES, FL	190.9	23.8	122.5	32.0	9.5	10.1
NASHVILLE, TN	1088.3	10.0	799.9	26.5	14.6	28.9
NASSAU SUFFOLK, NY	2659.4	1.9	1839.8	28.5	16.6	46.5
NEW BEDFORD FALL RIVER ATH FBORO, MA	533.8	5.4	286.6	17.6	10.9	33.5
NEW HAVEN WATERBURY MERIDEN, CT	853.4	6.0	558.9	20.8	15.9	29.6
NEW LONDON NORWICH, CT	272.1	6.7	169.9	15.0	14.7	21.2
NEW ORLEANS, LA	1223.2	−1.0	734.7	14.2	13.5	43.1
NEW YORK, NY	8876.5	3.8	6785.9	38.9	32.7	106.2
NEWARK, NJ	1825.4	0.2	1356.7	20.2	20.0	29.1
NIAGARA FALLS, NY	210.9	−4.5	108.1	6.6	10.0	17.5
NORFOLK-VA, BEACH NEWPORT NEWS, VA	1571.3	12.0	1078.2	29.4	15.2	43.7
OAKLAND, CA	2348.6	12.2	1506.2	33.8	17.1	46.6
OCALA, FL	233.2	18.4	110.9	31.1	6.7	17.2
ODESSA, TX	112.0	−5.6	32.6	−41.8	9.2	15.2
OKLAHOMA CITY, OK	1027.0	7.0	618.3	11.7	12.5	30.2
OLYMPIA, WA	188.1	15.4	104.6	24.3	8.8	7.3
OMAHA, NE-IA	648.5	4.6	491.0	16.8	14.2	19.7
ORANGE COUNTY, NY	334.3	8.2	168.8	22.8	8.6	13.9
ORLANDO, FL	1357.0	25.1	995.8	42.7	15.5	35.4
OWENSBORO, KY	78.1	−10.6	45.3	−4.7	8.8	11.6
OXNARD-VENTURA, CA	776.3	15.2	429.5	34.2	10.4	19.0
PANAMA CITY, FL	136.5	6.9	78.9	15.4	8.6	11.8
PARKERSBURG-MARIETTA, WV-OH	133.3	−10.5	75.6	−0.8	9.6	13.2
PASCAGOULA, MS	103.0	−10.5	52.2	−3.1	10.1	13.2
PENSACOLA, FL	372.0	7.4	208.3	21.6	9.9	20.5
PEORIA, IL	306.3	−9.7	173.9	−4.8	12.0	13.1
PHILADELPHIA, PA-NJ	5040.8	3.6	3558.0	33.0	21.9	84.3
PHOENIX, AZ	2578.6	20.9	1708.5	38.6	16.5	55.1
PINE BLUFF, AR	72.1	−15.6	37.6	−10.8	9.3	12.6
PITTSBURGH, PA	1982.9	−3.5	1268.4	16.8	15.2	47.7
PITTSFIELD, MA	137.8	−0.9	84.6	4.7	12.1	16.4
PORTLAND, ME	272.2	11.6	228.8	19.9	15.7	13.8
PORTLAND, OR	1371.8	9.8	986.0	24.6	15.6	34.9
PORTSMOUTH-DOVER ROCHESTER, NH	406.7	15.9	247.2	27.0	11.6	27.7
POUGHKEEPSIE, NY	267.0	2.8	167.1	16.5	13.2	9.6
PROVIDENCE PAWTUCKET WOONSOCKET, RI	969.1	5.6	590.0	19.1	13.9	41.3
PROVO OREM, UT	277.4	4.8	141.0	22.3	6.4	7.3
PUEBLO, CO	106.7	−13.3	54.8	−2.4	7.5	10.4
RACINE, WI	159.2	−9.3	75.8	−11.9	10.0	5.5
RALEIGH-DURHAM, NC	865.9	16.9	658.3	30.1	16.1	23.4
RAPID CITY, SD	82.7	1.1	52.5	−4.1	10.2	8.7
READING, PA	351.3	4.1	213.5	14.6	12.3	15.6
REDDING, CA	167.5	13.1	81.4	20.1	7.8	7.2
RENO, NV	291.1	12.6	204.3	20.6	14.2	16.7
RICHLAND KENNEWICK PASCO, WA	155.1	3.0	86.5	7.2	11.4	14.8

Table 4   (Cont.)

	Population in 000s	Population Growth in %	Employment in 000s	Employment Growth in %	Wages in 000s	Wages Growth
RICHMOND PETERSBURG, VA	947.0	8.9	717.5	22.8	16.5	25.7
RIVERSIDE SAN BERNARDINO, CA	3363.2	28.2	1562.4	61.0	13.5	110.7
ROANOKE, VA	221.0	−1.5	172.5	10.5	13.0	10.0
ROCHESTER, MN	113.9	6.5	87.1	7.8	15.9	5.7
ROCHESTER, NY	1036.5	3.3	693.5	20.5	15.4	27.5
ROCKFORD, Il	271.3	4.5	162.9	0.2	12.3	6.9
SACRAMENTO, CA	1782.9	19.4	1128.8	39.4	14.9	42.8
SAGINAW-BAY CITY-MIDLAND, MI	369.2	−7.6	195.0	1.8	11.1	8.5
ST. CLOUD, MN	210.5	9.7	120.5	17.7	7.8	5.0
ST. JOSEPH, MO	79.7	−4.1	48.0	−1.5	9.4	1.7
ST. LOUIS, MO IL	2523.9	3.1	1819.4	25.7	17.2	45.6
SALEM, OR	291.7	4.2	138.3	−3.9	7.9	5.5
SALINAS SEASIDE MONTFREY, CA	394.9	10.5	203.6	4.4	9.6	9.5
SALT LAKE CITY OGDEN, UT	1201.7	11.6	749.6	28.0	12.5	35.2
SAN ANGELO, TX	106.1	7.3	54.1	4.7	8.0	10.1
SAN ANTONIO, TX	1481.0	13.2	864.3	30.9	12.2	41.8
SAN DIEGO, CA	2997.6	19.0	1955.3	41.1	17.4	65.5
SAN FRANCISCO, CA	1737.8	8.1	1503.8	21.3	24.0	28.8
SAN JOSE, CA	1668.6	10.9	1192.3	21.6	21.5	22.2
SANTA BARBARA-SANTA MARIA-LOMPOC, CA	425.1	14.4	262.0	23.6	11.6	14.2
SANTA CRUZ, CA	247.8	7.3	147.1	20.6	8.9	8.9
SANTA FE, NM	126.2	7.1	86.8	16.0	12.3	8.9
SANTA ROSA-PETALUMA, CA	447.4	14.4	263.2	30.0	9.6	16.7
SARASOTA, FL	334.6	19.4	211.5	30.3	8.9	7.3
SAVANNAH, GA	253.9	4.5	167.5	17.3	11.3	9.4
SCRANTON-WILKES-BARRE, PA	723.1	−1.6	415.2	11.0	9.0	14.6
SEATTLE, WA	2288.4	14.8	1757.3	30.3	20.0	41.4
SHARON, PA	105.5	−12.8	50.5	−7.8	9.0	22.8
SHEBOYGAN, WI	99.6	−4.3	55.0	−6.5	10.7	8.9
SHERMAN DENISON, TX	90.8	−4.6	43.1	−10.1	9.2	9.5
SHREVEPORT, LA	314.2	−5.8	166.4	−3.2	9.5	10.7
SIOUX CITY, IA NE	114.2	0.9	75.5	3.7	9.7	6.0
SIOUX FALLS, SD	118.6	−4.4	83.5	−6.7	11.2	2.7
SOUTH BEND MISHAWAKA, IN	255.9	3.4	152.6	11.8	12.2	27.5
SPOKANE, WA	371.6	2.3	218.9	12.0	10.2	18.8
SPRINGFIELD, Il.	187.1	−1.4	133.1	5.0	12.1	8.2
SPRINGFIELD, MO	259.5	7.4	182.7	14.3	10.2	12.6
SPRINGFIELD, MA	616.2	2.2	370.5	14.6	11.4	17.3
STATE COLLEGE, PA	125.8	1.3	77.9	9.1	9.9	4.9
STEUBENVILLE-WEIRTON, OH-WV	111.3	−21.6	42.8	−29.9	9.6	9.6
STOCKTON, CA	576.7	19.1	271.7	32.3	9.3	28.2
SYRACUSE, NY	677.2	2.6	450.4	19.5	13.3	19.0
TACOMA, WA	665.3	12.4	353.3	28.7	9.5	25.7
TALLAHASSEE, FL	256.4	9.0	180.6	21.2	11.2	8.9
TAMPA-ST. PETERSBURG CLEARWATER, FL	2407.7	15.6	1596.0	41.1	14.5	63.7
TERRE HAUTE, IN	109.3	−16.5	52.2	−23.7	8.3	2.4
TEXARKANA, TX-TEXARKANA, AR	113.7	−5.5	60.2	1.1	8.4	11.6
TOLEDO, OH	600.0	−2.4	370.9	8.8	12.2	13.7
TOPEKA, KS	161.5	0.2	115.4	3.5	13.5	9.4
TRENTON, NJ	342.2	4.9	261.3	16.7	17.8	6.9
TUCSON, AZ	755.8	12.9	385.8	19.6	9.4	19.8

Table 4 *(Cont.)*

	Population in 000s	Population Growth in %	Employment in 000s	Employment Growth in %	Wages in 000s	Wages Growth
TULSA, OK	743.8	4.8	440.5	7.6	12.5	22.0
TUSCALOOSA, AL	149.1	−1.3	81.7	10.1	9.2	8.6
TYLER, TX	159.6	5.1	69.5	−17.4	9.2	4.2
UTICA-ROME, NY	309.3	−2.2	174.4	10.6	9.4	14.0
VALLEJO-FAIRFIELD NAPA, CA	536.4	17.9	257.3	34.3	9.2	19.9
VANCOUVER, WA	271.5	12.9	132.5	28.2	7.6	9.4
VICTORIA, TX	70.0	−6.0	16.6	−55.0	7.9	4.2
VINELAND-MILLVILLE BRIDGETON, NJ	135.6	−1.9	74.6	5.2	10.3	9.1
VISALIA TULARE PORTERVILLE, CA	356.8	13.7	167.2	21.8	6.7	20.1
WACO, TX	193.5	2.0	80.6	−16.3	7.8	3.6
WASHINGTON, DC-MD VA	4495.1	14.1	3888.3	39.8	28.4	65.5
WATERLOO-CEDAR FALLS, IA	120.2	−18.0	65.2	−22.3	10.4	9.6
WAUSAU, WI	101.5	−12.3	52.0	−19.1	8.7	−0.2
W. PALM BH BOCA RATON DELRAY BH, FL	1069.8	22.6	688.4	39.8	13.4	33.1
WHEELING, WV OH	131.2	−17.4	66.2	−9.4	8.3	16.7
WICHITA, KS	515.4	6.0	315.6	4.3	13.1	15.0
WICHITA FALLS, TX	116.4	−5.0	68.2	−8.7	10.2	14.8
WILLIAMSPORT, PA	112.9	−5.0	62.4	1.4	9.3	10.4
WILMINGTON, DE-NJ-MD	624.4	7.5	423.0	22.9	15.9	19.3
WILMINGTON, NC	122.7	1.6	83.1	10.6	10.5	9.5
WORCESTER-FITCHBURG LEOMINSTER, MA	766.0	7.7	434.1	21.2	13.2	37.0
YAKIMA, WA	200.3	5.4	111.3	11.9	7.3	9.3
YORK, PA	441.0	5.2	257.4	17.3	11.0	20.7
YOUNGSTOWN-WARREN, OH	449.9	−8.5	234.3	−0.1	10.3	13.8
YUBA CITY, CA	134.2	8.9	55.8	9.8	6.8	10.4
YUMA, AZ	132.4	9.1	41.6	−24.4	6.7	3.7

Appendix: Econometric Estimation

We started with the model

$$y_t = y_t\Gamma + x_tB + u_t \qquad (1)$$

where y_t is a 1×3 vector of transformed dependent variables at time t, x_t is the $1 \times s$ vector of predetermined variables, u_t is the 1×3 vector of structural errors, Γ is the 3×3 matrix of parameters to be estimated and whose diagonal elements are normalized to zero, and B is the $s \times 3$ matrix of additional parameters to be estimated. Note that x_t contains the lagged variables y_{t-1}, the squared lagged valued, and the dummy variables for regions.

The error u_t is assumed to be distributed with mean zero and variance-covariance $\sum_{tm}$, i.e., both heteroskedasticity at the cross-sectional dimension and autocorrelation are allowed.

Preliminary estimation based only on combinations of levels and logs showed the need for an exploration of intermediate Box–Cox transformations. Hence the values included in y_t and the lagged part of x_t are based on the well-known transformation

$$y_{it} = \frac{v_{it}^{\lambda_i}}{\lambda_i} \qquad (2)$$

where $\lambda_i \varepsilon [0, 1]$, is the index associated with population, employment or wage and v_{it} is the actual data on population, employment, or wage. In practice we chose a grid of values for λ and ran the estimation procedure adopted for each combination of λs and dependent variables.

We chose to use 2SLS because we wanted to avoid the problem of corruption of all the estimates in case of misspecification of a single equation associated with system estimation approaches, such as the 3SLS.

We ran three layers of estimations. The first regression was used to test for the presence of autocorrelation. This was a critical step since the presence of lagged variables combined with autocorrelation leads to inconsistent estimates. It came out clearly that for all the possible combinations of λs, there was always a significant autocorrelation (as measured by the Durbin–Watson statistics).

We then used the quasi-differencing method to wash out the autocorrelation by running the regressions on variables transformed as

$$\begin{aligned} \tilde{y}_{it} &= y_{it} - \alpha_i y_{it-1} \\ \tilde{x}_{it} &= x_{it} - \alpha_i x_{it-1} \end{aligned} \qquad (3)$$

The second equation of (3) refers to the variables in x_t involved in equation i. α_i is the autocorrelation coefficient. In order to use the 2SLS procedure after the transformation introduced in (3), it is necessary to accommodate the fact that every time-varying variable transformed according to (3) using two different αs yields two non-collinear variables that should be included in the list of variables to be used in the computation of the instruments. Even though we have potentially three distinct αs (from three different series of residuals), only two can be used since any third variable obtained by using (3) with a third α is always a perfect linear combination of the first two.

We then used the estimates obtained by 2SLS at this stage (which are hence consistent) to obtain residuals and used them for the estimation of heteroskedasticity following the model

$$\log(u_{it}^2) = Z_t \Theta + \varepsilon_{it}$$

where Z_t is the matrix of predetermined variables and instruments used in the last 2SLS procedure run.

Let $h_{ij} = \hat{u}_{ij}^2$ (i.e. the projected squared errors). We proceed with the third layer of 2SLS estimation after transforming all the variables by dividing them by the corresponding h_{ij}. This multiplies the number of predetermined variables by 3.

Notes

1   In 1990, there were 320 Primary Metropolitan Statistical Areas and 17 Consolidated Metropolitan Statistical Areas. CMSAs consist of groups of related and contiguous PMSAs. Definitions are in census volumes. All the data analyzed in this paper refer to PMSAs.

2 All the data analyzed in this paper are from diskettes containing the data in [8]. Employment is total full and part time workers; wage data are real earnings in 1987 dollars, including worker contributions for social insurance.

3 Alternative estimates are available from the senior author upon request.

References

1 A. Anas, (1992) "On the birth and growth of cities: Laissez faire and planning compared," *Regional Science and Urban Economics*, 22, 243–258.

2 M. Fujita, (1989) *Urban Economic Theory*, Cambridge University Press, New York.

3 M. Greenwood, (1981) *Migration and Economic Growth in the United States*, Academic Press, New York.

4 J. V. Henderson, (1988) *Urban Development* Oxford Univ. Press, New York.

5 J. V. Henderson, and Y. Ioannides, (1981) "Aspects of growth in a system of cities," *Journal of Urban Economics*, 10, 117–139.

6 E. Mills, and J. McDonald, (1992) (Eds.), *Sources of Metropolitan Growth*. Rutgers Center for Urban Policy Research, New Brunswick, NJ.

7 U.S. Department of Commerce, Bureau of Economic Analysis, (1985) *1985 OBERS BEA Regional Projections*. U.S. Government Printing Office, Washington, DC.

8 Woods and Poole, (1992) *1992 MSA Profile*, Woods and Poole, Inc. Washington, DC.

Further Reading Samples

Conclusion from *Are Cities Dying?*

EDWARD GLAESER

Source: Journal of Economic Perspectives, 12(2), Spring 1998, 139–60. Reprinted by permission of American Economic Association.

This paper has presented a panoramic view of the primary economies and diseconomies of urban size. Even though the advantages that cities once gained from being manufacturing centers have disappeared, I believe that agglomeration economies will ultimately continue to be large. Information spillovers will continue to be important and telecommunications may end up helping, rather than hurting, cities.

Nevertheless, cities have major costs and some of these may significantly increase. The likeliest possibility is that the future will be bright for the relatively homogeneous and low density agglomerations of the western United States, which can offer many of the economic advantages of agglomeration while also reducing the costs of congestion and crime. The poorer, more heterogeneous, older cities, however, will have more of a struggle. The future may be one where very specialized agglomerations filled with very particular income groups are the norm. If this vision comes to pass, then I am also sure that our society and economy risks losing a great deal. If it is true that the innovation and growth potential of cities depends on unplanned contacts between diverse individuals, these homogenous cities may prove much less innovative. Moreover, cities already have considerable segregation, and decentralized cities may lead to even less contact between different income and racial groups.

Beyond analyzing trends that affect the cities, economists do have some policy advice they can add. Most cities are far from pricing congestion effectively. Most cities still have land use and building regulations that are completely unconnected with any clear externalities. Many cities still try to redistribute income, despite the costs in terms of attracting the poor and repelling the rich that redistribution at such a micro-level within a metropolitan area can precipitate. A city which wishes to prosper should focus on pricing externalities correctly, protecting property rights and ensuring that human capital can be developed within its borders.

Conclusion from *Cities, Information, and Economic Growth*

EDWARD GLAESER

Source: Cityscape: A Journal of Policy Development and Research, 1, August 1994.

This article has emphasized the role of information in influencing urban form. Many important papers on growth have found that disembodied knowledge and human capital play major roles as engines of growth. This important role in economic growth suggests that any informational role that cities play may be crucial for America's future.

Cities and the spread of population across space interact importantly with information, deriving some of their natural advantages as centers for the flow of new ideas. Cities also have some of their greatest failings when their informational advantages fail to function. It seems that among the most crucial policy issues for the next century is the elimination of the informational barriers between downtown areas and ghettoes.

Abstract from *Industrial Development in Cities*

VERNON HENDERSON, ARI KUNCORO, AND MATT TURNER

Source: Journal of Political Economy, 103(5), 1995, 1067. © 1995 The University of Chicago Press. All rights reserved.

This paper uses data for eight manufacturing industries in 1970 and 1987 to test for and characterize dynamic production externalities in cities. We find evidence of both MAR externalities, which are associated with past own industry employment concentration, and Jacobs externalities, which are associated with past diversity of local total employment. More specifically, for mature capital goods industries, there is evidence of MAR externalities but none of Jacobs externalities. For new high-tech industries, there is evidence of Jacobs and MAR externalities. These findings are consistent with notions of urban specialization and product cycles: new industries prosper in large, diverse metropolitan areas, but with maturity, production decentralizes to smaller, more specialized cities. For mature industries, there is also a high degree of persistence in individual employment patterns across cities, fostered by both MAR externalities and persistence in regional comparative advantage.

Abstract from *Productivity Gains from Geographic Concentrations of Human Capital: Evidence from the Cities*

JAMES E. RAUCH

Source: Journal of Urban Economics, 34, 1993, 380–400. © 1993 Academic Press, Inc. All rights of reproduction in any form reserved.

Based on recent theoretical developments the argument is made that the average level of human capital is a local public good. Cities with higher average levels of human capital should therefore have higher wages and higher land rents. After conditioning on the characteristics of individual workers and dwellings, this prediction is supported by data for Standard Metropolitan Statistical Areas (SMSAs) in the United States, where the SMSA average levels of formal education and work experience are used as proxies for the average level of human capital. The alternative explanations of omitted SMSA variables and self-selection are evaluated. An estimate of the effect of an additional year of average education on total factor productivity is computed.

Discussion Questions

1   *The Draw of Downtown: Big Growth Predicted for Many U.S. Cities* and the *State of the Cities: Downtown is Up* suggest that empty nesters and others are settling downtown to soak up urban buzz and culture. There is a "taste for sports, culture, and entertainment, all of which can be found in town centres." These statements are directly relevant to three of the four factors that Quigley describes in his Table 1 as agglomeration implications of size and diversity. Describe why this is so.

2   Quigley identifies four periods of intense study of cities by economists. Briefly describe each period and the increased understanding of the economics of urban areas that resulted from each.

3   Pick one of the empirical articles that Quigley offers in support of the economic advantages of increased size and diversity in a city and read it. In more detail than given in Quigley's summary, describe why this empirical piece supports Quigley's argument.

4   Are there any disadvantages to increased size and diversity in a city? Describe what they are.

5   As a check on the metropolitan area projections for population given in Mills and Lubuele, find the most recent population figures (for the year 2000 or less) for all metropolitan areas in your state of residence. Compare these actual population figures to the forecasts made in their paper. How accurate are their forecasts? Does their accuracy differ by metropolitan area in your state? What could Mills and Lubuele have accounted for in their regression model to improve their forecast accuracy of metropolitan area population in your state?

PART II:

Location, Land Use, and Urban Sprawl

The only way you could tell you were leaving one community and entering another was when the franchises started repeating and you spotted another 7-Eleven, another Wendy's, another Costco, another Home Depot.

Tom Wolfe

CHAPTER SIX

Dreams of Fields: The New Politics of Urban Sprawl

Timothy Egan

Source: The New York Times, 15.11.98. © 1998 New York Times Company. © 1999 Dow Jones & Company, Inc. All rights reserved.

Seattle – What the author Tom Wolfe did for radical chic in the 1960s, narcissism in the 70s, and greed in the 80s, he may now be doing for runaway real estate development in his new novel on America at century's end. Urban sprawl, with all its strip-mall excess and soul-deadening homogeneity, is not just a central backdrop, but almost a character in "A Man in Full," the author's latest pen poke at contemporary life.

"The only way you could tell you were leaving one community and entering another was when the franchises started repeating and you spotted another 7-Eleven, another Wendy's, another Costco, another Home Depot," Mr. Wolfe writes. He was describing the Bay Area of California, but it could have been any metro area in the country.

On election day, voters from Southern California to New Jersey showed that the sprawl issue may have become a political driving force no less than a narrative function in the fictional world of Mr. Wolfe. Voters across the country and across party lines, from desert suburbs in the West to leafy cul de sacs in the East, voted to stop the march of new malls, homes and business parks at the borders of their communities, and to tax themselves to buy open space as a hedge against future development.

For Vice President Al Gore, who has been ratcheting up the sprawl issue as a top green concern, edging aside more contentious and somewhat abstract environmental concepts like global warming, the votes are seen as the start of a winning national campaign. Who, after all, could be against what the Sierra Club now describes as an attempt to return to Beaver Cleaver's America, albeit with smaller lot sizes?

Paving Paradise

"I've come to the conclusion that what we really are faced with here is a systematic change from a pattern of uncontrolled sprawl toward a brand new path that makes quality of life the goal of all our urban, suburban and farmland policies," Mr. Gore said in an interview. But Republicans like Gov. Christine Todd Whitman of New Jersey, have also listened to the same complaints around the barbecue. At the very edge of what the author Joel Garreau famously labeled "Edge Cities," people say their new communities have become too dependent on the automobile, too removed from nature, too close to the clutter of boxy retail stores.

Paving paradise, almost a reflex reaction in Southern California, was halted by a huge majority in Ventura County, where voters approved a series of urban boundaries around the fast-growing new cities wedged between Los Angeles and Santa Barbara, and stripped their elected supervisors of the power to approve new subdivisions and put it in the hands of voters instead.

Developers now will have to get voter approval to push the flood of tile-roofed subdivisions any further into land that has some of the last big lemon groves in California. About 80 percent of the county will be off-limits to developers, unless voters say differently, supporters of the measure said. The Los Angeles Times heralded the vote as a "revolution." In New Jersey, the most-densely populated state in the nation, voters in 43 cities and six counties decided to raises their taxes to buy and preserve open space. Statewide, by a two-to-one margin, voters also approved spending nearly $1 billion over 10 years to buy half of the Garden State's remaining garden space.

Grass Roots

Nationwide, voters approved nearly 200 state and local ballot initiatives on curbing sprawl.

The idea of Al Gore talking growth management for the next two years and beyond may be no more appealing than hearing another flat tax speech from Steve Forbes. The Vice President has been pounding the anti-sprawl bully pulpit for months, proclaiming the dawn of "an American movement to build more liveable communities." The issue is seen by his supporters as a key to all those Jeep Cherokee driving suburbanites with few political passions beyond the afternoon traffic jam. The elections earlier this month, based largely on grass-roots initiatives, have only bolstered Mr. Gore's case, his aides say.

But before Mr. Gore tries to lay a Democratic claim to an issue that cuts beyond most political lines, he will have to go through the Republican Governor of New Jersey. Just five years ago, Mrs. Whitman was held up by her party as a young Margaret Thatcher, with tax cuts as her banner. Now, a year into a second term, Mrs. Whitman has made protecting open space the primary issue – and perhaps her legacy – for the state. In what may be an act of heresy to the tax-cutting wing of her party, the Governor has been campaigning for tax increases to keep land out of the hands of developers. Initially, she proposed an increase in the gas tax, but has settled on the kind of selective property tax increases that were approved across New Jersey on election day. "We have got to understand that once land is gone, it's gone forever," said Mrs. Whitman while pushing the new open space measures. She could have been just another doorbeller from the Sierra Club, which, in response to a survey of members, has put sprawl at the top of its list of environmental concerns. The club says 400,000 acres of open space are lost to development every year.

The successful anti-sprawl campaigns steered away from talk of Government control or zoning arcana. They dwelled instead on images of lemon groves and tawny hills in Southern California, pumpkin patches and horse farms in New Jersey, and wind-whipped dunes in Cape Cod – all just beyond the exurban fringe. "We're not trying to subvert the

American dream – we're trying to get back to it," said Larry Bohlen, co-chairman of the Sierra Club's national campaign to fight sprawl. "It's that 'Leave it to Beaver' town where all the kids walk to school."

Opponents of these measures, led in California by home builders and developers, say the new political calculation could change in the blink of an eye if the economy turns bad. In bad times, people are less likely to vote to restrict growth. But in Oregon, which pioneered boundaries around all its major cities in the 1970s, voters have upheld the state's far-reaching anti- sprawl laws even during the depths of two recessions over the last 20 years. Developers say the votes this month were not so much an anti-growth chorus as they were a reflection of the frustration people feel over traffic and crowded schools. Still, the opponents say they are stunned by how quickly suburban growth has become a pejorative. "We seem to be at a point now where the word sprawl has been totally demonized," said Clayton Traylor, vice president for political issues for the National Association of Home Builders, which has 195,000 members.

Washington politicians may find it difficult to nationalize what is basically a local issue. Mr. Gore has raised the possibility of using the Federal tax code or major transportation bills to discourage growth that goes against community planning goals. "In the past, we adopted national policies that spend lots of taxpayer money to subsidize out-of-control sprawl," Mr. Gore said. "They suck the life out of urban areas, increase congestion in the suburbs and raise taxes on farms."

Mr. Gore is vague on what, precisely, could be done on a national level. But whatever he attempts to do will be met by stiff opposition if it ends up slowing development, Mr. Traylor said. Building lobbies for highways and some conservatives were outraged that the $217 billion transportation bill that was just approved by Congress contained a small amount of money for bike paths. "To the extent that the Vice President or anyone else at the Federal level tries to turn off the spigot for new infrastructure, we'll be there to fight them," Mr. Traylor said.

In Maryland, however, turning off the spigot proved to be a winning political cry, as supporters of new developments were hastily dispatched on election day. A Republican who favored two huge projects in Anne Arundel County, County Executive John G. Gary, was voted out of office, while Republicans who vowed to pull the plug on new water and sewage systems in neighboring Calvert County took control of the Board of Commissioners.

Homebuilders Heartened

In other states, developers have tried to co-opt the anti-sprawl movement. Arizona voters narrowly approved a measure, sponsored by the state's banking and building industry, that would set aside $20 million a year for 11 years to buy open space. But in return, the law would ban development fees and urban growth restrictions. The homebuilders were heartened by at least one of the sprawl votes that went the other way. In Georgia, voters turned down a measure to use a real estate transfer tax to preserve historical sites and open space. Georgia is the main setting for Mr. Wolfe's novel, a place where a huge, troubled development at the far edge of suburban Atlanta is at the core of one man's decline.

CHAPTER SEVEN

Al Gore Has a New Worry: "Smart Growth" to Cure "Suburban Sprawl" is the Newest Rationale for Government Growth

GEORGE F. WILL

Source: Newsweek, 15.2.99

IT IS BACK TO THE 1950S FOR LIBERALISM. ITS NEXT PALADIN, Al Gore, is alarmed about suburban "sprawl." That issue is the political equivalent of a 45 rpm record of The Platters' "The Great Pretender," or a stroll down memory lane in white-and-black saddle shoes with red rubber soles. It is so old it may seem new, and is fresh evidence of Gore's propensity for muddy, hackneyed and semihysterical thinking.

He has a talent – no, a virtuosity – for alarm, having pronounced our entire civilization "dysfunctional." Bill Clinton, too, is alarmed. His State of the Union Message – speaking of unregulated sprawl – advocated a "Livability Agenda" to control growth. But Gore is the real revivalist of the aesthetic politics that blossomed in the 1950s, when liberalism began to look askance at middle-class America.

He proposes $10 billion of "Better America Bonds" to prod communities to enhance their "livability" by planning "smart growth," particularly to preserve green space. This will prevent what a Gore enthusiast at the Sierra Club calls "low-density, habitat-globbling, traffic-creating growth."

Well. Seventy-five percent more families live in suburbs than in cities because they like using the freedom conferred by the automobile to make their habitats in low-density communities. This preference has long dismayed many liberals, who rather resent the automobile, which allows ordinary people to move around without the supervision of liberals. In the 1950s, liberals identified suburbanization with soulless bourgeois conformity, and flight from the stimulating social conditions (crime, poverty, filth, inferior schools, etc.) of the cities that liberals governed.

Now, green space is good and, within reason, government's business. But Gore's environmentalism seems to make *everything* government's business: Society is manageable and so should be managed by the far-seeing and fastidious political class.

"Bad planning," he says, "has too often distorted our towns and landscapes out of all recognition." Wait. What exactly has been "distorted"? Who cannot recognize what?

"Ill-thought-out sprawl," he says, has turned "what used to be friendly, easy suburbs into lonely cul-de-sacs" where "kids learn more about Nintendo and isolation than about fresh air and taking turns."

A "livable" suburb is one to which one commutes quickly. (More highways? Environmentalists will get the vapors.) Gore is alarmed that Americans waste time in congestion. (But the average commute has not appreciably increased in any urban area in 20 years. Steven Hayward of The Heritage Foundation says congestion has increased largely because vehicle miles traveled have increased four times faster than the population, and that is largely because of women joining the work force and minorities joining the middle class and getting cars.) Gore says "coordinated" growth (will the coordinators of our lives be nice?) preserves "some family farms" and a "natural ecosystem." Otherwise, growth will be "unsustainable," meaning...

Meaning is not Gore's forte. Does he worry that unsustainable growth will be sustained? Is a suburb without a family farm *un*livable? Gore worries about traffic into and out from central cities, but most commutes are between suburbs, where most jobs are now created. And here we go again: President Johnson's administration worried (Harry McPherson's memoir tells us) about "middle-class women, bored and friendless in the suburban afternoons."

Government – highways and subsidized mortgages – fostered the suburbanization Gore deplores. Now he wants government, author of the disaster known cheerily as "urban renewal," to inflict suburban renewal. So liberalism is about to suffer an acute case of Portland Envy. Hayward says the Oregon city is using zoning and other measures to produce high-density living by promoting multifamily housing such as row houses and shrinking the average lot size. To preserve land for high-density housing, "big box" retailers are discouraged. These include Wal-Mart, Price Club, Home Depot, but affluent liberals, including government planners, do not shop there. Predictably, housing costs are rising much faster in Portland than in rapidly growing but less regulated Western cities such as Phoenix, Las Vegas and Salt Lake.

At the beginning of this millennium, the world's largest city may have been Cordoba, Spain, with a population of 450,000. If so, an Iberian Gore was probably alarmed by the sprawl of it all. Gore says America "is losing 50 acres of farmland to development each hour." Gracious. But suburban expansion consumes just 0.0006 percent of the continental United States annually. And Gore's government says the amount of farmland has been fairly constant – more than 450 million acres – since 1945. To support commodity prices in the face of soaring agricultural productivity, Gore's government pays more than $1.7 billion annually to make cropland idle – more land than is devoted to *all* the nation's urban uses.

Analysts James D. Riggle and Jonathan Tolman note that New England woodlands now cover what once were thousands of family farms that could not compete with the more productive farms of the Midwest and Great Plains. Does that woodland depress Gore? The Department of Agriculture says: "Loss of farmland poses no threat to U.S. food and fiber production."

Economic analyst Irwin Stelzer says that as 30,000 people migrate to Phoenix every year, lawns replace desert at the rate of about an acre an hour. Is that alarming? When about 20 new houses go up every day in one of America's fastest-growing metropolitan areas, Las Vegas, does Gore grieve for the gobbled-up "habitat" of arid southern Nevada?

"In America," Gertrude Stein said, "there is more space where nobody is than where anybody is – that is what makes America what it is." That is still true, and so is this:

The purpose of "smart," "coordinated" growth is to prevent the masses, in their freedom, from producing democracy's byproducts – untidiness and even vulgarity. And the bland notion of "planning" often is the rubric under which government operates when making its preferences and prophecies – often meaning its arrogance and its mistakes – mandatory.

CHAPTER EIGHT

Urban Spatial Structure

ALEX ANAS, RICHARD ARNOTT AND KENNETH A. SMALL*

Source: Journal of Economic Literature, 36, September 1998, 1426–64.
Reprinted by permission of American Economic Association.

1. Introduction

AN INTERVIEW WITH Chicago's current mayor, Richard M. Daley:

> "New York is too big this way," the mayor says, raising a thick hand over his head. Stretching both arms out at his sides, he adds, "Los Angeles is too big this way. All the other cities are too small. We're just right." (Jeff Bailey and Calmetta Coleman 1996, p. 6)

Mayor Daley's remarks reflect a widespread fascination with the roles that urban size and structure play in people's lives. Academic as well as other observers have long sought explanations for urban development patterns and criteria by which to judge their desirability. Furthermore, as we shall see, understanding the organization of cities yields insights into economy-wide growth processes and sheds light on economic concepts of long-standing interest: returns to scale, monopolistic competition, vertical integration, technological innovation, innovation diffusion, and international specialization. Cities also are prime illustrations of some newer academic interests such as complex structural evolution and self-organization.

In this essay we offer a view of what economics can say about and learn from urban spatial structure. In doing so, we reach into neighboring disciplines, but we do not aspire to a complete survey even of urban economics, much less of the related fields of urban geography, urban planning, or regional science. Our focus is on describing and explaining urban spatial structure and its evolution.

This is a particularly interesting time to study urban structure because cities' growth patterns are undergoing qualitative change.[1] For two centuries at least, cities have been spreading out. But in recent decades, this process of decentralization has taken a more polycentric form, with a number of concentrated employment centers making their mark on both employment and population distributions. Most of these centers are subsidiary to

* The authors would like to thank John Pencavel, three referees, Robert Bacon, Amihai Glazer, Peter Gordon, Robert Johnston, Cassey Lee Hong Kim, and David Pines for helpful comments on earlier drafts, and Alexander Kalenik for assistance in the preparation of Figure 1. We also thank the University of California Transportation Center for financial assistance.

an older central business district (CBD), hence are called "subcenters." Some subcenters are older towns that gradually became incorporated into an expanded but coherent urban area. Others are newly spawned at nodes of a transportation network, often so far from the urban core as to earn the appellation "edge cities" (Joel Garreau 1991). There is some evidence, discussed later, that the employment centers within a given urban region form an interdependent system, with a size distribution and a pattern of specialization analogous to the system of cities in a larger regional or national economy.

At the same time, rampant dispersion of economic activity has continued outside centers altogether, prompting Peter Gordon and Harry Richardson (1996) to proclaim that Los Angeles, at least, is "beyond polycentricity." But even sprawl is far from homogeneous, and geographers have perceived patterns that conform to the mathematics of highly irregular structures such as fractals. Whether such irregularity is really new, or even increasing, is not so clear, as we shall see in the next section; but urban economics helps us understand the order that may be hidden in such patterns.

An important source of current change in urban structure is the changing economic relationships within and between firms. Telecommunications, information-intensive activities, deregulation, and global competition have all contributed to changes in the functions that firms do in-house, and in how those functions are spatially organized. Some internal interactions can now be handled via telecommunications with remote offices which already perform routine activities such as accounting. Some vertical interactions are now more advantageously made as external transactions among separate firms, possibly requiring even more frequent face-to-face communications because of the need for contracting. Allen Scott (1988, 1991) describes how such "vertical disintegration" has shaped the geographical structure of a number of industries in southern California, including electronics, animated films, and women's clothing. Meanwhile, firms are developing new interactive modes which are neither market nor hierarchy, but rather constitute what Walter Powell (1990) calls a "network" organizational form, characterized by "relationship contracting" and having unknown implications for locational propensities.

The research agenda that emerges from these observations is heavy on economies of agglomeration, a term which refers to the decline in average cost as more production occurs within a specified geographical area. One class of agglomeration economies is intra-firm economies of scale and scope that take place at a single location. Another class is positive technological and pecuniary externalities that arise between economic agents in close spatial proximity[2] due, for example, to knowledge spillovers, access to a common specialized labor pool, or economies of scale in producing intermediate goods. Agglomeration economies may be dynamic as well as static, and are suspected of giving cities a key role in generating aggregate economic growth (Jane Jacobs 1984; Edward Glaeser et al. 1992).

Any agglomerative or "centripetal" force, even one caused just by a unique resource such as a harbor, places a premium on land at certain locations. This encourages spatially concentrated capital formation (buildings) and accentuates the need to produce at discrete points in space because of increasing returns to scale in production (David Starrett 1974). Because of these pervasive externalities and nonconvexities, economic analysis when applied to urban geography yields results that differ in important and interesting ways from results of other branches of economics. Agglomeration economies also create first-mover advantages and regional specializations that are important in international trade (Paul Krugman 1991a), and some first-mover disadvantages that prevent optimal dynamic growth paths from being realized. We discuss these in Section 5.

Agglomeration economies are, of course, not new. As eloquently exposited by Raymond Vernon (1960) and Benjamin Chinitz (1961), they are at the heart of our current understanding of central business districts. But recent changes in the technology of agglomeration, due to advances in information processing and telecommunications, may profoundly alter the pattern of spatial development (Jess Gaspar and Glaeser 1998). Understanding these new forces will help us understand newly emerging forms of urban structure as well as basic determinants of industrial structure and interregional and international trade.

While our focus is on explaining urban spatial structure as a result of market processes, we touch on two related issues as well. The first concerns the role of government. Government policies – notably land-use controls and the provision of transportation infrastructure – play a major role in shaping cities. What can we say about optimal policy? The second issue concerns the importance of space in economics. Accounting for location yields new insights into economic phenomena that are normally analyzed in aspatial models. But what is the level of spatial resolution at which such phenomena are best analyzed?

2. History and Description of Urban Spatial Structure

We begin with a sketch of how urban form has evolved in modern times, followed by some observations on how to measure its characteristics.

2.1. Recent evolution of urban form

The spatial structure of modern cities was shaped, in large measure, by advances in transport and communication. The history of urban development in North America since colonial times allows us to document aspects of this process (Charles Glaab and Theodore Brown 1967).

Prior to about 1840, most cities were tied to waterways such as harbors, rivers, and canals. The average cost of processing freight fell sharply with the quantity processed at a particular port, creating substantial scale economies at harbors or river junctions with access to the sea. Similarly, as railroads competed with waterways later in the 19th century, scale economies in rail terminals created accessibility advantages near them as well. Meanwhile intra-urban freight transport took place mainly by horse and wagon, which was time consuming and unreliable in bad weather. These conditions favored the growth of a single manufacturing district located near the harbor or railhead, with residences surrounding it (Leon Moses and Harold Williamson 1967).

In the last quarter of the century, the telegraph greatly speeded the flow of information from city to city (Alexander Field 1992). But economies of scale prevented it from being used much within a city – instead, messengers remained the primary means of intra-city business communication. The high cost of intra-urban communication meant that even light manufacturing and service industries tended to concentrate within the central manufacturing core, as shown for New York by Chinitz (1960). But this small core area was far from homogeneous; rather, it was divided into districts, each specialized in an activity such as commercial banking, pawnbrokerage, or light or heavy manufacturing. In late nineteenth-century Chicago, four-fifths of the city's jobs were located within four miles of State and Madison streets, according to Raymond Fales and Moses (1972), who go on to show how a pattern of specialized districts arose due to agglomerative forces within industries and the linkages among them.

Before 1850, personal transport within the city was mainly by foot and horse-drawn carriage, causing the great majority of rich and poor alike to live close to the city center. For the most part, the rich outbid the poor for the most central and hence most convenient sites, so that income declined markedly with distance from the CBD, as is documented in studies of Milwaukee, Pittsburgh, and Toronto (Stephen LeRoy and Jon Sonstelie 1983).

Between 1850 and 1900, the advent of horse-drawn and then electric streetcars enabled large numbers of upper- and middle-income commuters to move further out. This migration gave rise to "streetcar suburbs," residential enclaves organized around a station on a radial streetcar line (Sam Warner 1962). Toward the turn of the century, subways further contributed to this pattern in the largest cities. Thus developed a spatial structure now known as the "nineteenth century city," consisting of a compact production core surrounded by an apron of residences concentrated around mass transport spokes.

The next big changes were the dissemination of the internal combustion engine and the telephone in the early twentieth century. Gradually the horse and wagon were replaced by the small urban truck, and the messenger by the telephone. For example, in the single decade from 1910 to 1920, truck registrations in Chicago increased from 800 to 23,000, while horse-drawn vehicle registrations dropped almost by half. Moses and Williamson (1967) estimate that variable costs and travel time for the truck were less than half those for the horse and wagon. The truck and the telephone allowed businesses to spread outward from the center, thereby taking advantage of lower land values while maintaining their links to the central port or railhead. Thus central business districts expanded. In Chicago, firms that moved in 1920 located on average 1.5 miles from the core, as opposed to 0.92 miles in 1908 (Moses and Williamson 1967).

The automobile, at first restricted to richer families, rapidly increased in importance with assembly-line production of the Model T Ford starting in 1908. Cars broadened the coverage of motorized personal transport, causing the areas between the streetcar suburbs to be settled and the residential apron to expand. The automobile competed successfully with mass transit, despite transit fares remaining flat in nominal terms from the beginning of the century until approximately World War II; it did this mainly by providing speed, privacy, and convenience, although it was also facilitated by an active program of building and upgrading public roads (Paul Barrett 1983).

As assembly-line production became widespread, the lower capital–land ratios charac-terized by flat buildings increased the attractiveness of locations where land was cheap. Nevertheless, even at mid-century many producers outside the core were bound to the central harbors and rail terminals for inter-city shipments. Eventually, however, this link was weakened by the creation of suburban rail terminals and the declining cost of inter-city trucking, the latter facilitated by the interstate highway system. These developments, coming primarily after World War II, enabled manufacturing to leapfrog out to the outermost suburbs. Central cities began their painful transition from manufacturing to service and office centers.

Due to the durability of the urban capital stock and urban infrastructure, cities in the modern American landscape bear proof of the lasting impacts of these developments. Large cities of the eastern seaboard and the midwest, such as Boston or Detroit, still contain streets and buildings dating from the heyday of their harbor and rail operations and from the subsequent era of radial mass transportation systems. Even Chicago, the great metropolis of the midwest, was first established as one of the last and western-most of the waterway cities – its later importance as a rail and air hub derived from its already well established position by the beginning of the rail era (William Cronon 1991). Further west, however, the spatial pattern of many urban settlements was first shaped by the railroad. Major cities, such as Oklahoma City, Denver, Omaha, and Salt Lake City, grew up around rail nodes and developed compact CBDs centered on rail terminals. In contrast, the even later automobile-era cities such as Dallas, Houston, and Phoenix have spatial structures determined mainly by the highway system. Los Angeles is an intermediate case: partly a western rail terminus and partly a set of residential communities populated by rail-based migration from the American midwest, its many towns became connected to each other by high-speed highways and eventually merged into one vast metropolis.

The most recent phase is the growth of "edge cities" in the suburban and even the outermost reaches of large metropolitan areas, both old and new (Garreau 1991). An edge city is characterized by large concentrations of office and retail space, often in conjunction with other types of development, including residential, at the nodes of major express highways. Most are in locations where virtually no development, possibly excepting a small town, existed prior to 1960. In many cases, the initial design and construction was the product of a single development company, even a single individual. Edge cities are made possible by ubiquitous automobile access, even when they are located at a transit station, as occasionally happens.[3]

Cities in western Europe have evolved somewhat differently. Being much older, many still have centers which started out as medieval towns. There is a greater mixture of residences and businesses in the core, possibly because of the rich cultural amenities there. Apartment buildings are more common and public transportation more important. Nevertheless, as in North America, there has been massive suburbanization and the emergence of edge cities.

2.2. Describing urban structure

Using basic land-use data, scholars have sought to describe the regularities and irregularities of urban structure. We are particularly interested in the degree of spatial concentration of urban population and employment. We distinguish between two types of spatial concentration. At the city-wide level, activity may be relatively *centralized* or *decentralized* depending on how concentrated it is near a central business district. The degree of centralization has been studied mainly by estimating monocentric density functions, and is discussed in Section 3. At a more local level, activities may be *clustered* in a polycentric pattern or *dispersed* in a more regular pattern. It is this clustering that has captured the recent attention of both theoretical and empirical economists.

Defining such clusters precisely, however, is not so easy. If one uses three-dimensional graphics to plot urban density across two-dimensional space, one is struck by how jagged the picture becomes at finer resolutions. An example is presented in Figure 1, which plots 1990 employment density in Los Angeles County (a portion of the Los Angeles urban region) using a single data set plotted at three different degrees of spatial averaging.[4] A

Figure 1.   Employment density, Los Angeles County, 1990, at different resolutions.
Source: Authors' plots of data from Southern California Association of Governments.

similar lesson from the fractal approach discussed below is that within a fixed area, development that appears relatively homogenous at a coarse scale may actually contain a great deal of fine structure. Where fine structure is present, it becomes somewhat arbitrary to say how large a concentration of employment is required to define a location as a subcenter. Even an isolated medical office has a high employment density when viewed at the scale of the building footprint, but we would not call it a subcenter. What about a cluster of twenty medical offices? What if this cluster is adjacent to a hospital and a shopping center? The distinction between an organized system of subcenters and apparently unorganized urban sprawl depends very much on the spatial scale of observation.

We consider three approaches to describing the fine structure of urban development. The first two are ways of mathematically describing distributions of points in space. The third is the basis for extensions of monocentric density functions to a polycentric pattern.

The first approach, called *point pattern analysis*, defines various statistics involving distances between observed units of development (R. W. Thomas 1981). These statistics are then compared with theoretical distributions. One such comparison distribution is that resulting from perturbations of a regular lattice, such as is postulated by one variant of central place theory (Walter Christaller 1933) in which development occurs in a hierarchy of centers, each with a hexagonal market area. Another comparison distribution is that resulting from purely random location, which can be described as a Poisson process. An example of the use of point pattern analysis is the search for population clusters in the Chicago area by Arthur Getis (1983).

A more recent approach to describing urban spatial patterns is based on the idea that they resemble *fractals*, geometric figures which display ever-finer structure when viewed at finer resolutions. Mathematically, a fractal is the limiting result of a process of repeatedly replicating, at smaller and smaller scales, the same geometric element. Thus the fractal has a similar shape no matter what scale is employed for viewing it. If the original element is one-dimensional, the fractal's length becomes infinite as one measures it at a finer and finer resolution; the classic example is a coastline. One plus the elasticity of measured length with respect to resolution is known as the *fractal dimension*. For example, a coastline might have length L when measured on a map that can just resolve 100-meter features, and $L \times 10^{D-1}$ when 10-meter features can be seen; its fractal dimension would then be D, at least within that resolution range. A perfectly straight coastline has fractal dimension one, since its length does not increase with the level of resolution.

Geographers have used fractals to examine the irregularity of the line marking the outer edge of urban development in a particular urban region. Michael Batty and Paul Longley (1994, pp. 174–79) use data on land development in Cardiff, Wales, to define such a boundary to an accuracy as fine as 11 meters. Their best estimates of the fractal dimension of this boundary are between 1.15 and 1.29. (By way of comparison, Britain's coastline has fractal dimension 1.25, Australia's 1.13.) Surprisingly, they find that the fractal dimension of Cardiff's outer edge of development declined slightly over the time period examined (1886 to 1922), a period of significant transport improvements, mainly in the form of streetcars. They conclude that "the traditional image of urban growth becoming more irregular as tentacles of development occur around transport lines is not borne out" (p. 185).

More significantly, one can use fractals to represent two-dimensional development patterns, thereby capturing irregularity in the interior as well as at the boundary of the developed area. For example, a fractal can be generated mathematically by starting with a large filled-in square, then selectively deleting smaller and smaller squares so as to create self-similar patterns at smaller and smaller scales. Such a process simulates the existence of undeveloped land inside the urban boundary. The fractal dimension D for this situation can be measured by observing how rapidly the fraction of zones containing urban development falls as zonal size is decreased, i.e., as resolution becomes finer. (More precisely, D is twice the elasticity of the number of zones containing any development with respect to the total number of zones into which the fixed urban area is divided.) We call this dimension the *areal fractal dimension*; it can vary from 0, indicating that nearly all the interior space is empty when examined at a fine enough resolution, to 2, indicating that each coarsely-defined zone that contains development is in fact fully developed. Long narrow development would have $D = 1$ (since as we increase the total number N of zones into which a well-defined region is divided, the number of zones containing any development would grow only as $\sqrt{N}$).

Batty and Longley (1994, Table 7.1) report estimated areal fractal dimensions for many cities around the world, with the result most often in the range 1.55 to 1.85. For Paris in 1981 the estimate is 1.66. For Los Angeles in the same year, it is 1.93, tied with Beijing for the highest among the 28 cities reported. This latter estimate implies that the fraction of area developed is almost constant at different scales, indicating a relative absence of fine-structure irregularities in development patterns. Apparently Los Angeles has grown in a more homogeneous manner than Cardiff or Paris.

Time series observations of London from 1820 to 1962, and of Berlin from 1875 to 1945, suggest that the areal fractal dimension has been increasing steadily throughout these time periods. This lends further support to the conclusion that urban growth during the industrial era has made development patterns somewhat more regular, at least in western Europe. Batty and Longley suggest that a possible reason is the more extensive imposition of land-use controls and other forms of urban planning.

Unfortunately, the estimated areal fractal dimension of a city is quite sensitive to just how the land-use data are summarized (Batty and Longley, p. 236). Another problem is that in such a measurement, a city's fine structure is assumed to look like a miniature of the coarse structure, whereas in fact the processes operating at the micro and macro scales are probably very different: fine structure may reflect local zoning rules or developers' detailed design strategies, while coarse structure may reflect regional planning, regional transportation facilities, or land speculation based on anticipated regional growth. Nevertheless, the fractal approach highlights the inadequacy of a deterministic view of development, adopted especially in earlier economic models, in accounting for the irregularities in urban structure. As we discuss in Section 5, more recent advances such as random utility theory enable us to deal with irregularities in a way that is better suited to economic modeling.

Most urban economists have used more intuitive, if simplified, depictions of urban structure, identifying one or more *employment centers* and estimating how these centers affect employment and population densities around them. Much of the early literature on subcenters used criteria based on local knowledge in planning organizations or real estate firms. More recent work has used objective definitions based on employment data for a large number of zones within a metropolitan area (John McDonald 1987). Genevieve Giuliano and Kenneth Small (1991) define a "center" – either a main center (the one containing the CBD) or a subcenter – as a cluster of contiguous zones, all with gross employment density exceeding some minimum $\bar{D}$, and together containing total employment exceeding some minimum $\bar{E}$. Thus a center contains a peak of employment density, yet substantial intermixing of population is not precluded. This definition facilitates comparisons across cities and among the various centers within a city, including the main center. But as we shall see in Section 4, where we describe some empirical uses of such definitions, the exact pattern of centers so defined may be quite sensitive to the choice of cutoff values $\bar{D}$ and $\bar{E}$. Once again, we find that urban structure is inconveniently irregular and scale-dependent – features that are important clues to the scale-dependent processes governing agglomeration in the modern world.

3. The Monocentric City Model

The monocentric city model was the most influential depiction of urban structure for at least two decades, following its formulation by William Alonso (1964) as an adaptation of Johann von Thünen's (1826) theory of agricultural land use. The model was quickly broadened to include production, transport, and housing, and has been generalized in many ways since.[5] It has proved extremely fertile because it provides a rigorous framework for analyzing the spatial aspects of the general-equilibrium adjustments that take place in cities, and for empirically measuring and comparing the degree of centralization across cities and time periods. In this section we present the basic model and illustrate how it can be used to explain historic trends in the suburbanization of households.

3.1 The basic model

In the model's simplest form, the city is envisaged as a circular residential area surrounding a central business district (CBD) of radius x_c, in which all jobs are located. The theory distinguishes between an *open* city with perfectly elastic population size (due to costless migration) and a *closed* city with fixed population. We deal here with the closed case. Each of N identical households receives utility $u(z, L)$ from a numeraire good z and a residential lot of size L.[6] A household located x miles from the CBD incurs annual transport cost $T(x)$, normally interpreted as commuting cost to the CBD. Each household has exogenous income y which must cover expenditures on the numeraire good, land at unit rent $r(x)$, and transport. Normally $T(x)$ is interpreted as including the value of travel time, so y must include the value of some time endowment.

We define the residential *bid rent* $b(x, \bar{u})$ at location x as the maximum rent per unit land area that a household can pay and still receive utility $\bar{u}$:

$$b(x, \bar{u}) = \max_{z, L} \frac{y - T(x) - Z}{L} \text{ s.t. } u(z, L) \geq \bar{u} \tag{1}$$

By the envelope theorem, the slope of the bid-rent function is

$$\frac{db(x, \bar{u})}{dx} = -\frac{T'(x)}{L[y - T(x), \bar{u}]} \tag{2}$$

where $L[.]$ is the solution to the maximization in (1). Equation (2) is one of the most basic results of the monocentric model, and is entirely intuitive. A household located a small additional distance dx from the CBD incurs additional transport cost $T'(x)dx$. To keep this household indifferent between the two locations, lot rent must be lower at the more distant location by the same amount: that is, $L db = -T'(x)dx$.

For each household, there is a family of residential bid-rent functions, indexed by $\bar{u}$. Households are treated as identical and costlessly mobile. Hence, they all obtain the same utility in equilibrium, and the equilibrium rent function $r(x)$ coincides with one of these bid-rent functions. To determine which one, two conditions are needed. First, there is an arbitrage condition at the city boundary (whose value x^* is yet to be determined): residential rent there must equal the rent on land in non-urban use, r_A. (This opportunity cost of land, often called "agricultural rent," is assumed not to vary with location.) Second, all households must be accommodated, which means the integral of household density $(1/L)$ over the residential area must equal the number of households:

$$\int_{x_c}^{x^*} \frac{\varphi(x)}{L[y - T(x), \bar{u}]} dx = N \tag{3}$$

where $\varphi(x)dx$ is the residential land area between x and $x + dx$.[7] These two conditions provide two equations in the unknowns x^* and $\bar{u}$; we denote the solution for $\bar{u}$ by u^e.

The land rent at any location is the maximum of the bid rents there:

$$r(x) = \max [b(x, u^e), r_A] = \begin{cases} b(x, u^e) & \text{for } x \leq x^* \\ r_A & \text{for } x > x^* \end{cases} \tag{4}$$

This expresses the principle that, in the land market, each piece of land goes to the highest-bidding use. This principle is the basis for generalizing the model to more than one type of household or to other sectors bidding on land outside the CBD; in such generalizations, the market rent function is the upper envelope of applicable bid-rent functions.

The comparative statics of the model were first fully worked out by William Wheaton (1974). To illustrate their derivation, consider the case of an increase in household population, N. This causes no change in the family of bid-rent functions (1) or in the lot-size function L[.] corresponding to any given net income and utility. But from (3) the higher population would create excess demand for land if the solution were unchanged. Equilibrium is reestablished with higher densities, lower utility, a steeper rent function, and an expanded outer boundary.

Land use in the simple monocentric model is efficient – that is, the equilibrium density pattern is Pareto optimal (Fujita 1989). This is basically because there are no externalities; land-use decisions are based entirely on trade-offs between desire for space and recognition of commuting costs, both of which are purely private. The need for commuting is exogenous in the model, so no agglomerative effects are present. Of course, these nice properties disappear in more realistic models with congestion, air pollution, neighborhood quality effects, and economies of agglomeration – the last being of prime interest in this essay.

Several comments are in order about the limitations of the monocentric model. The model implicitly assumes that businesses have steeper bid-rent functions than residents, so that all jobs are centrally located. But most of its results can follow from the weaker assumption that employment is dispersed in a circularly symmetric manner, so long as it is less dispersed than residences – that is, within any circle there are more jobs than resident workers. In this case the wage varies over location so as to offset differences in commuting costs (Robert Solow 1973; Michelle White 1988), and commuters still choose to travel radially inward to work.

The model is also easily extended to incorporate different groups of residents. For example, it can predict the pattern of residential location by income. In order to do this, marginal transport cost $T'(x)$ has to be reinterpreted to include the shadow value of time, which turns out to be its dominant component in modern developed nations. (Deriving this shadow value endogenously would require adding leisure and a time budget to the model.) Because this shadow value rises with income, so does marginal transport cost. If $T'(x)$ is less elastic with respect to income than is lot size $L[.]$, equation (2) predicts that rich households will have flatter bid-rent functions than poor households and hence will locate more peripherally. Whether this condition holds for a typical U.S. city is under some dispute (Wheaton 1977).

A more fundamental limitation is that the model is static. Two interpretations are possible, both unrealistic. One is that the model describes a stationary state with durable housing, which a real city would approach asymptotically. The other is that the model describes short-term equilibrium at a point in time, with perishable housing being continuously replaced. The trouble with both interpretations is that the typical life-times of buildings greatly exceed the time over which the model's parameters can be expected to remain unchanged.

3.2 Explanations of post-war suburbanization

What has the monocentric model enabled us to say about the dramatic changes in urban structure over the last century and a half? It obviously throws no light on the trend toward polycentricity. If it applies to anything, it should help explain the broad population decentralization that has occurred in most cities of the world (Mills and Jee Peng Tan 1980). To see how the model performs, we need to quantify the empirically observed trends and provide some plausible parameters for the model.

Pioneered by Colin Clark (1951), researchers have estimated urban population density functions for an enormous range of places and times.[8] In most of this work, a negative exponential function is assumed: $D(x) = D_0 e^{-\gamma x}$ where $D(x)$ is population density at distance x from the CBD and D_0 and γ are positive constants. The negative exponential function is convenient because it is easy to estimate after taking logarithms. The constant $\gamma \equiv -D'/D$ is the proportional rate at which population density falls with distance and is known as the *density gradient*. It is a useful index of population centralization.

Two of the strongest empirical regularities relating to urban spatial structure can be concisely stated using the gradient as defined earlier. First, density declines with distance from the center – the density gradient is positive. Second, virtually all cities in the developed world and most others elsewhere have decentralized over the last century or more – the density gradient has declined over time. Table 1 provides just a tiny sampling of empirical support for these assertions; corroborating evidence is provided for Japan by Mills and Katsutoshi Ohta (1976), for Latin America by Gregory Ingram and Alan Carroll

Table 1 Some estimates of population density gradients

City	Year	Density Gradient (per mile)
London	1801	1.26
	1841	0.93
	1901	0.37
	1931	0.27
	1939	0.23
	1961	0.14
Paris	1817	2.35
	1856	0.95
	1896	0.80
	1931	0.76
	1946	0.34
Frankfurt	1890	1.87
	1933	0.92
Birmingham, UK	1921	0.80
	1938	0.47
Rangoon	1931	1.16
	1951	0.55
New York	1900	0.32
	1940	0.21
	1950	0.18
Chicago	1880	0.77
	1900	0.40
	1940	0.21
	1956	0.18
Los Angeles	1940	0.27
Boston	1900	0.85
	1940	0.31
Sydney	1911	0.48
	1954	0.26
Christchurch	1911	1.61
	1951	1.34

Source: Clark (1967, pp. 349–51), converted from km to miles.

(1981), and for a number of developing nations by Mills and Tan (1980). Any persuasive theory of urban spatial structure should accord with these facts.

Urban economists' standard explanation for decentralization is a combination of rising incomes and declining transport costs, both of which cause the density gradient to decline according to the monocentric model. The second part of this explanation is not entirely satisfactory, however, because the largest portion of transport cost is user time, whose value tends to rise with wages, creating a strong force counteracting improvements in travel speeds. It is therefore worth taking a closer look at the magnitudes of the parameters governing the density gradient.

In order to most conveniently match theory with empirical measurement, we first consider a specific set of assumptions that lead to the negative exponential population density function.[9] Suppose the utility function is Cobb–Douglas, $u(z, L) = z^\alpha L^{1-\alpha}$. Suppose also that the ratio of marginal transport cost to income net of transport cost, $T'/(y - T)$, is constant across locations – reflecting the fact that congestion is least in peripheral locations from which total commuting cost is greatest. Then the population density function is negative exponential with gradient

$$\gamma = \frac{\alpha T'/y}{(1 - \alpha)[1 - (T/y)]} \tag{5}$$

.

Land rent is also negative exponential, with gradient γ/α, while net income $y - T$ and marginal transport cost T' are each negative exponential with gradient $(1 - \alpha)\gamma/\alpha$.

Using empirically plausible point estimates for the right-hand side of (5), from parameters appropriate for U.S. cities around 1970, we can calculate a gradient of $\gamma = 0.234$ per mile.[10] By way of comparison, Edmonston (1975, Table 5.5) and Mills and Ohta (1976) report average values of 0.38 and 0.12, respectively, for various samples of U.S. cities in 1970. So our "guesstimate" of (5) is near the average of their estimates.

How does (5) do in explaining decentralization in U.S. cities? Comparisons across decades are tenuous, but we can very roughly ask whether changes in incomes and transport costs could account for the changes in γ observed between 1950 and 1970. According to our model, from 1950 to 1970 the gradient should have fallen from 0.318 to 0.234 or by 26 percent.[11] By comparison, Edmonston reports a 41 percent decline in the density gradient for a sample of cities over that period. Again, the simple model appears to be in the right ball park.[12]

However, there are some unsatisfactory aspects to the attempt to explain density gradients in this way. Peter Mieszkowski and Mills (1993) give a cogent account. First, attempts to explain differences in gradients across cities and across times have not been very successful at isolating transport costs as an explanatory factor; this may be because such costs are inaccurately measured and are strongly correlated with income. Second, many of the density gradient estimates are based on just two observations, population in the central city and in the suburbs, along with the area covered by the central city; but this method appears to be highly inaccurate in certain cases, particularly in smaller cities. Third, because of lack of land-use data at a fine scale, most of the empirical work uses gross density (population divided by total land area) although the theory would be better represented by net density (population divided by residential land area); unfortunately, using gross density may drastically overstate the size of density gradients because the outer reaches of an urban area contain much higher proportions of undeveloped land (Mieszkowski and Barton Smith 1991). Finally, a strong negative correlation is observed between the density gradient and total population, with larger cities more decentralized; whereas the monocentric model predicts either no correlation or, in our version, a mild positive correlation.[13] Mills and Tan (1980) suggest that the observed negative correlation, "though not a consequence of the model, is strongly suggested by common sense" because larger cities support outlying employment subcenters (p. 315). This of course is an appeal to forces outside the monocentric model.

Probably the most serious deficiency of the monocentric model as an explanation of urban decentralization is its failure to account for the durability of housing. David

Harrison and John Kain (1974) observed that cities tend to grow outward by adding rings of housing at a density which reflects contemporaneous economic conditions, with the density of earlier rings remaining unchanged due to housing durability. The same phenomenon is demonstrated by Mieszkowski and Smith (1991), who show that the density of developed residential land (i.e. net density) in Houston is approximately constant all the way to the outer edge of the metropolitan area. A variety of dynamic versions of the monocentric model with durable housing has been constructed. In such models, the density gradient depends not only on the past time path of income and transport costs, but also on developers' expectations and the prospects for redevelopment. Explanations for observed density gradients are correspondingly complex.

Employment density functions can be estimated in the same way as population density functions, although data on the location of jobs are less readily available and less reliable than those for population. The general conclusion from the empirical literature is that the density gradient is larger for jobs than for households, but has been falling faster (Mieszkowski and Mills 1993). This evidence weakly supports the hypothesis that jobs have been following people; but there are many other reasons for jobs to have decentralized, as described in Section 2.

Other possible explanations of population decentralization, especially in the U.S., include variants of a "flight from blight" hypothesis. First is deteriorating central housing quality, due to style or technological obsolescence combined with rational decisions by owners to run down housing quality. Second is the existence of racial preferences combined with the tendency of poorer African-Americans to live in central cities. Third is negative neighborhood externalities associated with many poor neighborhoods. Fourth is the working out of Tiebout mechanisms for providing local public goods (Charles Tiebout 1956), resulting in better-off residents with high demands for local public goods abandoning the central city and excluding the poor from the suburbs through minimum lot-size zoning. All these explanations imply that the poor live near downtown and the rich are pushed or pulled out to the suburbs. The implied effect on the value of density gradients is, however, ambiguous.

4. The Polycentric City: Empirical Descriptions

We now turn to one of the most interesting features of modern urban landscapes – the tendency of economic activity to cluster in several interacting centers of activity. This section describes empirical findings. The next reviews theoretical models of polycentricity. Throughout, we use "center" to mean either the main center or a subcenter.

It is not hard to discover subcenters lurking in spatial employment or population data for most large cities. Giuliano and Small (1991) provide a review of studies, and new ones are steadily appearing. Here we consider some tentative generalizations about the nature and role of subcenters in U.S. cities, for which polycentricity has been examined in greater detail than anywhere else.

(i) SUBCENTERS ARE PROMINENT IN BOTH NEW AND OLD CITIES. Evidence is emerging that in each of the largest metropolitan areas in the United States, twenty or so subcenters can be identified using the criteria described in Section 2 with minimum gross density ($\bar{D}$) of 10 employees per acre and minimum total employment ($\bar{E}$) of 10,000. Giuliano and Small (1991) find 29 such centers in Los Angeles in 1980, and add three smaller outlying centers with prominent density peaks. Daniel McMillen and McDonald (1998b) find 15 sub-centers outside the city limits of Chicago meeting an identical criterion, using a combination of 1980 and 1990 data. Cervero and Wu (1997) find 22 such centers in the San Francisco Bay Area for 1990.

Each of these studies covers a Consolidated Metropolitan Statistical Area (CMSA), a census concept that is the most inclusive of the various types of metropolitan areas defined in official U.S. statistics. For example, San Francisco's CMSA includes nine counties, from the Napa Valley wine country in the north to San Jose and Silicon Valley in the south.[14]

(ii) THE NUMBER OF SUBCENTERS AND THEIR BOUNDARIES ARE QUITE SENSITIVE TO DEFINITION. Both the Los Angeles and the Chicago studies mentioned above find that with changes in density cutoffs, certain employment clusters could be viewed either as several large subcenters or as one mega-center. In the Chicago data, for example, the criteria just listed produce a huge subcenter near O'Hare Airport, with 420,000 employees,[15] whereas doubling the density cutoff breaks this subcenter into five smaller ones. The Los Angeles case, discussed in the next subsection, shows even more sensitivity to subcenter definition.

Such sensitivity is not surprising considering the observations made in Section 2. The urban landscape is highly irregular when viewed at a fine scale, and how one averages these local irregularities determines the look of the resulting pattern. It may be that the patterns that occur at different distance scales are influenced by different types of agglomeration economies, each based on interaction mechanisms with particular requirements for spatial proximity. This observation applies also to clustering at a regional scale such as the U.S. eastern seaboard and the core industrialized complex of northwestern Europe.

(iii) SUBCENTERS ARE SOMETIMES ARRAYED IN CORRIDORS. In the 1980 Los Angeles data, the four largest centers and one smaller one form an arc extending through the downtown area, Hollywood, and Century City all the way to the Pacific Ocean. The five centers are tenuously separated by zones just failing the density cutoff; a slight lowering of the cutoff causes the centers to become joined into one 19-mile-long center containing over 17 percent of the entire region's employment.

There is even an example where a corridor, rather than a set of point centers, seems to best explain surrounding density patterns. This is the Houston Ship Channel, a 20-mile-long canal lined by manufacturing plants and connecting central Houston (starting just two miles from the CBD) to Galveston Bay (Steven Craig, Janet Kohlhase and Steven Pitts 1996).

Both these examples of corridor development follow older established transportation facilities. Indeed, the corridor shape is quite familiar from urban history: as we have already seen, "streetcar suburbs" were prominent a century ago and less. Some of these communities and their associated transportation facilities later became the focus for development and redevelopment that were more automobile-oriented and more job-intensive. Similarly, at a regional scale, large metropolitan areas have sometimes grown together into a corridor-like "megalopolis" following an older inter-regional travel corridor, such as that between Boston and Washington.

(iv) Employment centers help explain surrounding employment and population. Several studies have established that point or corridor subcenters, as described above, help explain surrounding patterns of employment density, population density, and land values.

Three functional forms have been suggested as appropriate to generalize monocentric formulations to a polycentric structure (Eric Heikkila et al. 1989). All generalize the negative exponential function $D(x) = Ae^{-\gamma x}$ of Section 3.2, but each uses a different assumption about how the occupant of a given land parcel values access to multiple centers. They are:

$$D_m = Max_n\{A_n\exp(-\gamma_n x_{mn})\} \tag{6}$$

$$D_m = A\prod_{n=1}^{N}\exp(-\gamma_n x_{mn}) \tag{7}$$

$$D_m = \sum_{n=1}^{N}A_n\exp(-\gamma_n x_{mn}) \tag{8}$$

where D_m is density at location m, x_{mn} is distance of location m to center n, and A, A_n and γ_n are coefficients to be estimated.

The first, (6), assumes that centers are viewed as perfect substitutes; each center therefore generates its own declining bid-rent function for surrounding land, and land-use density at any point is determined by the highest of these bid-rent functions. In other words, what matters at any location is only the center with the largest influence at that point, and space is divided into strictly separate zones of influence as in the model of White (1976). We are not aware of any empirical support for this form, however, and it is rarely used in applied work.

The assumption in (7) is that centers are complements. The occupant of a given location requires access to every center in the area. This specification is easy to estimate after taking logarithms. It seems rather robust in practice, although it has a rather extreme property, that great distance from even one subcenter can entirely prevent development at location m. A modification of (7) that replaces $-\gamma_n x_{mn}$ by γ_n/x_{mn} overcomes this difficulty, and seems to fit even better.[16]

An intermediate case is the additive form (8), used by Gordon, Richardson, and H. L. Wong (1986) and by Small and Shunfeng Song (1994). It is based on the idea that the accessibility of a location is determined by the sum of exponentially declining influences from various centers. Here every center has an influence as in (7), but unlike in (7) a center's influence becomes negligible at large distances. Unfortunately, estimation of (8) requires nonlinear estimation and often produces convergence problems.

Considerable success has been attained using these models to explain density and land-value patterns in Los Angeles, Chicago, San Francisco, and a few other places. The pioneering studies were Daniel Griffith (1981) and Gordon, Richardson and Wong (1986). Small and Song (1994) are able to explain roughly 50 to 75 percent of the variance in employment or population density across the entire Los Angeles region using equation (8) with five centers for 1970 and eight centers for 1980. In all cases the special case of monocentricity is soundly rejected. The population density patterns fit well even though population data were not used to determine the locations of the centers used in the specification. Small and Song also show that monocentric density estimates fit poorly, especially in the later year, reinforcing the belief that polycentricity is an increasingly prominent feature of the landscape.

(v) SUBCENTERS HAVE NOT ELIMINATED THE IMPORTANCE OF THE MAIN CENTER.   Whenever a downtown center and one or more subcenters have been defined using the same criteria, downtown has more total employment, higher employment density, and usually a larger statistical effect on surrounding densities and land prices than does any subcenter. Because so many people believe that big-city downtowns are passé, it is worth reviewing this evidence in some detail.

Let us begin with Chicago. In explaining 1980 employment density patterns outside the city limits of Chicago, three large subcenters are found by McDonald and Prather (1994) to have exerted an important influence, but none has a t-statistic even one-fourth as large as does the CBD. In a remarkable study of land values over a century and a half, McMillen (1996) finds a clear and marked land-value peak at the CBD for each of 10 different years from 1836 to 1990, despite the steady rise in importance of centers several miles to the northwest.

In their study of San Francisco, Cervero and Wu (1997) list the sizes of the 22 centers emerging from the Giuliano–Small criterion described earlier. The largest and densest by far is the one containing downtown San Francisco. This center accounts for 15 percent of the region's employment. Silicon Valley is the second largest center, and the third (despite Gertrude Stein) is centered in downtown Oakland.

Now consider Los Angeles, famous for its sprawl. Garreau (1991) names more actual plus emerging "edge cities" there than in any other metropolitan area in the United States.[17] Yet of the centers identified by Giuliano and Small (1991), the one containing downtown Los Angeles dominates by nearly any measure. It contained 469,000 employees, more than double the next largest center and nearly ten times the size of the largest "edge city" in the region, known as South Coast Metro. The downtown center, much larger than the traditionally defined CBD, contained one-tenth of the region's employment and nearly one-third of the employment in all centers combined. Small and Song (1994) try alternative center locations in monocentric models of employment and population density, finding that the downtown center gives the best fit (although Los Angeles Airport comes close in the case of population).

(vi) MOST JOBS ARE OUTSIDE CENTERS.   Remarkably, centers account for less than half of all employment in the areas studied: 47 percent in San Francisco, one-third in Los Angeles, and less than one-fourth in suburban Chicago.[18] The polycentric pattern, interesting and important though it may be, coexists with a great deal of local employment dispersion. Furthermore, the population distribution can be explained much better by a model that accounts for distance to all employment rather than just to employment in centers, even if that model is constrained to have fewer parameters in total (Song 1994).

Nevertheless, we think Gordon and Richardson (1996) are premature in suggesting that dispersion has made the polycentric city a phenomenon of the past. Their results show that newer growth is more dispersed than earlier growth, but this has always been true. The crucial but unanswered questions are whether older centers remain vital and, when not, whether they are replaced by newer ones.

Another thing we do not know is whether subcenters fill essential niches in the local economy out of proportion to the sheer numbers of people working or shopping there. Certainly there is suggestive evidence that they do. Edge cities, for example, are well known as important sites of office location, indicating that they serve as nodes of information exchange. More generally, Giuliano and Small (1991) and McMillen and McDonald (1998b) find that different centers have quite different industry-mix characteristics, with some centers very specialized and others resembling the CBD in their diversity. Indeed, in Los Angeles, even the size distribution of centers closely follows the "rank-size rule" characterizing the distribution of city sizes within a nation.[19] Further empirical research on the economic roles that subcenters play would appear to us to have a high payoff.

(vii) COMMUTING IS NOT WELL EXPLAINED BY STANDARD URBAN MODELS, EITHER MONOCENTRIC OR POLYCENTRIC.   Bruce Hamilton (1982) was the first to note that the standard assumption of people commuting up a land-rent gradient cannot come close to explaining actual commuting patterns in the United States or Japan. Starting from the distributions of jobs and employee residences as functions of distance to the CBD, Hamilton calculates the average commuting distance when everyone commutes inward along a ray, as is implied by the monocentric model with dispersed employment. This procedure predicts average commutes of about one mile, understating actual average commutes by a factor of seven! Nor is the problem just monocentricity; letting density patterns be polycentric does not eliminate the discrepancy (Giuliano and Small 1993). In fact, even allowing for all the spatial irregularities of job and housing locations, average commutes are still three times as long, both in time and distance, as they would be if jobs and employees were matched so as to minimize average commuting distance as is implied by deterministic residential location models with identical individuals (Small and Song 1992).

It appears that at least in auto-dominated cities, there is more "cross-commuting," in which commuters pass each other in opposite directions, than there is commuting "up the rent gradient." Cross-commuting does not occur under standard assumptions, because if it did, people could reduce commuting costs without incurring higher rents, simply by interchanging houses. Naturally we don't expect the real world to fit the monocentric model perfectly, but being off by a factor of seven or even three is hard to swallow, considering the central role that commuting plays in the standard models.

There are several possible explanations for why people do not eliminate these extra commuting costs by moving. People have idiosyncratic preferences for particular locations, due to the different mixes of local amenities and to practical or sentimental attachments; two-worker households have to compromise between locations convenient to a job; frequent job changes and substantial moving costs cause people to choose locations convenient to an expected array of possible future jobs rather than just their current job; and racial and income segregation affect housing choices. All these explanations require job specialization, for otherwise people could get around the constraints by choosing a suitable job location. No one of these explanations is likely to explain the entire discrepancy, but perhaps all can together.

At a more fundamental level, these observations suggest that heterogeneity of prefer-ences and of job opportunities is extremely important in explaining urban residential location decisions. For example, adding idiosyncratic taste heterogeneity to a standard monocentric model results in greater decentralization (Anas 1990).

The upshot of the empirical work on subcenters is that some patterns stand out despite a great deal of irregularity and dispersion. Downtowns are still important; major employ-ment centers still exist and exert influence over surrounding population and employment distributions; but density and commuting patterns contain much randomness. We now turn to theoretical explanations of these facts. Because the theories could apply at regional as well as urban scales, the same analytical framework should also aid in the understanding of the regional clustering, both within and across national boundaries, that so vitally affects national cohesion and international trade.

5. Theories of Agglomeration and Polycentricity

Why do employment concentrations within cities exhibit the complex patterns discussed in the previous sections? To fix ideas, imagine first a "backyard economy" with no patterns – just a uniform distribution of economic activity over space. This would be the equilibrium under certain restrictive assumptions: land is homogeneous, production of each good exhibits constant returns to scale, goods and people are costly to transport, and there is no interaction over space. To understand agglomeration, we can ask, following Papageorgiou and T. Smith (1983): What are some alternative assumptions that would make this uniform distribution of activity unstable? The classical answers are spatial inhomogeneities and internal scale economies in production. More recent answers involve scale economies external to firms, including those arising from spatial contacts and imperfect competition. When any of these alternative assumptions holds in an environ-ment where transport and communication costs are not too high, spatial agglomeration can occur.

In this section we explore each of these alternative assumptions in turn. We then consider dynamics, and finally examine some approaches to agglomeration from outside economics.

5.1 Spatial inhomogeneities

Locations differ in factors such as soil, climate, mineral deposits, and access to waterways. Given such sources of Ricardian comparative advantage, trade arises and production specializes by location, unless transport costs are prohibitively high – in which case the backyard economy persists but with backyards that differ from one another.

Thus even with constant returns to scale in production, spatial inhomogeneities can give rise to towns (Marcus Berliant and Hideo Konishi 1996). An example is a mineral deposit which attracts workers to a mine. Miners have to be clothed and fed; depending on the structure of transport costs, some stages of the production or processing of clothing and food are performed locally. If the cost of shipping unprocessed ore is high, ore processing also occurs locally. A similar example is a town forming at a river rapids, since transshipment activity creates a demand for other goods causing local production – early Montreal is one such case.

Spatial inhomogeneities can create subcenters as well as central business districts. For example, a CBD may form on a harbor and a secondary employment center may form at the site of a river landing. The early model of White (1976) stressed such causes of subcenter formation.

5.2. Internal scale economies

The second classical explanation for agglomeration is economies of scale in some production process. An important example is scale economies in the loading and unloading of goods. Even in the absence of a natural advantage such as a protected harbor, port activities would tend to concentrate for this reason, a tendency which helped produce the port or railhead orientation of the nineteenth century city (Moses and Williamson 1967; Mills 1972). The advent of containerization has, if anything, intensified the economies of scale in port operations; trucking, by contrast, appears to require only small-scale loading and unloading equipment, so its terminal operations are widely dispersed along major highways.

Another source of scale economies is the production of local public goods (Joseph Stiglitz 1977), as suggested by many of the classic explanations for the historical origin of cities – the city as temple, citadel, capitol, marketplace, granary, or theater. Their counterparts in modern cities include civic buildings, water works, and monuments. Because such infrastructure is durable and lumpy, numerous man-made inhomogeneities emerge as an urban area grows and some become the sites around which new agglomerations form.

There are also scale economies in private production. A larger plant may have lower average production costs, but also higher average transport costs since inputs have to be gathered from, and outputs distributed to, a larger area. The efficient scale and hence the efficient market area are larger the greater is the degree of increasing returns and the lower are unit transport costs (Starrett 1974). The diseconomy from transport tends to balance the scale economies present in production, resulting in an equilibrium without the requirement that the production process itself have a U-shaped average cost curve – rather, the average production plus distribution cost is U-shaped.

5.3 External scale economies

We have seen that a public or private good produced under increasing returns can lead to agglomeration. Now suppose there are two private goods, each produced by a different firm, and that one of them, which is costly to ship, is used in the production of the other. This interindustry linkage may cause aggregate costs to be lower if the two firms co-locate. This is just one example of economies of scale that are external to individual firms, resulting in this case from transport costs. Other examples include contact externalities among consumers and market linkages between firms and consumers.

External scale economies between firms are called *economies of localization* if between firms in the same industry, and *economies of urbanization* if across industries. Economies of localization cause cities to be specialized; economies of urbanization cause them to be diversified. Empirical work has found strong evidence of localization economies and somewhat weaker evidence of urbanization economies.[20] Typically this work measures a production or cost function for firms in a given industry with a shift factor depending on local aggregate activity, either in the same industry (localization economies) or in all industries (urbanization economies).

External economies may also be dynamic, affecting not only the level of unit costs but also the rate at which they fall over time. An obvious example is technical progress spurred by knowledge transfer along the lines suggested by Paul Romer (1986). The prevalence of dynamic external economies is emphasized by Jacobs (1969) in describing the growth of cities, both early and modern, and by AnnaLee Saxenian (1994) in explaining the recent contest between Boston and Silicon Valley for dominance in computer electronics. There is some evidence that urbanization economies contribute to economic growth through endogenous technical change (Ó hUallacháin 1989; Glaeser et al., 1992).

One type of external economy that can be either localization or urbanization is *economies of massed reserves* (E. A. G. Robinson 1931; Hoover 1948), also called statistical economies of scale. In a world with firm-specific shocks, a firm with a specialized job vacancy is more likely to find a match with an unemployed worker when the labor market is larger; likewise, specialized capital that is unemployed due to a firm's closing is more likely to be successfully redeployed the larger the number of other firms using similar types of capital (Robert Helsley and William Strange 1991). Another type is *information exchange* within or between industries, for example, learning about the efficacy of new techniques by observing the successes and failures of competitors. Yet another type derives from *education*: because labor specialization encourages investment in human capital, larger cities have more educated work forces which may in turn result in more experimentation, more innovation, greater adaptability, and improved management skills.

How do inter-firm externalities affect spatial structure? We can learn a lot just by specifying how their strength varies with spatial proximity, even without describing their source. Using such a "pure externality" approach, Fujita and Hideaki Ogawa (1982) consider a closed market economy on a line segment with a fixed number of workers, each of whom consumes a single produced good and a residential lot of fixed size. They assume an equal number of firms, each employing one worker and occupying an industrial lot of fixed size. Workers commute to their jobs at a constant cost per unit distance. Firms benefit from proximity to other firms, as described by a *location potential function* in which the external productivity benefit conferred by one firm on another falls off with the distance between them according to a negative exponential function with a fixed decay rate. All agents are price takers. If commuting costs are very high, equilibrium entails a completely mixed land use pattern with all workers living adjacent to their job sites – the backyard economy again; if commuting costs are very low and the decay rate is small, agglomeration benefits dominate and firms cluster around one location giving rise to a monocentric city; and if commuting costs are moderate and the decay rate is high (so that a firm benefits a lot from nearby firms but not much from more distant firms) then equilibrium is polycentric. This model produces multiple equilibria – for example with one, three, or five centers – under the same set of parameter values, suggesting that a city's structure at a point in time may be path-dependent even when the durability of structures is ignored. Also, the comparative statics of this model are catastrophic – i.e., the solution changes discontinuously as parameter values are varied.

What might lie behind a location potential function? One possibility is simply *spatial contact*. Consider, for example, a very basic *fixed interaction model* in the spirit of Robert Solow and William Vickrey (1971) or E. Borukhov and Oded Hochman (1977). The city's geography is described by a finite space such as a line segment or a disc, with a geometric center but no predetermined economic center. The city is populated by homogeneous agents (either firms or households but not both), each of whom occupies a lot of unit size and interacts by traveling the same fixed number of times to visit every other agent. These abstract interactions can be interpreted as social contact, information acquisition, search, or exchange.[21]

Equilibrium is characterized by equal profits or, in the case of individuals, equal utilities. In equilibrium, the geometric center is the most accessible point; so rents peak there, declining monotonically towards the edge of the space. If the model is extended so that lot size is responsive to rent, population or employment density shows the same monotonic pattern. Unlike in the monocentric model of Section 3, however, this equilibrium is not efficient because interdependence among agents creates an externality. If an agent moves to a more accessible location, she imparts an external benefit on all other agents by reducing the average cost of their contacting her, which is in addition to the reduction in cost she obtains in contacting them[22] Since she does not value the benefit conferred on others, she will choose a less central location than is optimal. Hence, the city is too dispersed.

Presumably, the agents interact because they receive a benefit from doing so – for example, each pair of agents may exchange valuable but unpriced information. Then there is a second externality at the margin of the city's population, because adding a new agent confers a benefit on other agents that the new agent fails to capture. The city is therefore too small as well as too dispersed.

Contacts in the above models are non-market interactions between consumers or between firms. In Anas and Kim's (1996) general equilibrium model, contacts are instead market interactions and they occur between consumers and firms – specifically, purchases on shopping trips. Goods are differentiated by location. Each retail firm produces at a particular location under competitive conditions using land and labor, and sells its product on site. Having a taste for variety, a consumer shops everywhere products are sold, with the number of shopping trips to a particular location depending on its accessibility to that consumer's residence. Hence, this is a *flexible interaction model*, in which the attenuation of shopping trips with distance plays a role akin to that of the location potential function. Firms and consumers use varying amounts of land, and transportation is characterized by congestion. The model determines equilibrium rents, wages, and retail prices, all as functions of location with respect to the geometric center.

In the absence of external scale economies, firms and households in the Anas–Kim model are intermixed and dispersed around this geometric center, with commercial and residential densities declining with distance from it. But now suppose there is an external scale economy that operates within a particular shopping district. When the scale economy is large and congestion not too severe, there is a unique, stable equilibrium with firms in a single central district surrounded by consumers. As the cost of congestion increases, the monocenter becomes unstable and two or more smaller shopping districts emerge. Again we observe multiple equilibria, path dependence, and catastrophic transitions.

5.4 Imperfect competition

When firms compete imperfectly they impose a variety of pecuniary externalities on one another. In aspatial contexts this can create critical-mass effects as in some "big push" models of industrialization (Kevin Murphy, Andrei Schleifer and Robert Vishny 1989). In spatial contexts, imperfect competition can cause agglomeration in an analogous way. Indeed, from Harold Hotelling (1929) on, one of the central issues addressed by spatial competition theory is the circumstances under which firms have incentives to co-locate. Jean Gabszewicz and Jacques-François Thisse (1986) provide a review.

If economies of scale internal to the firm are large, the number of firms in the industry will be small. Given the resulting market power, determining equilibrium location patterns entails game-theoretic considerations. In such *spatial oligopoly models*, firms may compete in price, product quality, product mix, and location, conferring market advantages and disadvantages on each other. Such firms are typically conceived to be retailers or, more recently, developers (J. Vernon Henderson and Eric Slade 1993). Typically, product variety is assumed to be valued because of convex preferences, idiosyncratic preferences, or specialized intermediate goods. Such models easily produce externalities: suppose, for example, that expansion of the market occurs, causing one more firm to enter and the accessibility or variety of products to be thereby enlarged; this creates additional consumer surplus that is not fully captured by the entrant.

Agglomeration may arise in situations of spatial oligopoly, depending on the balance of advantages and disadvantages of clustering. In the model of Norbert Schulz and Konrad Stahl (1996), shoppers trade off the higher transport costs from traveling to a larger activity center (which on average is farther away from consumers) against the benefits from the increased product variety to be found there (which in their model lowers search costs). Retailers, in turn, trade off the larger potential volume of customers at a center offering the advantages of product variety against the lower degree of monopoly power achieved there. This type of model leads one to expect more homogeneous products to be sold in smaller centers, and more differentiated products, as well as big ticket items, to be sold in larger centers. The result is a hierarchy of centers analogous to the hierarchy of cities in the central place theories of Christaller (1933) and August Lösch (1940). The pattern is further complicated by complementarities that arise if consumers purchase multiple goods on a single trip, giving retailers of different goods an added incentive to locate in the same place (Robert Bacon 1984).

When economies of scale are less important but product variety is still valued, firms are more numerous and so may engage in *monopolistic competition*, in which strategic considerations are absent. One particular model of such a situation, by Avinash Dixit and Stiglitz (1977), has been used by others to derive results on agglomeration which can be interpreted as applying either at an intraurban or regional scale (e.g. Hesham Abdel-Rahman and Fujita 1990; Fujita and Tomoya Mori 1997). In two models by Krugman (1991b, 1993) co-location of all of the monopolistically competitive firms at a single point is a stable outcome when transport costs are low. Fujita (1988) has shown that introducing a land market into such models causes the agglomeration of firms to spread out as firms economize on rent, and generates a variety of possible equilibria in which residential and commercial land uses can be either mixed or segregated, monocentric or polycentric, depending on the structure of transport costs and consumer preferences.

5.5 Stability, growth, and dynamics

Recall that some of the static models we have discussed display multiple equilibria and catastrophic comparative statics. Adding a dynamic adjustment mechanism should then produce a model in which complex and interesting spatial patterns evolve over time.[23] The two-location model of Anas (1992) provides a simple illustration. Each location is a potential center, containing a fixed amount of land. Total population is N. Individuals at any location maximize a utility function depending on per-capita output at that location and on per-capita land consumption there. Per-capita land consumption at location i decreases with the number of people n_i there, but localization economies cause per-capita output at i to rise with n_i. Writing the resulting utility as $V(n_i)$, assume that $V(n_i)$ is inverted U-shaped with a maximum at n^*, and that $V(N) > V(0)$.

Our assumptions guarantee that the monocentric outcome, with all population in one center, is an equilibrium. So is the symmetric duocentric outcome with two centers, each of size $N/2$. A duocentric equilibrium is characterized by the condition $V(n_1) = V(N - n_1)$, so that no one has an incentive to move.

Consider, however, a dynamic adjustment mechanism in which migration occurs from a low- to a high-utility location. If $N < 2n^*$, the symmetric duocentric equilibrium is unstable because a small perturbation (i.e. a randomly sized group migration) that makes one center larger gives it a localization advantage, causing it to grow larger still until it absorbs all the population. Thus when the city is small, it is monocentric. But which of the two locations becomes the monocenter is determined by chance.

Larger cities are more interesting. If $N > 2n^*$ two things happen. First, the symmetric duocentric equilibrium is now stable and in fact Pareto superior to the monocentric one. Second, while the monocentric equilibrium remains locally stable, it is upset by a random migration of n' or more people from the monocenter to the other location, where n' is a number which depends on N. That is, it takes a certain threshold size n' to make a viable subcenter in the presence of an initial monocenter.[24] This suggests that some sort of coordination is required to move from the less efficient to the more efficient structure.

As it happens, n' is a decreasing function of N. We can now see what happens to a small city that grows. Suppose that in each time period, a randomly sized group migration from one location to the other occurs with probability proportional to the utility differential between the two locations. (The microfoundations for such fluctuations could, for example, include random migrations by small groups or herd behavior caused by signalling phenomena.) When total population is small, there will be just one center. As population grows, the one center remains but becomes less and less stable. Eventually a group migration produces a viable subcenter, which then grows rapidly until there are two equal-sized centers; but chances are this will not occur until well after the initial mono-center becomes inefficiently large. This suggests that a growing CBD can become too large because of coordination failures among potential outmigrants.

The process of "edge city" formation envisioned by Henderson and Arindam Mitra (1996) is one way in which subcenters can be sized and timed more efficiently. In their model firms decide whether to relocate from the monocenter to a new edge city. The essential innovation is the introduction of a developer who helps the migration process along by internalizing some of the external benefits that migrants to the edge city confer on each other. The developer is engaged in a game with the city government, which exercises influence over conditions in the original center. Henderson and Mitra examine the strategic considerations facing the developer, finding a rich set of possible decisions concerning the location and size for an edge city. The developer internalizes some of the externalities, but introduces new ones due to strategic effects. The role of developers is only just beginning to receive attention in the economic literature, but clearly it is quite important in practice.[25]

5.6 Non-economic dynamic models

The existence of multiple centers, the irregularity of spatial forms, and the unpredictability of how they evolve are important features of the modern urban landscape. Similar properties are also known to arise in a variety of nonlinear dynamic processes in chemistry, physics, and biology. As a result, some of the more interesting infusions of ideas into urban economics and urban geography are coming from those fields. In particular, urban structure is proving to be a fertile application of generalized concepts such as chaos, complexity, fractals, dissipative structures, and self-organization. All involve some form of positive feedback (W. Brian Arthur 1990), which in the urban growth context takes the form of development at one location somehow enhancing the development potential of nearby locations. This, of course, is just another description of agglomeration economies; the difference is that this strain of literature has emphasized the dynamic analytics of such feedback mechanisms rather than their economic underpinnings. In this sense it resembles many macroeconomic models.

These models typically explore systems that are out of equilibrium, an approach now also established in evolutionary economics (Richard Nelson 1995) and one that is amply justified by the durability of urban structures. Unfortunately, the models often lack prices and so may neglect forces tending toward the restoration of equilibrium. But are spatial interactions mediated through prices more important than unpriced spatial influences and externalities? Since unpriced externalities probably play a dominant role in shaping urban spatial structure, the challenge posed by the non-economic models cannot be easily dismissed. What follows is a sampler of these non-economic models from a quite eclectic literature centered mostly in geography and regional science. We attempt to extract some basic insights which are useful to economic models.

Markovian models explain the transitions of micro units from one state to another: development or redevelopment of a parcel of land, household migrations, and the birth or death of firms. Agglomeration effects imply that individual transition probabilities depend on the number of actors in each state, as in interactive Markov chain models (John Conlisk 1992). A model whose macro features depend on the particular realization of stochastic transitions is a model in which history matters, just as recent work has shown that it matters in other fields of economics (Paul David 1985; Arthur 1989) and just as it matters in the economic models with multiple equilibria discussed earlier.

Looked at more abstractly, positive feedback reinforces certain perturbations in the urban system and can therefore amplify some random fluctuations. Such fluctuations are driving forces in dynamic theories of *self-organization*. In some circumstances fluctuations result in sudden shifts from one relatively stable state to another, a phenomenon resembling punctuated equilibria in biological evolution (Niles Eldredge and Stephen Jay Gould 1972). Krugman (1996) uses Fourier analysis to decompose a random perturbation (such as the irregular spatial pattern of employment changes caused by building a large plant) into an infinite series of regularly spaced fluctuations at different spatial frequencies. A physical analogy is the decomposition of the sound of plucking a violin into a set of audible harmonic frequencies known as a tone and overtones. Just as the violin body amplifies some frequencies and dampens others, the urban system causes some of the regular spatial fluctuations to be magnified (as with an influx of new firms in a regular pattern) and others to be suppressed (as with the closing of unsuccessful firms due to unfavorable location patterns vis-à-vis their competitors). The result of selective amplification is recognizable macro spatial features such as a tendency toward a particular spacing among urban subcenters. By understanding the properties of the "amplifier," which is just a set of dynamic equations, we obtain insight into the varying spatial scales at which agglomeration or congestion effects occur. Some such effects are based on personal interaction, producing the classic CBD. Others are based on daily or weekly trip-making, yielding spatial structures at scales up to an hour or so of travel. Others are based on interregional or international trade, yielding size hierarchies of cities at a national, continental, or even global scale.

Diffusion and percolation are dynamic physical processes in which the evolution of a macro state, such as the flow of water through porous rock, is governed by microscopic obstructions whose precise locations are random. (An urban development analogy would be a new firm seeking to assemble a large land parcel in an area with many small parcels that are randomly occupied.) Relationships between such macro quantities as water pressure and average flow can be derived from the statistical properties of the obstructions, even though the exact pattern of pathways is random. Electrical conductivity and magnetization of minerals operate in somewhat similar ways (Armin Bunde and Shlomo Havlin 1996). A. Stewart Fotheringham, Batty and Longley (1989) propose that in an analogous way, discrete lumps of development arrive randomly at the edge of a metropolitan area and seek suitable vacant sites. Agglomeration is posited by requiring that a new lump may settle only on the edge of an existing cluster of development. The resulting patterns of developed land are fractals, and Batty and Longley (1994) use this model to derive the fractal patterns which, as noted in Section 2, they believe characterize urban development.

Hernan Makse, Havlin and Eugene Stanley (1995) propose a model with somewhat stronger agglomeration tendencies known as *correlated percolation*, in which the development probability for a given site increases with the proximity of other occupied sites and decreases with distance from an exogenous monocenter. Simulations yield growth patterns that resemble, at least impressionistically, the historical development of Berlin from 1875 to 1944, which especially in the later years showed a high degree of irregularity. Perhaps the main advantage of such models is the tools they offer for analyzing irregularity – for example, the fitting of power laws to the size distributions of local spatial fluctuations.

Per Bak and Kan Chen (1991) have shown that many dramatic physical phenomena, including avalanches and earthquakes, occur when the dynamics of a system push it to an ordered state that is just on the edge of breakdown. Given such a state of *self-organized criticality*, small fluctuations cause chain reactions whose sizes typically obey a power-law distribution. Krugman (1996) hints that the interactions among economic agents may produce similar states in cities, as well as in other economic situations, and that this may explain the prevalence of sudden transitions such as the extremely rapid growth of new edge cities. Extensions of economic models that produce sudden growth, such as those of Krugman (1996) and Anas (1992), could perhaps produce temporary states of self-organized criticality with testable statistical properties.

Regional scientists have long been interested in models in which the attractiveness of a location, for example a shopping center, is enhanced by large size. As already discussed, such models are capable of generating bifurcations, in which small shifts of parameter values produce qualitatively different equilibrium configurations, some stable and some not. Peter Allen and collaborators have put some of the same ideas into dynamic models intended to describe urban or regional growth processes that may be far from equilibrium. This work is part of a more general movement, inspired by Ilya Prigogine, to describe systems that maintain organized structure against the ravishes of entropy. Such systems are called *dissipative structures* (G. Nicholis and Prigogine 1977; John Foster 1993).

Allen's models are based upon interdependent growth equations for population and employment which incorporate both agglomeration economies and congestion diseconomies. For example, in the model of Allen and M. Sanglier (1981), employment S in a given region and sector obeys a dynamic equation in which dS/dt is proportional to S ($E-S$), where E is a measure of "potential employment demand." This potential demand is in turn determined by other equations in the system that account for the location's relative attractiveness, crowding, and a rather arbitrary "natural carrying capacity." Thus existing employment attracts new employment, but eventually the location becomes saturated. The authors create simulations in which random fluctuations cause the spontaneous creation of centers, which subsequently grow along a path resembling a logistic curve. Most simulations lead to a stable but not necessarily unique steady state. Constraints such as zoning regulations, if added early in the simulation, can affect which of the possible steady states occurs. This model and related ones have been calibrated for a number of cities and regions in Belgium, France, Senegal, and the United States (Allen 1997).

Most of the noneconomic models described here lack a price system and any explicit description of rational economic decision-making. Furthermore, their dynamic behavior is backward-rather than forward-looking. Thus, for all their tantalizing success in portraying the complexity in the dynamics of urban structure, they fail to incorporate economic explanations. Fortunately, they tend to be based on the behavior of individual units and so are not fundamentally incompatible with economic reasoning. This suggests that advances might be achieved by some merging of modeling techniques. Either economic behavior might be inserted rigorously into existing noneconomic models, or attractive analytical features from those models might be blended into existing models in urban economics.

An example of the first approach is by Hsin-Ping Chen (1996), who shows that a rigorous microeconomic model can generate macro-level equations like those of Allen and Sanglier. Chen's model contains land and labor prices, development and abandonment decisions, and other recognizable microeconomic constructs, all within a framework of agglomeration economies and congestion. She produces abstract simulations much like those of Allen and Sanglier, and in other work (Chen 1993) makes a plausible case for replicating the 1970–80 growth of the Los Angeles region with a calibrated version of the model.

6. The Welfare Economics of Urban Structure

In defense of the low-density development that increasingly characterizes modern cities, Gordon and Richardson (1997) have argued that the urban spatial structure generated by market forces reflects the will of the people – or more precisely, that it is a successful and largely desirable adaptation to the forces of urban growth and congestion. Planners, in contrast, typically have little faith in either the efficiency or the equity of market-determined outcomes, and advocate detailed land use planning. To evaluate these con-flicting points of view we need to explore the welfare economics of urban land use. In this section we attempt to show how some of the prominent policy questions can be illumin-ated, if not answered, by building on the theoretical models and empirical observations of the previous sections.

6.1 Can agglomeration economies be internalized?

We have seen that although agglomeration economies are the raison d'être of most cities, their exact nature is in flux and only partially understood. Our current understanding of them is based on a variety of factors including Smithian specialization, idiosyncratic matching, interaction, and innovation. Because these notions are broad ones, no one has really succeeded in coming to grips with how they affect the industrial organization of the modern city. Why, if there are economies of scale, is production not undertaken by a single large firm? Why do some forms of interaction occur within firms, while others operate through the market and yet others take place informally? And why do some interactions appear to require face-to-face contact while others can be effected via tele-communication? The answers given to these questions often refer to transactions costs, incomplete contracts, trust, and flexibility.

Does the market – broadly speaking – deal efficiently with agglomeration economies? The standard answer is negative. If scale economies are internal to firms, then efficient pricing cannot be supported by competition. If they are external, firms will under-employ those business practices that contribute social value to their neighbors. The standard argument, however, neglects that efficiency could be achieved by competition among private city-developers who would set up efficient cities, thereby internalizing the agglom-eration economies. Each city would operate at minimum average cost – a point of locally constant returns to scale – with increasing returns in the production of goods being balanced by decreasing returns in the production of accessible land, due to the higher costs of transport and communications in larger cities. Under marginal-cost pricing, the losses from production of goods would be just offset by profits on the production of accessible land, which are manifested as land rents – a variant of the Henry George Theorem (Richard Arnott and Stiglitz 1979). When developers make decisions concerning the internal structure of edge cities, they are to a limited extent playing this role. We do not, however, observe developers trading cities in a competitive market; so it is doubtful that agglomeration economies can be fully internalized in this way. Government intervention can help in principle, but until the sources of market failure are better understood it risks making things worse instead of better – as has also been argued in the international trade context (Krugman 1987).

6.2 How efficient is subcenter formation?

We have seen how agglomeration economies tend to create clusters of economic activity within a city and how these clusters influence surrounding residential densities. Given the rich nature of interactions within urban areas, such clusters play a variety of roles. What can we say about the optimality of the resulting pattern?

Our theoretical review suggests that urban subcenters, like cities themselves, are formed from the tension between agglomerative and dispersive forces. Both sets of forces entail strong externalities – external economies producing the agglomerative tendencies, and congestion or nuisance externalities limiting the size and density of the agglomeration that is achieved. The first set of externalities is largely positive, suggesting an inadequate private incentive to join an agglomeration and hence excessive dispersion. The second set consists of negative externalities, so may cause too many activities to locate close together. Since different externalities operate at different scales, it is quite possible for the spatial pattern of economic activity to be too centralized at one scale (e.g. cities that are too big) and too dispersed at another (e.g. sub-centers that are too small). To further complicate matters, the externalities are linked. For example, downtown congestion, along with the excessive residential decentralization caused by underpriced transport, may give rise to excessive employment decentralization (because jobs follow households), which may in turn spawn excessively large secondary agglomerations.

The two-location model of Anas (1992), reviewed in the previous section, illustrates these problems in a dynamic setting. As the population of the first center grows, there comes a time when it is optimal for a mass of population to move to the second location. Since, however, the social gains from relocation exceed the private gains, under atomistic migration the second center will not be established until probably much later. According to this reasoning, some collective action is needed not only to establish the second center at the right time but also to protect it until it becomes stable and self-sustaining. In principle, a private developer has a profit incentive to form the second center at the right time;[26] but in a more realistic model with multiple locations, the strategic rivalry among potential developers, each trying to create a subcenter, results in other inefficiencies (Henderson and Slade 1993). There may therefore be a role for government in assisting subcenter formation – for example by providing infrastructure, regulating or subsidizing developers, or subsidizing firm location. On a regional or national scale, analogous issues have been raised in the debates over France's "pôles de croissance," Britain's New Towns policy, and policies of less developed nations to divert growth away from their "primate" cities which contain large percentages of the national urban populations.

The comparison between optimal and market-determined spatial structure is further complicated by history dependence. The most obvious source is the durability of structures and infrastructure. But as we have seen, even in the absence of durability one can have multiple stable equilibria, with some more efficient than others and with history determining which obtains. On balance, therefore, it appears formidably difficult to ascertain how the actual size distribution and composition of subcenters differs from the optimum under realistic situations. While there is certainly scope for ameliorative government action, a precise prescription of good planning in this arena remains elusive.

6.3 Does traffic congestion cause excessive decentralization?

In the basic monocentric-city model, urban spatial structure is efficient. It is reassuring that the Invisible Hand can work with respect to the location of economic activities. Unfortunately, this efficiency property is not very robust theoretically, and is of questionable practical relevance because of the pervasiveness of externalities in actual cities. One of the most serious is traffic congestion.

The congestion externality arises because the user of a motor vehicle does not pay for its marginal contribution to congestion. Consequently, the private cost of travel during peak periods falls short of the social cost. Travel is misallocated across transport modes, routes, and times of the day, and overall travel may be excessive too. As is well known, this externality can be internalized by means of a congestion toll equal to the marginal congestion externality evaluated at the optimum. However, optimal congestion tolls are charged nowhere and congested travel is underpriced almost everywhere. Uncongested travel, by contrast, may be considerably overpriced, especially in nations with high fuel taxes.

What does this imply about urban form? Even in today's complex urban structures, the most severe congestion continues to occur on radial travel to and from the central business district (CBD), and it is here that underpricing is most severe. If urban structure is fundamentally shaped by commuting costs to the CBD, as postulated by the monocentric model, then such underpricing causes the city to be more spread out than is optimal. This excessive residential decentralization is compounded by a less obvious effect: underpricing travel distorts land values in a way that encourages planners to allocate too much downtown land to roads (Arnott 1979). To see why, suppose the only cost associated with a road is the opportunity cost of the land it uses. Now let the planner employ the following "naive" cost–benefit rule: at each location, expand the road until the incremental travel-cost saving from further expansion equals the residential market value of the incremental land required. However, the market value of residential land reflects only the *private* transport-cost savings from a more central location, not the *social* savings which – because of underpriced congestion – are greater. The market therefore undervalues downtown residential land, so that application of the naive rule results in too much land there being devoted to roads. Another way of viewing it is that the naive rule ignores the contribution to congestion of "induced traffic," i.e., traffic caused by land-use changes induced by the highway investment. Wheaton (1978) has argued that such a mechanism resulted in massive overbuilding of urban highways in the U.S. during the 1950s and 1960s.

This reasoning, of course, must be modified when one takes into account non-central employment. As congestion builds near the city center, some centrally located employers respond by moving out of the CBD and closer to their workers and customers, with agglomerative forces causing some of this employment to become clustered in subcenters. As the metropolitan area evolves from a monocentric to a dispersed or polycentric structure, average travel times and congestion levels are reduced. This phenomenon is empirically documented by Gordon, Ajay Kumar, and Richardson (1989) and Gordon and Richardson (1994), and occurs in simulations based on the theoretical model of Anas and Kim (1996).

Clearly, however, the process of decentralization does not occur efficiently because the congestion externality remains. Highly accessible land is still underpriced and hence is developed at inefficiently low density. So the resulting land use pattern is likely to be inefficiently dispersed (not clustered enough). It is more difficult to say if the pattern is also inefficiently decentralized (too spread out from the center) because the timing of polycentric development depends on how the land development industry is organized. If the industry is dominated by a few large developers, then timing is affected by strategic interdependence; whereas if there are instead many small developers, timing is influenced by coordination failure and the dynamics of herd behavior.

Possible second-best policies to correct excessive decentralization, if such is the case, include more sophisticated cost–benefit analysis of transport projects, minimum-density controls, and greenbelts. In fact, policies in the United States have worked in exactly the opposite direction, as emphasized by Anthony Downs (1992) and others. Subsidies for home ownership, subsidized highway construction and maintenance, and minimum-lot-size residential zoning are just some of the measures which have increased decentralization, even while keeping the poor excessively concentrated in the central cities. In response to the ongoing transformation in urban form, the planning community has tended to advocate policies aimed at reversing decentralization, reducing automobile use, and revitalizing the downtown core – for example building mass transit facilities or downtown convention centers. But because the pricing errors of the past have been cast in brick and asphalt, such policies are very expensive and have limited effectiveness.

6.4 When are land-use controls justified?

Given the many externalities revealed by our theoretical review, it is tempting to conclude that only very comprehensive and detailed planning can overcome the resulting inefficiencies. Because the externalities are so poorly understood, however, attempted cures may well do more harm than the disease. The brief discussion below illustrates the complexity of determining one aspect of optimal policy: land-use planning.

First, consider *incompatible land uses*. Cities are awash in very localized externalities, from the smells from a fish shop to the blockage of ocean views by neighbors' houses. Mills and Hamilton (1994, pp. 252–54) argue that they are not significant, but that may be because the worst have been eliminated by zoning. Because pricing solutions in this context would be extremely cumbersome, zoning is a potentially valuable tool for dealing with incompatible land uses. However, it can easily be overdone; for example, the complete separation of retail and residential land uses results in visual monotony and unnecessary auto travel.

Second, consider *preservation of open space*. Greenbelts and urban parks are potentially valuable public goods, and government intervention is probably the only viable way to ensure their provision. It is important to recognize, however, that *someone* is implicitly bearing the cost of designating areas off-limits to development. The increased scarcity of residential land induced by greenbelts drives up land rents and hence housing rents. So the bucolic landscapes surrounding London and Paris arguably come at the cost of miserable and badly overcrowded neighborhoods for the poor. Where such controls divert growth from the entire metropolitan area, they may improve the local environment but against this must be weighed the environmental cost of growth elsewhere. In other situations, greenbelts are likely to spawn exurban development further out, which raises another set of issues for growth management.

Third, consider *urban sprawl*, a pejorative term often used for leapfrogging in development. This appears inefficient at first glance. But what some planners see as haphazard development may well be the seeds of future agglomerations, and the land left vacant can be developed later at higher density than is justified today.

Another argument for greenbelts or growth boundaries is *maintenance of viable central cities*. Critics of current development patterns argue, with some justification, that misguided policies have produced excessively decentralized cities at great cost in duplicative infrastructure and with disastrous results for the poor who live in concentrations of blight (David Rusk 1993; Downs 1994; Myron Orfield 1997). Some of these authors argue for growth boundaries to force new development into the central cities in hopes of revitalizing them. But such gross restrictions may well have perverse distributional consequences: the prior owners of land within the boundary enjoy windfall gains at the expense of nascent businesses and new home buyers, while inner-city renters – who are disproportionately poor – must pay more for housing.

Finally, consider *exclusionary zoning*. Many suburban municipalities enforce minimum-lot-size restrictions, largely in order to exclude lower-income residents who would pay less in property taxes while receiving the full benefits of the local public goods. Such restrictions may also be designed to exclude undesired socioeconomic, racial, or ethnic groups. Exclusionary zoning probably adds considerably to decentralization as well as fostering social stratification, segregation in education, and racial division. By forcing the poor to live in central cities, it also limits their access to suburban blue-collar jobs, a phenomenon known as spatial mismatch (Kain 1968). These are all reasons why higher levels of government might want to encourage suburban municipalities to be more receptive to high-density housing targeted to lower-income residents.

6.5 Summary: The role of government policy

As in so much of economic policy analysis, it is hard to make overall recommendations about the scope of government intervention. Theory provides clear instances of market failure, against which must be balanced the likelihood and severity of government failure. An interesting object lesson is Paris, whose urban form has been strongly influenced by government intervention to limit central building heights and to channel exurban development towards planned satellite towns. The result is a city regarded by many as extremely attractive and vital. Others prefer the convenience, lower cost, and ease of interaction of Los Angeles, which Paris would probably come to resemble absent government policy.

What seems clear to us is that cities are complex entities in which market forces are both powerful and beneficial, and, in many ways, obvious and subtle. These market forces sometimes need to be controlled or channeled, yet they tend to find their own way of thwarting such restrictions. Whether a particular government policy is enlightened intervention or misguided meddling will inevitably be debated case by case.

7. Conclusion

And so we see that cities are strongly shaped by agglomeration economies, especially external scale economies. Cities teem with positive and negative externalities, all acting with different strengths, among different agents, at different distances. Some people need to interact frequently face to face; others carry out routine actions remotely via telecommunications but must meet periodically to create and renew trust; still others learn crucial information by overhearing conversations at restaurants, bars, parties, or meetings. Consumers want to purchase some goods often, other infrequently; some want to see and touch goods, others to hear about them from a friend; for some any variety will do, for others a specific variety is required. The pedestrian and car traffic generated by one firm as a side-effect can make or break another firm's business, as window shoppers stop at an intriguing display or as disreputable patrons scare away a neighbor's potential workers, residents, or customers. Together these many interactions, helped by history and a good deal of chance, produce the spatial structure that we see. Is it any wonder that spatial patterns are complex, that they occasionally display sudden change, or that tractable models can capture only a portion of their rich variegation?

Agglomeration economies have resisted attempts to fully understand their microfoundations. This is illustrated by urban economists' lack of confidence in forecasting the effects of the communications revolution on urban spatial structure. On the theoretical side, we do not know the scale at which the various forces work or what kinds of equilibria the simultaneous interaction of many forces will produce; nor do we have reliable models of dynamic growth paths with random shocks. We also do not know which external economies will be internalized through private initiative. On the empirical side, despite the increasing sophistication of studies relating a firm's productivity to the size and industrial composition of the city in which it is located, we do not really know the specific forces that produce these relationships, nor just how they depend on industry mix, industrial policy, local public goods, or zoning.

Complicating matters even more are the longevity of urban structures, including public infrastructure, and the stability of certain equilibria even when other equilibria exist that would make everyone happier. Urban structure locks in past forces that may have little bearing today. Precious little traffic now uses the locks on the Erie Canal that are the namesake of Lockport, New York; yet that is where its downtown remains. Other downtowns may be overcrowded because no developer has managed to assemble land or obtain zoning variances needed to establish a much needed satellite center.

We have seen that forces that are ascendant throughout the world are producing decentralization and dispersion at a citywide scale, and agglomeration at a local scale. Will Paris and Tokyo, then, go the way of Los Angeles? To a large extent they already have; in both, as in cities throughout the developed world, automobile-age development has created a vast periphery of residential suburbs with outlying commercial, office, and industrial centers. Apparently these patterns are not just the product of crazy Americans in love with their cars. Yet Paris and Tokyo have each preserved a distinctive city center, in part through strict zoning and by valuing historic preservation. In addition Paris, like other cities including London and Seoul, has seen the shape of decentralization and dispersion altered by central-government policies that zone large tracts of outlying land as greenbelts and create satellite cities. Our review suggests that such policies can in principle elicit more efficient growth paths; but that serious undesirable side-effects are likely. As for the city centers, whether the desire to maintain their special character can stave off the forces of economic change depends both on politics and on the ultimate preferences of the citizenry.

Notes

1 Throughout this essay we use the word "city," or the name of a particular city, to mean an entire urban region; other terms with similar meanings are "metropolitan area" and "urban area."

2 Some authors reserve the term "agglomeration economies" only for this second class.

3 The huge Walnut Creek office and retail complex 22 miles east of San Francisco, which developed in the 1970s and 1980s, has at its center a station of the Bay Area Rapid Transit system which opened in the early 1970s. Yet, the automobile accounts for 95 percent of commuting trips to the complex, and presumably an even higher proportion of other trips (Robert Cervero and Kang-Li Wu 1996, Table 5).

4 The data (available on request) are plotted on a 121×131 kilometer square locational grid, with a spatial smoothing function used to compute the smoothed average density at each grid point from the raw data for nearby zones. If zone i's centroid is distance D_i from the grid point, its density is weighted proportionally to $[1 - (D_i/R)]^2$, where R is the smoothing radius within which zone densities are allowed to affect a given grid point. In the three plots shown in the figure, R takes values equal to $2\sqrt{2}$, $4\sqrt{2}$, and $6\sqrt{2}$ kilometers respectively.

5 The key initial steps were taken by Edwin Mills (1967, 1972) and Richard Muth (1969). For an excellent synthesis see Masahisa Fujita (1989).

6 The model is readily extended to explicitly treat housing as a produced commodity, with lot size as one of its inputs. Jan Brueckner (1987) provides a nice analysis of the resulting comparative statics.

7 If all urban land is used for residential purposes and the city is circular, then $\phi(x) = 2\pi x$.

8 McDonald (1989) and Mills and Tan (1980) provide good surveys of methodology and results, respectively.

9 See Yorgos Papageorgiou and David Pines (1989) for a more complete discussion. The original derivation of the negative exponential relied on unitary price elasticity of demand for housing and Cobb–Douglas production of housing (Muth 1969 ch. 4). We instead provide conditions on the utility function and on transport costs, which to the best of our knowledge is novel. Alex Anas and Ikki Kim (1992) generate negative exponential densities by incorporating an income distribution.

10 Housing costs were probably around 20% of after-tax income net of commuting cost, and land costs about 20% of housing costs (Small 1981, p. 320), giving $1 - \alpha = 0.04$. We assume that each commuter had nine hours daily for commuting plus work, and that income was taxed at a constant rate τ. We assume that the average one-way commute was 10 miles and took place at a speed of 25 miles per hour, requiring 48 minutes of round trip per day. Suppose that the only cost of travel is time, valued at the after-tax wage rate. So total daily commuting cost averaged over x is $(48/60)w$, while marginal daily commuting cost (per mile of one way trip) is one-tenth as large. Figuring in taxes: $y = (1 - \tau)9w$, $T = (1 - \tau)(48/60)w$, and $T' = (0.10)T$. Hence $T/y = 0.0889$ and $T'/y = 0.00889$. (This implies that commuting time is, on average, about 9% of the consumer's time endowment, which is quite plausible.) Hence, $\gamma = (0.96/0.04)$ $(0.00889)/(1-0.0889) = 0.234$. To be better aligned with the empirical evidence (see Small 1992, pp. 44, 84), we would have to recognize that travel time is valued at $w/2$, or somewhat less

than the after-tax wage rate; and also that there is a variable money cost of automobile commuting equal to about half the time cost. These corrections happen to approximately cancel, so do not change the gradient estimate by much.

11   We assume that $1 - \alpha$ remained at 0.04 throughout the period. LeRoy and Sonstelie (1983, Table 4) estimate that real income rose approximately 88% over those two decades while real marginal transport costs (including the value of time) rose only 43%. (They give nominal figures which we deflated by the CPI. We have estimated the mean by interpolating between their figures for the 25th and 75th percentiles.) Then, the 1950 value of γ predicted by equation (5) is found by replacing the 1970 value of (T/y) by $[(T'/1.43)/(y/1.88)] = 1.315(T'/y)$, and similarly for T/y. The result is $\gamma = (0.96/0.04)\,(1.315)\,(0.00889)/[1-(1.315 \text{ times } 0.0889)] = 0.318$.

12   More refined predictions could be made using available extensions of the simple monocentric model. For example, accounting for income differences would increase the predicted density gradient if parameters are such that higher income people live more peripherally, since they also choose more land per dwelling for a given rent.

13   Looking at the outer boundary, rising population does not change marginal transport cost but it does increase total transport cost, hence lowering the denominator in (5) and causing γ to rise.

14   Smaller urban regions, and a few large ones like that surrounding Washington, D.C., are not classified as CMSAs but rather as Metropolitan Statistical Areas (MSAs). Both CMSAs and MSAs are collections of whole counties (except in New England) that are highly integrated; the MSA is closest to what before 1983 was defined as a Standard Metropolitan Statistical Area (SMSA). The CMSA typically combines several adjacent areas formerly classified as SMSAs, most of which are now called Primary Metropolitan Statistical Areas (PMSAs). For example, the New York–Northern New Jersey–Long Island CMSA consists of 11 PMSAs including New York (New York City plus three adjacent counties), Nassau-Suffolk (two counties constituting Long Island), and Newark (five counties in New Jersey). The Los Angeles–Anaheim–Riverside CMSA consists of four PMSAs: Los Angeles County, Riverside and San Bernardino Counties, Orange County, and Ventura County. See U.S. Bureau of the Census (1996, pp. 937–945). Because we are not interested in municipal boundaries, in this essay we generally designate a CMSA just by the name of its largest city.

15   O'Hare airport is annexed to the City of the Chicago, despite its being surrounded entirely by suburbs. For this reason employment at the airport itself is missing in these data, which cover only the suburbs.

16   McDonald and Paul Prather (1994), McMillen and McDonald (1998a, b). A different modification replaces the distances x_{mn} to specific centers n in (7) with distance to the nearest center, the second nearest center, and so forth. Rena Sivitanidou (1996) uses this form successfully to explain Los Angeles office and commercial land values.

17   Garreau's definition of an edge city includes five criteria: 5,000,000 square feet of office space; 600,000 square feet of retail space; a daily inflow of commuters; a "local perception as a single end destination for mixed use"; and a location that was residential or rural thirty years previously (Garreau 1991, p. 425). He allows for some element of judgment in deciding on boundaries and on when two nearby edge cities should be counted as one. An "emerging" edge city is an area showing signs that it will soon become an edge city.

18   This last statement is for 1990 employment using the more restricted definitions for the subcenters near O'Hare and Evanston, as preferred by McMillen and McDonald (1998b). Total 1990 employment in suburban subcenters was 558,600, from their Table 1. Total 1990 suburban employment was 2,381,900, from Daniel McMillen, private correspondence. Unfortunately certain data sources are incompatible between the City of Chicago and the rest of the CMSA; as a result many studies have used one or the other, making us unable to make statements for the entire CMSA.

19   This rule, also known as Zipf's law, postulates that the cumulative fraction of cities of size N or greater is proportional to $1/N$. See Kenneth Rosen and Mitchel Resnick (1980) for a thorough empirical investigation. See Krugman (1996) for a thoughtful discussion of possible reasons for this amazingly robust empirical relationship.

20   Randall Eberts and McMillen (1999) provide a good review. Glenn Ellison and Glaeser (1997) derive a general index of the geographical concentration of an industry that distinguishes between that due to the random distribution of finite-sized plants and that due to agglomerative forces other than internal scale economies. They find that for the U.S., roughly half the observed employment concentration is due to such randomness and internal scale economies; as to the other half, most industries show a mild degree of agglomeration while a few show a marked degree.

21   In actual cities, many such interactions are face to face. Because formal contracting is costly, much contracting takes place informally; this requires honest dealing, and honesty is communicated by body language and eye contact. The fact that humans have developed unconscious signals of their intentions, as well as the ability to decipher those signals, can be explained by theories of evolutionary stable strategies as postulated by John Maynard Smith (1976). See also Robert Frank (1988). Another reason for face-to-face interaction is that much creative activity is facilitated by conversation in a social setting (Jacobs 1969; Saxenian 1994).

22   That is, the benefit from lowering the cost of a given contact is mutual, so both agents cannot capture it fully through transaction prices. This easily misunderstood point is made by Tjalling Koopmans and Martin Beckmann (1957). It is true that any transactions that are socially desirable could be elicited by sufficient side payments – but this amounts to internalizing the externality. Short of that, any pricing rule that allocates the cost of the interaction in a specified way leaves one or both parties short of the full incentive to interact.

23   The multiplicity of equilibria, their stability, and the patterns of path dependence are analyzed explicitly in Fujita and Ogawa (1982) and in Anas and Kim (1996). These properties are implicitly present in the models of Papageorgiou and Smith (1983), Fujita (1988), Krugman (1991b, 1993) and Fujita and Mori (1997).

24   Hence two cities of size n' and $N - n'$ are another duocentric equilibrium, this one asymmetric; but it is locally unstable.

25   It is also important for equilibrium in Tiebout models of local public goods, as demonstrated by Henderson (1985).

26   On a smaller scale, James Rauch (1993) shows how the developer of an industrial park, in which there are production complementaries between firms, can achieve efficiency by subsidizing the first firms moving into the park in order to attract additional tenants. Shopping centers employ a similar strategy by giving rental discounts to anchor stores.

References

Abdel-Rahman, Hesham and Masahisa Fujita (1990) "Product Variety, Marshallian Externalities, and City Sizes," *Journal of Regional Science*, 30(2), 165–83.

Allen, Peter M. (1997) *Cities and Regions as Self-Organizing Systems: Models of Complexity*. Amsterdam: Gordon and Breach Science Pub.

——and M. Sanglier (1981) "A Dynamic Model of a Central Place System-II," *Geographical Analysis*, 13(2), 149–64.

Alonso, William (1964) *Location and Land Use*. Cambridge, MA: Harvard University Press.

Anas, Alex (1990) "Taste Heterogeneity and Urban Spatial Structure: The Logit Model and Mono-centric Theory Reconciled," *Journal of Urban Economics*, 28(3), 318–35.

——. (1992) "On the Birth and Growth of Cities: Laissez-Faire and Planning Compared," *Regional Science and Urban Economics*, 22(2), 243–58.

Anas, Alex and Ikki Kim (1992) "Income Distribution and the Residential Density Gradient," *Journal of Urban Economics*, 31(2), 164–80.

——. (1996) "General Equilibrium Models of Polycentric Urban Land Use with Endogenous Congestion and Job Agglomeration," *Journal of Urban Economics*, 40(2), 232–56.

Arnott, Richard J. (1979) "Unpriced Transport Congestion," *Journal of Economic Theory*, 21(2), 294–316.

——and **Joseph E. Stiglitz** (1979) "Aggregate Land Rents, Expenditure on Public Goods, and Optimal City Size," *Quarterly Journal of Economics*, 93(4), 471–500.

Arthur, W. Brian (1989) "Competing Technologies, Increasing Returns, and Lock-In by Historical Events," *Economic Journal*, 99(394), 116–31.

——. (1990) "Positive Feedbacks in the Economy," *Scientific America*, 262(2), 92–99.

Bacon, Robert W. (1984) *Consumer Spatial Behavior*. Oxford, UK: Clarendon Press.

Bailey, Jeff and Calmetta Y. Coleman (1996) "Despite Tough Years, Chicago Has Become a Nice Place to Live," *Wall Street Journal*, Aug. 21, 135(37), 1, 6.

Bak, Per and Kan Chen (1991) "Self-Organized Criticality," *Scientific America*, 264(1), 46–53.

Barrett, Paul (1983) *The Automobile and Urban Transit: The Formation of Public Policy in Chicago, 1900–1930*, Philadelphia: Temple University Press.

Batty, Michael and Paul Longley (1994) *Fractal Cities: A Geometry of Form and Function*. London: Academic Press.

Berliant, Marcus and Hideo Konishi (1996) "The Endogenous Foundations of a City: Population Agglomeration and Marketplaces in a Location-Specific Production Economy," working paper, U. Rochester.

Borukhov, E. and Oded Hochman (1977) "Optimum and Market Equilibrium in a Model of a City without a Predetermined Center," *Environment & Planning* A, 9(8), 849–56.

Brueckner, Jan (1987) "The Structure of Urban Equilibria: A Unified Treatment of the Muth-Mills Model," in *Handbook of Regional and Urban Economics, Vol. II: Urban Economics*. Edwin S. Mills, ed. North-Holland, Amsterdam, 821–45.

Bunde, Armin and Shlomo Havlin (1996) "Percolation I," in *Fractals and Disordered Systems*. Armin Bunde and Shlomo Havlin, eds. Berlin: Springer-Verlag, 59–113.

Cervero, Robert and Kang-Li Wu (1996) "Subcentering and Commuting: Evidence from the San Francisco Bay Area, 1980–1990," working paper, Inst. of Urban & Regional Development, U. C. Berkeley.

—— (1997) "Polycentrism, Commuting, and Residential Location in the San Francisco Bay Area," *Environment and Planning A*, 29(5), 865–86.

Chen, Hsin-Ping (1993) *Theoretical Derivation and Simulation of a Nonlinear Dynamic Urban Growth Model*. PhD dissertation, Dept. of Econ., U. California Irvine.

—— (1996) "The Simulation of a Proposed Nonlinear Dynamic Urban Growth Model," *Annals of Regional Science*, 30(3), 305–19.

Chinitz, Benjamin (1960) *Freight and the Metropolis*, Cambridge, MA: Harvard University Press.

—— (1961) "Contrasts in Agglomeration: New York and Pittsburgh," *American Economic Review, Papers & Proceedings*, 51(2), 279–89.

Christaller, Walter (1933) *Central Places in Southern Germany*, C. W. Baskin. Trans. London: Prentice-Hall [1966].

Clark, Colin (1951) "Urban Population Densities." *Journal of The Royal Statistical Society: Series A*, 114(4), 490–96.

—— (1967) *Population Growth and Land Use*. London: Macmillan.

Conlisk, John (1992) "Stability and Monotonicity for Interactive Markov Chains," *Journal of Mathematics and Sociology*, 17(2–3), 127–43.

Craig, Steven G., Janet E. Kohlhase and Steven C. Pitts (1996) "The Impact of Land Use Restrictions in a Multicentric City," working paper, University of Houston.

Cronon, William (1991) *Nature's Metropolis: Chicago and the Great West.* NY: Norton.

David, Paul A. (1985) "Clio and the Economics of QWERTY," *American Economic Review*, 75(2), 332–37.

Dixit, Avinash K. and Joseph E. Stiglitz (1977) "Monopolistic Competition and Optimum Product Diversity," *American Economic Review*, 67(3), 297–308.

Downs, Anthony (1992) *Stuck in Traffic: Coping with Peak-Hour Traffic Congestion.* Washington, D.C.: Brookings Institution.

—— (1994) *New Visions for Metropolitan America.* Washington, D.C. and Cambridge, MA: Brookings Institution and Lincoln Institute of Land Policy.

Eberts, Randall W. and Daniel P. McMillen (1999) "Agglomeration Economies and Urban Public Infrastructure," chapter 38 in: *Handbook of Regional and Urban Economics, Volume 3: Applied Urban Economics*, Paul Cheshire and Edwin S. Mills, eds. Amsterdam: North-Holland.

Edmonston, Barry (1975) *Population Distribution in American Cities.* Lexington, MA: D.C. Heath.

Eldredge, Niles and Stephen Jay Gould (1972) "Punctuated Equilibria: An Alternative to Phyletic Gradualism," in *Models in Paleobiology*. T. J. M. Schopf, ed. San Francisco: Freeman, Cooper & Co., 82–115.

Ellison, Glenn and Glaeser, Edward L. (1997) "Geographic Concentration in U.S. Manufacturing Industries: A Dartboard Approach," *Journal of Political Economy*, 105(5), 889–927.

Fales, Raymond and Leon N. Moses (1972) "Land Use Theory and the Spatial Structure of the Nineteenth Century City," *Papers and Proceedings Regional Science Association*, 28, 49–80.

Field, Alexander J. (1992) "The Magnetic Telegraph, Price and Quantity Data and the New Management of Capital," *Journal of Economics and History*, 52(2), 401–13.

Foster, John (1993) "Economics and the Self-Organisation Approach: Alfred Marshall Revisited," *Economic Journal*, 103(419), 975–91.

Fotheringham, A. Stewart, Michael Batty, and Paul A. Longley (1989) "Diffusion-Limited Aggregation and the Fractal Nature of Urban Growth," *Papers and Proceedings Regional Science Association*, 67, 55–69.

Frank, Robert H. (1988) *Passions Within Reason: The Strategic Role of the Emotions.* NY: Norton.

Fujita, Masahisa (1988) "A Monopolistic Competition Model of Spatial Agglomeration: Differentiated Products Approach," *Regional Science and Urban Economics*, 18(1), 87–124.

—— (1989) *Urban Economic Theory: Land Use and City Size*, Cambridge, UK: Cambridge University Press.

—— **and Tomoya Mori** (1997) "Structural Stability and Evolution of Urban Systems," *Regional Science and Urban Economics*, 27(4–5), 399–442.

Fujita, Masahisa and Hideaki Ogawa (1982) "Multiple Equilibria and Structural Transition of Non-monocentric Urban Configurations," *Regional Science and Urban Economics*, 12(2), 161–96.

Gabszewicz, Jean Jaskold and Jacques-François Thisse (1986) "Spatial Competition and the Location of Firms," in *Location Theory*, by Jean Jaskold Gabszewicz, Jacques-François Thisse, Masahisa Fujita and Urs Schweizer. Vol. 5 of *Fundamentals of Pure and Applied Economics* series. Chur, Switzerland: Harwood Academic Publishers, 1–71.

Gaspar, Jess and Edward L. Glaeser (1998) "Information Technology and the Future of Cities," *Journal of Urban Economics*, 43(1), 136–56.

Garreau, Joel (1991) *Edge City: Life on the New Frontier.* NY: Doubleday.

Getis, Arthur (1983) "Second-Order Analysis of Point Patterns: The Case of Chicago as a Multi-Center Urban Region," *Professional Geographer*, 35(1), 73–80.

Giuliano, Genevieve and Kenneth A. Small (1991) "Subcenters in the Los Angeles Region," *Regional Science and Urban Economics*, 21(2), 163–82.

—— (1993) "Is the Journey to Work Explained by Urban Structure?" *Urban Studies*, 30(9), 1485–500.

Glaab, Charles N. and Theodore Brown (1967) *A History of Urban America*, London: Macmillan Press.

Glaeser, Edward L. et al. (1992) "Growth in Cities," *Journal of Political Economy*, 100(6), 1126–52.

Gordon, Peter, Ajay Kumar, and Harry W. Richardson (1989) "The Influence of Metropolitan Spatial Structure on Communting Time," *Journal of Urban Economics*, 26(2), 138–151.

Gordon, Peter and Harry W. Richardson (1994) "Congestion Trends in Metropolitan Areas," in *Curbing Gridlock: Peak-Period Fees to Relieve Traffic Congestion, Volume 2: Commissioned Papers*, Transportation Research Board *Special Report* 242. Committee for Study on Urban Transportation Congestion Pricing, National Research Council. Washington, D.C.: National Academy Press, 1–31.

—— (1996) "Beyond Polycentricity: The Dispersed Metropolis, Los Angeles, 1970–1990," *Journal of American Planning Association*, 62(3), 289–95.

—— (1997) "Are Compact Cities a Desirable Planning Goal?" *Journal of American Planning Association*, 63(1), 95–106.

——and H. L. Wong (1986) "The Distribution of Population and Employment in a Polycentric City: The Case of Los Angeles," *Environment and Planning A*, 18(2), 161–73.

Griffith, Daniel A. (1981) "Evaluating the Transformation from a Monocentric to a Polycentric City," *Professional Geographer*, 33(2), 189–96.

Hamilton, Bruce W. (1982) "Wasteful Commuting," *Journal of Political Economy*, 90(5), 1035–53.

Harris, B. and A. G. Wilson (1978) "Equilibrium Values and Dynamics of Attractiveness Terms in Production-Constrained Spatial-Interaction Models," *Environment and Planning A*, 10(4), 371–88.

Harrison, David, and Kain, John F. (1974) "Cumulative Urban Growth and Urban Density Functions," *Journal of Urban Economics*, 1(1), 61–98.

Heikkila, E. et al. (1989) "What Happened to the CBD-Distance Gradient?: Land Values in a Policentric City," *Environment and Planning A*, 21(2), 221–32.

Helsley, Robert W. and William C. Strange (1991) "Agglomeration Economies and Urban Capital Markets," *Journal of Urban Economics*, 29(1), 96–112.

Henderson, J. Vernon (1985) "The Tiebout Model: Bring Back the Entrepreneurs," *Journal of Political Economy*, 93(2), 248–64.

——and Arindam Mitra (1996) "The New Urban Landscape: Developers and Edge Cities," *Regional Science and Urban Economics*, 26(6), 613–43.

—— and Eric Slade (1993) "Development Games in Non-monocentric Cities," *Journal of Urban Economics*, 34(2), 207–29.

Hoover, Edgar M. (1948) *The Location of Economic Activity*. NY: McGraw-Hill.

Hotelling, Harold (1929) "Stability in Competition," *Economic Journal*, 39(1), 41–57.

Ingram, Gregory K. and Alan Carroll (1981) "The Spatial Structure of Latin American Cities," *Journal of Urban Economics*, 9(2), 257–73.

Jacobs, Jane (1969) *The Economy of Cities*. NY: Random House.

—— (1984) *Cities and the Wealth of Nations: Principles of Economic Life*. NY: Random House.

Kain, John (1968) "Housing Segregation, Negro Employment, and Metropolitan Decentralization," *Quarterly Journal of Economics*, 82, 175–97.

Koopmans, Tjalling C., and Martin Beckmann (1957) "Assignment Problems and the Location of Economic Activities," *Econometrica*, 25(1), 53–76.

Krugman, Paul (1987) "Is Free Trade Passé?" *Journal of Economic Perspectives*, 1(2), 131–44.

—— (1991a) *Geography and Trade*. Cambridge, MA: M.I.T. Press.

—— (1991b) "Increasing Returns and Economic Geography," *Journal of Political Economy*, 99(3), 483–99.

—— (1993) "First Nature, Second Nature and Metropolitan Location," *Journal of Regional Science*, 33(2), 129–44.

—— (1996) *The Self-Organizing Economy*. Cambridge, MA: Blackwell.

LeRoy, Stephen F. and Jon Sonstelie (1983) "Paradise Lost and Regained: Transportation Innovation, Income, and Residential Location," *Journal of Urban Economics*, 13(1), 67–89.

Lösch, August (1940) *The Economics of Location*, W. H. Woglom and W. F. Stolper. Trans. New Haven: Yale University Press [1954].

Makse, Hernan A., Shlomo Havlin, and H. Eugene Stanley (1995) "Modelling Urban Growth Patterns," *Nature*, October, 377, 608–12.

Maynard Smith, John (1976) "Evolution and the Theory of Games," *American Scientist*, 64(1), 41–45.

McDonald, John F. (1987) "The Identification of Urban Employment Subcenters," *Journal of Urban Economics*, 21(2), 242–58.

—— (1989) "Econometric Studies of Urban Population Density: A Survey," *Journal of Urban Economics*, 26(3), 361–85.

——and Paul J. Prather (1994) "Suburban Employment Centres: The Case of Chicago," *Urban Studies*, 31(2), 201–18.

McMillen, Daniel P. (1996) "One Hundred Fifty Years of Land Values in Chicago: A Nonparametric Approach," *Journal of Urban Economics*, 40(1), 100–24.

——and John F. McDonald (1998a) "Population Density in Suburban Chicago: A Bid-Rent Approach," *Urban Studies*, 55(7), 1119–30.

—— (1998b) "Suburban Subcenters and Employment Density in Metropolitan Chicago," *Journal of Urban Economics*, 43(2), 157–80.

Mieszkowski, Peter and Edwin S. Mills (1993) "The Causes of Metropolitan Suburbanization," *Journal of Economic Perspectives*, 7(3), 135–47.

——and Barton Smith (1991) "Analyzing Urban Decentralization: The Case of Houston," *Regional Science and Urban Economics*, 21(2), 183–99.

Mills, Edwin S. (1967) "An Aggregative Model of Resource Allocation in a Metropolitan Area," *American Economic Review*, 57, 197–210.

—— (1972) *Studies in the Structure of the Urban Economy*. Baltimore: Johns Hopkins Press.

——and Bruce W. Hamilton (1994) *Urban Economics*, New York: Harper Collins.

Mills, Edwin S. and Katsutoshi Ohta (1976) "Urbanization and Urban Problems," in *Asia's New Giant: How the Japanese Economy Works*. Hugh Patrick and Henry Rosovsky, eds. Washington: Brookings Institution, 673–751.

Mills, Edwin S. and Jee Peng Tan (1980) "A Comparison of Urban Population Density Functions in Developed and Developing Countries," *Urban Studies*, 17(3), 313–21.

Mirrlees, James A. (1972) "The Optimum Town," *Swedish Journal of Economics*, 74(1), 114–35.

Moses, Leon and Harold F. Williamson, Jr. (1967) "The Location of Economic Activity in Cities," *American Economic Review*, 57(2), 211–22.

Murphy, Kevin M., Andrei Schleifer, and Robert W. Vishny (1989) "Industrialization and the Big Push," *Journal of Political Economy*, 97(5), 1003–26.

Muth, Richard F (1969) *Cities and Housing*. Chicago: The University of Chicago Press.

Nelson, Richard R. (1995) "Recent Evolutionary Theorizing About Economic Change," *Journal of Economic Literature*, 33(1), 48–90.

Nicholis, G., and Ilya Prigogine (1977) *Self-Organisation in Non-equilibrium Systems: From Dissipative Structures to Order through Fluctuations*. NY: John Wiley.

Ó hUalláchin, Breandán (1989) "Agglomeration of Services in American Metropolitan Areas," *Growth and Change*, 20(3), 34–49.

Orfield, Myron (1997) *Metropolitics: A Regional Agenda for Community and Stability*. Washington, D.C. and Cambridge: Brookings Institution and Lincoln Institute of Land Policy.

Papageorgiou, Yorgos Y. and David Pines (1989) "The Exponential Density Function: First Principles, Comparative Statics, and Empirical Evidence," *Journal of Urban Economics*, 26(2), 264–68.

—— and **T.R. Smith** (1983) "Agglomeration as Local Instability in Spatially Uniform Steady-States," *Econometrica*, 51(4), 1109–19.

Powell, Walter W. (1990) "Neither Market nor Hierarchy: Network Forms of Organization," in *Research into Organizational Behavior*, 12, 295–336.

Rauch, James E. (1993) "Does History Matter Only When It Matters Little? The Case of City-Industry Location," *Quarterly Journal of Economics*, 108(434), 843–67.

Robinson, E. A. G. (1931) *The Structure of Competitive Industry*. Cambridge, UK: Cambridge University Press.

Romer, Paul M. (1986) "Increasing Returns and Long-Run Growth," *Journal of Political Economy*, 94(5), 1002–37.

Rosen, Kenneth T. and Mitchel Resnick (1980) "The Size Distribution of Cities: An Examination of the Pareto Law and Primacy," *Journal of Urban Economics*, 8(2), 165–86.

Rusk, David (1993) *Cities Without Suburbs*. Baltimore: Johns Hopkins University Press.

Saxenian, AnnaLee (1994) *Regional Advantage: Culture and Competition in Silicon Valley and Route 128*. Cambridge, MA: Harvard University Press.

Schulz, Norbert and Konrad Stahl (1996) "Do Consumers Search for the Highest Price? Oligopoly Equilibrium and Monopoly Optimum in Differentiated-Products Markets," *Rand Journal of Economics*, 27(3), 542–62.

Scott, Allen J. (1988) *Metropolis: From the Division of Labor to Urban Form*. Berkeley: University of California Press.

—— (1991) "Electronics Assembly Subcontracting in Southern California: Production Processes, Employment, and Location," *Growth and Change*, 22(1), 22–35.

Sivitanidou, Rena (1996) "Do Office-Commercial Firms Value Access to Service Employment Centers? A Hedonic Value Analysis within Polycentric Los Angeles," *Journal of Urban Economics*, 40(2), 125–149.

Small, Kenneth A. (1981) "A Comment on Gasoline Prices and Urban Structure," *Journal of Urban Economics*, 10(3), 311–22.

—— (1992) *Urban Transportation Economics*, Vol. 51 of *Fundamentals of Pure and Applied Economics* series. Chur, Switzerland: Harwood Academic Publishers.

—— (1994) "Population and Employment Densities: Structure and Change," *Journal of Urban Economics*, 36(3), 292–313.

—— and **Shunfeng Song** (1992) "'Wasteful' Commuting: A Resolution," *Journal of Political Economy*, 100(4), 888–98.

Solow, Robert M. (1973) "On Equilibrium Models of Urban Location," in *Essays in Modern Economics*. Michael Parkin with A. R. Nobay, eds. London: Longman, 2–16.

—— and **William S. Vickrey** (1971) "Land Use in a Long Narrow City," *Journal of Economic Theory*, 3(4), 430–47.

Song, Shunfeng (1994) "Modelling Worker Residence Distribution in the Los Angeles Region," *Urban Studies*, 31(9), 1533–44.

Starrett, David A. (1974) "Principles of Optimal Location in a Large Homogeneous Area," *Journal of Economic Theory*, 9(4), 418–48.

Stiglitz, Joseph E. (1977) "The Theory of Local Public Goods," in *The Economics of Public Services*. Martin S. Feldstein and Robert P. Inman, eds. London: Macmillan. 274–333.

Thomas, R. W. (1981) "Point Pattern Analysis," in *Quantitative Geography: A British View*. N. Wrigley and R. J. Bennett, eds. London: Routledge and Kegan Paul, 164–76.

Tiebout, Charles M. (1956) "A Pure Theory of Local Expenditures," *Journal of Political Economy*, 64(5), 416–24.

U.S. Bureau of the Census (1996) *Statistical Abstract of the United States: 1996* Washington, D.C.: U.S. Government Printing Office.

Vernon, Raymond (1960) *Metropolis 1985*. Cambridge, MA: Harvard University Press.

von Thünen, Johann Heinrich (1826) *Der Isolierte Staat in Beziehung auf Landwirtschaft und Nationalokonomie*. Hamburg: F. Perthes.

Warner, Sam Bass Jr. (1962) *Streetcar Suburbs: The Process of Growth in Boston: 1870–1900*, Cambridge, MA: Harvard University Press.

Wheaton, William C. (1974) "A Comparative Statics Analysis of Urban Spatial Structure," *Journal of Economic Theory*, 9(2), 223–37.

—— (1977) "Income and Urban Residence: An Analysis of Consumer Demand for Location," *American Economic Review*, 67(4), 620–31.

—— (1978) "Price-Induced Distortions in Urban Highway Investment," *Bell Journal of Economics*, 9(2), 622–32.

White, Michelle J. (1976) "Firm Suburbanization and Urban Subcenters," *Journal of Urban Economics*, 3(4), 323–43.

—— (1988) "Location Choice and Commuting Behavior in Cities with Decentralized Employment," *Journal of Urban Economics*, 24(2), 129–52.

CHAPTER NINE

How America's Cities are Growing: The Big Picture

Anthony Downs

Source: The Brookings Review, Fall 1998. Brookings Institution Press, Washington DC.

Suburban sprawl has been the dominant form of metropolitan-area growth in the United States for the past 50 years. This article analyzes the nature of such sprawl, why it occurs in U.S. metropolitan areas, the problems it causes or aggravates, and some alternative possible forms of future metropolitan-area growth.

What Is Suburban Sprawl?

Suburban sprawl is not *any form* of suburban growth, but a *particular form*. The definition I will use was not developed deductively from some coherent underlying concept of "sprawlness." Rather, I looked inductively at all the criticisms of sprawl in the literature and derived ten specific traits that seemed most likely to cause them:

- Unlimited outward extension of new development
- Low-density residential and commercial settlements, especially in new-growth areas
- Leapfrog development jumping out beyond established settlements
- Fragmentation of powers over land use among many small localities
- Dominance of transportation by private automotive vehicles
- No centralized planning or control of land uses
- Widespread strip commercial development
- Great fiscal disparities among localities
- Segregation of specialized types of land uses in different zones
- Reliance mainly on trickle-down to provide housing to low-income households

Why Sprawl Has Been So Dominant

Opponents of suburban sprawl are quick to point out its problems and social costs. But they are loathe to admit that sprawl also produces many benefits for large numbers of metropolitan citizens – probably a majority in most regions. Those benefits include low-density residential lifestyles, relatively easy access to open space both at one's own home and in the countryside, a broad choice of places to work and live, relatively short commuting times for most of those who both live and work in the suburbs, ease of movement except in peak periods, the ability of middle- and upper-income households to separate themselves spatially from problems associated with poverty, and their ability to exercise strong influence on their local governments. Persuading those who receive these benefits to support future limits on sprawl will require proving to them that its costs to society as a whole – and therefore to them – outweigh their own gains.

Sprawl's Negative Impacts

Suburban sprawl generates, or at least aggravates, two different sets of economic and social problems that reduce the quality of life for millions of Americans.

The first set of problems occurs mainly in fast-growing areas, but spreads to other areas too. It includes traffic congestion, air pollution, large-scale absorption of open space, extensive use of energy for movement, inability to provide adequate infrastructures to accommodate growth because of high costs, inability to locate certain region-serving facilities like new airports that have negative local spillover effects, and suburban labor shortages because of inadequate low-income housing near new jobs. Low-density growth also tempts governments to spend too much of their limited resources on building highly visible new infrastructures rather than on the nearly invisible process of properly maintaining older existing ones. So we finance growth by gradually undermining the sustainability of the existing infrastructure inventory.

All these directly growth-related problems are essentially regional, not purely local. Therefore, purely local growth management policies adopted by individual municipalities cannot succeed without some strong regionwide mechanism for coordinating them.

The second set of problems affects mainly big cities, inner-ring suburbs, and a few outer-ring suburbs. These problems arise because suburban sprawl concentrates poor households, especially poor minority households, in certain high-poverty neighborhoods. Those neighborhoods then suffer from high crime rates, poor-quality public schools, other poor-quality public services, and fiscal resources that are inadequate for the services needed. These problems soon spread to inner-ring suburbs too. And many outer-ring suburbs with low commercial tax bases but a lot of relatively low-cost housing have inadequate taxable resources to pay for decent schools and other services, so they have high tax rates and poor services.

Sprawl and Concentrated Poverty

How sprawl generates directly development-related problems is obvious. How it concentrates poor people within the boundaries of many large cities and inner-ring suburbs and undermines their fiscal strengths is more complex.

Since 1950, some type of peripheral new development around American metropolitan areas has been inevitable because of their tremendous population growth. Cities had to expand outward from the center. Mainly vertical expansion would have required increases in density inconsistent with rising real household incomes and innovations in both transportation and communications.

But the particular form of U.S. peripheral growth has resulted in intensive concentration of very poor households, especially those in minority groups, in the older, more central portions of our metropolitan areas. This development is not inevitable. Similar mainly core-area concentrations of the poor do not arise in either most developed Western European nations or most still-developing nations. They have been caused in the United States by specific policies adopted to produce them.

The first American policy generating core-area poverty concentrations is the requirement that all new housing meet quality standards that are so high that most poor households cannot afford them. Unable to live in newly built housing, very poor people become concentrated in older neighborhoods found mainly toward the central part of each metropolitan area.

A second policy combines fragmented control over land uses in many small outlying municipalities with exclusionary zoning and other strategies designed to raise local housing costs. Suburban residents want to exclude poor people from their neighborhoods to protect their housing investments, to maintain their social status, and to isolate themselves spatially from what they see as undesirable traits of low-income households. So suburban behavior is partly responsible for the core-area concentration of the poor, even though most suburbanites claim no connection with central-city problems.

The third cause of inner-core poverty concentrations is racial segregation in housing markets. Repeated and recent studies of realtor and homeowner behavior prove that racial discrimination is still widespread in housing transactions. Reducing racial segregation is hard because even if both whites and blacks desire racially integrated living, the different ways they define it cause almost total segregation to emerge from free choice of locations. African Americans regard a neighborhood containing about half blacks and half whites as desirably integrated, whereas most whites regard desirable integration as involving less than one-third or one-fourth blacks. Given these disparate views, blacks will continue moving into a partly integrated neighborhood beyond the fraction that keeps the neighborhood desirable to whites. That causes other whites to stop moving in, and the inevitable annual turnover in neighborhood residents (about 16–20 percent in most areas) results in more blacks moving in but no more whites doing so. Eventually, the neighborhood becomes almost entirely black – thus racially segregated – even without anyone's explicitly desiring such segregation. Racial segregation against Hispanics is less pervasive but real.

Results of Concentrated Poverty

Core-area poverty concentrations contribute to adverse neighborhood traits that "push" many businesses and middle-and upper-income households of all races – mainly households with children – out of central cities into suburbs. When these firms and households leave core areas, they take their fiscal resources with them. Because our fragmented governance system does not permit core-area cities to tap into most suburban tax bases, core areas are left disproportionately burdened with providing costly services to many poor households. A self-aggravating downward fiscal spiral weakens the ability of core-area governments to provide quality public services and results in grossly unequal environments across our metropolitan areas. Such disparities in the neighborhoods in which children are raised make a mockery of the American ideal of equality of opportunity.

How is this process related to suburban sprawl? In theory, sprawl's specific traits have many roles in producing core-area concentrations of poverty. Unlimited extension into space removes new jobs from accessibility by unemployed inner-core residents; fragmented controls over land uses permit exclusionary zoning policies; and heavy dependence on private vehicles deprives poor people and non-drivers of mobility. However, when I have tried to verify these linkages empirically for 162 large metropolitan areas, most of the 10 traits of sprawl exhibit no statistically significant relationship to measures of urban decline. Even so, I believe the core-area concentration of minority poverty built into the American metropolitan development process aggravates urban decline. But that relationship may be inherent in all forms of American peripheral suburban growth, not just suburban sprawl, or it may be based on just a few of sprawl's basic traits.

Other Growth Strategies

What other forms of metropolitan-area growth might avoid or reduce the problems generated by sprawl? Two possibilities exist. One involves major alternative overall development strategies, the other, specific tactics to overcome sprawl's deficiencies. I will discuss both briefly, defining sprawl as unlimited low-density development.

There are three major alternative development strategies. The first, tightly bounded higher-density development, is typical of many Western European metropolitan areas. It features close-in urban growth boundaries, prohibition of almost all urban development outside them, high-density residential and other development within the boundary, greater stress on public transit for movement, centralized coordination of land use plans drawn up by local governments, and widely scattered new housing for low-income households. This alternative is such a radical change from existing American practices that it is unrealistic to believe that anything like it might even be considered in most U.S. metropolitan areas.

The second strategy, loosely bounded moderate-density development, lies between unlimited sprawl and tightly bounded high-density development. It has a loosely drawn growth boundary, permits some development outside the boundary, raises densities somewhat above sprawl levels, has some increase in public transit and carpooling, has centralized coordination of local land use planning, and provides some new low-income housing in growth areas. This strategy would nevertheless be a very great change from the unconstrained, low-density, auto-oriented growth now prevalent in most U.S. metropolitan areas.

The third strategy is new outlying communities and green spaces. It has a tightly drawn urban growth boundary, can incorporate the other features of either of the other strategies, but permits substantial growth outside the boundary within designated new communities centered on existing outlying towns. This alternatives sounds nice but has gained little political support in areas that have actually considered it.

It is obvious that continuation of suburban sprawl will surely not solve the serious problems I have described. In fact, it would make them worse. But it is not theoretically obvious, nor has it been decisively proven in practice, that any of these alternative strategies will largely solve the problems either. In theory, these alternative strategies would at least ameliorate them, as compared to continuing sprawl. Yet the advantages of these strategies have not been powerfully enough demonstrated to the American people to persuade them to give up the advantages they perceive in sprawl.

Specific Anti-sprawl Tactics

The other way to attack the problems is with specific tactics aimed at them. The first such tactic is some type of urban growth boundary to limit the outward draining of resources from core areas. This boundary need not be airtight to produce benefits. It should, however, be linked to public provision of key infrastructures, which should not be publicly financed outside the boundary. But no growth boundary will have any significant impact unless strong controls limit growth outside it. Moreover, an urban growth boundary that is the "accidental" sum of many separate boundaries adopted by individual communities is not likely to work. If there are no constraints on development in counties lying just outside the growth boundary, developers will leapfrog into those areas and put new growth there. That will simply accelerate sprawl, as has happened in the Twin Cities and around Toronto. In the San Francisco Bay area, several communities have adopted local growth boundaries and several others are considering doing so. But unless these efforts are coordinated, they will not be effective in solving the problems of the region as a whole.

The second tactic is regional coordination and rationalization of local land use planning, done by some regional planning body, such as the Metropolitan Council in the Twin Cities. Relying solely on individual communities to adopt growth management plans without any overall planning or coordination is like relying on a group of subcontractors to build a house with no overall blueprint. Yet very few U.S. metropolitan areas have been willing to adopt this tactic. Local officials universally resist it, because they claim it would reduce their "local sovereignty." In reality, they have no real control – and thus no true sovereignty – concerning growth-related problems, because those problems are all regional, and no purely local policies can solve them.

Experience suggests that communities individually responding to growth-related problems will adopt plans that lock in low density locally. Each locality will try to shift multi-family housing elsewhere to avoid the fiscal burdens such housing loads on to local taxpayers. Each locality will also adopt other exclusionary policies to protect single-family home values and keep poorer people out. These beggar-thy-neighbor plans will force growth either to more outlying areas less hostile to new development or into inner-city areas through illegal overcrowding. As a result, purely localized growth management will cause sprawl to become worse, not better. Growth will then be shifted to more outlying communities when existing ones refuse to permit higher densities.

The third tactic is some form of regional tax-base sharing, with all additions to commercial and industrial tax bases shared among all communities in the region, not just captured by the places where those developments are built. Such tax-base sharing would reduce fiscal disparities among local governments and thereby provide more equal opportunities for citizens across the entire area.

The fourth tactic is regionwide development of housing for low-income households, either by regional vouchers or regional new subsidies or by requiring developers to build a share of affordable housing in each new project. This tactic is controversial, but our society must begin by breaking down the concentration of poverty. David Rusk has recently proven that focusing on improving core-area poverty neighborhoods through community development has almost universally failed to prevent such neighborhoods from falling further and further behind the region. Yet most suburbanites who support any policies to ameliorate the problems of concentrated poverty would rather try to upgrade inner-city neighborhoods than help the residents there move into better neighborhoods. They prefer the failed upgrading tactic because it does not require them to face the prospect of accepting more poor residents into their neighborhoods and schools. In the long run, however, such acceptance is probably essential to reducing the serious national problems generated by concentrated inner-core area poverty.

A fifth tactic is regional operation of public transit systems and highways, including new facility construction. Several metropolitan areas have adopted this tactic, although whether their transportation systems produce results superior to those elsewhere has not yet been proven.

A final tactic is vigorous regional enforcement of laws against racial discrimination. Very few American metropolitan areas have carried out this tactic or seem about to do so.

Effectively adopting any of these tactics, or certainly most of them together, would likely require a strong regionwide implementing body. Yet hardly any U.S. metropolitan areas have been willing to consider doing this. Even if all these tactics were adopted, it is not certain that they would overcome the ill effects of core-area concentrations of poverty. The best that can be said is that they have a chance of doing so if they are carried out at a large enough scale over a very long time. Nor is it certain that these tactics would overcome a region's growth-related problems. For example, I am positive that traffic congestion will get worse almost everywhere, no matter what tactics anyone adopts.

Gaining Political Support

Until advocates of limited future sprawl can overcome the metropolitan majority's belief that the benefits of sprawl outweigh its social costs, they are not likely to notably reduce sprawl's dominance. How can they overcome that political resistance? Dealing with this critical issue is beyond the scope of this article. Some discussion of it is presented in the article by Myron Orfield (1998).

Most of the few states that have adopted effective growth management programs have been motivated by some crisis — usually an environmental issue such as new subdivisions disrupting Florida's Everglades. It is neither easy, nor desirable, to generate such crises on demand! Therefore, until more crises occur spontaneously, advocates of checking sprawl will have to grind away at the slow task of educating the majority of citizens who believe sprawl is good that its costs outweigh its benefits, even for them. I hope this article contributes some ammunition for that long struggle.

References

Orfield, Myron (1998) "Conflict or Consensus," *The Brookings Review*, Fall, 16(4), 31–4.

CHAPTER TEN

Prove It: The Costs and Benefits of Sprawl

Peter Gordon and Harry W. Richardson

Source: The Brookings Review, Fall 1998. Brookings Institution Press, Washington DC.

Cities have been generating suburbs for as long as records have existed. Most of the world's large cities are growing outward now, and very likely the pace will accelerate in the new age of information networking. Unpopular as the word is in some quarters, it is hard to avoid concluding that "sprawl" is most people's preferred life-style. Because no one wants to appear to contradict popular choices and interfere with the principle of consumer sovereignty, the critics of sprawl instead blame distorted prices, such as automobile subsidies and mortgage interest deductions, and claimed but unregistered costs of sprawl, such as unpaid-for infrastructure, lost agricultural output, congestion, and dirty air.

The cost position, however, is encumbered with at least two problems. First, most of us are not cost minimizers. Rather, we trade off costs for perceived benefits. And second, the costs argument is empirically shaky. Traffic "doomsday" forecasts, for example, have gone the way of most other dire predictions. Why? Because suburbanization has turned out to be the traffic safety valve. Increasingly footloose industry has followed workers into the suburbs and exurban areas, and most commuting now takes place suburb-to-suburb on faster, less crowded roads. The last three surveys by the Nationwide Personal Transportation Survey (NPTS) show increasing average work trip speeds – 28 mph in 1983, 32.3 mph in 1990, and 33.6 mph in 1995.

The alleged loss of prime farmlands is, in the words of the late Julian Simon, "the most conclusively discredited environmental–political fraud of recent times." U.S. cropland use peaked in 1930. Each year American farmers grow *more* crops using *less* land and labor.

As for the "compactness equals efficiency" argument, technological change takes us in the direction of efficient small-scale provision, weakening the old idea that scale economies of utility generation are there to be exploited by more compact urban forms. Large retail establishments, for example, can now keep low-kilowatt natural gas turbines on the premises.

U.S. public policies do not have a singular spatial thrust. Some policies, such as subsidized downtown renewal, subsidized and downtown-focused transit, subsidized downtown convention centers, sports stadia, and similar facilities, favor centralized settlement. Others, including inflexible zoning codes and the deductibility of mortgage interest and real estate property tax, favor dispersal.

The much vaunted subsidies to the auto-highway system consist mainly of decisions by government policymakers not to tax drivers to recover the cost of such externalities as congestion and environmental damage. And that issue recedes in importance as highway speeds increase and internal combustion engines become cleaner. The mortgage interest tax deduction raises land values throughout the metropolitan region. It has contributed much less to central-city decline than have suburban minimum lot size restrictions and poorer central-city amenities. In any event, reducing subsidies makes more sense than equalizing them, as, for example, through trying to equate automobile and transit subsidies.

The evidence that has been assembled on the difficult issue of infrastructure services costs is, at best, mixed. Even if it could be conclusively demonstrated that suburban and exurban infrastructure costs are higher than central-city costs, the solution is not to ban suburbanization and low-density development or introduce strict growth management controls. A better approach is to use developer impact fees (fees per residential unit imposed on new development) to recoup any difference between the fiscal costs and revenues from residential development.

The Need for Clarity

The sprawl discussion is distorted by a high degree of misinformation. To take one example, state and local growth management, "smart growth," and anti-sprawl protagonists frequently cite Los Angeles as the sprawl capital of the United States, with a land use pattern to be avoided at all costs. In fact, the urbanized area of the Los Angeles metropolitan region has the highest residential densities in the United States – higher even than the New York urbanized region – largely the result of its high land prices.

Casual observers have been deceived by looking at only the gross densities based on all the land area, much of which consists of vast unbuildable areas such as mountains and peripheral deserts. Another false conception is that suburban areas are dominated by single-family homes on large lots. In fact, the suburban and exurban "attached house" share of the metropolitan housing stock is about 50 percent. Of the nation's presumably higher-density attached housing, then, half is located outside central cities.

Increasingly, the attack on sprawl is being justified by the need to achieve the goal of "sustainable urbanization." But no one has defined the term satisfactorily. Rather, the talk is of recycling, increasing densities, and promoting transit as instruments for preserving resources for future use. The concern for future generations that sustainability implies gives insufficient weight to today's problems of poverty and inequality. In the words of Nobel Prize-winning economist Robert Solow, "There is at least as strong a case for reducing contemporary inequality (and probably stronger) as for worrying about the uncertain status of future generations." In our view, these problems cannot be alleviated significantly via the social engineering of urban space.

Some observers see compact and high-rise development as an accommodation to inferior forms of transportation that have been eclipsed by the automobile. The universal choice is for the freedom and flexibility that come only with personal transportation. Collective transportation loses in any head-to-head contest, as the widespread operations of large numbers of clandestine "gypsy" cabs and vans above one of the world's premier subway systems in New York City make clear. Even in New York, many origins and destinations are too dispersed to be serviced by fixed-route systems. The record of conventional transit throughout the United States is the same theme writ large. After hundreds of billions of dollars of public subsidy, transit use per capita is now at a historic low. The evolution of American cities and life-styles has outgrown 19th-century-style urban transit. Ironically, the mass transit favored by anti-sprawl activists – street cars, subways, and urban rail systems of earlier days – was the prime instrument of suburbanization. The automobile merely diversified its radial pattern.

And though mass transit supporters argue for higher densities to reduce congestion and improve air quality, in fact the relationship between density and traffic congestion is positive rather than negative, and the link between congestion and air quality is very complex and highly technical.

In the end, the goals of the anti-sprawl position are unattainable. Opportunities for infill development in central cities exist, but they are limited. There is a small, if growing, scattering of compact new developments in the suburban and, more often, exurban environments, but their impact on anti-sprawl goals is minimal. There is, for example, no evidence that they reduce off-site trips. Any reasonable assumptions about the extent of future compact developments must yield the conclusion that their influence on tomorrow's urban landscape is minuscule.

Proponents of the New Urbanism claim the ability to design community-friendly neighborhoods, thus joining the movement to revive communitarianism. While there is a lively debate over the current state of civil society (as the contributors to this *Review's* fall 1997 issue make clear), the case of the New Urbanists is much less clear. Residential developments and whole neighborhoods are being supplied by market-savvy builders attentive to the trade-offs that their customers are eager to make. People in compact communities live as privately as those in low-density suburbs. Were people to demand cozier spatial arrangements, they would soon get them. Moreover, the public's demand for "community" is being met in other ways, facilitated by the auto and even Internet access. In terms of transportation, we know that the overwhelming amount of travel is nonwork travel. About one-fifth of person-trips are for work-related purposes, one-fifth are for shopping, and three-fifths are for "social" reasons (including the NPTS categories "other family and personal business," "school/church," "visit friends or relatives," and "other social or recreational" purposes).

Dealing with the Costs of Sprawl

We are not advocating a "laissez-faire" approach to the development of our cities. Cities are, almost by definition, the cause of myriad unintended costs. Many problems (not all) can, and should, be resolved by low-cost negotiation between the affected parties (for example, developers and environmentalists) or by the exchange of expanded property rights (using such measures as emission fees, congestion prices, and development credits). The more radical measures proposed by critics of American cities – maximum densities, restrictions on automobile use, and mandatory fees and taxes to pay for transit – are grounded in misconceptions and are unlikely to achieve their stated goals.

The principle of consumer sovereignty has played a powerful role in the increase in America's wealth and in the welfare of its citizens. Producers (including developers) have responded rapidly to households' demands. It is a giant step backward to interfere with this effective process unless the benefits of intervention substantially exceed its costs. Bans on the amount of land that individuals can consume, or even worse, on driving, are extremely difficult to justify. In fact, when households purchase a single-family home in the suburbs, they are not consuming land per se. Rather, they are buying a number of attributes – good public schools, relative safety from crime, easy access to recreation and shopping opportunities, low taxes, responsive public services. Lot size is rarely crucial to the decision. In any event, lot sizes are becoming smaller as a result of rising land prices, and there may be opportunities for developers through creative design to reduce lot sizes still further while preserving privacy. But smaller lots are not going to revive the central city or alter significantly the consequences of suburban and exurban development.

Paradoxically, as the U.S. political system increasingly emphasizes deregulation and market processes at the federal, and sometimes the state, level, command-and-control restrictions and interest-group impositions at the local level are growing and are frequently being reinforced by actions in the courts. Much of this shift, exemplified by the expansion of land use regulations, reflects a retargeting of regulatory activity from economic sectors to such social concerns as education, health, and the environment. But for the cost–benefit calculus advocated by the anti-sprawl protagonists to prevail, the quality of their empirical evidence must be improved.

CHAPTER ELEVEN

Comment on Carl Abott's "The Portland Region: Where Cities and Suburbs Talk to Each Other – and Often Agree"

WILLIAM A. FISCHEL

Source: Housing Policy Debate, 8(1). © 1997 Fannie Mae Foundation. The copyrighted material is used with the permission of the Fannie Mae Foundation.

The Portland, OR, area's urban growth boundary is an idea whose benefits to the region may depend on a willingness to expand the boundary occasionally. The parable contained in this comment suggests that the declared unwillingness to expand the urban growth boundary could have contributed to Portland's recent sudden increase in housing prices. It further suggests that an inflexible attitude toward the boundary could cause long-run losses in employment in the Portland region, with few if any offsetting environmental benefits. Other regions should be aware of the potential drawbacks of installing such a boundary.

In the old days, when there was labor-union strife, people used to ask, "Why can't business and labor get together?" To this, Mr. Dooley (the voice of humorist Peter Finley Dunne) used to respond, "If business and labor ever do get together, it's good night for the rest of us."

Nowadays, a similar question is perennially asked about central cities and suburbs: Why can't they get together to solve their common problems? Carl Abbott has described the remarkable collaboration between the city of Portland, OR, and its suburbs. It does seem that Portland has performed the trick of uniting the interests of its suburban and central-city residents, at least as far as land use issues are concerned. As an outsider and an economist, I can hardly gainsay the political analysis of a long-time professor of urban studies at Portland State University. I propose instead to employ economic principles, offered in the form of a parable, to ask whether Portland's accomplishment is in the long-run interests of Portlanders and the rest of us. Readers are invited to draw their own conclusions as to whether there is any resemblance between the following story and Professor Abbott's account of Portland.

An island called Zeeland (figure 1) is surrounded by an ocean from which fish are taken and sold to both Zeelanders and people on other islands. However, 96 percent of Zeeland's economy consists of services and manufactured goods, which the inhabitants trade among themselves and with people on other islands.

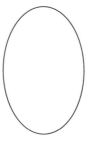

Figure 1   Zeeland, Phase 1

Zeeland is a pleasant island, and when its economy is doing well, it tends to grow in population as people arrive from other islands to take jobs. Growth traditionally took place in the following manner. When people arrived, they initially crowded into the existing housing stock. Since this caused prices to rise, developers of new housing saw a profit opportunity, and eventually more housing was built. Most of the new housing was initially built on newly created islets near Zeeland (figure 2); that is, developers would fill in the surrounding shallows with little islands. Eventually, enough little islands were created that they merged together (figure 3).

This process of development worried Zeelanders. The more naive said the ocean would eventually be filled in and they would run out of fish. (They somehow failed to notice that most of the fish they ate came from other islands and that the ocean was rather large.) The more sophisticated said the pattern of development made it harder for people on the outer islets to get to the island center, where jobs had traditionally been located, and for people in the center to get to the edges, where many new jobs were located. And many just disliked the messy pattern by which offshore development was taking place.

In response to these concerns, Zeelanders passed a law freezing for several years the island's borders where they were. It prohibited anyone from filling in any more shallows to create more islets. Housing for any net growth in the island's population in the next few years would have to be in homes built in spaces on the existing island.

The establishment of the new island growth boundary (IGB) did not cause any serious problems initially. Yes, some developers who formerly had the right to fill in shallows did complain, but the existing shores of Zeeland still encompassed much vacant, developable land. Newcomers had little trouble buying housing built on such lots and living pretty much like the old-timers on the island. It helped that immigration to Zeeland was not especially strong for many years, as the Zeeland economy was not expanding very rapidly.

It also helped a lot that owners of undeveloped land on Zeeland understood that the IGB would eventually be loosened. When growth began to push up prices so that land and housing were less affordable to newcomers, the government was supposed to allow new land to be added to the island. It would not be added in the traditional "leapfrog" way, though. There would be no more little islets popping up in the shallows. Instead,

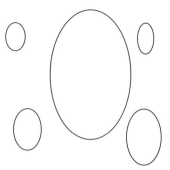

Figure 2   Zeeland Phase 2

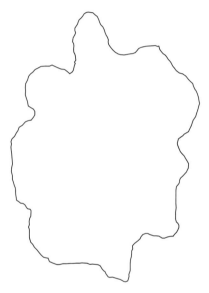

Figure 3   Zeeland Phase 3

all new infill would be contiguous to the island, so that it would expand like a balloon. Leapfrog growth was out; orderly, contiguous growth was in.

After 20 years, much of the previously undeveloped land in Zeeland had been occupied. The Zeeland economy had picked up, and more and more immigrants were arriving. Developers then pointed out that the IGB should be expanded, as had been planned long ago. But Zeelanders could not bring themselves to do it. Instead, they decided to try to accommodate all new development within the existing confines of the island, requiring developers to use the existing vacant lots.

The decision not to expand the IGB was the trigger for a land price explosion. Owners of vacant land had formerly expected that the government would expand the IGB and thus add more vacant land. Now they realized that they were in the catbird seat. Their land acquired a value they hitherto had not anticipated. Developers who had been waiting for newly created land outside the IGB to be added to the market now desperately sought to buy existing land to satisfy newcomers' demands for housing. But landowners were reluctant to sell very much. They saw that their undeveloped land was suddenly a much better financial asset than it had been just a few years before. Why should they sell for $50,000 an acre when they could get $100,000 in a few years? Now confident that the IGB would not add any more land to complete with their sites, owners sat and watched their land's value skyrocket.

As a result of the land price inflation, many newcomers, who formerly would have bought new houses built on vacant land, now turned to the existing stock of housing. They bid up the price of existing homes. Other newcomers settled for less spacious homes on much smaller lots on the few acres of land available to be developed.

None of this displeased most of the longtime residents of Zeeland. The value of their homes was going up considerably, and they were getting rich as a result (especially after they voted themselves a few property-tax cuts). When newcomers complained about the price of housing, the longtime residents pointed out how nice their island was and said that having the newcomers live in the new densely packed little huts – the only housing most could afford – would make Zeeland even more picturesque. They also pointed out that most people's trips to work would be a few minutes shorter because things were closer together in Zeeland.

But eventually some cracks developed in the plan. The reason is that the Zeelanders had overlooked another picture of their island. Zeeland was just one little island in the ocean. From 80 miles overhead, it looked something like figure 4.

Businesses that had moved to Zeeland and had created the immigration boom by offering more jobs began to have a problem. They were finding it increasingly difficult to induce new employees to move to Zeeland. When they were recruiting on other islands, they showed pictures of how nice Zeeland looked, but prospective employees soon realized that there was a rather stiff price tag attached. Either they would have to spend a fortune to live in houses like those on other islands, or they would have to live much more modestly (in the picturesque little huts).

To offset the higher housing costs, prospective employees insisted on higher wages in order to move to Zeeland. At first, businesses agreed, since business on all the islands was booming. But eventually they found that they could no longer compete with businesses on other islands. Their labor costs – about 70 percent of costs for most businesses – were so high that they could not sell their products at competitive prices.

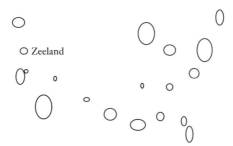

Figure 4 Zeeland from Space

After a while, businesses began to leave Zeeland for islands where it was not so costly to live. Even many native Zeelanders decided to sell their homes and move away in order to take advantage of the lower housing prices and better-paying jobs elsewhere. Zeeland was eventually left with a large stock of densely packed little huts in which few people wanted to live.

What Zeelanders had neglected to see was that Zeeland, though itself a sizable island, was only one of hundreds of pleasant islands in the sea. What looked like an unstoppable deluge of people mad to live in Zeeland was, in the larger picture, just a temporary trickle. Zeelanders had thought they could harness the flow to create a new style of island life, but they succeeded only in diverting it to other islands.

When the islanders finally decided to expand the IGB, it did no good. Few people were eager to move to Zeeland without a job, and prospective businesses were skeptical of the Zeelanders' promise that from now on, the IGB would be expanded to meet job seekers' demand for housing. The business folk muttered to themselves as they walked away from Zeeland officials at trade fairs, "Fool me once, shame on you; fool me twice, shame on me."

I offer this parable with mixed feelings. Portland's has been an interesting social science experiment, and one hates to suggest changes that would stanch the flow of research on the effects of metropolitanwide land use controls. The experiments abroad are hard to read because of the cultural and institutional differences. One of the great things about having 50 more-or-less autonomous states is that we can try experiments in places with a common background of law and politics.

So let Portland be Portland. That's easy to say, since I know it won't choose to be anything else. But for the rest of the nation's metropolitan areas, some caution is warranted. It might be better to see how the Portland experiment plays out, since there is some reason to believe that the downside of Portland's experiment is yet to come, and turning back is hard to do. The enthusiasm with which other areas, such as Seattle and San Jose, are importing the idea of metropolitanwide growth boundaries should be tempered by the fact that Portland's is a work in progress.

The second reason for my ambivalence about criticizing Portland's plan is that I have been an advocate of the idea that U.S. metropolitan areas are too spread out and that local zoning has contributed to that sprawl (Fischel 1985, chap. 12). My scenario has the suburbs developing only partially and then independently (that is, without the permission of the state or other communities in the metropolitan area) pulling up the gangplank to newcomers. This is accomplished with a host of land use controls that make new housing more costly to build. New development is then pushed either back to the city or still farther out into the countryside. It mostly goes farther out because employment has been shifting to the suburbs.

The economic drawback of this peculiarly American pattern is not so much that there is too much commuting. Commuting times have hardly risen in the past 20 years, largely because employment has followed residences into the far suburbs (Gordon, Kumar, and Richardson 1989). Nor is it the case that the new development does not pay its own way. Nearly all suburbs have in place the planning tools to be sure that development is not a fiscal burden, and, if anything, they use the tools too vigorously. The main problem with suburban zoning is that the overall pattern leaves the metropolitan area insufficiently dense to take advantage of economies of agglomeration.

The proper cure for all this is not to prohibit developers from building in the country-side. It is to prevent the suburbs from imposing unreasonably high standards for building housing in them. By inducing the close-in suburbs to accommodate development that is consistent with early, moderate-density patterns (we're talking quarter-acre lots here), much of the excessive decentralization could be avoided. The question is how to get the suburbs to change their ways.

It is here that Portland appears to be (figuratively) breaking new ground by not being willing (literally) to break new ground outside its urban growth boundary. It uses a metropolitanwide body to order the suburbs to rezone land to accommodate higher-density development – a situation unparalleled in the United States. Other metropolitan federations of local governments have come up with regional plans, but none has required individual municipalities to accept uses or densities they do not want. The Minneapolis–St. Paul area has a program of regional tax sharing (which is still unique after 20 years), but it still allows local governments to determine what type and density of development they want.

Most statewide land use controls impose a double-veto system. The state can reject projects that local governments want, but it hardly ever forces local governments to accept developments they do not want. The few exceptions – the Massachusetts anti-snob zoning law (Stockman 1992) and the New Jersey Supreme Court's *Mount Laurel* doctrine (Haar 1996) – only tell local governments they have to accept a certain socioeconomic mix of housing. After the proper mix is reached, both allow the local governments to be as exclusive as they want, which does nothing to address the problem of excessively low density development.

As much as I admire Portland's resolve to do something about excessive suburbaniza-tion, though, I cannot help but express some skepticism about how it will play out. Because of its current reluctance to extend the urban growth boundary – a reluctance that seems inconsistent with its original rationale of *orderly* suburban growth – metro-politan Portland has to impose density requirements on new development that are entirely out of scale with the size of the city and contrary to the experience of almost all other American metropolitan areas. The extremely high population density that Portland appears to envision as its future is beyond that of all but the largest cities in the United States.

Residents of very large cities put up with high density not because density itself is good, but because high density in those places is productive (Ciccone and Hall 1996). In big cities, the higher productivity of labor results in higher wages and incomes for residents, which offsets the higher price of housing and the other residential disadvantages of high-density living. Portland planners perhaps hope to attract high-wage industries to their high-density city, but they are unlikely to succeed if, as most urban economists believe, economies of agglomeration are achieved not solely by density, but also by the population size of the city (Mills and Hamilton 1994, 20). Herding all half-million Vermonters into a small area to achieve a Manhattan Island density would not make them sufficiently productive to warrant paying them Manhattan wages. Big-city wages prevail because the cities are both dense and large.

My own cure for excessive suburbanization would be to restore the rights of develop-ment-minded landowners (Fischel 1995, chap. 9). Many suburban zoning regulations do not conform to a historical standard of "normal behavior." Undeveloped land is subject to far more stringent standards than earlier developments were, so that much of it is developed at wasteful, estate-like densities. If the landowners who are subject to unreasonable ("supernormal") standards had an enforceable remedy (whether given by the courts or by state legislation), excessive suburbanization would be curbed.

The advantages of this more decentralized remedy for sprawl over the Portland plan are chiefly the same as the advantages of a decentralized market system over a centralized, planned economy. Central planning is problematic because planners cannot possibly acquire sufficient information to rationally balance all demands. Individual landowners have an effective incentive – personal profit – to acquire the information needed to balance present and future demands for their land. By judicious restoration of the rights of landowners, the larger public purpose of a reasonably compact urban area would be achieved at a lower cost.

References

Ciccone, Antonio, and Robert E. Hall (1996) "Productivity and the Density of Economic Activity." *American Economic Review* 86, 54–70.

Fischel, William A. (1985) *The Economics of Zoning Laws: A Property Rights Approach to American Land Use Controls*. Baltimore, MD: Johns Hopkins University Press.

Fischel, William A. (1995) *Regulatory Takings: Law, Economics, and Politics*, Cambridge, MA: Harvard University Press.

Gordon, Peter, Ajay Kumar, and Harry W. Richardson (1989) "Congestion, Changing Metropolitan Structure, and City Size in the United States." *International Regional Science Review* 12, 45–56.

Haar, Charles M. (1996) *Suburbs under Siege: Race, Space, and Audacious Judges*. Princeton, NJ: Princeton University Press.

Mills, Edwin S., and Bruce W. Hamilton (1994) *Urban Economics*, 5th edn. New York: HarperCollins.

Stockman, Paul, K. (1992) "Anti-Snob Zoning in Massachusetts: Assessing One Attempt at Opening the Suburbs to Affordable Housing." *Virginia Law Review* 78(2), 535–80.

CHAPTER TWELVE

Do Suburbs Need Cities?*

Richard A. Voith

Source: Journal of Regional Science, 38(3), 445–64. © 1998 Blackwell Publishers.

In this paper I examine the relationship between city and suburban growth over the last three decades for a sample of U.S. metropolitan areas. I develop a structural empirical model relating city income growth to suburban growth in income, population, and house values. The model allows for bidirectional effects of cities on suburbs and suburbs on cities, as well as for unobserved factors affecting both city and suburbs. The simultaneous, latent-variable model is identified using a combination of exclusion and covariance restrictions. Instrumental estimation results indicate that income growth in large cities enhances suburban growth; but income growth in small cities has little effect.

1. Introduction

The rapid growth of American suburbs and the coincident decline of cities raises new questions about the relationships between cities and suburbs. Are city and suburban economies still interdependent? Should suburban residents be concerned with central city decline? Is city decline and suburban growth a zero-sum gain, or are there externalities associated with cities that yield increasing returns to city growth at the metropolitan level? To the extent that there are positive externalities associated with city growth, suburbs of cities suffering the worst decline should have relatively slow rates of economic growth compared with suburbs surrounding growing cities. At the regional level, these positive externalities, if economically significant, suggest the possibility of gains from cooperation among city and suburban jurisdictions. On aggregate, increasing returns to city growth would imply that the current decline in American cities adversely affects the rate of national economic growth.

The processes of suburbanization, urban decline, and metropolitan growth have been studied extensively in recent years, but less attention has been paid to the relationships

* Vince Montemurro and Julie Northcott-Wilson provided excellent research assistance. Timothy Bartik, Gerald Carlino, Ted Crone, Andrew Foster, Joseph Gyourko, Robert Inman, Peter Linneman, James McAndrews, David Merrimann, Leonard Nakamura, and Ken Small all provided useful comments on an earlier draft. Three anonymous referees also provided comments that greatly improved the paper. The views expressed here are solely those of the author and do not necessarily represent the views of the Federal Reserve Bank of Philadelphia or of the Federal Reserve System.

among city and suburban economies.[1] Although there is considerable evidence that city and suburban economies are interdependent in the sense that long-run changes in population, employment, and measures of urban distress in cities and suburbs tend to be correlated, there is relatively little evidence that declining cities adversely affect surrounding suburbs.[2] Some recent work is, however, suggestive of a negative impact of central-city decline. Adams et al. (1996), for example, examine central-city distress and suburban growth and find that central-city distress reduces intermetropolitan in-migration to surrounding suburbs. At the micro level, Voith (1993, 1996) finds that employment decline in the city of Philadelphia adversely affects suburban house values controlling for changes in suburban employment. These effects decline with distance from the center of the city. Using data from California, Goetzmann, Spiegel, and Wachter (1996) also find that city and suburban house-price appreciation are closely linked for relatively near suburbs, but less so for more distant suburbs.

Although the results of Adams et al., Goetzmann, Spiegel, and Wachter, and Voith are suggestive of a causal link, they do not address two fundamental issues necessary for interpreting the measured relationships. The first is one of simultaneity – correlations between city and suburban economic phenomena could reflect the effects of suburban economies on the city. This poses a serious identification problem because there are few factors that affect city economies that do not also affect suburban communities and vice versa. Relative city and suburban tax rates, services and amenity levels, for example, affect people's and firms' choice of city or suburbs, and hence do not aid in the identification of the effects of a city's economy on its suburbs from those running in the reverse direction. The second problem is caused by unobserved common factors that affect both city and suburban economies. Secular decline in a metropolitan area's major industry, for example, may affect both city and suburbs and result in a correlation between city and suburban economies, even in the absence of a causal relationship between the two.

To overcome these problems, I specify a structural empirical model relating city income growth and suburban income growth, house-value appreciation, and population growth. By using three measures of suburban growth we can construct a structural model that is formally similar to those used to estimate the returns to schooling in the presence of unobserved ability; this structure allows the estimation of the effects of cities on suburbs purged of the correlations induced by unobserved common factors. The model is identified by a combination of exclusion and covariance restrictions. Annexation is one important source of identification as it affects city growth but does not directly affect suburban growth in those areas that do not lose land through annexation. Further, the panel structure of the data set allows covariance restrictions that identify parameters independently of unobserved common factors. Using census data on city and suburban growth over the last three decades for most U.S. metropolitan areas, I provide evidence that city income growth enhances suburban growth in income, house-price appreciation, and population, especially in metropolitan areas with large central cities.

2. Theoretical Considerations: Equilibrium and Growth

Models pioneered by Roback (1982) in which wages and rents adjust so that people and firms are indifferent to location, provide a useful starting point for examining the relationship between city and suburban economies. In the simplest form of these models, locations are good substitutes for one another, and population decline in less attractive areas is simply an adjustment toward an efficient equilibrium with more people and firms in desirable and productive areas. More recent equilibrium location models allow for the possibility of cross-jurisdictional externalities among local communities. Blomquist, Berger, and Hoehn (1988) present a model with regional agglomeration economies in production that results in the interdependence of local areas within a metropolitan area. In a similar vein, Voith (1991), presents a model in which regionally-valued attributes that are tied to a single locality generate cross-jurisdictional interdependence. Examples of this type of locally provided, regionally-valued amenities include waterfront parks, cultural districts, or even vibrant, pedestrian-oriented city streets.[3] In both models, changes in the attributes of one locality affect the equilibrium outcomes in the rest of the region. If the quantity of regionally-valued, productivity or welfare-enhancing attributes provided by cities increases with income, it should be expected that city income growth has a positive effect on suburban income and land value, as additional people are attracted to the region. To the extent that agglomeration economies and market size play a role in the quantity of regionally-valued attributes associated with a city, it is expected that larger cities would have more significant impacts on their suburbs than would smaller cities.

None of the above models focuses on Tiebout-type sorting behavior on the basis of income, education, or race that may increase the likelihood of undesirable locational equilibria.[4] Because many local attributes are produced using local resources, sorting by, say, income, may cause changes in the attributes of the location itself. As pointed out by Bradbury, Downs, and Small (1980), if out-migration lowers the attractiveness of the declining community, falling land prices may not be sufficient to stem the population outflow. Further, suburban communities seeking to avoid the costs of central-city problems may engage in exclusionary zoning which exacerbates fiscal disparities across jurisdictions (Inman and Rubinfeld, 1979). Sorting may result in urban concentrations of low income populations with insufficient resources to maintain social, human, and physical infrastructure. Benabou (1993), suggests that geographic sorting may have a negative impact on regional output because the benefits of complementarity between high-and low-skill workers in human-capital production are lost. Costs associated with sorting may initially be borne by the city itself (thus causing further decline), but ultimately, the increased costs will probably affect higher levels of government and will be unavoidable by other residents of the region.

The short- and long-run consequences of city decline, however, are likely to be quite different. Initially, city decline is likely to reduce city amenities, providing further impetus to move to the suburbs, and hence spurring suburban growth. In the long run, the entire region may be adversely affected, reducing the rate of suburban growth until a new long-run equilibrium is achieved. In the new equilibrium, the city is but a fraction of its former size, and the suburbs, though larger, are smaller than they would have been in the absence of externalities. Because the effects of city decline are likely to differ in the short and long run, an investigation of the relationship between city and suburban economies should examine the evolution of metropolitan areas over fairly long time periods.

In the framework of equilibrium location models, metropolitan, suburban, and city growth rates of income, land prices, and population can differ only while the system is adjusting to a new equilibrium. Because the attributes of a region change over time, the adjustment toward equilibrium is an ongoing process and growth rates within and across regions are likely to differ until equilibrium is achieved. Declining cities that have fewer regionally-valued amenities, diminished agglomeration economies, or high social costs may result in lower growth in income, house values, and population in their suburbs for extended periods.

Recently there has been increasing interest in models of endogenous metropolitan growth (see, for example, Lucas, 1988; or Krugman, 1991). In these models, sustained higher rates of growth in a metropolitan area occur because of external returns to human-capital accumulation (Rauch, 1991) or some other externality. Similarly, differences in metropolitan growth could persist if there are increasing returns to city growth at the metropolitan level; that is increases in city growth have externalities that cause increases in suburban growth. Correlations arising from increasing returns are likely to be difficult to distinguish from those consistent with long-run adjustment to new equilibria. I make no attempt to empirically distinguish between the two hypotheses.

3. Growth Rates and Raw Correlations

In this section, I describe the patterns of growth in income, house prices, and population in cities and suburbs. I focus on these variables because they are the variables that adjust to achieve locational equilibrium. Data on population, per capita real income, and median real house value for virtually all MSAs for 1960, 1970, 1980, and 1990 were assembled. In addition, average real house prices for most MSAs for 1970, 1980, and 1990 are used.[5] Using county-level data MSAs were broken into main central cities (MCC), counties that contained all or part of the MCC (designated CWMCC), and metropolitan counties that did not contain any part of the MCC (designated NOMCC).[6] Growth rates for cities and suburbs in each MSA, for each decade were calculated.

City, suburban, and metropolitan growth rates

Table 1 presents mean growth rates for central cities, suburbs, and metropolitan areas. The data summarized in this table are metropolitan-level observations. Table 2 provides a further breakdown of the suburban data using county-level observations. It is clear from Table 1 that suburban population and per-capita income outpaced city growth in every decade. Cities, therefore, now have a smaller share of total population, and their population is poorer relative to the suburbs than in the past. Aggregate income in the city grew much more slowly than in the suburbs, contributing to the fiscal distress observed in many cities today. The only area in which the city outperformed the suburbs was in house-value growth in the 1980s, which occurred only after very weak city appreciation in the 1970s. Table 2 displays the same information as above, but for suburban counties, separated into CWMCC counties (the growth data are for the suburban part of the county only) and NOMCC counties. Counties without the central city had faster population growth, higher income growth and faster average house-value growth than the suburban part of counties containing the central city.

Table 1 Growth rates: metropolitan-level observations

	Central City Mean Std. Dev.		Suburbs[a] Mean Std. Dev.		Metro Area Mean Std. Dev.	
Population Growth						
1960–1970	0.119	(0.220)	0.162	(0.211)	0.160	(0.133)
1970–1980	0.019	(0.155)	0.229	(0.186)	0.139	(0.135)
1980–1990	0.043	(0.132)	0.105	(0.141)	0.089	(0.117)
Real, Per Capita Income Growth						
1960–1970	0.193	(0.071)	0.283	(0.085)	0.241	(0.066)
1970–1980	0.071	(0.094)	0.163	(0.096)	0.125	(0.069)
1980–1990	0.143	(0.101)	0.190	(0.129)	0.181	(0.100)
Median Real House-Value Growth						
1960–1970	0.015	(0.110)	b		b	
1970–1980	0.211	(0.200)	b		b	
1980–1990	0.019	(0.298)	b		b	
Average Real House-Value Growth[c]						
1970–1980	0.162	(0.179)	0.295	(0.156)	0.233	(0.140)
1980–1990	0.050	(0.284)	0.042	(0.280)	0.052	(0.265)
Number of MSAs	281		281		281	

[a] Includes all of the MSA except the central city.
[b] Data available only for city and entire counties on a consistent basis over the sample period. Medians were not averaged to obtain metropolitan area totals, nor were transformations computed to obtain the suburban area.
[c] There are fewer observations for average house-value growth because data were not available for central cities of population less than 50,000. For central cities, the numbers of observations are 227 and 280 for 1970–1980 and 1980–1990 respectively. For suburbs and metro areas, the numbers of observations are 224 and 279 for 1970–1980 and 1980–1990, respectively.

City and suburban growth: raw correlations

Raw correlations suggest that city and suburban growth tend to move together. Table 3 presents the raw correlations of city growth with metropolitan growth and three measures of suburban growth in population, income, and house value during the last three decades. I focus primarily on city and suburban growth correlations, but include the city–metropolitan area correlations to be consistent with earlier studies.[7]

Table 3 reveals a somewhat surprising trend toward higher correlation of city and suburban variables over time, despite decentralization in metropolitan areas. Suburban population growth in the 1960s was negatively and significantly correlated with city population growth whereas in the 1970s and 1980s the correlation turned significantly positive. For the sample of CWMCC counties, the increases in the correlation between city and suburban population over time are more striking, rising from −0.32 in the 1960s to 0.40 in the 1980s. One reason for the large negative correlation in the 1960s is the high rate of annexation in that decade. Annexation induces a negative correlation between city and suburban population growth. Also, if cities annex the wealthier parts of the surrounding

Table 2 Suburban growth rates: county-level observations

	All Counties[a] Mean Std. Dev.		Counties with no Central Cities Mean Std. Dev.		Counties with Central Cities[a] Mean Std. Dev.	
Population Growth						
1960–1970	0.173	(0.275)	0.210	(0.165)	0.118	(0.378)
1970–1980	0.242	(0.218)	0.246	(0.196)	0.237	(0.247)
1980–1990	0.124	(0.160)	0.143	(0.162)	0.096	(0.154)
Real, Per-Capita Income Growth						
1960–1970	0.314	(0.107)	0.335	(0.106)	0.282	(0.099)
1970–1980	0.173	(0.101)	0.180	(0.101)	0.162	(0.100)
1980–1990	0.206	(0.117)	0.218	(0.105)	0.188	(0.131)
Median Real House-Value Growth						
1960–1970	b		0.201	(0.159)	b	
1970–1980	b		0.361	(0.170)	b	
1980–1990	b		0.047	(0.240)	b	
Average Real House-Value Growth[c]						
1970–1980	0.314	(0.173)	0.327	(0.175)	0.291	(0.166)
1980–1990	0.059	(0.264)	0.075	(0.250)	0.037	(0.282)
Number of counties[d]	656		391		265	

[a] Includes all of the county except the central city.

[b] Median house values were not computed separately for suburban parts of counties that contained central cities.

[c] The number of observations for average house value for the 1970s are, reading across, 569, 359, 210. For the 1980s, the numbers are 651, 388, and 263.

[d] Note that there are fewer suburban counties with main central cities than MSAs because 16 main central cities are independent, that is they are not part of a county.

suburbs, annexation is likely to induce a negative correlation between city and suburban growth in income and house values. However, this is not the whole story because, even in the sample of counties that do not contain the MCC, and hence are unaffected by annexation, the correlation is negative, though insignificant in the 1960s.

City and suburban per capita real income growth were highly correlated in each decade, and the magnitude of the correlation increased by about one third from the 1960s to the 1980s. The pattern of increasing correlation is more pronounced for real house values, whether measured by medians or averages. For medians, correlation in city and suburban growth more than doubled from the 1960s to the 1980s. The correlation in averages increased by more than 60 percent from the 1970s to the 1980s.

The finding that the correlation between city and suburban growth in income, population, and house value increased in the three decades following 1960 runs counter to many people's expectations. The negative or low correlations in the 1960s may reflect high substitutability between city and suburban growth simply because suburban areas were relatively undeveloped and there was high investment in infrastructure promoting suburban accessibility in the 1960s. On the other hand, higher correlations between city and

Table 3 Correlations for central city with metro area and suburbs

	Metropolitan Areas	All Suburban Counties[a]	Counties with no Central Cities	Counties with Central Cities[a]
Population Growth				
1960–1970	0.609	−0.188	−0.041	−0.322
1970–1980	0.729	0.261	0.233	0.317
1980–1990	0.709	0.273	0.239	0.401
Real, Per-Capita Income Growth				
1960–1970	0.815	0.456	0.398	0.503
1970–1980	0.872	0.552	0.479	0.686
1980–1990	0.835	0.605	0.603	0.599
Median Real House-Value Growth				
1960–1970	b	b	0.411	b
1970–1980	b	b	0.573	b
1980–1990	b	b	0.897	b
Average Real House Value Growth[c]				
1970–1980	0.906	0.525	0.480	0.706
1980–1990	0.939	0.849	0.820	0.887
Number of Observations (MSAs or counties)	281	656	391	265

Note: All correlations are significantly different from zero except for population growth of cities and counties with no central cities in the 1960s.

[a] Includes all parts of the county except the central city.

[b] Median house values were not computed for metropolitan areas or for suburban parts of counties that contained central cities.

[c] City and suburban average house value correlations have fewer observations; reading across, the numbers of observations for the 1970s are 224, 569, 359 and 210, and for the 1980s the numbers are 279, 651, 388, and 263.

suburban growth in the 1970s and 1980s may reflect increasing costs of suburbanization as development increased land prices and congestion increased public expenses in the suburbs as well as the city. Continued suburban growth may have become increasingly dependent on the overall desirability of the region, rather than simply shifting population from the central city. Metropolitan areas not plagued with the problems associated with declining cities appear to have had more robust suburban growth in the 1970s and 1980s.

4. Model Specification, Identification, and Estimation

The theoretical considerations described in Section 2 and raw correlations presented in Section 3 are consistent with the hypothesis that city growth positively affects suburban growth, but they are far from proving this hypothesis. Even if city and suburban economies were not interdependent, their economic performance may be correlated because they are subject to similar external forces. Also, suburbs are becoming more like cities so they may respond to external forces in ways that are increasingly similar to the responses of city economies over time. Additionally if the correlations do reflect causal relationships, the direction of causality may be from suburb to city rather than city to suburb.

To test whether city growth causes suburban growth I specify a structural model relating city growth in income to suburban growth in income, population, and house values. The model is consistent either with the view that cities' production of regionally-valued, productivity and welfare enhancing amenities increases as their income increases, or with the endogenous-growth perspective that increases in city productivity – as reflected in income growth – have external effects on suburban income growth. The model explicitly addresses the issues of potential simultaneity in city and suburban income determination and unobserved common factors resulting in spurious correlations across city and suburban economies. In addition, the model addresses the issue of city scale because larger cities are likely to have greater impacts on their suburban neighbors than smaller cities.

Specifically, I hypothesize that income growth in the city income in city i at time t, y_{it}^c, depends on the rate of contemporaneous suburban income growth, y_{it}^s, observable characteristics affecting city and suburbs, X_{it}, observed characteristics affecting only the city, X_{it}^c, and a set of unobservable factors common to the city and the suburbs, d_{it}. Adding a white-noise error term and assuming a linear functional form yields

$$(1) \quad y_{it}^c = \alpha_0 + \alpha_1 y_{it}^s + \alpha_2 X_{it} + \alpha_3 X_{it}^c + \alpha_4 d_{it} + \varepsilon_{it}^{y^c}$$

The equation for suburban income growth is similar to that for city income growth except that the effects of city income growth are allowed to vary by the size of the city, S_{it}.[8]

$$(2) \quad y_{it}^s = \beta_0 + \beta_1 y_{it}^c + \beta_2 y_{it}^c S_{it} + \beta_3 X_{it} + \beta_4 X_{it}^s + \beta_5 d_{it} + \varepsilon_{it}^{y^s}$$

I expect growth in both city and suburban income to be positively related to suburban population growth and house-price appreciation so the suburban population and house-price appreciation equations also include suburban income growth.

$$(3) \quad p_{it}^s = \gamma_0 + \gamma_1 y_{it}^c + \gamma_2 y_{it}^c S_{it} + \gamma_3 y_{it}^s + \gamma_4 X_{it} + \gamma_5 X_{it}^s + \gamma_6 d_{it} + \varepsilon_{it}^{p^s}$$

$$(4) \quad h_{it}^s = \delta_0 + \delta_1 y_{it}^c + \delta_2 y_{it}^c S_{it} + \delta_3 y_{it}^s + \delta_4 X_{it} + \delta_5 X_{it}^s + \delta_6 d_{it} + \varepsilon_{it}^{h^s}$$

A linear specification with no city income–city size interaction is also investigated separately for small, medium and large cities. As is discussed later, this avoids difficulties associated with nonlinear two-stage least-squares estimations as well as provides additional information on both the role of city size and the appropriateness of the identifying restrictions.

Identification

The model shown above is identified by a combination of exclusion and covariance restrictions. The city and suburban income equations are theoretically identified by exclusion restrictions on X^c and X^s. There are however, few justifiable exclusion restrictions because decisions by people and firms are likely to depend on *relative* values between city and suburb. For example, the relative density of the city to the suburbs should affect intrametropolitan location decisions, and hence city and suburban density should appear in both city and suburban equations.

Fortunately, there are some variables for which exclusion restrictions are appropriate, and these variations serve to identify the suburban income equation and, in some cases, both the city and suburban equation. These variables are (1) whether or not the city annexed land, which clearly can affect city growth, but cannot directly affect suburban growth in counties that do not lose land; (2) whether or not the city is part of a county, which may affect the fiscal performance of the central city, but cannot affect counties not containing the central city;[9] (3) whether or not the county contains a central city, which may differentially affect counties with and without central cities but should not affect central city growth; and (4) whether a county lost land to annexation, which can have differential impacts on county growth within the same MSA but should not differentially affect city growth.

The clearest identification of the suburban income-growth equation comes from the city annexation variable. Annexation, which for my purpose is defined as a binary yes/no variable, is useful in identification because it is common in all U.S. regions, except the Northeast. There is a great deal of variation in the occurrence of annexation across metropolitan growth. As is shown in Table 4, nearly 64 percent of all central cities annexed in the 1960s, 35 percent in the 1970s, and 40 percent in the 1980s. Annexation was most common in the West where almost 70 percent of all cities annexed in the 1980s.

The ability of cities to annex is largely dependent on state laws and there is considerable variation across states in the hurdles cities must overcome in order to annex suburban land. For many cities, state law makes a city's choice to annex or not largely exogenous to local consideration.[10] Concerns about endogeneity of annexation are further mitigated by the geography and the nature of our sample. Because many counties in SMSAs do not contain any part of the central city (most cities are completely surrounded by suburbs in a single county), and because cities generally cannot annex land that is not adjacent, suburban income growth in these counties (NOMCC counties) cannot be affected directly by central-city annexation. Most of the discussion of the model estimates is based on the

Table 4 Percent of central cities that annexed land in each decade

	1960s	*1970s*	*1980s*
Northeast	4.3	0.0	0.0
Midwest	73.0	33.7	30.3
South	73.7	44.4	52.5
West	84.8	50.0	69.6
United States	63.7	34.5	39.5

NOMCC sample. Note that in the NOMCC sample, the dummy variables that identify the city income-growth equation have no variation, so the city income equation cannot be identified.

In the presence of unobserved latent variables, the population-growth and house-appreciation equations are not identified with respect to the suburban income equation without covariance restrictions. Note that the population and house-value equations would be identified if the error terms of Equations 2, 3, and 4 were uncorrelated, so that the population and house-value equations would be recursive with respect to the suburban income equations. Since the unobserved part of the equations includes a common factor, d_{it}, it is unrealistic to assume no correlation.

Exploiting the panel structure of the data, reasonable assumptions about d_{it} can be used to identify the model. In particular, assume that d_{it} has a variance components structure such that $d_{it} = \varphi_i + \upsilon_{it}$, where φ_i does not vary over time and υ_{it} is uncorrelated with φ_i and is uncorrelated across i and t. Further assume that ε_{it} is uncorrelated across Equations 1 though 4. As shown in Hsiao (1986), the structural parameters in a model of the form shown in Equations 1–4 are identified given the above assumptions.[11] It should be noted that, even in the absence of valid exclusion restrictions that idenitfy the suburban income equation, the suburban population and house-equations are identified.

Estimation

Because the city and suburban income equations are identified by exclusion restrictions, they can be estimated by nonlinear two-state least-squares (NL2SLS). The predicted values for the endogenous variables are, by construction, uncorrelated with unobserved common factors. Thus, we need not be concerned with omitted variables bias on the coefficients on. the dependent variables. The major issue in NL2SLS is the choice of instrument set. The reduced form of the model is highly nonlinear in both variables and parameters. It contains interaction terms between city size and all other variables. Following Greene (1990) I expand the instrument set by including a second-degree polynomial of the interaction of the exogenous variables and city size to capture the nonlinearity in the reduced form. Of course, in the linear specification reported for small, medium, and large cities, we avoid the issue of instrument choice inherent in NL2SLS.

The key to obtaining consistent estimates of the structural parameters for the population and house-value equations is to create instruments for the endogenous variables that are uncorrelated with the unobserved variable, d_{it}. For the city income-growth and city income-growth $\times$ city size variables, the obvious choices are the predicted values based on the same instrument set as used in the NL2SLS estimation. Unfortunately, the analogous predicted value based on the suburban reduced form equation is a less attractive choice because there are no exogenous variables excluded from the suburban equations to identify the population and house-value equations, as was the case with the city variables. As suggested by Hsiao, satisfactory instruments can be obtained for suburban income growth using a purged instrumental variable technique. First, estimate the reduced-form equations for y_{it}^c, and form the residual, call it $z1_{it}$. $z1_{it}$ is correlated with d_{it} by construction. Use $z1_{is}$, $s \neq t$ is , as an instrument for d_{it} in the reduced-form estimations for y_{it}^s. Note that $z1_{is}$ is uncorrelated with the residual in the reduced form of the suburban income equation because υ_{it} is uncorrelated with υ_{is}. From the reduced-form suburban income equation, compute the residuals, denoted $z2_{it}$, which are uncorrelated with d_{it} and ϵ_{it} but correlated with y_{it}^s. Thus $z2_{it}$ can be used as an instrument for y_{it}^s in the structural equation for population and house values.[12]

5. Estimation Results

In this section two sets of results are reported. The first set consists of estimations of the model that allows for city income growth to have an effect that varies by city size. The second set consists of separate estimates of a linear model for small, medium, and large cities. These estimates provide additional insight into the role of city size, but also yield confirming evidence on the validity of the identifying restrictions. The model was estimated using three separate samples: (1) NOMCC counties for all three decades; (2) NOMCC counties for the 1970s and 1980s only; and (3) all suburban counties for the 1970s and 1980s. The results are qualitatively similar across samples although quantitatively the strongest city effects are found in the all-suburban-county sample and the weakest effects are found in the NOMCC sample using all three decades.[13] To conserve space, only the findings using the NOMCC sample for the 1970s and 1980s are presented. The NOMCC sample was chosen because this sample has the cleanest identification. The 1960s decade was excluded because of the relatively small raw city–suburban correlations and, as discussed in Section 3, there are reasons to expect the city–suburban relationships to be weak in the 1960s.

All of the estimations contain a number of control variables (corresponding to the X variables above). Population and population squared in the city, suburb, and metropolitan area at the start of the decade were included to control market-size effects. Population density of both city and suburb and their squares were included as a measure of growth potential and to control for changes in preferences for open space. Finally a set of dummy variables for census division and for decade were included. Since I have no expectation about the signs of the coefficients on the control variables I do not discuss them here. The dummy variables for census division are not reported to conserve space.

Models with city effects that vary with city size

Table 5 displays the instrumental variable estimations for suburban per-capita income growth, house-value appreciation, and population growth, respectively. All of the equations include city growth and city growth × city size as dependent variables.

PER-CAPITA REAL INCOME GROWTH.   Nonlinear two–stage least-squares estimations of the suburban income-growth equation are shown in column 1 of Table 5.[14] The coefficients on city income growth and city income growth interacted with city size are positive and significant.[15] These estimates imply that a 1 percentage point increase in the rate of city income growth in a moderate size city of one half million people would result in an increase in the rate of suburban income growth of 0.45 percentage points. In a very large city of 3 million, the increase in suburban income growth would be 0.60 percentage points.

Table 5 Suburban income, house-value, and population growth estimations with fixed effects for census divisions

	Income Growth		House Value Growth		Population Growth	
	Coefficient	T-Statistic[a]	Coefficient	T-Statistic[a]	Coefficient	T-Statistic[a]
Intercept	0.099*	(3.53)	0.030	(0.67)	−0.022	(−0.45)
City Income Growth	0.422*	(5.27)	0.764*	(5.95)	0.331*	(2.40)
(City Income Growth × City Size)/100,000	0.006*	(2.38)	0.024*	(6.02)	−0.005	(−1.09)
Suburban Income Growth			1.054*	(16.79)	0.694*	(10.29)
City Density/1000	0.018*	(4.39)	0.018*	(2.74)	0.004	(0.59)
(City Density/1000)^2	−0.001*	(−2.96)	−0.001	(−1.47)	−0.001	(−1.47)
Suburban Density/1000	−0.025	(−1.38)	−0.027	(−0.94)	−0.082*	(−2.60)
(Suburban Density/1000)^2	0.002	(0.84)	0.006	(1.40)	0.005	(1.05)
City Size/1,000,000	0.069*	(2.83)	0.118*	(3.03)	0.089*	(2.13)
(City Size/1,000,000)^2	−0.004	(−1.43)	−0.016*	(−3.32)	0.006	(1.11)
Suburb Size/100,000	−0.019*	(−2.82)	−0.036*	(−3.35)	−0.029*	(−2.51)
(Suburb Size/100,000)^2	0.002*	(3.67)	0.004*	(4.35)	0.002*	(2.33)
Metro Size/1,000,000	−0.014	(−1.09)	−0.028	(−1.39)	0.113*	(5.28)
(Metro Size/1,000,000)^2	−0.001	(−0.38)	0.001	(0.32)	−0.020*	(−5.36)
Dummy for 1970s	0.007	(0.72)	0.406*	(25.62)	0.140*	(8.19)
Adjusted R^2	0.386		0.620		0.467	
Number of Observations	782		782		782	

[a] All t-statistics are adjusted for the two stage estimation.
* Denotes significance at the 95% level.

REAL HOUSE-VALUE APPRECIATION.   In the real house-value appreciation estimations shown in column 2 of Table 5, city income, city income interacted with city size, and suburban income all significantly and positively affect suburban house-value appreciation.[16] The magnitude of the city income effects is quite large, and the gradient with respect to size is steep. A 1 percentage point increase in city income for a city of a half a million people would increase suburban appreciation by 0.88 percentage points. For a large city of 3 million, the same increase would increase suburban appreciation by 1.48 percentage points. As one would expect, an acceleration in the rate of suburban income growth has a large effect on suburban appreciation. A 1 percentage point increase in suburban income growth increases the appreciation rate by 1.05 percentage points.

POPULATION GROWTH.   The estimated effects of city income growth on suburban population growth, shown in column 3 of Table 5, are much smaller than the impact on house value. The interaction term is insignificant, and its sign is negative. The smaller estimated effect on population is not surprising because increased city income may make the city more attractive relative to the suburbs as well as make the metropolitan region relatively more attractive than others. Suburban income growth, on the other hand, has a substantially larger positive effect on suburban population growth.

Linear city effects: small, medium, and large cities

Estimating models with linear effects for city size separately for small, medium, and large cities is useful for at least three reasons. First, the relationship between city and suburbs may be qualitatively different for small and large cities. Second, it avoids the use of nonlinear two-stage least-squares in which the choice of instruments is as much art as science. Third, differences across the three samples provide insight into the validity of exclusion restrictions used to identify the suburban income equation. Again I focus on the NOMCC sample. The sample of MSAs with large cities consist of cities with a population of more than 500,000 in 1990, medium-sized cities are assumed to between 300,000 and 500,000, and small cities are assumed to have less than 300,000 people.[17]

Before examining the estimations for the three samples, it is useful to first examine the raw correlations between city income growth and suburban income, house-price, and population growth – these are shown in Table 6. Small, medium, and large cities all have significant, relatively large correlations in city and suburban income growth. Whereas the correlation is highest for large cities at 0.70, the correlation in small cities is also high at 0.54. Raw correlations among city income growth and suburban house-price appreciation are much smaller. Both large and small cities have significant, positive correlations between city income growth and suburban house-price appreciation, but these correlations are relatively small. There is an insignificant, though negative correlation in medium-sized cities. Finally, there is no significant correlation between city income growth and suburban population growth. Thus, even though one would expect large cities to exert a larger influence on their suburbs than would a small city, the raw correlations are very similar across small, medium, and large cities.

Turning to the model estimates, I show the estimated coefficient on city income growth for the equations for suburban income, house-value, and population growth for each sample in Table 7.[18] The estimates of the structural model paint a picture that is quite different from that of the raw correlations. For large cities, the estimated effect of city income on suburban income is highly significant and roughly the same magnitude as the raw correlation. The coefficient in the house-price-growth regression is also highly significant but much larger in magnitude. Finally, the population coefficient is insignificant and near zero, as is the raw correlation. These findings are consistent with a world in which housing is supplied relatively inelastically and income growth is capitalized into housing prices, which is probably the case in the largest cities. To see the economic

Table 6   Raw correlations with city income growth for small, medium, and large cities

Sample: 1990 Population	Income	House Price	Population	# Cities	# Counties
< 300,000	0.54*	0.09*	0.06	233	438
300,000–500,000	0.42*	−0.17	0.02	25	188
> 500,000	0.70*	0.25*	0.07	23	156

* Denotes significance at the 95% level.

Table 7 Effects of city income growth on suburban growth for small, medium, and large cities

Sample: 1990 Population	Income	House Price	Population	# Cities	# Counties
< 300,000					
Coefficient	−0.55	−0.17	1.65	233	438
T-statistic[a]	(−0.77)	(−0.21)	(1.51)		
300,000–500,000					
Coefficient	0.21	0.43	0.06	25	188
T-statistic[a]	(1.06)	(1.42)	(0.16)		
> 500,000					
Coefficient	0.70*	2.01*	−0.004	23	156
T-statistic[a]	(4.16)	(5.45)	(−0.01)		

[a] T-statistics are adjusted for the two-stage estimation.
*   Denotes significance at the 95% level.

importance of the income and house-value coefficients for large cities, it is possible to compute the cumulative gain to a suburban worker that would have accrued if city income growth in the decade had matched the suburban rate of 19 percent instead of the actual city rate of 14 percent. A suburban worker earning $50,000 per year and owning a $150,000 house in 1980 would have earned an additional $9560 and reaped $15,075 in additional house value appreciation, totaling $24,635 if the city income growth rate equaled the observed suburban rate.[19]

At the metropolitan level, suburban gains from even very small increases in income growth in large cities are very large. For example, consider the suburban impact of a 1 percentage point (an increase in the compound annual growth rate of less than 0.1 percentage points) in the decade growth rate of central-city income in the Philadelphia metropolitan area. Based on 1980 census data, total aggregate suburban income in 1982–4 constant dollars was $30.3 billion and the aggregate value of owner-occupied housing was $44.2 billion. Given these magnitudes, our estimates imply that a 1 percentage point increase in the decade city income growth rate would result in an additional $1.2 billion in cumulative suburban income and $0.9 billion in aggregate house value for a total benefit of $2.1 billion.

Even though the raw correlations for small cities are similar to those of the large cities, very different relationships emerge from the model estimates. City income growth is estimated to have a negative, though very insignificant effect on suburban income and house-price growth, and an insignificantly positive effect on suburban population growth. Medium-sized cities have positive, though insignificant impacts on suburban growth. The large difference in impacts between very large cities and small cities is consistent with the idea that large cities potentially offer unique benefits to their suburban neighbors, but small cities do not offer opportunities that are not already available in the suburbs. The positive, though insignificant effects for medium-sized cities are consistent with the increasing relevance of cities to suburbs as city size increases.

The large differences in the estimated relationships between the large-city and small-city samples, despite the similarity in their raw correlations, suggest that restrictions used to identify the model and the chosen instruments are valid. If the restrictions used to identify the model were not valid, one would simply expect to find estimated model coefficients that mimic the raw correlations. Rather the estimation seems to be capable of purging the correlation resulting from reverse causality and unobserved common trends.

Taken together, both the whole sample estimates and the estimates based on small, medium, and large cities strongly suggest that city income growth positively affects suburban growth in income, house value, and, to a lesser extent, population. These findings are driven, however, primarily by the effects of large cities on their suburbs; small cities have little measurable impact on their suburbs. The estimations imply that the slow rate of income growth in our large central cities has a significant negative impact on the aggregate wealth of metropolitan areas.

6. Conclusion and Conjectures

In this paper I have outlined the reasons why city growth might have a positive impact on suburban growth. Using data on cities and suburban counties I examined the relationship of city and suburban growth in income, population, and house values. Simple raw correlations suggest that the correlation between city growth rates and suburban growth rates have been increasing over the last three decades. These correlations suggest a positive relationship between city and suburbs. That is, healthy, growing cities foster faster-growing suburbs. Of course, the raw correlations could be the result of at least two alternative hypotheses: suburban growth could cause city growth or the correlation could be the result of unobserved common factors.

Because the correlations between city and suburban growth rates could be spurious, rather than indicative of a causal relationship between city and suburban growth, I developed a structural model to assess the relationship. The framework allows the identification of the effects of city growth on suburban growth independent of the effect of suburban growth on city growth and independent of unobserved common factors. The estimations suggest that city income growth results in higher suburban income growth, house-value appreciation, and to a much lesser extent, population growth. The effects of cities on suburbs arise primarily in metropolitan areas with larger cities; there appears to be little, if any, measurable relationship between small-city growth and suburban growth.

The statistical evidence that city income growth has positive external effects on suburban income and house-price growth is important because the long-run, gradual nature of the negative effects of urban decline make it difficult for people to observe casually, let alone mobilize support for policies to prevent urban decline. In particular, the negative impact may be unrecognized by suburban residents because the suburb is performing so much better than its declining central city counterpart. Thus, suburban residents may perceive themselves as relatively better-off when compared with their city neighbors, even though their incomes, populations, and house values are adversely affected by the city decline.

The implications of these findings for urban policies are very important. In particular, these results imply that suburban residents, and by extension, the nation, have important stakes in the prosperity of large central cities. Large central cities perform valuable functions that are not replaced when they decline. The evidence of a positive causal relationship suggests the possibility that both cities and suburbs could improve their welfare through cooperative actions to arrest urban decline. These actions might include regional financing of social service programs, regional efforts to improve educational opportunities for children in poor-quality school districts, and the elimination of large differences in local tax rates, especially taxes on mobile factors such as labor. Policies that require cooperation to achieve long-run objectives, however, may be difficult to forge, since there are likely to be short-run benefits for suburban areas from central city decline. Moreover, even if there are potential net benefits to the region as whole, it may not necessarily be the case that the benefits to suburban residents outweigh their costs.

Notes

1 Bradbury, Downs, and Small (1982) provide a detailed picture of the extent of urban decline, 1960–1975. Meiszkowski and Mills (1993) review the basic causes of suburbanization, including basic economic factors such as transportation costs and income growth and flight from fiscal and social problems associated with Tiebout-type sorting of people and firms.
2 Using various measures of distress, Bradbury, Downs, and Small (1982), find that city and metropolitan area distress move together over time. Mills (1990), finds that city population growth was correlated with overall metropolitan population growth in the 1960s and 1970s. Linneman and Summers (1990) find that city and suburban population growth were positively correlated in the 1970s and 1980s. Summers and Linneman (1990) find a similar relationship pertained for employment in the 1980s but not in the 1970s. Voith (1992) finds increasing correlation in city and suburban population and income growth over the last three decades for a sample of Northeast and North Central cities. None of the studies attempted to establish causal relationships.
3 Cities and suburbs provide very different sets of local attributes. Suburbs are characterized by widely dispersed development and privately controlled space. Cities, on the other hand, have dense development with a considerable amount of publicly accessible space. In the event of city decline, it is unlikely that city-style amenities would be replicated in the suburbs.
4 Most equilibrium models assume that all people are identical and that utility equalizes across locations, so geographic concentrations of less-advantaged people are not observed. One exception is Roback (1988) who analyzes equilibrium distributions of high-and low-skilled populations.
5 Population, income, and house-value data are from the *County and City Data Book Consolidated File 1947–77* (tape), *County and City Data Book 1983* (tape), and *County and City Data Book 1994* (CD ROM). All dollar values are deflated using the national CPI with 1982–4 = 100.
6 The definitions of MSAs change over time. In this analysis, I use the 1990 definitions of metropolitan areas. Thus for data in the 1960s, 1970s, and 1980s, additional counties were added to the published data. Note that I also examined the relationships between city and suburbs using 1960 MSA definitions and found qualitatively similar results. In all cases, I used MSA rather than CMSA definitions. In the case of New York, the five counties comprising the city of New York were treated as a single central city.
7 Bradbury, Downs, and Small (1982) report city and metropolitan correlations. However, as is evident in Table 2, relatively high city-metropolitan correlations can result even when city and suburban growth correlations are quite low.
8 I examined a specification in which the effect of city income growth varied with a city's population share, but unlike the case with city size, I found no significant link. I believe that city size is a better measure of a city's ability to provide unique opportunities to a metropolitan area than is the city's population share. Additionally, I estimated a model in which the effect of

suburban income on city income varied by suburban size; the results were not qualitatively different.

9   There are 16 central cities that are either independent jurisdictions or have congruent city and county boundaries. These cities must provide services typically provided by county governments in addition to those normally provided by the city. On the other hand, they have greater control over the services that are usually provided by counties.

10   For cities without insurmountable obstacles to annexation, there is some endogeneity in annexation choices; annexing cities systematically choose to annex higher-income suburban areas (Austin 1995).

11   The system is similar to a classic latent-variable problem analyzed by Chamberlain and Griliches (1975). They analyzed the effects of education on test scores and earnings in the presence of an unobserved variable ability and showed that if there are multiple indicators of success, then covariance restrictions can be used to identify the effect of education purged of the contribution of ability. In my problem, I have multiple indicators of suburban economic performance, and used covariance restrictions to identify the contribution of city growth to suburban growth, independent of unobserved common factors.

12   Even if there were no valid variables to exclude from the suburban income equation, and hence I could not get direct instruments for y^c, I could obtain instruments for y^c by using an analogous procedure to that used for y^s. In that case, neither the city nor suburban income equation would be identified, but consistent estimates of housing and population equation parameters could be obtained.

13   I would expect that the all-suburban-county sample would show the strongest effects because it includes counties containing the central city. These suburbs are geographically closer to the city and probably institutionally more tightly linked than are NOMCC counties. Given the relatively small raw city–suburban correlations in the 1960s, and as discussed in Section 3, given that there are reasons to expect weak city–suburban relationships in the 1960s, it is not surprising that the NOMCC sample including all three decades would show the weakest link between city and suburb.

14   For the equations to be empirically identified, the variables excluded from the suburban income equation – city annexation and whether or not the city is part of a county – must be significant in the city reduced-form equation. F-tests indicate that the excluded variables are jointly significant in the reduced-form city equation and indicate that the expanded instrument set is preferable to the instrument set that would be implied by a linear model. Recent work by Angrist and Krueger (1995) and others suggests that 2SLS estimates may be biased towards OLS in small samples if instruments are poor. They suggest a split sample estimator that is not subject to this bias even in small samples; rather it is biased towards zero. I also estimated the income equations with the split-sample estimator and obtained estimates that were qualitatively similar to the 2SLS estimates.

15   I also estimated a linear version of the model. In the linear 2SLS estimations, the coefficient on city income growth was approaching significance at the 10 percent level. Although F-tests suggest that the expanded instrument set implied by the nonlinear model is appropriate, an alternative hypothesis is that the model is linear in parameters, but the functions of the exogenous variables should be included in the structure. To this end, I estimated the linear model with the exogenous variables plus the interaction terms and their squares. In this estimation, city income is positively and significantly related to suburban income growth in each sample.

16   The strong effect of city income growth on suburban appreciation is evident in all three samples. The greatest measured effect is in the sample that includes the counties containing the central city and lowest for the estimation based on NOMCC counties and including the 1960s system.

17 These groupings are somewhat arbitrary and were chosen because the relationship between city and suburb in each grouping appears to be similar. Most MSAs (233, or 83 percent) have small central cities, but small central cities account for only 36 percent of the total central city population in the sample. Small cities have 438 NOMCC counties associated with them. By contrast, 23, or 8 percent of all MSAs have large central cities. These central cities, however, contain 48 percent of all central city population in the sample, and, despite their relatively small number, have 156 associated NOMCC counties. Finally, there are 25 MSAs with medium-sized central cities, with 16 percent of the total population in central cities and 188 associated NOMCC counties.

18 The complete estimations are available on request.

19 Calculation of the cumulative increase in income resulting from an increase in city income growth is computed as follows. An increase in decade city income growth by 5 percentage points and the 0.70 coefficient value imply a decade increase in suburban growth of 3.5 percentage points or an increase in the compound annual growth rate of 0.34 percentage points. In the first year of the decade, the income of the suburban resident increases by $1.0034 \times 50,000$ or \$170. This increases to $1.0034^{10} \times 50,000$ or \$1,726 by 1990. Cumulating these increases for each year, the total stock of additional income over the decade is about is about \$9,560. The increase in house value is simply the coefficient times the increase in city income growth times the house value: $2.01 \times .05 \times 15000 = 15075$.

References

Adams, Charles F, Howard B. Fleeter, Mark Freeman, and Yul Kim (1996) "Flight From Blight Revisited," mimeo, School of Public Policy and Management, Ohio State University.

Angrist, Joshua D. and Alan B. Krueger (1995) "Split-Sample Instrumental Variables Estimates of the Return to Schooling," *Journal of Business and Economic Statistics*, 13, 225–235.

Austin, D. Andrew (1995) "Politics vs. Economics: Evidence from Municipal Annexation," working paper, Department of Economics, University of Houston.

Benabou, Roland (1993) "Workings of a City: Location, Education, and Production," *The Quarterly Journal of Economics*, August, 619–55.

Blomquist, Glen C., Mark C. Berger, and John P. Hoehn (1988) "New Estimates of the Quality of Life in Urban Areas," *American Economic Review*, 78, 89–107.

Bradbury, Katharine, Anthony Downs, and Kenneth A. Small (1980) "Dynamics of Central City–Suburban Interactions," *The American Economic Review*, 70, 410–14.

—— (1982) *Urban Decline and the Future of American Cities.* The Brookings Institution, Washington, D.C.

Chamberlain, G. and Z. Griliches (1975) "Unobservables with a Variance-Components Structure: Ability, Schooling and the Economic Success of Brothers," *International Economic Review*, 16, 422–50.

Goetzmann, William N., Matthew Spiegel, and Susan Wachter (1996) "Suburbs and Cities," mimeo, Wharton School Real Estate Department, University of Pennsylvania.

Greene, William H. (1990) *Econometric Analysis.* New York: Macmillan Publishing Company.

Hsiao, Cheng (1986) *Analysis of Panel Data.* New York: Cambridge University Press.

Inman, Robert P. and Daniel Rubinfeld (1979) "The Judicial Pursuit of Local Fiscal Equity," *Harvard Law Review*, 92, 1662–750.

Krugman, Paul (1991) "Increasing Returns and Economic Geography," *Journal of Political Economy*, 99, 483–99.

Linneman, Peter D. and Anita A. Summers (1990) "Patterns of Urban Population Decentralization in the United States 1970–1987," working paper, Wharton Real Estate Center, University of Pennsylvania.

Lucas, Robert E. (1988) "On the Mechanics of Economic Development," *Journal of Monetary Economics*, 22, 3–42.

Meiszkowski, Peter and Edwin Mills (1993) "The Causes of Metropolitan Suburbanization," *Journal of Economic Perspectives*, 7, 135–47.

Mills, Edwin S. (1990) "Do Metropolitan Areas Mean Anything? A Research Note," *Journal of Regional Science*, 30, 415–19.

Rauch, James E. (1991) "Productivity Gains from Concentration of Human Capital: Evidence from the Cities," working paper no. 3905, Cambridge, MA: National Bureau of Economic Research.

Roback, Jennifer (1982) "Wages, Rents and the Quality of Life," *Journal of Political Economy*, 90, 1257–78.

—— (1988) "Wages, Rents and Amenities: Differences Among Workers and Regions," *Economic Inquiry*, 26, 23–41.

Summers, Anita A. and Peter D. Linneman (1990) "Patterns and Processes of Urban Employment Decentralization in the U.S., 1976–1986," working paper, Wharton Real Estate Center, University of Pennsylvania.

Voith, Richard P. (1991) "Capitalization of Local and Regional Attributes into Wages and Rents: Differences across Residential, Commercial and Mixed-Use Communities," *Journal of Regional Science*, 31, 127–45.

—— (1992) "City and Suburban Growth: Substitutes or Complements?" *Business Review*, Federal Reserve Bank of Philadelphia, September/October.

—— (1993) "Changing Capitalization of CBD-Oriented Transportation Systems: Evidence from Philadelphia, 1970–1988," *Journal of Urban Economics*, 33, 361–76.

—— (1996) "The Suburban Housing Market: Effects of City and Suburban Employment Growth," working paper No. 96-15, Federal Reserve Bank of Philadelphia, Pennsylvania.

Further Reading Samples

Abstract from *Subcenters in the Los Angeles Region*

GENEVIEVE GIULIANO AND KENNETH A. SMALL

Source: Regional Science and Urban Economics, 21, 1485–500. © 1991 Elsevier Science.
Reprinted with permission from Elsevier Science.

We investigate employment subcenters in the Los Angeles region using 1980 Census journey-to-work data. A simple subcenter definition is used, based solely on gross employment density and total employment. We find a surprising dominance of downtown Los Angeles and three large subcenters with which it forms a nearly contiguous corridor. Two-thirds of the region's employment, however, is outside any of the 32 centers we identify. Most centers have high population densities in and near them, and their workers' commutes are just 2.4 miles longer than other workers' commutes. A cluster analysis of employment by industry reveals several distinct types of centers, and a wide dispersion of sizes and locations within each type.

Abstract from *U.S. Suburbanization in the 1980s*

STACY JORDAN, JOHN P. ROSS, AND KURT G. USOWSKI

Source: Regional Science and Urban Economics, 28, 611–27. © 1998 Elsevier Science.
Reprinted with permission from Elsevier Science.

This paper measures and analyzes differences in rates of suburbanization during the 1980s among U.S. metropolitan areas which fit a monocentric urban model. Three findings are of interest: (1) the average rate of suburbanization for U.S. metropolitan areas was the same in the 1980s and the 1970s; (2) the monocentric urban model provides a good description of population distribution for a diminishing number of urban areas; and (3) variables that characterize the entire metropolitan area as well as those that measure disparities between the central city and its suburban ring are important in explaining differences in rates of decentralization.

Opening paragraph of *Space: The Final Frontier*

PAUL KRUGMAN

Source: Journal of Economic Perspectives, 12(2), Spring 1998, 161–74. Reprinted by permission of American Economic Association.

The title of this article was suggested by the back of a T-shirt, which I received as a gift from students at the University of Pennsylvania's regrettably vanished Department of

Regional Science. On the shirt's front was a portrait, not of James T. Kirk, but of Walter Isard, who for many years – most notably in his 1956 book *Location and Space-Economy* – tried to get his fellow economists to give the spatial aspects of the economy their proper due. Despite Isard's efforts, however, one must say that until the early 1990s the traditional neglect of spatial economics, of where economic activity takes place and why, remained pretty much intact. Even now, not one of the best-selling introductory textbooks in economics contains a single index entry for "location," "space," or "regions." (Most do not even contain an entry for "cities").

In the last six or seven years, however, interest in spatial economics has surged. In this article I will try to summarize briefly the reasons for that surge; the key elements of the so-called "new economic geography;" the current state of research; and the prospects and difficulties facing this subfield of economics.

Opening paragraphs of *The Causes of Metropolitan Suburbanization*

PETER MIESZKOWSKI AND EDWIN S. MILLS

Source: Journal of Economic Perspectives, 7(3), Summer 1993, 135–47. Reprinted by permission of American Economic Association.

In the United States, 69 percent of the population lived in what the government statisticians call metropolitan statistical areas (MSAs) in 1970, 75 percent in 1980, and 77 percent in 1990. But while a greater proportion of the population is living in urban areas broadly defined, a smaller proportion is living and working in the central cities. In the 1950s, 57 percent of MSA residents and 70 percent of MSA jobs were located in central cities; in 1960, the percentages were 49 and 63; in 1970, they were 43 and 55; in 1980, they were 40 and 50; in 1990, they were about 37 and 45. The United States is approaching the time when only about one-third of the residents within an MSA will live in central cities and only about 40 percent of MSA jobs will be located there.

Many popular discussions are written as if suburbanization were a postwar U.S. phenomenon, induced by circumstances peculiar to the period. For example, during the 1950s, it was claimed that home mortgage insurance by the federal government was responsible for suburbanization. In the 1960s, the interstate highway system and racial tensions were popular explanations of decentralization. More recently, crime and schooling considerations have been prominent explanations of urban decentralization. While all of these factors have played some role in causing suburbanization, they are all postwar phenomena, and are mostly provincial U.S. problems. In reality, the trend toward suburbanization has been prewar as well as postwar, and has been international in scope.

Abstract from *Analyzing Urban Decentralization: The Case of Houston*

PETER MIESZKOWSKI AND BARTON SMITH

Source: Regional Science and Urban Economics, 21, 183–99. © 1991 Elsevier Science. Reprinted with permission from Elsevier Science.

Decentralization in the Houston region is analyzed in this paper by the estimation of population density functions. The study is novel in that it uses actual land utilized for residential activity at different locations rather than using total land area. Also we analyze population density by regressing lot size of individual homes on their distance from the CBD. The development of Houston is also analyzed with reference to competing theories of urban development and explanations of decentralization.

Discussion

1 The Egan a
    lines." The
    something
    have beco
    close to th
    different
    Will's N

2 From a
    his col
    in the
    vulga
    gover
    its a

3 As
    des
    an

4 D
    u

5 C
    States is dis
    they are referring to. It
    sprawl end, or are there still points tha

6 According to Downs, how has sprawl produced a
    core of most U.S. metropolitan areas? What are the results o
    poverty?

7 Rewrite the Zeeland parable, that Fischel describes in his article regarding an urban
    growth boundary, beginning at the point of twenty years after its establishment.
    Produce this rewrite under two different scenarios. The first is that the urban
    growth boundary is allowed to expand at a rate of one mile per year. The second is
    that the urban growth boundary is eliminated.

8 Compare the specific anti-sprawl tactics advocated by Downs with the ones sug-
    gested by Fischel at the close of his article. How are they different? How are they
    similar?

9 Based on Voith's regression results, how would a one-percent increase in a central
    city's income growth effect a suburban city's income growth, house value growth,
    and population growth? Does this effect vary by population size of the central city?
    Calculate these effects with a central city size of 100,000; 500,000; 1,000,000; and
    3,000,000. What is a theoretical reason for a difference in suburban effects based on
    differences in central city population?

PART III:

Local Economic Development Incentives

For decades, we've heard scary stories of immense sums of our money spent – outright grants or taxes uncollected – so a state or locality can snare a factory, underwrite an enzterprise zone, build an industrial park, or finance some private owner's ballpark.

Neal R. Peirce

CHAPTER THIRTEEN

Ohio Looks Hard at What's Lost Through Business Subsidies

NEAL R. PEIRCE

Source: The Sacramento Bee, 5.6.97.

Three cheers for Ohio. In a move no other state's yet had the smarts (or guts) to undertake, Ohio is launching a full-bore study of the subsidies and pay-offs its governments give away to lure industries.

For decades, we've heard scary stories of immense sums of our money spent – outright grants or taxes uncollected – so a state or locality can snare a factory, underwrite an enterprise zone, build an industrial park or finance some private owner's ballpark. The national total, some experts believe, easily tops $5 billion a year.

But the Ohio subsidy study conceived and now chaired by state Sen. Charles F. Horn, a Republican from suburban Dayton, will go a lot further. Horn says the time's arrived to measure both benefit and cost of government subsidies: What's their net impact on a state's economy and welfare? What is the effect on tax rates, budgets, air and water quality, public safety?

For example: When communities provide tax subsidies to "win" a plant, do the local taxpayers gain or lose financially? How many new jobs are actually added? And who pays for the new roads, sewers, schools for employees' children? And what if the new, industry's lured from another community – often an inner-ring suburb or center city? What about the added costs – for welfare, social service, crime and justice, economic redevelopment – that the losing community incurs, or suddenly begs the state to help pay?

Then there's the land question. Ohio, not atypical among states, lost 10 percent of its farmlands in the 1980s. Are state or county programs subsidizing industries to move from multistory buildings in cities already serviced by infrastructure, to build sprawled facilities on prime agricultural land?

One has to ask: Why would any politician ask such prickly and challenging questions? America's army of economic developers, on hire to any locality ready to go smokestack chasing for new plants, will be annoyed. Land speculators and big-scale developers – who already have thousands of local councils in their pockets through campaign-giving – might try to knock off the questioner in the next election.

The delightful thing about Horn is that none of these perils frightens him. He already has a long, successful career behind him in the law, as founder of a high technology company, as mayor of Kettering and as veteran of 12 years in the Ohio Senate. He's an expert on defense-funded research and has served on presidential and National Science Foundation boards, headed the National Association of Regional Councils and played a key role in the Council of State Governments.

Today, Horn is America's one-man nerve center on the perils of excessive public subsidies. He has an e-mail network of 1,700 legislators, think tanks, university leaders and technology brokers.

Horn has had an uphill fight: Not until last year did he finally persuade Ohio to provide significant funding ($500,000) for the big subsidy study.
"Localities naturally think they have to compete to survive and think the whole states economy is someone else's business," Horn said. "I practically get booed off the platform when I talk to county commissioners."

But Horn believes Ohio, and other states, are ripe for a sea shift on subsidies. The excesses – topped by sports team owners' recent blackmail demands – have begun to arouse the public. What's more, people are starting to ask about investments needed now for 21st century survival in the global market.

"We have enormous technological resources in each metropolitan region," notes Horn. "Think of the promising alternative uses of these public funds, the potential new products and economic breakthroughs, if we were to identify and network the technology and science sources of each region, and then get the universities and laboratories and private industries working together."

Or in the words of a Horn ally, Christopher Coburn, head of technology partnerships for the Battelle Memorial Institute: "By 2015 more than the GDP [gross domestic product] of the world will be generated by countries that aren't even in the Big Seven today. We have limited public assets in America. We're in tough global competition. We can't afford to waste a single asset skewing the market with subsidies that don't cause net wealth production."

It's too early to say with confidence, of course, how convincing Horn's Ohio study will be in proving waste and bad judgment in today's industrial subsidy practices. But he's attracting broad attention in his lonely fight against government subsidies to footloose industries. He has a vision of what smart, technology-based investment can do to boost the economies of our metropolitan regions. He grasps the perils and opportunities in the global economy. And with the Internet, he's building a remarkable network for radical change.

CHAPTER FOURTEEN

Jobs, Productivity, and Local Economic Development: What Implications Does Economic Research Have for the Role of Government?*

Timothy J. Bartik

Source: National Tax Journal, XLVI, 1994.

Introduction

State and local "economic development programs" – programs that assist individual businesses with tax or financial subsidies, or special public services, in order to increase local jobs or improve local businesses' competitiveness – have become prominent and controversial. I receive several phone calls a month from reporters about the latest round in the state subsidy wars – such as Alabama's 1993 subsidies of $250 million for a new Mercedes plant, or South Carolina's 1992 subsidy package of $100 million for a new BMW plant. (Schweke, Rist, and Dabson, 1994, p. 23). The reporters seem most interested in criticisms that this is a waste of government resources. Is economic development, as argued by the Illinois Tax Foundation, "the newest form of pork"? (Ylisela and Conn, 1990).

Can economics research say anything useful about whether economic development policies can be effective? My answer is yes. Economics research suggests that traditional economic development policies of "buying growth," using various financial and tax subsidies, have a high cost per job created. Benefits large enough to justify such costs are more likely in economically distressed areas, in which the unemployed are more desperate for jobs and much of the existing public infrastructure is underutilized. Newer economic development policies, which provide services to enhance business productivity, may improve economic efficiency, but need careful evaluation. Such productivity-oriented services may make sense for low unemployment as well as high unemployment areas.

* I appreciate the helpful comments of Joel Slemrod, Randy Eberts, Paul Courant, and George Erickcek on earlier versions of this paper. Claire Vogelsong and Ellen Maloney provided their usual superb secretarial assistance.

I will consider the implications for economic development policies of three types of economics research. First, there are the implications of economists' philosophy about what justifies government intervention in private business decisions. Second, there has been extensive empirical research on how local economic growth responds to taxes, and how local growth affects local labor markets. Third, there are several recent studies on the effectiveness of specific economic development programs.

What are Economic Development Programs Today?

Most of the public resources for economic development go to tax subsidies and other financial subsidies to encourage firms to locate or expand in a particular governmental jurisdiction. Examples of such subsidies include: property-tax abatements; low-interest loans; tax exempt bonds to finance business expansion; wage subsidies; free land and infrastructure. Reliable statistics on these subsidies are rare. Data on the magnitude of economic development tax expenditures are only available for three states: Michigan, New York, and Louisiana. In Michigan, annual revenue foregone through property-tax abatements exceeds $150 million, over $16 *per capita* (Citizens Research Council of Michigan, 1986). In New York State, state and local tax breaks promoting economic development exceed $500 million annually, over $27 *per capita* (Regan, 1988). In Louisiana, industrial business property-tax exemptions cost over $270 million annually, over $60 *per capita*. (Schweke, Rist, and Dabson, 1994).

These tax expenditures vastly exceed government spending for economic development. Surveys indicate that annual city government spending for economic development averages around $3 *per capita* (National Council for Urban Economic Development, 1991; Poole, Kennedy, and Butler, 1993). Total state economic development agency spending in the United States is around $1.3 billion annually, around $5 *per capita* (National Association of State Development Agencies, 1992). Some government spending for economic development also is devoted to financial subsidies for business location or expansion.

This emphasis on tax breaks for large new facilities and expansions has a strong political rationale. A ribbon cutting at a new plant or plant expansion attracts attention. Providing a tax break allows a governor or mayor to take credit for good news. Much of the cost of this tax break may be deferred to the future.

State and local efforts to buy growth have intensified over time. For example, Kentucky in 1988 began a 6 percent wage subsidy program for new firms locating in high unemployment counties. Kentucky has since expanded the geographic scope of this program. Kentucky's aggressive wage subsidy has been imitated by Ohio, Oklahoma, Mississippi, and Alabama (Schweke, Rist, and Dabson, 1994, pp. 14, 38).

Although the spotlight is on "smoke-stack chasing," many state and local governments, since the early 1980s, have devoted resources to a new approach to economic development, which emphasizes providing customized services to help businesses improve their competitiveness. Such "new wave services" include: providing businesses with advice and technical assistance on modernization options; helping businesses figure out how to export; helping businesses with worker training; helping potential entrepreneurs and small businesses develop better business plans and locate financing. Such services are usually focused on small and medium sized businesses, which have the greatest needs for such services. Examples of "new wave" services include the following:

(1) the Edison Technology Center program in Ohio, in which local technical centers associated with universities provide manufacturers with advice on technology innovation and upgrading;

(2) Pennsylvania's Industrial Resources Center program, in which the state has contracted with quasi-private centers to help manufacturers with a variety of modernization, training, and management issues;

(3) the many community colleges in the United States that are aggressively creating customized training programs to serve business needs, usually with some state subsidy – the community colleges in the Carolinas are the most well-known examples;

(4) the export assistance offices in virtually every state economic development agency and many local economic development agencies – the Port Authority of New York and New Jersey runs a well-known program;

(5) efforts to encourage "industrial networks" in which businesses cooperate to solve their problems – for example, the Northern Economic Initiatives Corporation in northern Michigan helped a group of furniture manufacturers to cooperatively hire a productivity consultant and share shipping costs;

(6) the over 500 Small Business Development Centers around the United States, initially funded by the U.S. Small Business Administration, which provide small businesses with management advice and help in locating financing;

(7) the many entrepreneurial training programs around the country, often targeted at women (the Women's Self-Employment Project in Chicago), welfare recipients (the Self Employment Investment Demonstration sponsored by the Corporation for Enterprise Development), or the unemployed (demonstrations run by the states of Washington and Massachusetts).

These "new wave" economic development services are modestly funded. Although exact figures are scarce, only a small part of the $8 *per capita* in state and local economic development spending goes to such programs. Even if such economic development services were enormously expanded, they would still be minuscule compared to the United States economy. These programs face the problem of scale: how can these programs, with such limited resources, significantly affect the overall United States economy?

Market Failure and Economic Development Programs

As Courant discusses in his article in this symposium, economists have a well-developed philosophy about when government should intervene to affect local job growth. Economists presume that government should *not* intervene unless job growth is "mispriced" because of "market failure," the failure of private markets to work efficiently. In a perfectly efficient world, when an additional job is created, the worker in that job is paid wages equal to the value he or she places on their time in their alternative activities if that job had not been created – *e.g.*, child care, looking for another job, attending school or training programs, leisure. In addition, in this imaginary perfectly efficient world, the new job will generate tax revenues exactly equal to the additional roads, public schools, and other public services associated with this job growth. In the real world, job growth may often be "mispriced" in that its benefits and costs are unbalanced – workers may be substantially better off from becoming employed, and state and local governments may receive fiscal benefits or costs from additional job growth. Additional job growth is more likely to have social benefits in persistently high unemployment, economically declining areas. In high unemployment areas, many unemployed individuals will be desperate for a job, but unable to obtain one. These individuals will receive substantial benefits from obtaining the jobs provided by growth. In low unemployment areas, most individuals who desperately want a job can obtain one without additional job growth. The remaining unemployed will on average be less intense in their desire for a job. The benefit from employing such individuals in the jobs provided by growth will be less.[1]

Areas that have declined in employment and population will also have greater fiscal benefits from job growth. Such areas will have underutilized public infrastructure and services. Adding jobs or preventing further decline may require little additional public spending. In rapidly growing areas, additional job growth will require investments in roads, schools, and other infrastructure. Case studies have indicated that such infrastructure costs often exceed the tax revenues from new job growth. For example, a 1989 study of Montgomery County, Maryland indicated that each new office job produced county revenues per year of $410, whereas the new highways required for that job would cost $347. Altshuler and Gomez-Ibanez comment that "with such a slim margin, little tax revenue was left over to fund other county services that the office building might require (such as sewer, water, solid waste, police protection, or fire protection), let alone those required by the households of employees" (Altshuler and Gomez-Ibanez, 1993, p. 85).

There may also be a "market failure" rationale for government intervention to provide "new wave" economic development services, which target the productivity of small and medium-sized businesses. Private markets in information and training are imperfect. Such imperfections may impede productivity growth. Small businesses and potential entrepreneurs may have inadequate training in starting up and managing a business. Small and medium-sized business may not know enough about their options in technology, worker training, and exporting. Small businesses may also underinvest in worker training because of worker turnover.

There are private markets in information and training – consultants for example. But information is a peculiar commodity because it is difficult to evaluate the quality of information before one has consumed it. Uncertainty about quality may inefficiently restrict demand. In addition, training for managers and workers may sometimes be difficult to finance.

Claiming a "failure" in markets in information and training for small and medium-sized businesses does not justify every government-sponsored service that claims to correct these problems. Maybe some firms that lack information deserve to fail. Propping these firms up with free services would be a mistake. In addition, such programs face the challenge of providing services that firms value. Providing such services to firms is only efficient if the value of the information and training exceeds the costs of these services. Evaluating whether this is the case is important.

The nature of the potential market failure in information and training markets suggests that firms should be required to pay for some of the costs of such services, rather than being given free services. If the service is valuable, the firm should be willing to pay part of the costs. Fees also help stretch limited public dollars further. A given public budget for economic development can then support services to more firms.

Geographic Spillovers of Economic Development Programs

Another standard "welfare economics" issue for any state or local government policy, including economic development, is what are the spillover effects or "externalities" on other states or local areas. For state and local policies that buy job growth, the success of one area causes negative externalities for other areas. Extra job growth in one local area will *in part* (not necessarily totally) come at the expense of reduced job growth in other local areas.[2] This tradeoff is obvious when two states are competing for a Mercedes plant. But even when a state or local area attracts small business growth, that additional growth will usually reduce the sales of businesses located elsewhere, hurting their job growth.

These negative externalities reduce the national economic benefits of local competition for jobs. But even if national employment is unaffected, there may still be some net national benefits – or costs – of local competition for jobs. Net national benefits are more likely if the local areas that most aggressively "buy growth" are high unemployment areas. Even though greater job growth in high unemployment areas comes at the expense of low unemployment areas, this redistribution of jobs will yield net employment and fiscal benefits. The extra jobs in high unemployment areas will go to individuals who desperately need jobs, whereas the reduced jobs in low unemployment areas will be taken away from individuals who could easily obtain a job anyway. Reallocating growth from booming areas to declining areas allows greater use of existing infrastructure, and less spending on new infrastructure. In contrast, if low unemployment, booming areas are the most aggressive in "buying growth," job competition will have net national costs. Redistributing jobs from declining to booming areas will take jobs away from individuals who desperately need jobs, and provide jobs for individuals who could have obtained jobs anyway. This redistribution will also require more infrastructure spending.

Because the benefits of extra growth are lower for already booming areas, one could argue that high growth areas will not aggressively pursue growth. But political and economic elites may have strong private reasons for preferring pro-growth policies. Greater job growth will increase land prices and the prices charged by firms serving local markets (Bartik, 1991a)[3] Local banks, newspapers, and real estate developers will benefit from growth and have political clout (Logan and Molotch, 1987).

Economic development policies that enhance business productivity may also increase the efficiency of the national economy. Consumers throughout the nation benefit if businesses in one area can provide better-quality products at a lower price.

One might mistakenly think that improving local business productivity lacks national benefits because a more productive local economy will attract business activity from other local areas. But reallocating resources toward more productive uses increases national economic efficiency. Business competition also can appear to lack national benefits, because some businesses lose. For example, if Gateway Computers develops a cheaper way to make higher quality computers, it will take sales away from Compaq, but there would be net benefits even if total computer sales are unchanged. Reallocating resources toward better, cheaper computers enhances economic efficiency. Similarly, if Pittsburgh economic development agencies do a better job than Milwaukee agencies in improving the productivity of local small businesses, and as a result economic activity shifts from Milwaukee to Pittsburgh, this increases national economic efficiency.

Jobs to People Versus People to Jobs

I have argued that one rationale for local economic development policies in high unemployment areas is that such policies bring jobs to the persons who most need them. An alternative to bringing jobs to people is bringing people to jobs. Is promoting economic development in high unemployment areas preferable to encouraging unemployed workers to move to low unemployment areas?

It makes sense to give unemployed workers better information on job opportunities in other cities and states. But if workers have or are given good information, it is unclear that subsidizing them to move makes sense. Workers suffer large psychological costs from moving out of their home labor market, with its familiar people and places (Bartik, 1991a, pp. 64–66). If workers know the alternatives but reject moving, a policy of subsidizing workers to move seems unduly paternalistic.

Subsidizing firms to provide jobs in high unemployment areas also distorts a particular type of location decision, those of businesses rather than workers. But in this case we are subsidizing firms in order to have them recognize the effects of their job creation on another group, unemployed workers. This is different from subsidizing someone to change their behavior for their own good.[4]

Research on State and Local Fiscal Policy and Economic Growth

Although there is little research on the effects of state and local tax incentives and other *special* financial incentives for economic development, there has been extensive research on how *general* state and local taxes and public services affect local economies. This research suggests that economic development incentives may be costly per net new job created.

Most of this research has focused on how differences in taxes and public services across states or metropolitan areas affect the growth of states or metropolitan areas. My 1991 book, *Who Benefits from State and Local Economic Development Policies?*, summarizes 48 studies of taxes and growth in different metropolitan areas and states (Bartik, 1991a). Based on these 48 studies, if a state or metropolitan area reduces state and local business taxes by 10 percent, without changing its public services, and without other states or metropolitan areas changing their fiscal policies, then business activity in that state or metropolitan area on average seems to increase in the long run by around 3 percent. (In other words, the long-run elasticity of state or metropolitan area economic activity, with respect to state and local business taxes is on average estimated to be around −0.3.) Because studies differ, there is some uncertainty about this estimated effect of taxes. I argue in my book that the "true" average effect of a 10 percent reduction in state and local taxes is likely to be somewhere in between a 1 percent increase in business activity and a 6 percent increase in business activity (*i.e.*, the long-run elasticity is between −0.1 and −0.6).[5]

State and local spending on public services has a positive effect on local economies. This positive effect is large enough that some studies have found that a balanced budget increase in taxes, and spending on education or roads, will boost a state's economy (Bartik, 1989; Helms, 1985; Munnell, 1990). For business tax cuts to boost a state economy, they must be financed by increases in personal taxes or reductions in spending that does not provide services valued by business.

There has also been some research on how differences in property-tax rates within a metropolitan area affect the growth of suburban communities. Based on this research, a 10 percent reduction in an individual community's local business property taxes – for example, a reduction from 2.0 percent of property value to 1.8 percent – will, assuming other communities leave their property-tax rates unchanged, increase business activity in the community by around 20 percent. (In other words, the elasticity of a local community's business activity with respect to property taxes is around −2.0.) (Bartik, 1991a, b). How can the large effects of taxes on one community be reconciled with the modest effects of taxes on a metropolitan area? The most plausible reconciliation is that most of the increase in one community's business activity due to lower property taxes comes at the expense of other communities in the metropolitan area.

What implications does this research on the effects of *general* state and local taxes have for programs that target *special* incentives on a few firms and companies? The implications depend on whether development agencies can target incentives on firms that are the most responsive to local costs. My own view is that such targeting is usually a failure. Economic development agencies cannot read the minds of firms to tell whether a subsidy is really needed. The political pressure to extend incentives to all firms that qualify is great. [This has been termed the "reverse potato chip rule: when it comes to tax breaks, it is hard to give away just one." (Glastris, 1989, cited in Schweke, Rist, and Dabson, 1994).] Finally, there is no evidence from research that new branch plants, the most common targets of state and local incentives, are any more responsive in the long run to state and local taxes than are existing, smaller firms.

Hence, it seems plausible that the cost per job created from incentive programs is quite similar to the cost per job created from reducing overall state and local business taxes. Based on the average estimated effect reported above – an elasticity of around −0.3 for studies of metropolitan areas or states – general tax reductions or special tax incentives will have an *annual* cost to state and local governments per job created of $4,000. This calculation takes into account the extra tax revenue gained from firms for whom the tax reduction or subsidy did affect the location decision, as well as the cost of giving tax reductions or subsidies to firms that would have located or expanded in the area anyway.[6] The $4,000 annual cost is conservative in that it ignores the extra public service costs caused by new jobs.

It is important to understand the meaning of this estimated $4,000 annual cost per job created. First, this is an ongoing cost. Each year the job is in existence, the state or local government will have to pay a subsidy or give up tax revenue of $4,000. The present discounted value of the cost per job created would be much greater than $4,000. Second, although the average job created pays more than $4,000 annually, this need not imply that the benefits of job creation exceed the costs. Unemployed workers place value on their time, so being hired for a job will have benefits less than the wages paid. In addition, a portion of the jobs created by economic development subsidies will go to inmigrants, reducing the benefits to the original residents who pay for development subsidies. The benefits of local job creation are discussed later in this article.

There is uncertainty in this cost estimate. Some studies show greater tax effects on location decisions, whereas other studies show no effects whatsoever. As Courant (1999) points out in his article in this symposium, the costs per job created may vary from one local economy to another. We could provide better policy advice if we had more precise estimates of the effects of specific tax incentives in different local economies.

But despite the uncertainty, most evidence is consistent with the belief that economic development subsidies, in most state or metropolitan areas, are likely to have significant costs per job created in a metropolitan area. Contrary to some claims, tax and financial incentives are *not* a free lunch for a state or metropolitan area. These programs do not create enough jobs and new tax revenue that the programs have little or no net cost. Some states or metropolitan areas may perceive sufficient benefits from new jobs that a $4,000 annual cost of creating a new job could seem reasonable. But this cost is high enough that a state or metropolitan area should think carefully about whether aggressively using tax subsidies to attract new business activity will have net benefits.

Another implication of this research is that small communities within metropolitan areas may be tempted to engage in incentive wars, with little net benefit to the metropolitan area. If a 10 percent reduction in a community's business property tax rates increases local business activity by 20 percent, then a community can raise revenue by lowering business property taxes – if no other community in the metropolitan area responds by lowering its property taxes. In the real world, other communities in the metropolitan area will respond. Communities will lose more tax revenue and gain fewer jobs then they initially expected.

Research on Effects of Job Growth on Local Labor Markets

There is much evidence that stronger local job growth has significant long-run labor market benefits for local residents. A 10 percent increase in jobs in a metropolitan area in the long run increases local employment rates by 2 percent. To put it another way, in the long run, around one in five of the new jobs created go to the original local residents, and the other four go to in-migrants. A 10 percent increase in metropolitan employment also increases long-run real wages in the metropolitan area by around 2 percent. This increase in real wages occurs because individuals in a growing local economy are able to get and keep jobs in higher-paying occupations. (See Bartik, 1991a for a review and estimates, and Bartik, 1993c for more recent evidence.)

Local residents are able to sustain these real income gains in the long run even though local job growth leads to significant in-migration. In the short run, with limited in-migration, local residents are able because of growth to obtain jobs they otherwise would not have obtained. These jobs provide job skills. Because of these job skills, local residents are permanently better off because of a one-time surge in local job growth.

The percentage increase in income from local job growth is greater for disadvantaged groups. High school dropouts gain more than college graduates, African-Americans gain more than whites, and the lowest-income quintile families gain more than the average family (Bartik, 1991a, 1993a, 1994).

A worker's labor market fortunes are more affected by the job growth of his or her metropolitan area than the job growth of the particular city or county in which the worker resides (Bartik, 1993b). Metropolitan areas are the best definition of a "labor market," within which job-related opportunities tend to equalize for similar individuals.

The benefits of metropolitan job growth are significantly greater for jobs with a high wage premium, that is jobs that pay well relative to the skills required (Bartik, 1993b, 1994).[7] A shift in a metropolitan area's industry mix toward higher-wage-premium industries not only increases wages, but also increases labor force participation.

Research on Economic Development Programs to Improve Productivity

There have been few evaluations of economic development programs that seek to improve business productivity. Those evaluations that have been done, however, suggest that such programs can be effective.

Several studies suggest that *industrial extension services* and *small business development centers*, which provide businesses with information and training about modernization, exporting, worker training, or management, can be helpful. A survey of business clients of Ohio's Edison Technology Center Program found that one-third of the businesses believed that assistance from the Edison program had helped them to increase sales, profits, market share, or employment (Mt. Auburn Associates, 1992). A survey of business clients of Pennsylvania's Industrial Resource Center program found that 20 percent of the businesses reported increased revenue because of the program, and almost half reported cost reductions due to the program (KPMG Peat Marwick, 1993). A survey of clients of Oregon's Small Business Development Center program found that one-fourth believed that the program had greatly increased their profits (Public Policy Associates and Brandon Roberts Associates, 1992).

A word on evaluation methodology. Economists are suspicious that survey respondents may lie about their evaluations. But several features of these surveys and programs suggest that these evaluations are reliable. There is no requirement that businesses must claim services were essential in order to get the service. Furthermore, if the service was useless, what is the incentive for businesses to claim it was useful? These surveys allowed respondents to be anonymous. Finally, both the Ohio and Oregon evaluations supplemented surveys with business focus groups, which confirmed the survey results.

Surveys of clients of business assistance programs can be helpful with program design if different programs are evaluated using the same survey. Survey results from different programs can be compared to see which approach is most effective.

Comparisons of surveys suggest that business information programs are more effective when programs are *locally run*, with extensive *business involvement*. For example, the most effective Edison Centers are those with extensive business influence over program design, whereas those Centers dominated by university administrators get lower ratings from their business clients. In Oregon, the 19 locally run Small Business Development Centers were more highly rated by business clients than Oregon's other small business service programs, which delivered services through a single state office.

A recent study suggests that *entrepreneurial training* programs can significantly increase the rate at which potential entrepreneurs start up new businesses. The U.S. Labor Department has sponsored experiments in the states of Washington and Massachusetts in entrepreneurial training for unemployment insurance recipients. In these experiments, UI recipients interested in entrepreneurship were randomly assigned to treatment and control groups. The treatment groups received training and assistance in developing a business plan, and a lump-sum payment of their remaining UI benefits if they achieved business planning goals. In Massachusetts, 47 percent of the treatment group entered self-employment, compared to 29 percent of the controls, whereas in Washington State, 52 percent of the treatment group entered self-employment, compared to 27 percent of the controls (Benus, Wood, and Grover, 1994).

Another study indicates that *customized job training* assistance can improve business productivity (Holzer *et al.*, 1993). Holzer *et al.* evaluated Michigan's industrial training grant program for manufacturing firms undergoing modernization. The evaluation compared firms that received training grants with firms that applied for grants too late in the fiscal year. The state program awarded grants on a "first come–first serve" basis to all firms that met eligibility criteria. Holzer *et al.* found that firms that received grants did more job training afterwards than nongrantees, and their product scrappage rates declined more. Product scrappage rates declined enough that the training seemed cost-effective. A key issue is why firms did not pursue such training on their own.

Holzer's study could be criticized on the grounds that firms that applied too late for grants may also be less capable in other ways. This criticism is not supported by the data, which suggest that assisted and unassisted firms were quite similar.

Conclusion: Advice to Policymakers

To summarize the implications of research for economic development policy, I will conclude with two memos: one to a governor or mayor, the other to the President.
To: Governor or Mayor of Jurisdiction X. Re: three things you can do to improve your jurisdiction's economic development policies.

(1) *Target tax/financial subsidies for economic development more carefully.* Because tax and financial subsidies for economic development are expensive per job created, they should be used more thoughtfully then they are at present. Such expensive subsidies make more sense for high unemployment areas. Because the unemployed are more desperate for jobs in high unemployment areas, even expensive subsidies may have benefits exceeding costs. In low unemployment areas, many persons obtaining jobs because of an economic development program could have obtained

jobs anyway. Adding jobs in a boom area will also require expensive new infrastructure. The high costs of subsidizing new jobs may not be worth it in low unemployment, fast growing areas. Tax and financial subsidies for new jobs make more sense if the jobs pay a high *wage premium*, that is, they pay well relative to the skills required. High-wage-premium jobs will provide more desirable jobs for local residents. In addition, higher-wage jobs will have greater multiplier effects on the local economy, as the higher wages lead to a greater boost to local consumer demand.[8]

Tax and financial subsidies should have rules to guide when subsidies are to be given and their amount. For example, the rules might increase the subsidy for a higher-wage plant that employs more local residents. Without rules, political pressures may lead to excessive subsidies for large projects.

(2) *Economic development policies should place more emphasis on improving business productivity.* Because research suggests that economic development services to improve business productivity can be effective, state and local governments should place more emphasis on this area. More effort should be devoted to programs to train entrepreneurs, provide advice to small and medium-sized businesses, and help small and medium-sized businesses with worker training. Such programs may be more cost-effective than tax subsidies to large companies, even if they do not allow for high-publicity ribbon cuttings.

These productivity-related services to business should be regularly evaluated, by surveys of business clients and comparisons of assisted and unassisted firms, to monitor their effectiveness and suggest program improvements. Program managers should focus these programs on filling gaps where private markets have problems providing information for improving productivity. Where possible, fees should be charged to business clients to partially cover the cost of these services: this stretches limited public dollars and shows whether these services are valued.

(3) *Metropolitan cooperation in economic development programs is essential.* Competition for jobs among jurisdictions within the same metropolitan area uses public resources without changing overall labor market opportunities in the metropolitan area. A metropolitan area is one labor market. If the goal of economic development policy is to improve labor market opportunities, economic development should be coordinated within a labor market area.

To: President Clinton.
Re: two things you can do to improve the effectiveness of government economic development efforts.

(1) *Use limited federal resources to expand and standardize evaluations of economic development programs.* Because of the budget deficit, the federal government is unlikely to devote sufficient resources to economic development services to make a significant different in the overall United States economy. Furthermore, there is some evidence that locally controlled economic development services are more effective.

With limited federal dollars, it would be more effective to encourage improvements in the quality of local economic development programs, particularly economic development programs that improve productivity. Local governments lack sufficient incentive to support evaluations. The benefits of high-quality evaluation accrue to governments around the nation, not just the government conducting the evaluation. Federal funding should support evaluations of state and local economic development programs, and support disseminating the results of such evaluations.

Evaluations would be more useful if they were done similarly for different states and cities, so that the effectiveness of different programs could be compared. For standardization of our national leadership and funding, one first step would be to develop a standard survey form for business clients of economic development programs.

(2) *The national interest would be served by discouraging state and local governments in areas with low unemployment rates and booming economies from providing large financial and tax subsidies for economic development.* Political pressures lead to large tax subsidies and financial subsidies for large companies making location decisions. In low unemployment areas, the local employment benefits from these subsidies are more than offset by the losses to high unemployment areas that do not succeed in attracting the large company.

It is undesirable to eliminate all economic development programs, because some of these programs help promote business productivity. It also is undesirable to prevent high unemployment areas like Detroit from competing for new business. What we should try to do is discourage low unemployment, prosperous areas from offering excessive financial subsidies to new business.

It is infeasible to eliminate all financial subsidies for economic development, given the many thousands of jurisdictions and companies involved in such subsidy programs and the enormous political pressures encouraging such subsidies. What may be desirable and feasible is to *limit* – not eliminate – the *types* of subsidies provided to a few large companies. For new plant location decisions or expansion decisions that exceed some number of workers or dollar amount of investment, federal community development block grant assistance or industrial development bond authority could be reduced if an area provides "unproductive" subsidies to affect that location or expansion decision. The penalty for providing such subsidies would be greater for low unemployment areas. "Unproductive" subsidies would be defined as discretionary subsidies provided to one firm that would not have any permanent effect on the local economy if the firm leaves. Under this definition, a tax abatement or free land for a company would be an "unproductive" subsidy. On the other hand, building a new access road or training a firm's workers would not be considered an unproductive subsidy, because some benefit from this spending would still continue if the firm left the area. A proposal similar to this was reportedly included in an early draft of Vice President Gore's Reinventing Government Task Force on the Commerce Department.

Such a proposal might be welcomed by many governors and mayors. This limited federal intervention would enable more states and cities to resist the political pressures of trying to claim credit, by using large subsidies, for large companies' location or expansion decisions. The limitation of such subsidies would free up some state and local resources for more productive approaches to economic development, whether through productivity-oriented economic development programs, general improvements in public services, or general tax reductions. Finally, this approach would still give considerable latitude to high unemployment areas to help create new jobs for local residents.

Afterword: Comments on Courant's Perspective

Although this might not be apparent to some readers, Paul Courant and I are in general agreement in our perspective on local economic development policy. Both of us emphasize that policymakers and researchers should spend more time thinking about and measuring the *ultimate benefits* of local economic development policy. Policymakers and researchers need to focus on the benefits of such programs for the unemployed, different groups of workers, the local fiscal situation, and the productivity of the local economy. Job creation in and of itself should not be seen as the ultimate goal of economic development programs.

Where Courant and I differ is my greater emphasis on the value of research on the costs and effectiveness of economic development programs in creating jobs and enhancing productivity. Although there is uncertainty in current research, I would argue that we do know some useful things: tax incentives for economic development are not self-financing, but have significant costs per job created; some programs that promote productivity appear to be effective. We need to continue this line of research. Even as we learn more about the labor market and fiscal effects of job growth, we will need to have more precise information about how different economic development programs in different cities affect job growth. Furthermore, we need much more research on the "new wave" economic development programs, which seek to promote business productivity. Can such programs play a significant role in increasing the competitiveness of American industries? How can such programs be best designed? The answers to such questions may be important to the long-term performance of the United States economy.

Notes

1   Using economic jargon, in high unemployment areas the gap between wages actually paid and the "reservation wage" of the unemployed will be greater. The "reservation wage" of an individual is the lowest wage for which that individual would be willing to work.

2   Whether national job growth on net goes up or down is a complicated issue. If local governments compete by subsidizing labor demand, and national labor supply is not completely inelastic, a partial equilibrium analysis would lead us to expect some increase in equilibrium national employment. Whether a general equilibrium analysis would also make such a prediction depends on the macroeconomic model used. Furthermore, as Courant points out, most local development subsidies are nominally subsidies to capital. But because the subsidies are conditioned on the number and quality of jobs provided, they also have some of the character of a labor demand subsidy.

3   From an economic efficiency perspective, these increases in local land prices and other local prices are a transfer of resources between different groups, and do not represent a net gain for society.

4   Formally, suppose unemployed workers in city X have benefit W from getting a job and moving costs M from moving to get one. We reduce a typical firm's profit by D by inducing them to create one more job in city X. If workers have full information, M must exceed W, and no

subsidy can be efficient. But it is possible that W can exceed D, and a subsidy for firm job creation may be efficient. Some economists will argue that workers and firms on their own should be able to make such a deal to create jobs. In an imperfect world, however, government may sometimes be the best available mechanism to reach such deals.

5   These elasticity estimates combine studies that look at business taxes with studies that look at overall taxes. Elasticity estimates do not seem to depend on the tax measure. It is reasonable to assume that the effects estimated for overall taxes are attributable to the business taxes included in that overall tax measure.

   These elasticity estimates also combine results from studies that use different measures of business activity, for example total local employment, gross state product, and plant starts. These differences in dependent variable do not lead to systematic differences in estimated tax effects, so I refer in the text simply to effects on local business activity.

6   The calculation is as follows. The tax elasticity of private employment with respect to state and local business taxes (E) is defined as $(d\mathcal{J}/\mathcal{J})/(dT/T)$, where $\mathcal{J}$ is the number of jobs, $d\mathcal{J}$ is the change in the number of jobs, T is the tax rate, and dT is the change in the business tax rate. The percentage change in revenue from a tax cut, dR/R, will approximately equal $dT/T + d\mathcal{J}/\mathcal{J}$. Substituting and rearranging, one obtains $dR/d\mathcal{J} = (R/\mathcal{J})[1 + (1/E)]$. $R/\mathcal{J}$ is state and local business tax revenue per job, which is about \$1,620 per job in the United States With a value of -0.3 for E, one obtains $dR/d\mathcal{J} = -\$3,780$.

   The figure of \$1,620 for state and local business taxes per private employee comes from three sources. Total state and local tax revenue in fiscal year 1989 was \$469 billion (U.S. Bureau of the Census, 1988–89). The most recent estimate of the business share of state and local taxes is 31 percent (U.S. ACIR, 1981). Private nonagricultural employment in the United States averaged 89 million during fiscal year 1989 (U.S. Department of Commerce Bureau of Economic Analysis, 1991).

7   These "wage premia" are often referred to by economists as "efficiency wage premia." Wage premia are estimated by relating wages to a worker's education, experience, and other character-istics, and dummy variables for industry. These industry wage differentials are large and persistent over time (Krueger and Summers, 1988; Katz and Summers, 1989).

8   *National* targeting of high-wage industries, or any particular industry type, is controversial among economists [see, for example, the debate over the paper by Katz and Summers (1989)]. Local development policy that targets industry is somewhat different, for three reasons. (1) We already are targeting at the local level, and the question is whether to do so randomly or by some rational formula. (2) There are clearly greater benefits for local residents from higher-wage-premia jobs, in wages, employment rates, and multiplier effects. The national benefits of such targeting are more unclear. (3) The diversity of different local jurisdictions limits the damage from mistaken targeting.

References

Altshuler, Alan A. and Jose A. Gomez-Ibanez. (1993) *Regulation for Revenue: The Political Economy of Land Use Exactions*. Washington, D.C.: The Brookings Institution.

Bartik, Timothy J. (1989) "Small Business Start-Ups in the United States: Estimates of the Effects of Characteristics of States." *Southern Economic Journal*, April, 1004–18.

Bartik, Timothy J. (1991a) *Who Benefits from State and Local Economic Development Policies?* Kalamazoo, Michigan: W. E. Upjohn Institute for Employment Research.

Bartik, Timothy J. (1991b) "The Effects of Property Taxes and Other Local Public Policies on the Intrametropolitan Pattern of Business Location." In *Industry Location and Public Policy*, edited by Henry W. Herzog, Jr. and Alan M. Schlottmann, 57–80. Knoxville, TN: The University of Tennessee Press.

Bartik, Timothy J. (1992) "The Effects of State and Local Taxes on Economic Development: A Review of Recent Research." *Economic Development Quarterly*, 6(1), February, 102–10.

Bartik, Timothy J. (1993a) "The Effects of Local Labor Demand on Individual Labor Market Outcomes for Different Demographic Groups and the Poor." *W. E. Upjohn Institute for Employment Research working paper 93–23*. Kalamazoo, Michigan: W. E. Upjohn Institute for Employment Research.

Bartik, Timothy J. (1993b) "Economic Development and Black Economic Success." *Upjohn Institute technical report No. 93–001*. Kalamazoo, Michigan: W. E. Upjohn Institute for Employment Research.

Bartik, Timothy J. (1993c) "Who Benefits From Local Job Growth, Migrants or the Original Residents?" *Regional Studies*, September 1993c, 27(4), 297–311.

Bartik, Timothy J. (1994) "The Effect of Metropolitan Job Growth on the Size Distribution of Family Income." *Journal of Regional Science*, 34(4), 483–501.

Benus, Jacob M., Michelle Wood, and Neelima Grover. (1994) *A Comparative Analysis of the Washington and Massachusetts Ul Self-Employment Demonstrations*. Report prepared for U.S. Department of Labor, ETA/UIS by Abt Associates, Inc. Bethesda, MD, January.

Citizens Research Council of Michigan. (1986) "Municipal Government Economic Development Incentive Programs in Michigan." *Citizens Research Council of Michigan report no. 280*. Detroit, MI, February.

Courant, Paul (1999) "How would you know a Good Economic Development Policy if you Tripped over one? Hint: Don't just Count Jobs", *National Tax Journal*, 47(4), 863–81.

Glastris, Paul. (1989) "Holdup in the Windy City." *U.S. News and World Report*, July 17, 41.

Helms, Jay L. (1985) "The Effect of State and Local Taxes on Economic Growth: A Time Series Cross Section Approach." *The Review of Economics and Statistics*, February, 574–82.

Holzer, Harry J., Richard N. Block, Marcus Cheatham, and Jack H. Knott. (1993) "Are Training Subsidies for Firms Effective? The Michigan Experience." *Industrial and Labor Relations Review*, 46(4), July, 625–36.

Katz, Lawrence and Lawrence Summers. (1989) "Industry Rents: Evidence and Implications." *Brookings Papers on Economic Activity* (Microeconomics issue), 209–90.

KPMG Peat Marwick. (1993) *Customer Satisfaction Survey of the Pennsylvania Industrial Resource Centers*. Harrisburg, PA: Pennsylvania Department of Commerce.

Krueger, Alan and Lawrence Summers. (1988) "Efficiency Wages and the Inter-Industry Wage Structure." *Econometrica*, 56, March 259–64.

Logan, John and Harvey Molotch. (1987) *Urban Fortunes: The Political Economy of Place*. Berkeley, CA: University of California Press.

Mt. Auburn Associates. (1992) "An Evaluation of Ohio's Thomas Edison Technology Centers." Final report submitted to the Ohio Department of Development. Somerville, MA, December.

Munnell, Alicia H. (1990) "How Does Public Infrastructure Affect Regional Economic Performance?" *New England Economic Review*, September/October, 11–33.

National Association of State Development Agencies. (1992) *NASDA 1992 State Economic Development Expenditure Survey*. Washington, D.C.: National Association of State Development Agencies.

National Council for Urban Economic Development. (1991) *Trends in Economic Development Organizations: A Survey of Selected Metropolitan Areas*. Washington, D.C.: National Council for Urban Economic Development.

Poole, Kenneth E., Tanya Kennedy, and Elizabeth Butler. (1993) *Survey of Public Economic Development Agencies: Summary of Results*. Washington, D.C.: National Council for Urban Economic Development.

Public Policy Associates and Brandon Roberts & Associates. (1992) *Oregon Small Business Services Evaluation*. Lansing, MI. Final Report.

Regan, Edward V. (1988) *Government, Inc.: Creating Accountability for Economic Development Programs.* Chicago: Government Finance Officers Association.

Schweke, William, Carl Rist, and Brian Dabson. (1994) *Bidding for Business: Are Cities and States Selling Themselves Short?* Washington, D.C.: Corporation for Enterprise Development.

U.S. ACIR (Advisory Commission on Intergovernmental Relations). (1981) *Regional Growth: Interstate Tax Competition.* Report A-76 (March), revised version of Table A-1, Figures for 1977. Washington, D.C.

U.S. Bureau of the Census. *Government Finances: 1988–89.* Washington, D.C.: U.S. Government Printing Office, 21.

U.S. Department of Commerce, Bureau of Economic Analysis. (1991) *Survey of Current Business*, January: S-10.

Ylisela, James, Jr. and Sandra Conn. (1990) *Helping Small Business: DCCA's Promise and Failure.* Springfield, IL: Illinois Tax Foundation.

CHAPTER FIFTEEN

Sports, Jobs, and Taxes: Are New Stadiums Worth the Cost?

ROGER G. NOLL AND ANDREW ZIMBALIST

Source: *The Brookings Review*, Summer, 1997. Brookings Institution Press, Washington DC, 1998.

America is in the midst of a sports construction boom. New sports facilities costing at least $200 million each have been completed or are under way in Baltimore, Charlotte, Chicago, Cincinnati, Cleveland, Milwaukee, Nashville, San Francisco, St. Louis, Seattle, Tampa, and Washington, D.C., and are in the planning stages in Boston, Dallas, Minneapolis, New York, and Pittsburgh. Major stadium renovations have been undertaken in Jacksonville and Oakland. Industry experts estimate that more than $7 billion will be spent on new facilities for professional sports teams before 2006.

Most of this $7 billion will come from public sources. The subsidy starts with the federal government, which allows state and local governments to issue tax-exempt bonds to help finance sports facilities. Tax exemption lowers interest on debt and so reduces the amount that cities and teams must pay for a stadium. Since 1975, the interest rate reduction has varied between 2.4 and 4.5 percentage points. Assuming a differential of 3 percentage points, the discounted present value loss in federal taxes for a $225 million stadium is about $70 million, or more than $2 million a year over a useful life of 30 years. Ten facilities built in the 1970s and 1980s, including the Superdome in New Orleans, the Silverdome in Pontiac, the now–obsolete Kingdome in Seattle, and Giants Stadium in the New Jersey Meadowlands, each cause an annual federal tax loss exceeding $1 million.

State and local governments pay even larger subsidies than Washington. Sports facilities now typically cost the host city more than $10 million a year. Perhaps the most successful new baseball stadium, Oriole Park at Camden Yards, costs Maryland residents $14 million a year. Renovations aren't cheap either: the net cost to local government for refurbishing the Oakland Coliseum for the Raiders was about $70 million.

Most large cities are willing to spend big to attract or keep a major league franchise. But a city need not be among the nation's biggest to win a national competition for a team, as shown by the NBA's Utah Jazz's Delta Center in Salt Lake City and the NFL's Houston Oilers' new football stadium in Nashville.

Why Cities Subsidize Sports

The economic rationale for cities' willingness to subsidize sports facilities is revealed in the campaign slogan for a new stadium for the San Francisco 49ers: "Build the Stadium – Create the Jobs!" Proponents claim that sports facilities improve the local economy in four ways. First, building the facility creates construction jobs. Second, people who attend games or work for the team generate new spending in the community, expanding local employment. Third, a team attracts tourists and companies to the host city, further increasing local spending and jobs. Finally, all this new spending has a "multiplier effect" as increased local income causes still more new spending and job creation. Advocates argue that new stadiums spur so much economic growth that they are self-financing: subsidies are offset by revenues from ticket taxes, sales taxes on concessions and other spending outside the stadium, and property tax increases arising from the stadium's economic impact.

Unfortunately, these arguments contain bad economic reasoning that leads to over-statement of the benefits of stadiums. Economic growth takes place when a community's resources – people, capital investments, and natural resources like land – become more productive. Increased productivity can arise in two ways: from economically beneficial specialization by the community for the purpose of trading with other regions or from local value added that is higher than other uses of local workers, land, and investments. Building a stadium is good for the local economy only if a stadium is the most productive way to make capital investments and use its workers.

In our Brookings book, *Sports, Jobs, and Taxes* (1997), we and 15 collaborators examine the local economic development argument from all angles: case studies of the effect of specific facilities, as well as comparisons among cities and even neighborhoods that have and have not sunk hundreds of millions of dollars into sports development. In every case, the conclusions are the same. A new sports facility has an extremely small (perhaps even negative) effect on overall economic activity and employment. No recent facility appears to have earned anything approaching a reasonable return on investment. No recent facility has been self-financing in terms of its impact on net tax revenues. Regardless of whether the unit of analysis is a local neighborhood, a city, or an entire metropolitan area, the economic benefits of sports facilities are de minimus.

As noted, a stadium can spur economic growth if sports is a significant export industry – that is, if it attracts outsiders to buy the local product and if it results in the sale of certain rights (broadcasting, product licensing) to national firms. But, in reality, sports has little effect on regional net exports.

Sports facilities attract neither tourists nor new industry. Probably the most successful export facility is Oriole Park, where about a third of the crowd at every game comes from outside the Baltimore area. (Baltimore's baseball exports are enhanced because it is 40 miles from the nation's capital, which has no major league baseball team.) Even so, the net gain to Baltimore's economy in terms of new jobs and incremental tax revenues is only about $3 million a year – not much of a return on a $200 million investment.

Sports teams do collect substantial revenues from national licensing and broadcasting, but these must be balanced against funds leaving the area. Most professional athletes do not live where they play, so their income is not spent locally. Moreover, players make inflated salaries for only a few years, so they have high savings, which they invest in national firms. Finally, though a new stadium increases attendance, ticket revenues are shared in both baseball and football, so that part of the revenue gain goes to other cities. On balance, these factors are largely offsetting, leaving little or no net local export gain to a community.

One promotional study estimated that the local annual economic impact of the Denver Broncos was nearly $120 million; another estimated that the combined annual economic benefit of Cincinnati's Bengals and Reds was $245 million. Such promotional studies overstate the economic impact of a facility because they confuse gross and net economic effects. Most spending inside a stadium is a substitute for other local recreational spending, such as movies and restaurants. Similarly, most tax collections inside a stadium are substitutes: as other entertainment businesses decline, tax collections from them fall.

Promotional studies also fail to take into account differences between sports and other industries in income distribution. Most sports revenue goes to a relatively few players, managers, coaches, and executives who earn extremely high salaries – all well above the earnings of people who work in the industries that are substitutes for sports. Most stadium employees work part time at very low wages and earn a small fraction of team revenues. Thus, substituting spending on sports for other recreational spending concentrates income, reduces the total number of jobs, and replaces full-time jobs with low-wage, part-time jobs.

A second rationale for subsidized stadiums is that stadiums generate more local consumer satisfaction than alternative investments. There is some truth to this argument. Professional sports teams are very small businesses, comparable to large department or grocery stores. They capture public attention far out of proportion to their economic significance. Broadcast and print media give so much attention to sports because so many people are fans, even if they do not actually attend games or buy sports-related products.

A professional sports team, therefore, creates a "public good" or "externality" – a benefit enjoyed by consumers who follow sports regardless of whether they help pay for it. The magnitude of this benefit is unknown, and is not shared by everyone; nevertheless, it exists. As a result, sports fans are likely to accept higher taxes or reduced public services to attract or keep a team, even if they do not attend games themselves. These fans, supplemented and mobilized by teams, local media, and local interests that benefit directly from a stadium, constitute the base of political support for subsidized sports facilities.

The Role of Monopoly Leagues

While sports subsidies might flow from externalities, their primary cause is the monopolistic structure of sports. Leagues maximize their members' profits by keeping the number of franchises below the number of cities that could support a team. To attract teams, cities must compete through a bidding war, whereby each bids its willingness to pay to have a team, not the amount necessary to make a team viable.

Monopoly leagues convert fans' (hence cities') willingness to pay for a team into an opportunity for teams to extract revenues. Teams are not required to take advantage of this opportunity, and in two cases – the Charlotte Panthers and, to a lesser extent, the San Francisco Giants – the financial exposure of the city has been the relatively modest costs of site acquistion and infrastructural investments. But in most cases, local and state governments have paid over $100 million in stadium subsidy, and in some cases have financed the entire enterprise.

The tendency of sports teams to seek new homes has been intensified by new stadium technology. The rather ordinary cookie-cutter, multipurpose facility of the 1960s and 1970s has given way to the elaborate, single-sport facility that features numerous new revenue opportunities: luxury suites, club boxes, elaborate concessions, catering, signage, advertising, theme activities, and even bars, restaurants, and apartments with a view of the field. A new facility now can add $30 million annually to a team's revenues for a few years after the stadium opens.

Because new stadiums produce substantially more revenues, more cities are now economically viable franchise sites – which explains why Charlotte, Jacksonville, and Nashville have become NFL cities. As more localities bid for teams, cities are forced to offer ever larger subsidies.

What Can Be Done?

Abuses from exorbitant stadium packages, sweetheart leases, and footloose franchises have left many citizens and politicians crying foul. What remedy, if any, is available to curb escalating subsidies and to protect the emotional and financial investments of fans and cities?

In principle, cities could bargain as a group with sports leagues, thereby counter-balancing the leagues' monopoly power. In practice, this strategy is unlikely to work. Efforts by cities to form a sports-host association have failed. The temptation to cheat by secretly negotiating with a mobile team is too strong to preserve concerted behavior.

Another strategy is to insert provisions in a facility lease that deter team relocation. Many cities have tried this approach, but most leases have escape clauses that allow the team to move if attendance falls too low or if the facility is not in state-of-the-art condition. Other teams have provisions requiring them to pay tens of millions of dollars if they vacate a facility prior to lease expiration, but these provisions also come with qualifying covenants. Of course, all clubs legally must carry out the terms of their lease, but with or without these safeguard provisions, teams generally have not viewed their lease terms as binding. Rather, teams claim that breach of contract by the city or stadium authority releases them from their obligations. Almost always these provisions do not prevent a team from moving.

Some leases grant the city a right of first refusal to buy the team or to designate who will buy it before the team is relocated. The big problem here is the price. Owners usually want to move a team because it is worth more elsewhere, either because another city is building a new facility with strong revenue potential or because another city is a better sports market. If the team is worth, say, $30 million more if it moves, what price must the team accept from local buyers? If it is the market price (its value in the best location), an investor in the home city would be foolish to pay $30 million more for the franchise than it is worth there. If the price is the value of the franchise in its present home, the old owner is deprived of his property rights if he cannot sell to the highest bidder. In practice, these provisions typically specify a right of first refusal at market price, which does not protect against losing a team.

Cities trying to hold on to a franchise can also invoke eminent domain, as did Oakland when the Raiders moved to Los Angeles in 1982 and Baltimore when the Colts moved to Indianapolis in 1984. In the Oakland case, the California Court of Appeals ruled that condemning a football franchise violates the commerce clause of the U.S. Constitution. In the Colts case, the condemnation was upheld by the Maryland Circuit Court, but the U.S. District Court ruled that Maryland lacked jurisdiction because the team had left the state by the time the condemnation was declared. Eminent domain, even if constitutionally feasible, is not a promising vehicle for cities to retain sports teams.

Ending Federal Subsidies

Whatever the costs and benefits to a city of attracting a professional sports team, there is no rationale whatsoever for the federal government to subsidize the financial tug-of-war among the cities to host teams.

In 1986, Congress apparently became convinced of the irrationality of granting tax exemptions for interest on municipal bonds that financed projects primarily benefiting private interests. The 1986 Tax Reform Act denies federal subsidies for sports facilities if more than 10 percent of the debt service is covered by revenues from the stadium. If Congress intended that this would reduce sports subsidies, it was sadly mistaken. If anything, the 1986 law increased local subsidies by cutting rents below 10 percent of debt service.

Last year Senator Daniel Patrick Moynihan (D-NY), concerned about the prospect of a tax exemption for a debt of up to $1 billion for a new stadium in New York, introduced a bill to eliminate tax-exempt financing for professional sports facilities and thus eliminate federal subsidies of stadiums. The theory behind the bill is that raising a city's cost from a stadium giveaway would reduce the subsidy. Although cities might respond this way, they would still compete among each other for scarce franchises, so to some extent the likely effect of the bill is to pass higher interest charges on to cities, not teams.

Antitrust and Regulation

Congress has considered several proposals to regulate team movement and league expansion. The first came in the early 1970s, when the Washington Senators left for Texas. Unhappy baseball fans on Capitol Hill commissioned an inquiry into professional sports. The ensuing report recommended removing baseball's antitrust immunity, but no legislative action followed. Another round of ineffectual inquiry came in 1984–85, following the relocations of the Oakland Raiders and Baltimore Colts. Major league baseball's efforts in 1992 to thwart the San Francisco Giants' move to St. Petersburg again drew proposals to withdraw baseball's cherished antitrust exemption. As before, nothing came of the congressional interest. In 1995–96, inspired by the departure of the Cleveland Browns to Baltimore, Representative Louis Stokes from Cleveland and Senator John Glenn of Ohio introduced a bill to grant the NFL an antitrust exemption for franchise relocation. This bill, too, never came to a vote.

The relevance of antitrust to the problem of stadium subsidies is indirect but important. Private antitrust actions have significantly limited the ability of leagues to prevent teams from relocating. Teams relocate to improve their financial performance, which in turn improves their ability to compete with other teams for players and coaches. Hence, a team has an incentive to prevent competitors from relocating. Consequently, courts have ruled that leagues must have "reasonable" relocation rules that preclude anticompetitive denial of relocation. Baseball, because it enjoys an antitrust exemption, is freer to limit team movements than the other sports.

Relocation rules can affect competition for teams because, by making relocation more difficult, they can limit the number of teams (usually to one) that a city is allowed to bid for. In addition, competition among cities for teams is further intensified because leagues create scarcity in the number of teams. Legal and legislative actions that change relocation rules affect which cities get existing teams and how much they pay for them, but do not directly affect the disparity between the number of cities that are viable locations for a team and the number of teams. Thus, expansion policy raises a different but important antitrust issue.

As witnessed by the nearly simultaneous consideration of creating an antitrust exemption for football but denying one for baseball on precisely the same issue of franchise relocation, congressional initiatives have been plagued by geographical chauvinism and myopia. Except for representatives of the region affected, members of Congress have proven reluctant to risk the ire of sports leagues. Even legislation that is not hampered by blatant regional self-interest, such as the 1986 Tax Reform Act, typically is sufficiently riddled with loopholes to make effective implementation improbable. While arguably net global welfare is higher when a team relocates to a better market, public policy should focus on balancing the supply and demand for sports franchises so that all economically viable cities can have a team. Congress could mandate league expansion, but that is probably impossible politically. Even if such legislation were passed, deciding which city deserves a team is an administrative nightmare.

A better approach would be to use antitrust to break up existing leagues into competing business entities. The entities could collaborate on playing rules and interleague and postseason play, but they would not be able to divvy up metropolitan areas, establish common drafts or player market restrictions, or collude on broadcasting and licensing policy. Under these circumstances no league would be likely to vacate an economically viable city, and, if one did, a competing league would probably jump in. Other consumer-friendly consequences would flow from such an arrangement. Competition would force ineffective owners to sell or go belly up in their struggle with better managed teams. Taxpayers would pay lower local, state, and federal subsidies. Teams would have lower revenues, but because most of the costs of a team are driven by revenues, most teams would remain solvent. Player salaries and team profits would fall, but the number of teams and player jobs would rise.

Like Congress, the Justice Department's Antitrust Division is subject to political pressures not to upset sports. So sports leagues remain unregulated monopolies with de facto immunity from federal antitrust prosecution. Others launch and win antitrust complaints against sports leagues, but usually their aim is membership in the cartel, not divestiture, so the problem of too few teams remains unsolved.

Citizen Action

The final potential source of reform is grassroots disgruntlement that leads to a political reaction against sports subsidies. Stadium politics has proven to be quite controversial in some cities. Some citizens apparently know that teams do little for the local economy and are concerned about using regressive sales taxes and lottery revenues to subsidize wealthy players, owners, and executives. Voters rejected public support for stadiums on ballot initiatives in Milwaukee, San Francisco, San Jose, and Seattle, although no team has failed to obtain a new stadium. Still, more guarded, conditional support from constituents can cause political leaders to be more careful in negotiating a stadium deal. Initiatives that place more of the financial burden on facility users – via revenues from luxury or club boxes, personal seat licenses (PSLs), naming rights, and ticket taxes – are likely to be more popular.

Unfortunately, citizen resistance notwithstanding, most stadiums probably cannot be financed primarily from private sources. In the first place, the use of money from PSLs, naming rights, pouring rights, and other private sources is a matter to be negotiated among teams, cities, and leagues. The charges imposed by the NFL on the Raiders and Rams when they moved to Oakland and St. Louis, respectively, were an attempt by the league to capture some of this (unshared) revenue, rather than have it pay for the stadium.

Second, revenue from private sources is not likely to be enough to avoid large public subsidies. In the best circumstance, like the NFL's Charlotte Panthers, local governments still pay for investments in supporting infrastructure, and Washington still pays an interest subsidy for the local government share. And the Charlotte case is unique. No other stadium project has raised as much private revenue. At the other extreme is the disaster in Oakland, where a supposedly break-even financial plan left the community $70 million in the hole because of cost overruns and disappointing PSL sales.

Third, despite greater citizen awareness, voters still must cope with a scarcity of teams. Fans may realize that subsidized stadiums regressively redistribute income and do not promote growth, but they want local teams. Alas, it is usually better to pay a monopoly an exorbitant price than to give up its product.

Prospects for cutting sports subsidies are not good. While citizen opposition has had some success, without more effective intercity organizing or more active federal antitrust policy, cities will continue to compete against each other to attract or keep artificially scarce sports franchises. Given the profound penetration and popularity of sports in American culture, it is hard to see an end to rising public subsidies of sports facilities.

References

Noll, Roger G. and Andrew Zimbalist (eds) (1997). *Sports, Jobs, and Taxes: The Economic Impact of Sports Teams and Stadiums*. Washington, DC: Brookings Institution Press.

CHAPTER SIXTEEN

Can Local Incentives Alter a Metropolitan City's Economic Development?*

ROBERT W. WASSMER

Source: Urban Studies, 31(8), 1994, 1251–78. Taylor & Francis Ltd.

Cities in the US and Europe have chosen increasingly to offer incentives designed to attract and retain local economic development. The increased use of local incentives has occurred with little or no empirical test of their effectiveness. This paper contains a statistical method that can be applied to any group of cities to measure the 'additive effect', or lack of it, that incentives exert on local economic development. Regression analysis applied to cities in the Detroit metropolitan area indicates that incentive efficacy depends on city-specific characteristics and how economic development is measured. Although there are situations where incentive offers exert an additive effect on local economic development, in a majority of situations this is not the outcome.

1. Introduction

Communities in the US and Europe have increasingly used local development incentives. The increased use of these incentives is attributable to the relative decline of many urban communities and to local policy-makers' inherent desire to reverse the decline. Some say support for this activist agenda has come from empirical research that confirms the statistically significant effects that sub-national fiscal variables exert on intra-regional firm location. More convincing support for intervention requires corroborating research on the effectiveness of targeted local economic development incentives. To date, this research has been less determinant.

Previous to the 1980s, empirical researchers had determined that sub-national measures of taxation and expenditure exerted little or no influence on business location. This consensus was based on regression analysis that ignored the market relationship inherent to firm location and hence ignored the corresponding simultaneity problem in estimating a single regression equation. In the 1980s, regression analyses began accounting for the local

* This research received financial assistance from CULMA (the College of Urban, Labor, and Metropolitan Affairs at the Wayne State University) and benefited from data assistance provided by Priya Rajagopalan. John Anderson, Donald Coffin, Kenneth Small, Michael Wolkoff, and two anonymous referees offered valuable comments. Any remaining errors are the author's own.

supply of firm sites and firms' demand for these sites. Fox (1981) found that a 1 per cent increase in a community's effective property tax rate in the Cleveland area of the US reduced the long-run industrial percentage of a city's property tax base by 4.43 per cent. A 1 per cent increase in local business services in the Cleveland area increased the same percentage by 2.78 per cent. Although magnitudes differ, the direction of these results has been confirmed by numerous other US based studies (see Wassmer, 1990: and Bartik, 1991).[1]

If sub-national fiscal variables influence business location, then a targeted alteration of local taxes or expenditure may be used to attract a firm to a community. Many local policy-makers accept this logic and vigorously pursue local development incentives. The problem with such vigorous pursuit is that there has been little empirical testing of whether local incentives can alter the trend in a community's economic development. In other words: can a city put together a package of targeted incentives that effectively increases its rate of economic growth or decreases its rate of economic decay?

Much of the previous research on local incentives has evaluated its impact on job creation by assessing its cost per job created. Willis (1985) assumed that a portion of the employment increase observed after an incentive went into effect would have occurred regardless of the incentive. On this basis, he concluded that local incentives are not cost effective. In a survey of firms in North East England that received local government assistance, Wren (1987) found that nearly two-thirds of the projects would have been completed without it. The difficult attribution problem of identifying only the additive effect of local incentives has been discussed by Storey (1990) and in much of this research. Storey defined the 'additive effect' as the amount of positive local economic development that could be attributed solely to the offering of a local incentive package. Regretfully, there have been few attempts to quantify this pure additive effect. Coffin (1982) examined development in the city of Indianapolis, before and after a property-tax-abatement programme, and found that the decline in various economic measures slowed roughly two years after incentives began. His data set was not large enough to test the significance of this slowdown. In recent surveys, both Boviard (1992) and Foley (1992) recognised that regression analysis is one of the most appropriate procedures for isolating the additive effects of local incentives.

Wolkoff (1985), Anderson (1990) and Wassmer (1992) have completed some of the few regression investigations of the effectiveness of local development incentives in the US. Through an examination of how property tax abatements modify the cost of firm capital, Wolkoff concluded that a 50 per cent reduction in property taxes has a small marginal impact on business costs and hence on encouraging local economic development. Anderson found that growing cities are more likely to adopt tax increment financing. (Tax increment financing allows a city to capture the additional tax revenue generated by a firm and use it specifically for projects that directly benefit the firm.) Wassmer determined that cities offering property tax abatements experienced an increase in property tax base, but at local costs (decreased home values and increased property tax rates) and state costs (increased state subsidies) that are sometimes disregarded. These studies did not directly address the additive effect of offering local incentives, though all three researchers agreed upon the need for it to be done.

Papke (1991) has completed a regression analysis that does effectively measure the additive effect of the state of Indiana's urban enterprise zone programme. Enterprise zones in the US are established by state governments that designate a fixed number of areas that are economically depressed and may benefit from a wide range of subsidies and tax cuts. Papke found that the establishment of an urban enterprise zone permanently increased firm inventories within the region that contains the zone by approximately 8 per cent and reduced unemployment claims. She also found that the value of taxable capital within the average zone declined approximately 13 per cent. Papke made no attempt to measure the separate effects of the different components of Indiana's enterprise zone programme.

An empirical method that yields evidence on the separate additive effects exerted by specific local incentives on a city's economic development is given here. This paper has two purposes: to present a needed regression technique that isolates the additive effects of local incentive programmes; and to provide the results of this method applied to a sample of cities drawn from a US metropolitan area. The intended audience for this paper is both practitioners and researchers. The methodology should interest practitioners as a different technique to assess the efficacy of development assistance. The technique should interest researchers as a method to investigate local development issues.

So that the methodology may be applied to cities in any region, the derivation of the empirical procedure is given in general terms. The procedure is then applied to a group of cities in the Detroit metropolitan area. Section 2 contains a basic theory of what determines a city's economic development over time. A brief description of local development incentives available in the Detroit metropolitan area and how they compare with what is available in the US is provided in Section 3. Section 4 consists of a description of the econometric method. The regression results from the sample of Detroit area cities are given in Section 5. Section 6 contains the summary and conclusion.

2. Determinants of a City's Economic Development over Time

Local economic development is defined here as the level of business activity in a community. Although some local policy-makers like to evaluate business activity based on employment (the familiar phrase 'jobs, jobs, jobs'), it may be more appropriately measured by a broader gauge such as value added, sales or receipts. This is pertinent when considering that most forms of local development assistance raise the relative price of labour and effectively discourage its use.[2] A city's economic development is measured in one of six ways: manufacturing employment, manufacturing value added, retail employment, retail sales, service employment, or service receipts. These development measures are chosen because local incentives are easily classified into industrial and non-industrial categories. Manufacturing measures are expected to be influenced by industrial incentives. Retail and service measures are expected to be influenced by non-industrial incentives.

Given the size of the available data set, the goal is to try to account for as many factors as possible that influence the level of a city's economic development measured over time. One factor that affects local development is exogenous structural change in the macro-economy. For example, a structural change that causes a national decline in manufacturing could also cause a local decline in manufacturing activity. A second exogenous factor that intertemporally influences local economic development is the national business cycle. As the economy moves through recession and recovery, business activity in a city should also move negatively and postively away from its long-term trend in development.

Local economic and demographic factors, which are likely to be endogenously determined with local development, are also expected to influence a city's economic development. After controlling for these factors, there may still be a temporal inclination in a city's economic development. This inclination could be due to changes in consumer preferences, incomes and transport options. Varying local land cost, initial economic development, initial population, etc. could also generate differences between city development paths.

A final factor that may alter local economic development is the incentive package offered by the city. Ideally, a local development incentive should only be offered if it exerts a positive influence on local economic development. If this is the case, after controlling for structural, cyclical and other local influences, local incentives should exert a separate additive effect on a city's economic development. Since this paper investigates this issue in regard to cities in the Detroit metropolitan area, a discussion of local development incentives available in the state of Michigan and how they compare with programmes offered throughout the US is given next.

3. Local Development Incentives in Michigan

Michigan cities have been able to offer locally initiated development incentives for nearly 20 years. The four local programmes that have been available are industrial development bonds, manufacturing property tax abatements, commercial property tax abatements, the establishment of a downtown development authority, and/or a tax increment financing authority district.

Industrial development bonds (IDBs) are issued by local governments and the funds are used to acquire land, buildings and machinery that is then leased back to a private firm. The revenue from the lease is used to service the debt, while the privately held land and capital act as the debt's collateral. These bonds are most often used with regard to industrial firms. The benefit of an IDB comes from the tax-free status that interest income enjoys from both the federal personal income tax and the locality's state personal income tax if the bond-holder lives in the state. Investors thus accept a lower interest rate than demanded from a comparable private bond. A city passes these interest savings to a firm to encourage its location within the city's boundaries.

The first industrial development bond in the Detroit metropolitan area was issued in 1967.[3] Between the late 1960s and early 1980s, IDBs were increasingly used by all US local governments. Federal restrictions have curtailed their more recent use. In 1986, 45 of the 50 states continued to allow local governments the regulated option of some form of IDB as a development tool (National Association of State Development Agencies, 1986).

Manufacturing property tax abatements have been available to Michigan communities since 1974. Under an almost non-binding state restriction, the legislative body of a local government can establish plant rehabilitation and industrial development districts in which local property tax abatements can be granted to industrial firms. (In 1984 the restrictions on plant rehabilitation and industrial development districts only applied to 2.6 per cent of the cities, townships and villages in Michigan. This, and other facts on

Michigan development programmes, are given in detail in Citizen's Research Council of Michigan (1986) and Southeast Michigan Council of Governments (1990).) For renovation, the property tax reduction freezes taxable value at pre-rehabilitation value. For new construction, the assessed taxable value of real and personal property is cut in half. A city has the discretion to grant this abatement for up to 12 years and then it can be renewed. Abatement programmes similar to this are popular throughout the US. In 1986, local governments in 28 of the 50 states had the ability to grant some form of property tax reduction to manufacturing firms.

Commercial property tax abatements were available to Michigan cities between 1978 and 1988. In 1988 the Michigan legislature determined the commercial programme ineffective and failed to renew legislation that allowed it. The institutional details of this programme were analogous to the manufacturing abatement programme. The feeling that commercial property tax abatements are less warranted than manufacturing abatements is reflected in only 21 states offering similar incentives to non-industrial firms in 1986.

Michigan cities have also been able to create a downtown development authority (DDA) since 1974. The creation of a DDA is left entirely to local discretion. The stated goal of such an authority is to promote business development and prevent deterioration in a city's central business district. Downtown development authorities are authorised to draw up and to implement development plans, to acquire and dispose of property, and to establish tax levies to support their activities.[4]

In a tax increment financing authority (TIFA) district, additional property tax revenue after the establishment of the district is diverted to the specific purpose of financing development-related costs within the designated area. This frees the area from relying on outside funds for special development needs. A TIFA district is intended to revitalise an area of a city through the creation and implementation of a development plan. This plan is arranged by a local development authority – which can be a DDA – that uses TIFA-generated funds to maintain its own office and to purchase additional infrastructure and services for the district. Michigan cities have been allowed to create TIFA districts since 1980 and have largely employed them for encouraging non-industrial economic development. Tax increment financing in the US began in California in 1952 and its popularity has never waned. In 1982, 28 states allowed some form of TIFA financing (Huddleson. 1984).[5]

Industrial development bonds, manufacturing and commercial property tax abatements, downtown development authorities and tax increment financing represent nearly the entire menu of incentives that US local governments have been granted the right to exercise at their own discretion.[6] Michigan allows, or has allowed, all these incentives. A data set gathered from its largest urban area consequently offers a natural test of their effectiveness.

4. Empirical Specification

Section 2 contained a basic theory of what factors determine the level of local economic development. For a given city, this theory can be represented in general functional form as:

$$DEV = DEV\ (STR,\ CYC,\ LOC,\ TRD,\ PAC) \tag{1}$$

where, STR = economy-wide structural variable; CYC = economy-wide cyclical variable; LOC = specific local variables; TRD=time-trend; PAC=package of development incentives offered.

As discussed earlier, local economic development (DEV) is gauged in six different ways: manufacturing employment (MEMP), value-added in manufacturing production (MVAL), retail employment (REMP), retail sales (RSAL), employment in service industries (SEMP), or gross receipts earned in service provision (SREC). DEV is always measured as a level and not a change. All dollar values are deflated by an appropriate index.[7] The economy-wide structural effect is alternatively measured by the percentage of US gross national product (GNP) earned in manufacturing production (MAN%), retail and wholesale production (RET%), or service production (SER%). The economy-wide cyclical effect is measured by the US employment rate (UNEM%).[8]

The variables chosen to represent local factors that influence economic development are housing density (HDEN), percentage of housing built more than 30 years ago (H30% – which proxies for the age of property in general in the city), percentage of population that is African American (AFAM%), and the number of major crimes divided by population (CMPOP). The choice of these particular variables is based on their statistical significance in earlier studies of local employment growth (see, for example, Bradbury *et al.*, 1982; Palumbo *et al.*, 1990). All local right-side variables are lagged one period to control for their possible endogeneity with the dependent variable. Since firms make development decisions well in advance of hiring labour or selling a product, lagged values may also better represent the actual variables observed by firms to make the decision to expand locally or contract locally in the current period.

Local incentives that apply to manufacturing development are industrial development bonds and manufacturing property tax abatements. Commercial property tax abatements, downtown development authorities and tax increment financing apply to encouraging retail and service development.

The level of industrial development bonds (IDB%) in a city is accounted for by the cumulative real face value of total IDBs issued in a city up to time $t - 1$, divided by the real market value of the city's manufacturing property tax base at time $t - 1$.[9] This, and all incentive measures, are lagged one period to control for their likely endogeneity with the different measures of economic development. The use of lagged measures allows for the fact that development incentives likely have a cumulative effect that is not realised instantaneously. The cumulative incentives offered in period $t - 1$, rather than the incentives in period t, are likely to be a better proxy for the marginal incentives available to firms in period t.

The degree of local manufacturing property tax abatement is measured as the cumulative real market value of manufacturing property tax base abated away in the previous period divided by the real value of the city's manufacturing property tax base in the previous period if all were fully taxed (MABAT%). An analogous value is calculated for commercial property tax abatements (CABAT%). The presences of a downtown development authority (DDA), and of a tax increment financing authority (TIFA), are respectively represented by the number of years that either of these two types of district has existed in the city up to the previous period under consideration. It is hypothesised that the longer a district has been in existence, the greater its effect should be.[10]

The empirical estimation of what determines local economic development over time requires a city data base consisting of all variables in equation (1). As Foley (1992, p. 575) has pointed out, the scarcity of such data makes regression analysis of this type rarely possible. For US cities, a time-series of the desired economic development variables is available in the *Economic Census of Manufacturers, Economic Census of Retail Trade*, and *Economic Census of Service Industries*. These data have been published quinquennially since 1967 for incorporated places whose population is greater than 2500. Before 1967, comparable data are available for 1947, 1954, 1958 and 1963. Economic censuses also provide information on the percentage of the US GNP coming from manufacturing, retail and service sectors. HDEN and AFAM% are available in every US decennial census. The US decennial census of housing began collecting H30% in 1960. A city's CMPOP is derived from the yearly US Federal Bureau of Investigation's *Uniform Crime Report* that is available from the mid 1960s onwards.

Over time, there are therefore nine observations on a city's manufacturing, retail and service development. A regression estimation of equation (1) for a single city would therefore have only one or two degrees of freedom. The consistency of an ordinary least-squares estimate calculated from such a small sample would face severe criticism – see Pindyck and Rubinfeld (1991. ch. 2), for example. The solution to this problem is to pool a time-series of the required data for a city with cross-sections from many different cities. Given the variables included in each cross-section, it is reasonable to assume that cross-section parameters are constant over time. The act of pooling provides more efficient parameter estimates.

A pooled version of equation (1) looks like:

$$\text{DEV}_{i,t} = DEV_{i,t}(STR_t, \, LOC_{i,t-1}, \, \text{TRD}_{i,t}, PAC_{i,t-1}) \tag{2}$$

where, $i = 1, 2, \cdots, N$ (number of cities in sample); $t = 1, 2, \cdots, T$ (last period observed).

In equation (2), it is assumed that structural, cyclical and local variables influence all cities' economic development in the same manner. Each city is allowed a separate constant and a specific time-trend to its economic development.[11]

A second issue related to the paucity of data is finding the desired measures of local development incentives. Data on local incentives are rarely publicly reported and sometimes not even recorded by a central state agency. Michigan's Tax Commission maintains records on the value of property tax abatements offered by all local communities. Figures on tax abatements offered in the Detroit metropolitan area were previously gathered for Wassmer (1992). Michigan's Treasury Department keeps record of all local IDBs. Information on the creation date of a city's DDA and TIFA district is taken from the Southeast Michigan Council of Governments (1990).

Since the effect of a local incentive on a given measure of economic development is constrained to be constant across all cities, an attempt was made fully to interact incentives with the chosen local characteristics. (For a discussion of the interaction model, see Pindyck and Rubinfeld, 1991, p. 103.) Interaction results are reported if the interactive variables as a whole exerted a statistically significant influence on the regression.

The results of this experiment should be of interest to policy-makers because they show whether the incentive exerts the same effect in any type of city, or whether the incentive exerts a distinct effect in different types of city.

In regard to the chosen measures of local characteristics, housing density (HDEN) and the percentage of the population that is African American (AFAM%) are available for every cross- section. The percentage of housing over 30 years old (H30%) and the number of serious crimes per population (CMPOP) are only available from 1960 onwards.[12] It is possible to include HDEN and AFAM% in every cross-section of the different economic development regressions and to interact HDEN and AFAM% with the incentive variables. It is not possible to include H30% and CMPOP in every cross-section. Instead, H30% and CMPOP are only interacted with the incentive variables. Variable designations and means are given in Table 1.[13]

The basis for selection of cities in the manufacturing (retail or service) data set is that the Detroit area city had to be large enough to be recorded in the relevant census of industry publication and firm-specific employment had also to be a small enough percentage not to violate the confidentiality standard of the US Census. These exogenously imposed selection criteria narrowed the manufacturing sample to 8 cities and the retail or service sample to 25 cities.[14] Given nine years of observation, the pooled manufacturing and retail or service samples respectively contain 72 and 225 observations. Due to a significantly smaller data set for manufacturing, and the probable occurrence that race and crime play less of a role in the location decisions of industrial firms, AFAM% and CMPOP are excluded from the manufacturing development regressions.

The six regressions to be calculated are based on the following general functional forms:

$$MEMP_{i,t}; MVAL_{i,t} = MEMP_{i,t}; MVAL_{i,t} (MAN\%_t, UNEM\%_t, HDEN_{i,t-1}, TRD_{i,t},$$
$$MABAT\%_{i,t-1}, HDMAB_{i,t-1}, H3MAB_{i,t-1}, IDB\%_{i,t-1}, HDIDB_{i,t-1}, H3IDB_{i,t-1}) (3)$$

$$REMP_{i,t,}; RSAL_{i,t,}; SEMP_{i,t,}; SREC_{i,t} = REMP_{i,t}; RSAL_{i,t}; SEMP_{i,t,}; SREC_{i,t}$$
$$(RET\%_t, UNEM\%_t, HDEN_{i,t-1}, AFAM\%_{i,t-1}, TRD_{i,t}, CABAT\%_{i,t-1},$$
$$HDCAB_{i,t-1,}; AACAB_{i,t-1}, H3CAB_{i,t-1}, CRCAB_{i,t-1}, DDA_{i,t-1}, HDDDA_{i,t-1}, \qquad (4)$$
$$AADDA_{i,t-1}, H3DDA_{i,t-1}, CRDDA_{i,t-1}, TIFA_{i,t-1}, HDTFA_{i,t-1}, AATFA_{i,t-1},$$
$$H3TFA_{i,t-1}, CRTFA_{i,t-1})$$

The pooled econometric specifications in equations (3) and (4) require the estimation of city-specific linear time-trends. This is accomplished by creating a separate trend variable (TRD) for each city by setting it equal to 1 for the 1947 observation, 8 for the 1954 observation, ..., up to 41 for the 1987 observation. City-specific TRD is equal to zero for all other cities observations. The estimation of a separate constant term is attained by including a constant variable for each city that is equal to one for the city's observations and zero elsewhere.

An additional specification issue is whether a city's development relates to the causal variables in a linear or non-linear manner. Plotting the development variables against time for each city revealed that these relationships are unlikely to be linear. On this basis, the decision was made to try a linear and log-linear specification and to test formally which is

Table 1 Descriptions and means of regression variables

Name (t =1954–87)	Description	Mean (24 observations)	Mean (75 observations)
Dependent variables			
$MEMP_t$	Manufacturing employment	28 886.00	
$MVAL_t$	Manufacturing value added (1982 \$s based on US GNP deflator)	1 086 913 763.00	
$REMP_t$	Retail employment		4949.00
$RSAL_t$	Retail sales (1967 \$s based on Detroit CPI deflator)		162,762, 128.00
$SEMP_t$	Service employment		2 785.00
$SREC_t$	Service receipts (1967 \$s based on Detroit CPI deflator)		42,360,095.00
Right-side variables			
$MAN\%_t$	Percentage US GNP from manufacturing	25.60	
$RET \%_t$	Percentage US GNP from retail wholesale		16.84
$SER\%_t$	Percentage US GNP from service		11.62
$UNEM\%_t$	US unemployment rate	6.02	6.02
$HDEN\%_{t-1}$	Total dwelling units/square miles	2613.00	2057.00
$AFAM\%_{t-1}$	(African-American population/total population) $\times$ 100		9.27
TRD_t	Equals 1 for 1947, 8 for 1954, ..., up to 41 for 1987	–	–
$MABAT\%_{t-1}$	(Total manufacturing property tax abatements/Property tax base) $\times$ 100	(3.02)	
$CABAT\%_{t-1}$	(Total commercial property tax abatements/Property tax base) $\times$ 100		(0.31)
$IDB\%_{t-1}$	(Total value of industrial development bonds/Property tax base) $\times$ 100	(2.42)	
$DDA\%_{t-1}$	Number years that downtown development authority existed		(0.45)
$TIFA\%_{t-1}$	Number years that tax increment financing authority existed		(0.11)
$H30\%_{t-1}$	(Dwellings greater than 30 years old/ Total dwellings) $\times$ 100	(57.28)	(48.64)
$CMPOP_{t-1}$	Number of series crimes/Population		(0.08)
$HDMAB_{t-1}$	HDEN $\times$ MABAT%	(3672.90)	
$HDIDB_{t-1}$	HDEN $\times$ IDB%	(2451.87)	
$HDCAB_{t-1}$	HDEN $\times$ CABAT%		(1070.44)
$HDDDA_{t-1}$	HDEN $\times$ DDA		(1591.35)
$HDTFA_{t-1}$	HDEN $\times$ TIFA		(445.36)
$H3MAB_{t-1}$	H30% $\times$ MABAT%	(87.77)	
$H3IDB_{t-1}$	H30% $\times$ IDB%	(80.13)	
$H3CAB_{t-1}$	H30% $\times$ CABAT%		(29.38)
$H3DDA_{t-1}$	H30% $\times$ DDA		(38.34)

Table 1 (*Cont.*)

Name ($t = 1954$–87)	Description	Mean (24 observations)	Mean (75 observations)
H3TFA$_{t-1}$	H30% × TIFA		(11.01)
AACAB$_{t-1}$	AFAM% × CABAT%		(6.15)
AADDA$_{t-1}$	AFAM% × DDA		(16.76)
AATFA$_{t-1}$	AFAM% × TIFA		(3.35)
CMCAB$_{t-1}$	CMPROP × CABAT%		(0.040)
CMDDA$_{t-1}$	CMPOP × DDA		(0.062)
CMTFA$_{t-1}$	CMPOP × TIFA		(0.017)

the more appropriate using a Box–Cox Test (see Pindyck and Rubinfeld, 1991, pp. 240–243). For all measures of economic development, the non-linear visual evidence was confirmed by the formal test and a log-linear specification used in the final regression estimation. An added advantage of this specification is that the estimated coefficient on TRD represents the continuous rate of growth or decay in the measure of economic development.[15] First-order autocorrelation and heteroskedasticity were detected in the initially estimated residuals, corrected using the three-stage time series autocorrelation model described in Pindyck and Rubinfeld (1991. pp. 228–229).[16]

5. Empirical Results

Figure 1 is a map of the Detroit area showing the location of all cities included in the samples. Cities included in each sample and information on variable values are given in the Appendix in Tables A1 and A2. Tables A1 and A2 also illustrate city differences in employment trends in the manufacturing, retail and service sectors. Between 1947 and 1987, manufacturing employment increased in only three of the eight cities included in the industrial sample. Manufacturing employment in Detroit decreased by nearly 70 per cent. Between 1947 and 1987, retail employment decreased in five of the 25 cities included in the sample. Confirming the tie between the central city's retail and manufacturing sector, an approximate 70 per cent reduction in retail employment also occurred in the central city of Detroit and its enclaves of Hamtramck and Highland Park. Following national structural changes, service employment increased in every city in the sample.

Three of the seven Detroit area cities that offered manufacturing property tax abatements also used IDBs (for a further examination of the incentives used in the Detroit area, see Wassmer, 1993). River Rouge's 1987 use of IDBs was 71 per cent of existing manufacturing property tax base and was due to its heavy reliance on the steel industry for employment, the drastic restructuring and decline in US steel manufacturing, and the city's attempts to aid in firm capital replacement through assisted bond financing. The percentage of industrial property granted an abatement increased for all cities that offered abatements in 1977. For all cities that granted abatements in the commercial sample, except Birmingham and Hamtramck, this increase was also observed between 1982 and 1987. The magnitudes of the commercial property tax abatement increases were much smaller than the manufacturing property tax abatement increases. Sixty per cent of the

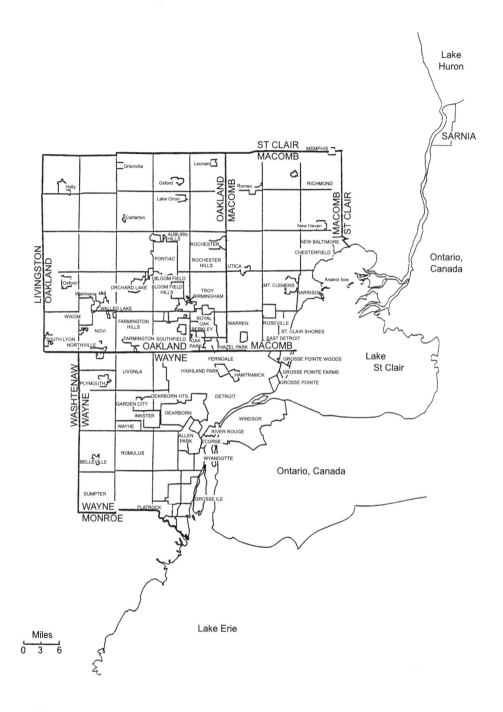

Figure 1 Communities in the metropolitan Detroit area

cities that offered commercial abatements also utilised downtown development authorities in 1987. This may be compared with a figure of 35 per cent for cities that offered commercial property tax abatements and had also established a tax increment financing authority district by 1987. Of the cities that had a DDA in 1987, 45 per cent also had a TIFA.

Tables A3–A8 in the Appendix contain the regression results. Statistical significance is defined throughout the paper as being at the 80 per cent or greater confidence level in a two- tailed test.[17] *Ceteris paribus*, the results in Tables A3 and A4 indicate that between 1954 and 1987 Mount Clemens's manufacturing employment increased by a continuous rate of 7.7 per cent, while real value added increased by a rate of 10.9 per cent. Reflecting capital for labour substitution that generally occurred during this period in all cities, with the exception of Highland Park, the rate of increase of real manufacturing value added was greater than manufacturing employment. Holding all else constant, a one percentage-point increase in US GNP earned in manufacturing caused approximately a 13 per cent increase in a Detroit area city's manufacturing employment and an even larger 15 per cent increase in real manufacturing value added. As expected, a Detroit area city's manufacturing employment moved counter to the national unemployment rate. A city's lagged housing density had a negative influence on both manufacturing employment and real value added. An increase of one dwelling unit per square mile reduced MEMP by 0.05 per cent and reduced MVAL by a slightly smaller 0.04 per cent. Residential activity likely reduces manufacturing activity due to limited land in a city.

A tabular description of how the full interaction model works in the manufacturing employment and value added regressions is given in Table 2. Over and above the abatement variable itself, the full interaction model applied to manufacturing property tax abatements did not exert a significant influence on Detroit area manufacturing employment.[18] The remainder of the full interaction effects were significant in the manufacturing regressions. An appropriate place to evaluate the effect of an incentive where the full interaction model is significant, is at the mean values of lagged local housing density (HDEN) and lagged percentage of housing greater than 30 years old (H30%). The calculated full effect of a change in an incentive on manufacturing employment or value added is given in the appropriate element of the second row of Table 2.[19] Evaluated at mean local characteristics, only the use of industrial development bonds exerted the desired additive effect on local manufacturing value added.

Conclusions based on only the mean evaluation of the full interaction effect of incentives would be deceiving. As given in the third row of Table 2, interactive incentive effects can change sign if local characteristics change. Cities where an increase in local use of incentives exerts an effect different from that calculated at mean local characteristics are listed in the fourth row of Table 2. Using 1987 local characteristics, a one percentage-point increase in local industrial property granted an IDB would result in a 0.02 per cent increase in Highland Park's manufacturing employment and 0.04 per cent increase in River Rouge's manufacturing employment. Although these effects are small, they are positive. Sign reversal in these cities is being driven by a much larger than mean lagged percentage of local capital stock that is over 30 years old.

Again using 1987 characteristics, an increase in the percentage of manufacturing property granted an abatement would have a positive effect on Detroit's, and Highland Park's manufacturing value added. Respectively a one percentage-point increase in

Table 2 Information on full-interaction incentive effects for manufacturing regressions

Information	MEMP regression		MVAL regression	
	MABAT% interacted with HDEN and H30%	IDB% interacted with HDEN and H30%	MABAT% interacted with HDEN and H30%	IDB% interacted with HDEN and H30%
F-statistic for interaction inclusion	1.251 (probability 70.3 per cent)	2.049 (probability 85.8 per cent)	19.803 (probability 99.9 per cent)	3.613 (probability 96.4 per cent)
Total incentive effect at means[a]	−0.021*[b]	−0.002*	−0.133***	0.607**
Could Total incentive effect change sign?	No	Yes[c]	Yes[d]	Yes[e]
Cities,[f] Total incentive effect, (HDEN), and [H30%]	None	(1) Highland Park, 0.0002, (3949), [78.70] and (2) River Rouge, 0.0004, (2020), [79.08]	(1) Detroit, 0.030, (3371), [76.44] and (2) Highland Park, 0.081, (3949), [78.70]	(1) Detroit, −0.057, (3371), [76.44] and (2) Highland Park, −0.189, (3949), [78.70]

Two-tailed statistical significance: *** = 99–100 per cent; ** = 90–98 per cent; * = 80–89 per cent.

[a] Percentage increase in MEMP or MVAL caused by a 1 percentage–point increase in MABAT% or IDB%, evaluated at means of interaction variables.

[b] The reported total effect is only the coefficient on the incentive variables because the full interaction model was not statistically significant at a greater than 80 per cent confidence level.

[c] Sign can change if: HDEN remains at mean (or less) and H30% rises to greater than 77 per cent (or less).

[d] Sign can change if: HDEN remains at mean (or greater) and H30% rises to greater than 80 per cent (or less); or H30% remains at mean (or greater) and HDEN rises to greater than 4698 (or less).

[e] Sign can change if: HDEN remains at means (or greater) and H30% rises to greater than 77 per cent (or less); or H30% remains at mean (or greater) and HDEN rises to greater than 8131 (or less).

[f] Where total incentive effect does change sign using 1987 values instead of median.

MABAT% would raise MVAL by 3.0 and 8.1 per cent in these cities. These sign deviations are being driven by both a lagged housing density and lagged housing age that is much larger than mean values. The influence of a larger than average local value of housing density or housing age on the effect that industrial development bonds exert on manufacturing value added is just the opposite. In the cities of Detroit and Highland Park, a 1 per cent increase in 1987 IDB% would reduce MVAL respectively by 5.7 and 18.9 per cent.

The effect local incentives have on economic development is dependent both on how development is measured and the characteristics of the city offering the incentive. Holding other relevant causal variables constant, property tax abatements can exert a positive additive effect on manufacturing value added in a city with high housing density and an old capital stock. High housing density probably serves as a proxy for less land being available for firm sites. An older local housing stock is likely to be negatively related to the availability of the 'green fields' preferred by new manufacturing firms for development. Property tax abatements perform their desired role providing that these negatives are large enough. Elastic responses in manufacturing value added from an increase in abatements have been found for certain cities.

The case of industrial development bond offers and manufacturing development is interesting. In regard to increasing value added, IDBs are effective only in cities with a low housing density and a newer capital stock. In regard to increasing employment, IDBs are effective only in cities with just the opposite characteristics. In the case of an old city (with high housing density and an old capital stock) like Highland Park, a city's financing help may be enough to preserve employment but it is not enough to compensate for the aged capital stock producing less and less value added. On the other hand, in a newer city, IDB offers are negatively related to employment and positively related to value added. In a newer city, financing assistance is more likely to be used for high-tech capital improvements that reduce employment but increase value added.

A significant positive coefficient on an incentive measure, or on an incentive interacted with local characteristics, indicates that the incentive had the desired additive effect on local manufacturing development. Controlling for cyclical, structural and some local influences, the incentive would have pulled the economic development positively away from the city's long-term trend in growth or decay. Following the same reasoning, a significant negative coefficient would indicate that the incentive caused a decline in manufacturing development. This is difficult to believe. A significant negative coefficient for an incentive is likely to be the result of only correlation and not causation.

A theory behind the correlation argument is that if a city experiences a decline in its economic development it responds by offering local incentives. As the decline gets even worse, the city offers even more incentives. The city's economic decline cannot be attributed to the act of offering local development incentives. Although offering development incentives without proper evaualation may be a symptom of generally poor city management practices, the offering of an incentive is only positively correlated to other factors that have caused the decline in local economic development. Why not a similar correlation argument for a significant positive coefficient on an incentive variable? For this to occur, as factors cause development to increase, the city would have to decide to offer incentives. Furthermore, as these positive factors encourage even further development, the city would have to offer even greater incentives. This correlation argument is much less plausible than the causation argument put forth earlier.[20] An additional concern is that endogeneity between local incentive and development measures may cause a derived positive coefficient to be smaller than it really is. This problem has been greatly reduced by lagging all incentive variables five years previous to when development variables are measured.

A visual representation of the Wyandotte portion of the manufacturing value added result is given in Figure 2. The actual value of Wyandotte's 1954–87 real manufacturing value added is represented by the lighter bars. 'WYNMVAL' (Wyandotte Manufacturing Value Added). The darker bars, TRD (TREND), represent the fitted value from only the city-specific constant and the time-trend. The line TSCL (Trend-Structural-Cyclical-Local) also includes the fitted effects of the national structural and cyclical variables, and the effects of local variables excluding the incentive package. The additional fitted effects of property tax abatements and industrial revenue bonds are included in the final line FIT. Similar diagrams were created for other cities and generally support the chosen econometric specification. In Figure 2, and these other diagrams, the fitted equation does a fair-to-good job of tracking actual development measures. The city-specific constant and proportional growth rate pick up the general trend, while the structural and cyclical proxy variables pick up most of the peaks and troughs in a city's development trend. As Figure 2 shows, without local incentives the predicted value of Wyandotte's real manufacturing value added in 1982 and 1987 is much higher than it actually was. The inclusion of the effect of property tax abatements and industrial development bonds lowers the fitted value of WYNVAL to near its actual value and subsequently exhibits the undesired negative effect.

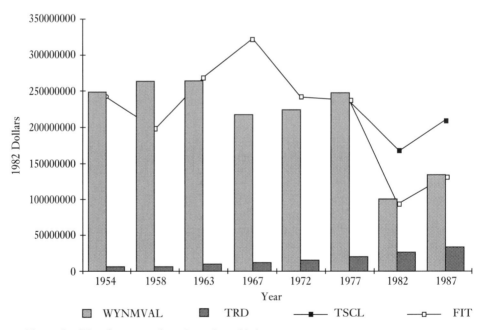

Figure 2   Wyandotte manufacturing value added.

Tables A5 and A6 in the Appendix contain the pooled regression results for retail employment and real retail sales. Coefficients on TRD were less likely to be statistically significant in the retail regressions than in the manufacturing regressions. A 1 per cent increase in US GNP earned in the retail/wholesale sector led to a 8.4 per cent increase in real retail sales and no significant effect on retail employment for these metropolitan Detroit cities. A 1 per cent increase in the US unemployment rate led to an elastic 2.8 per cent decrease in local Detroit area retail employment and a very elastic 8.0 per cent decrease in real retail sales. The difference in elasticity could be caused by a core group of retail employees that firms retain even when sales fall during a recession.

Opposite to its effect on manufacturing development, a city's lagged value of housing density exerted a positive influence on both retail employment and retail sales. An additional house per square mile increased retail employment and real retail sales by approximately 0.03 per cent. As to be expected, retail firms are more likely to develop in cities with larger markets as proxied by local housing density. *Ceteris paribus*, a 1 per cent increase in the lagged percentage of the population that is African-American had a statistically insignificant effect on real retail sales, but decreased retail employment by 1.1 per cent. This may just be the result of the type of retail firms in communities with a greater African-American presence employing fewer people.

Turning to the measures of local development incentives, the variables representing commercial property abatement, a downtown development authority, and a tax increment financing authority fully interacted with local characteristics did not exert a statistically significant effect on either form of retail economic development. This finding is summarised in Table 3.

Due to the insignificance of the interaction model, only the coefficients on CABAT%, DDA and TIFA are reported in the Appendix's Tables A5 and A6. The only significant additive effect of a locally initiated incentive on retail development was the use of a TIFA on retail employment. *Ceteris paribus*, for the average city in this sample a 1-year increase in the time a tax increment financing authority is in place raised retail employment by 7.4 per cent. The number of years a TIFA has been present also exerted a positive influence on real retail sales though the coefficient was only statistically significant at a 55 per cent degree of confidence. On the other hand, holding all else constant, a 1-year increase in the number of years a local downtown development authority was in place resulted in a significant 3.7 per cent decrease in retail sales. Also, a 1 per cent increase in the percentage of commercial property granted an abatement resulted in a 5.5 per cent decrease in retail sales.

The retail regression results show that the effect locally initiated incentives have on local retail development depends again on both how development is measured and the type of incentive used. In regard to local retail economic development, incentives did not exert measurably different influences in different types of city. No matter the type of city, commercial property abatements and downtown development authorities appear ineffective at increasing local retail development in this sample of cities. A tax increment financing authority is the only incentive found to exert a positive additive effect on local retail economic development. It is informative to note that in regard to commercially motivated incentives, 'less is more' in that the average city would be better off only granting a TIFA as opposed to granting all three commercial incentives.

Table 3 Information on full-interaction incentive effects for retail regressions

Information	REMP regression			RSAL regression		
	CABAT% interacted with HDEN, H30%, AFAM% and CMPOP	DDA interacted with HDEN, H30%, AFAM% and CMPOP	TIFA interacted with HDEN, H30%, AFAM% and CMPOP	CABAT% interacted with HDEN, H30%, AFAM% and CMPOP	DDA interacted with HDEN, H30%, AFAM% and CMPOP	TIFA interacted with HDEN, H30%, AFAM% and CMPOP
F-statistic for interaction inclusion	0.206 (probability 6.5 per cent)	1.225 (probability 69.7 per cent)	0.155 (probability 3.9 per cent)	0.416 (probability 20.5 per cent)	0.234 (probability 8.1 per cent)	0.229 (probability 7.8 per cent)
Total incentive effect at means[a]	−0.020[b]	−0.006[b]	0.0740*[b]	−0.055**[b]	−0.037**[b]	0.032[b]

Two-tailed statistical significance: ** = 90–98 per cent or * = 80–89 per cent.

[a] Percentage increase in REMP or RSAL caused by a 1-year increase in TIFA or DDA, or by a 1 percentage-point increase in CABAT%.

[b] The reported total effect is only the coefficient on the incentive variable because the full interaction model was not statistically significant at a greater than 80 per cent confidence level.

The fact that retail firms are more inclined to be tied to a location because of customer base probably explains why the offering of commercial abatements and the presence of a downtown development authority does not exert a positive additive effect. A tax increment financing authority may exert its positive additive effect on retail employment by providing a method, which private markets fail to do, by which to organise and raise revenue for the refurbishment of a declining business district. A downtown development authority can do the same, but it appears that the tax increment form of financing is more effective (probably less bureaucratic) than levying a city-wide property tax that is then funnelled through a development agency. A TIFA district need not turn a local business district into a boom area, but only needs to slow down the trend in abandonment to exhibit an additive effect.

The last set of regression results relates to local economic development in the service sector and is contained in Tables A7 and A8 in the Appendix. There was a significant positive trend in these cities' real service receipts and less of a significant positive trend in service employment. The percentage of US GNP earned in the service sector had a positive influence on service employment and an insignificant influence on real service receipts. The national rate of unemployment exerted the expected negative influence on service receipts and a statistically insignificant negative influence on service employment. Similar to the retail regressions, a lagged one dwelling unit increase per square mile increased both service employment and real service receipts by approximately 0.02 per cent. Again, similar to the retail regressions, a lagged 1 per cent increase in African-American population had no significant effect on service receipts, but did decrease service employment by 2.6 per cent.

In both service regressions, more of the variables that account for local incentives and their interaction with local characteristics were statistically significant than in the analogous retail regressions. As recorded in Table 4, the full interactive effect of any incentive was only significant in regard to commercial property abatements and service employment.

In regard to commercial property tax abatements and service employment, a higher lagged local housing density, a higher lagged local percentage of the housing greater than 30 years old, and a higher lagged local crime rate all had the effect of making commercial property tax abatements less effective in their positive effect on service employment. The higher the lagged local percentage of the population that is African-American, the greater the positive effect of abatement on local service employment. As shown in row three of Table 4, it is possible for the total incentive effect of abatements to change from the positive additive effect exhibited at mean values of local variables to a negative effect exhibited at location specific 1987 values. The values of local characteristics at which a sign change occurs are extreme. Simulation shows that the direction of the 1987 effect of CABAT on SEMP only changes for the city of Hamtramck. In Hamtramck, a 1 per cent increase in commercial property tax abatements in 1987 would have been related to a 4.4 per cent decrease in local service employment. The negative effect was driven by the city's higher than average housing density, percentage of housing greater than 30 years old, and crime rate. If a city exhibits enough negative characteristics, the offer of commercial property tax abatements do nothing to alter its trend in service employment. Commercial property tax abatements only produce additive effects when a city is not too badly off.

In all types of cities, the offering of commercial property tax abatements had a statistically insignificant effect on real service receipts. An additional year of existence

Table 4 Information on full-interaction incentive effects for service regressions

Information	SEMP regression			SREC regression		
	CABAT% interacted with HDEN, H30%, AFAM% and CMPOP	DDA interacted with HDEN, H30%, AFAM% and CMPOP	TIFA interacted with HDEN, H30%, AFAM% and CMPOP	CABAT% interacted with HDEN, H30%, AFAM% and CMPOP	DDA interacted with HDEN, H30%, AFAM% and CMPOP	TIFA interacted with HDEN, H30%, AFAM% and CMPOP
F-statistic for interaction inclusion	2.106 (probability 91.7 per cent)	1.416 (probability 76.8 per cent)	1.052 (probability 3.9 per cent)	0.675 (probability 39.0 per cent)	0.669 (probability 38.9 per cent)	0.511 (probability 27.2 per cent)
Total incentive effect at means[a]	0.320**	−0.091**[b]	0.398**[b]	0.030[b]	−0.026**	0.185**[b]
Could Total incentive coefficient change sign?	Yes[c]	No	No	No	No	No
Cities,[d] Total incentive effect, (HDEN), [H30%], {AFAM%}, and <CMPOP>	Hamtramck, −0.044, (4949), [92.9], {12.94}, <0.130>	None	None	None	None	None

Two-tailed statistical significance: ** = 90–98 per cent or * = 80–89 per cent.

a   Percentage increase in SEMP or SREC caused by a 1 year increase in TIFA or DDA, or by a 1 percentage point increase in CABAT%.

b   The reported total effect is only the coefficient on the incentive variable because the full interaction model was not statistically significant at a greater than 80 per cent confidence level.

c   Sign can change if: other means constant and HDEN rises to greater than 7541; or other means constant and H30% rises to above 502.55 per cent; or other means constant and CMPOP rises to above 0.160.

d   Where total incentive effect does change sign using 1987 values instead of median.

for a tax increment finance authority exerted a significant additive effect in all cities on both measures of service related economic development. TIFA increased local service receipts by 18.5 per cent and local service employment by approximately 40 per cent. The presence of a downtown development authority for an additional year reduced service receipts by 2.6 per cent and service employment by 9 per cent. The direction of influence of TIFAs and DDAs was the same for all retail and service measures of development. Reasons given for why this occurred in the retail sector also apply to the service sector. This further substantiates the validity of this reasoning.

Figure 3 is a visual representation of the econometric results in regard to service employment in the city of Royal Oak. Up to 1977, TSCL (Trend-Structural-Cyclical-Local) tracks ROYSEMP (Royal Oak Service Employment) very well. After 1977, TSCL rises above the actual level of Royal Oak's service employment. FIT, which includes the effect of commercial abatements, a DDA and a TIFA district, serves to bring the predicted values very close to the actual values for 1982 and 1987. As shown earlier for Wyandotte manufacturing value added, the presence of local incentives exerts the undesired negative effect on Royal Oak's service employment.

6. Summary and Conclusion

This paper contains a relatively simple regression technique that can be applied to any city, or group of cities, to measure the separate effect that incentives have on local

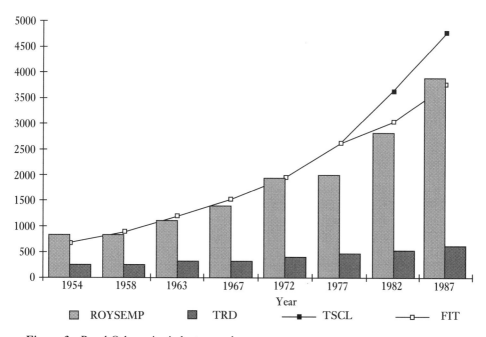

Figure 3 Royal Oak service industry employment.

economic development. It has been shown that cities in the Detroit metropolitan area offer most of the locally initiated incentives that are available in the US. The Detroit metropolitan area was therefore chosen as a natural place to apply the regression technique.

As to whether local incentives can alter the trend in a Detroit metropolitan city's economic development, the regression results suggest that it is wrong to assume that the offering of incentives can be characterised as always having the same effect. After controlling for structural, cyclical and local influences, the effects of local incentives on measures of local economic development exhausted all possibilities.

Evaluated at the mean value of local characteristics, there were no statistically significant effects in 4 of the 16 possibilities (25 per cent) in regression estimation where an incentive could exert an influence on economic development. Of the remaining 12 significant cases. there were 7 instances (44 per cent) of a negative relationship between an incentive offer and local development. As discussed earlier, it is unlikely that a negative relationship indicates that the incentive caused a decline in economic activity, but only that it was correlated with it. In only 5 instances (31 per cent). the incentive, evaluated at the mean, caused the desired additive effect on local economic development.[21] These findings are far different from the usual policy-maker's presumption that the offering of a local incentive always exerts an additive effect on local economic development. In fact, the results indicate that a more reasonable premise is that city incentives exert no effect, or are only positively associated with further economic decline.

It is also wrong for policy-makers to assume that incentives always exert the same effect in any city. The use of the interaction model has demonstrated that in many cases local characteristics determine the aftermath of an incentive offer. This was no better confirmed than for local manufacturing development. In the average metropolitan Detroit community, industrial property tax abatements do not exert the desired positive effect on the two local manufacturing measures. But, in communities where characteristics (i.e. housing density and age of capital stock) that repel industrial firms are large enough, industrial property tax abatements can induce an elastic response in real manufacturing value added. In addition, it was discovered that industrial development bonds exert a slight negative effect on local manufacturing employment in the average community. But again, IDBs can exert the desired additive effect if housing density and capital stock age are large enough. Finally, in the average city, industrial development bonds exert a positive influence on real manufacturing value added. Again, however, this can change to a negative influence if local housing density or capital stock are large enough.

In the one case where the interaction of local characteristics with an incentive produced a significant influence on non-industrial economic development, an increase in commercial property tax abatements was shown to be positively related to an increase in service employment for the average Detroit area city. Opposite to the manufacturing situation, the two local characteristics thought to repel non-industrial investors (an old capital stock and high crime rate) work to make commercial incentives less effective. A city's high housing density, which in terms of a market proxy should be an advantage for a commercial firm, also works against the success of commercial property tax abatements. If these local measures were large enough, it was possible for service employment to be negatively related to commercial property tax abatement use. Since commercial development is so closely tied to the existence of a local market, a non-industrial firm can be compensated with an incentive for a slight lapse in local market characteristics, but it appears that the same firm is not willing to substitute an incentive for a large degeneration in the local market.[22]

For measures of non-industrial local economic development, it was shown that incentives are much more likely to exert the same influence no matter the type of city. With the exception of certain applications of tax increment financing, this constant influence was either negative or statistically insignificant. This finding is consistent with *a priori* thinking that non-industrial economic development is tied more to the existence of a local market and hence is less likely to be swayed by local incentive offers. TIFA districts may offer a positive additive effect because in the least bureaucratic way they primarily preserve existing commercial business districts.

Dependent on the type of city, then, local incentive offers can: (1) be negatively associated with local economic development; (2) exert no effect on local economic development; or (3) exert a positive influence on local economic development. This finding probably indicates that this group of cities was offering local incentives with few questions asked. A similar conclusion in regard to local property tax abatements in the Detroit area has already been given by Wolkoff (1985) and Wassmer (1992, 1993). If this is the case, there is a need for a systematic method by which to judge when a community should be allowed to offer local incentives.

A criterion that most would agree upon is that a city should only grant an incentive when the expectation is that the offer is likely to have a positive effect on local development. This research has perhaps shown a way in which the city itself, or more probably a regional or state regulatory agency, could determine what the expectation is for a particular type of city in regard to the offering of a specific form of incentive. If property tax abatements, industrial development bonds, downtown development authorities or tax increment finance authorities have had no positive effect on a certain type of city's development in the past, they are unlikely to have an additive effect in the future. Even when one form of incentive exerts a positive influence in a city, other incentives may not exert the desired influence.

Results from regressions of the type presented here could therefore be used by policymakers to decide which incentives are most effective in a city, which incentives the city should not use, and even which incentives should be abandoned by all cities. The proposed 'additive effect' criterion is only a necessary, but not a sufficient, condition for an incentive offer. The criterion does not consider the additional requirement that the benefit of the additive effect exceed the incentive's cost. Additional research still needs to be completed on measuring the benefits of local economic development against incentive costs.

Notes

1 The extent of a fiscal variable's effect on business location increases as the range of location choices diminishes (i.e. intra-regional to intra-metropolitan).

2 Due to labour being a complement to capital in production, development incentives tied to capital use (property tax abatements, capital and land acquisitions, bond assistance, etc.) can still increase employment. The point is that employment would be less than if incentives were targeted directly at job creation.

3 For the purpose of this paper, the Detroit metropolitan area is defined as Macomb, Oakland and Wayne counties. This is the US Census's 1970 definition of the Detroit Standard Metropolitan Statistical Area (SMSA). See Figure 1.

4 In a Michigan city of less than 1 million, the DDA's yearly tax levy may be as high as 0.10 per cent of total city property value. In the city of Detroit, whose population is currently greater than 1m, a DDA's property tax levy is restricted to a maximum 0.05 per cent of the city's total property value.

5 Local incentives that are not evaluated here are local zoning ordinances, land acquisitions and regulatory relief. These incentives are not included because it is either difficult to get information on them, or difficult to quantify them in a comparable manner. To the degree that these are constant in a city, their influence on development is measured by the city-specific time-trend.

6 Enterprise zones are also available in US cities and can include the offering of the described incentives within a specific area and the forgiveness or reduction of some state taxes. These are not discussed here because US enterprise zones are entirely state-determined. See Papke (1991) for a more complete description.

7 Since manufacturing output is sold in a national market, manufacturing value added is measured in 1982 dollars based on the US GNP deflator. Retail sales and service receipts are more locally based and are given in 1967 dollars based on the Detroit consumer price index.

8 As pointed out by a referee, it would be reasonable to explore alternate lagged relationships between different right-side variables and economic development. As will be shown, it is not pursued here because of the limited degrees of freedom available in the relatively short time-series.

9 Since the earliest IDBs were issued in the late 1960s and early 1970s, and the productive life of most business capital is greater than 20 years, it is appropriate to use a cumulative measure of local IDBs as opposed to IDBs issued in a given period. The same argument applies to a cumulative measure of property tax abatements. Since they are calculated in percentage terms, these measures are fully comparable across cities.

10 The presence of a DDA or TIFA could be represented with just a dummy variable. This specification was tried and in three out of four cases the sum of squared residuals declined. The decision was made to keep the cumulative measure because of this result and because the measure is consistent with how other forms of incentives are gauged.

11 Another specification that may interest local officials, or state officials attempting to regulate them, is to allow an incentive to exert a distinct effect in each city. This would enable a definite conclusion to be made as to whether the incentive had the desired additive effect in a city, but would say nothing about the effects of local incentives in general. This alternate specification was tried using this data set. Similar to the results given later, incentives were effective at increasing economic development in some cities and ineffective in other cities.

In Papke's (1991) research, an econometric specification similar to equation (1) is referred to as "the most basic model". She also tries three other specifications that, in alternate ways, controls for possible sample selection bias. Papke concludes that the estimated effect of an enterprise zone is similar across all specifications and elaborate controls for selection bias are not necessary. The limited time-series available here did not allow for a matching series of specification tests and Papke's finding is taken as support for the basic specification used here.

12 The desired values of HDEN, AFAM% and H30% are calculated from decennial census values through linear interpolation.

13 With the exception of industrial development bonds first used in 1967, other forms of local incentive were not introduced into this area until the late 1970s. This is why even though observations on H30% and CMPOP are only available from 1960 onwards, H30% and CMPOP can still be fully interacted with all incentive variables. The mean values for all incentives are only calculated for observations from 1970 onwards. Means calculated from a limited sample are given in parenthesis in the body of Table 1. The number of observations used to calculate the means are given in parenthesis at the top of this table.

14 In Macomb, Oakland and Wayne counties in 1987 there was a total of 72 cities. Selection bias in regression estimation is expected to be limited because a separate trend is derived for each city. Some of the cities in the sample did not offer any amount of a particular local development incentive in the period under consideration.

15 The estimated coefficients on all right-side variables represent the relative change in the dependent variable given an absolute change in the right-side variable.

16 In the first stage of this model, the regression is estimated and a value of ρ_1 (which represents the degree of autocorrelation) calculated for each city in the sample. In the second stage, ρ_i is used to calculate a generalised-difference form of the initial regression that is then re-estimated. This procedure necessarily reduces the regression sample size by the number of cities in a cross-section. In the final stage, heteroskedasticity is corrected by using White's heteroskedastic consistent covariance matrix in the regression estimation.

17 A 'Type II error' occurs if a coefficient is interpreted to be statistically insignificant when in fact it does exert the calculated effect. As exhibited by previous behaviour, local policy-makers appear to desire to err on the side of incentives exerting a measurable effect. Therefore the possibility of commiting a Type II error was thought to be more worrisome to the typical policy-maker than the opposite. Since three significance levels are recorded in the regression results, readers who disagree with this strategy can make their own evaluations of significance.

18 The statistical significance of the full interaction was determined by re-running the regressions excluding the interaction variables for an incentive and comparing the restricted and un-restricted residuals using an F-test (see Pindyck and Rubinfeld. 1991. pp. 110–112). The relevant F- statistics are given in the first row of Table 2.

19 As an example, the full interaction coefficient on IDB% in the MEMP regression is:

$$-0.010 \div (-6.691\text{E-}08 \times 2613) + (0.000133 \times 57.28)$$

or approximately -0.002.

20 It is possible that a city with an improving economic climate may choose to offer economic development incentives just because other cities are offering them and the city does not wish to jeopardise its economic growth. If this is the case, incentives have not necessarily caused the improving economic climate and instead are only correlated with it. Wassmer (1993) has found evidence that cities may offer incentives just because they are offered by competing firms in a metropolitan area.

21 There were also three different cities for which the result of industrial development bond and property tax abatement offers had a positive effect – as opposed to the negative effect if evaluated at mean values of local characteristics.

22 With the exception of River Rouge, all the cities where the effect of an incentive displayed a different sign from that of the effect in a city with average characteristics were contained within the boundary of the area's central city. This is a strong clue that incentives exert different effects in a metropolitan area's central city as compared to its suburbs.

References

Anderson, J.E. (1990) "Tax Increment Financing: Municipal Adoption and Growth," *National Tax Journal*, 43, June, 155–164.

Bartik, T.J. (1991) *Who Benefits from State and Local Economic Development Policies?* Kalamazoo. MI: W. E. UpJohn Institute for Employment Research.

Boviard, T. (1992) "Local Economic Development and the City," *Urban Studies*, 29, 343–68.

Bradbury, K.A., Downs, A. and Small, K.A. (1982) *Urban Decline and the Future of American Cities*. Washington, DC: Brookings Institution.

Citizens Research Council of Michigan (1986) *Municipal Government Economic Development Incentive Programs in Michigan*. Detroit, MI.

Coffin, D.A. (1982) "Property Tax Abatement and Economic Development in Indianapolis." *Growth and Change*, April, 18–23.

Foley, P. (1992) "Local Economic Policy and Job Creation: A Review of Evaluation Studies." *Urban Studies*, 29, 557–98.

Fox, W.F. (1981) "Fiscal Differentials and Industrial Location: Some Empirical Evidence," *Urban Studies*, 18, 105–111.

Huddleson, J.R. (1984) "Tax Increment Financing as a State Development Policy," *Growth and Change*, April. 11–17.

National Association of State Development Agencies (1986) *Directory of Incentives for Business Investment and Development in the United States: A State-By-State Guide*, 2nd edn. Washington, DC: The Urban Institute.

Palumbo, G., Sacks, S. and Wasylenko, M. (1990) "Population Decentralization within Metropolitan Areas: 1970–1980," *Journal of Urban Economics*. 27, 151–67.

Papke, L.E. (1991) *Tax Policy and Urban Development: Evidence from an Enterprise Zone Program*. National Bureau of Economic Research working paper no. 3945. Cambridge, MA.

Pindyck, R.S. and Rubinfeld, D.L. (1991) *Econometric Models and Economic Forecasts*, 3rd edn. New York: McGraw-Hill, Inc.

Southeast Michigan Council of Governments (1990) *Tax Incentives/Tax Abatements in Southeast Michigan*. Detroit, MI.

Storey, D.J. (1990) "Evaluation of Policies and Measures to Create Local Employment." *Urban Studies*, 27, 669–84.

Wassmer, R.W. (1990) "Local Fiscal Variables and Intrametropolitan Firm Location: Regression Evidence from the United States and Research Suggestions," *Environment and Planning C: Government and Policy*, 8, 283–96.

Wassmer, R.W. (1992) "Property Tax Abatement and the Simultaneous Determination of Local Fiscal Variables in a Metropolitan Area," *Land Economics*, 68, August, 263–82.

Wassmer, R.W. (1993) "The Use and Abuse of Economic Development Incentives in a Metropolitan area," *Proceedings of the Eighty-Sixth Annual Conference*. National Tax Association–Tax Institute of America. Columbus. OH.

Willis, K.G. (1985) "Estimating the Benefits of Job Creation from Local Investment Subsidies," *Urban Studies*, 22, 163–71.

Wolkoff, M.J. (1985) "Chasing a Dream: The Use of Tax Abatements to Spur Urban Economic Development," *Urban Studies*, 22, 305–15.

Wren, C. (1987) "The Relative Effects of Local Authority Financial Assistance Policies." *Urban Studies*, 24, 268–78.

Appendix

Table A1   Manufacturing values for Detroit metropolitan cities included in sample

City	MEMP 1947	MEMP 1987	IDB% 1972	IDB% 1987	MABT% 1977	MABT% 1987
Detroit	338373	102200	1.28	9.20	1.74	25.30
Ferndale	3404	2900	0.00	0.00	1.72	11.56
Highland Park	19701	9300	0.00	0.00	0.00	12.57
Mount Clemens	1848	3900	0.00	0.00	0.00	5.87
River Rouge	2952	500	0.00	71.12	0.00	1.49
Royal Oak	857	2200	0.00	0.00	0.00	26.57
St Clair Shores	215	2400	0.00	0.00	0.00	0.00
Wyandotte	7621	2800	0.00	3.82	4.97	34.00

Table A2   Retail and service values for Detroit metropolitan cities included in sample

City	REMP 1947	REMP 1987	SEMP 1947	SEMP 1987	CABAT% 1982	CABAT% 1987	DDA 1987	TIFA 1987
Allen Park	168	2425	25	2161	0.79	0.91	0	0
Berkley	381	1661	37	1431	0.00	0.00	0	0
Birmingham	1042	5407	145	5709	1.69	1.17	0	0
Dearborn	5303	14250	469	10687	0.26	0.76	7	6
Detroit	114038	38529	32429	53411	3.52	5.79	12	6
East Detroit	582	2802	48	2164	0.81	2.90	2	0
Ecorse	501	613	40	371	0.60	1.76	0	0
Ferndale	1429	2204	142	1692	0.00	2.55	8	0
Garden City	266	2216	17	1095	0.22	2.59	7	0
Grosse Pointe Farms	177	685	16	325	6.98	7.38	0	0
Gross Pointe Woods	171	1001	13	945	0.00	0.00	0	0
Hamtramck	2848	897	593	475	1.29	1.02	0	7
Hazel Park	566	1287	71	747	2.54	3.41	0	0
Highland Park	4104	1144	655	1591	0.00	0.09	0	4
Inkster	291	844	24	442	0.00	0.00	0	0
Mount Clemens	1375	2817	174	3206	1.29	3.26	3	0
Oak Park	31	2978	120	3696	0.00	1.59	0	0
Plymouth	591	1798	47	2308	1.20	8.28	5	0
Pontiac	4889	4275	752	4271	0.30	2.61	11	7
River Rouge	685	256	95	115	0.00	0.00	0	0
Rochester	361	1979	56	1915	0.00	0.00	0	0
Roseville	258	7063	28	2636	0.26	0.51	7	0
Royal Oak	2452	5165	297	3903	0.17	2.38	12	6
St Clair Shores	668	1610	48	1562	1.37	1.46	7	0
Wyandotte	2063	1394	191	1388	1.17	1.33	1	6

Table A3   Pooled ordinary least-squares regression results with autocorrelation and heteroskedastic correction: manufacturing employment, 1954–87
Dependent variable: log $(MEMP_t)$ – 64 observations

City	Constant	TRD_t		
Detroit	11.163***	−0.015**	MAN%$_t$	0.132***
	(1.030)	(0.008)		(0.038)
Ferndale	5.574***	0.040***	UNEM%$_t$	−0.038*
	(1.131)	(0.013)		(0.024)
Highland Park	8.029***	0.019**	HDEN$_{t-1}$	−0.0005***
	(1.087)	(0.008)		(0.0002)
Mount Clemens	3.813**	0.077***	MABAT%$_{t-1}$	−0.021*
	(1.178)	(0.013)		(0.013)
River Rouge	6.209***	−0.017	IDB%$_{t-1}$	−0.010
	(1.140)	(0.022)		(0.015)
Royal Oak	4.529***	0.053***	HDIDB$_{t-1}$	−6.691E-08**
	(1.273)	(0.019)		(3.944E-08)
St Clair Shores	2.322***	0.106***	H3IDB$_{t-1}$	0.000133*
	(1.304)	(0.018)		(0.000083)
Wyandotte	5.854***	0.031**		
	(1.153)	(0.016)		

Notes: Adjusted $R^2 = 0.997$; F- statistic = 1012.85; standard errors are in parenthesis.
Two-tailed statistical significance: *** = 99 per cent or greater; ** = 90–98 per cent; and * = 80–89 per cent.

Table A4   Pooled ordinary least-squares regression results with autocorrelation and heteroskedastic correction: real manufacturing value added, 1954–87
Dependent variable: log $(MVAL_t)$ – 64 observations

City	Constant	TRD_t		
Detroit	20.261***	0.010	MAN%$_t$	0.152**
	(1.762)	(0.009)		(0.067)
Ferndale	15.115***	0.052*	UNEM%$_t$	−0.037
	(2.081)	(0.021)		(0.046)
Highland Park	19.393***	−0.099**	HDEN$_{t-1}$	−0.0004**
	(2.289)	(0.037)		(0.0002)
Mount Clemens	12.883***	0.109***	MABAT%$_{t-1}$	−0.644***
	(2.237)	(0.024)		(0.038)
River Rouge	15.825***	−0.005	HDMAB$_{t-1}$	6.393E-05**
	(1.999)	(0.026)		(3.121E-05)
Royal Oak	13.377***	0.095***	H3MAB$_{t-1}$	0.0060***
	(2.211)	(0.024)		(0.0013)
St Clair Shores	9.190***	0.130**	IDB%$_{t-1}$	2.630***
	(2.226)	(0.025)		(0.577)
Wyandotte	15.345***	0.048**	HDIDB$_{t-1}$	−0.00011**
	(2.169)	(0.023)		(0.00005)
			H3IDB$_{t-1}$	−0.0303***
				(0.0067)

Notes: Adjusted$R^2 = 0.999$; F-statistic= 1879.21; standard errors are in parenthesis.
Two-tailed statistical significance: *** = 99 per cent or greater; ** = 90–98 per cent; and *= 80–89 per cent.

Table A5 Pooled ordinary least-squares regression results with autocorrelation and heteroskedastic correction: retail employment. 1954–87
Dependent variable: $\log(REMP_t)$ – 200 observations

City	Constant	TRD_t		
Allen Park	6.940***	0.031***	$RET\%_t$	−0.030
	(0.565)	(0.006)		(0.031)
Berkley	6.251***	0.027*	$UNEM\%_t$	−0.028***
	(0.990)	(0.018)		(0.008)
Birmingham	7.819***	0.021***	$HDEN_{t-1}$	0.00026***
	(0.533)	(0.004)		(0.00006)
Dearborn	9.019***	0.019***	$AFAM\%_{t-1}$	−0.0108**
	(0.579)	(0.007)		(0.0051)
Detroit	11.137***	−0.003	$CABAT\%_{t-1}$	−0.0199
	(0.565)	(0.009)		(0.0221)
East Detroit	7.300***	0.015***	DDA_{t-1}	−0.0061
	(0.527)	(0.003)		(0.0189)
Ecorse	7.041***	−0.007*	$TIFA_{t-1}$	0.0740*
	(0.550)	(0.004)		(0.0515)
Ferndale	7.679***	−0.007		
	(0.536)	(0.006)		
Garden City	6.619***	0.034***		
	(0.541)	(0.006)		
Grosse Pointe Farms	6.394***	0.014**		
	(0.526)	(0.007)		
Gross Pointe Woods	7.050***	0.001		
	(0.753)	(0.017)		
Hamtramck	7.230**	−0.026***		
	(0.592)	(0.003)		
Hazel Park	6.934***	0.004		
	(0.550)	(0.005)		
Highland Park	7.551***	0.0003		
	(0.599)	(0.0134)		
Inkster	7.700***	−0.003		
	(0.558)	(0.007)		
Mount Clemens	7.811***	0.006**		
	(0.535)	(0.003)		
Oak Park	7.257***	0.023**		
	(0.521)	(0.012)		
Plymouth	6.845***	0.019***		
	(0.529)	(0.004)		
Pontiac	9.179***	−0.004		
	(0.536)	(0.005)		
River Rouge	6.440***	−0.007		
	(0.546)	(0.006)		
Rochester	6.066***	0.045**		
	(0.570)	(0.006)		
Roseville	7.422***	0.043***		
	(0.536)	(0.005)		

Table A5 *(Cont.)*

City	Constant	TRD$_t$
Royal Oak	8.522***	0.001
	(0.524)	(0.004)
St Clair Shores	7.128***	0.037***
	(0.535)	(0.005)
Wyandotte	8.047***	−0.023**
	(0.644)	(0.009)

Notes: Adjusted $R^2 = 0.995$; F-statistic $= 650.16$; standard errors are in parenthesis.
Two-tailed statistical significance: *** $= 99$ per cent or greater; ** $= 90$–98 per cent; and * $= 80$–89 per cent.

Table A6 Pooled ordinary least-squares regression results with autocorrelation and heteroskedastic correction: real retail sales, 1954–87
Dependent variable: log (RSAL$_t$) – 200 observations

City	Constant	TRD$_t$		
Allen Park	15.881***	0.016	RET%$_t$	−0.084*
	(1.061)	(0.008)		(0.061)
Berkley	15.229***	0.003	UNEM%$_t$	−0.080***
	(1.106)	(0.007)		(0.012)
Birmingham	16.822***	0.008	HDEN$_{t-1}$	0.00034**
	(1.075)	(0.006)		(0.00014)
Dearborn	17.679***	0.020***	AFAM%$_{t-1}$	−0.0040
	(1.049)	(0.005)		(0.0083)
Detroit	19.258***	0.001***	CABAT%$_{t-1}$	−0.0551**
	(1.338)	(0.013)		(0.0224)
East Detroit	16.218***	0.012*	DDA$_{t-1}$	−0.0370**
	(1.066)	(0.008)		(0.0187)
Ecorse	15.830***	−0.030**	TIFA$_{t-1}$	0.0316
	(1.166)	(0.012)		(0.0520)
Ferndale	16.389***	−0.003		
	(1.334)	(0.004)		
Garden City	15.580***	0.030***		
	(1.052)	(0.009)		
Grosse Pointe Farms	15.202***	0.012*		
	(1.054)	(0.009)		
Gross Pointe Woods	15.848***	−0.010		
	(1.145)	(0.016)		
Hamtramck	15.333***	−0.018***		
	(1.459)	(0.004)		
Hazel Park	15.391***	0.003		
	(1.221)	(0.006)		
Highland Park	16.047***	−0.012***		
	(1.386)	(0.022)		
Inkster	15.670***	0.029***		
	(1.137)	(0.009)		

Table A6 *(Cont.)*

Mount Clemens	16.390***	0.008
	(1.095)	(0.006)
Oak Park	15.724***	0.027***
	(1.015)	(0.009)
Plymouth	15.741***	0.016**
	(1.060)	(0.006)
Pontiac	17.635***	0.002
	(1.051)	(0.009)
River Rouge	15.390***	−0.030*
	(1.319)	(0.018)
Rochester	15.237***	0.023***
	(1.085)	(0.006)
Roseville	16.118***	0.040**
	(1.026)	(0.008)
Royal Oak	17.121***	0.007
	(1.049)	(0.007)
St Clair Shores	15.566***	0.074**
	(1.032)	(0.014)
Wyandotte	16.743***	−0.028***
	(1.122)	(0.006)

Notes: Adjusted $R^2 = 0.995$; F-statistic $= 736.25$; standard errors are in parenthesis.
Two-tailed statistical significance: *** $= 99$ per cent or greater; ** $= 90$–98 per cent; and * $= 80$–89 per cent.

Table A7   Pooled ordinary least-squares regression results with autocorrelation and heteroskedastic correction: service employment, 1954–87
Dependent variable: $\log (SEMP_t)$ – 200 observations

City	Constant	TRD_t		
Allen Park	4.212***	0.042***	SER%	0.089**
	(0.355)	(0.015)		(0.046)
Berkley	4.605***	0.015	$UNEM\%_t$	−0.011
	(0.383)	(0.014)		(0.014)
Birmingham	5.089***	0.036***	$HDEN_{t-1}$	0.00023***
	(0.360)	(0.012)		(0.00009)
Dearborn	5.712***	0.043***	$AFAM\%_{t-1}$	−0.0255***
	(0.355)	(0.012)		(0.0072)
Detroit	9.088***	0.032***	$CABAT\%_{t-1}$	0.7035*
	(0.623)	(0.011)		(0.4579)
East Detroit	4.514***	0.026**	$HDCAB_{t-1}$	−5.835 E-05
	(0.348)	(0.013)		(0.0001207)
Ecorse	3.500***	0.025	$AACAB_{t-1}$	0.00961***
	(0.547)	(0.021)		(0.00291)
Ferndale	4.589***	0.026**	$H3CAB_{t-1}$	−0.00705
	(0.432)	(0.013)		(0.00644)
Garden City	3.404***	0.046***	$CMCAB_{t-1}$	−3.9831*
	(0.332)	(0.014)		(2.8221)

Table A7   (*Contd.*)

City	Constant	TRD$_t$		
Grosse Pointe Farms	2.804***	0.043***	DDA$_{t-1}$	−0.0908**
	(0.427)	(0.015)		(0.0400)
Gross Pointe Woods	4.016**	0.022*	TIFA$_{t-1}$	0.398**
	(0.314)	(0.014)		(0.160)
Hamtramck	4.365***	−0.011		
	(0.690)	(0.010)		
Hazel Park	3.996***	0.034**		
	(0.421)	(0.014)		
Highland Park	4.661***	0.052***		
	(0.684)	(0.019)		
Inkster	4.603***	0.027*		
	(0.362)	(0.016)		
Mount Clemens	4.849***	0.040***		
	(0.356)	(0.012)		
Oak Park	3.919***	0.075***		
	(0.388)	(0.015)		
Plymouth	3.908***	0.043***		
	(0.425)	(0.015)		
Pontiac	6.152***	0.026**		
	(0.390)	(0.013)		
River Rouge	3.747***	0.005		
	(0.559)	(0.014)		
Rochester	2.569***	0.072***		
	(0.390)	(0.018)		
Roseville	3.619***	0.067***		
	(0.328)	(0.014)		
Royal Oak	5.312***	0.027**		
	(0.381)	(0.011)		
St Clair Shores	3.829***	0.061***		
	(0.320)	(0.014)		
Wyandotte	4.674***	0.006		
	(0.456)	(0.013)		

Notes: Adjusted $R^2 = 0.992$; *F*-statistic $= 424.73$; standard errors are in parenthesis.
Two-tailed statistical significance: *** $= 99$ per cent or greater; ** $= 90$–98 per cent; and * $= 80$–89 per cent.

Table A8   Pooled ordinary least-squares regression results with autocorrelation and heteroskedastic correction: real service receipts, 1954–87
Dependent variable: log (SREC$_t$) – 200 observations

City	Constant	TRD$_t$		
Allen Park	13.876***	0.089***	SER%	−0.020
	(0.338)	(0.016)		(0.048)
Berkley	14.668***	0.052***	UNEM%$_t$	−0.035**
	(0.473)	(0.018)		(0.014)
Birmingham	15.506***	0.065***	HDEN$_{t-1}$	0.00019*
	(0.406)	(0.017)		(0.00012)

Table A8 *(Cont.)*

Dearborn	15.809***	0.079***	AFAM%$_{t-1}$	−0.0128
	(0.376)	(0.012)		(0.0102)
Detroit	19.826***	0.033***	CABAT%$_{t-1}$	−0.0297
	(0.825)	(0.019)		(0.0381)
East Detroit	14.437***	0.068***	DDA$_{t-1}$	−0.0262**
	(0.388)	(0.016)		(0.0297)
Ecorse	13.163***	0.073***	TIFA$_{t-1}$	0.1853**
	(0.540)	(0.016)		(0.0951)
Ferndale	14.880***	0.053***		
	(0.497)	(0.014)		
Garden City	13.542***	0.082***		
	(0.355)	(0.018)		
Grosse Pointe Farms	12.610***	0.073***		
	(0.421)	(0.013)		
Grosse Pointe Woods	14.192**	0.059*		
	(0.327)	(0.015)		
Hamtramck	14.580***	0.011		
	(0.882)	(0.009)		
Hazel Park	15.578***	0.037***		
	(0.458)	(0.013)		
Highland Park	14.738***	0.067**		
	(0.883)	(0.030)		
Inkster	14.015***	0.087***		
	(0.552)	(0.016)		
Mount Clemens	14.617***	0.080***		
	(0.402)	(0.012)		
Oak Park	13.767***	0.116***		
	(0.767)	(0.033)		
Plymouth	13.800***	0.083***		
	(0.362)	(0.015)		
Pontiac	16.106***	0.057***		
	(0.398)	(0.015)		
River Rouge	13.962***	0.033**		
	(0.668)	(0.016)		
Rochester	12.744***	0.107***		
	(0.415)	(0.018)		
Roseville	13.592***	0.102***		
	(0.405)	(0.019)		
Royal Oak	15.477***	0.062***		
	(0.394)	(0.013)		
St Clair Shores	13.472***	0.134***		
	(0.402)	(0.017)		
Wyandotte	14.683***	0.040***		
	(0.467)	(0.015)		

Notes: Adjusted $R^2 = 0.996$; F-statistic $= 884.49$; standard errors are in parenthesis.
Two-tailed statistical significance: *** $= 99$ per cent or greater; ** $= 90$–98 per cent; and * $= 80$–89 per cent.

Further Reading Samples

Abstract from *Enterprise Zones and Employment: Evidence from New Jersey*

MARLON G. BOARNET AND WILLIAM T. BOGART

Source: *Journal of Urban Economics*, 40, 198–215. © 1996 Academic Press, Inc. All rights of reproduction in any form reserved.

This paper presents new evidence on the effectiveness of urban enterprise zones as an economic development tool. The results reported here are from an econometric analysis of the New Jersey urban enterprise zone program using data at the municipal level from 1982 to 1990. We find no evidence that the urban enterprise zone program in New Jersey had a positive effect on total municipal employment, on employment in various sectors, or on municipal property values. We conclude that the program was ineffective in achieving its goal of improving the economic conditions in and around the zones.

Abstract from *Amenities as an Economic Development Tool: Is There Enough Evidence?*

PAUL D. GOTTLIEB

Source: *Economic Development Quarterley*, 8(3), August 1994, 270–85.
© 1994 Sage Publications Inc. Reprinted by permission of Sage Publications Inc.

The argument for using amenities as an economic development tool appears to be a powerful one. Even if such a strategy failed to attract industry, constituents presumably would benefit. Outside of the survey literature, however, there is little hard evidence that firms actually react to "quality of life" in their location decisions. This article reviews the theoretical, survey, and econometric literatures on amenity-oriented firm location and employment growth. Though limited, the existing literature suggests that an amenities strategy for development should be regional; that jurisdictions should focus on basics like schools, environment, crime, and congestion; and that amenities should be managed in the broader context of trends in urbanization.

Abstract from *Quality of Life in Central Cities and Suburbs*

MARK J. JENSEN AND CHARLES L. LEVEN

Source: *Annals of Regional Science*, 1997, Springer-Verlag, Heidelberg.

This study shows that there has been a statistically significant shift in the quality of life (QOL) in central cities of the 25 largest metro areas relative to their suburbs since 1980.

This follows actual improvement of central cities in the 1950s, followed by steady degradation in the 1960s and 1970s. These conclusions are based on a statistical analysis of key variables derived from a revealed preference conception of QOL. This is an important methodological advance, since relevant variables for directly constructing hedonic measures of QOL normally are unavailable for central cities. The basic Census data used in the analysis also indicate that the observed "turnaround" is evident without respect to size of metro area within the set of 25 largest and without respect to region of the country.

Abstract from *Tax Increment Financing: Municipal Adoption and Effects on Property Value Growth*

JOYCE Y. MANN AND MARK S. ROSENTRAUB

Source: *Public Finance Review*, 26(6), November, 523–47. © 1998 Sage Publications Inc. Reprinted by permission of Sage Publications Inc.

Tax increment financing (TIF) has been adopted widely by municipalities in the United States as an economic development tool. Despite the large number of state initiatives and TIF's increasing popularity, few statistical studies have been conducted to examine the direct effect of the TIF program from an economic perspective. This article analyzes the effect of TIF plans on property value growth by comparing pre-TIF to post-TIF property value changes in a first-difference model. The empirical results from a panel of Indiana cities indicate that the TIF program has increased median owner-occupied housing values in a TIF-adopting city by 11% relative to what it would have been without TIF. This finding suggests that the TIF program effectively stimulates property value growth in an entire community.

Abstract from *Tax Policy and Urban Development: Evidence from the Indiana Enterprise Zone Program*

LESLIE E. PAPKE

Source: *Journal of Public Economics*, 54(1), 37–49. © 1994 with permission from Elsevier Science.

This paper analyzes the effect of the Indiana enterprise zone (EZ) program on local employment and investment using a panel of local taxing jurisdictions. As in other EZ programs, Indiana's incentives favor capital relative to labor, but the target of the capital incentive is unusual – the stock of inventories. Using various estimation methods, I estimate that zone designation initially reduces the value of depreciable personal property by about 13 percent, but also reduces unemployment claims in the zone and surrounding community by 19 percent. The value of inventories in Indiana zones is 8 percent higher than it would be without the program.

Abstract from *New Strategies for Inner-City Economic Development*

MICHAEL E. PORTER

Source: Economic Development Quarterly, 11, February. © 1997 Sage Publications Inc. Reprinted by permission of Sage Publications Inc.

Revitalizing America's inner cities requires an economic strategy to build viable businesses that can provide sorely needed, nearby employment opportunities. Economic development in inner cities will come only from recognizing the potential advantages of an inner-city location and building on the base of existing companies, while dealing frontally with the present disadvantages of inner cities as business locations. The economic potential in inner cities has been largely unrecognised and untapped. The private sector, which must play a central role in inner-city economic development, is just beginning to recognise this potential and has already begun investing. By improving perceptions and tackling long-neglected problems in the inner-city business environment, this trend can be accelerated. Government and community-based organizations have continuing, vital roles, but their efforts must be refocused from direct intervention to preparing and training the inner-city workforce and creating a favorable environment for business.

Discussion Questions

1 In his column, Peirce raises important questions:
   - When communities provide tax subsidies to 'win' a plant, do local taxpayers gain or lose financially?
   - How many new jobs are actually added?
   - What about the added costs – for welfare, social service, crime and justice, economic redevelopment – that the losing community incurs, or suddenly begs the state to pay?

   Why do local policymakers avoid asking such questions?

2 Economists believe that public intervention is justified in private markets only when a market failure is detected. Describe the type of market failures that Bartik cites to justify the offering of economic development incentives by government to private firms.

3 Find out what local economic development incentives are offered in your community. In the style of Bartik's memo to a mayor, write your own memo to your Mayor that relates Bartik's suggestions specifically to reforming the way that local incentives are offered in your community. Do you think your suggestions will ever be implemented? Is there a problem if only your community, and not surrounding communities, implements them?

4 According to Noll and Zimbalist, what is the bad economic reasoning that is present in most private consultant's evaluation of the economic effect of a sport's stadium in a metropolitan area? Are there any reasonable economic justifications for why a city should subsidise a professional sports team?

5 In his regression study, Wassmer notes that: "A criterion that most would agree upon is that a city should only grant an incentive when the expectation is that the offer is likely to have a positive effect on local economic development." Briefly describe all of the situations that he found for the Detroit Metropolitan Area where a specific type of local incentive, in a specific type of city, had a significant positive influence on a specific type of economic activity. Is a positive effect on local economic development the only criterion that should be used by a policymaker in deciding whether to offer a local incentive?

PART IV:

Race, Employment, and Poverty in Urban Areas

The largest American cities are becoming home to a larger and larger share of the national welfare burden.

Brookings Center on Urban and Metropolitan Poverty

CHAPTER SEVENTEEN

Big U.S. Cities Carry Welfare Burden: Deep Poverty, Isolation from Suburbs Keep Many from Independence

Laura Meckler

Source: The Detroit News, 19.2.99

Washington – As welfare rolls plummet in virtually every state, families on welfare increasingly are concentrated in large cities like Detroit, where deep poverty and isolation from suburban jobs makes for a tougher road to independence. Welfare caseloads are dropping in and out of cities, but they are dropping most slowly in the nation's largest, oldest urban areas, particularly in the Northeast, Midwest and South, the Brookings Institution said in a study released Thursday. It's an important, if somewhat disturbing, trend for state officials giddy from four years of unprecedented welfare declines but now increasingly focused on those who remain on the rolls. "Caseload decline does not tell the whole story of welfare reform in America," said the report by Brookings' Center on Urban & Metropolitan Policy. "The largest American cities are becoming home to a larger and larger share of the national welfare burden."

For instance, Wayne County houses 48 percent of Michigan's welfare families, up from 42 percent in 1994. Michigan officials say they are trying to address the problems, most notably lack of transportation to get people to suburban jobs. "There is no countywide transportation system in the Detroit area," said Karen Smith, spokeswoman for Michigan's welfare department. "It is very difficult for people who do not own their own vehicles to get from where they live to where a job might exist."

Researchers say the findings in the Brookings report has implications for local, state and federal governments, suggesting they must come up with new ways to get people in cities to jobs in the suburbs and address the hard-core problems of deep poverty. "This is ultimately where welfare reform succeeds or fails at the end of the day," said Bruce Katz of Brookings.

Between 1994 and 1998, welfare rolls fell 35 percent in the counties that contain the nation's 30 largest cities. That compares with a 44 percent drop nationwide. Nationwide, a third of the nation's welfare families lived in these counties in 1994. That rose to 40 percent by last year. These counties are home to just 20 percent of the total population.

The study found cities with a growing portion of the welfare population shared some characteristics: They were likely to be in the South, Northeast and Midwest. They were likely to have higher unemployment rates. They were more likely to have high rates of concentrated poverty – meaning areas where at least 40 percent of the people are poor. And concentrated poverty is associated with a host of other problems that make it tough to get off welfare: illiteracy, drug and alcohol abuse, school dropouts, teen pregnancy and out-of-wedlock births. The study found of the nation's 30 largest cities:

- 14 saw their caseloads drop more slowly than their state's caseload.
- In six, the declines were about even with the state.
- And in nine cities, welfare rolls fell faster in the city than in the rest of the state.
- Washington, D.C., one of the largest cities, has no state to compare itself to.

CHAPTER EIGHTEEN

Race Panel Divided Over Poverty: Experts Disagree on Causes, Cures of Urban Problems

LOUIS FREEDBERG

Source: San Francisco Chronicle, 12.2.98. © 1998 The San Francisco
Chronicle. Reprinted with permission.

A day after fending off irate hecklers, President Clinton's advisory board on race took on
the tougher challenge of how to overcome widespread poverty in minority communities.
Several experts told the board that urban poverty is caused by multiple factors, ranging
from a changing job market to pure discrimination, but they could not agree on the best
strategy to tackle the problem.

Yesterday's gathering in San Jose of President Clinton's Race Initiative Advisory Board
was far calmer than the tense and occasionally raucous town meeting at Independence
High School the night before, where ordinary citizens spoke with passion that sometimes
boiled over to boisterous and divisive anger. Yesterday it was the turn of policy wonks
[experts] and community activists to weigh in on the complex relationship between
economics and skin color. William Julius Wilson, one of the nation's leading sociologists
on urban poverty, said racism is what originally forced many blacks into low-skilled jobs in
the nation's urban centers and trapped them there with little chance for escape. "There is
no way to explain the disproportionate number of minorities who are poor without taking
the legacy of race into account – and the legacy of racism is the urban ghetto," he said. But
he said profound economic transformations – such as the decline in demand for low-
skilled jobs – have contributed to keeping blacks in poverty. He said government-inspired
remedies are needed to address the changing nature of the job market which hampers all
races. "The best thing for these economically depressed neighborhoods would be if we
could extend this (national) economic recovery for next several years," said Wilson.

But John Hope Franklin, the African American historian who is chairman of the
advisory group, took issue with Wilson. "If I were on the unemployment line, I would
not want to wait until the unemployment rate came down until I had the opportunity to
work," he said. Robert Woodson, director of the National Center for Neighborhood
Enterprise and the only conservative on the panel, thought otherwise. Woodson discounted the importance of race. "Why are poor blacks suffering in cities run by blacks?"
he asked. "And why are Latinos suffering in poor areas run by Latinos? It is not just race

and economics that determines one's behaviour and values," said Woodson. "We have to recognize that culture is also a factor." One strategy, Woodson said, would be to remove bureaucracy and other obstacles for poor inner-city residents who wish to start their own small businesses.

But Doug Massey, a University of Pennsylvania expert on segregated housing, said a major cause of poverty for blacks is that they historically live in more segregated neighborhoods than any other minority group. Discrimination is the cause of much of that segregation, Massey said, and active government intervention is needed to prevent it. "It's not to say that the economy is not important, or culture is not important, but there is still discrimination out there," he said.

Matthew Snipp, a sociologist at Stanford University, pointed out that Native Americans face special challenges in overcoming poverty. He said explanations like housing segregation are inadequate to explain persistent unemployment rates of nearly 40 percent in some Native American communities. "Reservations have become desegregated. We now have tribal governments operated by tribal people, but Indian people are no better off," he said.

Raquel Rivera Pinderhughes, a professor of urban studies at San Francisco State University, said another key factor that is seldom taken into account was what she called "anti-immigrant sentiment" in California. "We have to deal with anti-immigrant climate, which is making all immigrant populations and native-born ethnic populations more vulnerable to labor exploitation, civil rights violations, pitting groups against one another," she said. Because of these influences and others, all panelist agreed that "monolithic strategy" to deal with poverty would be a mistake.

Despite the conflicts, the experts found signs of hope. And Massey said that perhaps what was most hopeful was that "we're having this conversation on race, and the Clinton administration is now turning to the unfinished business of the civil rights movement."

CHAPTER NINETEEN

No Easy Way Out: Study Finds Urban Poverty Digs Heels In

JAMIE WOODWELL AND SUSAN ROSENBLUM

Source: Nation's Cities Weekly, 17.8.98. Reprinted by permission of National League of Cities, Washington DC.

A new study, issued by the U.S. Census Bureau, concludes that poverty is a "transitory condition" for many, but only chronic for some. The report found that while one in three Americans lived in poverty for at least two consecutive months, only one in 20 people stayed poor for two years. Boston Mayor Tom Menino called even this "transitory" condition an "outrage." "The fact that in any one year, over one-fifth of our population lived in poverty for two straight months is unacceptable," he said. "The strength of our communities is measured in the well-being of our children and families."

The report, *Dynamics of Economic Well-Being, Poverty 1993–1994: Trap Door? Revolving Door? Or Both?*, uses multiple measures of poverty to show that it is "complex" and affects people differently. The report studies how long people stay poor, as well as how often they move in and out of poverty. The government considers a family of four poor if their income is less than $16,450 a year. Other findings include:

- Central cities have the highest poverty rates and suburbs have the lowest rate;
- Central cities had more people (per capita) enter poverty and fewer people (per capita) leaving poverty than did either suburbs or nonmetropolitan areas;
- African Americans and Hispanics had higher poverty rates than whites, but African Americans stayed poor 60 percent longer (6.8 months) than whites (4.2 months); and
- Poor households headed by a female stayed poor longer (7.2 months) than households headed by a married-couple (3.9 percent).

According to Menino, who chairs the National League of Cities (NLC) Task Force on Youth, Education, and Families, "The best insurance against poverty is education. In Boston, I have made education my number one priority. A good education, including early childhood education and lifelong learning, holds the key to the future of our children and our economies."

Another key to reducing urban poverty is to adopt policies and programs that link economic development with workforce development. "We need to promote more public-private sector collaboration that results in connecting poor people with better-paying jobs," notes Task Force Vice-Chair Mayor Michael Morrison, Waco, Texas. "Workforce development means building systems that not only educate and train people for work, but also transport them to where the jobs are," he said. "It also means providing supports and benefits necessary for people to keep the jobs they have." One of these "supports" is affordable health insurance. Two parents working full-time at minimum wage jobs that offer no health insurance can quickly plunge a family of four into poverty if someone falls ill or has an accident. The Federal Agency for Health Care Policy and Research reports that while more employers offer health benefits, the proportion of workers accepting these offers has declined due to high costs. The largest declines were found among the working poor – people earning less than $7 an hour.

NCL Efforts

To learn more about what the National League of Cities is doing to help cities reduce poverty through workforce development, contact Susan Rosenblum, Project Manager, Workforce Development, by phone: 202/6263030, or by e-mail: rosenblum@lc.org.

CHAPTER TWENTY

Inner Cities

EDWIN S. MILLS AND LUAN' SENDE LUBUELE

Source: Journal of Economic Literature, 35, June 1997, 727–56. Reprinted by permission of American Economic Association.

1. Introduction

This essay interprets and generalizes studies and data related to economic and social issues in inner cities of U.S. metropolitan areas (MSAs).

What are inner cities? Generically, they are the oldest parts of MSAs. Practically, all are incorporated cities, and most of the data on inner cities relates to incorporated cities or to the counties in which they are located. (Some MSAs contain two or three inner cities.) The central business district (CBD) of an inner city is typically the business center of the MSA. We use the term "inner city," to mean the same places as the somewhat official term "central city." However, "central city" is losing official status, and we will employ the more familiar term "inner city." Our usage is to be distinguished from an alternative usage sometimes employed to mean poor parts of central cities.

Why do social scientists study inner cities? First, inner cities are important components of the spatial organization of MSAs. Places we now refer to as inner cities once constituted entire MSAs, and city boundaries tended to move outward as MSAs grew and decentralized. Boundary movement has slowed during this century, whereas MSA growth and decentralization have continued at rapid paces. In the 1990s, many more people live in MSA suburbs (parts of MSAs outside inner cities) than in inner cities and about as much employment is located in suburbs as in inner cities. Nevertheless, inner cities are typically near the geographical centers of MSAs; certain production sectors are concentrated there; CBDs are typically the focus of the MSA's transportation system; and MSA population and employment densities are highest in inner cities. The MSA's highest land values are found in CBDs in most MSAs. All recent studies conclude that inner cities remain important and integral parts of their MSAs (see Mills 1990; Keith Ihlanfeldt 1994; and Richard Voith 1994).

Second, and much more important in terms of both recent scholarly literature and government interventions, inner cities contain large concentrations of low income people and of almost every index of social dysfunction and alienation. The tale of inner city woes

* The authors are indebted to James Quane, William Julius Wilson, and other participants in the seminar on urban inequality, Irving Harris Graduate School of Public Policy Studies, University of Chicago, at which an earlier draft of this paper was presented. We are especially indebted to Charles Becker, Rebecca Blank, and Christopher Jencks for valuable comments. We are also indebted for comments on earlier drafts to referees of the Journal.

will be spelled out and documented in subsequent sections, but it is important at the outset to establish balance. By no means everybody in inner cities is poor and alienated. Nor are all the schools bad or all neighborhoods crime ridden. Most inner cities contain high, and some very high, income neighborhoods, and many contain large, stable, and racially mixed and congenial middle class neighborhoods. Even census tracts (which typically contain about 5,000 people each) in which at least 40 percent of residents are below the poverty line contain impressive mixtures of conventional and stable nonpoor families (see Paul Jargowsky 1996.)

Although the two issues identified above are mostly studied in different publications, an important goal of this essay is to examine the relationships between them. What are the important spatial relationships between inner cities and suburbs, and how and why have they changed? Does the United States have a disproportionate share of poor and alienated people? Are the poor and alienated disproportionately concentrated in inner cities compared with the implications of a reasonable null hypothesis? If so, why? And how does spatial concentration relate to relationships between inner cities and suburbs as both cause and effect?

The outline of the paper is as follows. Section 2 presents theory and evidence about the spatial and sectoral organizations of U.S. MSAs. Section 3 introduces the study of the socio-economic status of inner city residents in comparison with suburban residents. Section 4 presents a brief international comparison of social indicators. Section 5 analyzes the evidence about the causes and consequences of the concentration of poverty and social pathology in inner cities. Section 6 draws conclusions from the analysis.

2. Spatial and Sectoral Organization of U.S. MSAs[1]

Three issues are addressed in this section. First, why are inner cities the focus of employment and production in metropolitan areas, and why has the concentration of people and employment in inner cities diminished in recent decades? Second, why are poverty and alienation so concentrated in inner cities? Third, how are the first two issues related?

In 1990, about 78 percent of the U.S. population lived in MSAs, and a somewhat larger percentage of workers worked there. (There is modest net commuting into MSAs on the way to work.) The percent of the population living in MSAs has increased steadily since data became available, from 55 percent in 1940. Although they are not the same people, the percentage of the population that lives in urban areas has been about the same as that in MSAs since 1940, and the percentage increased from 5 in 1790 to 57 in 1940.[2] The growth rates of both U.S. and MSA populations have slowed in recent years, but the MSA population grew about 40 percent faster than the national population from 1980 to 1990, about 1.4 compared with about 1.0 percent per year.

Why do so many people live and work in MSAs? The important part of the question is why employment and earnings opportunities are better in MSAs than elsewhere.[3] The answer is proximity, although urban theorists do not use the term;[4] proximity of workers to jobs, of firms to customers, of firms to other firms with whom they do business, and of workers and firms to information generating and dispersing institutions. Not only are traditional economies of scale and scope important in producing large concentrations of workers and producers, but also the lower costs of moving people, goods, and information because of proximity within large MSAs than elsewhere result in greater output per unit of input in large MSAs. Urban specialists refer to this as agglomeration economies. A typical estimate is that MSA output per unit of input increases 4–6 percent for each doubling of MSA size (see J. Vernon Henderson 1988).

In the simplest theoretical model, referred to as the monocentric model, which is literally realistic for 19th and early 20th century MSAs and still has many realistic implications, there is a transshipment node through which all goods shipments from or to the MSA must pass. Railheads and ports are the best examples. Because goods movement within the MSA is costly, all firms in the MSA that bring goods to or ship goods from the MSA locate in contiguous spaces around the node. This space defines the CBD. Residences of workers who commute to the CBD are located in contiguous places surrounding the CBD, because noncontiguous locations would entail needless commuting expense. Firms that produce goods and services for local consumption locate near the housing inhabited by their customers. Under minimal assumptions, no goods produced in the MSA, whether they are for export or for local consumption, are shipped away from the CBD, and no workers commute outward from their residences on the way to work.

If all workers have the same earnings and housing demand equations, equilibrium land rents and housing user costs in the residential area fall just rapidly enough with distance from the CBD so that workers are indifferent as to residential location. Because commuting is costly, workers residing farther from the CBD are compensated for their higher commuting costs by lower dwelling rents or ownership user costs. Thus, real housing consumption per worker increases with distance from the CBD, even through workers are equally well off wherever they live.

Commuting entails both time and money costs. Money costs are vehicle costs or transit fares. Time costs occur because time spent commuting has valuable alternative uses. Estimates suggest that commuters value per hour driving time at about one-third of the wage rate and that MSA commuting costs are divided about equally between time and money costs for typical commuters.[5] Other evidence indicates that the income elasticity of housing demand is somewhat less than one. These conditions, plus substitutability between land and structure inputs in producing housing, imply that the function showing the decline of residential density with distance from the center within the residential area flattens as earnings rise or as the per mile money or time cost of commuting declines (see Jan Brueckner 1987). Thus, suburbanization or decentralization, defined as flattening of the residential density-distance function, occurs as real earnings rise and as commuting cost per mile falls or as commuting speed increases.

Figure 1 shows typical MSA density–distance functions. $D(x)$ is population density at distance x from the MSA center $\underline{x}$ is the radius of the CBD and $\bar{x}$ is the radius of the MSA. $D_o(x)$ shows the density pattern when incomes are low or commuting costs are high. $D_1(x)$ shows the pattern after incomes have risen or commuting costs have fallen.

$$p = \int_{\underline{x}}^{\bar{x}} \pi x D(x) dx$$

is the MSA total population if the MSA is circular.

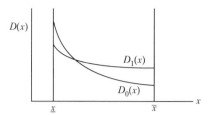

Figure 1

The same conditions imply that high earnings workers live farther from the CBD than low earnings workers. The intuition is that, if all workers value commuting time at the same fraction of wages and have the same income elasticity of housing demand, the inexpensive housing at more distant residential locations is worth more to high than to low earnings workers, because high earnings workers consume more housing.

This analysis ignores several important issues, but I believe it provides the first important insight into MSA suburbanization and residential segregation by income. The plausible assumptions of the monocentric model imply that residential density–distance functions flatten as earnings rise and commuting improves and that workers voluntarily segregate themselves, with higher earnings workers residing at greater distances from the CBD. Nobody knows how much explanatory power the simple model has. William Wheaton (1977) has argued that it may not be much (see also Peter Mieszkowski and Mills 1993). Nevertheless, the facts are clear. Suburbanization, defined as flattening density-distance functions, has pervaded United States MSAs for at least 50 years and has characterized every metropolitan area in the world for which density patterns and trends have been measured, during a half century of pervasively rising incomes and transportation improvements in MSAs. By the 1990s about two-thirds of the U.S. MSA population lived in suburbs and about half of MSA jobs were located there. Those percentages increase each decade and there is neither theoretical reason nor data to indicate that they will not continue to increase in future decades. Indeed, suburban population growth is somewhat faster than MSA population growth, so most inner city populations decrease somewhat. Rising incomes with distances of residences from the CBD have characterized U.S. MSAs for decades and have become increasingly prominent in recent decades; and characterize metropolitan areas elsewhere in the world at least to a considerable extent.

What other phenomena provide plausible hypotheses to explain suburbanization and income segregation by distance from CBDs? There are several.

Start with the most obvious defect of the monocentric model described above: the assumption that the MSA makes use of only one transshipment node for goods entering or leaving the MSA and that, as a result, all jobs related to handling and processing such goods are located in the resulting CBD. (The accuracy of that pattern during the period of rapid industrial growth from 1850 to 1900 is dramatically demonstrated for Chicago by William Cronon (1991; see also Charles Glaab and Theodore Brown 1967). For at least 75 years, manufacturing sectors have been moving from CBDs. At first, many such moves were from CBDs to more distant parts of inner cities, as when the stockyards moved from the Chicago River to the southwest side of Chicago. Since World War II, most such moves have been to suburbs, then to distant suburbs and, to some extent, outside MSAs altogether (see Gerald Carlino 1985).

There have been several pervasive causes of manufacturing suburbanization, but the first and most important has been the modal shift in goods movement from rail and ship to road. The advent of the internal combustion engine and of improved roads and trucks enabled manufacturers to move goods from and to the MSA directly from and to suburban locations without using CBD terminals. Circumferential highways have permitted producers located in almost any suburb to move goods economically between the MSA and other places in almost any direction.

In fact, for several decades, retailing and service-producing office activities have dominated CBD land use. The advent of electrically powered elevators and structural steel buildings has made rents per square foot of space almost as low in 80-story as in 5-story office buildings. This ability to make much more productive use of land would have enabled skyscrapers to outbid manufacturing for CBD land even if no changes had occurred in modes of goods shipment.

Economical production of services in skyscrapers and the high cost of moving workers over substantial distances are necessary conditions for the modern CBD, but the advantages to businesses of proximity to related businesses are the sufficient condition. Only the need for intensive interaction with related businesses can justify CBD land values that are an order of magnitude greater than those a few miles away. Partly cause and partly consequence of such concentration is that MSA road and rail commuting systems tend to be radial from the CBD.[6]

Some CBD office activities produce services for local use and some for export from the MSA. Nobody knows the shares, but an export share of one-third has been conjectured. In both production for local and for export sale, the need to interact with related businesses justifies CBD locations, especially because most service exports from MSAs are by electronic means.

In fact, not only manufacturing but also offices and retail shops have suburbanized during the last half century. In 1950, about 70 percent of MSA employment was in inner cities, and in 1980 it was somewhat more than 50 percent. By 1990, it was certainly somewhat less than half. Shops mostly serve local residents and are dispersed throughout suburbs. Offices, whether they produce services for MSA use or for export, are found in suburban clusters similar to but mostly smaller than CBD clusters. Once again, the need for proximity to related businesses is the reason for clustering. Since the 1970s, some suburban clusters of offices and retailing have become very large, and Joel Garreau (1991) has coined the term "edge city." Most are not located at the edges of MSAs, but the suggestion that they are of near-city size is accurate.[7]

Suburbanization of all kinds of production interacts with residential suburbanization. Jobs attract residents to suburbs and residents attract jobs, whether they are producing for local use or for export.

There are other reasons that offices have moved from CBDs to suburban clusters. One is that some CBDs may have become so large that they have exhausted economies of scale and scope. That may not be important in that total CBD employment has been falling for a couple of decades in some MSAs. A second reason may be that congestion has increased in and near CBDs because of the expense and political difficulty of increasing the capacity of the transportation system in high density CBDs. A third may be that modern methods of communication have reduced the need for face-to-face communication among office workers (see Mills 1995). A fourth is that pervasive use of cars permits inexpensive commuting between low density origin–destination pairs, making cars cheaper than public transit for workers who both live and work in suburbs. A fifth, related to the purposes of this essay, may be that offices tend to employ well educated and well paid workers; if such employees have moved to suburbs for reasons given above, it increases the motivation of employers to follow. A sixth reason, also related to the purposes of this essay, undoubtedly is to escape the disamenities of crime for employees and of crime and poor schools for employees' children in inner cities.

All the factors just discussed have contributed to the flattening of land rent and population density-distance functions. The negative relationship between land values or rents and distance from the CBD would persist in the presence of almost all of the factors just discussed. This subject is discussed further below.

A final comment on this issue is that there is little that is uniquely advantageous about a CBD as a location for an office cluster.[8] To the extent that office workers export services outside the MSA, they do so by electronic and printed means, with little need to be near inter-MSA transportation terminals. Proximity to the airport is more important for export of office services than proximity to rail and ship terminals. However, proximity to CBD electronic infrastructure may be important, although it too is being replicated in suburban office centers. In an approximately circular MSA, location of an office cluster in the CBD minimizes mean commuting distance for workers whose residences are scattered throughout the MSA. But that is unlikely to be important if most workers commute by car, if downtown streets are congested, and if there are good circumferential and other highways in suburbs.

Employment suburbanization is an important and interesting issue.[9] The important issue in this essay is how employment suburbanization interacts with inner city problems. Employment suburbanization gave rise to the "mismatch" hypothesis. First analyzed in John Kain (1968), a substantial literature has developed on the subject. The hypothesis is that employment suburbanization has caused an increasing mismatch between locations of jobs that are increasingly in suburbs and locations of the residences of low income and, especially, minority residents who live in inner cities. The inference is that such people have lower earnings, more unemployment, and perhaps lower rates of labor force participation than they would if they lived closer to suburban employment clusters.[10]

Employment suburbanization does not by itself provide an explanation of inner city problems. Workers can and do suburbanize in large numbers. The important issue, discussed further below and in Section 5 below, is why black workers have followed jobs to suburbs in much smaller numbers than white workers have. The more dispersed are given MSA employment and workers' residences, the shorter commute trips can be. However, shorter commuting times but not distances appear to have resulted from business and residential suburbanization in U.S. MSAs in recent decades. In addition, dispersed employment and residences make possible within an MSA context the small town life styles that U.S. residents say they prefer. That indeed has occurred in many edge cities. Finally, Mills (1985), presented a simple calculation that suggests that suburban dispersal of blacks might increase white population and employment in inner cities.[11] If that is so, suburbanization by inner city minorities would not "empty out" inner cities, as is widely feared. Whatever the causes or consequences, whites have been deterred from location in communities with large minority populations.

Many reasons have been put forth by advocates of the mismatch hypotheses as to why employment suburbanization disadvantages inner city minorities. Racial discrimination in suburban housing heads the list. Beyond doubt, it was more important in the 1960s, when Kain first put forward the mismatch hypothesis, than it has been in recent years. Evidence will be reviewed below. Racial discrimination in suburban employment has been hypothesized but not carefully tested. Higher costs of commuting and job search are also hypothesized. Some of these hypotheses appear to be clutching at straws. Writers forget that, during the decades preceding 1970, hundreds of thousands of desperately poor blacks migrated hundreds of miles from southern farms to northern cities in search of better lives. Despite limited employment opportunities and blatant discrimination in destination cities, better lives were indeed found. That dramatic historical episode makes the hypothesized deterrent effect of a ten mile bus trip to the suburbs in search of a job appear a little thin. We still do not have convincing analyses as to why relatively low income minorities have not followed jobs to suburbs in larger numbers.

So far, it has been shown that population and employment suburbanization have been massive in the United States during the last half century. Basic theoretical models provide plausible reasons, which not all scholars find persuasive, to expect voluntary income segregation, with income levels generally increasing with distance from the CBD. The massive suburbanization of employment and population reinforce each other, but employment suburbanization should be expected to reduce segregation by income, not increase it, although segregation by income has actually increased. Edge city employment clusters are small suburban CBDs, and the conditions that generate income segregation by distance from the CBD should also generate income segregation by distance from suburban employment clusters; but the suburbs as a whole should have greater proportions of low income workers the greater is employment suburbanization. Thus, substantial and increasing income segregation between suburbs and inner cities remains a mystery.

Almost no one believes that the concentration of low income population and social pathology in inner cities is entirely voluntary. The issue is in what sense and for what reasons it is involuntary. A large and disparate literature has appeared on the subject. (See Mieszkowski and Mills, 1993, for a brief survey.) The basic idea of this analysis, which I will refer to somewhat inaccurately as the "flight-from-blight" model, can be stated briefly. Perhaps for the reasons previously discussed, relatively high income residents are the first to move from inner cities to suburbs as MSAs grow and expand beyond inner city boundaries. It is important to note that flight-from-blight may have been among the reasons for the early exodus of high income residents from inner cities. Between the 1920s and the 1960s there was a massive migration of low income black citizens from the rural south, mostly to inner cities in the north. For a variety of reasons, probably including those discussed above, most settled near CBDs of inner cities. The result has been higher crime rates, poorer schools, and more turmoil in inner cities since the early postwar years and even before the war. Indeed, net migration of low income minorities into inner cities has continued to the present, although most such migrants have been Hispanics, not blacks, since about the mid-1970s.

Whatever the weights to be given to the causes, large numbers of middle and upper middle income whites have moved from inner cities for at least half a century, and nearly all MSA population growth has taken place in suburbs. Some suburban communities were already incorporated, but suburban residents obtained incorporation for many others in order to provide local government services. Considerable sorting of residents by demand for local government services, willingness to pay local taxes, and income, followed. The sorting process has led to the enormous literature referred to as the Tiebout Theory and Club Theory. People vote on local issues with both their feet and their ballots, not to mention with lobbying. Tiebout and Club models hypothesize that in equilibrium sub-urban voters sort themselves into communities in each of which voters have similar demands for housing and local government services (and willingness to pay taxes to produce the services). How closely the actual distribution of residents among suburban communities approximates the Tiebout hypothesis characterization is debatable, but there can be no doubt that the sorting by Tiebout-like mechanisms has been considerable in suburbs. On strong assumptions, a Tiebout equilibrium is socially efficient, or nearly so at least among voluntary location patterns, but few scholars regard it as equitable. Certainly, most inner cities cannot be regarded as approximations to Tiebout equilibria. They exhibit considerably more earnings inequality than do typical suburbs. More important, in most analyses, Tiebout-like suburban communities cannot engage in substantial income redis-tribution, which must be left to state or national governments.

Why have low income black residents actually or potentially eligible for jobs that have moved to suburbs not followed such jobs to suburbs? Some have, but most have not. The reasons are complex and only imperfectly understood. First, the poorest inner city residents receive substantial parts of their incomes from government transfers and many would do so even if they lived in suburbs, under existing eligibility criteria. Whether stiffer eligibility criteria being proposed, especially since fall 1994, would increase labor force participation of transfer recipients and induce significant numbers to move to suburbs is an open question. At present, inner city residents mostly dependent on transfers have little reason to migrate to suburbs. Highly subsidized dwellings and facilities that disburse transfer payments and services are likely to be more accessible in poor inner city neighborhoods. The group at issue here can be approximately character-ized as the actual or potential "working-poor."

One important reason that the working poor have not followed jobs to suburbs in larger numbers than they have is racial discrimination and hostility in suburban housing and employment. Both kinds of discrimination have been historically documented. Both have been illegal since the mid-1960s and have certainly become much less virulent since then. Nevertheless, a series of reports concludes that racial discrimination in the sale, rental, and financing of housing has continued into the 1990s. Analyses in the 1990s have benefited from much larger and more detailed data sets collected by government agencies, than were available in earlier years. Alicia Munnell et al. (1996) analyzed Boston data and concluded that minority mortgage applications were approved much less frequently than other applications even if income, wealth, and credit history were taken into account. James Berkovec et al. (1996) analyzed a massive FHA data set and concluded that blacks have higher default rates than whites even taking into account a richer set of characteristics data than Munnell had available. Both studies have been criticized (see the comments by John Quigley and others in the issue of *Cityscape* in which the Berkovec et al. paper appeared). John Yinger (1995) has analyzed results of audits in applications to buy or rent dwellings. Audits assemble pairs of black and white applicants artificially matched by characteristics and record carefully approval rates and other ways that applicants are received. Several careful audits have been executed and all conclude that racial discrimination in the sale and rental of housing has persisted into the 1990s. Audits provide excellent evidence in civil and criminal suits regarding housing discrimination. Whatever their deepest feelings may be, it is ironic that those charged with renting and selling dwellings continue to risk subjecting themselves to ruinous civil and criminal suits. A recent study by Joseph Gyourko, Peter Linneman, and Susan Wachter (1996) concludes that there are no racial differences in homeownership rates among those who are similarly qualified and who can meet underwriting requirements for downpayments and closing costs. However, among those who are downpayment constrained, minority ownership rates are lower than those of whites.

What is the nonspecialist to make of the recent welter of conclusions? Analyses of mortgage approval and default rates appear to have reached the point of strained differences, without firm conclusions. Audit analyses, however, appear to have conclusions that are as definitive as those of laboratory experiments.

The intellectual trip from dozens of housing audits to minority suburbanization is quite long. Some audits have been conducted in inner cities, although most have presumably been conducted in suburbs. In addition, there is no easy correlation between discrimination revealed by audits and failure of minorities to locate suburban housing. Undoubtedly, the more adverse treatment minorities receive from housing agents, the thicker skinned they must be to find adequate suburban housing. Each person has a limit as to how long he is willing to persist in the face of mistreatment. Finally, minorities may interpret mistreatment by agents as forecasts of mistreatment by neighbors, and that may be intentional on the part of agents.

Tiebout (see David Wildasin, 1987, for a survey) did not include land use controls in his model. However, Hamilton (1976) and others, including Mills (1979), have claimed that land use controls are employed to prevent people with low incomes and modest housing demands from residing in suburban communities that are dominated by higher income residents who suburbanized earlier and for whom the land use controls are mostly not binding. Lower income people might inhabit modest housing in such communities, pay the modest taxes that local tax rates would imply for them and consume the education and other local government services that the higher taxes paid by the higher income majority can provide. Suburban real estate taxes are not necessarily lower relative to dwelling values than inner city taxes, but a modest dwelling located in a high income suburb would pay less taxes than the cost of the high quality local government services that can be provided in the jurisdiction. In addition, because income is correlated with skin color, exclusion of low income people also excludes minorities who may be regarded as undesirable, either because of their skin color or because their children are expensive to educate.

This is the "free-loader" problem and land use controls can provide an approximate solution to it. Communities cannot legally zone out low income or minority people, but they can and do zone out the only housing such groups can afford. Many suburban communities zone out multi-family housing and place severe restrictions on single-family detached units: minimum lot size, set-backs, minimum square feet of floor space, architectural controls, etc. A host of studies shows that the benefits of high quality schools, security, and exclusiveness are capitalized into land values in suburban communities.

The result is to enable communities to exclude people by income level with considerable precision. With a few pyrotechnic, but practically minor, exceptions, the courts have not interfered with exclusionary controls by communities.[12] Although exclusionary zoning is more genteel than burning crosses on minorities' lawns, the result is equally coercive.

Flight-from-blight is thought by many writers to be self-reinforcing. The more higher income people leave inner cities for suburbs, the worse the concentration of poverty and social pathology in inner cities becomes. And the worse inner cities become, the more higher income residents move to suburbs. Nevertheless, the facts are that most MSAs have some highly exclusionary suburbs but also many suburban communities that place no more than minimal restrictions on housing.

This tidy analysis has recently been brought into question in an important paper by Dennis Epple and others (see Glenn Cassidy and Epple, 1994, and references therein). Their analysis is nonspatial. A fixed and finite number of communities, say N, is big enough to house a fixed and exogenous number of MSA residents. The MSA income distribution is exogenous. MSA residents are mobile among the communities and choose their community of residence in Tiebout-like fashion so as to maximize personal utility. Housing is built endogenously to house workers who choose to reside in each community. Land values and therefore housing costs are endogenous. In each community, the two parameters of a linear (in income) local government tax-transfer function are chosen by the median voter among the equilibrium residents.[13] There are no land use or other controls on places of residence. Cassidy and Epple prove the following remarkable result: in equilibrium, the N communities can be numbered from one to N in such a way that the nth community contains a continuous segment of the MSA income distribution, incomes rise monotonically with the number assigned to the community, residents at the ends of the income distribution segment within the nth community are indifferent between living in it and the $(n - 1)$th or $(n + 1)$th community, and no resident wants to live in any other community. In other words, segregation by income among communities is voluntary and complete. The intuition is that in perfect Tiebout equilibrium, the median voter chooses a tax-transfer function that makes the community the optimum residence for a continuous segment of the MSA income distribution. Whether the equilibrium is socially efficient is an open issue; it presumably is among noncoercive allocations of residents to communities. The paper is remarkable in that it implies perfect and voluntary income segregation among suburban communities in a model without land use controls and with a median voter-controlled local government.

Inner cities and suburban communities do not actually consist of single segments of the MSA income distribution, as the Cassidy–Epple model implies. Bringing into the model the fact that MSA residents are by no means indifferent as to the locations of their residences would vastly complicate the model, but presumably would help to account for the mixtures of incomes within communities. In addition, land use controls on residences certainly exist, and are fought over bitterly not only in suburbs but also even in inner cities. Why are land use controls guarded so jealously if lower income people stay away voluntarily? The Cassidy–Epple paper reopens the question. One possible answer is that residents want land use controls because they do not understand the force of voluntary segregation, or because they want to reinforce the effects of voluntary segregation. A second answer may be that residents place value on kinds of residential conformity within a community that are not guaranteed by similarity of incomes. A third may be that controls reinforce each other; if many nearby communities have controls, each perhaps having relatively small distorting effects on the Cassidy–Epple outcome, it may be dangerous to be the only high income community without controls. A fourth is that, in MSAs where employment is dominated by suburban clusters, spatial considerations may so dominate residential choices that land use controls are crucial to the protection of community homogeneity. Some combination of the four explanations may be correct.

The conclusions of this section can be summarized easily. Suburbanization of people and production has occurred naturally as MSAs have grown, real incomes have risen, and as both intra- and inter-MSA transportation have improved. It is also natural that relatively high income residents have suburbanized first and most. Contrary to the formal analysis, employment suburbanization has not shortened commuting distances in general, and low earnings minority workers have not moved close to suburban jobs in as large numbers as might be expected. One common explanation for the slowness of minority workers to suburbanize is racial discrimination in suburban housing and employment, but it is difficult to believe that racial discrimination remains a powerful force.[14] A second explanation is that suburban land use controls exclude low income residents from suburban communities. However, the Cassidy–Epple analysis implies that residents segregate themselves voluntarily by income among suburban communities, even in the absence of land use controls. Presumably, land use controls reinforce the tendency to voluntary segregation, but the conceptual analyses do not appear to add up to a satisfactory explanation of the strong and increasing segmentation of U.S. MSAs by income. In most MSAs, a few high income suburbs have powerful and exclusionary land use controls, but many provide only minimal restrictions on housing.

3. Introduction to Inner City Problems

This section provides a systematic introduction to inner city problems that have been referred to in cavalier fashion in the previous section.

It is not intended in this paper to provide an etiology of socio-economic problems. That task would go far beyond the goals of this paper and would be inconclusive because of conflicting theories, data, techniques of analysis, and conclusions of analysts. Instead, the goal is to indicate the differences in the incidence of socio-economic problems between MSA inner cities and suburbs. In addition, evidence will be reviewed as to the extent to which socio-economic problems are worsened by their concentration in inner cities. Socio-economic problems and the literature that addresses them are too complex to be addressed here. Our goal is to document and interpret information related to their spatial patterns.

The first question is what problems are to be the focus of the discussion. As a practical matter the choice is relatively easy. There is a long history of systematic analysis by social scientists of socio-economic problems. Interacting with that analysis is a history of data collection and publication regarding such problems. Choice of problems to discuss is dictated by the set of problems that specialists have analyzed and that governments have documented. In recent years, this *Journal* has published several surveys of positive and normative analysis of a range of problems that define inner city-suburban differences and that have interested economists and other social scientists.[15] Although some surveys refer to inner city concentrations of problems, spatial incidence within MSAs is not the focus of any of the surveys. Such surveys do, however, define relevant problems and provide important background analyses.

Based on the foregoing criteria, attention will be focused on health and vital statistics, poverty and income distribution, housing, crime, and local government finances and services. No attempt will be made here to provide comprehensive data on the incidences of these problems in inner cities and suburbs. Instead, the goal will be to provide enough data to indicate how bad the plights of inner city residents are relative to those of suburban residents. Indeed, it will be found that most data tell a consistent story.

Although poverty and income distribution are by no means sufficient statistics as measures of well being, they are correlated with virtually every other measure. In addition, they are well documented and well studied, so considerable emphasis will be placed on them. Health and vital statistics are perhaps the most important measures of well being and they are only imperfectly correlated with income. Real housing consumption is strongly correlated with income, so it will not be discussed in detail. Crime is the social pathology most strongly associated with inner cities in the minds of many. In addition, data are plentiful, although controversial as to accuracy. Finally, local government finances are well documented and studied in the United States. Local government service qualities, especially public schools, are widely thought to be much better in suburbs than in inner cities, although school quality is notoriously difficult to measure.

Social scientists are honor bound to state that more and better data are needed, and that is certainly true of the subjects of this essay. Nevertheless, an enormous volume of data is available for both domestic and international comparisons. It is unlikely that more data would alter the basic conclusions.

It is widely appreciated that the United States suffers in comparison with other industrialized countries in almost every measure of social well being. Although almost no other countries present such data by inner city and suburb or by race, it will be useful to start with a brief set of international comparisons. That will place bounds on the United States inner city-suburb comparisons, and will permit at least crude estimates as to what parts of the U.S. problems are really racial problems and what parts are broader social problems. We thus start, in the next section, with a brief international comparison.

The two criteria for choice of data to study – data availability and professional opinion as to importance of specific problems – interact. Especially in the United States, social scientists and those directly concerned with government policy have a substantial influence on what data are collected and published by government agencies.

4. A Brief International Comparison[16]

This section provides a brief international comparison of easily and widely available measures of social ills. The purpose of the presentation is to place bounds on the extent to which high United States incidences of social ills are associated with inner city problems. Data are first presented to demonstrate how much worse United States measures are than those in other countries. International data are not presented for inner cities. However, most United States data are presented by race. It is thus possible to make comparisons between measures for other countries and those for whites in the United States. Because blacks are heavily concentrated in U.S. inner cities, the comparison will indicate whether adverse U.S. measures are mostly associated with racial disparities in the United States. Then, in the next section, comparisons will be made for U.S. data by race and by inner city and suburban residence.

It is pointless to compare U.S. measures with those in much lower income countries. Most measures of well being are at least moderately correlated with per capita income, and U.S. measures inevitably compare well with those in countries whose per capita incomes are no more than a small fraction of the United States level. The comparison is thus restricted to OECD countries, the 23 countries with about the world's highest per capita incomes. Using the World Bank's Purchasing Power Parity measure of income, income per capita nevertheless varies by a factor of three or four in recent years among the 23 OECD countries. All the data reported in this section are from OECD, United Nations, and World Bank publications. The sources present average data for two periods involving many years, the 25–30 years and the 15–20 years ending about 1990, depending on data availability. Comparison between the two averages provides an index of progress with the social indicators that is not accounted for by increases in per capita income.

Table 1 shows the data analyzed in this section. The social indicators included are shown at the tops of columns. For each country, the first line shows data for the longer period and the second line shows data for the shorter and more recent period. Inspection of the table makes clear that the U.S. performance is among the worst of the countries included for most of the social indicators. To make the comparisons more precise, each of the social indicators was regressed on a plausible set of determinants, in each case including GDP per capita, percent of the population that is urban, and a dummy that is one for the more recent period. In the regressions related to health and mortality indicators, doctors/1000 population was included as an explanatory variable. Only GDP per capita and the time dummy have coefficients that tend to be significant, so regressions that include other independent variables are not shown. Also, it should be noted that the low birth weight,[17] illegitimacy, and all three crime-related regressions have positive GDP coefficients, so the United States ranking is better using the regressions than those using the raw data for those dependent variables.

Results are shown in Table 2. For each regression and each country, the ratio of the realized value of the social indicator to the value calculated from the sample regression was calculated. The table shows the United States rank for that statistic. The rank and ratio calculations are carried out just for the more recent period, i.e., when the dummy takes the value one. The intuition for the statistic is that it indicates how much better or worse the country performed than would be predicted by the determinants included in the regression. In other words, the calculation indicates how the United States compares with other sample countries in terms of how far its social indicators are from values that are predicted from the independent variables in the regressions.

The dummy coefficients show that, for most measures, progress during the 30 year period has exceeded what can be explained by the independent variables included. The

Table 1 International social indicators data

Country	GDP per Capita	Life Expectancy	Urban Share of Population	Share of Income of bottom 20%	Ratio Population per Doctor	Ratio Pupil to Teacher	% of Pupils Reaching Grade 4
USA	3,650*	70	0.719	4	670	29	
	7,400	73	0.737	4		23	95
Australia	2,090	71	0.83	7	720	28	
	7,110	73	0.859			21	76
Japan	900	70	0.673	5	970	29	
	4,520	74	0.757			26	100
New Zealand	2,120	71	0.789		820	22	
	4,620	72	0.828	8		18	
Austria	1,270	70	0.508		720	20	
	4,730	71	0.532			19	94
Belgium	1,730	71	0.934		700	21	
	5,930	72	0.946			19	80
Denmark	2,060	73	0.77	4	740	11	
	6,900	74	0.818	7		8	100
Finland	1,760	69	0.439	3	1300	23	
	5,390	72	0.583	7		19	98
France	2,030	71	0.671	2	830	30	87
	5,980	73	0.73	5		23	94
Germany	1,930	70	0.78	6	680	27	91
	6,670	71	0.81	7		23	100
Iceland	2,290	73	0.827			22	
	6,350	75	0.868			19	100
Ireland	920	71	0.487		950	33	
	2,640	72	0.536	7		31	99
Italy	1,260	70	0.618		1854	22	
	3,690	73	0.656	6		19	
Luxembourg	2,090	69	0.63			24	
	7,460	71	0.737			19	90
Netherlands	1,610	74	0.856	4	850	19	
	6,140	74	0.884	9		16	98
Norway	1,840	74	0.576	5	790	21	
	6,600	75	0.682			8	99
Spain	710	71	0.613	6	800	34	
	2,770	73	0.696	6		21	95
Sweden	2,760	74	0.771	5	910	20	
	8,300	75	0.827	7		20	99
Switzerland	2,380	72	0.528		710		
	7,940	75	0.557				93
U.K.	1,830	71	0.871	7	870	25	
	3,900	72	0.887			20	
Canada	2,620	72	0.729	7	770	26	
	7,250	73	0.756	4		10	96
Greece	700	70	0.475		710	35	
	2,370	73	0.553		600	30	96
Portugal	410	65	0.239	6	1240	32	
	1,540	69	0.277	7	1061	20	91

*   1st row: 25 to 30 years ending about 1990; 2nd row: 15 to 20 years ending about 1990.

Table 1 (*Cont.*)

Country	Infant Mortality in 1991	% of Low Birth Weight Babies in 1990	Homicide Rates in 1975 and 1986	Prisoner Rates in 1975 and 1986	Drug Crime Rates in 1975 and 1980	Illegitimate Birth Rates 1975 and 1985 in % of Births
			(per 100,000 persons)			
USA	8.9	7	9	374	278	11
			9	381	234	25
Australia	7.1	6				
Japan	4.6	6				
New Zealand	8.3	6	1	175	94	4
			2			4
Austria	7.4	6	3			
			2	167		
Belgium	8.4	6	1	139		3
			3	149		7
Denmark	7.5	6			73	
			1		94	
Finland	5.8	4				
France	7.3	5	1	98	7	9
			4	83	20	
Germany	7.1		4	172		8
			4	153		13
Iceland	5.5					
Ireland	8.2	4	1	47	9	
				28		5
Italy	8.3	5	3	104	6	8
			4	43	14	
Luxembourg	9.2					
Netherlands	6.5					
Norway	7	4				
Spain	7.8	4	0	42	4	6
			2		15	
Sweden	6.1	5			269	
Switzerland	6.2	5				
U.K.	7.4	7	2	102		9
			1	129		
Canada	6.8	6	3	64	244	7
			2		306	
Greece	9	6	1	60		
			2	78		13
Portugal	10.8	5				

Sources:
- Social Indicators of Development 1993, World Bank.
- Report on the World Social Situation 1993, United Nations.
- Several World Development Reports, World bank.
- Several OECD Economic Surveys Reports, OECD.

Table 2 Regressions for international social indicators data

	Infant Mortality in 1991	Life Expectancy	Pupil per Teacher Ratio	% of Low Birth Weight Babies ('90)	Homicides Rates in '75 and '86	Prisoners Rates in '75 and '86	Drugs Crimes Rates in '75 and '80	Illegitimate Birth Rates '75 and '85
Constant	32.1	71.3	24.3	−3.07	−6.4E-16	1.49E-15	−4.5E-16	−8.6E-16
	(9.92)	(.295)	(1.11)	(7.64°)	(.189°)	(.201°)	(.189°)	(.26°)
Log GDP	−2.54	0.556	−2.36	0.88	0.461	0.557	0.683	0.347
	(1.02)	(.209)	(.786)	(.79°)	(0.189)	(.201)	(.189)	(.26°)
Dummy		1.71	−5.2					
		(.417)	(1.57)					
R^2	0.19	0.349	0.315	0.013	0.177	0.27	0.431	0.053
F-stat	6.17	12	9.96	1.24	5.95	7.65	13.1	1.78
Prob(F-stat)	0.02	0.00	0.00	.28°	0.024	0.014	0.003	0.209
D.F	21	39	37	17	22	17	15	13
U.S. ratio	1.3451	0.9926	1.3863	1.2216	2.1768	1.8225	0.8701	1.6537
Rank U.S.	2	7	1	3	2	2	3	2
out of	23	21	20	19	12	8	8	6

The standard deviations of the estimates are shown in parentheses. The ° indicates failure to be significant at 10%. Log GDP was used for infant mortality, life expectancy, and pupil/teacher. Standardized Log GDP was used for the rest. Ranking is from the worst standing to the best. The larger ranking numbers indicate better performance.

adjusted R^2s indicate that GDP and the time dummy are far from the complete set of variables that determine values of the social indicators. By almost every social indicator, the United States has almost the worst rank of its performance relative to the prediction on the basis of the independent variables.

It is easy to show that, for most social indicators, the poor U.S. performance relates strongly to the racial composition of the population. Comparing data for the white U.S. population with national data for other OECD countries yields the following results: for life expectancy, the United States ranks third from the best; for the incidences of low birth weight, illegitimacy, and infant mortality, it is in the middle of the OECD ranking; for the homicide rate, the United States is still the worst among the OECD countries.[18] Thus, for one of the social measures, the white U.S. population ranks among the most favorable measures in the OECD; for three, it is near the middle; and for one, it has the worst measure. Thus, a substantial part, but by no means all, of the poor U.S. performance is racially correlated.

5. Comparisons Among U.S. National, Inner City, and Suburban Trends

This section begins with a brief survey of national trends in poverty and other forms of social distress. It then turns to a more detailed analysis of inner city-suburban trends and differences.

Table 3 presents data for U.S. trends in the social indicators that were analyzed in Table 2. The first two columns show real GDP per capita and its annual compound growth rates between the adjacent years indicated. The dramatic deceleration of the

United States real growth rate is well known. (If first quarter 1990 to first quarter 1995 is used for the 1990s figure, the annual growth rate is 1.3 percent instead of the 1.0 percent shown.) It is also well known that the poverty rate fell rapidly from 1959 (the first year for which the official index was calculated) until the early 1970s and that it has risen since then. Indeed the incidence of poverty decreased every year from 1959 to 1969, increased in the early 1970s, dropped to its lowest point ever in 1973, trended upward until 1983, fell each year from 1983 to 1989, and has risen steadily since then.[19] The deceleration in per capita real income growth was accompanied by a widening in the earnings distribution since the mid-1970s. Trends in other social indicators are mixed. Life expectancy has increased steadily, the homicide rate is trendless, infant mortality has fallen steadily and dramatically, the incidences of prisoners and drug arrests have increased alarmingly, active physicians per capita have increased rapidly, illegitimacy has soared, the incidence of low birth weight babies has increased, and pupils per teacher have decreased.

It is well known that incidences of social ills are much higher among blacks than among whites. Table 4 presents some comparisons. U.S. blacks have always had lower per capita incomes than whites. Many studies have shown what the first column of Table 4 confirms, that the gap has narrowed since 1960. The black–white ratio was .539 in 1960 and .641 in 1990. Indeed, the ratio narrowed even during the 1980s, when overall earnings inequality increased, the black–white ratio having been .580 in 1980.

Racial differences between poverty rates have not narrowed, however. Black poverty incidences have exceeded three times those of whites during the 30-year period. Until the

Table 3 U.S. economics and social indicators for selected years, 1960–1994

Year	Real GDP per capita (000 dollars)	Real GDP Annual Growth	Poverty (% of Population)	Life Expectancy (Years)	Homicides (per 100,000 Population)	Infant Mortality (per 1,000 live births)
1960	11.2		22.2			
		2.3				
1970	14.0		12.6	70.8	9.0 (1972)	20.0
		1.8				
1980	16.6		13.0	73.7	10.2	12.6
		1.7				
1990	19.6		13.5	75.4	9.4	9.2
		1.0				
1994	20.5		15.1 (1993)	75.7 (1992)	9.8 (1992)	8.9 (1991)
34 year period		1.9				
1970	96.7	1.52	26.4		22.4	
1980	139.2	1.82	29.4	6.8	18.6	256
1990	295.0	2.19	43.8		16.9	435
1994	330.2 (1992)	2.27 (1992)	45.2 (1991)	7.1 (1991)	17.0 (1992)	401 (1991)

Sources: Economic Report of the President, Poverty in the United States, Statistical Abstract of the United States, Uniform Crime Statistics.

1990s the black incidence fell each decade, whereas the white incidence increased after 1970. These data indicate that the growth in income inequality has characterized both races. Life expectancy has increased steadily for both races, and the gap has narrowed slightly. The percent of the adult population that has attended four years of high school has increased rapidly for both racial groups, dramatically for blacks.

Black illegitimacy rates have been much higher than those of whites throughout the period covered by the table and reached the alarming rate of two-thirds by 1991.[20] Infant mortality rates fell steadily and substantially for both races during the 21 years covered by the table, but the black–white ratio increased during the period. The United States government does not publish data on the races of those who commit crimes, because criminals' races may be unknown or uncertain.[21] The FBI *Uniform Crime Reports* do, however, publish arrest rates by race for recent years. For 1991 the ratio of total arrest rates relative to the sizes of the racial groups was about 2.5 times as great for blacks as for whites. For homicide arrests, the ratio was greater than 8.

Freeman (1994) has compiled data from several sources and reports some of the most extraordinary social data ever assembled. Define "under supervision of the criminal justice system" as people incarcerated, on probation, or on parole. His subject is labor market effects, so he reports data as percentages of the number of the relevant group that is in the labor force. For all males, those under the supervision of the criminal justice system are 6.6 percent of the male labor force. For males 18–34 years old, the figure is 11 percent. For all black males 18–34 years old, the figure is 59.4 percent. Those figures should bring tears to the eyes of the most cynical criminologist. Of course, some people under the supervision of the criminal justice system are also in the labor force, and some are employed. The figures are presented by Freeman to show that male criminality is likely to have large labor force effects, but they also represent an appalling social commentary.

We turn now to inner city-suburban comparisons. The percentage of the U.S. population that is black has risen slowly in recent decades, from 11.7 in 1980 to 12.1 in 1990. The

Table 4   Racial Comparisons of U.S. Economic and Social Indicators

Year	Real Income per capita (000 dollars)		Poverty Rate (Percent)		Life Expectancy (Year)		Educational Attainment (Percent of population 25 and older completed 4 years of high school)		Illegitimacy (Percent of all births in groups)		Infant Mortality (per 1,000 births)	
	Black	White	Black	White	Black	White	Black	White	Black	White	Black	White
1960	5.5	10.2	55.1	17.8			20.1	43.2				
	(1967)		(1959)									
1970	6.3	11.3	33.5	9.9	65.3	71.7	31.4	54.5	38.0	6.0	32.6	17.8
1980	7.6	13.1	32.5	10.2	69.5	74.4	51.2	66.8	55.0	11.0	21.4	11.0
1990	9.8	15.3	31.9	10.7	71.2	76.1	66.2	79.1	65.0	20.0	18.0	7.6
1994			33.3	11.6	71.8	76.5	70.4	81.5	68.0	22.0	17.6	7.3
			(1992)		(1992)		(1993)		(1991)		(1991)	

Sources: See Table 3.

percentage of the MSA population that is black has also risen slowly, from 12.7 in 1980 to 13.7 in 1990. The percentage of inner city populations that is black has risen at about the same rate, from 22.5 in 1980 to 23.6 in 1990. Thus, the percentages of MSA and inner city populations that are black have risen about in proportion to their slight percentage increase in the national population. Net inmigration of blacks to MSAs and inner cities has virtually ceased since about the mid-1970s. The key observation is that twice as many whites live in suburbs as in inner cities, whereas half as many blacks live in suburbs as in inner cities. That fact, in addition to the large disparities in economic and social indicators between the races that have already been presented, makes certain that large inner city-suburban disparities will also be found. In addition, high income people of both races tend to locate in suburbs much more than low income people.

It must be emphasized that U.S. suburbs are by no means any longer "lily white." Of the 27 million blacks who live in MSAs, one-third live in suburbs (1992). A few suburban places, illustrated by Prince Georges county, a Maryland suburb of Washington, D.C., are predominantly black. But at least a sprinkling of blacks live in most suburban communities.

If residents suburbanize in decreasing order of their incomes, then mean suburban income exceeds mean inner city income regardless of the percentages of the MSA population that live in suburbs and central cities. Suburban/inner city income disparities are greatest when a very small or very large percentage of the MSA population lives in suburbs. The ratio of suburban to central city mean income is smallest when the population is divided about equally between central city and suburbs. (The income ratio would be minimized at an exactly even central city/suburban population division if the MSA income distribution were symmetrical.)

The implication is that differences between black and white suburban/central city ratios must be interpreted with care. If high income people suburbanize before low income people and regardless of race, then, given that whites' average income is higher than blacks, whites will be more suburbanized than blacks and, in the vicinity of a 50/50 white suburban/inner city division, whites' suburban/inner city income disparities will be smaller than blacks. The result implies nothing about racial discrimination in suburban housing or employment.

Table 5 (Tables 5–7 are data from the 1990 census) shows per capita income of whites and blacks in inner cities for the United States and for nine Census regions. For whites, suburban incomes exceed those in inner cities by only five percent, whereas for blacks suburban incomes are 25 percent greater than those in inner cities. These ratios presumably reflect the more nearly even distribution of whites than blacks between suburbs and inner cities, with the effect suggested in the previous paragraph, and perhaps the greater use of suburban locations by whites than by blacks, especially those of modest incomes. For whites, suburban incomes exceed those in inner cities in only five of the nine regions, whereas black suburban incomes are greater in all regions. For both races, the largest suburban-inner city disparities are found in the northeastern and industrial north central regions. Reasons for this regional pattern are unknown.

The 1990 Census presents a remarkably rich data set classified by race and by location of residence within MSAs. Table 6 shows data on percentage of adult residents who have obtained a bachelor's degree, in the same format as Table 5. By this measure, white inner city residents are better educated than their suburban counterparts not only for the

Table 5   U.S. and regional 1990 income per capita of whites and blacks, inner cities, and suburbs

(Per Capita Income)

Region	Inner City		Suburbs	
	White	*Black*	*White*	*Black*
United States	16,424	8,713	17,326	10,934
New England	16,297	10,224	19,988	14,890
Middle Atlantic	18,000	9,736	18,462	12,716
East North Central	14,369	8,266	16,811	11,808
West North Central	14,530	7,798	16,369	11,338
South Atlantic	17,478	8,561	17,283	10,540
East South Central	15,518	7,137	17,730	7,401
West South Central	15,615	7,432	14,549	8,226
Mountain	15,081	9,614	15,132	10,512
Pacific	18,628	10,876	18,573	12,423

Source for Tables 5–7: 1990 U.S. Census of Population, Washington, D.C. U.S. Dept. of Commerce, Economics and Statistics, 1992.

country as a whole but also for six of the nine regions, indeed for all regions except the two northeastern and the eastern part of the industrial north central region. That is certainly contrary to popular impressions. Blacks fit the popular impression much better than whites, as suburbanites are better educated for the country as a whole and for all regions except the east south central.

Table 7 shows 1970 poverty rates in the same format. For the U.S., black poverty rates are, and have been for several decades, two to three times those of whites. Again perhaps contrary to popular impression, for the country as a whole, the relative poverty incidence in inner cities to suburbs is somewhat greater for whites than for blacks. These patterns vary somewhat among regions.

Dividing MSAs into four size categories – less than 250,000, between 250,000 and 500,000, between 500,000 and 1,000,000, and greater than 1,000,000 – nearly every statistic varies systematically by MSA size. The percentage of the population that is white decreases and the percentage that is black increases as MSA size increases for MSAs, inner cities and suburbs; the poverty rate decreases uniformly as MSA size increases for both races and in both inner cities and suburbs; per capita income increases with MSA size in all four racial-locational categories; and commuting times (not available by race) increase uniformly with MSA size in MSAs, inner cities and suburbs. Although the percentage of the population with a bachelor's degree generally increases with MSA size in all four racial–locational categories, the increases are not all monotonic in MSA size. They are monotonic for both races in suburbs, but not in inner cities.

Everyone knows that crime rates are greater in inner cities than in suburbs.[22] The FBI's index of crimes known to the police shows that the incidence of crimes is about twice as great in inner cities as in suburbs. Inner city residents are about five times as likely to be homicide victims as suburban residents. Nationwide, blacks are nearly ten times as likely as whites to be homicide victims. Homicides are not only the most serious crimes, but are also the crime for which police records are likely to be most accurate.

Table 6 U.S. and regional percentage of adult residents with bachelor's degrees, 1990

Region	Inner City		Suburbs	
	White	Black	White	Black
United States	17.7	7.5	16.5	10.9
New England	15.9	8.1	20.4	15.0
Middle Atlantic	15.1	7.5	16.5	10.9
East North Central	14.5	5.9	14.9	11.4
West North Central	18.5	7.2	18.1	13.5
South Atlantic	19.1	7.5	16.5	10.8
East South Central	17.7	7.8	12.3	7.0
West South Central	19.8	8.2	15.6	10.0
Mountain	19.1	9.8	17.4	11.7
Pacific	20.0	9.8	17.4	11.9

Source: See Table 5.

Table 7 U.S. and regional poverty rates, 1990

Region	Inner City		Suburbs	
	White	Black	White	Black
United States	12.0	31.1	6.6	19.5
New England	10.5	24.5	4.4	9.4
Middle Atlantic	13.1	27.7	5.4	15.3
East North Central	12.9	35.1	5.6	19.0
West North Central	11.1	34.7	5.5	17.3
South Atlantic	10.3	29.7	6.7	18.6
East South Central	11.0	34.7	9.9	31.7
West South Central	14.3	35.2	10.4	29.3
Mountain	11.8	27.0	8.0	20.5
Pacific	11.0	24.4	7.6	16.2

Source: See Table 5.

The easy conclusion is that inner city, especially minority, residents have lower incomes and more social problems than suburban residents by almost every available measure.

Until now, almost nothing has been said about the roles of governments in MSAs. It is widely appreciated that local governments provide most of the government services that have immediate impacts on residents' lives: public education, police and fire protection, local criminal justice, some health services, public transportation, water and sanitation, and some transfer payments.

A considerable literature exists on expenditures and taxes of local governments in MSA inner cities compared with suburbs. General magnitudes can be summarized briefly.[23] Total local government spending is about 50 percent more per capita in inner cities than in suburbs. Inner city governments spend more per capita than suburban governments on every major service category except public education, on which per capita spending is similar. The inner city–suburban disparity in per capita spending increased considerably from the 1950s to the 1980s. Per capita local government taxes are about 25 percent greater in inner cities than in suburbs. Because incomes are lower in inner cities, the disparities in both expenditures and taxes per dollar of residents' incomes are greater than the disparities per capita. The tax disparity narrowed between the 1950s and the 1980s. Excesses of local government expenditures over taxes are made up mostly by transfers from federal and state governments, and local governments in inner cities receive about 53 percent more per capita in such transfers than suburban governments receive.

Although local taxes per resident are greater in inner cities than in suburbs, it is not clear that taxes per resident levied on residents are greater. By far the largest local tax in MSAs is the property tax. About half of MSA employment is in inner cities, but only one-third of MSA residents live in inner cities. Thus, nonresidential real estate per capita is greater in inner cities than in suburbs. Because most commercial real estate is subject to local real estate taxes (in many inner cities at higher percentages of market value than residences), a larger fraction of real estate taxes must be levied on commercial property, and a smaller fraction on residences, in inner cities than in suburbs.[24] Why do local governments spend more per capita and relative to residents' incomes in inner cities than in suburbs? The accounting answer is that they spend more because federal and state government transfers enable them to spend more. The deeper answer is that federal and state transfers are greater because people are needier and social problems are worse in inner cities than in suburbs. It is patent that federal and state transfers have not eliminated the gaps in income and social problems between inner cities and suburbs or between blacks and whites during the last 30 years. Whatever the combination of reasons, most measures of the gaps between blacks and whites have narrowed, but most measures of the gaps between inner cities and suburbs have widened, during the period in which government spending on poverty and social problems has been large and rising.

The most important question that can be asked about government spending in inner cities is whether it has been effective. The issues are beyond the scope of this paper, and only peripheral comments will be made here.

First, the fact that inner city–suburban gaps have widened despite higher government spending in inner cities does not imply that inner city spending has been ineffective. Government spending should help people, not places, and blacks who have benefited from government spending in inner cities may have moved to suburbs, reducing black–white gaps but increasing blacks' inner city–suburb gaps. It is the fact that poverty rates remain high and that so many indexes of social problems have worsened during the last 30 years that makes skeptics doubt the efficacy of government spending.[25] The bothersome aspect of the local government inner city–suburban nexus is not on the tax side. Although inner city taxes per capita are higher, taxes per resident levied on residences are probably no more than negligibly higher in inner cities than in suburbs. Instead, the skeptics' weapon is that the ostensible quality of local government services is demonstrably worse. Public schools, crime, health, and poverty are patently worse in inner cities than in suburbs, despite greater local government spending on most such problems in inner cities.

Debate remains lively in part because the ostensible measures of the quality of local government services are not appropriate measures. Children of poor or poorly educated parents or of single parent families are more expensive and more difficult to educate and more prone to crime and welfare dependency than children of parents who do not have such problems. Almost beyond doubt, such problems are transmitted from one generation to the next. Skeptics believe that the easy availability of welfare and other transfers tempts men and unmarried teenage women to parent illegitimate children. That is an important and hotly debated subject, because children of unmarried teenage women do worse than others by almost any measure, but the issue is how people respond to incentives, and it has little to do with inner cities vs suburbs.

The above is germane to the flight-from-blight concept. A poorly documented tenet of those who emphasize the syndrome is the alleged cumulative nature of the flight. Middle class people are thought to leave inner cities because of crime, schools, taxes, etc., and their flight worsens such measures, leading to more flight and worse measures. For middle class residents, it is unlikely that taxes differ enough between inner cities and their suburbs to induce significant migration. It is more likely that the inducement to sub-urbanize relates to the quality of local government services: public school quality and crime rates to be precise.[26] Businesses are affected indirectly by the same service qualities in that poor schools and high crime rates make it difficult to attract middle class em-ployees. In most cases, middle class employees can protect their families by living in suburbs and commuting to inner city jobs, but they are nevertheless exposed to dangers of street crime where they work. Businesses may in many cases be exposed to higher taxes and more regulations in inner cities than in suburbs. If, in addition, their employees fear street crime near their work places, businesses may be induced to locate in suburbs. There is intuitive appeal to the idea that flight-from-blight may be cumulative, but evidence is sparse.

One aspect of the great debate is germane to the inner city–suburb nexus: the effects of the spatial concentration of the poor on their children. For given family income and other socio-economic characteristics, do children of such families fare worse if they live in neighborhoods of mostly poor people? Most noneconomists have believed that the answer is "yes" since the famous Coleman report, and based on cumulating evidence.[27] Studies conclude that other things equal, children of poor parents with given characteristics, perform worse in school, are less likely to complete high school, are more likely to have illegitimate children, and are less likely to obtain good jobs the more of their neighbors are poor. In a fine survey, Haveman and Wolfe (1995) conclude, with carefully stated reservations, that growing up in a poor or distressed family, or in a poor neighborhood imparts most of the widely reported disadvantages to children, at least to some extent. In an ingenious recent paper, Michael Kremer (1996) concludes that, not only are Americans not becoming increasingly segregated by ability or accomplishments within families or neighborhoods, but also that what we know about intergenerational transmission of such traits creates doubts that modest additional sorting among parents or neighborhoods would have much effect on children.

The description of inner city dysfunction and alienation is not bleak by historical standards. U.S. inner cities have for at least 150 years been the chaotic destinations of masses of poor migrants from abroad and from domestic farms. Migrants have dramatic-ally improved their living standards, at least within a generation, and continue to do so.

And they have moved to better locations as their living standards have risen. One difference from earlier times is that the better places have been in suburban jurisdictions during the last 50 years or so. Jurisdictional concentration of the poor and alienated apparently matters, but how much is unclear. A second difference has been the slowing of overall earnings increases and the widening disparity in the national earnings distribution during the last 15 to 25 years. Whatever the direct effects of government policies, the slowing growth and widening inequality of earnings have reduced the abilities of poor inner city residents to climb out of poverty.

6. Conclusions and Parting Thoughts

The important conclusions of this paper can be briefly summarized.

1. Although the United States has the highest per capita real income among OECD countries using the World Bank's measure, it has among the worst measures of most social indicators in the industrialized world. Careful international comparisons of poverty measures would tell the same story.
2. Much, but not all, of the poor United States performance is racially correlated. The white United States population compares much more favorably with other OECD countries than does the total United States population.
3. The U.S. black–white gap is large but has diminished considerably since the mid-1960s by most measures. Illegitimacy is the dramatic exception.
4. Blacks have suburbanized in smaller proportions than whites, but blacks have followed whites to the suburbs in substantial numbers. We are inclined to judge that many inner city blacks could improve their lives, at least in terms of schools and safety, by migrating to suburbs. Many of the poorest inner city blacks probably could not, and many middle class blacks either have suburbanized or live quite comfortably in inner cities.
5. Inner city–suburban gaps in social indicators are large and have increased by most measures during the last 30 years.
6. The previous finding probably results mainly from the tendency of not only higher income whites but also of higher income blacks to suburbanize more than their lower income counterparts.

A dramatic and deeply disturbing phenomenon to people who were socially and intellectually concerned in the mid-1960s is the paucity of progress that has been made in solving socio-economic problems and in reducing racial tensions during the subsequent 30 years. One can argue that governments have done too much or too little, but one cannot argue that the effort has been negligible. Many trillions of dollars have been spent to aid inner cities, improve low income housing, finance wars on drugs and poverty, subsidize low income health care, prosecute and incarcerate criminals, improve the nutrition of the poor, improve the education and training of the poor, and reduce racial tensions.

The largest federal, state, and local government expenditures have gone to fight poverty and drugs, and to improve housing and health care. Since the late 1960s, the tendency of governments has been to tinker with programs: add a little money here, subtract a little there, introduce yet another job training program, make minor changes in incentives for means-based transfer programs. The tendency of scholars has been to accept the proposition that programs have been well-intentioned, but have been badly designed or administered and to suggest changes that will improve performance. A rising tide of skeptics, starting well before November 1994, claims that government programs are part of the problem, not part of the solution, and that many programs should be swept away, not reformed.

Here we will content ourselves with a few observations about spatial aspects of programs.

First, we offer a conjecture as to why so many poor blacks remain in inner city slums. The conjecture is a supplement to explanations that rely on the natural tendency of higher income residents to suburbanize before lower income residents and on whatever effect remains of racial and class discrimination in suburban housing and employment. Some hedonic analysis (Edwin Mills and Ronald Simenauer 1996) indicates that constant quality housing prices are lower in inner cities than in suburbs. That is contrary to the implication of the basic monocentric model discussed earlier, but it is probably because of other causes of suburbanization discussed in Section 2. The effects of high crime rates and poor public schools in inner city slums must be to lower land values there, but such disamenities are not included in the hedonic analysis. That conclusion is supported by analysis of studies of capitalization of local government taxes and services provision in dwelling values, by housing abandonment in inner cities, and by direct evidence on market values and rents of slum dwellings. In addition, the oldest housing in most MSAs is found in inner city slums, and old housing is cheap housing, other things equal. The implication is that much of the worst inner city housing must be cheaper than any housing to be found in suburbs. Poor quality housing can be built in some suburbs, but old housing cannot, and better quality schools and lower crime rates keep land values high in suburbs. Thus, the cheapest market value housing is found in inner city slums. Add the fact that government owned-and-subsidized housing is much more plentiful in inner cities than in suburbs.[28] The result is that the cheapest housing in the MSA must often be found in inner city slums, even if land use controls impose almost no limits on the supply of low income housing in suburbs.

Many government programs have been proposed both to improve the living standards of the poor and to enable them to relocate from inner city slums. Housing vouchers, school vouchers, or a negative-income tax would have some such effect provided they were useable anywhere in the MSA.[29] However, any such proposal would meet the powerful objection of the two-thirds majority of MSA residents who live in suburbs. They would complain loudly that government was using their tax dollars to subsidize the poor to move into their communities. The introduction of local governments with MSA-wide jurisdictions is an even more radical proposal. It would enable local governments to reduce inequalities in local government service provision and tax rates between inner cities and suburbs. The terror sometimes induced by the proposal should be attenuated by the fact that MSA-wide local governments are indeed the norm in most countries in the world, and that they have been instituted in a few U.S. MSAs, without dire consequences. However, it is unclear to what extent the result would be to disperse the poor from inner city slums.

Notes

1 Nearly all MSAs consist of a county or counties that contain one or more incorporated cities (a subset of which are inner cities) with populations of at least 50,000 people, and contiguous counties that are predominately urban in character and relate to the city or cities by substantial commuting. The basic metropolitan concept is officially designated a Primary Metropolitan Statistical Area (PMSA), of which there were 361 in 1994. The government also defines a Consolidated Metropolitan Statistical Area (CMSA). A CMSA consists of a set of contiguous and related PMSAs. In 1994, there were 34 CMSAs. Unless otherwise stated, the term "metropolitan area" or MSA will refer to PMSAs in this paper.

2 People are urban if they live in a place that has a population of at least 2,500 people and most of the workers are nonagricultural. There are many urban places outside MSAs and some rural people live in MSAs. Because MSAs include only entire counties, there is considerable rural land beyond their urban fringes, but inside the MSAs.

3 The other part of the question is the extent to which people prefer to live in MSAs for consumption and social purposes. The answer appears to be, "to some extent." The range of consumer goods and services available within a few miles of home is much greater in MSAs and many goods are cheaper there. Popular surveys conclude that people regard an MSA of 50,000 to 100,000 residents as ideal. But such surveys do not ask about preferences contingent on earnings and employment opportunities. It is much better to look at earnings and employment data. Employment rates per working age adult are greater in MSAs; and real wages are somewhat greater in MSAs. If preferences for MSA living were much stronger than preferences for rural living, wage rates would be lower in MSAs. In fact the issue is moot in contemporary terms. Contemporary MSAs are so dispersed that residents can find "city," "edge city," "small town," and rural life styles within MSAs. The subject is discussed at greater length below.

4 The most comprehensive theoretical exposition of reasons for urban concentration is Masahisa Fujita (1989). A more recent but less comprehensive survey of urban economic theory is Geoffrey Turnbull (1995).

5 See Mills and Bruce Hamilton (1994) and Kenneth Small (1992). About 90 percent of United States workers commute by car. The other 10 percent are divided about equally between those who commute by transit and those who work at home or walk to work.

6 In the Chicago MSA, about 0.5 million of 4.4 million employees work in the CBD. About 10 percent of an MSAs employment located in the CBD appears to be typical.

7 A few high quality papers have analyzed suburban employment clusters. See David Hotchkiss and Michelle White (1993) and Robert Helsley and Arthur Sullivan (1991), and references therein.

8 Some edge cities in large MSAs are about as large as inner cities in smaller MSAs, and are gradually replicating not only the office clusters but also the retail and entertainment facilities of the inner city.

9 No papers have yet appeared that make suburban employment clusters fully endogenous. Models are needed that explain why, when, where, and how many suburban clusters appear, and how they interact with the CBD and with each other. Most existing papers analyze their interactions just with residential patterns. See Brueckner and Richard Martin (1995).

10 For a recent survey of the mismatch literature, see the paper by Harry Holzer (1991). See also Brueckner and Martin (1995), and Kain (1992).

11 The calculation assumes that whites and blacks must choose between residential locations in inner cities and suburbs. Inner cities have advantages to both in terms of locations of employment and amenities. If whites are deterred from residential locations by large concentrations of

blacks, then the greater the concentration of blacks in suburbs, and therefore the less their concentration in inner cities, the more whites are willing to live in inner cities. The same considerations might induce more businesses to locate in inner cities.

12   New Jersey provided the most dramatic litigation, in the 1970s and 1980s. The state supreme court issued several decisions collectively referred to as the Mt. Laurel decisions. With remarkably perceptive economic analysis, it concluded that land use controls that unreasonably restricted low and moderate income housing violated the state constitution. The court required communities to permit enough such housing for low and moderate income workers to be able to live within reasonable commuting distances of their jobs. However, the effects have been minor. In addition, some communities effectively zone out jobs that would employ low income workers. See Robert Burchell, Patrick Beaton, and David Listokin (1983). When the court's edicts became threatening, the state legislature finally legislated on the issue. It modified the quotas the court had set and, incredibly, permitted communities to buy and sell up to half their quotas. A nearby high income community could sell up to half its quota to Trenton at a negotiated price. The result was presumably to improve the housing, if not the schools and security, of low income residents, but it hardly contributed to integration of suburbs or to increases in affordable housing close to suburban work places. This episode illustrates a view that has since become conventional wisdom among experts in state–local politics; in a system that grants enormous powers to local governments to manage their jurisdictions, it is almost impossible to prevent them from accomplishing what powerful local forces want them to do.

13   There are no local government services in the model. However, if it is assumed that all residents of a given community receive the services provided by the community and that taxes are adequate to pay for the services, the model can be interpreted to include services implicitly. Housing is a private good in the model: residents receive utility only from their own housing consumption, not from that of their neighbors.

14   Jencks has suggested in correspondence that racial hostility in many activities may deter all but thick-skinned minorities from locating in suburbs even if discrimination is not a powerful force. For example, racial tensions are high even in schools with large groups of minority students.

15   Chronologically, recent surveys include Lawrence Smith, Kenneth Rosen, and George Fallis (1988), Isabel Sawhill (1988), James Smith and Finis Welch (1989), Mieszkowski and George Zodrow (1989), Burton Weisbrod (1991), John Donohue and James Heckman (1991), Robert Moffitt (1992), Nicholas Barr (1992), Frank Levy and Richard Murnane (1992), and Robert Haveman and Barbara Wolfe (1995). Some concepts are poorly measured. For example, despite an outpouring of literature, we have only moderately better understanding of the production function for elementary and secondary education than we had a quarter century ago. See Heckman, Anne Layne-Farrar, and Peter Todd (1995) and Eric Hanushek and Steven Rivkin (1996). Nevertheless, our judgment is that applied research has made as perceptive judgment about variables to measure as can be reasonably expected.

16   Timothy Smeeding, Michael O'Higgins, and Lee Rainwater, eds. (1990) provide a fine analysis of poverty and income distribution in seven countries: Canada, Israel, Norway, Sweden, United Kingdom, United States, and West Germany.

17   The United States and other high income countries make greater efforts to save babies that are premature than do many other countries. Because such efforts are not always successful, both the infant mortality and low birth weight data may be affected. We are indebted to Becker for pointing this out to us, and to Jencks.

18   The comparisons are for 1990 or 1991 data. United States data for the white population are taken from the *Statistical Abstract of the United States 1994*. Other OECD countries also have racial minorities, but their black populations are much smaller percentages of total population than in the United States, and few data are reported by race.

19 The correct measure of poverty has always been controversial. The measured rate is probably no less accurate for recent than for earlier years, except that the income measure excludes non-cash transfers, such as Medicaid, which have grown rapidly during recent decades. Consumer surveys have long shown that the poor spend considerably more than their incomes. That may be partly asset depletion, but also that some income is not revealed to government investigators.

20 The illegitimacy rates in Table 4 are not inconsistent with the declining birth rates among black women shown by Randall Olsen (1994, table 5). The figures in Table 4 are percentages of black and white babies born to unmarried women, whereas Olsen's figures are births per unmarried woman.

21 Victimization surveys report race for violent crimes. They indicate similar disparities to those indicated by arrest rates.

22 A referee has insisted that we point out that FBI data are reported by the place where the crime is committed, and suggests that some inner city crimes are committed by suburban residents. The referee did not refer to evidence and did not refer to the possibility that some suburban crimes may be committed by inner city residents.

23 See Roy Bahl, Jorge Martinez-Vasquez, and David Sjoquist (1992). The most comprehensive recent analysis of inner city government finances is Helen Ladd and Yinger (1989).

24 The best judgment is that residential real estate taxes per capita are about the same in inner cities as in suburbs. Inner city sales and payroll taxes are higher than in suburbs, but unknown amounts of such taxes are paid by suburban commuters and visitors to inner cities. We are indebted to William Oakland for enlightenment on this issue.

25 Richard Herrnstein and Charles Murray (1994) is the fullest and most articulate skeptical view. However, academic commentators have discovered serious flaws in the analysis and re-analyses of the Herrnstein and Murray data have reached conclusions that are contrary to those of the authors. See Arthur Goldberger and Charles Manski (1995) and Heckman (1995).

26 The behaviorally relevant issues are whether middle class children learn as much in inner city as in suburban schools and whether children and adults are exposed to as much danger from crime in inner cities as in suburbs. The issues cannot be in doubt. Whether the government services are better or worse in inner cities than in suburbs in a deeper sense may be very much in doubt.

27 For recent contributions and references to earlier literature, see Susan Mayer (1991), and Mayer and Jencks (1991). See also White (1993) and James Rosenbaum (1995).

28 Michael Schill and Wachter (1995) conclude that inner city biases of federal housing and other programs are an important cause of inner city problems.

29 The negative income tax and housing voucher experiments that were conducted in the 1960s and 1970s had little effect in inducing inner city poor beneficiaries to suburbanize. However, the period of eligibility may have been too short to induce substantial movements of residents.

References and Further Reading

Bahl, Roy Martinez-Vasquez, Jorge and Sjoquist, David L. (1992) "Central-City Suburban Fiscal Disparities," *Public Finance Quart*, October, 20(4), 420–32.

Barr, Nicholas (1992) "Economic Theory and the Welfare State: A Survey and Interpretation," *Journal of Economic Literature*, June, 30(2), 741–803.

Berkovic, James, Cannes, Glenn B, Gabriel, Stuart A., and Hannan, Timothy N. (1996) "Mortgage Discrimination and FIHIA Loan Performance," *Cityscape*, 2(1), 9–24.

Brueckner, Jan (1987) "The Structure of Urban Equilibria: A Unified Treatment of the Muth-Mills Model," in *Handbook of Urban Economics*. Eds.: Edwin Mills. Amsterdam: North-Holland.

Brueckner, Jan and Martin, Richard (1995) "Spatial Mismatch: An Equilibrium Analyses." mimeo.

Burchell, Robert W. Beaton, Patrick and Listokin, David (1983) *Mount Laurel II*. Center for Urban Policy Research. New Brunswick, NJ: Rutgers U.

Carlino, Gerald (1985) "Declining City Productivity and the Growth of Rural Regions," *Journal of Urban Economics*, July, 18(1), 11–27.

Cassidy, Glenn and Epple, Dennis (1994) "Property Ownership and Tax Structure." mimeo, July.

Coleman, James (1966) *Equality of Educational Opportunity*. Washington, DC: U.S. GPO.

Cronon, William (1991) *Nature's Metropolis*. New York: W. W. Norton.

Danziger, Sheldon and Gottschalk, Peter (1987) "Continuing Black Poverty: Earnings Inequality, the Spatial Concentration of Poverty, and the Underclass." *American Economic Review*, May, 77(2), 211–15.

Donohue, John J. III and Heckman, James (1991) "Continuous Versus Episodic Change: The Impact of Civil Rights Policy on the Economic Status of Blacks," *Journal of Economic Literature*, December, 24(4), 1603–43.

Eberts, Randall W. (1995) "Urban Labor Markets." staff working paper. Kalamazoo, MI: Upjohn Institute, January.

Fischel, William A. (1992) "Property Taxation and the Tiebout Model: Evidence for the Benefit View from Zoning and Voting," *Journal of Economic Literature*, March, 30(1), 171–77.

Freeman, Richard (1994) "Crime and the Job Market." Cambridge, MA: National Bureau of Economic Research working paper 4910.

Freeman, Richard B. and Holzer, Harry J. (1986) (eds) *The Black Youth Employment Crisis*. Chicago: University of Chicago Press.

Fujita, Masahisa (1989) *Urban Economic Theory*. New York: Cambridge University Press.

Galster, George and Killen, Sean. (1995) "The Geography of Metropolitan Opportunity: The Segregation of the Poor in the U.S.," *Housing Policy Debate*, 6(1).

Garreau, Joel (1991) *Edge City*. New York: Doubleday.

Glaab, Charles N. and Brown, Theodore, A. (1967) *History of Urban America*. New York: Macmillan.

Goldberger, Arthur S. and Manski, Charles F. (1995) "The Bell Curve: Review Article," *Journal of Economic Literature*, June, 33(2), 762–76.

Gyourko, Joseph, Linneman, Peter and Wachter, Susan (1996) "Analyzing the Relation Among Race, Wealth and Homeownership in America." mimeo.

Hamilton, Bruce W. (1976) "Capitalization of Intrajurisdictional Differences in Local Tax Prices," *American Econonomic Review*, December, 66(5), 743–53.

Hanushek, Eric and Rivkin, Steven (1996) "Understanding the 20th Century Growth in U.S. School Spending." Cambridge, MA: National Bureau of Economic Research working paper 5547.

Haveman, Robert and Wolfe, Barbara (1995) "The Determinants of Children's Attainments: A Review of Methods and Findings," *Journal of Economic Literature*, December, 33(4), 1829–78.

Heckman, James (1995) "Lessons from the Bell Curve," *Journal of Political Economy*, 103(5), 1091–1120.

Heckman, James, Layne-Farrar, Anne and Todd, Peter (1995) "Does Measured School Quality Really Matter? An Examination of the Earnings-Quality Relationships." Cambridge: National Bureau of Economic Research, working paper 5274, September.

Henderson, J. Vernon (1988) *Urban Development*. New York: Oxford University Press.

Helsley, Robert W. and Sullivan, Arthur M. (1991) "Urban Subcenter Formation," *Regional Science and Urban Economics*, July, 21(2), 255–75.

Herrnstein, Richard J. and Murray, Charles (1994) *The Bell Curve*. New York: Free Press.

Holzer, Harry J. (1991) "The Spatial Mismatch Hypothesis: What Has the Evidence Shown," *Urban Studies*, February, 28(1), 105–22.

Hotchkiss, David and White, Michelle J. (1993) "A Simulation Model of a Decentralized Metropolitan Area with Two-Worker, 'Traditional,' and Female-Headed Households," *Journal of Urban Economics*, September, 34(2), 159–85.

Ihlanfeldt, Keith (1994) "The Importance of the Central City to the Regional and National Economy: A Review of the Arguments and Empirical Evidence." research paper No. 44, June Georgia State University, College of Business Administration.

Jargowsky, Paul (1996) *Poverty and Place*. New York: Russell Sage Foundation.

Kain, John (1968) "Housing Segregation, Negro Employment and Metropolitan Decentralization," *Quarterly Journal of Economics*, May, 82(2), 175–97.

——. (1992) "The Spatial Mismatch Hypothesis: Three Decades Later," *Housing Policy Debate*, 3(2), 371–460.

Kremer, Michael (1996) "How much Does Sorting Increase Inequality?" Cambridge, MA: National Bureau of Economic research working paper 5566.

Ladd, Helen F. and Yinger, John (1989) *America's Ailing Cities*. Baltimore: Johns Hopkins University Press.

Levy, Frank and Murnane, Richard J. (1992) "U.S. Earnings Levels and Earnings Inequality: A Review of Recent Trends and Proposed Explanations," *Journal of Economic Literature*, September, 30(3), 1333–81.

Mayer, Susan (1991) "How Much Does a High School's Racial and Socioeconomic Mix Affect Graduation and Teenage Fertility Rates?" in *The Urban Underclass*. Eds.: Christopher Jencks and Paul Peterson. Washington, DC: Brookings Institution, 321–41.

Mayer, Susan and Jencks, Christopher (1991) "Growing Up In Poor Neighborhoods: How Much Does It Matter?" in *The Urban Underclass*. Eds.: Christopher Fenchies and Paul Peterson. Washington, DC: Brookings Institution, 321–41.

Mieszkowski, Peter and Mills, Edwin S. (1993) "The Causes of Suburbanization," *Journal of Economic Perspectives*, Summer 7(3), 135–47.

Mieszkowski, Peter and Zodrow, George R. (1989) "Taxation and the Tiebout Model," *Journal of Economic Literature*, September, 27(3), 1098–146.

Mills, Edwin S. (1979) "Economic Analysis of Urban Land-Use Controls," in *Current Issues on Urban Economics*. Eds.: Peter Mieszkowski and Mahlon Straszheim. Baltimore: Johns Hopkins University press, 511–41.

——. (1985) "Open Housing Laws as Stimulus to Central City Employment," *Journal of Urban Economics*, March, 17(2), 184–8.

——. (1990) "Do Metropolitan Areas Mean Anything? A Research Note," *Journal of Regional Science*, August, 30(3), 415–19.

——. (1995) "Crisis and Recovery in Office Markets," *Journal of Real Estate Finance Economics*, January, 10(1), 49–62.

Mills, Edwin and Hamilton, Bruce W. (1994) *Urban Economics*. 5th edn. New York: Harper-Collins Pub.

Mills, Edwin and Simenauer, Ronald (1996) "New Hedonic Estimates of Regional Constant Quality House Prices," *Journal of Urban Economics*, March, 39(2), 209–15.

Moffitt, Robert. (1992) "Incentive Effects of the U.S. Welfare System: A Review," *Journal of Economic Literature*, March, 30(1), 1–61.

Munnell, Alicia et al. (1996) "Mortgage Lending in Boston: Interpreting HMDA Data," *American Economic Review*, March, 86(1), 25–53.

OECD. *Economic Surveys*. Paris: OECD, Periodical.

Olsen, Randall J. (1994) "Fertility and the Size of the U.S. Labor Force," *Journal of Economic Literature*, March, 32(1), 60–100.

Rosenbaum, James (1995) "Changing the Geography of Opportunity by Expanding Residential Choice: Lessons from the Gatreaux Program," *Housing Policy Debate*, 6(1), 2–69.

Sawhill, Isabel (1988) "Poverty in the U.S.: Why Is It So Persistent?" *Journal of Economic Literature*, September, 26(3), 1073–119.

Schill, Michael and Wachter, Susan (1995) "The Spatial Bias of Federal Housing Law and Policy: Concentrated Poverty in Urban America," *University of Pennsylvania Law Rev.*, 143(5), 1285–1342.

Small, Kenneth (1992) *Urban Transportation Economics*. Philadelphia: Harwood Academic Pub.

Smeeding, Timothy M., O'Higgins, Michael and Rainwater, Lee (eds) (1990) *Poverty, Inequality and Income Distribution in Comparative Perspective*. Washington, DC: Urban Institute Press.

Smith, James P. and Welch, Finis R. (1989) "Black Economic Progress After Myrdal," *Journal of Economic Literature*, June, 27(2), 519–64.

Smith, Lawrence B., Rosen, Kenneth T. and Fallis, George (1988) "Recent Developments in Economic Models of Housing Markets," *Journal of Economic Literature*, March, 26(1), 29–64.

Struyk, Raymond and Fix, Michael (1993) *Access Denied; Access Constrained*. Washington, DC: Urban Institute Press.

Turnbull, Geoffrey K. (1995) *Urban Consumer Theory*. Washington, DC: Urban Institute Press.

United Nations (1993) *World Social Situation 1993*. New York: United Nations.

U.S. Bureau of the Census (1994) *Statistical Abstract of the United States 1994*. Washington, DC: U.S. GPO.

U.S. Council of Economic Advisers *Economic Report of the President*. Washington, D.C.: U.S. GPO, Annual.

U.S. Dept. of Commerce Bureau of the Census *Poverty in the United States*. Washington, DC: U.S. GPO, Annual.

U.S. Federal Bureau of Investigation *Uniform Crime Reports*. Washington, D.C.: U.S. GPO, Annual.

Voith, Richard (1994) "Do Suburbs Need Cities?" Working Paper No 93–27, Federal Reserve Bank of Philadelphia, September.

Weisbrod, Burton A. (1991) The Health Cure Quadrilemma: An Essay on Technological Change, Insurance Quality of Care, and Cost Containment, *Journal of Economic Literature*, June, 29(2), 523–52.

Wheaton, William (1977) "Income and Urban Residence: An Analysis of Consumer Demand for Location," *American Economic Review*, September, 67(4), 620–.

White, Michelle (1993) "Measuring the Benefits of Homeowning: Benefits to Children." mimeo, December.

Wildasin, David (1987) "Theoretical Analysis of Local Public Economics," in *Handbook of Regional and Urban Economics*. Vol. 2. Eds.: Edwin Mills. New York: North-Holland, 11–78.

Wilson, James Q. and Herrnstein, Richard J. (1985) *Crime and Human Nature*. New York: Simon & Schuster.

Wilson, William Julius (1987) *The Truly Disadvantaged: The Inner City, The Underclass, and Public Policy*. Chicago: University of Chicago Press.

World Bank (1993) *Social Indicators of Development, 1993*. Washington, DC: World Bank.

———. *World Development Report*. Washington, DC: World Bank, Annual.

Yinger, John (1995) *Closed Doors, Opportunities Lost*. Washington, DC: Russell Sage Foundation.

CHAPTER TWENTY-ONE

Information on the Spatial Distribution of Job Opportunities within Metropolitan Areas*

KEITH R. IHLANFELDT

Source: *Journal of Urban Economics*, 41, 218–42. © 1997 Academic Press.

This paper investigates the knowledge that people have of the spatial distribution of job openings within their metropolitan area. Respondents to a survey conducted in Atlanta in 1993 were asked to rank areas within the Region based on the number of job openings for workers without college degrees. To judge the accuracy of the answers, a variety of methods are employed to obtain the true rankings. Results indicate that both whites and blacks have poor information, with blacks the worse informed, and that the black disadvantage is entirely attributable to residential segregation.

1. Introduction

A substantial amount of evidence has accumulated which indicates that the spatial distribution of job opportunities and wage rates for less educated workers is nonuniform within metropolitan areas. In general, both wages and job openings have been found to be greater in white suburban areas than within central cities and black suburban areas.[1] This evidence has been taken as support for the spatial mismatch hypothesis, which states that the suburbanization of low-skill jobs and continued housing market segregation have acted together to create a surplus of less educated workers within central cities and a shortage of these same workers within suburban areas.

An unresolved issue is why the labor market disequilibrium represented by spatial mismatch is not eliminated by market forces. The movement of jobs from the central city to the

* Support for this project came from the Russell Sage Foundation and the Ford Foundation and the Research Committee, College of Business Administration, Georgia State University. The comments of David Sjoquist, Julie Hotchkiss, Jorge Martinez, Harry Holzer, John Bound, Barry Hirsch, and two anonymous reviewers improved this paper. Jessica Bye assisted in the collection of the data and Mary Beth Walker and Chris Bollinger provided econometric advice.

suburbs constitutes a geographic shift in labor demand, to which the supply of inner-city labor should eventually adjust. Most studies of labor market adjustments to sectoral or geographic demand shifts (Freeman[10]; Blanchard and Katz [5]) suggest that long-run labor supply is quite elastic and that fairly complete adjustments in employment occur over a number of years. If this adjustment does not occur for inner-city residents, then we need to identify the adjustment barriers and develop appropriate policies for overcoming them.[2]

One possible barrier that may explain the persistence of spatial mismatch is that inner-city residents may have poor information on the spatial distribution of job opportunities. That this is the case is suggested by two hypotheses that relate labor market information to "space"; that is, where the worker resides within the metro area. First, to find a job less educated workers rely heavily on friends and relatives and direct applications without referrals (Holzer [15]). The reliance on these informal methods of job search (rather than, for example, using an employment agency) suggests that information on available job opportunities may decay rapidly with distance from home (Ihlanfeldt and Sjoquist [20]). Second, space may affect labor market information if the amount of information varies across neighborhoods and workers rely on neighbors as a source of job market information. William Wilson [41] has argued that people living in underclass neighborhoods have poor information about legitimate jobs because they lack contact or interaction with individuals and institutions that represent mainstream society.

Since blacks disproportionately reside within inner-city and underclass neighborhoods, the above hypotheses imply that they possess less information on the spatial distribution of job opportunities than whites. However, it may also be the case that blacks invest less in obtaining such information because the expected return is less. If blacks believe they are excluded from suburban jobs because of either labor or housing market discrimination, blacks may possess less information of the spatial distribution of job opportunities even after controlling for space.

The empirical literature on labor market information consists of two types of studies: (1) those that have related the method of information acquisition (e.g., formal versus informal) to wage and employment outcomes (Ullman [37]; Reid [30]; Granovetter [11]; Corcoran et al. [9]; Allen and Keaveny [1]; Holzer [16]) and (2) those that have measured labor market ignorance as the difference between the actual and potential or frontier wage (Hofler and Polachek [14]; Hofler and Murphy [13]). Surprisingly, no previous research could be found on the knowledge that workers have of the spatial distribution of job opportunities or openings within their local labor market.

The issues to be addressed in this paper are threefold. First, what knowledge do less educated workers have of the intra-metropolitan spatial distribution of job opportunities? Second, how does this knowledge vary between blacks and whites and how much of this difference can be attributed to residential segregation? Third, what personal and locational factors account for the amount of labor market information possessed by the individual worker?

The results indicate that (1) both whites and blacks have poor information, with blacks being the worse informed; (2) the black advantage is entirely attributable to residential segregation; and (3) people living in underclass neighborhoods are not poorly informed relative to those living outside of these areas.

In the next section, the methods employed to document the spatial distribution of jobs within the study area (Atlanta, Georgia) are described and the distributions yielded by these methods are presented. In Section III, the Atlanta component of the Multi-City Study of Urban Inequality (MCSUI) along with the results presented in Section II are employed to investigate Atlantans' knowledge of the local labor market. A theoretical model that seeks to explain individual variation in knowledge is developed in Section IV and the results from estimating equations that are based upon this model are presented in Section V. Conclusions and suggestions for further research are found in the final section.

2. The Spatial Distribution of Jobs Within the Atlanta Region

Study area

The study area is the Atlanta Region (see Fig. 1) with includes the central city of Atlanta and the nine counties comprising the inner suburban ring.[3] During the 1980s, the Region experienced a strong northside shift in the spatial distribution of jobs (see Table 1). The share of the Region's jobs located in the northern suburbs grew from 40% in 1980 to 52%

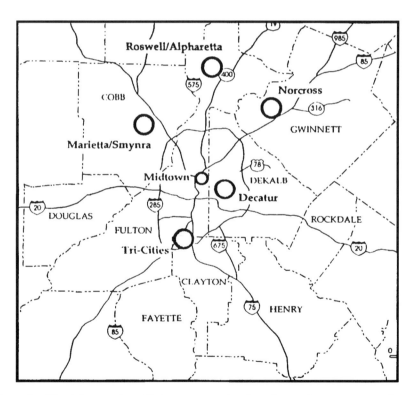

Figure 1   The Atlanta region. Circles represent the six major employment centers that survey respondents were asked to rank based on job opportunities or openings for people without college degrees.

in 1990. The share of jobs located in the City of Atlanta declined from 40% to 29% over the same period. The southern suburbs' share of the Region's jobs declined over the decade from 20 to 19%.

The northside bias in the suburbanization of jobs might suggest that the northern suburbs offer the greatest job opportunities for people without college degrees. However, there was also disproportionate population growth on the northside of the Region during the 1980s (see Table 1). The share of the Region's population located in the northern suburbs grew from 44% in 1980 to 52% in 1990. Nevertheless, despite the strong population growth that accompanied the strong employment growth on the Region's northside, there is reason to believe that there are more job openings for less educated workers in the northern suburbs in comparison to the rest of the Region. Relative to the City and the southern suburbs, the northside is much more affluent, with an average household income in 1989 that is 38% higher than in the City and 30% higher than in the southern suburbs (see Table 1). Hence, there may be a imbalance between the number of jobs for less educated workers and the number of people who reside on the northside who are willing to work at these jobs.

There are two data sets that can be used to investigate this possibility. In 1989, a survey was conducted of the managers of 102 fast-food restaurants located throughout the Region.[4] The advantage of this survey is that job tasks are essentially identical across

Table 1 Data on the Atlanta Region

	Northern suburbs	Central city	Southern suburbs
Percentage share of region's population			
1980	44	23	33
1990	52	16	32
Percentage share of Region's jobs			
1980	40	40	20
1990	52	29	19
Percentage share of region's whites			
1980	57	10	32
1990	65	7	28
Percentage share of region's blacks			
1980	8	60	33
1990	18	39	43
1989 average household income	$52,238	$37,756	$40,236
Data from fast-food restaurant sample			
Average difficulty finding workers	2.63	1.95	2.06
Average number of walk-ins/week	5.7	12.7	9.8
Average starting wage	$4.39	$3.84	$3.80
Number of observations	35	21	46
Data from MCSUI employer survey			
Average job vacancy rate	0.048	0.016	0.022
Number of oberservations	214	176	209

Sources: Income and population, the 1990 Census; jobs, the Atlanta Regional Commission's Employment Survey.

restaurants and therefore differences in required skill levels are unlikely to affect comparisons between geographic areas. Among the questions that were asked are the following:

(1) How difficult is it for you to find new employees? (very difficult, 4; somewhat difficult, 3; moderately difficult, 2; not difficult at all, 1).
(2) In an *average* week, if you did not advertise for help in any way (such as putting up a sign in the store window or asking current employees to recruit friends), how many *walk-ins* would normally come into the restaurant asking about a job?
(3) A new employee has just graduated from high school, has no previous work experience in fast food, and will work over the lunch hour Monday–Friday. What is the *starting wage* this new employee receives?

Table 1 reports the average response to each of the above questions for each of the three areas. While the difference in mean values are small and statistically insignificant between the City and the southern suburbs, the differences between these areas and the northern suburbs are large and statistically significant (at the 1% level by a two-tailed test). On the northside, it is more difficult to find workers, the average number of walk-ins per week is half as large as for the other two areas, and the average starting wage rate is 16% higher. These data therefore suggest that the northside of the Atlanta Region offers both higher wages and greater job availability for people without college degrees.

The other data set can be used to document the northside advantage in job availability for less educated workers is The Multi-City Study of Urban Inequality (MCSUI) Survey of Employers.[5] These data are an employee-weighted sample of firms interviewed in 1993. Among the questions asked of a person within the firm who is responsible for hiring are the number of job vacancies within each of five occupational groups and the number of employees currently working for the firm in each of these groups. To construct a job vacancy rate for each firm relevant to less educated workers, the number of vacant jobs in clerical, blue-collar, and service occupations was summed and divided by the total number of positions (both filled and unfilled) in these three occupational groups. If jobs are more plentiful relative to the available labor supply on the northside of the region, this area should have a higher vacancy rate. As show in Table 1, the estimated job vacancy rates are 0.048, 0.016, and 0.022 for the northern suburbs. City, and southern suburbs, respectively. The difference between the northern suburbs and the City is statistically significant at the 1% level, while the difference between the northern and southern suburbs is significant at the 10% level. The vacancy rates for the City and southern suburbs are not significant different.

In addition to the above survey data, there is anecdotal evidence that the northside offers greater job availability for less educated workers. A number of stories have appeared in Atlanta's newspapers reporting worker shortages in the northern suburbs, with some employers responding by providing shuttle service to inner-city workers (Vessey [38]; McCosh [24]; Beasley [3]; Walston [39]).

The racial composition of the Atlanta population varies dramatically across the City, the southern suburbs, and the northern suburbs. According to the 1990 Census of Population, the City contains 39% of the Region's blacks but only 7% of the Region's whites. The northern suburbs contain 65% of the whites, but only 18% of the blacks. The southern suburbs hold 43% of the Region's blacks, but only 28% of the white population.

In summary, the study area is characterized by rapid employment growth on the northside of the Region, which evidence suggests has resulted in relatively more job openings and wage premia for lower-skill workers. The racial composition of the northern suburbs is disproportionately white.

The MCSUI questions

The Atlanta component of the Multi-City Study of Urban Inequality consisted of 1528 in-home interviews, which occurred between June 1993 and November 1993. These interviews were conducted by Mathematica Policy Research, with funding provided by the Russell Sage Foundation and Ford Foundation. Blacks and residents of low-income neighborhoods were oversampled.

Those respondents who indicated that they were not retired and had at some time searched for employment were shown a map of the Atlanta Region which identified six employment centers (see Fig. 1): Marietta/Smyrna, Roswell/Alpharetta, Norcross, Midtown, Decatur, and the Tri-Cities area. The first three areas are major employment centers located in the northern suburbs, Midtown has become the *de facto* central business district of the City of Atlanta, and Decatur and the Tri-Cities area are in the southern suburbs. Respondents were asked two questions:

(1) Which area has the fewest job opportunities or openings for a person without a college degree?
(2) Of these six areas, which one do you believe has the most job opportunities or openings for a person without a college degree?

In order to judge the accuracy of the respondent's answers, three methods are employed to obtain "true" rankings of the six areas. First, the managers of the five public employment offices located within the study area were separately interviewed. They were asked to rank the six areas in terms of the number of available jobs for people without college degrees. Each manager was given sufficient time (1 to 2 weeks) to review his/her files in order to provide a more accurate ranking. The rankings provided are remarkably similarly (see Table 2). All but one manager ranked Roswell/Alpharetta as best (he ranked it second best) and all five ranked the Tri-Cities area as worst. In all cases the three northern suburban areas are ranked higher than the other areas.

The second method used to determine the true ranking of job availability among the six areas involves using employment data from the Atlanta Regional Commission (ARC) for each of the six areas and the 1990 Public Use Micro-data Sample (PUMS). These data are used to compute the change in the number of jobs not requiring a college degree over the period December 1990 to December 1993. It was toward the end of this period when the MCSUI surveys were administered. For each census tract ARC publishes annual employment estimates for eight major industry groups: construction; manufacturing; transportation, communication, and utilities; wholesale trade; retail trade; finance, insurance, and real estate; services; and government.[6] Estimates of the number of jobs in each group by area that did not require a college degree are obtained by using the PUMS to cross tabulate industry group, level of education, and county. The total number of jobs not requiring a college degree is obtained by summing across industry groups. The results are

Table 2   Rankings of employment centers based upon the number of job opportunities for workers without college degrees

	Manager Number					Change in jobs 1990–1993		Job vacancy rate
	(1)	(2)	(3)	(4)	(5)			
Roswell/Alpharetta	1	2	1	1	1	6501	(31.8)[a]	0.117 [19][b]
Marietta/Smyrna	2	1	3	2	3	2967	(3.7)	.041 [54]
Norcross	3	3	2	3	2	3756	(7.8)	.007 [30]
Decatur	4	4	5	4	5	582	(9.0)	n.a.
Midtown	5	5	4	5	4	132	(0.6)	0.002 [14]
Tri-Cities	6	6	6	6	6	1420	(−6.0)	0.005 [9]

Sources: Interviews with managers of state employment offices and employment data from the Atlanta Regional Commission and the MCSUI Survey of Employers.
[a]   The numbers in parentheses are percentage changes.
[b]   The numbers in brackets are the number of sampled firms located in each area.

reported in the second to last column of Table 2. The increase in the number of jobs for less educated workers is greatest in Roswell/Alpharetta, where the absolute increase is 6501 jobs. The other two northern suburban areas, Marietta/Smyrna and Norcross, also experienced positive growth with the number of jobs increasing 2967 and 3756, respectively. In contrast, there is negligible job growth in Midtown over the 3-year period and *negative* growth in Decatur and the Tri-Cities area.

The final method involves using the MCSUI Employer Survey to compute an average job vacancy rate for each area in the same manner as before. While the number of firms within each area is small, the highest average vacancy rate is for the Roswell/Alpharetta area and the rates for the Marietta/Smyrna and Norcross areas are higher than for the other two areas (Midtown and Tri-Cities) for which an average could be computed (see last column of Table 2).

In summary, the three methods used to determine the true ranking of job availability across areas are consistent with one another and substantiate the conclusion that the northern suburbs offer the greatest job opportunities for people without college degrees.

3. Respondents Knowledge of the Atlanta Labor Market

Table 3 reports the percentages of blacks and whites who named each area as having the fewest and most job opportunities or openings for a person without a college degree. Separate sets of percentages are given for all respondents, respondents without bachelor's degrees, respondents without bachelor's degrees who are labor force participants, and the unemployed among the latter group.

The results indicate that while blacks have worse knowledge of the labor market than whites, both racial groups are very poorly informed. Blacks most frequently list Roswell/ Alpharetta as having the fewest opportunities, when in fact it has the most opportunities, while whites most frequently rank the Tri-Cities area as having the most opportunities, when in fact it has the fewest opportunities. These results hold for all four of the groups

Table 3 Percentage of respondents naming each area as having the fewest and most job openings for people without college degrees

	All respondents		No college degree		No college degree, labor force participant		No college degree unemployed	
	Black	White	Black	White	Black	White	Black	White
Percentage naming area as worst								
Roswell/Alpharetta	37.2	23.1	36.5	23.1	38.1	24.4	26.2	25.0
Norcross	8.9	9.1	8.4	8.5	8.3	9.1	15.4	9.4
Marietta/Smyrna	14.0	6.6	15.3	6.4	15.8	6.3	23.1	9.4
Midtown	12.3	27.3	13.4	28.5	14.3	30.8	21.5	40.6
Decatur	6.7	3.6	6.8	3.1	7.0	2.8	4.6	0.0
Tri-Cities	6.1	7.6	4.4	6.4	4.8	5.9	3.1	3.1
Do not know	14.8	22.7	15.4	24.1	11.8	20.9	6.2	12.5
Percentage naming area as best								
Roswell/Alpharetta	4.8	4.7	5.0	5.1	5.5	3.5	4.6	6.3
Norcross	8.1	9.5	7.2	8.8	7.5	9.5	10.8	12.5
Marietta/Smyrna	7.1	12.9	7.8	15.9	7.3	16.9	10.8	15.6
Midtown	29.1	17.8	29.7	16.3	31.8	16.9	35.4	12.5
Decatur	22.9	8.7	23.5	8.1	23.6	8.3	21.5	6.3
Tri-Cities	14.8	26.5	13.0	24.8	13.5	26.8	15.4	34.4
Do not know	13.3	19.9	13.9	21.0	10.8	18.1	1.5	12.5
Percentage naming a northern area as best	19.9	27.1	19.9	29.8	20.3	29.9	26.2	34.4
Percentage naming a northern area as best and a nonnorthern area as worst	10.9	17.6	11.0	19.0	12.0	18.9	12.3	21.9
Observations	608	472	502	295	399	254	65	32

identified in Table 3. Clearly, people are not just uninformed, they are misinformed concerning the whereabouts of available jobs.

The bottom of Table 3 reports two summary measures of the information respondents have of the spatial distribution of job opportunities: (1) the percentage that named one of the employment centers in the northern suburbs as having the most opportunities and (2) the percentage that named one of the northern suburbs' employment centers as having the most opportunities and named one of the employment centers located in either the City of Atlanta or the southern suburbs as having the fewest opportunities.

Among all the respondents, only 19.9% of blacks and 27.1% of whites named a northern employment center as having the most opportunities, despite the phenomenal job growth that has occurred on the northside of the Atlanta Region. The percentage who named a northside center as having the most and a non-northside center as having the fewest opportunities is only 10.9% for blacks and 17.6% for whites.

As one moves from left to right across the columns of Table 3, the expectation is that information on the spatial distribution of jobs for less educated workers would improve, since each successive group identified at the top of the column presumably would experience a greater average benefit from possessing such information. For example, those without bachelor's degrees should have a better idea of where non-college graduates should look for work than those with bachelor's degrees. While the magnitudes of the summary measures do increase as one moves across the columns, the increases are very small. Even among the group who has the most to gain from the labor market information – namely, those who are unemployed without bachelor's degrees, only 26.2% of blacks and 34.4% of whites are aware of the northside advantage.

4. A Model of Knowledge of the Spatial Distribution of Job Opportunities

Theoretical framework

The acquisition of labor market information is considered a type of investment behavior. In the present context, labor market information is the ability to accurately rank subareas of the metropolitan region in terms of job opportunities (openings) for workers without college degrees.

Assume that the region consists of two subareas, the central city and the suburbs, and that job opportunities are spatially uniform within these areas but are more plentiful in the suburbs. If the individual is to have more than a 0.50 probability of providing an accurate ranking, information must be acquired about jobs in *both* the central city and the suburbs. Investment theory suggests that the individual will obtain information about jobs in a particular area if the present value of the benefits is greater than the costs. Information about jobs in any area is assumed to yield no benefits to people who are not interested in working or who are not dependent on job opportunities for non-college graduates. Hence, groups who have lower rates of labor force participation (e.g., women with children) and workers with college degrees or special talents are expected to invest less frequently in information about jobs for non-college workers. They are, therefore, less likely to provide an accurate ranking of subareas.

By definition, labor force participants invest in information about jobs in at least one of the two subareas. Since transportation costs are nontrivial, it is reasonable to assume that all labor force participants invest in information about jobs located in the subarea within which they reside. Knowledge of the spatial distribution of job opportunities therefore depends on whether the individual acquires information about jobs in the subarea that is not lived in. The present value of the benefits of this information can be expressed as

$$B = \int_0^l [\bar{W}_I(t) - \bar{W}_{NI}(t)]e^{-rt}dt \tag{1}$$

where $\bar{W}_I$ and $\bar{W}_{NI}$ represent expected wages with and without the information, respectively, l is the time horizon, and r is the discount rate. The expected wage is the product of the wage rate and the probability of employment ($P(\mathcal{J})$) and is defined net of commuting costs:

$$\bar{W} = (W - TV).P(\mathcal{J}),\tag{2}$$

where T is the round trip commute time and V is the value of travel time.

$\bar{W}_I$ will be higher for individuals who are geographically mobile between the two subareas, where the latter is defined as being able to residentially relocate to the other subarea (in order to reduce T) or being willing to commute to the other subarea (i.e., the individual has a relatively low V). There are four factors that can readily be linked to the individual's geographic mobility: race, gender, housing tenure, and health status.

Because of housing and mortgage market discrimination, blacks may be less able to move between subareas than whites. In addition, T may be higher for blacks because of their greater dependence on public transit.[7] Public transit vehicles generally move more slowly than automobiles. More importantly, the former requires more walking and waiting time, especially for those workers making a reverse commute. In fact, the length of the walk required to get to many suburban job sites from the nearest public transit stop may be prohibitive. For reasons related to both discrimination and transportation, therefore, blacks are expected to invest less frequently in information about jobs located in the non-home subarea.

A number of reasons suggest that women are less geographically mobile than men. First, women are more dependent on public transit than men (Pisarski [29]). Second, because of their lower wage rates and shorter work hours, women's transportation costs are a higher percentage of their earnings for any given journey-to-work (Madden [23]). Third, because of their greater home and child care responsibilities, women may place a higher value on their commuting time.[8] Fourth, it is generally the husband's rather than the wife's work location that has the greater influence on the residential location of married couples. For these reasons, the expectation is that women will invest less in information about jobs located in the non-home subarea, especially if they are married or have children still living at home.

Moving and transaction costs are higher for homeowners than for renters, while poor health may make it difficult to move or make a long commute. Homeowners and people with poor health are therefore less geographically mobile and therefore are expected to less frequently make the investment in information about non-home area jobs.

Having considered how the benefit of acquiring information about jobs for less educated workers in the non-home subarea may vary across individuals, the remaining issue is how the cost of acquiring such information may vary. Residential location is hypothesized to be an important influence, with cost varying across subareas and within subareas across neighborhoods. Costs are expected to be lower for suburban residents for two reasons. First, the propensity to travel outside the home subarea and thereby gain information on jobs in the other subarea varies between central city and suburban residents. Suburbanites come to the city more often than city residents travel to the suburbs on non-work related trips (e.g., for personal business or entertainment) or on trips that combine job search with other purposes. Second, the local media represents an inexpensive source of information on economic growth and development within the region. The media's coverage, however, is biased in favor of the central city for obvious reasons. Hence, suburban residents possess a cheap source of information on the City that central city residents do not share, at least to the same extent, on the suburbs.[9]

Within subareas, neighborhood may affect the cost of acquiring information in the manner suggested by Wilson [41], who argues that people living in underclass neighborhoods have poor information about legitimate jobs because they lack contact or interaction with individuals and institutions that represent mainstream society. In the present context, Wilson's hypothesis can be couched in terms of the investment in information condition. In underclass neighborhoods fewer people make the investment in information about jobs in either the home or the non-home subarea because fewer people choose to participate in the labor force. There is, therefore, a lower probability that one's neighbors will have accurate information to share on the spatial distribution of available jobs. However, the influence of neighborhood is more complicated than Wilson's hypothesis suggests. While labor force participation is lower in underclass neighborhoods, among those who do participate the investment in information about jobs in the non-home subarea may be more likely to occur simply because these workers are highly dependent on jobs that do not require a college degree. The issue, therefore, of whether information on the spatial distribution of job openings for less educated workers is collectively better or worse in underclass neighborhoods is *a priori* ambiguous and can only be addressed empirically.

Empirical model

To investigate how the above factors impinge on the knowledge MCSUI respondents have of the spatial distribution of job opportunities, the summary measures (KNOW1, KNOW2) are regressed on variables describing the individual and his/her residential location (see Table 4 for variable means and definitions). KNOW1 equals one if the respondent named one of the northside employment centers as having the most job opportunities or openings for a person without a college degree and equals zero otherwise. KNOW2 equals one if the respondent named one of the northside centers as having the most and one of the other centers as having the fewest job opportunities or openings for a person without a college degree and equals zero otherwise.

If the respondent is a non-Hispanic black, the dummy variable BLACK equals one. The reference group consists of non-Hispanic whites. There are too few Hispanics living in Atlanta and therefore in the sample to include them in the analysis.

CITY and SSUB are dummy variables which indicate whether the respondent lives in the City of Atlanta or the southern suburbs, respectively. The reference category is people residing in the northern suburbs.

Various approaches have been used to identify underclass neighborhoods (Sjoquist [33]). One common approach involves using a concentrated poverty criterion (Reischauer [31]; Nathan [27]; Greene [12]; Bane and Jargowsky [2]. Based upon this approach, census tracts are stratified into those having a poverty rate of 30% or higher (HPOV), those having a poverty rate of less than 30% but greater than 10% (MPOV), and those with a poverty rate of 10% or less (reference category).

In addition to BLACK, other variables that measure the geographic mobility of the respondent include whether the respondent said his/her health is poor (PHEALTH),

Table 4 Variable definitions and means

	Definition	All respondents	No bachelor's degree	No bachelor's LF participant
Dependent variables				
KNOW1	Named one of the northside employment centers as having the most job opportunities or openings for a person without a college degree	0.248	0.253	0.256
KNOW2	Named one of the northside centers as having the most and one of the other centers as having the fewest job opportunities or openings	0.151	0.153	0.159
Independent variables				
BLACK	Respondent is black	0.560	0.624	0.614
CITY	Respondent resides in City of Atlanta	0.281	0.314	0.291
SSUB	Respondent resides in southern suburbs	0.458	0.478	0.492
HPOV	Lives in a census tract that has a poverty rate of 30% or higher	0.174	0.211	0.186
MPOV	Lives in census tract that has a poverty rate less than 30% but greater than 10%	0.402	0.452	0.458
EXPER	Years respondent has worked	16.628	17.474	17.213
HS	High school diploma	0.439	0.598	0.617
COLLEGE	Associate or Bachelor's degree	0.429	0.223	0.236
RENTER	Rents home	0.536	0.589	0.573
PHEALTH	Respondent reported poor health	0.035	0.040	0.011
OINC	Family income minus respondent's income	25,063	27,386	28,704
MM	Married male	0.202	0.172	0.192
MF	Married female	0.225	0.223	0.213
FNC	Female, no children at home	0.334	0.333	0.327
FWC	Female, with children at home	0.275	0.298	0.278

whether the respondent rents his/her home (RENTER), whether the respondent is a married female (MF) or married male (MM), and whether the respondent is a woman without (FNC) or with (FWC) children living at home. The reference category for MF and MM is single people and for FNC and FWC is males.

The respondent's level of education is represented by two variables. HS indicates whether he/she has only a high school degree. COLLEGE indicates that he/she has an associate or bachelor's degree. The reference group is people with less than a high school education.

Family income minus the respondent's earnings (OINC) and years spent working (EXPER) are included since these variables are known to be related to labor force participation. The inclusion of a number of the variables already mentioned can also be justified on this basis (education, health status, and the gender/children variables).

Eight variables indicating the current or most recent occupation of the respondent were also included in preliminary runs to investigate whether workers with "special talents" have less knowledge of the spatial distribution of jobs for less educated workers. Since these variables are jointly insignificant in all cases, they are excluded from final regressions.

Separate equations are estimated for all respondents, respondents without bachelor's degrees, and those among the latter group who are labor force participants.

Econometric issues

Three estimation issues are addressed: (1) the appropriate functional form, (2) the possible endogeneity of some of the regressors, and (3) the cluster design of the sample.

Since there is no *a priori* expectation regarding the appropriate functional form to use to estimate the knowledge equations, both dichotomous logit and linear probability function models are estimated. Although logit is the more common approach. Stoker [34] has shown that the linear probability model is a way to estimate a well-defined partial derivative that may be the best in a broad variety of circumstances. In addition, the Hausman tests and the random effects estimation discussed below are only possible for the linear model.

Another issue is whether the location variables, CITY and SSUB, are endogenous. While these variables may affect KNOW in the manner hypothesized above, it is also possible that people who are aware of the fact that jobs are more plentiful on the northside of the region may choose to locate there. If this is the case, a more sophisticated estimation technique would be required, such as two-stage least squares or instrumental variables. To test for the endogeneity of the location variables Hausman tests are conducted. For both of the dependent variables, KNOW1 and KNOW2, the null hypothesis of exogeneity cannot be rejected at the 5% level.[10]

Finally there is an issue concerning the sampling design. For reasons of cost containment, the MCSUI data were not collected using simple random sampling. Instead, a cluster design was employed that included 120 primary sampling units each of which is located in a different census tract. To accommodate the design of the sample, it is reasonable to assume that the error term of the regression equation (μ_{ij}) has the following properties:

$$\mu_{ij} = \alpha_i + \epsilon_{ij} \tag{3}$$

$$E(\alpha_i) = E(\epsilon_{ij}) = E(\alpha_i \epsilon_{ij}) = 0 \tag{4}$$

$$E(\alpha_i^2) = \sigma_\alpha^2 \quad \text{and} \quad E(\epsilon_{ij}) = \sigma_\epsilon^2 \tag{5}$$

where α_i is a random (*iid*) cluster effect and ϵ_{ij} is a random (*iid*) individual effect. Because the μ_{ij} are not independent, the OLS estimator yields unbiased but inefficient estimates of the slope coefficients. More importantly, the usual standard errors and test statistics for the slope coefficients can be seriously biased (Moulton [26]). The random effects model (also known as the error components model), however, is asymptotically efficient under the above assumptions. This model involves first obtaining estimates of σ_α^2 and σ_ϵ^2 and then using the general least squares estimator. There are a large number of estimators available that yield consistent estimates of the variance components. The one selected is the maximum likelihood estimator, which is recommended by Moulton [25] when the number of groups (i.e., clusters) is large.

5. Results

The results from estimating the knowledge equations are reported in Table 5 (logit) and Table 6 (random effects). The implied partial derivitives (evaluated at the means of the independent variables) and the associated asymptotic t statistics obtained from the logit estimation are highly similar to the estimated coefficients and t statistics obtained from the random effects estimation. Also, the results are qualitatively consistent between the two alternative dependent variables, KNOW1 and KNOW2. For all equations, estimated coefficients are collectively found to be significantly different from zero at better than the 1% level as measured by the likelihood ratio test.

BLACK is statistically insignificant by a one-tail test at the 5% level in all estimated equations. This contrasts with the results obtained from simple regressions of KNOW on BLACK. In all cases, the coefficient on BLACK is negative and statistically significant in the latter equations. The lower mean information values reported for blacks in Table 3, therefore, reflect the fact that BLACK is correlated with other explanatory variables. This issue will be addressed in greater detail below.

Across the estimated equations the variables having the strongest influence on the respondent's knowledge of the labor market are CITY and SSUB. Living in either one of these areas reduces the probability that the respondent is aware of the northside advantage in job availability, with city residents being the worst informed. To illustrate the magnitude of the location effects, which are generally significant at the 1% level, consider the KNOW1 results obtained for people without bachelor's degrees. The probability of knowing that jobs are more plentiful in the northern suburbs is 0.29 lower for city residents and 0.23 lower for residents of the southern suburbs in comparison to people living on the northside of the Region. These results suggest that space plays an important role in explaining the acquisition of labor market information.

The neighborhood variables, HPOV and MPOV, have positive signs. HPOV, but not MPOV, is sometimes significant at the 10% level (two–tailed test). These results are contrary to Wilson's hypothesis that people living in underclass neighborhoods have relatively poor information. As suggested in Section IV, information may be collectively better in poorer neighborhoods because these people are more dependent on jobs that do not require college degrees. This conclusion is strengthened by the results obtained with the education variables. The variable indicating whether the respondent holds a college degree (COLLEGE) is negative and statistically significant at the 10% level (two–tailed test) in all estimated equations.

Table 5 Estimated coefficients of the labor market knowledge equations obtained from logit models[a]

	Dependent Variable:		KNOW1	Dependent Variable:		KNOW2
	All respondents	No bachelor's degree	No bachelor's LF participant	All respondents	No bachelor's degree	No bachelor's LF participant
BLACK	−0.060	−0.073	−0.017	−0.324	−0.291	−0.200
	(0.28)	(0.28)	(0.06)	(1.30)	(0.97)	(0.62)
	[−0.011]	[−0.014]	[−0.003]	[−0.041]	[−0.038]	[−0.027]
CITY	−1.220	−1.525	−1.503	−1.028	−1.084	−0.954
	(4.13)	(4.31)	(3.90)	(2.85)	(2.57)	(2.11)
	[−0.227]	[−0.288]	[−0.285]	[−0.131]	[−0.141]	[−0.127]
SSUB	−0.879	−1.184	−1.195	−0.489	−0.556	−0.547
	(4.06)	(4.40)	(4.21)	(1.96)	(1.83)	(1.68)
	[−0.163]	[−0.224]	[−0.227]	[−0.063]	[−0.072]	[−0.073]
HPOV	0.559	0.697	0.629	0.652	0.556	0.509
	(1.72)	(1.87)	(1.53)	(1.67)	(1.27)	(1.07)
	[0.104]	[0.132]	[0.119]	[0.083]	[0.072]	[0.068]
MPOV	0.231	0.301	0.298	0.169	0.056	0.049
	(1.05)	(1.13)	(1.07)	(0.65)	(0.18)	(0.15)
	[0.043]	[0.057]	[0.057]	[0.022]	[0.007]	[0.007]
EXPER	−0.011	−0.008	−0.008	0.005	0.010	0.014
	(1.46)	(0.97)	(0.81)	(0.59)	(1.01)	(1.27)
	[−0.002]	[−0.002]	[−0.002]	[0.001]	[0.001]	[0.002]
HS	−0.392	−0.384	−0.543	−0.108	−0.119	−0.191
	(1.64)	(1.56)	(1.96)	(0.37)	(0.40)	(0.59)
	[−0.073]	[−0.073]	[−0.103]	[−0.014]	[−0.015]	[−0.025]
COLLEGE	−0.825	−0.972	−1.064	−0.511	−0.757	−0.816
	(3.19)	(3.09)	(3.07)	(1.63)	(1.98)	(1.95)
	[−0.153]	[−0.184]	[−0.202]	[−0.065]	[−0.098]	[−0.109]
RENTFR	0.048	0.111	0.051	0.236	0.322	0.333
	(0.26)	(0.51)	(0.21)	(1.08)	(1.24)	(1.15)
	[0.009]	[0.021]	[0.010]	[0.030]	[0.042]	[0.045]
PHEALTH	0.011	0.133	0.322	−1.111	−1.659	−0.067
	(0.02)	(0.28)	(0.35)	(1.48)	(1.59)	(0.06)
	[0.002]	[0.025]	[0.061]	[−0.142]	[−0.216]	[0.009]
OINC	4.4E-07	5.3E-07	IOE-06	6.8E-07	6.6E-07	2.0E-06
	(0.77)	(0.64)	(0.19)	(0.50)	(0.54)	(0.25)
	[8.1E-08]	[1.0E-07]	[1.9E-07]	[8.7E-08]	[8.6E-08]	[2.7E-07]
MM	−0.160	−0.122	−0.123	−0.236	−0.327	−0.375
	(0.65)	(0.42)	(0.40)	(0.81)	(0.94)	(1.04)
	[−0.030]	[−0.023]	[−0.023]	[−0.030]	[−0.043]	[−0.050]
MF	0.414	0.331	0.361	0.445	0.302	0.265
	(1.85)	(1.26)	(1.24)	(1.66)	(0.96)	(0.75)
	[0.077]	[0.062]	[0.069]	[0.057]	[0.039]	[0.035]
FNC	−0.727	−0.806	−0.775	−0.572	−0.638	−0.725
	(3.11)	(2.94)	(2.57)	(2.07)	(2.01)	(2.11)
	[−0.135]	[−0.152]	[−0.147]	[−0.073]	[−0.083]	[−0.097]

Table 5   (Cont.)

	Dependent Variable:		KNOW1	Dependent Variable:		KNOW2
	All respondents	No bachelor's degree	No bachelor's LF participant	All respondents	No bachelor's degree	No bachelor's LF participant
FWC	−0.658	−0.632	−0.483	−0.658	−0.681	0.523
	(2.67)	(2.29)	(1.62)	(2.19)	(2.05)	(1.50)
	[−0.122]	[−0.119]	[−0.092]	[−0.084]	[−0.089]	[−0.070]
Constant	0.433	0.535	0.625	−0.917	−0.865	−0.973
	(1.13)	(1.23)	(1.27)	(2.00)	(1.69)	(1.68)
2 log likelihood	57	59	51	37	36	26
Obs	969	712	605	969	712	605

[a] Absolute value of symptotic t statistic is in parentheses and implied partial derivative is in brackets. Implied partial derivatives are computed at the means of the independent variables.

The estimated coefficients on whether the respondent is a married male all have negative signs, but the associated t statistics are very small. In contrast, the estimated coefficients on whether the respondent is a married female all have positive signs and are statistically significant about one-third of the time. These results are inconsistent with the hypothesis that married women invest less in information about distant jobs because they are less geographically mobile. A possible explanation for these unexpected results is that married women can rely on their husbands as an inexpensive source of information on the labor market.

The results obtained with the gender variables, FNC and FWC, strongly suggest that women's knowledge of the spatial distribution of available jobs for less educated workers is worse than men's. In all cases, these two variables have negative and statistically significant coefficients (frequently at the 1% level, but always at the 10% level, by a one-tailed test). The similarity in the magnitudes of the FNC and FWC estimated coefficients suggests that whether the woman lives with children has little effect on her acquisition of labor market knowledge.

The other variables entering the estimated equations generally have little explanatory power. RENTER is always positive, as expected, but is consistently insignificant. PHEALTH has the expected sign and is statistically significant at the 10% level for all respondents and those without bachelor's degrees in the KNOW2 equations. EXPER is generally not significant. The estimated coefficients on OINC are always positive. OINC is included as a measure of the propensity of the individual to be interested in working. The expected sign is therefore negative. However, like the marital status of women, higher values of OINC signify that there are other family members who are working and therefore there may be an inexpensive source of information within the household. The OINC estimated coefficients are significant in the random effects but not the logit models.

As documented in Table 3, there is a sizable racial difference in the values of the information summary measures. However, as noted, BLACK is not found to have an independent influence on KNOW after accounting for the other independent variables

Table 6 Estimated coefficients of the labor market knowledge equations obtained from logit models[a]

	Dependent Variable:		KNOW1	Dependent Variable:		KNOW2
	All respondents	No bachelor's degree	No bachelor's LF participant	All respondents	No bachelor's, degree	No bachelor's LF participant
BLACK	−0.008	−0.011	−0.002	−0.038	−0.037	−0.025
	(0.23)	(0.24)	(0.05)	(1.22)	(0.96)	(0.60)
CITY	−0.222	−0.291	−0.289	−0.128	−0.146	−0.133
	(4.16)	(4.44)	(4.19)	(2.76)	(2.66)	(2.22)
SSUB	−0.165	−0.229	−0.234	−0.070	−0.084	−0.081
	(4.03)	(4.47)	(4.43)	(1.99)	(2.03)	(1.75)
HPOV	0.093	0.117	0.107	0.073	0.064	0.065
	(1.59)	(1.71)	(1.46)	(1.44)	(1.11)	(1.02)
MPOV	0.040	0.051	0.052	0.024	0.011	0.008
	(1.02)	(1.06)	(1.06)	(0.69)	(0.28)	(0.20)
EXPER	−0.002	−0.001	−0.001	0.001	0.001	0.002
	(1.43)	(0.88)	(0.76)	(0.57)	(1.02)	(1.33)
HS	−0.075	−0.073	−0.104	−0.016	−0.017	−0.031
	(1.69)	(1.64)	(2.01)	(0.42)	(0.45)	(0.76)
COLLEGE	−0.147	−0.162	−0.183	−0.065	−0.085	−0.098
	(3.13)	(3.04)	(3.04)	(1.65)	(1.89)	(1.90)
RENTER	0.006	0.020	0.011	0.024	0.037	0.040
	(0.20)	(0.53)	(0.27)	(0.89)	(1.16)	(1.15)
PHEALTH	0.001	0.026	0.058	−0.093	−0.113	0.008
	(0.02)	(0.32)	(0.36)	(1.48)	(1.65)	(0.06)
OINC	6.7E-08	6.9E-08	7.4E-08	7.8E-08	7.9E-08	8.3E-08
	(1.59)	(1.64)	(1.75)	(2.21)	(2.24)	(2.28)
MM	−0.034	−0.025	−0.024	−0.032	−0.045	−0.052
	(0.74)	(0.48)	(0.41)	(0.85)	(1.00)	(1.08)
MF	0.067	0.047	0.059	0.050	0.029	0.032
	(1.75)	(1.06)	(1.20)	(1.53)	(0.79)	(0.77)
INC	−0.126	−0.134	−0.130	−0.070	−0.078	−0.092
	(3.07)	(2.83)	(2.53)	(2.03)	(1.96)	(2.10)
IWC	−0.116	−0.110	−0.085	−0.078	−0.083	−0.070
	(2.65)	(2.25)	(1.61)	(2.12)	(2.02)	(1.56)
Constant	0.546	0.572	0.592	0.273	0.287	0.276
	(7.71)	(7.20)	(6.77)	(4.59)	(4.30)	(3.68)
Log of the likelihood function	−530	−384	−329	−357	−262	−234
Obs	988	726	614	998	726	614

[a] Absolute value of t statistic is in parentheses.

To investigate the importance that each variable plays in explaining the gross differential in information between blacks and whites, the estimated coefficients are used to predict the probability that the representative black (B) and white (W) is informed:

$$\hat{P}_W = \hat{a} + \bar{X}_W\hat{\alpha} \tag{6}$$

$$\hat{P}_B = \hat{a} + \hat{\beta} + \bar{X}_B\hat{\alpha} \tag{7}$$

where $\hat{a}$ is the estimated intercept, $\hat{\beta}$ is the estimated coefficient on BLACK, X are the other explanatory variables, and $\hat{\alpha}$ are the estimated coefficients on these variables.[11] The subtraction of (7) from (6) yields

$$\hat{P}_W - \hat{P}_B = -\hat{\beta} + \hat{\alpha}(\bar{X}_W - \bar{X}_B) \tag{8}$$

which reveals the contribution that each explanatory variable makes in explaining the difference in predicted probabilities between whites and blacks. Since the results are not sensitive to choice of model, sample group, or information measure, only those based on the random effects KNOW1 equations estimated for people without bachelor's degree are reported in Table 7.

The results indicate that CITY explains the entire gap in the probability of being informed between blacks and whites. That is, the much higher tendency of blacks to reside in the City of Atlanta (approximately 6.5 times greater than whites) accounts for their relative disadvantage in knowledge concerning the spatial distribution of available jobs for less educated workers. The other variables have relatively small and offsetting influences.

Table 7   The contribution of each variable to the difference in knowledge between whites and blacks

	White mean	Black mean	Contribution to difference
KNOW1	0.322	0.216	–
BLACK	–	–	0.011
CITY	0.073	0.459	0.109
SSUB	0.447	0.497	0.013
HPOV	0.048	0.309	−0.031
MPOV	0.260	0.567	−0.017
EXPER	17.522	17.446	0.000
HS	0.586	0.604	0.001
COLLEGE	0.275	0.192	−0.013
RENTER	0.432	0.682	−0.005
PHEALTH	0.018	0.053	−0.001
OINC	19.165	10.397	0.003
MM	0.225	0.141	−0.002
MF	0.348	0.148	0.009
FNC	0.360	0.320	−0.005
FWC	0.225	0.340	0.012

6. Conclusions

The key finding of this paper comes not from the regression equations but from the simple descriptive statistics presented in Table 3, which show that people, regardless of their race or labor force status, have very poor information on the spatial distribution of jobs for less educated workers. From a policy perspective, this finding may actually be encouraging. For it suggests that disseminating information on the whereabouts of jobs might have handsome paybacks in reducing inner-city poverty and unemployment and eliminating worker shortages in suburban areas. In comparison to alternative remedies for the spatial mismatch problem, such as suburban dispersal of blacks or better transportation for reverse commuters, information dissemination is a far less expensive proposition.

The Federal Transit Administration and local transit authorities have conducted reverse-commuting experiments, while the Department of Housing and Urban Development is currently analyzing the effects of its "Moving to Opportunity" demonstration, which involves relocating housing subsidy recipients from the city to the suburbs. But there have been no demonstrations that focus on providing less educated people, especially those living in inner-cities, with better labor market information. In light of this paper's results, such experiments are worthy of consideration.

The only other paper that has focused on the persistence of the spatial mismatch problem is Holzer et al. [17]. In that paper we found that black and white central city residents do not offset greater job decentralization with greater distances travelled, either for search or work. The negative effects of decentralization on travel were found to persist even after controlling for the time costs of travel. This suggests that barriers unrelated to transportation play a relatively more important role in explaining the perpetuation of the spatial mismatch problem.

Holzer et al. identify information limitations, perceived hostility, weak skills, and employer discrimination as possible hurdles inner-city residents face in finding work in the suburbs. The results of this paper lend some support to the importance of the first factor, without precluding the possible importance of the others.

Notes

1 For evidence that wage rates are higher in suburban areas, see Ihlanfeldt and Young [21], Hughes and Madden [18], and Straszheim [35], [36]. Studies showing that jobs are more available within suburban areas are more sparse. Nevertheless, there is mounting anecdotal evidence that this is the case (Biddle [4]; Brownstein [7]; Congbolay [8]; McCosh [24]; Peirce [28]; Roberts [32]; Wartzman [40]).

2 The ideas expressed in this paragraph were originally stated in Holzer, Ihlanfeldt, and Sjoquist [17], p. 321.

3 The Atlanta Region is defined by the Atlanta Regional Commission, which is Atlanta's metropolitan planning organization. In 1990 the Atlanta Region accounted for 83 and 92% of the MSA's people and jobs, respectively.

4 This survey was conducted by Madelyn Young as part of her dissertation research. For details, see Young [42].

5 This survey was developed and administered by Harry Holzer at Michigan State University.

6 The ARC employment estimates are based on commercially available business lists and confidential ES-202 data obtained from the Georgia Department of Labor.

7 According to the 1990 Census of Population and Housing STF3A, 39% of the black households living in the City of Atlanta had no auto, van or truck at home for use by household members.

8 For empirical evidence that women value their travel time at a higher fraction of the wage rate than men, see Ihlanfeldt [19].

9 In the empirical model, residential location is actually divided into the City of Atlanta, the northern suburbs, and the southern suburbs. The arguments in the text suggest that northern suburban residents are likely to possess information about jobs in the northern suburbs and the City, City residents are likely to possess information only about City jobs, and southern suburban residents are likely to possess information about jobs in the southern suburbs and the City. Residents of both the City and the southern suburbs are therefore expected to have relatively poor knowledge of the northside advantage in job availability.

10 The omitted variables version of the Hausman test is employed (Maddala [22], pp. 510, 513). This test involves regressing CITY and SSUB on the other explanatory variables and a set of instrumental variables. KNOW is then regressed on CITY and SSUB, the other explanatory variables, and the predicted values of CITY and SSUB. The null hypothesis of exogeneity is rejected if the predicted value variables are jointly significant. The instruments used include the respondent's stated attitudes toward living in neighborhoods with varying numbers of blacks and whites, total household income, household size, whether the respondent had lived in the greater Atlanta area all of his/her life, whether the respondent is a Democrat or a Republican, and whether the respondent was born outside the United States. One indicator of the quality of these instruments is whether they are jointly significant in the CITY and SSUB regressions (Bound, et al. [6]). The F statistic for the test of the joint statistical significance of the instruments is significant at the 1% level for both equations. The F statistics for the Hausman tests are 0.084 and 1.70 with 2 and 951 degrees of freedom for KNOW1 and KNOW2, respectively. The 5% significance point for the F distribution with these degrees of freedom is 3.00.

11 The actual and predicted values of KNOW1 are very close. Actual values are 0.322 and 0.216 and predicted values are 0.320 and 0.218 for whites and blacks, respectively.

References

1 Allen, R. E. and Keaveny, T. J. (1980) "The Relative Effectiveness of Alternative Job Sources." *Journal of Vocational Behavior*, 16, 18–32.

2 Bane, M. J. and Jargowsky, P. A. (1990) Ghetto Poverty: Basic Questions, in *Inner-City Poverty in the United States* (L. E. Lynn, and M. McGeary, Eds.), National Academy Press, Washington, DC.

3 Beasley, D. (1990) "Cobb Busses Take City Workers to Jobs," *Atlanta Constitution*, March 14, A1.

4 Biddle, F. M. (1987) "Suburban Jobs Throw Commute in Reverse" *Chicago Tribune*, November 8, 1.

5 Blanchard, O. and Katz, L. (1992) "Regional Evolutions," *Brookings Papers on Economic Activity*, 0, 1–61.

6 Bound, J., Jaeger, D. A. and Baker, R. (1993) *The Cure Can Be Worse Than the Disease: A Cautionary Tale Regarding Instrumental Variables*, National Bureau of Economic Research, technical paper no. 137.

7 Brownstein, V. (1989) "A Growing Shortage of Workers is Raising Inflation Risks," *Fortune*, 10, 33–34.

8 Congbolay, D. (1989) "Bay's Summer Job Scene – Help Wanted in the Suburbs." *San Francisco Chronicle*, June, 19, A7.

9 Corcoran, M., Datcher, L. and Duncan, G. J. (1980) "Information and Influence Networks in Labor Markets, in *Five Thousand American Families–Patterns of Economic Progress Volume III* Institute of Social Research, Ann Arbor, MI.

10 Freeman, R. B. (1977) "Fixed coefficient and manpower requirement models: A synthesis," in *Research in Labor Economics* (R. Ehrenberg, Ed.) JAI Press, Greenwich, CT.

11 Granovetter, M. (1974) *Getting A Job: A Study of Contacts and Careers* Harvard University Press, Cambridge, MA.

12 Greene, R. P. (1989) *Poverty Concentration in Large American Cities: Factors Accounting for the Emergence and Changing Spatial Patterns of Extreme Poverty Areas*, PhD thesis, University of Minnesota.

13 Hofler, R. A. and Murphy, K. J. (1992) "Underpaid and Overworked: Measuring the Effect of Imperfect Information on Wages." *Economic Inquiry*, 30, 511–29.

14 Hofler, R. A. and Polachek, S. W. (1985) "A New Approach for Measuring Wage Ignorance in the Labor Market," *Journal of Economics and Business*, 37, 267–76.

15 Holzer, H. J. (1987) "Informal Job Search and Black Youth Unemployment," *American Economic Review*, 77, 446–52.

16 Holzer, H. J. (1988) "Job Search Methods used by Unemployed Youth," *Journal of Labor Economics*, 5, 1–20.

17 Holzer, H. J. Ihlanfeldt, K. R. and Sjoquist, D. L. (1994) "Work, Search, and Travel among White and Black Youth," *Journal of Urban Economics*, 35, 320–45.

18 Hughes, M. A. and Madden, J. F. (1991) "Residential Segregation and the Economic Status of Black Workers: New Evidence For an Old Debate," *Journal of Urban Economics*, 29, 28–49.

19 Ihlanfeldt, K. R. (1992) "Intraurban Wage Gradients: Evidence by Race, Gender, Occupational Class, and Sector," *Journal of Urban Economics*, 32, 70–91.

20 Ihlanfeldt K. R. and Sjoquist, D. L. (1990) "Job Accessibility and Racial Differences in Youth Employment Rates," *American Economic Review*, 80, 267–76.

21 Ihlanfeldt, K. R. and Young, M. (1996) "The Spatial Distribution of Black Employment between the Central City and the Suburbs," *Economic Inquiry*, 64, 693–707.

22 Maddala, G. S. (1992) *Introduction to Econometrics*, second edn. MacMillan, New York.

23 Madden, J. F. (1981) "Why Women Work Closer to Home," *Urban Studies*, 18, 181–94.

24 McCosh, J. (1990) "Business Counting on Mass Transit to Boost Labor Pool," *Atlanta Journal and Constitution*, November 5, J1.

25 Moulton, B. R. (1989) *Using SAS to Estimate a Regression with Two Variance Components* mimeo, Division of Price and Index Number Research. U.S. Bureau of Labor Statistics September.

26 Moulton, B. R. (1990) "An Illustration of a Pitfall in Estimating the Effects of Aggregate Variables on Micro Units", *Review of Economics and Statistics*, 72, 334–8.

27 Nathan, R. (1987) "Will the Underclass Always be with us?" *Society*, March/April, 57–62.

28 Pierce, N. R. (1988) "Can the Suburban Jobs Boom Reach the Ghetto?" *National Journal*, August 13, 2108.

29 Pisarski, A. E. (1992) *Travel Behavior Issues in the 90's* U.S. Department of Transportation: Federal Highway Administration, Washington, DC.

30 Reid, G. L. (1972) "Job Search and the Effectiveness of Job-finding Methods," *Industrial and Labor Relations Review*, 25, 479–95.

31 Reischauer, R. D. (1987) *The Size and Characteristics of the Underclass*, Brookings Institution, Washington, DC.

32 Roberts, S. (1990) "Migrant Labor: The McShuttle to the Suburbs," *New York Times*, June 14, B1.

33 **Sjoquist, D.** (1990) *Concepts, Measurement, and Analysis of the Underclass: A Review of the Literature*, Research paper no. 7, Policy Research Center, Georgia State University, Atlanta, GA.

34 **Stoker, T. M.** (1986) "Consistent Estimation of Scaled Coefficients" *Econometrica*, 54, 1461–81.

35 **Straszheim, M. R.** (1980a) "Discrimination and the Spatial Characteristics of the Urban Labor Market for Black Workers," *Journal of Urban Economics*, 7, 119–40.

36 **Straszheim, M. R.** (1980b) "Urban Labor Markets and their Consequences for Black Employment," *Annual Housing Surveys*, 11, Department of Housing and Urban Development, Office of Policy Development and Research.

37 **Ullman, J. C.** (1968) "Interfirm Differences in the Cost of Clerical Workers," *The Journal of Business*, 41, 153–65.

38 **Vessey, S.** (1994) "Jobs Plentiful, Workers Scarce," *Atlanta Constitution*, May, 14, DI.

39 **Walston, C.** (1987) "Reverse Commuting: City Dwellers Working in Suburbs a Growing Trend," *The Atlanta Constitution*, December, 24, G1.

40 **Wartzman, R.** (1993) "Good Connections: New Bus Lines Link the Inner-city Poor with Jobs in Suburbia," *The Wall Street Journal*, September, 24, 1.

41 **Wilson, W.** (1987) *The Truly Disadvantaged*, University of Chicago Press, Chicago, IL.

42 **Young, M. V.** (1991) Wage rate differentials in the fast food industry: An Atlanta labor market study, unpublished dissertation, Georgia State University, College of Business Administration.

Further Reading Samples

Abstract from *Political Economy of Urban Poverty in the 21st Century: How Progress and Public Policy Generate Rising Poverty*

TIMOTHY BATES

Source: *Review of Black Political Economy*. Reprinted by permission of Transaction Publishers. © 1995 Transaction Publishers. All rights reserved.

Increasing the incidence of poverty is rarely the primary purpose of public policy decisions, but it is often a byproduct. When HUD Secretary Henry Cisneros calls upon local governments to improve their business climates by "lowering operating costs, reducing unreasonable regulatory burdens...", his objective is job creation generally, but achievement of that objective may entail increasing the ranks of the urban poor (Cisneros, 1995, p.5). Rising poverty in urban America is increasingly rooted in the fact that officially sanctioned economic development policies are working. Understanding why this is true is a precondition for formulating pragmatic political-economic strategies for attacking the causes of this tragic situation.

References

Cisneros, Henry (1995) "Urban Entrepreneuralism and National Economic Growth," *U. S. Department of Housing and Urban Development Essay*, September.

Abstract from *Local Labor Markets and Local Area Effects on Welfare Duration*

JOHN M. FITZGERALD

Source: *Journal of Policy Analysis and Management*, 14(1), 43–67. © 1995 Association for Public Policy Analysis and Management. Reprinted by permission of John Wiley & Sons Inc. New York.

The Survey of Income and Program Participation (SIPP) has become an important tool for studying how long people stay on welfare programs because it has monthly data on a variety of welfare programs. This article presents estimates of duration models for unmarried women with children who are on the Aid to Families with Dependent Children program (AFDC) using the 1984 and 1985 panels of SIPP. A weakness in previous welfare duration studies is that they do not include local labor market conditions or other local area effects; this omission may bias the estimated effects of policy variables (such as benefit levels) and labor market variables. This article incorporates relevant local area information from the City County Data Book and links this to SIPP welfare recipients based on county of residence. I find that local variables such as unemployment rates or per capita sales affect welfare exit rates, especially for blacks. Living in an urban area lengthens welfare spells for both whites and blacks.

Abstract from *Moving Into and Out of Poor Urban Areas*

EDWARD GRAMLICH, DEBORAH LAREN AND NAOMI SEALAND

Source: Journal of Policy Analysis and Management, 11(2), 273–87. © 1992 Association for Public Policy Analysis and Management. Reprinted by permission of John Wiley & Sons Inc. New York.

Newly available geographical information from the Panel Study of Income Dynamics (PSID) is used to estimate a variety of relationships involving high-poverty metropolitan census tracts. The longitudinal data from the PSID show a great deal of geographical mobility even for persistently poor adults, with as many as one fourth of certain groups of these entering and leaving poor urban census tracts in a year. At the same time, solution of the transition matrices for various group – whites and blacks of various income classes, in families with and without children, living in different types of census tracts – in the early 1980s shows the gradual emptying out of poor urban tracts, particularly of whites and blacks in families without children. As a consequence, despite the great degree of geographical "churning," poor urban areas gradually become poorer, blacker, and the home of a larger share of black families with children. Some of these aggregate trends had been noticed by researchers comparing these areas in the 1970 and 1980 censuses; our more up-to-date results demonstrate the relationships between the micro and macro data.

Abstract from *Black Employment Problems: New Evidence, Old Questions*

HARRY J. HOLZER

Source: Journal of Policy Analysis and Management, 13(4), 1994, 699–722. Association for Public Policy Analysis and Management. Reprinted by permission of John Wiley & Sons Inc. New York.

This article attempts to review and synthesize some new evidence on the employment problems of young blacks, especially relating to the issues of skill and spatial mismatch, racial discrimination, crime, and immigration. I also discuss various interpretations of these phenomena and highlight the fact that both shifts in demand (that is, employers and jobs) and the characteristics and responses of supply (that is, workers) in the labor market appear to be responsible for recent trends in employment and earnings among young blacks. This implies that government policy should focus directly on demand-side issues (such as job availability) in the short term, and especially on improving the adjustment of the black labor force to these shifts in demand over time.

Abstract from *The Los Angeles Rebellion: A Retrospective View*

JAMES H. JOHNSON, JR., CLOYZELLE K. JONES, WALTER C. FARRELL, JR., AND MELVIN L. OLIVER

Source: *Economic Development Quarterly*, 6(4), November, 356–72. © 1992 Sage Publications Inc. Reprinted by permission of Sage Publications Inc.

The Los Angeles rebellion of 1992 is evaluated from an urban political economy perspective. After discussing the anatomy of the rebellion and assessing retrospectively the outcome of the police brutality trial, the civil unrest is situated within the broader context of the recent demographic, social, and economic changes occurring in Los Angeles society. This is followed by a critical review of existing policies and proposals advanced to rebuild Los Angeles. An alternative strategy for rebuilding south central Los Angeles, which seeks to address the real "seeds" of the rebellion, is proposed.

Abstract from *Neighborhood Exposure to Toxic Releases: Are There Racial Inequities?*

WARREN KRIESEL, TERENCE J. CENTNER AND ANDREW G. KEELER

Source: *Growth and Change*, 27, Fall, 479–99. © 1996 Center for Business and Economic Research, University of Kentucky. Published by Blackwells Publishers.

This paper explores the use of empirical evidence to determine whether the exposure of minorities to environmental risks constitutes aversive racism. Connections are drawn between definitions of aversive racism and statistical approaches to research into the relationship between race and risk, paying particular attention to the influence of both non-racial discrimination and industrial location factors. Federal judicial and executive remedies to aversive racism are examined in light of the standards of evidence presented. An empirical study of the connection between race and exposure to toxic releases is then presented for Census block groups in Georgia and Ohio. It was found that the significance of race depends on the breadth of the explanatory model used in the analysis. A model of overall exposure to toxic releases shows that race is significant in a narrow model of discrimination but not in a broader model including industrial location factors. However, a model of targeting of minorities in the recent location of toxics-emitting facilities fails to show discrimination in any of the regression analyses. These findings support the view that environmental justice concerns cannot be addressed through reform of siting processes; broader remedies involving more stringent protection of exposure to toxic emissions are more likely to be effective.

Abstract from *The Impact of Welfare Reform on Local Labor Markets*

LAURA LEETE AND NEIL BANIA

Source: Journal of Policy Analysis and Management, 18(1), 509–76. © 1998 Association for Public Policy Analysis and Management. Reprinted by permission of John Wiley & Sons Inc. New York.

We develop a local labor market information system to assess the labor market effects of recently adopted welfare reform laws. Using the Cleveland-Akron metropolitan area as a prototype, we develop an occupationally and geographically specific inventory of projected job openings and measure the skill mismatch between projected job openings and the welfare population likely to enter the labor market. We find the skill mismatches are quite large: Following implementation of reform, welfare recipients entering the labor force would initially have to claim anywhere from 34 to 61 percent of expected low-skill job openings in order to become fully employed. Labor market opportunities are further diminished if one takes into account the effect of gender and space in limiting job accessibility. Welfare recipients entering the labor market as a result of reform would require from 40 to 75 percent of jobs remaining if predominantly male occupations are removed from consideration. The AFDC recipients who depend on public transportation, even in extraordinarily long commutes, can access only 40 to 44 percent of entry-level job openings.

Discussion Questions

1 As reported in the Meckler article, between 1994 and 1998, welfare rolls throughout the country fell 44 percent. This compares to a 35 percent average drop in the counties that contain the United State's 30 largest cities. Describe the reasons that have been offered for this difference.

2 Robert Woodson, Director of the National Center for Neighborhood Enterprise points out in the Freedberg article: "It is not just race and economics that determines one's behavior and values. We have to recognize that culture is also a factor." Whereas, William Julius Wilson, a leading urban sociologist, said that: "There is no way to explain the disproportionate number of minorities who are poor without taking the legacy of race into account – and the legacy of racism is the urban ghetto." What does Woodson mean by "culture"? Does economics ever take culture into consideration in the decision to look for work and then accept a job? Could both Woodson and Wilson be right in that there is a cause and effect relationship between racism and culture? Is there a tie to spatial mismatch theory here?

3 Find out how poverty is defined and calculated in the United States. Knowing this, do you agree or disagree with Boston Mayor Tom Menino's statement in the Woodwell and Rosenblum article: "The fact that in any one year, over one-fifth of our population lived in poverty for two straight months is unacceptable." Why?

4 Mills and Lubuelle discuss the important issue as to what degree the concentration of low-income population and social pathology in inner cities is involuntary. A theory that supports its involuntary nature, and thus it not necessarily being the fault of central city policies, is the flight-from-blight model. Describe the basic thinking behind this model. Can this model be reasonably offered as the sole reason for inner-city disparities?

5 Mills and Lubuelle use a regression method and data from 23 OECD countries to conclude that the USA has almost the worst rank of its performance relative to what is predicted it should be based on the independent variables. Describe the method used to come up with this finding.

6 In Table 7 of his paper, Ihlandfeldt presents the contribution of each explanatory variable to the differences in employment knowledge exhibited by Whites and African Americans. Describe how this table is derived. How does he conclude that CITY explains the entire probability of being informed between Whites and African Americans?

PART V
Urban Public Education

Despite a 15-year-long national school-improvement movement, many urban public schools are still falling apart physically and produce dismal results when it comes to teaching students.

Arthur Levine

CHAPTER TWENTY-TWO

Why I'm Reluctantly Backing Vouchers

ARTHUR LEVINE

Source: *The Wall Street Journal Reprinted 15.6.98. with permission of The Wall Street Journal.*

Throughout my career, I have been an opponent of school voucher programs. I disapproved of them because I feared they would undermine public schools. They also threatened to diminish the teaching of universal democratic values by supporting parochial and ideologically based schools. Studies of the limited experiments conducted with vouchers and school choice in the U.S. showed these options were used disproportionately by relatively affluent families, raising the concern that vouchers could turn our public schools into ghettos for the poor. In addition, the research showed vouchers produce little if any improvement in student achievement, but result in higher educational costs.

However, after much soul-searching, I have reluctantly concluded that a limited school voucher program is now essential for the poorest Americans attending the worst public schools. Despite a 15-year-long national school-improvement movement, many urban public schools are still falling apart physically and produce dismal results when it comes to teaching students. These schools show no signs of improving; some are even deteriorating. They are the worst schools in America. Walking through their halls, one meets students without hope and teachers without expectations. These schools damage children; they rob them of their futures. No parent should be forced to send a child to such a school. No student should be compelled to attend one.

Today these schools are effectively reserved for the urban poor. More-affluent parents have other options – private schools, suburban schools or better public schools. As never before in American history, we live in an age in which the future of our children is inextricably tied to the quality of the education they receive. In the past, a school dropout or a less-educated American could find a job in manufacturing or in one of the service professions, earning wages adequate to support a family. Those jobs have all but disappeared. Today, to force children into inadequate schools is to deny them any chance of success. To do so simply on the basis of their parents' income is a sin.

What I am proposing is a rescue operation aimed at reclaiming the lives of America's most disadvantaged children. This would involve a limited voucher program focusing on poor, urban children attending the bottom 10% of public schools. Their families would be reimbursed an amount equal to the cost per student of public education (a national average of roughly $6,500) to allow them to attend a better school. These schools could be nonsectarian private schools or better public schools in the suburbs. The money could even be used to create better urban public-school alternatives.

The voucher rescue would aim to accomplish three goals. Most important, it would offer poor children a way out of the worst schools. If the research on vouchers is correct, not nearly as many as one would hope will choose this option. However, many will – and that is all that matters. Second, it will become possible to shut down some of the poor schools abandoned by students with vouchers. This will permit urban public school districts to concentrate their resources on more promising and effective schools. Third, the vouchers could encourage the creation of strong urban schools. This could happen as entrepreneurs and private companies such as the Edison Project follow the dollars and establish private inner-city schools. It could happen if urban public school districts decide to replace old schools with better ones so that they can compete for students. In any case, schools receiving voucher funding should be required to meet serious performance standards. They need to be accountable both fiscally and academically.

This is a painful proposal for me to offer. In making it I am departing from the views of most of my colleagues at Teachers College and of educators across the nation, whom I deeply respect. I do so only in response to a desperate situation. I offer it not as a convert to vouchers, but as an individual who thinks in this one instance they may be the only way to save the most disadvantaged children. I offer this proposal not as a detractor of public schools, but as a champion who wants them to be as strong as they can be.

CHAPTER TWENTY-THREE

Current Issues in Public Urban Education

LAWRENCE O. PICUS

The 100 largest school districts in the United States educate 22.9 percent of our nation's K–12 students, yet they represent a mere 0.6 percent of the school districts serving these children. Often faced with older buildings and more children who are "at risk" for various reasons, urban districts face tremendous challenges in educating these youngsters.

A number of educational reforms taking hold across the country offer promise for improvement. Implementation of site-based management, which allows officials and teachers at the school level to focus on the specific needs of the children for whom they are responsible, offers promise for improving schools across the nation, particularly in urban areas. Other reforms are not as well tested but also show promise. Today there are a number of successful schools in urban areas, giving hope that, in the future, more children in our largest cities will attend schools that offer them greater opportunities.

Introduction

Although there are over 15,000 school districts in the United States, nearly one-fourth of the nation's public elementary and secondary students attend classes in the 100 largest districts.[1] Despite, or perhaps because of, their tremendous size, these districts face a number of intractable problems in providing educational services to their student populations. Metropolitan school districts frequently serve large concentrations of children who come from low-income families, are minorities, or speak limited English. The dropout rate is often considerably higher in central city districts. Most of these districts have higher concentrations of disabled students who require access to specialized, and hence extensive, services. These and other factors often lead to lower student achievement in these large districts.

Funds to improve schools in urban areas frequently seem limited, and many state school finance formulas do not provide funds to compensate these districts for the additional costs associated with greater service demands and higher costs of providing educational services. Moreover, urban school districts face considerable pressures from constituents. Taxpayers express concern over increasing property taxes, while teachers seek higher wages and smaller classes. Parents of children with disabilities seek more services for their children, while state funds for special education decline. Test scores in urban districts are often lower than in surrounding suburbs, leading to calls for breaking up the district or for establishing choice or voucher programs. These pressures often work at cross purposes, leading to breakdowns in management and organization, thus limiting the effectiveness of urban school personnel to provide a quality education for the children enrolled in the district.

This article provides a brief description of urban school systems in the United States and identifies the special problems these districts face in educating the children within their boundaries. It discusses current reform efforts that appear to show promise in improving not only urban schools but hopefully all schools.

Characteristics of Urban School Districts

Because school districts are organized in different ways in each of the 50 states, it is difficult to establish a statistical portrait of urban school districts. States such as California, Illinois, and Texas each have approximately 1,000 school districts, and even suburban areas have a number of large districts that exhibit urban characteristics. Other states such as Florida, where the 67 districts are coterminous with county borders, have a number of large school districts centered around relatively smaller cities. Among the more than 15,000 school districts in the United States, there are 22 districts with over 100,000 students. In 1990–91, these districts enrolled 5.2 million students, or 12.4 percent of the total number of children in public schools across the country. That year, almost half (47.3 percent) of the nation's students were enrolled in the 683 school districts with enrollments exceeding 10,000 students (Sietsema 1993).

Student characteristics

The 100 largest districts in the United States include all of the major urban areas in the country. They range in size from nearly 1 million students and 1,000 schools in New York to almost 40,000 students and 82 schools in Pittsburgh. In 1990–91, the most recent year for data on urban districts, these 100 districts enrolled 9,627,140 students, or 22.9 percent of the 42,095,467 students enrolled in public schools across the nation (figure 1). These districts represent less than 1 percent of the total number of school districts, yet they contain 16.5 percent of the nation's schools and 22.6 percent of the nation's teachers. Just over 19 percent of the nation's high school graduates received their diplomas from these 100 districts (Sietsema 1993).

The 100 largest districts have an average of 96,271 students, 5,147 teachers, and 142 schools. This results in a pupil/teacher ratio of approximately 19 to 1 and an average school size of 678 students. Across the entire nation, the average school district has about 5 schools, 137 teachers, and 2,521 students (National Center for Education Statistics 1994). This leads to a pupil/teacher ratio of about 18 to 1 and an average school size of 504 pupils. Thus, urban school districts tend to have slightly larger classes and bigger schools.

Urban districts also have a disproportionate share of minority students. In the 89 districts for which data were available, 43 reported that 50 percent or more of their students were white, non-Hispanic. Fifteen of those 43 reported minority representation

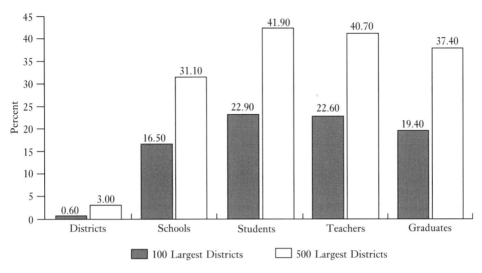

Figure 1 Characteristics of the 100 and 500 largest school districts as a percent of all U.S. school districts, 1990–91
Source: Sietsema (1993).

of less than 25 percent, and 10 had less than 20 percent. In the remaining 46 districts, more than half of the students were ethnic minorities. In 19 of these districts, more than half the students were African-American. Another six districts reported that a majority of their students were Hispanic, and one district reported a majority of Asian/Pacific Islanders. In the remaining 20 districts, no single racial/ethnic group constituted more than 50 percent of the student population (Sietsema 1993).

Spending patterns

Few data are available on how per-pupil expenditures in urban districts compare with expenditures in all school districts. Recent work by researchers at the Finance Center of the Consortium for Policy Research in Education (CPRE) has looked closely at the question of how school districts spend their funds and allocate resources. While the overall findings indicate that school districts are remarkably consistent in the proportion of total resources devoted to various functions (e.g., instruction, administration, maintenance and operations, transportation, instructional support), some findings related to large urban school systems are noteworthy.

In analyzing data from the Schools and Staffing Survey and the census of governments of the U.S. Bureau of the Census, Picus (1993a) concluded that per-pupil spending tends to be higher in urban than rural areas. In general, as the community gets larger, per-pupil spending increases. However, spending in the suburbs surrounding a city typically exceeds spending in the central city itself. Moreover, Picus (1993b) found that the average pupil/teacher ratio tends to be somewhat higher in urban areas than in other districts.

Detailed analyses of national data and of state databases in Florida, New York, and California indicate that, on average, school districts spend 60 percent of their resources on instruction (Picus and Fazal 1995). Many have used this finding to argue that public schools, in large urban districts in particular, suffer from an "administrative blob." However, CPRE research (Picus and Fazal 1995) indicates that administrative expenses tend to be in the range of 12 to 14 percent of total expenditures, half of that at the school site and half in the central office. Moreover, the research summarized in the Picus and Fazal (1995) study shows that costs for central administration in the largest districts in all three states – Florida, New York, and California – are well below the state average. Thus, despite the considerable size of the bureaucracy engaged in the operation of the Dade County, New York City, and Los Angeles schools, there are sufficient economies of scale to allow each of these districts to devote a smaller portion of total resources to central administration than other districts do in their respective states.

Revenue patterns

There is substantial evidence that urban school districts face considerably higher costs of education than rural and suburban school districts. Often the cost of living in urban areas is higher than in other parts of the nation, requiring districts to pay teachers higher salaries and increasing the costs of other staff as well as supplies and materials (Nelson 1991). Moreover, urban areas frequently have higher concentrations of children from low-income families or children requiring special education services (Odden and Picus 1992). In addition, urban districts often face substantial transportation costs either to meet integration requirements or simply because urban traffic conditions make bus travel more expensive in large cities (Wood et al. 1995).

Despite these considerable cost factors, most state school finance formulas do not take urban needs into consideration in the distribution of funds to the schools. Most school aid programs provide assistance to school districts in inverse relation to district property wealth per pupil. Despite low household incomes, most large cities generally are not "property poor" and thus do not generate large amounts of state aid through traditional school finance formulas (Odden and Picus 1992). Some states offer additional aid through categorical programs, and there are federal programs for compensatory education (Title I), bilingual education, special education, and a host of other special needs. However, these programs often are inadequate to meet the needs of the children in urban school systems (Goertz 1988).

Meeting the Needs of Urban Schools

Despite all of the difficulties facing urban school systems, a number of educational reform efforts and policy initiatives are under way that show promise in improving the quality of education and raising student outcomes in urban areas.

School finance

The two most common approaches to meeting urban school district needs through state school finance formulas are cost-of-education indices and categorical grants to fund programs for children with special needs (Odden and Picus 1992). Although the concept of a cost-of-education index is straightforward, developing an index that can be used to adjust the amount of aid to which a school district is entitled is both complex and fraught with political pitfalls. While a number of states rely on such indices in distributing state aid, the indices are frequently determined through political compromise rather than based on measured differences in educational costs across school districts in a state. Florida bases its cost index on a cost-of-living index, without regard to how this index corresponds to the costs of educational inputs (Nakib 1995); Texas has created an index based more directly on educational resources. However, the study on which the Texas index was based has not been updated in a number of years, and the current formula allows only half of the index to be used in the distribution of some of the funds (Picus and Toenjes 1994).

In addition to these difficulties, state school finance formulas do not account for other demands on local property tax dollars. As Levin, Muller, and Sandoval (1973) argued over 20 years ago, there are often more competing demands for property tax resources in urban areas, making it more difficult for big city school districts to garner support for higher school taxes. This "municipal overburden" is rarely addressed in the distribution of state funds to school districts.

One way this problem has been resolved in the past has been through the use of categorical grants. California is the only state that has actually provided assistance to districts on the basis of their "urbanness," although many states provide a range of categorical funding schemes for districts with high concentrations of students with special needs (Gold 1993). While generally a successful way to ensure that the needs of children in urban school districts are being met, many of these programs are underfunded, or the eligibility requirements are so loosely stated that many other districts in a state are also eligible for funds. This looseness is often necessary to garner enough political support in the legislature to pass the program in the first place.

A number of states rely on pupil weighting programs to meet the needs of special children (Gold 1993). In these states, children in certain categories are given a special weight. The weighted number of students is then used to calculate the amount of funding a district receives. Thus, urban districts that have high concentrations of children with special needs can receive additional funds to finance the education of those youngsters.

Clune (1994) suggested that school finance should shift its focus from ensuring equity across school districts to making sure that all students have access to adequate funds so they will be able to perform at a high level. While data are limited on how much it would cost to reach Clune's goal of adequacy, he has estimated that implementing an adequacy system in the districts where most of the nation's poor children live (which are largely urban) would cost $30 billion a year more than we are currently spending.

Even if state school finance formulas are able to provide additional resources to urban schools, there is no guarantee that these funds will make a difference in improving student performance. A number of other reforms have been attempted to improve urban schools in recent years. Some of the more important ones are discussed below.

Site-based management

The emergence of site-based management as a major component of school reform requires that it be given particular attention in any discussion of urban school systems. Site-based management places greater authority in the hands of school-site personnel and not surprisingly has been implemented in a number of different ways across the United States (Malen, Ogawa, and Kranz 1990; Wohlstetter and Odden 1992). The rationale for site-based management is a belief that the closer to the student a decision is made, the better that decision is likely to serve the student. In addition, movement to more decentralized management of school systems is believed to reduce unnecessary layers of administration and middle management.

Site-based management is a particularly powerful tool in large urban districts where there are a large number of schools. To date, schools have been given authority over some combination of three areas – budget, curriculum, and personnel (Clune and White 1988). Budget authority varies by school district, with some districts granting school sites only limited authority over marginal spending decisions, and others granting sites the flexibility to trade personnel positions and vary the composition of the staff at the school. In settling a lawsuit aimed at equalizing school district expenditures within the Los Angeles Unified School District, district officials have agreed to establish a management information system that will give site administrators adequate information to consider salary levels in hiring new staff. It is hoped that once the system is fully implemented, spending differences based on teacher experience and education (which drive the level of teacher salaries) will be substantially reduced across the district, thus virtually eliminating differences in per-pupil spending across schools.

Many districts have also granted school sites more autonomy over curriculum decisions. Rather than telling sites what the curriculum for each subject will be, districts are beginning to grant the school sites greater latitude in deciding what will be taught when and what materials to use. In some models, links between school levels are required to ensure adequate articulation as students move from one level to the next.

Finally, many districts are granting school sites more autonomy in personnel decisions regarding who will be hired and what kinds of positions will be filled. Such autonomy gives schools the flexibility to trade an assistant principal for additional teachers to reduce class size, or to accept slightly larger classes in exchange for a guidance counselor to help problem children. Each site is given the authority to decide for itself what organization will work best in meeting its established educational goals (Wohlstetter and Van Kirk 1995).

A number of management approaches are used by local school sites as they take more responsibility for the management and operation of their schools. A model pioneered by the Edmonton, Alberta, school district grants school-site authority to the site principal, who is empowered to make many decisions. Moreover, the district has given spending authority for 95 percent of the budget to local sites (Wohlstetter and Buffett 1992). A second model, used in a number of districts and required in all Texas school districts for the past two years, requires authority to be shared among the members of a school-site council composed of the principal, schoolteachers, and community members (Picus and Hertert 1992). In Los Angeles, the Los Angeles Educational Alliance for Restructuring Now has developed a similar authority-sharing model that is being implemented in a number of schools across the district. A third model grants control to the local community. In Chicago, school-site councils are elected by voters in the school attendance area, and councils have the authority to hire and fire the school principal. Little evidence exists about which of these models is most effective (Wohlstetter and Odden 1992).

Recent work by researchers in the private sector offers a conceptual framework for site-based management that may help districts decentralize important decisions. Lawler (1991) establishes a framework for shifting decision making to the production level, a procedure that may be applicable to the local management of school sites as well. Lawler suggests that four components are essential to the successful implementation of site-based management:

1. Information: The site must have access to adequate information about the inputs (resources) and outputs (student outcomes) of the system.
2. Knowledge: Individuals at each site must have adequate knowledge of educational research to know what methods and which curricula will work best in their particular circumstances.
3. Power: The local site must have the power to implement the programs it decides are appropriate to its circumstances.
4. Rewards: A reward structure must be established that rewards teams for successfully achieving their goals.

Current research sponsored by the Department of Education's Office of Educational Research and Improvement is studying the extent to which districts that have implemented successful site-based management programs use this framework.

Charter schools

A logical leap from site-based management is charter schools. Charter schools are independent public schools that choose to break away from their school district and operate on their own. Following Minnesota's lead, about half of the states have authorized the establishment of charter schools. These schools must prepare a charter describing their educational goals and how they will be achieved. Charter status typically must be granted by the school's district and by the state Board of Education. Schools that are granted a charter can waive state rules and regulations to the maximum extent, and they are supposed to receive the same level of per-pupil funding that is available to their former district. The charters often expire after a stated period of time, and state policy requires that these schools show they have achieved their goals or are making progress toward achieving them.

Although charter schools are relatively new, a total of 10 charters have been granted to schools in the Los Angeles Unified School District. Two of the charter schools have been granted complete autonomy from the school district for budget and operations. Seven others maintain independent status only for curriculum, having chosen to remain with the district for fiscal management functions. Preliminary analyses of these schools by the author indicate that the basis for deciding whether to stay with the district or provide fiscal services on their own was determined mostly by the relative costs of teachers in the schools. Schools with average teacher salaries above the district average are at a considerable fiscal disadvantage if they opt out of the school district, whereas schools with relatively low teacher salaries can use the savings for other purposes when the district provides level per-pupil funding to all charter schools as required by state law. One charter school in Los Angeles recently had its charter revoked by the district's Board of

Education because of administrative mismanagement that resulted in a deficit of $1.3 million.

School choice

The solutions discussed so far for improving the quality of urban (and all other) schools have focused on self-determination of the school site. Another option is to let parents decide which school offers the best program for their children. While voucher programs have been proposed in a number of different forms for the past 20 years, a more recent innovation is public school choice. Under most choice proposals, parents are able to select which school their child will attend, regardless of where they live and whether or not they live in that school district. Parents are typically responsible for transporting their children to the school.

In some states, notably Minnesota, the only limits on school choice are based on school capacity and parental willingness to transport their children. In California, options are somewhat more limited. Parents may enroll their children in a school located in a district where they are employed if they are not satisfied with their local school or if they wish to be closer to their children during the workday. While interdistrict choice is a restricted privilege granted to Californians, many districts in the state have begun choice programs within the district boundaries.

Proponents of choice models believe that schools will compete with one another for children and thus be forced to improve or close down due to lack of enrollments. While this market-based strategy has certain appeal, it seems unlikely that it will succeed in its pure form. Many parents choose to send their children to the local school because it is more convenient, and they expect the district to offer a quality program in all schools. Moreover, in a district that has no excess capacity at any of its schools, choice is a moot question since a school will have room for additional children only if some elect to attend alternative schools. Therefore, it is unlikely that choice models will succeed in weeding out poorly performing schools, although they may have some impact on the improvement of schools that are forced to compete for children.

Vouchers

Another issue that has gained considerable attention in recent years is school vouchers. Despite efforts to establish school voucher programs in many states, most notably California's failed effort in 1993, there are just two voucher programs in existence today. In Milwaukee, Wisconsin, the state provides vouchers to some 1,500 low-income students that can be used in private schools in the city. The value of the vouchers is the roughly $2,500 of state aid provided to the Milwaukee school district. While participation in the program has been extensive, no evidence exists that the quality of education in these private schools is better than that in the public schools, and efforts to expand the program in Milwaukee have run into considerable opposition both among district officials and teachers and in the state legislature. In Cleveland, a similar voucher program that began in the fall of 1996 includes religious schools.

Recent polling in California indicates that if another voucher proposal had been on the ballot in 1996, it would most likely have been defeated by the voters. Given the strong opposition of the education community to vouchers, it is unlikely that this alternative will become a major funding mechanism in the near future.

Employee relations and professional development

Another important element to consider in improving urban schools is the teachers. Teacher salaries and benefits account for 60 percent of total educational expenditures nationally. The direct contact between teachers and students provides the greatest impact on student learning. Therefore, if a district aims to improve student performance, the teachers will play a crucial role in determining whether or not it succeeds.

Today, teacher compensation is based on the number of years a teacher has been teaching and the education he or she has attained since beginning to teach. There is no salary boost for performance, and merit pay and career-ladder programs have been unsuccessful in both raising average teacher salaries and improving the quality of teachers. Odden and Conley (1992) argue that teacher compensation should be based instead on what teachers "know and can do," suggesting that increases in salary be tied to demonstrable knowledge of methods that lead to improved student achievement. Odden and Conley also suggest that to achieve a system where pay is tied to some measure of what teachers know and can do, and to ensure that local sites have adequate knowledge to manage themselves well, districts and schools need to devote substantially more resources to professional development. Odden and Conley argue that schools should spend as much as 2 to 4 percent of their budgets on professional development activities, rather than the less than 1 percent that is the norm today. Rewarding teachers who demonstrate knowledge of successful educational practices is at the heart of the national teaching certificate being developed by the National Board for Professional Teacher Standards.

Conclusion

Improving urban education will require more than the application of additional money. Current research on how schools allocate and use fiscal resources shows that regardless of the level of resources available to a school district, funds are spent for functions such as instruction, administration, and operations and maintenance in almost exactly the same proportions. Thus it seems safe to expect that if additional dollars are allocated to urban school systems, they will continue doing more of the same. Recent research by Hedges, Laine, and Greenwald (1994) questions earlier work by Hanushek (1986, 1989), which argued that additional money did not lead to improved student outcomes. It seems that if money makes a difference, it will have a larger impact if districts and schools find alternative, better ways to use additional funds.

For example, teachers frequently argue that salaries have to be improved to attract more highly qualified individuals to the teaching profession. While this is no doubt the case, increasing the salaries of all teachers seems an expensive way to recruit new individuals and by itself does little to improve the quality of schools in the short and medium term. A more effective strategy might be to improve salaries for beginning teachers and provide opportunities for both new and current teachers to reach the highest levels of the salary schedule more quickly if they can demonstrate knowledge of teaching methods that research indicates will lead to improved student outcomes.

The single biggest resource available to urban school districts for staff development is the funds used to pay teachers for the education they receive. It is estimated that this amounts to $260 million a year in Los Angeles alone. By changing the way teachers earn these funds, the district can create substantial incentives toward improving schools with little or no additional investment.

While urban schools face a tremendous number of problems in meeting the educational needs of the children living within their boundaries, there are many reasons to be optimistic about the future of the schools in our largest cities. Despite the continued barrage of negative discussion focused on urban schools, there are many examples of excellent schools in our cities as well. *Money* magazine may have said it best: "By and large, public schools are not lacking in experienced topnotch teachers, challenging courses or an environment that is conducive to learning.... If they [teachers] find an industrious student who is eager to learn, more often than not they will give him or her all of the personal attention that private tuition money could buy" (Topolnicki 1994, 112).

Notes

1   Although the focus of this article is on urban school districts, national data are available only for the 100 largest districts. While virtually all of the 100 largest districts are in urban areas, some of those districts do not exhibit the characteristics of a truly urban district. Despite the slight differences between these two groups, the terms "100 largest districts" and "urban districts" are used interchangeably in this article.

References

Clune, William H. (1994) "The Shift from Equity to Adequacy in School Finance." *Educational Policy*, 8(4), 376–94.

Clune, William H. and Paula White (1988) *School-Based Management: Institutional Variation, Implementation and Issues for Further Research*. New Brunswick, NJ: Rutgers University, Consortium for Policy Research in Education.

Goertz, Margaret (1988) *School Districts' Allocation of Chapter 1 Resources*. Princeton, NJ: Educational Testing Service.

Gold, Steven (1993) *Public School Finance Programs of the United States and Canada*. Albany, NY: State University of New York, Rockefeller Institute on Government, Center for the Study of the States.

Hanushek, Eric (1986) "The Economics of Schooling: Production and Efficiency in Public Schools." *Journal of Economic Literature* 24(3), 1141–77.

Hanushek, Eric (1989) "The Impact of Differential Expenditures on Student Performance." *Educational Researcher* 18(4), 45–52.

Hedges, Larry V., Richard D. Laine and Rob Greenwald (1994) "Does Money Matter? A Meta-Analysis of Studies of the Effects of Differential School Inputs on Student Outcomes." *Educational Researcher* 23(3), 5–14.

Lawler, Edward (1991) *High Involvement Management*. San Francisco, CA: Jossey-Bass.

Levin, Betsy, Thomas Muller and Corazon Sandoval (1973) *The High Cost of Education in Cities*. Washington, DC: The Urban Institute.

Malen, Betty, Rod T. Ogawa and Judith Kranz (1990) "What Do We Know About School Based Management? A Case Study of the Literature – A Call for Research." In *Choice and Control in American Education*. Vol. 2, *The Practice of Choice, Decentralization and School Restructuring*, ed. W. H. Clune and J. F. Witte, 289–342. Bristol, PA: The Falmer Press.

Nakib, Yasser (1995) "Beyond District Level Expenditures: Schooling Resource Allocation and Use in Florida." In *Where Does the Money Go? Resource Allocation in Elementary and Secondary Schools*, ed. Lawrence O. Picus and James L. Wattenbarger, 85–105. Thousand Oaks, CA: Corwin Press.

National Center for Education Statistics (1994) *Digest of Education Statistics, 1994*. Report No. NCES 94–115. Washington, DC: U.S. Department of Education, Office of Educational Research and Improvement.

Nelson, F. Howard (1991) "An Interstate Cost-of-Living Index." *Educational Evaluation and Policy Analysis* 13(1), 103–12.

Odden, Allan R., and Sharon Conley (1992) "Restructuring Teacher Compensation Systems." In *Rethinking School Finance: An Agenda for the 1980s*, ed. Allan R. Odden, 123–47. San Francisco, CA: Jossey-Bass.

Odden, Allan R., and Lawrence O. Picus (1992) *School Finance: A Policy Perspective*. New York: McGraw-Hill.

Picus, Lawrence O. (1993a). *The Allocation and Use of Educational Resources: District Level Evidence from the Schools and Staffing Survey*, working paper no. 34, The Finance Center of Consortium for Policy Research in Education, Los Angeles, CA.

Picus, Lawrence O. (1993b). *The Allocation and Use of Educational Resources: School Level Evidence from the Schools and Staffing Survey*, working paper no. 37, The Finance Center of Consortium for Policy Research in Education, Los Angeles, CA.

Picus, Lawrence O., and Minaz B. Fazal (1995) "Why Do We Need to Know What Money Buys? Research on Resource Allocation Patterns in Elementary and Secondary Schools." In *Where Does the Money Go? Resource Allocation in Elementary and Secondary Schools*, ed. Lawrence O. Picus and James L. Wattenbarger, 1–19. Thousand Oaks, CA: Corwin Press.

Picus, Lawrence O., and Linda Hertert (1992) *CPRE Core Summary Report: Texas*. New Brunswick, NJ: Rutgers University, Consortium for Policy Research in Education.

Picus, Lawrence O., and Laurence A. Toenjes (1994) "Texas School Finance: Assessing the Equity Impact of Multiple Reforms." *Journal of Texas Public Education* 2(3), 39–62.

Sietsema, John (1993) *Characteristics of the 100 Largest Public Elementary and Secondary School Districts in the United States: 1990–91*. Report No. NCES 93–131. Washington, DC: U.S. Department of Education, National Center for Education Statistics, Office of Educational Research and Improvement.

Topolnicki, David M. (1994) "Why Private Schools Are Rarely Worth the Money." *Money*, October, 1994, 98–112.

Wohlstetter, Priscilla, and Tom M. Buffett (1992) "Promoting School-Based Management: Are Dollars Decentralized Too?" In *Rethinking School Finance: An Agenda for the 1980s*, ed. Allan R. Odden, 203–35. San Francisco, CA: Jossey-Bass.

Wohlstetter, Priscilla, and Allan Odden (1992) "Rethinking School-Based Management Policy and Research." *Educational Administration Quarterly* 28(4), 529–49.

Wohlstetter, Priscilla, and Amy Van Kirk (1995) "Redefining School-Based Budgeting for High Involvement." In *Where Does the Money Go? Resource Allocation in Elementary and Secondary*

Schools, ed. Lawrence O. Picus and James L. Wattenbarger, 212–35. Thousand Oaks, CA: Corwin Press.

Wood, R. Craig, David Thompson, Lawrence O. Picus, and Don I. Tharpe (1995) *Principles of School Business Management*, 2nd edn. Reston, VA: Association of School Business Officials, International.

CHAPTER TWENTY-FOUR

Why Is It So Hard to Help Central City Schools?

WILLIAM DUNCOMBE AND JOHN YINGER*

Source: *Journal of Policy Analysis and Management*, 16(1), 1997, 85–113. ©
1997 Association for Public Policy Analysis and Management. Reprinted by
permission of John Wiley & Sons Inc. New York.

Many states have implemented educational grant systems designed to provide more aid to
school districts that are, by some standard, in greater need. Nevertheless, many if not most
central city school systems continue to produce poor educational outcomes, as measured, for
example, by test scores and dropout rates. Using data from New York State, this article asks
why existing aid formulas fail to provide the assistance that central city school districts need to
bring their educational outcomes up to reasonable standards. Two principal explanations are
explored: the failure of existing aid programs to recognize the high cost of providing
education in central cities and the possibility that aid simply makes central cities less efficient
without raising educational outcomes. The article presents aid programs that account for
costs, but shows that these revised programs will do little to help central cities without at least
one politically unpopular provision, namely a large state budget or a high required local
property tax rate. The article also estimates the extent to which increased aid to central cities
leads to their less efficient operation, thereby undermining the objective of improved educational outcomes for central city students. The article concludes by listing the steps that a state
can take to help central city schools and by discussing the yet unresolved problems that arise
in helping these districts.

Despite decades of education reform efforts since the *Serrano* decision, school quality
remains distressingly low in many central cities. In New York State, for example, educational outcomes in the three large upstate central cities, as measured by the test-score-
based index we develop later in the article, are 60 percent below the state average.
Advocates of more aid for central city schools argue that existing aid programs fail to
recognize the unique features of these schools that make it expensive for them to provide
education. Opponents argue that more aid will make central city schools even less efficient
than they already are and will have little impact on educational outcomes. This article
explores these two views. In particular, we estimate, for both central city and other
districts, what would happen to some key educational outcomes and to the efficiency
with which they are provided if a state shifts to an aid program in which educational
outcomes, rather than expenditures, are the focus of equalization.

* The authors are grateful to Bob Inman and an anonymous referee for helpful comments.

Our objectives are to design outcome-based state aid programs and simulate their effects. We discuss the conceptual issues that arise in any attempt to meet these objectives and describe the steps a state would have to take in designing outcome-based aid. Although we have an unusually extensive data set for school districts in New York State, we cannot fully resolve all the conceptual and statistical issues that arise in this process. Instead, we examine relatively straightforward aid programs and draw on the existing literature to illustrate their likely effects on educational outcomes.

The analysis in this article builds on three relationships. The first two, cost and demand equations for education, are well known. The cost equation describes the relationship between educational spending, outcomes, and costs. We focus on a particular set of educational outcomes, including test scores and the dropout rate. The demand equation explores the factors affecting a district's choice of these educational outcomes, such as its income, tax price, and state aid. Our key innovation in estimating these equations is to include a variable, described more fully later, that measures, among other things, the efficiency with which these educational outcomes are delivered. The third relationship concerns the determinants of this "efficiency" measure. This analysis of "efficiency" must be interpreted with care, but it allows us to estimate the extent to which higher state aid results in less efficient delivery of educational outcomes.

The article begins with a presentation of the behavioral foundations. We explain our cost, demand, and efficiency equations and describe our estimation results, which are based on school districts in New York in 1991. We then bring in state aid reform. We focus on foundation aid formulas, which are designed to bring all districts up to a minimum spending or outcome level. Because central city districts tend to have relatively poor outcomes, a foundation aid plan can focus attention on them without bringing in stronger, more controversial equity standards, such as wealth neutrality, that may involve the relative position of various high-outcome districts.[1] We describe the types of foundation aid and explain our methodology for simulating the impact of a new aid plan on educational outcomes. Next we present our simulation results. We show how various types of districts, including central city districts, are affected both by our preferred foundation plan and by other plans based on the incomplete information a state is likely to employ. Our conclusion summarizes the key lessons from our simulations and, to the extent possible, answers the question in our title.

Behavioral Foundations: Costs, Outcomes, and Efficiency

The cost equation

Any production process uses available technology to translate inputs into outputs. In cost terms, the amount a production unit spends depends on the output level it chooses and on the price of inputs.[2] Analysts have long recognized that this process is particularly complicated with public production because outputs are difficult to define.[3] The translation of inputs, such as teachers and classrooms, into units of governmental activity, such as hours of mathematics instruction, looks like a standard production problem; however, measures of this activity are difficult to develop and the output parents ultimately care about is learning, not instruction. Measures of learning, such as standard achievement test scores, are sometimes controversial, but they are widely available and, as we will see, can be selected using statistical procedures.

The production of learning or any other final outcome depends on the environment in which it is provided. For example, a given amount of instruction delivered in a district where most of the pupils come from poor, single-parent families will, all else equal, result in less learning than if it is delivered where most of the pupils come from stable, middle-class homes. This difference reflects the fact that poverty and single parenthood not only make it difficult for a family to provide resources, such as books and computers, to reinforce lessons learned in school, but also because poverty and family breakup often result in stresses that distract children from their school work.

In short, spending in a school district depends not only on the educational outcomes the district provides and its input prices, but also on its cost environment. Thus, we estimate the cost equation with district spending per pupil as the dependent variable and educational outcomes (such as test scores), wages, and various environmental cost factors (such as district enrollment and poverty rate) as explanatory variables.[4]

This equation makes it possible to calculate two indexes that are crucial for the rest of our analysis. The first is a cost index, which indicates the amount each school district must spend to provide the same level of educational outcomes as the average district.[5] The second is an educational outcomes index. As discussed later, outcome-based aid programs generally require state policymakers to select the educational outcomes on which school performance will be based.[6] This choice has a significant impact on the distribution of aid, largely because it affects the estimated cost index. Our outcome index is a weighted average of the outcome variables included in the regression, where the weights, which are measured by the regression coefficients, indicate the value voters place on each outcome.[7] This approach provides an appealing replacement for an arbitrarily selected test score as a summary indicator of a district's performance because it is based on a variety of educational outcomes, which are selected and weighted based on statistical procedures.

Several scholars, particularly Hanushek (1986, 1996), argue that additional school spending has little impact on educational outcomes. Other scholars, including Ferguson (1991), Downes and Pogue (1994), and Ferguson and Ladd (1996), provide compelling evidence that spending matters. The approach used here makes it possible to estimate the relationship between spending and a set of educational outcomes selected on statistical grounds. Moreover, as explained later, we explicitly control for productive inefficiency, which is a common explanation for the lack of association between spending and outcomes.

The demand equation

Educational outcomes, measured by our index, reflect the decisions of voters and school officials in each school district. Following another long line of literature, educational outcomes are a function of a district's median income; its tax price, which is the amount of taxes the median household can expect to pay to raise educational outcomes by one unit; the aid it receives; and its preferences, as reflected by its demographic characteristic.[8] The tax price is the product of tax share and marginal cost. The tax share is the ratio of median house value to property value per pupil. It indicates how much the median voter must pay to raise one more dollar per pupil. The marginal cost indicates how much the district must spend to provide one more unit of educational outcomes. We estimate this demand relationship, therefore, by regressing our index of educational outcomes on district median income, tax price, state aid, and a few preference variables.

This demand equation also helps solve a problem in the cost equation, namely that the educational outcome variables are endogenous so that the estimated coefficients may be biased. The demand equation identifies exogenous instruments, such as income and tax share, that can be used in a simultaneous equations procedure for the cost equation.

Measuring district efficiency

Costs and outcomes also are influenced by a district's productive efficiency, that is, by its ability to translate its resources into outcomes given its cost environment. The problem, of course, is that efficiency is difficult to measure. Although we cannot measure efficiency directly, we can use a technique called data envelopment analysis (DEA) to compare the spending in each district with that in other districts providing the same level of the educational outcomes selected for the cost equation.[9] A DEA variable takes the form of an index that reaches 1.0 in the districts that spend the least, holding measured outcomes constant. However, this DEA variable cannot be interpreted as a measure of efficiency; at a given level of the selected outcomes, for example, districts that spend a relatively high amount might be inefficient in all their activities or might direct their spending toward other outcomes. Moreover, a district's spending might be higher (and hence its DEA index lower) than other districts with the same outcomes if it faces high costs. Nevertheless, the DEA variable does reflect productive efficiency, along with other things, and we can use it to bring efficiency into our analysis.

To begin, we include the DEA variable in our cost and demand equations to control for productive inefficiency. In the cost equation, this type of inefficiency could lead to higher spending, controlling for outcomes and cost factors, and in the demand equation, it effectively raises the price of educational outcomes and could lead voters to substitute away from them, holding income, tax price, and other factors constant. Thus, in both equations, a failure to account for productive inefficiency could bias the coefficients of other variables, and therefore bias the outcome and cost indexes, among other things. Including the DEA variable minimizes this bias. Because the DEA variable reflects costs and omitted outcome variables as well as productive inefficiency, including it in these two equations also may reduce the precision with which the coefficients of cost and outcome variables can be estimated (see Duncombe, Ruggiero, and Yinger, 1996). However, this loss of precision is a small price to pay for eliminating omitted variable bias.

The efficiency equation

Our third equation explores the determinants of school district efficiency, with the DEA measure as the dependent variable. Although not relevant in the cost and demand equations, the distinction between productive inefficiency and spending on unobserved outcomes is crucial here. Our objective is to estimate the impact of state aid on a district's productive efficiency. Simply regressing the DEA variable on state aid would not suffice, however, because the DEA variable is influenced by educational outcomes other than those included in the outcome index, and the aid coefficient is likely to be biased if the other outcomes are excluded from the regression. To minimize this bias, we include in our regression measures of other educational outcomes. Because the DEA variable also reflects cost factors, we include the input and environmental cost factor from our cost equation, along with a few others. Thanks to these controls, we interpret the coefficients of the state aid variables, which are discussed later, as measures of the impact of state aid on a district's productive efficiency.

The efficiency equation also includes three broad categories of exogenous factors that, according to existing theories about the behavior of public and private managers, might affect the productive efficiency of school district personnel.[10] Public choice scholars emphasize that competition in the delivery of a public service is likely to put external pressure on managers to be more efficient. Although we have no measure of competition from private schools, we can identify city districts that do not face extra electoral competition in the form of a required school budget referendum. Second, jurisdiction size is hypothesized to affect efficiency because larger governments "will be associated with decreased responsibility of local officials and decreased participation by citizens" (Ostrom, 1972, p. 487). Because potential economies of pupil scale are already controlled for through the cost variables, district population is used as a determinant of efficiency.

Finally, efficiency could be affected by external socioeconomic factors, such as the level of adults' education, that influence the ability and incentives of citizen/voters to monitor and put pressure on school officials. Leibenstein (1966) suggests a reverse relation between community wealth and the external pressure put on public officials: Residents of districts with higher property wealth or income may exert less pressure on school officials because inefficiency does not prevent high outcomes if enough resources are available.[11]

This discussion points to two ways in which state aid might influence efficiency. First, the Leibenstein hypothesis suggests that higher aid might lead to less efficiency as it loosens the constraints on school officials. Second, with interdistrict competition, districts that receive high aid relative to similar districts, with which they are likely to compare themselves, may face less pressure to improve their educational outcomes. School districts often compare themselves to other districts in the same property-value/enrollment class. As a result, we divide the school districts in New York into 16 such classes and define two basic aid variables: average aid in a district's class and the difference between a district's aid and the average aid in its class. The first variable, which we call the between-class aid variable, tests our first hypothesis about aid, and the second, the within-class aid variable, tests our second hypothesis. Finally, because the impact of aid may depend on a district's circumstances, we interact both of these variables with district income and (to keep the functional form flexible) district income squared.

Estimation results

The cost, demand, and efficiency equations are estimated for 631 school districts in New York State using data for 1991.[12] Table 1 presents the estimation results for the demand and cost equations.[13] The dependent variable for the cost equation is a district's approved operating expense per pupil.[14] The educational outcomes are the average share of students above a standard reference point on third and sixth grade maths and English tests; the average share of students who pass several state-run standardized tests in high school; and

Table 1　Education cost and demand equations, New York school districts, 1991

Variables	Coefficient	t-statistic
Cost equation[a]		
Intercept	−4.9550	−1.53
Third-and sixth-grade PEP scores (Average % above standard reference point)[b]	5.1106	2.50
Percent nondropouts[b]	4.4757	1.62
Percent receiving Regents diploma[b]	1.3449	3.19
Efficiency index (percent)[b]	−1.1670	−4.87
Log of teacher salaries[b]	0.6487	1.57
Log of enrollment	−0.5680	−3.54
Square of log of enrollment	0.0345	3.44
Percent of children in poverty	1.0109	3.93
Percent female-headed households	2.2260	3.85
Percent of students with severe handicaps	0.8584	1.29
Percent of students with limited English proficiency	4.0525	2.68
SSE	34.58	
Adj. R^2	0.32	
Number of observations	631	
Demand equation		
Intercept	−1.2428	−1.42
Log of median family income	0.8880	9.49
Ratio of operating aid to median income[c]	3.5723	2.55
Ratio of other lump-sum aid to median income[c]	3.0807	1.33
Ratio of matching aid to median income[c]	−8.2197	−1.58
Log of tax share	−0.3118	−6.39
Log of efficiency index[b]	0.4391	1.98
Percent owner-occupied housing	0.2322	1.51
Relative percent of adults with college education	0.1752	0.65
SSE	37.36	
Adj. R^2	0.47	
Number of observations	631	

[a]　The cost and demand models are estimated with linear 2SLS regression. The dependent variables are the logarithm of per-pupil operating expenditures for the cost model and of the outcome index for the demand model.
[b]　These variables are treated as endogenous. See footnote 6 for a discussion of the instruments.
[c]　Aid variables are multipled by the tax share.

the share of students who stay in school.[15] These three outcome variables all have the expected signs, two of the three are highly significant, and the third, the non-dropout rate, is significant at the one-tailed 5.3 percent level.[16] For these outputs, at least, higher spending and higher output go hand in hand. The DEA variable has the expected negative sign and is highly significant. The most significant cost coefficients indicate that per-pupil costs increase with poverty, single-parent households, and limited English proficiency, and are a U-shaped function of enrollment, with a minimum at about 3800 pupils. The wage elasticity, 0.65, is significant at the one-tailed 5.9 percent level.[17]

The cost index derived from these results indicates how much a district must spend, relative to the average district, to obtain services of a given quality, holding efficiency constant. It ranges from 0.74 to 2.61, although 75 percent of districts fall below 1.05 and 75 percent are above 0.89. The cost equation also leads to our index of educational outcomes.

The demand equation implies an income elasticity of 0.89 and a price elasticity of −0.31, which are both in the range of previous estimates for education and are highly significant. State aid is divided into three types.[18] The key aid variable, operating aid, has a large and significant coefficient. The variable for other lump-sum aid has a similar coefficient but is not statistically significant. The matching aid variable, which is an amount, not a matching rate, has a negative sign but is not statistically significant. The DEA variable has the expected sign and is significant, unlike the two preference variables.

Estimation results for the efficiency equation are presented in Table 2. As expected, district efficiency decreases with district property value, district income, the ratio of matching aid to income, and population density, and increases with the share of college educated parents. City districts and districts with large populations do not have significantly different efficiency from other districts, however. The DEA variable also does, as expected; reflect outcome and cost variables. The 14 outcome variables reflect the percentage of students taking specialized state examinations in various subjects and per-pupil levels of various types of special facilities and equipment. The nine cost variables include all those in the cost equation plus the weighted pupil measure used by New York to allocate its current aid and the percentage of students in high school.[19] Four outcome and four cost variables in Table 2 are statistically significant.

Table 2 also reveals the complexity of the link between aid and productive efficiency. As expected, the "within-class" coefficient, which is highly significant, indicates that districts with aid that is high relative to other districts in their value/enrollment class are less efficient, all else equal. Although not significant at conventional levels, the "between-class" coefficient suggests that districts in value/enrollment classes that receive a relatively high amount of aid are less efficient than districts in other classes.[20] Table 2 also reveals a nonlinear interaction between the impact of aid and district income. As discussed in more detail in the Appendix, the effect on efficiency of higher aid both relative to the average in a district's group and relative to other groups is at a minimum when district income is close to the statewide average and increases as income diverges from the average in either direction.

Aid Programs Aid Simulations

Because our focus is on central city schools, which have relatively low levels of educational outcomes, we restrict our attention to state aid programs, called foundation grants, that are designed to bring all districts up to some minimum quality level. About 80 percent of the states, including New York, currently use grants of this type.[21] This section describes foundation aid formulas and explains how we simulate their impacts.

Table 2 Determinants of school district efficiency, New York school districts, 1991[a]

Variables	Coefficient	t-statistic
Intercept	5.8247	5.84
Aid variables[b]		
Within-class variable	−1278.7540	−2.44
Between-class variable	−447.7361	−1.42
Within *log of income	243.4566	2.44
Within * log of income squared	−11.5955	−2.44
Between * log of income	84.2389	1.39
Between * log of income squared	−3.9711	−1.36
Other efficiency factors		
Log of per-pupil property value	−0.2786	−9.58
Log of median family income	−0.3245	−3.79
Ratio of matching aid to median income	−0.0719	−2.53
City district (1 = yes)	0.0005	0.02
Total district population (millions)	0.9210	1.16
Population density (thousands)	−0.0137	−2.77
Percent college educated parents	0.5071	3.28
Omitted outcome measures		
Percent of grade taking Regents exam in:		
English	0.0658	1.34
Earth science	0.1134	3.04
Global studies	−0.0312	−0.54
History	0.0144	0.23
Math I	−0.0073	−0.16
Math II	−0.0468	−0.66
Math III	0.3132	4.42
Biology	0.1999	3.49
Chemistry	0.0031	0.06
Physics	0.0374	0.61
Per-pupil art and music facilities	−5.2932	−4.35
Per-pupil video equipment	−0.0834	−0.61
Per-pupil personal computers	−0.5918	−1.36
Per-pupil network facilities	−11.3262	−1.36
Cost factors		
Log of teacher salaries	−0.1024	−1.44
Log of enrollment	0.3622	2.47
Square of log of enrollment	−0.0256	−2.42
Percent of children in poverty	−0.1286	−0.71
Percent female-headed households	0.1474	0.42
Percent of students with severe handicaps	−0.2215	−0.45
Percent of students with limited English	−1.5298	−2.24
Percent of students in high school	0.1125	0.56
Weighted pupil index	0.3443	4.53

Number of observations is 631.

[a] Estimated with a Tobit regression; OLS results are similar. The dependent variable is the logarithm of the efficiency index.

[b] Districts are divided into 16 classes based on per-pupil property value and enrollment; the aid variable is from the demand model (all lump-sum aid divided by income): "within-class" is the difference between a district's aid and the average aid in its class; "between-class" is the average aid in its class.

Foundation aid formulas

A standard foundation grant takes the following form:

$$A_i = E^* - t^* V_i \tag{1}$$

where the subscript indicates the school district, A is aid per pupil, E^* is the minimum spending per pupil set by the state, t^* is the minimum acceptable local property tax rate determined by the state, and V is property value per pupil. Intuitively, a foundation grant makes up the difference between the revenue a district can raise at a tax rate t^* and the revenue it needs to provide spending E^*.

Two policy questions arise in implementing equation (1). The first is that many low-wealth districts may not choose a tax rate as high as t^*, and therefore will not reach a spending level of E^*, even with a foundation grant. Although New York is a notable exception, many states deal with this issue by requiring a minimum effort from every district, defined as a local tax rate of at least t^*.[22] This step enlists the districts in the program to ensure that all districts provide an adequate education, as defined by E^*. We examine foundation grants with and without this minimum-effort requirement. Second, a literal application of equation (1) requires negative aid in districts with high property values. To the best of our knowledge, no state collects negative aid of this type, so we do not examine formulas with negative aid here.[23] Instead, all of our aid plans have minimum aid equal to zero.

The standard foundation formula contains a major flaw because it does not recognize that some districts have higher costs than others. A high-cost district that spends E^* per pupil will not receive the same educational outcomes as a low-cost district that spends the same amount. As shown by Ladd and Yinger (1994), this problem can be solved by introducing a cost index into equation (1). In particular, let C be an index of educational costs, defined to equal unity in the average district and let S be an index of educational outcomes, scaled so that $E_i = S_i$ in a district with average costs and perfect efficiency.[24] Now state policymakers must select a minimum educational outcome, S^*, and the foundation formula becomes:

$$A_i = S^* C_i - t^* V_i \tag{2}$$

Equation (2) implicitly assumes that all districts are perfectly efficient. Expecting perfect efficiency is unrealistic, however, and a perfect-efficiency standard ensures that few if any districts will actually achieve the target outcome level, S^*. Thus, we add one more policy parameter to this equation, namely the efficiency standard that state policy-makers expect school districts to meet. Let e be an index of district efficiency, with $e = 1$ in an efficient district, and let e^* be the standard state officials select. Now the foundation formula becomes:

$$A_i = \frac{S^* C_i}{e^*} - t^* V_i \tag{3}$$

This formula ensures that any district making at least the minimum effort, t^*, that is at least as efficient as the target level, e^*, will be able to provide the minimum outcome, S^*. Districts that levy lower tax rates (assuming they are allowed to do so) or that are less efficient will still fall short of the minimum outcome. Districts that are more efficient than the target are rewarded in the sense that they receive more money than necessary for them to reach S^* (at tax rate t^*).

The total aid a district receives equals its aid per pupil from equation (3) multiplied by its enrollment. The state aid budget, B, is the sum, across districts receiving aid, of this aid amount. Because district characteristics are fixed, setting S^*, e^*, and t^* therefore determines B. It follows that to hold B constant across aid formulas, one of the policy parameters must be made endogenous. Our strategy is to examine formulas with various values of S^*, holding e^* constant, and solving for the value of t^* that keeps B at its current level.

Simulation strategy

The cost, demand, and efficiency equations make it possible to simulate the impact of alternative foundation plans on educational outcomes in New York State. The first step, of course, is to estimate the amount of aid each district would receive under each foundation plan. As noted earlier, all simulations hold total state spending at the 1991 level of actual state operating aid plus other lump-sum aid, namely $3.65 billion or $2427 per pupil.

The demand equation can then be used to simulate educational outcomes. Because state aid appears in this equation, any change in state aid has a direct effect on the educational outcomes a district selects. However, state aid also appears in the efficiency equation and the DEA variable appears in the demand equation, so state aid also has an indirect impact on educational outcomes through its impact on efficiency.

To simulate the direct impact of aid on outcomes, we first subtract the effect of New York's existing aid programs, which, as explained earlier, fall into three categories: basic operating aid, other lump-sum aid, and matching aid. In particular, all our simulations start by calculating the decline in educational outcomes associated with eliminating current operating and other lump-sum aid, based on the coefficients of these two variables. However, because we lack information on matching rates and because matching programs are a very small part of the current state budget, our simulations assume that these programs remain untouched.

The next step is to calculate the impact of the new foundation plan on outcomes. We pool together all lump-sum aid to determine the available state aid budget, calculate the aid each district would receive under a new foundation plan, and then, using only the estimated coefficient of operating aid, determine the increase in educational outcomes that would occur if the district received this much aid.

The indirect impact of a new aid formula on outcomes is calculated in two steps. First, we use the coefficients in the efficiency equation to predict the efficiency level each district would achieve given the aid it would receive under each foundation plan. This procedure holds constant the nonefficiency determinants of the DEA measure, such as cost factors and educational outcomes other than those in the outcome index, so, as discussed earlier, it reveals the impact of aid on productive efficiency alone.[25] This step also leads to an estimated efficiency level in each district under each plan.[26] Second, we use the coefficient of the DEA variable in the demand equation to calculate the impact of the predicted change in efficiency on a district's educational outcome.

These calculations reveal the educational outcome in each district under each foundation formula. Once the educational outcome is known, we work backward, using the cost equation, to educational spending and, using district property value, to the tax rate levied to cover operating spending.[27] When the foundation plan imposes a minimum tax rate that exceeds a district's preferred rate, spending under the plan is set equal to state aid under the plan plus the property tax revenue at the required minimum tax rate, and the cost equation is used to estimate outcomes.[28]

Simulation Results

Our simulations are designed to show how various foundation aid formulas influence educational outcomes, particularly in central cities. This section describes the districts in our sample and presents the simulation results for our preferred outcome-based foundation programs and for other foundation programs based on less complete information.

District classes

To facilitate the presentation of our results, we divide the 631 school districts into six relatively homogeneous classes, which are described in Table 3. These classes distinguish between the New York City area, called downstate, and the rest of the state, called upstate, and within each broad region, between city, suburban, and rural districts. Moreover, the school districts for three large upstate central cities, Buffalo, Rochester, and Syracuse, are placed into a separate class. Unlike any other districts in the sample, these three school districts are part of a city government, instead of being independent. The sample does not include New York City itself, both because information on several key variables was missing, and because New York City is so unique that bringing it into the analysis would distract attention from general principles.

The three large upstate cities, which have the lowest property values and incomes and highest school tax rates of any class, are fairly typical of central city school districts throughout the Northeast and Midwest. They have very high costs, for example, reflecting their relatively high wages and high concentrations of poverty, female-headed households, and students with handicaps. To a lesser degree, small upstate cities also have incomes and property values that fall below, and school tax rates that fall above, the state average. However, school costs for these cities are not far above average. In contrast, the downstate small cities have relatively high incomes and house values and relatively low tax rates, but are second behind the upstate large cities in their school costs. These relatively high costs reflect both the relatively high wages in the New York City area and several other cost factors, such as a concentration of students with limited English proficiency. Although suburbs exhibit some of the same upstate–downstate differences, they tend not to be disadvantaged in resources or costs in either part of the state. Finally, rural districts fall between the upstate suburbs and small cities in both their resources and their costs.

Table 3   Average characteristics of school districts by region and type, New York school districts, 1991

Characteristic	State average	Downstate		Upstate			
		Small cities	Suburbs	Large cities	Rural	Small cities	Suburbs
Per-pupil expenditure							
Total expenditure	$8399	$12,135	$11,874	$8245	$7472	$7345	$7402
Operating expenditure	$6054	$8741	$9016	$5186	$5145	$5184	$5333
Fiscal capacity							
Per-pupil property value	$196,204	$329,178	$394,556	$112,903	$138,974	$135,567	$146,751
Median family income	$40,426	$54,635	$61,635	$26,527	$30,474	$32,455	$39,029
Local school property tax rate[a]	2	1.8	1.9	2.2	2.0	2.1	2.1
Cost and other Factors							
Cost index	100.0	131.9	107.3	197.9	100.9	109.6	91.1
Teacher salaries	$24,727	$30,101	$28,333	$26,205	$23,713	$23,627	$23,676
Enrollment	2383	4492	3277	33,054	1060	4100	2273
Percent of children in poverty	11.6	10.9	5.2	36.5	16.0	19.3	9.2
Percent female-headed households	8.8	12.3	9.3	19.1	8.2	11.8	8.2
Percent students with severe handicaps	4.5	7.1	5.3	7.8	4.1	5.6	4.0
Percent students with limited English	1.0	4.3	2.2	2.1	0.6	1.0	0.6
Population density	1093.1	7063.9	3061.7	6268.3	64.8	1805.9	532.9

The same sample of 631 districts was used in these calculations and in the other tables.
[a]   The local school tax rate equals local school revenue divided by full property value of a district: local revenue excludes state and federal aid.

Policy simulations for outcome-based foundation plans

Our basic simulations cover six outcome-based foundation aid plans. These plans are defined by three different values of S^* (the 25th, 50th, and 75th percentiles of the current outcome distribution), with and without the requirement that districts set a minimum tax rate of t^*. All the plans also set e^* at the 75th percentile of the current efficiency distribution.

The second column of Table 4 presents the aid amounts under our preferred outcome-based plan for the three values of S^*. Imposing a minimum tax rate does not alter the aid a district receives, so this table applies to foundation plans both with and without the minimum-tax-rate requirement. A comparison of the first two columns of this table reveals that an outcome-based plan would lead to dramatic increases in aid to the three large upstate cities and modest increases in aid to small upstate cities, at the expense of all other types of districts. With the most generous outcome-based foundation plan, the aid to large cities is well over three and a half times as high as it is now, $9635 per pupil compared with $2736. Even the least generous outcome-based plan would increase these cities' aid by two and a half times.

Table 4 Comparison of aid per pupil under different foundation formulas, New York school districts, 1991[a]

		Outcome-based aid system			
Aid system	Present aid[c]	Correct cost index – Efficiency correction	Incorrect cost index – Efficiency correction	Incorrect cost index – No efficiency correction	Expenditure-based aid system
Aid: S^* =25th percentile = 3628.2[b]					
Downstate					
Small cities	$2384.27	$1886.98	$2764.88	$3074.25	$947.12
Suburbs	1654.44	1037.88	1554.43	1934.01	922.24
Upstate					
Large cities	2736.18	7061.52	7686.14	6385.73	3181.01
Rural	2844.63	2594.74	2306.38	2237.49	2925.76
Small cities	2836.10	3087.84	2808.16	2596.32	3023.78
Suburbs	2847.44	2067.83	1803.36	1866.15	2798.34
Aid: S^* = 50th percentile = 4634.8[b]					
Downstate					
Small cities	2384.27	1558.23	2527.34	2762.11	880.70
Suburbs	1654.44	852.04	1365.71	1553.17	804.55
Upstate					
Large cities	2736.18	8375.10	9181.21	7660.25	3302.38
Rural	2844.63	2713.67	2359.43	2301.13	3022.54
Small cities	2836.10	3275.03	2933.71	2801.07	3116.74
Suburbs	2847.44	1971.26	1667.84	1800.47	2841.20
Aid: S^* = 75th percentile = 5719.2[b]					
Downstate					
Small cities	2384.27	1633.86	2384.77	2577.46	744.82
Suburbs	1654.44	789.45	1279.78	1381.42	657.91
Upstate					
Large cities	2736.18	9634.93	10,624.36	8940.12	3535.22
Rural	2844.63	2759.50	2331.99	2350.19	3234.07
Small cities	2836.10	3315.89	2902.81	2917.59	3288.27
Suburbs	2847.44	1823.29	1503.49	1687.93	2912.62

[a]   All grants require approximately the same state budget to fund as the actual aid system in 1991: $3.65 billion.
[b]   Percentiles refer to the current outcome distribution.
[c]   Total current lump-sum aid per pupil.

The impact of these aid programs on educational outcomes is presented in the second columns of Tables 5 and 6. The first column indicates outcomes under the current aid system, which includes several small lump-sum programs plus a foundation plan with the minimum expenditure (not outcome) level set at approximately the 25th percentile of the current expenditure distribution and with various hold-harmless and minimum-aid provisions. A comparison of the first and second columns of Table 5 reveals that, regardless of

Table 5 Comparison of predicted outcomes under different foundation formulas, New York school districts, 1991, no minimum tax rate[a]

| | | Outcome-based aid system | | | |
Aid system	Actual outcomes	Correct cost index – Efficiency correction	Incorrect cost index – Efficiency correction	Incorrect cost index – No efficiency correction	Expenditure-based aid system
Aid: S^* = 25th percentile = 3628.2[b]					
Average	4759.5	4686.4	4662.7	4654.5	4799.3
Downstate					
Small cities	3949.1	4058.2	4283.1	4287.7	3730.6
Suburbs	5641.7	5509.6	5634.4	5672.6	5537.2
Upstate					
Large cities	1891.6	2365.6	2428.3	2262.5	1947.6
Rural	4256.6	4220.9	4152.6	4120.9	4310.9
Small cities	3912.0	3940.8	3877.4	3826.5	3989.0
Suburbs	4954.0	4846.6	4778.6	4776.1	5062.5
Aid: S^* = 50th percentile = 4634.8[b]					
Average	4759.5	4694.6	4667.3	4661.5	4815.5
Downstate					
Small cities	3949.1	4008.6	4280.8	4281.5	3712.7
Suburbs	5641.7	5471.1	5631.5	5633.6	5513.8
Upstate					
Large cities	1891.6	2546.6	2635.1	2424.9	1964.4
Rural	4256.6	4262.5	4176.7	4151.4	4342.7
Small cities	3912.0	3990.7	3913.2	3875.7	4016.4
Suburbs	4954.0	4841.8	4761.1	4777.7	5085.7
Aid: S^* = 75th percentile = 5729.2[b]					
Average	4759.5	4695.7	4667.9	4665.9	4852.9
Downstate					
Small cities	3949.1	4030.9	4299.4	4281.6	3678.8
Suburbs	5641.7	5465.7	5675.9	5627.8	5481.5
Upstate					
Large cities	1891.6	2735.1	2853.1	2600.5	1998.9
Rural	4256.6	4286.6	4180.6	4173.2	4412.5
Small cities	3912.0	4010.9	3917.4	3908.2	4070.7
Suburbs	4954.0	4818.6	4729.6	4764.0	5131.9

[a] All grants require approximately the same state budget to fund as the aid system in 1991: $3.65 billion.
[b] Percentiles refer to the current outcome distribution.

the level of S^*, an outcome-based foundation plan would provide a substantial outcome boost to schools in the large upstate central cities. With the most generous plan, in the third panel, outcomes increase by about 45 percent. Even with S^* set at the 75th percentile, however, outcomes in these three cities still fall far short of even the current median outcome level of 4635. The shift to an outcome formula also would benefit small cities, both upstate and downstate, to a small degree. The losers, at least in terms of educational outcomes, would be suburbs, both downstate and upstate. Educational outcomes in rural areas would be largely unaffected by this shift, at least on average.

The second column of Table 6 presents results for an outcome-based foundation plan with a required minimum tax rate. This plan enlists the school districts in the efforts to bring districts up to S^*. Outcomes obviously are higher for all types of districts under this approach. As in Table 5, the most dramatic increases are for large, upstate central cities. The average outcome for these three cities with the most generous plan, 4588, is almost two and a half times as large as their current outcome, 1892. This new outcome level falls short of the target S^*, 5729 (and indeed is even a bit below the 50th percentile target of 4635), because the efficiency level in these districts falls below e^*.

Comparing Tables 5 and 6 reveals that a foundation plan with New York's current budget can do little to bring low-outcome districts up to a reasonable outcome target unless school districts are forced to contribute to the effort. This key point is examined further in Table 7, which describes the local tax rate devoted to school operating expenses (now called a local contribution rate to distinguish it from the overall school tax rate) when no minimum rate is imposed. The demand equation implies that an increase in operating aid results in both increased operating spending and a reduced local contribution to the operating budget. This result, which is well known from other studies (see, e.g., Inman, 1979), reflects the fact that aid allows a district to shift some of its own funds from operating spending to other school purposes, such as capital spending; to other public services, such as police; or to private consumption through tax cuts.[29] As shown in Table 7, this response is dramatic in large cities, which receive the largest increase in aid. In fact, without a required minimum tax rate (or, more literally, a minimum local contribution rate), the local contribution to operating spending in large cities actually goes negative, which implies that some of the aid intended for operating purposes is used for other things, such as school capital spending.

This result does not, of course, imply that the school property tax rate in large cities is negative. In fact, Table 3 shows that these cities start out with the highest school property tax rates in the state. Moreover, we do not estimate the extent to which property taxes for capital spending increase when operating aid increases, so it is possible that large cities have higher overall tax rates than other types of districts even after the cuts described in Table 7. This result simply shows that large cities, which face the constraints imposed by high costs and low wealth in providing all public services, respond to a large increase in state operating aid for education by shifting some of their own resources to other activities. This shift undercuts a state's efforts to ensure minimum educational outcomes.

Placing a minimum on the local contribution rate obviously raises local contributions. As shown in Table 7, the value of t^* for the most generous plan is above the average contribution rate that every type of district would choose without a required minimum rate. Even with the other two plans, which result in average local contribution rates above t^* for most types of districts, adding the requirement increases average local contribution rates because some districts of each type have rates below t^*.[30] In all cases, however, the increases are much larger in large cities than elsewhere. Local contribution rate increases of this magnitude help move large cities closer to the educational outcome targets, but they

Table 6 Comparison of predicted outcomes under different foundation formulas, New York school districts, 1991, required minimum tax rate[a]

		Outcome-based aid system			
Aid system	Actual outcomes	Correct cost index – Efficiency correction	Incorrect cost index – Efficiency correction	Incorrect cost index – No efficiency correction	Expenditure-based aid system
Aid: $S^* = $ 25th percentile $= 3628.2$[b]					
Average	4759.5	4884.1	4807.6	4747.8	4865.8
Downstate					
Small cities	3949.1	4058.2	4283.1	4287.7	3730.6
Suburbs	5641.7	5781.2	5898.1	5888.0	5656.3
Upstate					
Large cities	1891.6	3191.1	3307.8	2770.3	1947.6
Rural	4256.6	4464.1	4269.2	4206.7	4390.7
Small cities	3912.0	4201.8	4303.9	3912.3	4062.9
Suburbs	4954.0	4945.3	4840.5	4805.9	5088.3
Aid: $S^* = $ 50th percentile $= 4634.8$[b]					
Average	4759.5	5407.5	5233.5	5211.7	5274.5
Downstate					
Small cities	3949.1	4177.3	4423.6	4477.1	3723.4
Suburbs	5641.7	6371.4	6518.4	6537.0	6032.2
Upstate					
Large cities	1891.6	3944.1	4067.2	3659.9	2085.0
Rural	4256.6	5105.2	4787.9	4712.8	4898.8
Small cities	3912.0	4882.2	4576.2	4479.6	4461.1
Suburbs	4954.0	5300.0	5085.2	5107.2	5443.1
Aid: $S^* = $ 75th percentile $= 5729.2$[b]					
Average	4759.5	6251.7	6068.4	6136.3	6323.7
Downstate					
Small cities	3949.1	5223.7	5454.3	5572.1	4734.1
Suburbs	5641.7	7548.5	7830.4	7848.9	7122.5
Upstate					
Large cities	1891.6	4588.4	4729.2	4401.8	2643.9
Rural	4256.6	5940.6	5578.9	5601.7	5974.1
Small cities	3912.0	5635.6	5285.0	5336.4	5393.1
Suburbs	4954.0	5978.0	5711.2	5855.3	6476.7

[a] All grants require approximately the same state budget to fund as the aid system in 1991: $3.65 billion.
[b] Percentiles refer to the current outcome distribution.

also pull local resources away from other things that cities must do, such as provide educational facilities or police protection.

The implications for productive efficiency of outcome-based foundation plans are presented in Table 8. The first column presents current efficiency levels and the second

Table 7 Comparison of local contribution rate for operating expenditure under different foundation formulas, New York school districts, 1991, no minimum tax rate[a]

		Outcome-based aid system			
Aid system	Actual rate	Correct cost index – Efficiency correction	Incorrect cost index – Efficiency correction	Incorrect cost index – No efficiency correction	Expenditure-based aid system
Aid: $S^* = $ 25th percentile $t^* = 1.19\%$[b]					
State average	1.93	1.55	1.78	1.98	1.77
Downstate					
Small cities	1.95	1.76	1.83	1.89	2.09
Suburbs	2.30	1.96	2.14	2.13	2.31
Upstate					
Large cities	2.15	−0.44	−0.62	1.41	1.84
Rural	1.65	1.25	1.52	1.82	1.48
Small cities	1.86	1.21	1.47	1.80	1.68
Suburbs	1.99	1.67	1.90	2.11	1.75
Aid: $S^* = $ 50th percentile $t^* = 1.89\%$[b]					
State average	1.93	1.49	1.81	1.78	1.70
Downstate					
Small cities	1.95	1.82	1.95	1.83	2.08
Suburbs	2.30	2.02	2.48	2.14	2.31
Upstate					
Large cities	2.15	−0.93	−1.12	−0.61	1.74
Rural	1.65	1.11	1.42	1.52	1.37
Small cities	1.86	1.06	1.37	1.48	1.59
Suburbs	1.99	1.65	1.92	1.91	1.67
Aid: $S^* = $ 75th percentile $t^* = 2.64\%$[b]					
Average	1.93	1.51	2.00	1.80	1.56
Downstate					
Small cities	1.95	1.84	2.11	1.93	2.07
Suburbs	2.30	2.11	3.20	2.41	2.30
Upstate					
Large cities	2.15	−1.22	−1.37	−1.05	1.55
Rural	1.65	1.07	1.43	1.43	1.15
Small cities	1.86	1.02	1.38	1.38	1.41
Suburbs	1.99	1.71	2.00	1.91	1.53

[a] All grants require approximately the same state budget to fund as the aid system in 1991: $3.65 billion. The local contribution rate is calculated by subtracting per-pupil lump-sum aid from operating expenditures and dividing by per-pupil property value. A negative local contribution rate is possible because some aid may be spent on capital expenditures or on transportation (which is not included in operating spending here).

[b] The value of t^* applies to column 2.

Table 8 Comparison of predicted efficiency rates under different foundation formulas, New York school districts, 1991[a]

		Outcome-based aid system			
Aid system	Existing aid programs[b]	Correct cost index – Efficiency correction	Incorrect cost index – Efficiency correction	Incorrect cost index – No efficiency correction	Expenditure-based aid system
Aid: S^* = 25th percentile = 3628.2[c]					
Average	69.05	78.26	77.46	73.74	70.40
Downstate					
Small cities	50.36	57.36	54.88	52.09	53.89
Suburbs	51.39	59.10	57.31	54.13	53.62
Upstate					
Large cities	89.52	83.67	80.54	80.80	89.93
Rural	75.77	85.65	84.97	81.41	77.06
Small cities	74.22	82.98	82.22	78.88	75.42
Suburbs	72.05	81.84	81.00	77.24	72.94
Aid: S^* = 50th percentile = 4634.8[c]					
Average	69.05	78.51	77.60	77.25	70.72
Downstate					
Small cities	50.36	58.18	55.53	54.87	54.22
Suburbs	51.39	59.50	57.77	57.31	54.05
Upstate					
Large cities	89.52	79.84	76.37	80.61	90.20
Rural	75.77	85.65	85.12	84.97	77.29
Small cities	74.22	82.94	82.31	82.22	75.72
Suburbs	72.05	82.34	81.57	81.00	73.30
Aid: S^* = 75th percentile = 5729.2[c]					
Average	69.05	78.29	77.44	77.55	71.40
Downstate					
Small cities	50.36	57.85	55.60	55.38	55.02
Suburbs	51.39	59.44	57.65	57.72	54.88
Upstate					
Large cities	89.52	75.74	71.99	77.04	90.84
Rural	75.77	85.18	84.81	85.10	77.77
Small cities	74.22	82.54	82.05	82.30	76.37
Suburbs	72.05	82.33	81.58	81.48	74.08

[a] All grants require approximately the same state budget to fund as the aid system in 1991: $3.65 billion. This table presents estimates of actual efficiency rates using the model presented in Table 2. All cost factors and additional outcomes are held constant at the mean and the aid and other efficiency factors are allowed to vary. Predicted efficiency is then divided by the maximum efficiency to scale the variable up to a maximum of 1.0 (most efficient).

[b] Based on the existing aid system. The same method is used for calculating efficiency as for the other aid programs, with all current lump-sum aid categories combined into one.

[c] Percentiles refer to the current outcome distribution.

column presents efficiency levels for three different outcome targets. Efficiency is not affected by the local tax rate, so Table 8 applies to programs both with and without a minimum-tax-rate requirement. On average, the most generous outcome-based plan raises the average efficiency index in the state from 69.1 to 78.3 percent. Moreover, for all three outcome targets, these plans significantly raise efficiency in every type of district except the large upstate cities.

The decline in efficiency in large city districts is not surprising given their large boost in aid. With the most generous outcome-based plan, the efficiency index for these districts declines by about 15 percent, from 89.5 to 75.7. This decline works against the goals of the aid program; as aid goes up, the impact of each dollar of aid on outcomes goes down. However, the magnitude of this effect is moderate; without the decline in efficiency, the most generous plan would boost their educational outcomes by 45(1.15) = 52 percent, instead of 45 percent.

Policy simulations for simpler but less complete state policies

Implementing our aid plans requires an understanding of cost indexes, an explicit decision about the acceptable level of inefficiency, and the estimation of cost indexes controlling for efficiency. Existing state plans do not meet any of these requirements, so we simulate three alternative foundation plans based on less complete information than our own.[31]

The simplest foundation plan follows equation (1), with no recognition of costs or efficiency. The results for such a plan are presented in the last (fifth) column of Tables 4 through 8. Because the implicit expenditure target in the current New York foundation plan is set at about the 25th percentile of the current expenditure distribution, a comparison of the first and last columns in the first panel of these tables largely reflects the impact of eliminating hold-harmless and minimum-aid provisions and pooling all lump-sum aid into a foundation formula. These steps would modestly increase aid (and outcomes) in upstate cities, both large and small, and decrease aid substantially (with little impact on outcomes) in downstate cities and suburbs. The average impact on rural districts and downstate suburbs would be minimal.

Bringing in the results in the second column, we can see that an outcome-based foundation goes much farther than an expenditure-based foundation in shifting aid to large cities. It does not go nearly as far, however, in shifting aid away from downstate small cities and suburbs. Largely because they face very high labor costs, these downstate districts tend to have high costs, a fact that is missed by an expenditure-based plan. The current system of hold-harmless and minimum-aid provisions serves some of the same purpose as a cost correction by boosting aid to these districts, but it goes too far in this direction and does not ensure fair treatment either within these districts or between these districts and others.

These tables also reveal that even the most generous expenditure-based foundation plan leaves large cities far short of any outcome target, even with a required minimum tax rate. In fact, the most generous such plan, in the last panel of Table 6, helps large cities but still leaves them at an outcome level well below the 25th percentile of the current distribution! Moreover, Table 8 shows that these plans do little to increase efficiency in the average district.

The first step a state must take in moving toward a complete outcome-based foundation is to estimate a cost index. An aid program for municipal services, including education, based on an estimated cost index was implemented in Massachusetts (Bradbury et al., 1984), and school aid programs based on estimated cost indexes are presented in Ratcliffe, Riddle, and Yinger (1990), Downes and Pogue (1994), and Duncombe and Yinger (1996). Thus, we now examine outcome-based foundation programs that, like these, incorporate a cost index estimated without controlling for efficiency and that implicitly assume, following equation (2), that all districts are efficient. A cost index estimated in this way is biased by the omission of an efficiency variable, but it takes a large step toward recognizing the role of input and environmental cost factors.[32]

Results for these programs, presented in the fourth column of Tables 4 through 8, reveal that in most cases adding a cost index closes a large share of the gap between the expenditure-based foundation in column 5 and the outcome-based foundation in column 2. Under the most generous plan, for example, adding a biased cost index raises aid to large cities from $3535 per pupil (column 5 of Table 4) to $8940 (column 4), compared to the complete-information amount (column 2) of $9635.

In contrast, the foundation plan based on a biased cost index leads to much higher aid and higher outcomes (with little impact on efficiency) for downstate small cities and suburbs than either the expenditure-based foundation or the complete-information foundation in column 2. This result mainly reflects the large, negative correlation between efficiency and wage rates; because of this correlation, leaving efficiency out of the cost equation biases upward the coefficient of the wage variable and hence biases upward the cost index in places with high labor costs, particularly downstate districts.[33] In fact, the wage elasticity goes from 0.649 to 2.08 when the efficiency variable is left out.[34] In effect, therefore, an aid program based on a biased cost index rewards the downstate districts for their inefficiency. This is, of course, an inappropriate outcome.

This result poses a serious challenge to policymakers and researchers. Aid formulas based on simple cost indexes of the type that have been presented in the literature appear to be a big step in the right direction, but this step has a price. To the extent that efficiency is correlated with cost factors, a standard cost index will reflect inefficiency as well as costs, and an aid formula based on it will favor inefficient districts as well as high-cost ones. In New York, this effect does not boost aid to big cities, which despite their reputation are relatively efficient, but instead boosts aid to downstate small cities and suburbs, which tend to be inefficient.

Obviously the relevant correlations could vary from state to state, so these results cannot determine whether this type of plan would reward the same types of districts for inefficiency in other states. Nevertheless, the possibility that the plan rewards inefficiency clearly undercuts its appeal.

One simple step a state can take to recognize the role of efficiency is to bring in the concept of e^* using equation (3). All this step requires is identifying an efficiency level that is regarded as acceptable. This approach recognizes that virtually no districts will be able to achieve perfect efficiency so that spending greater than S^*C_i is needed to bring district i up to the S^* outcome target. Compared to the previous approach, therefore, this approach focuses more aid on higher need districts. The third column of Tables 4 through 8 show the impact of a foundation plan with a biased cost index but with a value of e^* set at the 75th percentile of the current efficiency distribution. This plan takes another small step toward the complete-information plan in column 2. In most cases, the entry in column 3 falls between the entry in column 2, which has no correction for e^*, and the entry in column 2, which is based on an unbiased cost index. Because this plan retains the biased cost index, however, it does little to eliminate the excess aid given to downstate districts. Moreover, it actually overcompensates central city districts to a small degree, compared to their aid with an outcome-based foundation, because they, too, face relatively high wages.

Conclusions

Our first conclusion, already expressed in previous studies, is that a state cannot ensure adequacy in educational outcomes without including a cost index in its foundation formula.[35] In New York, and, we suspect, in many other states, this lesson is particularly important for large cities, which tend to have relatively high costs. Even when minimum tax rates are imposed, an expenditure-based foundation plan set to bring districts up to the 75th percentile of the current expenditure distribution does not bring large cities in upstate New York up to even the 25th percentile of the current outcome distribution. This result provides a key part of the answer to the question in our title: The failure of existing state aid plans to accurately account for variation in educational costs across districts helps explain why educational outcomes in many central cities remain far below their state's average.

Estimating cost indexes also may help dispel the widespread and, by our calculations, incorrect perception that large cities are relatively inefficient, a perception that may constitute a political barrier to increases in their aid. In New York, and no doubt in many other places, the key reason why large cities have low outcomes despite their high spending is that, through no fault of their own, they face high costs. By our estimates, their current efficiency is above the state average, but they must spend twice as much as the average district to obtain the same educational outcomes.

A second lesson, also present in previous literature, is that a state cannot help low-outcome districts in general and large cities in particular without some combination of a larger state budget and required local property tax rate increases. The current New York budget for educational aid would have relatively modest impact on educational outcomes in large cities even if it were funneled through a formula that accounted for costs and set a high outcome target. The reason, of course, is that a foundation grant only ensures the outcome target under the assumption that districts set a minimum tax rate, which must be a high tax rate if the target is high or the budget is low. Stressed as they are by school debt expenses, nonschool expenditure demands, and declining tax bases, many central city districts are reluctant to impose tax rates for school operating expenses that are close to the minimum tax rates implicit in these plans.

This result does not imply that large cities are unwilling to tax themselves; indeed, their current overall tax rate for schools is higher than that of any other type of district. It simply emphasizes that large cities are likely to respond to increased operating aid for schools by shifting some of their own resources to other activities that are also in need of support. A state that is serious about bringing all districts up to a reasonable performance standard therefore must come up with new broad-based sources of revenue or new forms of revenue sharing, perhaps combined with modest required local tax increases.

A third lesson is that states are right to be concerned about districts' productive efficiency. In particular, we find three main reasons why this concern is justified. First, estimating a cost index without controlling for efficiency inappropriately rewards some inefficient districts. In New York, this approach leads to severe upward bias in the impact of wages on the cost index and unfairly rewards the relatively inefficient downstate districts that face high wage rates – at the expense of other districts. In another state the bias might work in another direction.

The second reason is that the presence of inefficiency interferes with a state's ability to reach a performance target in every district. If an outcome-based foundation formula implicitly assumes that all districts are perfectly efficient, it will fail to bring the vast majority of low-performance districts up to its target outcome. Thus, states must explicitly decide what level of inefficiency is acceptable and incorporate this level into their aid formulas. The trick here is to find a balance between efforts to reward efficiency and efforts to achieve performance standards. This lesson provides part of the explanation for poor outcomes in large cities in New York; an aid program that brings districts up to an outcome target if they are at the 75th percentile of the current efficiency distribution provides significantly more aid to large cities than an otherwise comparable program that expects all districts to be perfectly efficient.

The third reason is that aid programs themselves have a direct impact on productive efficiency. We find, for example, that relatively high aid leads to relatively low efficiency, all else equal. The aid programs examined here all shift aid toward large cities and therefore reduce efficiency there. This result provides another part of the answer to the question in our title; programs to increase aid to central city schools undermine themselves to some degree by lowering the efficiency of these districts. The importance of this point should not be exaggerated, however; switching to the most generous of our plans would cut efficiently in the three large upstate cities by only 15 percent.

Efficiency is, of course, a complex topic. We believe that the approach offered here is a step in the right direction, but it does not, by any means, answer all questions about the topic. It may be too complex for consideration by state policymakers. Moreover, it does not fully resolve the question of whether efficiency can be separated from other factors that might influence our DEA variable, such as educational outcomes not in our main index or unobserved cost factors. Nevertheless, we believe that this approach shows how crucial accounting for efficiency can be.

What can state policymakers do?

Some of these lessons suggest concrete steps that state policymakers could take to boost outcomes in central city schools: Phase out hold-harmless and minimum-aid provisions that steal aid from the neediest districts; estimate cost indexes and incorporate them into foundation aid formulas; make people aware of the importance of cost factors to combat the perception that central city schools are relatively inefficient and therefore undeserving of aid; and change the implicit efficiency target in foundation formulas to a realistic level, such as 0.75 or 0.8, instead of demanding perfect efficiency. These steps would, of course, increase the fairness of a foundation plan for other types of districts, as well.[36]

Other lessons presented here do not yet lead to clear policy actions. The method we propose to measure efficiency and control for it in a cost regression is both complicated and not yet widely known. Simpler methods that accomplish the same objectives have not been developed. Moreover, no one has yet designed an aid program that provides districts with clear incentives to be more efficient while at the same time bringing districts up to some outcome target or otherwise promoting equity. Solving this problem is beyond the scope of this article, but we hope to have provided a foundation that makes it possible for such an aid system to be designed by future research.

Despite these uncertainties, our main conclusion is that states could design aid programs that would dramatically boost educational outcomes in central city schools. The real reason that it is so hard to help central city schools may be that these programs lack political support.

Appendix

State aid and district inefficiency

The results in Table 2 concerning the relationship between aid and efficiency are summarized in Figure A1, for the within-class effect, and Figure A2, for the between-class effect. In both figures, e_i stands for efficiency in district i, A stands for the value/ enrollment class average aid per pupil, Y stands for income in the average district, and σ stands for the standard deviation in the distribution of income per pupil across districts. Figure A1 reveals that the within-class effect can be quite large. At the statewide average income, a district with the maximum positive difference between its aid and the average aid for its class has an efficiency index of about 0.65, compared to an efficiency

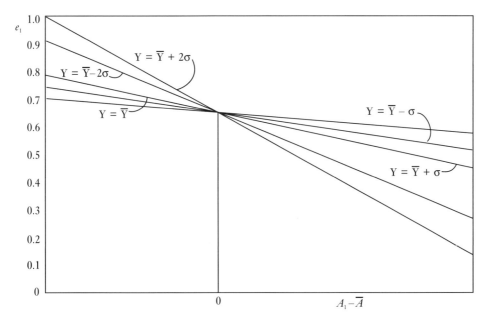

Figure A1 Efficiency and deviation in aid from class average

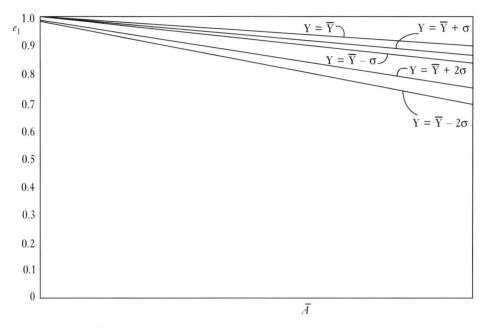

Figure A2   Efficiency and average aid for district class

index of about 0.75 for the district with the maximum negative difference, all else equal. As the steepest lines in Figure A1 indicate, this 10-point difference jumps to 60 points or more for districts with incomes far from the average. According to Figure A2, an average-income district in the class that receives the most aid has an efficiency index that is also about 10 points below that of an average-income district in the class that receives the least aid. In this case, however, the gap increases only to about 25 points for districts with incomes at either tail of the distribution.

Notes

1   Wealth neutrality is a situation in which educational outcomes are not correlated with district wealth per pupil. For more on alternative equality standards for school finance, see Berne and Stiefel (1984) Monk (1990), and Duncombe and Yinger (1996). For a recent discussion of the importance of adequacy, the standard behind a foundation plan, see Clune (1993).

2   The literature on educational production and educational costs is reviewed in Hanushek (1986) and Cohn and Geske (1990). For a comparison of production and cost analysis, see Duncombe, Ruggiero, and Yinger (1996), who point out that only the latter can provide a comprehensive picture of each district's relative costs, which, as we will see, is needed to design an outcome-based aid program.

3   Discussions of the unique features of educational production can be found in Bridge, Judd, and Moock (1979), Hanushek (1986), Ratcliffe, Riddle, and Yinger (1990), Ferguson (1991), Downes and Pogue (1994), Duncombe, Ruggiero, and Yinger (1996), and Ferguson and Ladd (1996). See also Ladd and Yinger (1991) and Duncombe and Yinger (1993).

4 Teacher wages are set by a school district and are therefore endogenous in this equation. See note 16.

5 A district's cost index equals its predicted spending per pupil, with all variables except the cost variables set at the state average, divided by average spending in the state (and with the predicted, not actual, value of the wage variable). For more on cost indexes, see the references in note 3.

6 It is possible to design an outcome-based aid program without selecting specific outcomes, but the required cost equation is more abstract and less compelling than the one used here. See Downes and Pogue (1994) or Duncombe, Ruggiero and Yinger (1996).

7 See Duncombe and Yinger (1996). Our form can be derived from a simple model in which a district tries to maximize a multiplicative outcome index, S, subject to a budget constraint in which each outcome, S_i, is produced at a constant cost c_i. (A cost-minimization version of this problem leads to the same result.) To be specific, a district with total spending, E, tries to select the set of outcomes, S_i to:

Maximize $S = \Pi_i (S_i)^u t$

Subject to $E = \Sigma_i c_i S_i$

The first-order conditions of this problem imply that:

$E = (\alpha_1 + \alpha_2 + \alpha_3) S / \lambda$

where λ is a Lagrangian multiplier to indicate the scale of spending. Moreover, the first-order conditions also can be used to express the coefficients from the output index, the α_i values in terms of the cost parameters. The result:

$$E = \frac{\Sigma_i c_i S_i}{S} S \equiv (\text{Average Cost}) S$$

where average cost is constant. This is exactly the form we estimate. Without the assumption of constant costs per unit of S, the estimated coefficients of the outcome variables might reflect production and demand, not just demand as in this model. As discussed in Duncombe and Yinger (1993) however, this strong assumption is impossible to avoid without very complicated techniques.

8 For reviews of this literature, see Inman (1979), Rubinfeld (1987), and Ladd and Yinger (1991). A detailed derivation of the specification used here is in Duncombe and Yinger (1996).

9 Data envelopment analysis (DEA) uses linear programming to determine a "best-practice frontier" for production. It was pioneered by Charnes, Cooper, and Rhodes (1978), and Färe and Lovell (1978). It has become popular in evaluating productive efficiency in the public sector because it handles multiple outputs, is nonparametric, and can be applied to both production and cost functions. See Grosskopf and Yaisawarng (1990) for an application of DEA to cost efficiency. For more on the application of DEA to education, see Färe, Grosskopf and Weber (1989), Duncombe, Ruggiero, and Yinger (1996), and Ruggiero (1996).

10 See, for example, Leibenstein (1966), Niskanen (1971), Migué and Bélanger (1974), Wyckoff (1990), and Ruggiero, Duncombe, and Miner (1995). Empirical work on efficiency is limited. Applications of DEA to education can be found in Bessent and Bessent (1980) and Färe, Grosskopf and Weber (1989). Tests of theories about efficiency can be found in Ruggiero, Duncombe, and Miner (1995). Duncombe, Miner, and Ruggiero (1997), and Borger et al. (1994).

11 High-income residents also may have a relatively high opportunity cost for their time.

12   For more information on these data, including sources, see Duncombe and Yinger (1996). There were 695 school districts in New York in 1991; our sample was limited because of missing data.

13   For more discussion of this cost model, including results for some alternative specifications, see Duncombe, Ruggiero, and Yinger (1996).

14   Approved operating expense, defined by New York State, includes salaries and fringe benefits of teachers and other school staff, other instructional expenditures, and all other expenditures related to operation and maintenance of schools. We exclude transportation expenditures because we have no measures of the relevant environmental cost factors. The average value of this variable is $6212 per pupil.

15   The elementary outcome is based on Pupil Evaluation Program (PEP) tests and the high school outcome on Regents exams. The process by which these variables were selected is described in Duncombe, Ruggiero, and Yinger (1996). We limited our analysis to variables that had correlations of 0.1 or higher with demand factors, combined related variables into averages, and checked our results using factor analysis.

16   The two equations are estimated with two-stage least squares. All the exogenous variables in the demand equation are used as instruments for outcomes in the cost equation. The cost equation also treats the DEA variable and the wage rate as endogenous. Instruments for the DEA variable, which come from the efficiency equation discussed later, are total district population and population density, percent of the private employees who are managers or professionals, and whether the district is a city district. County population and the county wage rate for manufacturing production workers are instruments for the wage variable. Finally, the DEA variable is treated as endogenous in the demand equation, using the same instruments.

17   The wage variable is average salary for teachers with five or fewer years of experience, adjusted for experience, education, type or certification, and tenure. See Duncombe and Yinger (1996).

18   Basic operating aid constitutes over 60 percent of the state aid budget. For details on the various aid programs, see Duncombe and Yinger (1996).

19   This measure gives extra weight to students with special needs or disabilities and to students in secondary school. The correlation between this measure and our cost index is only 0.14. See Duncombe, Ruggiero, and Yinger (1996). The percent of students in high school is a significant cost factor in some states where some districts only teach elementary students. See Ratcliffe, Riddle, and Yinger (1990). Although its coefficient is close to zero and statistically insignificant if it is included in our cost equation, we include percent in high school in the efficiency equation just in case it picks up some otherwise unexplained cost factor.

20   Although none of the "between" coefficients is significant by itself, the set of three coefficients is significant at the one-tailed 6.2 percent level.

21   See Gold et al. (1992). New York actually calls its operating aid a "power-equalizing" grant, and this usage leads Gold et al. to misclassify the New York program. In fact, New York uses an expenditure-based foundation formula that we define later.

22   Actually, there is a second choice here, too, namely whether to require all districts to levy the minimum tax rate, including those who already provide the minimum outcome. The plans evaluated in this article impose the minimum-tax-rate requirement on all districts (or on none).

23   Some states use aid plans that are equivalent to negative aid. For example, Kansas sets the property tax rate for all districts, collects the revenue, and then returns the same grant per weighted pupil to each district, regardless of the amount a district contributed. See Reschovsky (1994). For simulations of foundation (and other) plans with negative aid, see Duncombe and Yinger (1996).

24   The state aid formula requires S^*C_i to be the amount a district must spend to obtain the outcome level S^*. Our conceptual framework implies that $E = S'C'f/e$, where S' is the product of the (unlogged) outcome variables, each raised to the power indicated by its estimated

coefficients (as in note 7); C' is the product of the (unlogged) cost variables, each raised to the power indicated by its estimated coefficient; e is an unobserved index of productive efficiency; f is all other factors that influence spending; and the district subscript is implicit. Our cost index, C_i is C' divided by its average value across districts. Because e cannot be observed, we estimate $E = S'C'd\mu$, where d is our DEA variable multiplied by its estimated coefficient and exponentiated and μ is the error term exponentiated. It follows that $f/e = d\mu$ or $f = ed\mu$. Using the estimate of e obtained from our efficiency equation, which, as explained later, holds the nonefficiency aspects of d constant, we can obtain an estimate of f. Thus:

$$E = \frac{S'C'f}{e} = \frac{S'\overline{C'}\frac{C'}{\overline{C'}}f}{e} = \frac{S'\overline{C'}C_i f}{e}$$

Finally, holding f constant at its average value across districts, we define a scaling factor, γ, that transforms S' into our final outcome index, S, such that $S = E$ in a district with average cost ($C = 1$) and perfect efficiency ($e = 1$):

$$E = S = \gamma S' = \overline{C'}/S'$$

25 To be specific, we set the value of all nonefficiency variables at the state mean for every district.

26 To eliminate the impact of nonefficiency variables, we rescale the predicted index so that it has a maximum value of 1. This approach, which is equivalent to assuming that under all aid programs at least one district is perfectly efficient, is similar to that of McCarty and Yaisawarng (1993) and Ray (1991), in their method, a DEA efficiency measure is regressed on socio-economic factors affecting outcomes with a rescaled version of the residual used as the new measure of efficiency. We also control for possible omitted outcomes and include exogenous factors likely to affect variation in efficiency across districts.

27 To be specific, we use the equation:

$$E_i^n = E_i' + C_i \left(\frac{S_i^n}{e_i^n} - \frac{S_i'}{e_i'} \right)$$

where the superscripts indicate new (n) and existing (x) aid formulas.

28 To be specific, we use the equation:

$$S_i^n = \left(\frac{E_i^n - E_i'}{c_i} + \frac{S_i'}{e_i'} \right) e_i^n$$

where the superscripts are defined in note 27.

29 Because our measure of operating spending excludes transportation expenses, this effect also might indicate that general-purpose operating aid induces districts to shift funds to transportation. With the exception of the large city districts, school districts in New York are separate from municipal government, so increases in police or other spending require a cut in school taxes combined with an increase in municipal taxes.

30 A table comparable to Table 7 presenting average local contribution rates with a minimum rate requirement is available from the authors upon request. Under the most generous plan, 85 percent of districts are forced to impose the minimum t. This drops to 29 percent under the least generous plan.

31 To hold constant the level of required local effort (as well as the state budget), we hold the minimum required tax rate, where relevant, at its level in column 2 for all the other plans (columns) with the same value of S^*.

32 Some states use much more ad hoc methods for measuring costs. These are, of course, even more biased. See Duncombe, Ruggiero, and Yinger (1996).

33 All cost coefficients are biased when efficiency is left out, but in our equation the bias in the wage variable is particularly dramatic.

34 A value of 0.65, which implies that districts have some opportunities to substitute away from teachers when teacher salaries rise, appears reasonable. Any value above 1.0, let alone 2.08, is not reasonable, as it implies that a district cannot preserve its outcome level after a wage increase simply by hiring the same number of teachers at the new higher wage.

35 See, especially, Bradbury et al. (1984). Ratcliffe, Riddle, and Yinger (1990), Downes and Pogue (1994), and Duncombe and Yinger (1996).

36 These steps also would help meet equity objectives other than the minimum-adequacy objective of a foundation plan. See Duncombe and Yinger (1996).

References

Berne, Robert and Leanna Stiefel (1984) *The Measurement of Equity in School Finance*. Baltimore: Johns Hopkins University Press.

Bessent, Authella M. and E. Wailand Bessent (1980) "Determining the Comparative Efficiency of Schools through Data Envelopment Analysis," *Educational Administration Quarterly*, 16, 57–75.

Borger, B., K. Kerstens, W. Moesen and J. Vanneste (1994) "Explaining Differences in Productive Efficiency: An Application to Belgian Municipalities," *Public Choice*, 80, 339–58.

Bradbury, Katharine L., Helen F. Ladd, Mark Perrault, Andrew Reschovsky and John Yinger (1984) "State Aid to Offset Fiscal Disparities across Municipalities," *National Tax Journal*, 37, 151–170.

Bridge, R. Gary, Charles Judd, and Peter Moock (1979) *The Determinants of Educational Outcomes: The Impact of Families, Peers, Teachers, and Schools*. Cambridge, MA: Ballinger Publishing Company.

Charnes, Abraham, William W. Cooper, and Edwardo Rhodes (1978) "Measuring the Efficiency of Decision Making Units," *European Journal of Operational Research*, 2, 429–44.

Clune, William (1993) "The Shift from Equity to Adequacy in School Finance," *The World and I*, 8, 389–405.

Cohn, Elchanan and Terry Geske (1990) *The Economics of Education*, 3rd edn. New York: Pergamon Press.

Downes, Thomas and Thomas Pogue (1994) "Adjusting School Aid Formulas for the Higher Cost of Educating Disadvantaged Students," *National Tax Journal*, 47, 89–110.

Duncombe, William and John Yinger (1993) "An Analysis of Returns to Scale in Public Production, with an Application to Fire Protection," *Journal of Public Economics*, 52, 49–72.

Duncombe, William and John Yinger (1996) "School Finance Reform: Aid Formulas and Equity Objectives," Metropolitan Studies Occasional Paper No. 175, Center for Policy Research, Syracuse University, January.

Duncombe, William, Jerry Miner, and John Ruggiero (1997) "Empirical Evaluation of Bureaucratic Models of Inefficiency," *Public Choice*, 93, October, 1–18.

Duncombe, William, John Ruggiero, and John Yinger (1996) "Alternative Approaches to Measuring the Cost of Education," in Helen F. Ladd (ed.), *Holding Schools Accountable: Performance-Based Reform in Education*. Washington, DC: The Brookings Institution.

Färe, Rolf S., Shawna Grosskopf, and William Weber (1989) "Measuring School District Performance," *Public Finance Quarterly*, 17, 409–28.

Färe, Rolf S. and Knox Lovell (1978) "Measuring the Technical Efficiency of Production," *Journal of Economic Theory*, 19, 150–62.

Ferguson, Ronald (1991) "Paying for Public Education: New Evidence on How and Why Money Matters," *Harvard Journal on Legislation*, 28, 465–98.

Ferguson, Ronald and Helen Ladd (1996) "Additional Evidence on How and Why Money Matters: A Production Function Analysis of Alabama Schools," in Helen F. Ladd (ed.), *Holding Schools Accountable: Performance-Based Reform in Education.* Washington, DC: The Brookings Institution.

Gold, Steven, David Smith, Stephen Lawton, and Andrea C. Hyary (1992) *Public School Finance Programs of the United States and Canada, 1990–91.* Albany, NY: The Nelson A. Rockefeller Institute of Government.

Grosskopf, Shawna and Suthathip Yaisawarng (1990) "Economies of Scope in the Provision of Local Public Services," *National Tax Journal,* 43, 61–74.

Hanushek, Eric (1986) "The Economics of Schooling: Production and Efficiency in Public Schools," *Journal of Economic Literature,* 24, 1141–77.

Hanushek, Eric (1996) "School Resources and Student Performance," in Gary Burtless (ed.), *Does Money Matter: The Link between Schools, Student Achievement and Adult Success.* Washington, DC: The Brookings Institution.

Inman, Robert (1979) "The Fiscal Performance of Local Governments: An Interpretative Review," in Peter Mieszkowski and Mahlon Straszheim (eds.), *Current Issues in Urban Economics.* Baltimore: The Johns Hopkins University Press.

Ladd, Helen and John Yinger (1991) *America's Ailing Cities: Fiscal Health and the Design of Urban Policy,* updated ed Baltimore: The Johns Hopkins University Press.

Ladd, Helen and John Yinger (1994) "The Case for Equalizing Aid," *National Tax Journal,* 47, 211–24.

Leibenstein, Harvey (1966) "Allocative vs. X-Efficiency," *American Economic Review,* 56, 392–415.

McCarty, Therese A. and Suthathip Yaisawarng (1993) "Technical Efficiency in New Jersey School Districts," in Harold O. Fried, C. A. Knox Lovell, and Shelton S. Schmidt (eds), *The Measurement of Productive Efficiency: Techniques and Applications.* New York: Oxford University Press.

Migué, Jean-Luc and Gérard Bélanger (1974) "Toward a General Theory of Managerial Discretion," *Public Choice,* 17, 27–43.

Monk, David (1990) *Educational Finance: An Economic Approach.* New York: McGraw-Hill.

Niskanen, William A. (1971) *Bureaucracy and Representative Government.* Chicago: Aldine-Atherton.

Ostrom, Eliner (1972) "Metropolitan Reform: Propositions Derived from Two Traditions," *Social Science Quarterly,* 53, 474–93.

Ratcliffe, Kari, Bruce Riddle, and John Yinger (1990) "The Fiscal Condition of School Districts in Nebraska: Is Small Beautiful?" *Economics of Education Review,* 9, 81–99.

Ray, Sabhash C. (1991) "Resource Use in Public Schools: A Study of Connecticut," *Management Science,* 37, 1520–628.

Reschovsky, Andrew (1994) "Fiscal Equalization and School Finance," *National Tax Journal,* 47, 185–97.

Rubinfeld, Daniel (1987) "The Economics of the Local Public Sector," in Alan J. Auerbach and Martin Feldstein (ed.), *Handbook of Public Economics,* Vol. 2. New York: Elsevier Science Publishers.

Ruggiero, John (1996) "On the Measurement of Technical Efficiency in the Public Sector," *European Journal of Operational Research,* 90(3), 553–65.

Ruggiero, John, William Duncombe, and Jerry Miner (1995) "On the Measurement and Causes of Technical Inefficiency in Local Public Services: With an Application to Public Education," *Journal of Public Administration Research and Theory,* 5, 403–28.

Wyckoff, Paul G. (1990) "The Simple Analytics of Slack-Maximizing Bureaucracy," *Public Choice,* 67, 35–67.

Further Reading Samples

Opening paragraphs of *School Resources and Student Performance*

ERIC HANUSHEK

Source: From Gary Burtless (ed.) (1998) *Does Money Matter?* Brookings Institution Press, Washington DC, p. 43.

THE EFFECTIVENESS of school spending has been hotly debated for at least the past quarter century. Beginning with the Coleman report [Coleman et al. 1966] evidence has accumulated to suggest that simple views of what determines student achievement are wrong. Student achievement seems unrelated to standard measures of the resources going into schools. Interest in this research and the conclusions emanating from it derives from its direct implications for policy, thus elevating the subject from an arcane research discussion to a public debate.

The interest in schooling from a policy perspective comes from several sources. First, schooling is perceived as an important determinant of individual productivity and earnings. Thus it becomes an instrument for affecting both the national economy and the distribution of individual income and earnings. Second, while not often subjected to much analysis, schooling is assumed to generate various externalities, ranging from its effect on economic growth to its value for a well-functioning democracy, thus justifying an important component of public intervention. For assessments of what is known about externalities in education, see Hanushek (1996) and Poterba (1996). Third, school spending is itself significant, amounting to over 4 percent of gross domestic product and representing the largest expenditure in most state and local budgets. Combined, these factors point to a natural policy focus on the effectiveness of national expenditure on schools.

References

Coleman, James S., and others (1966) *Equality of Educational Opportunity*, GPO.

Hanushek (1996) "Rationalizing School Spending: Efficiency, Externalities, and Equity, and Their Connection to Rising Costs." In *Individual and Social Responsibility: Child Care, Education, Medical Care, and Long-term Care in America*, edited by Victor R. Fuchs, 59–91. Chicago: University of Chicago Press.

Poterba, James M. (1996) "Government Intervention in the Markets for Education and Health Care: How and Why?" In *Individual and Social Responsibility: Child Care, Education, Medical Care, and Long-term Care in America*, edited by Victor R. Fuchs, 277–304. Chicago: University of Chicago Press.

Abstract from *Information and Inner City Educational Attainment*

JENS LUDWIG

Source: Economics of Education Review, 18, 1999, 17–30. © 1998 Elsevier Science. Reprinted with permission from Elsevier Science.

Data from the National Longitudinal Survey of Youth (NLSY) are analyzed to examine whether adolescents living in low-income urban areas have less accurate information about labor market institutions than teens in more affluent communities, and whether information influences educational attainment. All adolescents seem to implicitly underestimate the educational requirements of their occupational goals, and teens (particularly males) in high-poverty urban areas have less accurate information than those in other neighborhoods. Information varies across neighborhoods in part because of the effects of family socioeconomic status on information, including the education and employment experiences of parents. The labor market information measures available with the NLSY are related to schooling persistence, even after controlling for AFQT scores and family background.

Abstract from *Race and the Structure of School Districts in the United States*

JORGE MARTINEZ-VAZQUEZ, MARK RIDER, AND MARY BETH WALKER

Source: Journal of Urban Economics, 41(2), March, 281–300. © 1997 Academic Press.

We believe that tastes for association could play an important role in determining the structure, conduct, and performance of the system of local governments in the United States. Accordingly, we incorporate racial discrimination into a model of jurisdiction formation. If one group is prejudiced, the model demonstrates that as the population of a region becomes more racially heterogenous a greater number of jurisdictions is required to satisfy their taste for disassociation. Using state and metropolitan area panel data, we test this implication of the model. We find that, controlling for other relevant variables, increasing racial heterogeneity of a state population increases the number of school districts. We discuss the robustness of our results. We compare the impact of racial heterogeneity on special districts with its impact on school districts. In sharp contrast to our school district result, we find no evidence that increasing racial heterogeneity affects the formation of special districts.

Discussion Questions

1   Economists are usually the first to expose the benefits of competition. But public economics also recognizes that seemingly competitive markets can fail if the good or service under consideration is public, or externalities are present in consumption or production of the good or service. Knowing this, present the economic arguments both in favor and against putting the urban public school voucher supported by Levine in place. What side of the argument do you support?

2   Of the three authors included in this section, Picus is the most optimistic that current problems in urban public school districts can be solved by working within the public system and without a large infusion of new spending. Describe the reforms that Picus sees as best helping the plight of urban public schools. Do you agree with his assessment? Why?

3   How do Duncombe and Yinger measure a school district's efficiency? What variables do they believe explain differences in this measure of efficiency observed across New York state school districts? Examine Table 2 in their paper and describe the theoretical arguments given in support of the statistically significant effects they find in this regression. Were you surprised by any of their regression findings?

4   Duncombe and Yinger conclude that: "states could design aid programs that would dramatically boost educational outcomes in central cities. The real reason that it is so hard to help central city schools may be that these programs lack political support." Could economic-based arguments be used to bolster political support for these programs? What would they be?

PART VI:
Urban Public Housing

Public housing in America is almost universally acknowledged as a policy failure of mammoth proportions.

S. C. Gwynne

CHAPTER TWENTY-FIVE

Miracle in New Orleans: What Do a Bunch of College Professors Know About Fixing Public-housing Projects? A Lot, it Turns Out

S. C. GWYNNE

Source: Time Magazine, 9.3.98. © 1998 Time Inc. Reprinted by permission. © 1999 Dow Jones & Co., Inc. All rights reserved.

Public housing in America is almost universally acknowledged as a policy failure of mammoth proportions. But in a nation of neglected, rat-infested and crime-ridden housing projects, New Orleans has always rated special notoriety. Its government-subsidized apartments were consistently rated among the country's worst. One of its biggest projects, an 1,800-unit catastrophe called Desire, was long reputed to be the very worst. The Housing Authority of New Orleans (HANO), a political hornet's nest of patronage and chronic mismanagement, was so inept at making repairs that tenants routinely waited years for simple services. Hundreds of tenements were literally falling down.

Things got so bad that two years ago the U.S. Department of Housing and Urban Development found itself with two choices: place the housing authority under jurisdiction of a federal judge or find an outside institution free of HANO's own dubious 58-year history to run it. Federal officials decided to hand the housing authority over to Tulane University – a highly selective, overwhelmingly white, old-line Southern school situated in a picturesque neighborhood in uptown New Orleans. It seemed an unlikely choice: What could Tulane know about fixing a bureaucracy that was rotting away as much as the buildings in its care? A lot, it turns out. According to the Federal Government's rating system, Tulane has pulled off one of the most dramatic turnarounds in the history of public housing. Says Tulane President Eamon Kelly: "The university is the last institution you would pick to run public housing, until you look at the alternatives."

Tulane first came to the attention of HUD with a proposal it submitted offering to use the resources of the university to help one housing project. What the university got instead, in a deal cut by then HUD Secretary Henry Cisneros and New Orleans Mayor Marc Morial, was full authority over the housing of 55,000 people – 10% of the city's population – in 10 projects. The agreement allowed Tulane senior vice president Ron

Mason, the new de facto head of HANO, to undertake a complete reorganization of the agency.

Wisely, Mason and Tulane first tackled nuts and bolts. They evicted criminals and drug users, reduced the backlog of work orders by 9,000 and improved response times for such things as plumbing repairs from months to days or hours. Just as important, they enlisted the support of citywide tenant groups who had once fought HANO bitterly.

At a 1,400-unit project called C. J. Peete, residents have been recruited to do maintenance and help with security and job placement. "It used to be nobody paid attention to what we were saying," says Augusta Kerry, head of C. J. Peete's resident council. "Now they listen, and we do things together."

That's one prong of the Tulane approach. The other is a series of ingenious ways Mason has found to put the brains and resources of the university to work in the city's poorest neighborhoods (average annual household income: $5,300). By recruiting large numbers of students and faculty to work in projects and by opening Tulane's campus to residents of public housing, Tulane has gone far beyond simple management of real estate. Some 150 faculty and 500 students from Tulane and nearby Xavier University now venture forth regularly to C. J. Peete, where they do everything from private tutoring to teaching courses on health, parenting, job training, teen pregnancy and high school equivalency. They help residents find jobs, and provide seed capital from the program's budget, as well as know-how, to help them start small businesses. So far, the program has helped 1,000 families.

In other Tulane-run tenant programs, 354 jobs have been found for residents, 600 youths have been placed in basketball and other sports programs, and 10 summer camps have been started.

Fully half of the city's 13,500 housing units will be torn down in the next five years. In their place will rise $750 million of new housing, planned by Tulane and HANO and financed by the Federal Government. In once forbidding places like Desire, new single-family units and community centers are already on the drawing board. "The stuff we are doing is cutting edge," says HANO executive director Michael Kelly, an architect. "We're going to be reshaping neighborhoods."

After only two years it may seem premature to call Tulane's stewardship an unqualified success. "They have a long way to go," says Kevin Marchman, HUD's Assistant Secretary for Public and Indian Housing. "But they have made more progress in the last two years than we have seen in the last 25. What is going on in New Orleans is a local miracle." That, at the least, ought to keep the money flowing.

How Tulane did it

- Thousands of homes were repaired, and criminals and drug users evicted
- Tenants were recruited to help run the projects they live in
- Students and faculty were enlisted to tutor and help with job searches

CHAPTER TWENTY-SIX

Urban Housing Policy in the 1990s

STUART A. GABRIEL*

Source: Housing Policy Debate, 7(4), 673–93. © 1996 Fannie Mae Foundation. The copyrighted material is used with the permission of the Fannie Mae Foundation.

Recent decades have witnessed some resolution of certain long-standing concerns of urban housing policy. Other issues, including the limited availability of affordable rental units, mortgage finance-related constraints on homeownership, reduced housing and income assistance to very low income populations, and problems of equal opportunity to housing and housing finance, remain at the forefront of the national policy debate.

A variety of initiatives provide opportunities for efficiency gains in the pursuit of housing policy goals. These include the reformation of the Federal Housing Administration, consolidation of U.S. Department of Housing and Urban Development programs, transformation of the public housing system, enhanced underwriting flexibility by government-sponsored enterprises, and their introduction of new mortgage instruments. However, sizable cuts in federal rental housing and income supports, together with the loss from the stock and the diminished production of low-income rental housing, will undoubtedly result in economic distress among the lowest income renter populations.

Introduction

Recent decades have witnessed some evolution in both the focus of and the approaches to urban housing policy. Certain housing problems have seen some resolution, and other issues remain at the forefront of the national policy debate. Some improvement has been recorded in the physical characteristics of the housing stock, overall housing conditions, and problems of residential overcrowding. However, the limited availability of affordable rental units, mortgage finance-related constraints on home-ownership, reduced housing and income assistance to very low income populations, problems of public housing and low-income housing preservation, and issues of equal opportunity in housing and housing finance markets remain at the forefront of the current housing policy debate.

* The author is grateful to Steve Hornburg for helpful comments on an earlier draft of this article.

Overview of Housing Conditions: Adequacy, Quality, and Overcrowding

By various measures, the adequacy of the nation's housing stock has registered significant improvement since World War II. For example, more than 40 percent of U.S. housing units were without complete plumbing facilities at the end of World War II; by 1980, such units had fallen to less than 1 percent of the U.S. housing stock.[1] According to the 1990 decennial census, approximately two-thirds of the U.S. housing stock was single-family units; the vast majority of homeowners lived in single-family units. In contrast, housing units in structures with four or more stories constituted only about 10 percent of all existing housing units. Census data indicate that some 16 million single- and multi-family units were added to the housing stock over the 1980s at an average pace of 1.7 million units per year. The average size of those newly constructed units increased by over one-fifth, from 1,720 to 2,080 square feet.[2]

Over the remainder of the 1990s, the National Association of Home Builders (NAHB) forecasts that the sum of single- and multifamily housing starts will average about 1.4 million units per year. That forecast provides for a moderate strengthening in housing starts from the average annual pace of 1.2 million units recorded over the 1990–94 period. The forecast roughly coincides with an average anticipated growth in households of about 1.3 million over the 1995–99 period.[3] While recent periods have witnessed some percept-ible improvement in multifamily housing starts from the relatively weak levels observed in the latter half of the 1980s and the early part of the 1990s, the anticipated strengthening in total starts derives largely from the single-family market, which should average about 1.1 million starts per year during the 1996–99 period (Megbolugbe and Simmons 1995).

Although measures of residential overcrowding trended downward over much of the century, evidence from the 1990 census reveals some slight increase in the incidence of overcrowding during the 1980s. In 1940, the first census of housing indicated that some 20 percent of all residential units were overcrowded, defined as more than one household member per room.[4] By 1980, that measure of overcrowding had decreased to about 4.5 percent, but then it rose slightly to about 5 percent in 1990. As would be expected, higher crowding rates are found in metropolitan areas with the large numbers of Hispanic and Asian immigrants, reflecting the tendency of those groups to surmount housing afford-ability difficulties by sharing quarters.[5]

Overall housing quality has been enhanced during recent decades not only by the addition of new, higher quality units to the stock, but also by the removal of deficient units. About 6 percent of substandard units were eliminated from the housing stock from 1974 to 1985; that period also witnessed a 46 percent decline in the number of inadequate units renting for under $300 (1988 dollars) (see Apgar 1991). In contrast, units renting for $350 or above (1988 dollars) increased by about 5 percent from the mid-1970s to the mid-1980s.

However, ongoing reductions in the number of low-quality rental units have exacer-bated the shortage of those units as well as problems of housing affordability among very low income populations. Between 1989 and 1993, the number of very low income renters with pressing housing needs (households paying more than half of their income in rent or residing in substantially substandard housing) rose by 700,000 to 5.6 million. As discussed below, housing assistance to very low income populations – including preservation of low-income rental housing and a rethinking of the role of public housing – remains a critical housing policy issue.

Homeownership Opportunities

Public opinion surveys repeatedly indicate strong household sentiment in favor of home-ownership. Homeownership is viewed as the key investment of typical U.S. households; further, it is widely believed that homeownership contributes to neighborhood quality and an improved residential environment. Homeownership goals are central to U.S. housing policy, and their achievement has been facilitated through a variety of policies affecting tax liability, mortgage finance instruments, and financial institutions. Those provisions are generally well known and include the federal income tax deductibility of mortgage interest as well as the availability of long-term, fully amortizing, and low down payment mort-gages, which facilitate homeownership through reductions in down payment and monthly mortgage servicing requirements. The availability of mortgage finance has been enhanced through the development of specialized housing finance institutions in the primary mortgage market; secondary mortgage market institutions also have served to greatly expand the liquidity of primary market lenders and hence the flow of funds to the housing sector. In so doing, the government-sponsored housing finance agencies have significantly reduced nonprice mortgage credit rationing and concomitant cyclical fluctuations in housing activity.

Partly because of those policies, homeownership rates trended upward throughout the post-World War II era to about two-thirds of all households during the early 1980s, but then eased downward during the mid-1980s. The decline was concentrated among younger and middle-aged households. Among cohorts in the 15–44 age range, homeownership rates declined by 4 to 7 percentage points during that period. In contrast, rates of homeowner-ship increased during the mid-1980s among older households. In general, younger house-holds are more mobile than older households and hence are more likely to change their tenure status in response to a change in the relative price of owning to renting. Further, younger households experienced a perceptible decline in real incomes during the first half of the 1980s. Those declines in real income resulted in greater difficulties in mortgage qualification for first-time buyers, in terms of both accrual of wealth for down payment and monthly mortgage servicing requirements. Rates of homeownership in 1992 remained below their 1982 levels for all age cohorts below 54 years. In contrast, homeownership rose in the groups over age 55. Rates of homeownership vary significantly by household race and ethnicity. In 1990, rates for white households were close to 70 percent: in contrast, black and Hispanic households had homeownership rates in the low to mid 40 percent range. The overall rate of homeownership started rising again in 1993, and for the third quarter of 1996 it reached 65.6 percent, nearly equal to its 1980 peak of 65.8 percent (U.S. Census Bureau 1996). An average of forecasts by Fannie Mae, Freddie Mac, the U.S. Department of Housing and Urban Development (HUD), and the NAHB had predicted that the homeownership rate would not return to its 1980 peak until the year 2000.

Research suggests that household tenure choice is driven by a variety of economic and demographic variables, including availability of liquid assets for down payment and, perhaps most important, the relative costs of owning to renting over the expected length of stay in the house. Economists calculate homeownership costs on a full after-tax or user-cost basis, which accounts for mortgage-servicing costs, fees, and closing costs of homeownership, maintenance, depreciation, opportunity costs associated with the down payment, expected housing asset appreciation, and the like. Of those components of homeownership user costs, expected housing asset appreciation typically displays the greatest volatility and is often the determining factor in the home purchase decision. For example, during the mid-to late 1980s, homeownership rates registered the largest increases in areas of high expected rates of housing asset appreciation. Conversely, during the early 1990s, the substantial house price declines recorded in many metropolitan area markets resulted in significantly dampened near-term expectations of housing investment returns as well as concomitant falloffs in the demand for owner-occupied housing.[6]

Even in cases of high expected rates of housing asset appreciation (and hence low homeownership user costs), homeownership may be impaired by low levels of nominal housing affordability, as reflected in onerous down payment or mortgage-servicing (debt-to-income) requirements. In urban areas that experienced house price runups during the mid- to late 1980s, nominal affordability requirements became an insurmountable barrier to homeownership for many potential home buyers.[7] Despite some retreat in house prices in many areas during the early 1990s and mortgage interest rates that remain at levels lower than those recorded during much of the 1980s, nominal housing affordability remains a barrier to homeownership among large segments of the renter population.[8]

Although homeownership rates have traditionally been depressed among immigrant and other underserved populations, immigrant groups have recently made significant progress in attaining ownership status. For instance, recent immigrant populations boosted their homeownership rate from about 24 percent in 1980 to almost 55 percent in 1990 (Joint Center for Housing Studies of Harvard University 1995). Among black and Hispanic households, however, homeownership rates fell during the 1983–93 period. Homeownership rates among black and Hispanic households remain substantially below those of white households, even after adjusting for variables such as income level.[9] As such, there remains significant potential for homeownership gains among minority and immigrant groups; it is estimated that if minority and immigrant households were to achieve home-ownership at the same rate as their U.S.-born white counterparts (adjusting for age, income, and family status), an additional 2 million households would become homeowners (Joint Center for Housing Studies of Harvard University 1995). In the context of continued macroeconomic expansion, the outlook for overall improvements in home-ownership is guardedly positive, but only in the context of public and private mortgage finance initiatives that meet the particular needs of these and other groups.

To that end, a variety of efforts are currently under way to address the nominal affordability constraints of lower income, first-time buyer, and underserved populations. Notable here are current efforts by the government-sponsored enterprises (GSEs) to support low down payment conventional loan programs to enhance access to homeowner-ship among households with limited accrued wealth but demonstrated mortgage-carrying capacity. Along with this effort is an attempt by the GSEs to generally enhance the flexibility of the conventional mortgage underwriting guidelines and qualify a broader spectrum of households. The new mortgage designs are consistent with the chartered responsibilities of the GSEs to service the full spectrum of the potential home-buying market, including lower and moderate-income households. Further, the promotion of innovative mortgage designs and marketing efforts on the part of the GSEs reflect their recognition of the ever-expanding diversity of households, lifestyles, and living arrangements in the 1990s. That diversity likewise creates new market opportunities for the secondary market agencies.

The GSEs and others continue to review the sensitivity of mortgage loan performance – relating to default, prepayment, and expected magnitude of loan losses in the event of early loan termination – to their loan underwriting guidelines. The analyses indicate the mortgage portfolio performance tradeoffs associated, for instance, with lower down payment and higher monthly payment-to-income ratio loans. Current efforts to reduce down payment burdens and to enhance the flexibility of secondary market mortgage underwriting come in the wake of a proliferation of variable-rate mortgages during the 1980s. The lower initial rate of those variable-rate loans enabled larger numbers of home buyers to surmount nominal qualification requirements. Other innovative mortgage designs – perhaps including price-level adjusted mortagages evaluated in recent years by HUD – would similarly provide higher levels of nominal housing affordability at interest rates well below those of conventional fixed-or adjustable-rate loans. The GSEs also are actively reviewing the effects of home buyer education programs in helping to mitigate default and loan losses among the new, lower down payment loan programs.

Homeownership also has been aided in recent years by new housing designs that target the first-time buyer and lower income markets with higher density and more affordable housing products. This is particularly true in high land price areas such as California, where builders are experimenting with such innovative designs as the placement of up to 18 single-family units per acre. The reduced land component of such high-density developments enables pricing at levels far below that of comparable single-family homes. Increasingly, nonprofit real estate development corporations and local redevelopment agencies seek to finance and develop affordable housing using a combination of public and private monies. In many cases, those organizations have succeeded in providing mortgage financing to borrowers not well qualified for conventional loans. For example, homeownership opportunities for lower income households can be enhanced through a variety of "soft second" programs, through which funds for a second mortgage can be acquired from a state, local, or not-for-profit agency. Repayment terms of those second mortgages are generally more lenient than those required by first-mortgage lenders. Such opportunities are limited in scope, however, and are often directed at younger, first-time buyers. Pent-up demand for affordable ownership units remains strong in many parts of the country, further suggesting a significant demand-side impetus to the development of affordable housing among traditional for-profit builders.

Housing Very Low Income Renters and Preserving Federally Assisted Low-income Housing Stock

Recent research indicates that roughly one-fourth of the nation's renters – some 4.4 million households – receive some form of government assistance and have low incomes (Wallace 1991). Of that number, about one-third are elderly and about one-half are minorities or families with children. A 1990 survey of tenants of 202 public housing authorities by the National Association of Housing and Redevelopment Officials further indicated that two-fifths of tenants were on welfare, whereas about one-half were classified as working poor or Social Security recipients.

Given this vast requirement for housing assistance among the nation's renter population, concern has focused on the preservation of the nation's federally assisted low-income housing stock. Preservation of existing assisted units became increasingly important in the wake of reduced production of those units during the 1980s; Apgar (1991) estimated a reduction by 2.8 million between 1974 and 1985 in the number of low-rent unsubsidized units affordable to a poverty-threshold family. During the 1980s, concerns about the mortgage prepayment and subsequent conversion to market rate use of approximately 600,000 assisted housing units led to the passage of emergency federal legislation in 1987 and 1990. That legislation recognized that mortgages on approximately 360,000 federally insured and financed units and 75,000 state-financed units would reach their 20-year prepayment date during the 1990s. Accordingly, the legislation established a program to refinance or sell some of those assisted and at-risk units to other "qualified" public, nonprofit, or tenant buyers.[10] A variety of factors, including reductions in the supply of unassisted low-rent housing units, decreased additions to and increased losses from the stock of assisted units, and reductions in federal government income supports of low-income households, together serve to place low-income renters in a precarious position.[11]

The 1990 Low-Income Housing Preservation and Resident Homeownership Act requires sizable commitments of federal funding for rehabilitation and preservation of eligible assisted housing units. In effect, substantial portions of the existing Section 236 housing inventory are being recapitalized. That effort constitutes one of the larger federal housing funding programs of the current decade. The federal funding enables improvements in capital infrastructure, financing, and property management to retain a large number of units in the assisted housing stock over the long term.

Another potentially fruitful direction for preservation of assisted housing involves the active participation of state and local governments (Koebel and Bailey 1992). Koebel and Bailey discuss the various elements of a comprehensive state and local strategy to preserve assisted units, such as assessing inventory, developing lists of potential priority buyers, providing state-level technical assistance, assisting in predevelopment and equity funding, training in property management, and providing buyers of last resort. In so doing, state governments seek to identify and to enhance the capacity of localities, nonprofit organizations, and tenant groups to participate in preservation activities. In general, an enhanced state role in preserving federally assisted housing is one element among a variety of innovative low-income state housing preservation programs enacted in the wake of the ongoing retrenchment in federal funding.[12]

Further, it is estimated that approximately 1.4 million public housing units may be in jeopardy due to aging and depreciation (Schnare 1991) According to Schnare, about one-third of the existing public housing stock is more than 25 years old; a recent estimate suggested that about 15 percent of all units have renovation needs of $20,000 or more. In many cases, maintenance and repair have been deferred since the date of construction. An estimated $12.2 billion (1990 dollars) would be required to put all public housing in an acceptable physical condition with all existing building systems operational. In many of the large metropolitan areas, those public housing units constitute 10 percent or more of the total rental stock.

Various strategies have been proposed to address the critical physical needs of public housing units to retain them in the low-income housing stock. Those approaches are based on the recognition that a significant infusion of funds is undoubtedly required to address public housing capital needs. However, the difficulties of many public housing authorities cannot be solved by money alone nor are all those units necessarily worth saving. According to HUD estimates, approximately $1.75 billion per year in expenses on mandatory needs (e.g., lead-based paint abatement, handicapped access, mandatory modernization) is required in addition to the approximately $12 billion necessary to put public housing units in an operational condition (U.S. HUD 1989). HUD further estimates that renovation is not cost-effective for about 10 percent of public housing units; in those cases, renovation expenses exceed the costs of new construction. HUD also compared the development and maintenance costs of public housing with the ongoing costs of a Section 8 certificate. Findings suggest that preservation of about 80 to 90 percent of all public housing units would be cost-effective relative to the ongoing budgetary commitment for a demand-side housing voucher. Units that fail the cost-effectiveness test could account for as much as 20 percent of required renovation expenditures for public housing.

As suggested above, infusion of financial capital for renovation and modernization of public housing is only a partial solution, since management improvements are required for a number of troubled public housing authorities. Further, those housing authorities must be provided a new set of management incentives for effective capital planning because the funding process has traditionally rewarded the accumulation of severe and pressing needs. Alternatively, the life-cycle needs of public housing units could be budgeted in response to anticipated maintenance and other requirements. Any such life-cycle allocations, however, must contain the proper incentives for cost containment. More fundamental, policy analysts and lawmakers must view preservation of public and assisted housing not as a one-time capital investment, but rather as one requiring infusions of capital at ongoing and predictable stages in the life of the property.

As will be discussed in greater detail below, HUD proposed a major initiative to transform public housing as part of its 1995 "reinvention plan." In 1996, the agency sought to consolidate public housing accounts into programs for capital management improvements and operations. Approximately 3,300 public housing agencies that were performing well were given substantial local autonomy to determine which units to demolish and which to modernize. At the other end of the spectrum, HUD sought new receivership powers to intervene aggressively with approximately 100 public housing authorities (PHAs) that have severe management and operational difficulties. Later, the capital and operating accounts will be converted to project-based assistance to expose the management of the PHAs to the rigors of local rental market conditions. Ultimately, HUD will seek to convert those project-based subsidies into tenant-based assistance and, in so doing, will require the PHAs to compete directly with rental housing supplied in the private sector. The HUD plan is both ambitious and costly: It seeks to phase out the highly inefficient centralized control of public housing while enabling residents of public housing to achieve higher levels of economic welfare through the choice of public or private units in a variety of locations.

As an alternative to public housing, existing tenant-based rental assistance in the form of certificate and voucher programs provides a mechanism by which to meet the housing needs of very low income households. In 1994, about 1 million households received assistance through HUD's Housing Certificate Program, and another 300,000 households were aided through the Housing Voucher Program (Goering, Stebbins, and Siewert 1995). These programs target households with incomes of less than 50 percent of the metropolitan area median level. The federal mandate gives priority to households that have been involuntarily displaced, are homeless or live in substandard housing, or pay over half of their income in rent. The Rental Assistance Program has been ongoing since 1974; the voucher program was established in 1987. The vouchers permit greater flexibility in household location by allowing households to use their rent subsidies in areas where rents exceed the market area's fair market rent (as determined annually by HUD).[13] HUD contracts with approximately 2,500 PHAs nationwide to administer these programs.

More recently, Section 153 of the Housing and Community Development Act of 1992 asked HUD to evaluate the potential efficacy of rental certificate and voucher programs in helping low-income households to move out of inner-city poverty areas. That inquiry seeks to build on results of a small number of dispersion programs (such as Chicago's Gautreaux program) that document a range of improved socioeconomic outcomes (higher employment rates and wages, improved rates of high school graduation, higher overall levels of household satisfaction) among households that succeeded in moving away from segregated and very low income inner-city areas. Results of a recent HUD study (Goering, Stebbins, and Siewert 1995) strongly support the desirability of expanding low-income household housing choice (beyond areas of concentrated poverty) through the HUD Rental Assistance Program. A variety of social, market, and other barriers continue to limit the choice sets of very low income and often minority households. Accordingly, HUD should be encouraged to assess (and offer policy proposals in response to) the variety of impediments to low-income housing choice. Similarly, it would be useful to ascertain the relative efficacy of various dispersion strategies currently used in particular metropolitan areas, including housing search counseling, outreach to landlords, and provision of information on rental housing opportunities. HUD has undertaken a demonstration program, entitled "Moving to Opportunity for Fair Housing," which attempts to relocate about 2,000 families away from areas of concentrated inner-city poverty through a combination of efforts, including rental certificates and vouchers, counseling, and help in moving. Evaluation of this experimental program, together with new research on the impediments to residential mobility and the factors that affect housing choice of low-income households, should figure importantly in future policy designs that will enable households to use their rental assistance to break from areas with high concentrations of poverty and limited economic opportunities.

Discrimination in Housing and Mortgage Markets

In recent years, there has been widespread controversy and policy debate concerning the fair and equal access of low-income and minority households and neighborhoods to housing opportunities and mortgage finance. On the housing side, the debate derives in part from the publication of numerous studies providing compelling statistical evidence of racial discrimination in rental housing markets.[14] On the mortage side, allegations of discrimination in mortgage lending stem in part from analyses of Home Mortgage Disclosure Act (HMDA) data, which reveal wide disparities in the volume of lending activity across individuals and neighborhoods stratified by race. Virtually identical racial disparities are revealed in the home mortgage purchase patterns of the secondary market agencies.[15]

Numerous recent studies, using more comprehensive data, seek to carefully evaluate discrimination hypotheses. Although results of those studies are far from uniform, virtually all studies of loan origination, loan performance, and loan instrument choice – controlling for objective indicators of mortgage default risk – find significant and sizable differences in mortgage market activity across applicants or borrowers stratified by race or neighborhood racial composition. In particular, a 1992 study by the Federal Reserve Bank of Boston found statistically dampened rates of mortgage loan origination among black applicants, after having controlled for a wide variety of borrower, loan, and locational default risk characteristics (Munnell et al. 1992). Results of that study provide support for allegations of discrimination in Boston loan markets. However, findings across a relatively large number of recent mortgage discrimination studies are far from uniform; it is often suggested that the significant race coefficients in studies of lending discrimination may reflect in part indicators of borrower creditworthiness that are correlated with borrower race but are omitted from the statistical analysis. For example, Berkovec et al. (1994) found higher rates of default and higher loan losses among minority borrowers, all things equal. Those results are not consistent with the hypothesis that marginally qualified minorities are systematically held to a higher standard of creditworthiness than other borrowers (Berkovec et al. 1994). Regardless, the widespread statistical evidence of racial and neighborhood disparities in mortgage lending has led regulators and policy makers alike to pursue more aggressive and proactive strategies aimed at the achievement of fair lending outcomes.[16] Policy initiatives focus on improved detection of discriminatory practices and better enforcement of existing fair housing and fair lending legislation. Various ongoing and proposed initiatives are discussed below.

Detection

The financial institution audit and examination process currently includes improved methods of detecting discrimination. New statistical models developed by the Federal Reserve Board allow bank auditors to test application files for systematic evidence of unwarranted disparities in mortage loan origination.

Discrimination in loan origination may also be evaluated through the application of statistical models to mortgage loan performance data. As mentioned above, such studies have been undertaken for the FHA-insured single-family loan portfolio by the Federal Reserve Board; also, a limited test of such models for conventional mortgage loans has been performed by Freddie Mac.

HUD and the U.S. Department of Justice have successfully applied tester methodologies in the detection of housing market discrimination. Large samples from tester studies have enabled HUD to indicate the incidence of housing discrimination across metropolitan areas.

Enforcement

The U.S. Department of Justice has demonstrated a willingness to prosecute cases of housing and lending discrimination. Some of those cases have been well publicized and may serve as a signal to those engaging in illegal discriminatory practices.

In recent years, the Federal Reserve Board has held up bank merger proposals because of the failure of lending institutions to fulfill requirements of the Community Reinvestment Act regarding the spatial, income class, and racial distribution of lending activity.

Other policy proposals

Secondary mortgage market agencies have pledged to evaluate the accuracy and appropriateness of their underwriting guidelines as well as the extent to which those guidelines have resulted in racial or neighborhood disparities in mortage loan origination. More generally, the GSEs are seeking to inject flexibility into their underwriting guidelines and to more fully ascertain how those guidelines are related to loan performance.

Similarly, the secondary market agencies have sought to provide liquidity for low down payment loan products that better serve the income and wealth constraints of low-income, inner-city, and minority populations. Origination of those loans is sometimes coupled with mandatory home buyer education and loan counseling to help the GSEs mitigate the risks associated with low down payment loans.

Initiatives sponsored by secondary market agencies such as Fannie Mae seek to enhance the training and participation of minorities in the mortgage lending, underwriting, and brokerage fields. The premise is that improved minority representation in these fields will reduce disparities in mortgage lending evident in the HMDA data.

Closing Remarks: The New National Housing Landscape

The priorities and directions of housing policy have undergone some evolution in the wake of the 1994 Republican ascendancy in Congress. Those same federal policies had previously come under review because of Clinton administration efforts both to rein in deficit spending and to improve the efficiency of government agency functions. The administration remains committed to the policy objectives outlined in earlier sections of this article, including preservation of low-income rental housing, enhancement of neighborhood choice among low-income assisted renters, transformation of the role of public housing, enhancement of homeownership opportunities among low-and moderate-income households, and enforcement of fair housing and fair lending legislation. However, HUD's ability to make good on those commitments may be severely constrained because of cutbacks in appropriations to the agency and an evolved political agenda.[17] While HUD continues to exist, reductions in federal government housing appropriations significantly reduce the number of poor and low-income households receiving housing and income assistance, raise rent levels in federally assisted housing, and deny home heating and cooling assistance to a large number of low-income households.[18]

Overall, the budgetary and political environment surrounding housing policy has largely evolved in the post-1994 context. Philosophically, the new legislative environment seeks to diminish the federal government role in (and funding of) housing policy and instead emphasizes enhanced flexibility in the control of the reduced funding commitments at the state and local levels. In addition, bipartisan support is expressed for initiatives that make government function in a less bureaucratic, more efficient, and more businesslike manner. The devolution in federal government control over housing programs (both programmatic and budgetary) presumes that lower levels of government have the knowledge and ability to make more efficient use of previously earmarked housing funds. While that sometimes may be the case, it also is true that such a policy will result in cuts to programs that are critical to needy households and communities. Much of the initial impetus for federal government housing intervention emanated from acknowledged and compelling individual and community needs coupled with the recognition that little in the way of expertise, resources, or initiatives was available or likely to be forthcoming at lower governmental levels. At a minimum, calls for devolution in federal government spending and controls should be accompanied by evidence of how state and local agencies might succeed in providing adequate local solutions to recognized local problems.

HUD policy makers have responded to the new political agenda and to critiques of agency operation through the development of a "blueprint" for reinvention of the agency (U.S. HUD 1995). In large measure, that document focuses on transformation of public housing, enhancement of homeownership opportunities among targeted populations, privatization of the Federal Housing Administration (FHA), and performance measurement of HUD programs. The HUD plan proposes to phase out direct subsidies to public housing and instead provide direct assistance to the residents of public housing, allowing them greater mobility and housing choice (as discussed above). The plan would also force public housing authorities to compete with private landlords for subsidized and unsubsidized tenants. Anticipating downsizing of the agency, the plan specifies other initiatives, including consolidation of 60 major HUD programs over the next few years into three performance-based funds: the Community Opportunity Fund, the Affordable Housing Fund, and the Housing Certificates Fund. The Community Opportunity Fund will focus on community economic revitalization and will encompass all current Community Development Block Grant and economic development initiatives. Consistent with congressional intent and with agency efforts to enhance program flexibility and reduce bureaucracy, HUD program grantees (states and localities) will have broad authority in the use of federal resources. The Affordable Housing Fund will encompass all HUD grant programs for the development of low-and moderate-income housing. Finally, the Housing Certificates Fund will combine all current housing assistance programs (including public housing, assisted housing, and Section 8 rental assistance), which will be administered largely through public housing agencies. HUD anticipates completing the consolidation activities by fiscal year 1998; public agencies will be given additional time if necessary to fully convert to tenant-based subsidies.

Also central to HUD's overall reform efforts are initiatives to restructure the FHA and to reform numerous multifamily operating procedures that pertain to portfolio restructuring, property disposition, preservation, and enforcement. The various FHA restructuring proposals and their implications are discussed in some detail in a collection of articles by Vandell (1995), Retsinas (1995), and Weicher (1995). Broad consensus exists regarding the set of fundamental issues to be addressed in the context of any FHA restructuring. In brief, a variety of government and research reports have indicated the critical lack of up-to-date FHA management control and data processing systems, related inefficiencies in important FHA functions of insurance processing and asset management, and the accrual of substantial losses to the FHA multifamily loan insurance fund. It is also widely appreciated that the basic FHA single-family program is actuarially sound. Also, con-sensus exists that the FHA should remain true to its basic mission of providing credit enhancements to expand housing opportunities among higher risk and low- to moderate-income households and that the agency requires greater autonomy to accomplish that broadly defined goal.

The HUD proposal is to reinvent the FHA in the form of a wholly government-owned corporation within HUD to be known as the Federal Housing Corporation (FHC). Because of its status as an entity of the federal government (and therefore its access to lower cost capital), the new FHC is expected to carry out its broadly defined mission without any government credit subsidy. Specifically, the FHC would attempt to maintain on going federal government housing finance commitments to low-and moderate-income households, particularly those households and areas deemed too risky to be served by the private sector. In so doing, it would also seek to smooth cyclical fluctuations in mortgage supply, demonstrate and introduce innovative mortgage products, and further enhance competition in the supply of mortgage funds. However, it would undertake those activities in a more efficient, business-oriented manner devoid of current FHA statutory constraints on mortgage offerings.[19]

The FHC will undertake a substantive review of all single-family, multifamily, and health care facility markets with the aim of defining appropriate instruments and strategic market share over the near to middle term. Regardless of the precise organizational and legal structure of the new government housing finance entity, the critical problems of the multifamily insurance and subsidy programs need to be addressed; in fact, numerous analysts and policy makers suggest the outright elimination of the multifamily insurance program. Such an argument may indeed be appropriate, given the inability of the multifamily program, with its lower cost of funds, to operate on an actuarially sound basis as required by statute. The magnitude of FHA multifamily insurance in force is about one-eighth of that in the single-family portfolio; in terms of overall market share, the FHA insured about 7 percent of all multifamily mortgage originations in 1994 (Weicher 1995).

The anticipated FHC market niche will continue to evolve, given the enhanced flex-ibility of underwriting and lower down payment loan products currently being promoted by the GSEs. Although the FHC will undoubtedly continue to emphasize loan products that facilitate homeownership opportunities for underserved populations and neighbor-hoods, the FHC will compete more directly with those new and more flexible conventional loan instruments currently being underwritten by the GSEs. However, to be true to and effective in its basic mission of promoting homeownership among risky and lower income borrowers, the new entity must maintain its status as a government agency. It is only in the context of the lower cost of funds afforded by such status that the FHC could continue to serve those underserved market segments. Any equivocation of the current federal government guarantee of FHA insurance would jeopardize attainment of those funda-mental and long-standing housing policy goals.

In the wake of this evolution in the priorities and pragmatics of federal housing policy, substantial uncertainty abounds concerning implications for housing outcomes. Enhanced flexibility of GSE underwriting and the introduction of new, lower down payment mortgage instruments similarly should support homeownership among minority, low-to moderate-income, and immigrant populations. Improved flexibility and local control in the management of public housing, together with the introduction of tenant-based subsidies and the increased utilization of rental subsidies outside inner-city poverty areas, should increase economic welfare among very low income renter populations. Consolidation of HUD programs will offer improved efficiency as well, and devolution of funding and programmatic responsibility to state and local levels may sometimes provide local solutions to local problems.

However, sizable cuts in federal government rental housing and income supports will undoubtedly result in economic distress among the lowest income renter populations. Those difficulties will be further reinforced by the loss from the stock and diminished production of low-income rental housing units. Given the scarcity of affordable rental units, the housing problems of very low income renter populations will spill over to increased homelessness and additional burdens on the criminal justice system. Overall, the combination of lower levels of housing funding and increased local control will likely substantially reduce a variety of long-standing federal housing commitments and services. It is hoped that the national commitment to the pressing housing needs of low-income renter populations is not too greatly eroded, and that the hoped-for efficiency gains at HUD become evident, to realize the long-standing housing policy goals of improved homeownership and rental housing opportunities for the large number of traditionally underserved American households.

Notes

1 In 1989, the median age of the housing stock was 26 years; about one-fourth of existing units were built before 1940, and some 30 percent were constructed after 1975.

2 The data cited in this paragraph are derived from Devaney (1991).

3 The discrepancy between the housing starts and household formation forecasts is roughly accounted for by anticipated changes in vacancies and net removals from the housing stock.

4 This measure counts all rooms except bathrooms, hallways, closets, and porches. For more information, see Baer (1976).

5 For additional discussion of this point, see Myers and Wolch (1994).

6 Of continuing interest here is the process by which households form expectations of housing investment returns and hence the appropriate time frame and weighting of prior-year house price fluctuations in the calculation of homeownership user costs.

7 For the nation as a whole, changes in quality-adjusted new home prices substantially exceeded the rate of growth in the Consumer Price Index for all urban consumers during 1986 and 1987. The opposite held true for the 1988–93 period.

8 For example, in 1989, only about 14 percent of Los Angeles households could afford the median-priced existing home in the county, which sold for approximately $200,000 or about twice the national average. Owing largely to house price declines during subsequent years, some 37 percent of households in Los Angeles could afford the median-priced home by 1995. Nationally, about half of all households could qualify to purchase the median-priced existing home.

9   In 1993, about 43 percent of all African-American and 40 percent of all Hispanic households were homeowners, compared with 70 percent of all white non-Hispanic households. Sizable racial disparities in homeownership remain after adjusting for household income levels.

10 See the Emergency Low-Income Housing Preservation Act of 1987 and Title VI – the Low-Income Housing Preservation and Resident Homeownership Act – of the National Affordable Housing Act of 1990. Incentives for the preservation of federally assisted low-income housing contained in the 1990 act include insured or direct capital improvement financing, provisions for an equity takeout loan, an 8 percent return on preservation equity, investor access to reserves, higher levels of Section 8 and non-Section 8 rents, and insured acquisition loans and grants to qualified purchasers.

11 For example, the Joint Center for Housing Studies of Harvard University (1995) estimates that in San Francisco some 51 percent of all low-income renters pay more than half of their incomes for rent. Many of those low-income renters receive no form of government assistance.

12 According to recent estimates, over 300 new state-level housing programs were implemented during the 1980s. See, for example, Nenno (1991).

13 The Rental Assistance Program provides a monthly payment to the landlord equal to the difference between the tenant's contribution (the greater of 30 percent of net income, 10 percent of gross income, and the portion of welfare assistance designated to housing) and the gross rent (including utilities). Certificates may be applied to any rental unit that meets HUD's quality standards and does not exceed the fair market rent (FMR) of the area. HUD calculates the FMR as the annual adjusted average rent of modest but unsubsidized units in the market area. In contrast, the newer Housing Voucher Program allows the tenant contribution to exceed the ceilings that govern the certificate program and in so doing provides opportunities in higher rent areas for families willing to take on that added burden.

14 For further information on this topic, see Yinger (1990) and Fannie Mae Office of Housing Policy Research (1992).

15 See, for example, Canner and Gabriel (1992).

16 It should be further noted that disparate treatment can and does arise at various other junctures in the housing search and loan origination process, including realtor racial steering, real estate advertising, loan product development and steering, loan underwriting, and attempts by lenders to "work out" problems in the credit report.

17 The new agenda was evident in the Federal Housing Reform and Local Empowerment Act, proposed by a task force of first-term Republicans and then-Senate Majority Leader Robert Dole, which sought to eliminate the U.S. Department of Housing and Urban Development.

18 Further targeted for sizable cutbacks are programs designed to fight violence and drug abuse in public housing.

19 Currently, each FHA mortgage product is labeled according to the section of the National Housing Act in which it is described. In contrast, it is anticipated that the design of mortgage products by the FHC would not be done by statute; the new entity would be given a broad authority to enhance credit consistent with its articulated financial and programmatic goals.

References

Apgar, William (1991) "Preservation of Existing Housing: A Key Element in a Revitalized National Housing Policy." *Housing Policy Debate*, 2(2), 187–210.

Baer, William C. (1976) "The Evolution of Housing Indicators and Housing Standards." *Public Policy*, 24(3), 361–93.

Berkovec, James, Glenn Canner, Stuart Gabriel, and Tim Hannon (1994) "Race, Redlining, and Residential Mortgage Loan Performance." *Journal of Real Estate Finance and Economics*, 9, 263–94.

Canner, Glenn, and Stuart Gabriel (1992) "Market Segmentation and Lender Specialization in the Primary and Secondary Mortgage Markets." *Housing Policy Debate*, 3(2), 241–329.

Devaney, John F. (1991) *Housing in America: 1989–1990*. Washington, DC: U.S. Department of Commerce, Bureau of the Census.

Fannie Mae Office of Housing Policy Research (1992) "Discrimination in Housing and Mortgage Markets." *Housing Policy Debate*, 3(2).

Goering, John, Helene Stebbins, and Michael Siewert (1995) *Promoting Housing Choice in HUD's Rental Assistance Programs*. Report to Congress. Washington, DC: U.S. Department of Housing and Urban Development, Office of Policy Development and Research.

Joint Center for Housing Studies of Harvard University (1995) *The State of the Nation's Housing*. Cambridge, MA: Harvard University.

Koebel, C. Theodore, and Cara L. Bailey (1992) "State Policies and Programs to Preserve Federally Assisted Low-Income Housing." *Housing Policy Debate*, 3(4), 995–1016.

Megbolugbe, Isaac F. and Patrick A. Simmons (1995) *An Overview of Demographic Trends and Housing Market Impacts: 1995–2000*. Internal Research Report. Washington. DC: Fannie Mae Office of Housing Research.

Munnell, Alicia, Lynn Browne, James McEnearney, and Geoffrey Tootell (1992) *Mortgage Lending in Boston: Interpreting HMDA Data*, working paper No. 92–7. Boston, MA: Federal Reserve Bank of Boston.

Myers, Dowell, and Jennifer Wolch (1994) *Housing*, mimeo. Los Angeles, CA: University of Southern California, School of Urban and Regional Planning and Department of Geography.

Nenno, Mary (1991) "State and Local Governments: New Initiatives in Low-Income Housing Preservation." *Housing Policy Debate*, 2(2), 467–97.

Retsinas, Nicolas P. (1995) Comment on "FHA Restructuring Proposals: Alternatives and Implications." *Housing Policy Debate*, 6(2), 395–415.

Schnare, Ann B. (1991) "The Preservation Needs of Public Housing." *Housing Policy Debate*, 2(2), 289–318.

U.S. Census Bureau (1996) *Housing Vacancy Survey: Third Quarter 1996*. World Wide Web page <http://www.census.gov/hhes/www/hvs.html> (last revised October 22).

U.S. (HUD) Department of Housing and Urban Development (1989) *Report to Congress on Alternative Methods for Funding Public Housing Modernization*. Washington, DC: U.S. Government Printing Office.

U.S. (HUD) Department of Housing and Urban Development (1995) *HUD Reinvention: From Blueprint to Action*. Washington, DC.

Vandell, Kerry D. (1995) "FHA Restructuring Proposals: Alternatives and Implications." *Housing Policy Debate*, 6(2), 291–393.

Wallace, James E. (1991) "Who Benefits from Preservation: The People behind the Numbers." *Housing Policy Debate*, 2(2), 219–44.

Weicher, John C. (1995) Comment on "FHA Restructuring Proposals: Alternatives and Implications." *Housing Policy Debate*, 6(2), 417–37.

Yinger. John (1990) *Estimates of the Incidence and the Severity of Unfavorable Treatment from the Housing Discrimination Study*. Washington, DC: The Urban Institute.

CHAPTER TWENTY-SEVEN

The Dynamics of Housing Assistance Spells

Thomas L. Hungerford*

Source: *Journal of Urban Economics*, 39, 193–208. © 1996 Academic Press, Inc.

Over the past several years many researchers have examined public welfare programs, but little of this research has examined housing assistance. This paper focuses on the duration of housing assistance spells. A hazard model is estimated using data from the Survey of Income and Program Participation. The results suggest that although some people leave housing assistance after brief spells, many will continue to receive assistance for relatively long periods. The results also present evidence of the absence of duration dependence in housing assistance spells. Furthermore, important interactions between housing assistance and receipt of other public assistance are found.

Over the past several years much research has focused on public welfare programs, but little of it has examined housing assistance. However, in recent years, social scientists have become increasingly concerned about rising crime rates in public housing projects and increasing social isolation of the residents of these projects (Kasarda [8] and Wilson [14, 15]). For example, Kasarda argues that because of place-oriented public housing "a large minority underclass has become anchored" in economically distressed inner-city areas, while Wilson argues that the social isolation excludes residents from the job network system that is important in learning about a job. Another concern is that families, once in a public housing unit, tend to stay there for years (GAO [13]). Policymakers have become alarmed at the rising number of people seeking to move into public housing units.[1]

The Federal Government has subsidized housing for low-income people since the 1930s. In 1991, the Federal Government budgeted almost $17 billion for housing programs to assist over 5.5 million households. Furthermore, throughout the 1980s and early 1990s, the Department of Housing and Urban Development (HUD) experimented with various programs designed to provide recipients of housing assistance with the skills necessary to obtain jobs.[2] The idea is to increase the earnings of housing assistance recipients so they will no longer need housing assistance. But, are few skills and

* I would like to thank Bruce Meyer for providing me with his FORTRAN routine to estimate the hazard models reported in this paper, and two anonymous referees and the editor for their comments. The views presented here do not necessarily represent the views of the U.S. General Accounting Office.

low-earnings the only barriers to leaving housing assistance? Will training funds be wasted on those who are already job ready and will leave housing assistance after brief stays?

This paper focuses on the duration of housing assistance spells. Given the policy emphasis of moving able-bodied people to self-sufficiency as quickly as possible, it is important to know what determines the length of time people receive housing assistance. Knowing who receives housing assistance for short periods has important implications not only for the residential composition of housing projects, but also for the targeting of scarce training funds through HUD's self-sufficiency programs.

Previous research on housing assistance, for the most part, has not examined the dynamics of the receipt of such assistance. One exception is research by Blank and Ruggles [2] who were concerned with the dynamics of multiple program participation. They estimated various hazard models using a sample of female household heads who received public assistance benefits. Among other things, they found that housing assistance spells tend to be longer than other types of welfare spells.

This paper differs from that of Blank and Ruggles in two respects. First, all household heads who receive housing assistance are included. Second, a variable was included that indicates the tightness of the local housing market. The results present evidence that some people leave housing assistance after brief stays. The rest of this paper is organized into three sections. The next section lays out the conceptual foundations for the analysis. The results are presented and discussed in section 2. Finally, section 3 contains a few concluding remarks.

1. Conceptual Foundations

1.1. Theoretical foundations

The government provides housing assistance in one of two forms: public housing or rental subsidies. In the case of public housing, the local public housing agency (PHA) provides recipients with a housing unit in a public housing complex. Recipients of a rental subsidy choose a housing unit in the private rental market and the local PHA pays part of the rent.

Public housing assistance, a means-tested program, is different from most other means-tested welfare programs in two important respects. First, public housing assistance is an in-kind benefit rather than a cash grant (like Aid to Families with Dependent Children (AFDC) or Supplemental Security Income (SSI)) or a near-cash benefit (such as food stamps). Typically, a public housing resident pays 30% of their family income for rent, and as long as the resident does not violate the lease they can remain in public housing indefinitely. Since there is no market rent for a public housing unit, it is difficult to calculate the amount of the housing subsidy or to determine if the in-kind nature of public housing forces families to over-consume housing.[3]

Second, housing assistance is not an entitlement as are AFDC, SSI, and food stamps. Therefore, public housing is rationed and many public housing agencies have long waiting lists. As a result, many residents may be reluctant to give up a public housing unit since they would go to the end of the queue should they wish to return to public housing.

The theoretical framework for analyzing the length of time living in a public housing unit is based on a model of choice and search or sequential statistical decision theory.[4] Previous analyses of the duration of welfare spells have started from choice models (see, for example, Blank [1] and Fitzgerald [5]). Recipients choose between staying on or getting off of welfare. However, there is more to leaving public housing than there is to getting off of welfare: the household must decide whether or not to leave public housing and search for suitable housing. Over time, both the returns to living in public housing and the external housing market can change, forcing the household to continually reevaluate available options. But information regarding the local housing market and the household's ability to pay full rent is imperfect. This information is collected and evaluated before the household is willing to move.

Rental subsidy assistance is also means-tested. There are various subsidy programs, but all have some common features. First, the recipient pays part of the rent and the local PHA pays the rest directly to the landlord. Second, the subsidy falls as the recipient's income increases to the break-even income level. Changes in family composition affect eligibility only to the extent that it changes the break-even income level. At the break-even income level the recipient is no longer eligible for the rental subsidy. The length of time a recipient receives a rental subsidy can be modeled in much the same way as welfare spells have been modeled.

In either case, the length of time a household receives housing assistance is a random variable. The distribution of this variable depends on the household's characteristics and the environment in which the household lives. The most obvious are the characteristics of the household head, such as marital status, number of children in the family unit, sex, race, and age. Another group of factors include those affecting the household head's labor force status: education, disabilities, receipt of assistance from other welfare programs, and the unemployment rate. Last, the conditions in the local housing market would affect housing decisions.

1.2. Econometric method

The unit of observation for this study is the individual (household head). The model used is the proportional hazards model (Cox and Oakes [3] and Kalbfleisch and Prentice [7]). In the present case, the hazard is the conditional probability that an individual will stop receiving housing assistance at time t given they have received such assistance until t. More formally it is defined as

$$\lim_{\Delta \to 0^+} \frac{\Pr(t \leq T_i < t + \Delta \,|\, T_i \geq t)}{\Delta} = \lambda_0(t)\exp(X_i(t)'\beta),$$

where $\lambda_0(t)$ is the baseline hazard common to all individuals, T_i is the time of failure for individual i (e.g., moving out of public housing), $X_i(t)$ is a vector of covariates for individual i, some of which vary over time, and β is a vector of parameters. The baseline hazard can be estimated either parametrically or nonparametrically and the model can include left-or right-censored observations.[5] The most common parametric model is the Weibull model, but the nonparametric model allows for greater flexibility by letting the baseline hazard be a step function. After some experimentation, five steps appear to fit the data, so the baseline hazard to be estimated is[6]

$$
\lambda_0(t) = \begin{cases}
\lambda_1, & \text{if } 1 \leq t \leq 4 \\
\lambda_2, & \text{if } 5 \leq t \leq 8 \\
\lambda_3, & \text{if } 9 \leq t \leq 12 \\
\lambda_4, & \text{if } 13 \leq t \leq 16 \\
\lambda_5, & \text{if } t \geq 17
\end{cases}.
$$

The empirical method used here builds on Meyer's [9] method by allowing for left-censored spells.

1.3. Data

The data used for the estimation of the hazard model come from the Survey of Income and Program Participation (SIPP) 1986, 1987, and 1988 Full Panel Microdata Research Files. The SIPP panels are longitudinal data sets that followed individuals for up to 28 months. The 1986 panel followed individuals from October 1985 to March 1988, the 1987 panel followed individuals from October 1986 to April 1989, and the 1988 panel followed individuals from October 1987 to December 1989. The overlapping design of the SIPP panels allows the use of multiple panels resulting in a larger number of cases. There are two advantages to using the SIPP. First, the SIPP sample follows housing assistance recipients rather than housing units. Second, unlike the Michigan Panel Study of Income Dynamics (PSID), the SIPP provides monthly information on a household's receipt of housing assistance as well as on welfare receipt.

Only household heads living in public housing units or receiving a rental subsidy were selected. Individuals whose housing assistance spells are both left-and right-censored (i.e., neither the start nor the end of the spell are observed) were eliminated from the sample. All in all, 2706 household heads in the SIPP sample had at least one housing assistance spell (public housing or rental subsidy). Of these individuals, 1480 or 55% of the spells were both left- and right-censored. The final sample used in this study contains 1226 household heads with housing assistance spells, of which 140 or 11% were right-censored and 380 or 31% were left-censored. A few individuals had more than one housing assistance spell. If the break between spells was one month and the individual did not move to another state then the two spells were coded as one long spell. Otherwise the first spell that was not left-censored was used.

The variables (and means) used in the analysis are listed in Table 1. Three time invariant dummy variables were included to indicate if the individual is female (FEMALE), black (BLACK), or disabled (DISABLED).[7] Eight time varying variables were also included. Three of these are dummy variables indicating if the individual is married with spouse present (MARRIED), over 64 years old (ELDERLY), or receiving in-kind (food stamps and/or Medicaid) welfare benefits (INKIND). Also included are years of education (EDUC), number of children less than 6 years old (KIDS6), and total real cash transfers (CASHTRNS). The SIPP panels only provide information on the respondent's state of residence, which forced the use of two state level variables. The first

Table 1 Variables and means

Variable	All	≤ 12 Months	> 12 Months	Censored at ≤ 12 months
		A. Means: Public Housing		
		Time constant		
FEMALE	0.522	0.398	0.661	0.528
BLACK	0.229	0.141	0.328	0.233
DISABLED	0.213	0.199	0.287	0.184
		Time varying		
MARRIED	0.318	0.403	0.240	0.306
ELDERLY	0.225	0.194	0.298	0.207
KIDS6	0.211	0.248	0.193	0.198
EDUC	9.503	8.830	9.690	9.813
INKIND	0.310	0.194	0.485	0.292
CASHTRNS	69.302	47.587	101.864	66.110
UR	6.264	6.714	6.259	5.997
FMR	387.996	384.770	386.472	390.692
DURATION	8.838	4.655	19.029	6.268
N	720	206	171	343
		B. Means: Rental Subsidy		
		Time constant		
FEMALE	0.597	0.449	0.727	0.592
BLACK	0.160	0.131	0.197	0.154
DISABLED	0.239	0.140	0.341	0.229
		Time varying		
MARRIED	0.259	0.355	0.189	0.255
ELDERLY	0.202	0.122	0.303	0.184
KIDS6	0.227	0.187	0.296	0.210
EDUC	9.652	9.000	9.561	9.959
INKIND	0.338	0.224	0.508	0.300
CASHTRNS	83.210	60.874	130.280	68.891
UR	5.921	5.579	6.232	5.905
FMR	399.885	404.89	401.953	396.856
DURATION	9.486	5.084	18.265	6.910
N	506	107	132	267

is the state unemployment rate (UR) which captures the state labor market conditions. The other is the average metropolitan real Fair Market Rent for a two-bedroom unit[8] (FMR). The interpretation of this variable is not straightforward. It not only proxies for local housing market conditions (Rosen and Smith [11]), but also is a proxy for the housing subsidy[9] and may indicate the length of the housing assistance waiting list.[10] Fortunately each of these leads to a larger Fair Market Rent having an expected negative effect on the hazard.

2. Results

The total sample was split into three groups and the mean of each variable for each group is shown in Table 1. The first group consists of individuals who received housing assistance for 12 months or less. The second group contains those individuals who received assistance for more than 12 months. The last group is composed of those with censored spells of 12 months or less. The most interesting differences are between "short-term" recipients ($\leq$ 12 months) and "long-term" recipients ($>$ 12 months). A much higher proportion of the long-term housing assistance recipients are female, black, disabled, elderly, and receiving welfare more than the short-term recipients. Also the short-term recipients are more likely to be married. For many of the characteristics, the means for the third group (censored with spells $\leq$ 12 months) are between the short-term and long-term groups.

The maximum likelihood estimation proceeds in two steps. In the first step, the total sample is used to estimate the effects of the covariates on the hazard. The second step focuses more narrowly on those spells that are not left-censored. The reason for this second step is to examine the most recent recipients of housing assistance since many self-sufficiency programs are targeted to newer recipients.[11] The maximum likelihood estimation results of the hazard models are listed in Tables 2 and 3. Various forms (parametric and nonparametric) for the baseline hazard were tried and the parameter estimates for the covariates were nearly the same for each specification. Furthermore, various covariates were tried before settling on those included in the tables.[12] A likelihood ratio test was performed to determine if the public housing and rental subsidy samples should be combined. The result for the total sample indicates that public housing spells are not different from rental subsidy spells; therefore the public housing and rental subsidy samples were combined.[13] However, for the subsample without the left-censored spells, the result indicates that they should not be combined,[14] suggesting that public housing spells are different from rental subsidy spells.

The results for the total sample are presented in column 1 of Table 2. The MLE coefficient estimates are in Panel A of the table, the baseline hazard estimates are contained in Panel B, and the marginal impacts on the hazard of variable changes are presented in Panel C. The hazard rate for exiting housing assistance spells is fairly small at 0.19. The most important variables affecting the hazard are the household head's sex, age,[15] education, receipt of in-kind public assistance benefits, and the state unemployment rate. Perusal of Panel C shows that female household heads, the elderly, and the less educated are less likely to leave housing assistance than males (by 20%),[16] prime-aged (working age) individuals (by 27%), and the more educated (6% for each year of education).

Interestingly, the coefficient estimate for the unemployment rate (UR) has an unexpected sign and is statistically significant. A possible explanation may be that individuals will leave a high unemployment area for areas where there are more employment opportunities. Unfortunately, using state level data does not allow testing this explanation. The parameter estimates for self-reported disability (DISABLED) has the "wrong" sign, but the estimate is very small and is not statistically significant. The coefficient estimate for the fair market rent (FMR) has the "right" sign but also is small and not statistically

Table 2 Results: Hazard model
(Standard errors in parenthesis)

Variable	Total sample (1)	Nonelderly, nondisabled (2)
	Panel A. Maximum Likelihood Results[a]	
FEMALE	−0.2264**	−0.2300***
	(0.1053)	(0.1320)
BLACK	−0.1705	−0.2177
	(0.1091)	(0.1381)
DISABLED	−0.0699	
	(0.1038)	
ELDERLY	−0.3137*	
	(0.1101)	
MARRIED	−0.0346	−0.1589
	(0.1137)	(0.1371)
KIDS6	0.0838	0.1077
	(0.0801)	(0.1058)
EDUC	0.0636*	0.0797*
	(0.0147)	(0.0187)
INKIND	−0.4505*	−0.6440*
	(0.1117)	(0.1610)
CASHTRNS/1000	0.0832	0.0727
	(0.1276)	(0.1929)
UR	0.0941*	0.0760**
	(0.0256)	(0.0326)
FMR/1000	0.3803	0.0961
	(0.7765)	(0.9700)
ln *L*	−1509.648	−950.806
N	1226	740
	Panel B. Baseline Hazard Estimates[b]	
Period 1	0.0512	0.0557
	(0.0210)	(0.0283)
Period 2	0.0237	0.0317
	(0.0099)	(0.0164)
	[1.183]	[0.734]
Period 3	0.0203	0.0230
	(0.0090)	(0.0127)
	[1.352]	[1.052]
Period 4	0.0131	0.0187
	(0.0069)	(0.0123)
	[1.726]	[1.198]
Period 5	0.0148	0.0315
	(0.0087)	(0.0211)
	[1.601]	[0.684]
	Panel C. Marginal Impacts[c]	
Base	0.1913	0.1921
FEMALE	−0.0388	−0.0395

Table 2 *(Cont.)*

Variable	Total sample (1)	Nonelderly, nondisabled (2)
BLACK	−0.0300	−0.0376
DISABLED	−0.0129	
ELDERLY	−0.0515	
MARRIED	−0.0065	−0.0282
KIDS6	0.0167	0.0218
EDUC	0.0126	0.0159
INKIND	−0.0694	−0.0912
CASHTRNS	0.0001	0.0001
UR	0.0189	0.0152
FMR	0.0028	0.0007

* Two-tailed t test significant at 1% level.

** Two-tailed t test significant at 5% level.

*** Two-tailed t test significant at 10% level.

[a] Estimated with a nonparametric baseline hazard, 5 steps.

[b] The numbers in brackets are t statistics testing the hypothesis that the particular baseline hazard estimate is equal to the estimate for period 1.

[c] Base case is the hazard in period 1 and is determined with all dummy variables (FEMALE, BLACK, DISABLED, ELDERLY, MARRIED, and INKIND) and KIDS6 set equal to zero, EDUC set to 9, CASHTRNS set to $70, UR set to 6.3, and FMR set to $388. Marginal impacts are determined by increasing CASHTRNS and FMR by 10%, and all other variables by 1, and taking the difference between the new hazard and the base case hazard.

Table 3 Results: Hazard model with left-censored spells deleted (standard errors in parenthesis)

Variable	Public housing (1)	Rental subsidy (2)	Nonelderly nondisabled (3)
	Panel A. Maximum Likelihood Results[a]		
FEMALE	−0.4338**	−0.3467	−0.4415*
	(0.2046)	(0.2666)	(0.1861)
BLACK	−0.4042***	−0.3701	−0.4923**
	(0.2376)	(0.3199)	(0.2226)
DISABLED	0.0567	−0.5492***	
	(0.2031)	(0.2957)	
ELDERLY	−0.4151**	−0.6715**	
	(0.2006)	(0.3225)	
MARRIED	0.0116	0.0282	−0.1496
	(0.2028)	(0.2714)	(0.1844)
KIDS6	0.2654***	−0.1017	0.1894
	(0.1357)	(0.2692)	(0.1515)
EDUC	−0.0141	−0.0028	−0.0012
	(0.0274)	(0.0338)	(0.0252)
INKIND	−0.8660*	−0.4208	−0.8361*
	(0.2240)	(0.2918)	(0.2353)
CASHTRNS/1000	0.3790**	0.0960	0.2249
	(0.1604)	(0.2606)	(0.1996)

Table 3 *(Cont.)*

Variable	Public housing (1)	Rental subsidy (2)	Nonelderly nondisabled (3)
UR	0.1052**	−0.1057	0.0380
	(0.0488)	(0.0808)	(0.0474)
FMR/1000	−0.7873	0.0217	−1.0309
	(1.4594)	(1.7564)	(1.3205)
In *L*	−755.041	−443.611	−796.786
N	504	342	513
	Panel B. Baseline Hazard Estimates[b]		
Period 1	0.1108	0.1817	0.1597
	(0.0819)	(0.1883)	(0.1121)
Period 2	0.0588	0.1175	0.1048
	(0.0432)	(0.1207)	(0.0737)
	[0.561]	[0.287]	[0.410]
Period 3	0.0546	0.1003	0.0813
	(0.0428)	(0.1054)	(0.0599)
	[0.608]	[0.377]	[0.617]
Period 4	0.0309	0.0687	0.0652
	(0.0272)	(0.0807)	(0.0543)
	[0.926]	[0.853]	[0.759]
Period 5	0.0391	0.0329	0.1081
	(0.0346)	(0.0479)	(0.0911)
	[0.807]	[0.766]	[0.358]
	Panel C. Marginal Impacts[c]		
Base	0.1432	0.0924	0.1367
FEMALE	−0.0504	−0.0271	−0.0488
BLACK	−0.0476	−0.0286	−0.0531
DISABLED	0.0084	−0.0390	
ELDERLY	−0.0486	−0.0452	
MARRIED	0.0016	0.0027	−0.0190
KIDS6	0.0435	−0.0089	0.0285
EDUC	−0.0020	−0.0002	−0.0002
INKIND	−0.0830	−0.0317	−0.0775
CASHTRNS	0.0004	0.0001	0.0002
UR	0.0159	−0.0092	0.0053
FMR	−0.0043	0.0001	−0.0054

* Two-tailed *t* test significant at 1% level.

** Two-tailed *t* test significant at 5% level.

*** Two-tailed *t* test significant at 10% level.

[a] Estimated with a nonparametric baseline hazard, 5 steps.

[b] The numbers in brackets are *t* statistics testing the hypothesis that the particular baseline hazard estimate is equal to the estimate for period 1.

[c] Base case is the hazard in period 1 and is determined with all dummy variables (FEMALE, BLACK, DISABLED, ELDERLY, MARRIED, and INKIND) and KIDS6 set equal to zero, EDUC set to 9, CASHTRNS set to $70, UR set to 6.3, and FMR set to $388. Marginal impacts are determined by increasing CASHTRNS and FMR by 10%, and all other variables by 1, and taking the difference between the new hazard and the base case hazard.

significant which could be due to the crudeness of the FMR variable. Those receiving other in-kind benefits (food stamps or Medicaid) are much less likely to leave housing assistance. It should be noted from Panel C that receipt of in-kind benefits has the largest marginal impact on the hazard, reducing the hazard by 36%, thus suggesting important interactions between housing assistance and receipt of other in-kind benefits.

The estimates for the baseline hazard implied by the step function are shown in Panel B of the table. Casual inspection of the estimates suggests the existence of duration dependence,[17] though there is a slight spike in period 5. However, the test of duration dependence is not whether the estimates are equal to zero, but rather whether the estimates are equal to one another. The numbers in brackets are the t statistics testing the hypothesis that the particular baseline hazard estimate is equal to the estimate for period 1. In each case, the null hypothesis cannot be rejected at the 5% level. These results, therefore, cannot reject the hypothesis that the baseline hazard is constant.

Column 2 of Table 2 focuses on those household heads who are nonelderly and nondisabled. Most self-sufficiency programs are targeted to those who are expected to work, and the concern over dependence on housing assistance is directed toward the able-bodied. While the results are not identical to those in column 1, many of the same trends are apparent. Male household heads and those with more education are more likely to leave housing assistance. The negative effect of the receipt of other in-kind public assistance benefits is stronger than for the total sample. Again, the state unemployment rate has a "perverse" effect on the housing assistance hazard. Last, casual inspection of the results shown in Panel B suggest the existence of duration dependence, but the t tests indicate that the hypothesis of a constant baseline hazard cannot be rejected.

The results for the subsample of household heads whose housing assistance spells recently started (those with spells that are not left-censored) are shown in Table 3. As mentioned above, a likelihood ratio test indicates that the public housing sample and the rental subsidy sample should not be combined. The results for public housing residents are shown in column 1. Some of the same results are apparent: females, the elderly, and those receiving in-kind benefits are less likely to leave public housing. However, the results also show that blacks are less likely to leave public housing (although the coefficient estimate is statistically significant only at the 10% level), and those with young children or receiving cash transfers are more likely to leave public housing. Since public housing units and environments may be inferior, one possible explanation for the coefficient estimate for the number of young children is parents want to take their children out of unfavorable living environments. Increases in cash transfers give families the means to move out of public housing and into private sector housing. The coefficient estimate for years of education is small and not statistically significant.

The results of the hazard model for rental subsidy spells are shown in column 2 of Table 3. In most instances, the signs of the coefficient estimates are the same as those for public housing spells but are not as precisely estimated. There are four estimates that are different from those for public housing. The coefficient estimate for DISABLED is negative and significant at the 10% level. Household heads with health conditions that limit work appear to receive rental subsidies longer. Neither the number of young children under 6 nor the state unemployment rate affect rental subsidy spells, in contrast to public housing spells. The coefficient estimate for cash transfers is small and not statistically significant. One possible explanation for this difference with public housing residents is that rental subsidy recipients already live in private sector housing and have no need to flee inferior public housing units. Last, the receipt of in-kind benefits from other public assistance programs has a much smaller and statistically insignificant impact on the hazard rate. As before, the results of the t test shown in Panel B indicate the absence of duration dependence in both public housing and rental subsidy spells.

The results for recently started housing assistance spells show that the elderly and disabled are less likely to leave housing assistance programs. Since training programs are targeted to prime-aged individuals, the hazard models were reestimated with the sample of nonelderly and nondisabled household heads; the results are shown in column 3 of Table 3. A likelihood ratio test was performed to determine if the public housing sample and the rental subsidy sample should be combined. The results show that the null hypothesis that the coefficient estimates for the two samples are the same cannot be rejected.[18] Therefore, public housing residents and rental subsidy recipients were combined into one sample. The results are pretty much the same as before. Female household heads, black household heads and families receiving in-kind public assistance benefits are less likely to stop receiving housing assistance. The coefficient estimate for the amount of cash transfers received is not statistically significant, as well as the coefficient estimate for years of education. The baseline hazard estimates (Panel B) show the same pattern as before and indicate that the baseline hazard is constant.

3. Concluding Remarks

The results presented in this paper, while not definitive, offer some insight into the barriers to leaving housing assistance. First, the results show that some people do move out of public housing or stop receiving rental subsidies after relatively short periods. These individuals appear to be more job ready than longer-term housing assistance recipients. However, the hazard rates for housing assistance spells are rather low, and although some individuals leave quickly, the results suggest that many will continue to receive assistance for long periods. A large proportion of the longer-term recipients are over 65 years old or disabled. Any program aimed at getting people to leave housing assistance by enhancing their job skills[19] needs to take into consideration the characteristics of the longer-term housing assistance recipients and the barriers they face moving into the economic mainstream.

Second, the evidence strongly suggests that leaving housing assistance is related to other welfare programs. Especially for recent recipients, moving someone out of public housing means not only overcoming any disincentives from public housing but also the disincentive effects from other in-kind benefit welfare programs, which confirms Blank and Ruggles' [2] finding.[20] Interestingly, this does not appear to be the case for recent recipients of rental subsidies. Even though rental subsidy recipients are slightly more likely to receive benefits from other public assistance programs than public housing residents, the receipt of these benefits do not appear to affect the probability of losing the rental subsidy. Receipt of cash government transfers increases the hazard for leaving public housing. Since these funds can be used for private sector housing, it may be that higher payments lead families to flee inferior public housing units.

Last, in a very careful examination of AFDC spells, Blank [1] found no evidence of duration dependence and the present results also show no evidence of duration dependence in housing assistance spells. However, these results do not necessary invalidate Wilson's [14, 15] social isolation hypothesis. Given the relatively short observation window, the effects of social isolation may not have had time to set in. The evidence suggests that public housing complexes will tend to become less diverse and less representative of the population over time. Furthermore, public housing units will tend to be occupied by those with few contacts to the labor market: the elderly, the disabled, and single female household heads.

Notes

1 Shawn G. Kennedy, in *The New York Times* (Dec. 27, 1992, p. 31), reports that applicants on the waiting list for public housing in New York city are nearly equal to the total number of units in the city's public housing projects.

2 These programs included Project Self-Sufficiency, Operation Bootstrap, and most recently the Family Self-Sufficiency program.

3 In a recent study, Schone [12] estimates that the budget constraint imposed by public housing is binding and concludes that "all participants would lower housing consumption ... if the program were replaced with an equally generous cash transfer."

4 See DeGroot [4] for an exposition of statistical decision theory and Mortensen [10] for an application to job search.

5 Right-censored observations are spells where the beginning is observed but have not ended by the time the individual leaves the sample, and left-censored observations are spells where the beginning is not observed but the end of the spell is observed.

6 The steps were chosen at four month intervals because of the seam problem. See Hill [6] for a discussion of the seam problem in the SIPP.

7 The disability variable is self-reported and indicates if the individual has a "physical, mental, or other health condition that limits the kind of work" he/she can do at any time during the 30 month SIPP sampling period.

8 The Fair Market Rent is determined annually by HUD and is set equal to the rent at the 45th percentile in each area.

9 The SIPP panels do not provide information on the rent paid by public housing residents, the amount of the rent subsidy, or information on the characteristics of the housing unit.

10 It is reasonable to expect that tight housing markets will have high Fair Market Rents and long waiting lists for public housing (e.g., New York city).

11 At one point, HUD considered providing Family Self-Sufficiency training funds only to new housing assistance recipients. The Job Opportunities and Basic Skills (JOBS) program for welfare recipients targets young potential long-term recipients, and President Clinton's proposed welfare reforms apply only to welfare recipients born after 1971.

12 The parameter estimates for the variables that were included in all specifications did not very much from specification to specification.

13 The test statistic is 16.106 and the critical value with 16 degrees of freedom at the 5% level is 26.296.

14 The test statistic is 28.27 and the critical value at the 5% level with 16 degrees of freedom is 26.296.

15 When age was entered as a continuous variable the coefficient estimate was negative, small, and not statistically significant. When both age and the elderly dummy variable were entered the

coefficient estimate for age was positive, very small, and not statistically significant. The coefficient estimate for the elderly dummy was approximately equal to that listed in Table 2.

16   The percentage changes are calculated by dividing the marginal impacts in Panel C by the base case hazard.

17   The length of time receiving housing assistance influences the probability of receiving future housing assistance. In the model, negative duration dependence would be indicated if the baseline hazard were to decline over time.

18   The test statistic is 14.35 and the critical value is equal to 23.685 at 14 degrees of freedom.

19   This is a function of HUD's new Family Self-Sufficiency program.

20   They found that food stamp receipt, but not AFDC, was negatively correlated with the duration of housing assistance spells.

References

1   Blank, R. M. (1989) "Analyzing the Length of Welfare Spells," *Journal of Public Economics*, 39, 245–73.

2   Blank, R. M. and Ruggles, P. (1992) *Multiple Program Use in a Dynamic Context: Data from the SIPP*. SIPP working paper 9301.

3   Cox, D. R. and Oakes, D. (1984) *Analysis of Survival Data*. London: Chapman and Hall.

4   DeGroot, M. H. (1970) *Optimal Statistical Decisions*. New York: McGraw-Hill.

5   Fitzgerald, J. (1991) "Welfare Durations and the Marriage Market," *Journal of Human Resources*, 26, 545–61.

6   Hill, D. H. (1988) "Response Errors Around the Seam: Analysis of Change in a Panel with Overlapping Reference Periods," in *The Seam Effects in Panel Surveys* Kalton, G. Hill, D. and Miller, M. (eds) SIPP working paper 9011.

7   Kalbfleisch, J. D. and Prentice, R. L. (1980) *The Statistical Analysis of Failure Time Data*. New York: Wiley.

8   Kasarda, J. D. (1985) "Urban change and minority opportunities," in *The New Urban Reality* Peterson, P. E. (ed.), Washington: The Brookings Institution.

9   Meyer, B. D. (1988) *Semiparametric Estimation of Hazard Models*, mimeo, Northwestern University.

10   Mortensen, D. T. (1986) "Job Search and Labor Market Analysis," in *The Handbook of Labor Economics* Ashenfelter, O. C. and Layard, R. (eds), Amsterdam: North-Holland.

11   Rosen, K. T. and Smith, L. B. (1983) "The Price-Adjustment Process for Rental Housing and the Natural Vacancy Rate," *American Economic Review*, 73(4), 779–86.

12   Schone, B. S. (1993) *Estimating the Distribution of Taste Parameters of Households Facing Complex Budget Spaces: The Effects of In-Kind Transfers*, mimeo, Agency for Health Care Policy and Research.

13   U.S. General Accounting Office (1992) *Public and Assisted Housing: Linking Housing and Supportive Services to Promote Self-Sufficiency*, GAO/RCED-92-142BR.

14   Wilson, W. J. (1985) "The urban underclass in advanced industrial society," in *The New Urban Reality* P. E. Peterson, (ed.), Washington: The Brookings Institution.

15   Wilson, W. J. (1987) *The Truly Disadvantaged*, Chicago: University of Chicago Press.

Further Reading Samples

Opening paragraphs from *Time for Revisionism on Rent Control?*

RICHARD ARNOTT

Source: Journal of Economic Perspectives, 9(1), Winter 1995, 99–120. Reprinted by permission of American Economic Association.

Economists have been virtually unanimous in their opposition to rent control. In a survey of economists' opinions, Alston, Kearl, and Vaughan (1992) asked a stratified random sample of 1990 American Economic Association members whether they "generally agree," "agree with provisions," or "generally disagree" with 40 statements related to economic theory and policy. The greatest degree of consensus on any question – 93.5 percent – was agreement or qualified agreement with the statement: "A ceiling on rents reduces the quantity and quality of housing available." This is hardly a discriminating question concerning economists' attitudes towards rent control, but is nonetheless suggestive. There has been widespread agreement that rent controls discourage new construction, cause abandonment, retard maintenance, reduce mobility, generate mismatch between housing units and tenants, exacerbate discrimination in rental housing, create black markets, encourage the conversion of rental to owner-occupied housing, and generally short-circuit the market mechanism for housing.

In recent years, however, there has been a wave (or at least a swell) of revisionism among housing economists on the subject of rent control. While few actually advocate controls, most are considerably more muted and qualified in their opposition. Perhaps a majority, at least among the younger generation, would agree with the statement that a well-designed rent control program can be beneficial.

References

Alston, Richard M., J. R. Kearl and Michael B. Vaughan (1992) "Is There a Consensus Among Economists in 1990s?" *American Economic Review*, 82(2), May, 203–9.

Abstract from *Default Rates and Mortgage Discrimination: A View of the Controversy*

Jan K. Brueckner

Source: Cityscape: A Journal of Policy Development and Research, 2(1), February 1996, 65.

This commentary evaluates the debate over interpretation of the empirical findings of Berkovec, Canner, Gabriel, and Hannan (BCGH), which show higher default rates for black FHA borrowers. It argues that BCGH's critics, who claim that the results cannot be used to infer the absence of mortgage discrimination, are right. However, since the critics' points are acknowledged in BCGH's original paper, BCGH are hardly guilty of over-stating their case.

Abstract from *Housing Price Dynamics Within a Metropolitan Area*

KARL E. CASE AND CHRISTOPHER J. MAYER

Source: Regional Science and Urban Economics, 26, 387–407. © 1996 Elsevier Science. Reprinted with permission from Elsevier Science.

This paper analyzes the pattern of house price appreciation in the Boston area from 1982 to 1994. The empirical results are consistent with the predictions of a standard urban model in which towns have a fixed set of amenities. The evidence suggests that changes in the cross-sectional pattern of house prices are related to differences in manufacturing employment, demographics, new construction, proximity to the downtown, and to ag-gregate school enrollments. These findings support the view that town amenities are not easily replicated or quickly adaptable to shifts in demand, even within a metropolitan area.

Abstract from *Evidence of Racial Discrimination in Different Dimensions of Owner-Occupied Housing Search*

CANOPY ROYCHOUDHURY AND ALLEN C. GOODMAN

Source: Real Estate Economics, 24(2), 1996, 161–78.

This paper examines the incidence and extent of racial discrimination in various dimen-sions of owner-occupied housing search. Audit data for sales units (1980–90) from the Fair Housing Center of metropolitan Detroit is used in an ordered probit framework. Agents' own prejudices and the prejudices of their customers are shown to be significant in explaining discrimination. Results also indicate that white home seekers are steered toward more white and affluent neighborhoods.

Discussion Questions

1 Do you agree with Gwynne's remark that public housing in America is a policy failure of immense proportions? In his review article, does Gabriel describe any policy successes that could be attributed to public housing?

2 *Empowerment* is now considered by many to be a key element in a successful government program designed to assist poor people. What does this term mean? Was empowerment present in Tulane's takeover of the Housing Authority of New Orleans? Are there any economic principles or concepts that would support empowerment as an essential ingredient in policies to assist the poor?

3 Is there any economic justification for federal, state, or local government to assist in the process of an individual securing a home mortgage? Do these justifications apply equally well to poor and rich people?

4 Describe some of the major new initiatives that HUD has put in place in the late 1990s? In your opinion, have they gone far enough with these initiatives, or, does more along these lines need to be done?

5 How do government investigators determine if discrimination has occurred in housing and mortgage markets? Can they just look at the percentage of loans granted to Whites who applied, and to minorities that have applied, and claim discrimination if the minority percentage is lower?

6 In simple language, describe the hazard regression model used by Hungerford. Interpret each of the regression coefficients provided in Hungerford's Table 2 in the Total Sample column. Any surprises?

PART VII:

Urban Crime

Increasingly, statistics are confirming an emerging perception among urban residents: Many of America's cities, in small ways and large, are safer now than they have been in decades

Leon Lazaroff and Jim Blair

CHAPTER TWENTY-EIGHT

The Mystery of the Falling Crime Rate

DAVID C. ANDERSON

Source: *The San Diego Union-Tribune*, 4.6.97. © 1997.

In the mid-1980s, crack and guns produced a surge of urban crime, and politicians responded to public fear and anger with tougher prisons, longer sentences and new limits on the discretion of judges and parole boards who might be tempted to reduce them. In the mid-1990s, the violent crime rate is declining. Did the stiffer punishments make the difference?

Stiffer punishments certainly swelled the prison population. Between 1984 and 1994, according to the federal Bureau of Justice Statistics, the number of convicts admitted each year to the nation's state and federal prisons grew by 120 percent, from 246,260 to 541,434. The taxpayers' bill for corrections also more than doubled to $31.5 billion. But what, in fact, was all this money buying? On this point, the statistics are hardly reassuring. The issue is one of scale. Perhaps half of serious crimes are reported to police. Of these, only about one-fifth result in an arrest, and less than two-thirds of those result in a conviction. In the end, while some 20 million serious crimes are committed each year, only about 500,000 criminals go to state or federal prison, many of them for nonviolent offenses.

Even if each convicted felon is responsible for multiple crimes, how can incarceration of so small a fraction of serious criminals have much effect on the crime rate, either directly or as a deterrent? And how to justify spending $31.5 billion – a third of the overall budget for police, courts and corrections – on punishing such a tiny percentage of serious crimes? Call it the "back-end/front-end" debate. Back-enders focus on the retribution dispensed at the conclusion of the criminal justice process; front-enders look for earlier interventions: more creative policing, gun control, drug treatment and other alternatives to prison. While back-enders talk about the crime they prevent by incarcerating criminals, front-enders point out that eventually most criminals are released and return to crime. Indeed, while 541,434 criminals were sent to prisons in 1994, 456,942 came out – for a net reduction of the at-large population that year of only 84,492 criminals. This does represent an increase over 1984, when there was a net reduction of 24,492. But it's hard to see how incapacitating 60,000 more criminals, a figure that includes nonviolent drug offenders, can have more than a modest impact on serious crime rates. Couldn't some of the $31.5 billion spent each year on locking them up be put to better use?

The most striking evidence that it could comes from New York City. The violent summer of 1990 prompted the city's first black mayor, David Dinkins, to push through a significant expansion of the police force – and a tax to pay for it. This was a gift of immeasurable value to Mayor Rudolph Giuliani, who defeated Dinkins in the next election, and to his new police commissioner, William Bratton. Bratton, who is now said to be among the top contenders to head the Los Angeles Police Department, took a new management approach, dispersing responsibility for crime fighting downward to precinct commanders and holding them strictly accountable for results. He ordered up reams of statistical data, and police computers began to map out crime and enforcement patterns with unprecedented precision and timeliness. At the same time, Bratton mounted a citywide campaign against "quality of life" offenses – drinking in public, urinating on the street, general rowdiness. Though the endeavor sounded like a public relations stunt, it was deadly serious – the mechanism for an aggressive form of "stop and frisk" patrolling targeted on youthful lowlifes. Bratton asserted that these measures caused a steep decline in New York City's homicide rate, and the evidence so far supports him. The nation's big-city homicide rate turned down after 1991 and has continued to fall through 1996. But New York City's decline far exceeds the national figure. San Diego, too, has seen big declines in crime, apparently the result of increased police presence and more aggressive patrolling. Such successes should encourage thinking about other front-end measures. For example, improving the nation's overcrowded and underfunded lower courts would give judges more power to intervene meaningfully after a first or second minor offense, rather than waiting for the offender to commit a serious crime. Making available more treatment for drug-involved offenders may wind up costing less overall than sending them to prison for short terms, then returning them to lives of addiction and crime, even if a sizable percentage does not make it through treatment programs. Getting serious about gun control might also make a bigger difference in violent crime rates, at lower cost, than the current practice focused so narrowly on prison.

The question should not be what is the most gratifying way to take revenge on criminals, but what are the most effective ways to fight crime?

Percent change by category from FBI preliminary 1996 crime report:

Overall crime	−3%
Violent crime	−7%
Murder	−11%
Rape	−3%
Robbery	−8%
Aggravated assault	−6%
Property crime	−3%
Burglary	−5%
Larceny-theft	−2%
Auto theft	−5%

CHAPTER TWENTY-NINE

Bright Lights, Big City, and Safe Streets: Urban Dwellers Bask in Greater Sense of Security, as Crime Rates Drop Even Further

LEON LAZAROFF AND JIM BLAIR

Source: Christian Science Monitor, 5.1.98. © 1999 Dow Jones & Company, Inc. All rights reserved.

This year, Denise Malick will joyfully go about the chore of removing Christmas lights strung outside her Los Angeles home. In years past, by this time they've been stolen. A few miles away, on Hollywood Boulevard, the prostitutes and drug dealers no longer hang out in front of Hamburger Hamlet. "People are coming down here again ... They feel more comfortable walking up and down the boulevard," says restaurant manager Robin Moor. In Manhattan, Greggor Petrovic is out walking his terrier on the Upper West Side and notices a different feel to the city. "It's definitely safer than {it was} a few years ago. There are more people out at night," he says.

Increasingly, statistics are confirming an emerging perception among urban residents: Many of America's cities, in small ways and large, are safer now than they have been in decades. Last week, the nation's two biggest cities, New York and Los Angeles, reported the fewest homicides in 30 years and 20 years, respectively. Chicago, New Orleans, Dallas, Baltimore, and San Francisco also reported a continued fall in murder rates. While Denver, Detroit, and Nashville bucked the trend, nationwide homicides dropped 11 percent.

Reasons for the decline – which in most cases extend to each of the seven major crime categories that cities report to the FBI – are varied. And perhaps because of public skepticism or media story selection, Americans' perception of urban safety is only beginning to catch up with a five-year-old trend in many places. Generally, surveys show that the public's fear of crime remains higher than it should be in light of such large drops in murder, assault, and robbery, says Eric Monkkonen, professor of public policy at the University of California at Los Angeles. "It may not be a rational response to a declining crime rate, but it may have something to do with putting more pressure on government and police to lower crime," says Mr. Monkkonen.

New York Mayor Rudolph Giuliani has certainly paid heed to such sentiments. Mr. Giuliani eagerly takes credit for the drop in murders from a 1990 peak of 2,245 to 756 last year. On Thursday, he vowed to redouble his efforts by hiring 1,600 more officers, bringing the size of the department to a record 40,000 police. In addition to force size, New York police credit the use of a computerized system that quickly determines the location of a crime by tracking emergency phone calls. It's a rapid-response program begun four years ago in conjunction with sweeping antidrug programs and vigorous enforcement of quality-of-life laws such as littering and panhandling. "Better policing won't solve everything, but it can't be denied that it has helped," says Tom Reppetto, director of the Citizen's Crime Commission, a private organization.

In Hollywood, the turnaround has come about since April, when area businesses hired off-duty police to patrol a six-block stretch of the boulevard, afflicted for years with drug dealing and illegal vendors. "We have people who haven't been to Hollywood for a couple of years, and they walk around and they're amazed {at the improvement}," says Kerry Morrison, executive director of the Hollywood Entertainment District.

Criminologists say the urban-crime drop is the result of several factors. More jobs have created fewer reasons to turn to crime, says Andrew Karmen, a sociologist at John Jay College of Criminal Justice in New York. Demographic trends also contribute to the homicide decline: There are fewer young men between 16 and 24. And there's the "little brother factor," which says that a generation of teenagers who witnessed personal traged-ies are turning away from crime. "We've noticed the drop in the percentage of funerals for teenagers here as a result of drive-by shootings," says the Rev. Leonard Jackson of the First African Methodist Episcopal Church in Los Angeles.

A waning of the crack epidemic that hit poorer urban neighborhoods in the mid-1980s is cited in a National Institute of Justice (NIJ) study as another key reason for the crime downturn. Tougher sentencing policies "would also suggest" another reason for less violent crime, says Pamela Lattimore, director of crime behavior at the NIJ. But while tougher sentencing may bring down the crime rate, police work "has actually gotten more difficult," says David Hepburn, president of the Los Angeles Police Protective League. The "three strikes" law, he says, makes criminals with previous offenses more aggressive when confronted by police. "They know that if they are caught that they're going back to prison, probably for the rest of their lives."

CHAPTER THIRTY

Urban Crime: Issues and Policies

ANN DRYDEN WITTE

Source: Housing Policy Debate, 7(4), 1996, 731–48. © 1996 Fannie Mae Foundation. All rights reserved.

Research suggests that some social and criminal justice policies can affect the crime rate. This article considers the major criminal justice and social policy issues related to urban crime, such as drugs, domestic violence, property values, and the underground economy.

Family disruption, drugs, limited economic opportunities, and unoccupied and unsupervised youth are all found to be associated with urban crime. The article concludes that major reductions in crime are likely to result only from increased economic and social opportunities for families and youth, particularly for young males. Intensive programs directed at families and at-risk youth are more likely to lower crime than are programs directed at people already heavily involved in illegal activities. It costs less to keep young people in education and training programs than to imprison them, and such programs are more likely to produce productive and well-adjusted adults.

Introduction

Urban crime is a major issue for Americans. This is true even though the most reliable evidence available, data from the National Crime Survey, indicates that the level of crime is lower today than it was in the late 1970s and early 1980s. The amount of crime is less for the most feared offenses, including rape, aggravated assault, burglary, and larceny, as well as for less serious offenses.[1]

The composition of crime has changed. While the overall murder rate in the United States has declined since the late 1970s, the murder rate for young males, particularly young black males, has increased. Beginning in 1985, the murder victimization rate for blacks aged 15 to 24 began to increase substantially. In the late 1980s, the victimization rate for young blacks exceeded the previous record levels of the early 1970s, and it has continued to increase during the 1990s. Murder victimization rates for white males aged 15 to 24 began increasing only in the late 1980s, and by the early 1990s they had returned to the rate of the late 1970s (Flanagan and Maguire 1994).

Between 1981 and 1990, arrests of those under 18 for murder and nonnegligent manslaughter rose by more than 60 percent. By 1990, 14 percent of all murders were committed by people under age 18. It appears that although we are not experiencing more violent crime, we are experiencing unusually high levels of violent crime committed by young males. In 1990, 70 percent of the people arrested in the United States were aged 16 to 34, and more than 80 percent were male (Flanagan and Maguire 1994).

The political response to the urban crime problem has been erratic and uncoordinated. During the 1980s, the federal government vigorously pursued a "war on drugs." Both states and the federal government passed laws that mandated long prison sentences without parole for many offenses. Three-strike laws (mandating severe penalties for offenders after three convictions) are the latest example of stringent sentencing policies. To house those sentenced under these tough new laws, state governments went on a prison-building spree, roughly tripling the number of jail cells between 1970 and 1990.

Getting tough on crime probably bought us a somewhat lower overall crime rate, but it did not secure an urban environment in which most citizens feel safer. The level of violent crime committed by urban youth increased substantially. The overall reduction in crime was bought at a high price. Many careful observers are now calling for a change in policy.[2]

Police are better educated and older; more diverse in gender, race, and ethnicity; and more unionized. They make increasing use of modern technology. Spending on police increased by approximately 50 percent in real terms between 1970 and 1990, but the number of police officers barely kept pace with the population (Flanagan and Maguire 1994). Police were increasingly assigned to communities rather than to patrol cars as "community policing" spread widely. Under community policing, police returned to walking a beat, but their range of activities was wider than that of the beat cops of the 1950s. The police in many urban areas became spokespeople for the neighborhood through local government bodies and assumed some roles normally reserved for social workers. They helped to clean up neighborhoods. They intervened in potentially crime-producing situations (e.g., mediating family disputes, closing down crack houses for code violations). They encouraged citizens, local businesses, and neighborhood social and educational institutions to become involved in crime control.

Policy Issues Arising from Urban Crime

Drugs and crime

In urban areas, it often appears that drugs and crime, particularly violent crime, are inextricably linked. Drugs are typically expensive and often reduce the user's eligibility and motivation to hold a job. The combination results in an increased proclivity to commit crimes, which may turn violent. Because drugs are traded in an underground economy, those who feel cheated in transactions have no legal recourse and must take matters into their own hands, often through violence. Turf wars break out between drug providers operating in a regulatory and legal vacuum, so the distribution of even relatively benign drugs such as marijuana may precipitate violence.

Not all crime is associated with drug use. For example, although the rise of crack cocaine during the 1980s appears to have increased the level of urban violence, the major rise in youth crime occurred after the crack epidemic had largely run its course. Empirical explanations for this low correlation include a report by Reuter, MacCoun, and Murphy

(1990), who found that only about a quarter of the dealers they studied were committing property crimes and only 3 percent engaged in violent crime. Reuter and his colleagues estimated that regular drug sellers have only a 1 percent chance of being killed and a 7 percent chance of being injured during a year, but a 22 percent chance of being imprisoned.

While the wave of imprisonments for drug use and possession that occurred during the 1980s has increased the riskiness of drug dealing and may have contributed to the decline in drug use that followed, this wave leveled off during the late 1980s (Flanagan and Maguire 1994). Imprisonment of drug users and drug dealers has bought us some decrease in crime, but at a high price. These expenditures have had no apparent effect on youth violence.

Drug-related crime remains primarily an urban problem. Even though many suburban-ites use drugs at rates equivalent to those of urbanites, the distribution of drugs often remains concentrated in cities. Neighborhoods like New York's Washington Heights, with access to the George Washington Bridge and the suburbs of New Jersey beyond, are plagued by visitors in search of drugs. Satisfying this suburban demand creates a major marketing opportunity for local drug dealers. Competition to supply the drugs can at times turn deadly and at the least erode the civility of community life (Williams 1989).

Drug dealing, like most other criminal activity, is a young man's game. For young men with poor education and job prospects, dealing illegal drugs is an attractive high-risk, high-return way of making money. However, recent research (e.g., Reuter, MacCoun, and Murphy 1990) suggests that many of the stereotypes of drug dealers are incorrect. For example, drug dealing is generally not a full-time activity. Selling is most common in the evenings and on weekends. Reuter, MacCoun, and Murphy estimate that three-quarters of drug dealers have legitimate employment and that less than 40 percent sell drugs daily.

The estimated median monthly earnings of drug dealers in Washington, DC, during the late 1980s were approximately $700 per month, the same as their earnings from legitimate employment (Reuter, MacCoun, and Murphy 1990). The distribution of earnings from drug sales is highly skewed. Most drug dealers earn little, but a few earn a great deal. The illegal drug industry is, however, big business. Carlson (1993) estimates that the illegal market for cocaine in the United States yielded income of more than $8 billion in 1991; the market for heroin, more than $6 billion; and the market for marijuana, almost $8 billion.

Although "solving" the drug problem may help to alleviate the crime problem, it will not end crime. Moreover, we must have realistic expectations regarding the extent to which public policy can solve the drug problem and the degree to which solving the drug problem will lower the crime rate in urban areas.

People will always use drugs. As long as we make some drugs illegal, illegal markets will arise to satisfy the demand. Public policy and social change decreased drug use during the 1980s, but substantial and lucrative markets for illegal drugs remain. Given current drug laws, public policy can hope only to control the size of the market and to mitigate the damage caused by the drug market and drug use.

Public debate regarding drug laws has ossified. Rather than carefully considering a broad range of drug polices, discussions tend to focus on the extremes of legalization and criminalization (e.g., see articles in Krauss and Lazear 1991). Fortunately, our choices are broader. Possible drug policies are arrayed along two spectra:

1. *Tax treatment.* Some drugs (e.g., prescription drugs and over-the-counter drugs) are subject to no special tax treatment, while others (alcohol and tobacco) are subject to excise taxes. Illegal drugs are, of course, untaxed.

2. *Governmental restrictions.* At one end are over-the-counter drugs that are subject to no restrictions on purchase or use. Next come drugs such as cigarettes and alcohol that have age restrictions on purchase. Other pharmaceuticals require prescriptions for purchase. Some drugs, such as marijuana, have either de facto or de jure freedom of use, but sale is illegal. Finally, there are drugs such as cocaine and heroin for which both use and sale are illegal.

We would be well advised when considering policy options for particular drugs to consider a broad range of options for both taxation and regulation.

The family and crime

The O. J. Simpson case focused public attention on domestic violence. National victimization surveys indicate that more than 40 percent of violent crimes occur between related or romantically involved individuals (Flanagan and Maguire 1994). The link between domestic problems and crime has long been a concern of the police, but it has not figured prominently in discussions of urban crime.

Violence within the family (e.g., husbands' assaults on wives, parents' assaults on children, children's assaults on elderly parents) is a major contributor to the urban crime problem. Research suggests that higher levels of employment, particularly for men, lead to lower levels of domestic violence. There are no firm data on trends in the level of domestic violence (Tauchen and Witte 1995; Tauchen, Witte, and Long 1991). More incidents of domestic violence are now reported, but it is impossible to say whether the level of domestic violence or only the level of reporting is increasing. Since levels of violence tend to be lower in intact families, the increase in divorce and remarriage may have led to an increase in domestic violence (Tauchen, Witte, and Long 1991).

Contrary to conventional wisdom, domestic violence does not appear to be more common in low-income households if the amount of employment is held constant. The Simpson case reflects two other important characteristics of domestic violence. First, domestic violence is common even in high-income households. Second, assaults by men on their romantic partners appear to be more frequent when the partner differs substantially in race, ethnicity, income, or education. Couples of mixed race or ethnicity appear more likely to experience violence than other couples. Also women who earn more or who are better educated than their male partners seem more likely to be victims, other things being equal (Tauchen, Witte, and Long 1991).

Many police departments adopted a presumptive arrest policy for domestic violence during the 1980s because an experiment in Minneapolis showed that individuals arrested for domestic violence were less likely to repeat their offense. The experiment compared the effectiveness of arrest, counseling, and getting the perpetrator out of the house for a cooling-off period. Arrest was shown to be more effective than the other two responses to domestic violence (Sherman 1992).

More recent work suggests that although arrest lowers the level of violence in some settings, it raises it in others. Individuals with strong ties to the community and more conforming lifestyles seem to be deterred by arrest, but individuals who are more alienated may increase their level of violence after arrest (see Garner, Fagan, and Maxwell 1995 or Sherman 1992 for details).

Property values and crime

Crime is one of the major negative externalities that depress property values in urban areas. Neighborhoods that experience large increases in either violent or property crime generally have declining property values. Housing prices also tend to decline in neighborhoods where markets for illegal goods flourish. Neighborhoods with depressed housing prices and abandoned buildings also frequently become havens for criminals and centers for the illegal drug trade.

The flip side of this coin is that people are willing to pay for safe homes and neighborhoods. They do this by choosing to live in suburban areas and by paying high property taxes for good police forces. They also increasingly do this by living in privately guarded compounds or "gated communities." Expenditures on private security personnel have grown rapidly in the United States since the 1960s.[3]

Crime and the ghetto

An important feature of U.S. urban areas is the existence of ghettos (generally inhabited by people of similar racial, ethnic, or national origins), where an underground economy tends to flourish. Indeed, in some cases underground economic activity is far more important than the legal economy in both the social and economic life of the ghetto. The underground economy in the ghetto, with its tenuous ties to legal institutions and its need for secrecy, provides a congenial environment for criminal activity.

The underground economy can be divided into an *informal* sector and an *illegal* sector. In the informal sector, perfectly legal good and services are bought and sold; however, the seller either is not properly registered or licensed or does not pay taxes. In the ghetto, such activity ranges from small factories producing clothing with the help of illegal Latin American or Asian immigrants to unlicensed barbers or beauticians cutting the hair of friends and neighbors. Such activity flourishes in distressed neighborhoods because the level of "unemployment" is high and because low incomes force ghetto residents to use low-cost providers. Inner-city markets are often wide open to informal suppliers because many firms in the formal sector do not wish to provide goods and services in low-income areas. The illegal sector of the underground economy consists of activities that are against the law, such as drug dealing, prostitution, or defrauding government benefit programs.

Studies indicate that the majority of economic activity in the Watts area of Los Angeles is either illegal or informal. Studies of New York City suggest that the informal economy grew rapidly during the 1980s.[4]

An important part of the illegal sector is the drug trade, often organized around urban gangs. Gangs maintain a complicated relationship with the neighborhoods where they deal drugs.

After a multiyear, multicity ethnographic study, Jankowski (1991, 210) concludes that "in those neighbourhoods where gangs operate, the gang and the community have established a working relationship." He further notes that "this relationship is predicated on a number of exchange relationships in which the gang and the community provide each other with certain services."

Gangs contribute countless dollars to local commerce and serve as local militias that attempt to control some of the spillover crimes associated with drug use, such as break-ins and muggings. Many inner-city communities, in turn, give gangs sanctuary from civil authority and often legitimize them by conferring status on their members. In short, the relationship between gangs and the ghetto may be more symbiotic than adversarial, and this relationship often hinders crime and drug prevention efforts.

Public Policies Affecting Crime

Public policies that affect urban crime are of two distinct types. First, there is a whole set of social policies (e.g., drug treatment policies, child welfare policies, jobs policies) that affect crime either directly or indirectly. Second, there is criminal justice policy aimed at preventing crime when possible and apprehending and punishing criminals.

Research suggests that some social policies and some criminal justice policies can reduce the crime rate. Among social policies, efforts to provide meaningful activities (e.g., jobs, schools, education) to young males, particularly minority males, and preventive or supportive programs, particularly programs directed to young children and their families, can reduce crime. There is also evidence that structured, community-oriented, and value-centered schools can improve educational performance and lower levels of juvenile delinquency (Mandel 1995; Witte 1996).

Among criminal justice policies, both police resources and police policies can deter crime, but the effect is not large (Tauchen and Witte 1994). Prisons can incapacitate offenders, but they do not appear to deter them significantly. The effect of this incapacitation on the crime rate depends on the rate at which new offenders take the places of incarcerated offenders on the street.

While early intervention appears most successful, some intensive programs for at-risk youth have been shown to be effective, and research suggests that keeping young people busy with legal activities can reduce crime (Witte and Tauchen 1994). The Job Corps, which places at-risk young people in residential, structured work and educational programs, has significantly reduced the level of crime of participants. Research suggests that good jobs, good education, and structured social (including religious) activities can lower the level of crime among the young. A strict, caring, value-centered learning environment such as that found in good parochial schools also seems to increase educational attainment and reduce juvenile delinquency.[5]

It is important to note that the term "criminal justice system" is a misnomer. No such system exists. Rather, there is a hodgepodge of criminal justice agencies at various levels of government. Crime prevention is largely a police function and the responsibility of local government. Punishment for crimes is meted out by the courts and correctional agencies, which are generally part of state government. The federal government has a limited role: It is responsible for interstate and international crimes, it supports research on the causes of crime and the operation of criminal justice agencies, and it provides funds and seeks to affect nationwide criminal justice policy.

Local government policies affecting crime

Many local governments have programs designed to keep young people busy, particularly during the summer. As far as I am aware, there has been no systematic evaluation of such programs. However, research suggests a number of reasons such programs might be successful and finds that young men who are busy working or going to school commit fewer offenses.

The British are using such programs explicitly for crime control. For example, the local council in Luton paid for youth clubs in its high-crime public housing and experienced a decline in crime while the rest of England experienced an increase. Bristol and Kirklees, West Yorkshire, set up summer programs for 11-to 16-year-olds in high-crime areas and found that crime declined about 30 percent from previous summers. A scheme in Bolton to encourage young street children to join sports, arts, or counseling groups greatly reduced nuisance calls to the police. In the United States, the Children at Risk (CAR) program keeps youth busy in after-school and summer programs that divert time and energy from delinquency. Preliminary results show significant decreases in juvenile arrests and convictions for the experimental group (Harrell 1995).

The effect of police departments on crime depends on both the level of police resources and the way resources are used. Apprehension is more likely when the police respond rapidly, and rapid apprehension is a stronger deterrent than apprehension long after the crime has been committed. Modern technology allows 911 calls to be handled far more expeditiously than in the past. Still, the proportion of crimes solved by the police (the clearance rate) remains low. For example, the police make an arrest for less than one-sixth of burglaries (Flanagan and Maguire 1994).

The 1980s saw a number of changes in policing:

1. As noted earlier, many police departments adopted community policing. Research shows that with community policing people feel safer and neighborhoods can improve. Yet community policing does not appear to decrease crime rates.
2. Computer analyses of police data identified "hot spots" from which there were frequent calls to the police. Police allocated more resources to those hot spots, and such calls declined. However, crime appears to have been displaced to other areas rather than suppressed.
3. As noted earlier, some police departments made arrest the presumptive response to domestic violence, but recent research has called this policy into question.

State policies affecting crime

The state generally provides substantial money for education, administers welfare programs, seeks to stimulate economic growth and development, regulates the provision of child care, decides what is illegal, and runs the courts and prisons. State social and development expenditures have not generally been aimed at reducing crime, and I am not aware of studies that assess their impact on crime.

State governments can most easily lower the crime rate by legalizing some things. For example, a number of states have effectively decriminalized the use of marijuana, but the current political atmosphere makes it unlikely that legalization will be pursued on any substantial scale.

Legalization is not a possibility for violent crimes or major property crimes such as burglary, robbery, and larceny. The state tries to deter such offenses by running a court system that determines who is guilty; setting punishments for convicted offenders: and running probation, prison, and parole departments to carry out sentences that restrict offenders' freedom.

During the past decade, we have moved from a system dominated by indeterminate sentences that allowed early release for prisoners who behaved well in prison to a system dominated by long, determinate sentences. This change has swelled our prison population with inmates who have longer sentences and no hope of parole. Between 1975 and 1990, the number of prison inmates with sentences of one year or more nearly tripled (Flanagan and Maguire 1994).

We have also radically changed the way we allocate the ever-growing number of prison spaces. In 1974, 52 percent of prisoners had been convicted for violent offenses, 31 percent for property offenses, and 10 percent for drug offenses. By 1988, 30 percent of new court commitments to prison were for violent offenses, 37 percent for property offenses, and 25 percent for drug offenses. We substantially increased the proportion of prison spaces allocated to drug offenders and decreased the proportion allocated to violent offenders. Although prison sentences do keep offenders off the streets, drug dealers, even at the wholesale level, are replaced quite quickly. Violent offenders are replaced more slowly. Allocating more prison resources to drug rather than violent offenders decreases the level of incapacitation obtained per dollar spent. Many states are now changing policy and reserving an increasing proportion of prison spaces for violent offenders (Flanagan and Maguire 1994).

More worrisome still is the fact that an increasing proportion of state expenditures is going to prisons and a declining proportion to higher education. During the 1970s and 1980s, total public expenditures on education grew by a factor of four and one-half, while expenditures on the criminal justice system grew by a factor of six (Flanagan and Maguire 1994). During the same period, public expenditure on public colleges and universities grew by 78 percent, while expenditures on corrections grew by almost 900 percent. In 1990, it cost an average of $9,442 per year to send a young person to a higher educational institution and $25,496 per year to keep a young person in prison. The states increasingly emphasize imprisoning rather than educating young people.

Federal policies affecting crime

The federal government provides substantial money for early childhood education and family interventions through its matching funds program and Head Start. Head Start has been expanded in recent years, but it still serves only 28 percent of eligible children, at a cost of $2.2 billion per year. Further, and more important from a crime control perspective, Head Start has not been shown to reduce juvenile delinquency, possibly because it is only a one-year program for many participants and because the family support part of the program has been weak (Zigler, Taussig, and Black 1992).

The federal government has also funded what might best be termed demonstration projects for juveniles, such as the Job Corps (discussed earlier).

The federal criminal justice system deals mainly with interstate and international offenses that have little relevance to the urban crime problem. Under the auspices of the war on drugs, the federal government has used the military and other resources to try to interdict international drug shipments (generally ineffectively) and has loaded the federal prisons with drug offenders. Today more than 50 percent of federal prisoners are in prison for drug offenses (Flanagan and Maguire 1994).

The federal government supports (at a declining level) research on crime, delinquency, and the criminal justice system. The results of such research may be important in determining state and local policies. For example, longitudinal studies have shown that a small number of high-rate offenders are responsible for a disproportionate number of offenses (Tauchen and Witte 1994), and experiments on police handling of domestic violence have altered the way police handle such incidents (Garner, Fagan, and Maxwell 1995).

Finally, the federal government provides funds to state and local criminal justice agencies. For example, the Violent Crime Control and Law Enforcement Act of 1994 proposes spending $9 billion to help local police departments hire 100,000 new officers (although the actual number hired is far lower). Research suggests that these federal initiatives may be fruitful avenues for criminal justice policy (Donohue and Siegelman 1994, Tauchen and Witte 1994).

New Directions for Public Policy toward Urban Crime

Criminal justice policies

During the past decade, we have greatly increased the proportion of criminal justice resources allocated to prisons. Between 1970 and 1990, while the number of prison cells roughly tripled, the number of police officers remained approximately constant (Flanagan and Maguire 1994).

Research suggests that building more prisons is not the most effective use of criminal justice dollars. Incarceration does not appear to significantly decrease either the post-release criminal activities of those incarcerated (specific deterrence) or the level of crime in most urban communities (general deterrence).

The crime-reducing effect of increased expenditures on police has more research support. Such increases do seem to deter young men from committing crimes, but the effect on crime is not large (Tauchen and Witte 1994). Still, increased spending on police will likely have a larger effect on crime than increased spending on prison cells.[6]

Most citizens do not like to see drug dealing in urban streets. Random violence among dealers and the vacant stares and hyperactivity of drug users make the streets more threatening. However, most citizens fear violent crime aimed at the general public far more than they fear drug dealing or the negative externalities it produces. Both these public attitudes and research suggest that it may be time to reallocate criminal justice resources from drug dealing to violent crime. Some states are now beginning to reallocate prison resources to violent offenders. There may be a hidden crime-reduction benefit in using more of the new prison cells to house violent offenders, who are not as quickly or completely replaced with new offenders as drug dealers are.

What are we going to do with convicted drug dealers if we do not put them in prison? I would suggest that many drug dealers, and indeed many property offenders, can best be punished with fines and electronic surveillance. With new monitoring technology, the movements of convicted offenders can be followed carefully while they are on the street. They can be picked up if they are found to be at the scene of a burglary or at known centers of drug distribution. Fines collected from the offenders could be used to pay surveillance costs or restitution for victims.

In the long run, we may want to rethink our laws regarding "victimless" crimes such as drug use. For example, we could consider decriminalizing the less virulent drugs, such as marijuana. There are precedents for this in the repeal of Prohibition during the 1930s and the more recent legalization, and state provision, of gambling.

Policies for at-risk youth

Growing up poor in U.S. urban areas has never been easy, but the situation facing young, urban Americans has deteriorated since the 1960s and early 1970s. Urban schools, particularly in distressed neighborhoods, are more often settings for violence and drug dealing than for education. Traditional education, even at its best, ill prepares young people for the high-tech, rapidly changing workplace of today. Respected authority, legitimate role models, supervision by adults, and close, caring relationships with adults are scarce in distressed neighborhoods. Structured, legal leisure activities are rare, but the streets provide a range of illegal and semilegal ways of killing time and even making money.

Few programs for at-risk youth have been shown to be effective, with the notable exception of the Job Corps (described earlier). Funds are unlikely to be available to remove a large proportion of at-risk youth from their neighborhoods. It is not even clear that this would be desirable on a large scale. What are we to do with the youth who remain in the difficult environment of the inner city? I think we have no choice but to make some changes in the environment, beginning with schools. Considerable research suggests that structured, value-oriented education and education that seeks close ties with families can improve the lives of at-risk youth. It may be time to invest in such education rather than traditional public high schools. New York City has experimented with alternative school settings, and the CAR program has shown preliminary success in diverse low- income settings (Harrell 1995).

Research also suggests that it is important to keep young people busy doing something legal that interests and engages them. Youth who spend more time working and at school have lower levels of criminal activity, even after controlling for a large number of other factors. Also, inner-city youth who are involved in church activities or who attend parochial schools have lower levels of criminal activity and are more likely to escape poverty than youth who are not so involved. The British experience and preliminary CAR results cited above suggest that well-structured summer programs may be effective both in making the streets more pleasant and in lowering crime. (See Witte and Tauchen 1994 for evidence regarding the effect of work and schooling on crime.)

Even intensive interventions with preadolescent or adolescent youth who already have problems can be expected to produce only limited benefits. Larger benefits may come only if we begin interventions much earlier.

A better start

Small-scale studies have shown that intensive early interventions that combine early childhood education with family support and education in parenting can reduce juvenile delinquency. Successful programs work with at-risk parents and children for at least two years before children enter school; provide high-quality infant, day-care, or preschool programs for children; provide informational and emotional support on child-development and child-rearing issues for parents; provide prenatal and postnatal health care; and either provide vocational counseling or training or make sure that they are available for parents.

Such programs are expensive, but not as expensive as effective programs for juveniles or the criminal justice system's costs of dealing with crime after it has occurred. The lesson here, as in other areas of policy, is that prevention works and is generally cheaper than dealing with problems after their inception.[7]

Head Start is a step in the right direction, but it is too small, has too few services, and is too brief to change the lives of the children it enrolls. Current research suggests that the most effective long-term programs to combat crime within the context of the existing health and welfare policies, the child's family life, and the current economic situation will be intensive programs for at-risk children and their families that begin before or shortly after a child is born.

Conclusions

Crime rates are now declining in U.S. urban areas. There is much debate as to why this is the case. Some claim that the decline is attributable mainly to the "get tough" crime policy of the 1980s, while others claim it is attributable mainly to a decline in the number of young people and to a calming of the drug turf wars. On balance, research suggests that most of the drop in crime stems from a decrease in the number of young people and from increased police effectiveness.

The rate of violent crime among young males has risen substantially in recent years. We do not know the reason for this increase, but it seems likely to have arisen from a number of sources: disorganized communities, dysfunctional families, and decreased economic and educational opportunities. An effective attack on the youth crime problem may involve the criminal justice system only as a backup. Intensive work with at-risk families, organized community activities, and better educational and economic opportunities may provide a more effective front-line attack. The relative costs of education and imprisonment certainly suggest that reallocation of resources from imprisonment to education and training is worthwhile.

Notes

1 See Donohue and Siegelman (1994) for a compilation of crime statistics and well-informed discussion of various types of data on crime.
2 The outline of one possible direction is reflected in the Violent Crime Control and Law Enforcement Act of 1994. A quite different outline appears in the congressional Republicans' *Contract with America* (Gillespie and Schellhas 1994).

3   See Flanagan and Maguire (1994) for police statistics and Long and Witte (1980) for a survey of
    the effect of crime on property values.
4   Pozo (1993, 1996) and Sassen-Koob (1989) discuss the underground economy in urban areas.
5   See Witte (1996) for a survey and Harrell (1995) for a preliminary report of a comprehensive
    program for at-risk youth.
6   Campbell (1994) discusses the effect of police on crime.
7   Zigler, Taussig, and Black (1992) discuss the effect of early childhood interventions.

References

Campbell, John (1994) "Policing Crime," *Federal Reserve Bank of Boston Regional Review*, 4, 6–11.
Carlson, Kenneth (1993) Income from Illegal Activities. Unpublished tables. Cambridge, MA: Abt
    Associates.
Donohue, John, and Peter Siegelman (1994) *Is the United States at the Optimal Rate of Crime?*
    working paper. Chicago: Northwestern School of Law.
Flanagan, Timothy J., and Kathleen Maguire (1994) *Sourcebook of Criminal Justice Statistics.*
    Washington, DC: U.S. Department of Justice.
Garner, Joel, Jeffrey Fagan, and Christopher Maxwell (1995) "Published Findings from the
    Spouse Assault Replication Program: A Critical Review," *Journal of Quantitative Criminology*, 11,
    3–28.
Gillespie, Ed, and Bob Schellhas, (eds) (1994) *Contract with America: The Bold Plan by Rep.
    Newt Gingrich, Rep. Dick Armey, and the House Republicans to Change the Nation.* New York:
    Times Books.
Harrell, Adele (1995) *Impact of the Children at Risk Program.* Washington, DC: The Urban
    Institute.
Jankowski, Martín Sánchez (1991) *Islands in the Street: Gangs and American Urban Society.*
    Berkeley, CA: University of California Press.
Krauss, Murray, and Edward Lazear (1991) *Searching for Alternatives: Drug-Control Policy in the
    United States.* Stanford, CA: Hoover Institution Press.
Long, Sharon, and Ann Witte (1980) "Evaluating the Effect of Public Policies on Land Prices in
    Metropolitan Areas: Some Suggested Approaches." In *Urban Land Markets: Price Indices, Supply
    Measures, and Public Policy Effects*, ed. J. Thomas Black and James Hoben, 133–59. Washington,
    DC: Urban Land Institute.
Mandel, Richard (1995) *Prevention or Pork? A Hard-Headed Look at Youth-Oriented Anti-Crime
    Programs.* Washington, DC: American Youth Policy Forum.
Pozo, Susan (1993) *Price Behavior in Illegal Markets.* Unpublished manuscript. Kalamazoo, MI:
    Western Michigan University, Department of Economics.
Pozo, Susan (1996) *The Underground Economy.* Kalamazoo, MI: Upjohn Institute.
Reuter, Peter, Robert MacCoun, and Patrick Murphy (1990) *Money from Crime: A Study of the
    Economics of Drug Dealing in Washington, DC.* Santa Monica, CA: Rand Corporation.
Sassen-Koob, Saskia (1989) "New York City's Informal Economy." In *The Informal Economy:
    Studies in Advanced and Less Developed Countries*, ed. Alejandro Portes, Manuel Castels, and
    Lauren Benton, 60–77. Baltimore, MD: Johns Hopkins University Press.
Sherman, Lawrence (1992) *Policing Domestic Violence.* New York: Free Press.
Tauchen, Helen, and Ann Witte (1994) "Criminal Deterrence: Revisiting the Issues with a Birth
    Cohort." *Review of Economics and Statistics*, 76, 399–412.
Tauchen, Helen, and Ann Witte (1995) "The Dynamics of Domestic Violence." *American
    Economic Review*, 85, 414–18.
Tauchen, Helen, Ann Witte, and Sharon Long (1991) "Domestic Violence: A Non-Random
    Affair." *International Economic Review*, 32, 1–21.

Williams, Terry (1989) *The Cocaine Kids: The Inside Story of a Teenage Drug Ring*. Reading, MA: Addison Wesley.

Witte, Ann (1996) "The Social Benefits of Education: Crime" In *The Social Benefits of Education*, eds Jere Behrman and Nevzer Stacey. Ann Arbor, MI: University of Michigan Press.

Witte, Ann and Helen Tauchen (1994) "Work and Crime: An Exploration Using Panel Data." *Public Finance*, 49, 155–67.

Zigler, Edward, Cara Taussig, and Kathryn Black (1992) "Early Childhood Intervention: A Promising Preventative for Juvenile Delinquency." *American Psychologist*, 47, 997–1006.

CHAPTER THIRTY-ONE

Estimating the Economic Model of Crime with Panel Data

CHRISTOPHER CORNWELL AND WILLIAM N. TRUMBULL*

Source: The Review of Economics and Statistics, 1994, 76.

Previous attempts at estimating the economic model of crime with aggregate data relied heavily on cross-section econometric techniques, and therefore do not control for unobserved heterogeneity. This is even true of studies which estimated simultaneous equations models. Using a new panel dataset of North Carolina counties, we exploit both single and simultaneous equations panel data estimators to address two sources of endogeneity: unobserved heterogeneity and conventional simultaneity. Our results suggest that both labor market and criminal justice strategies are important in deterring crime, but that the effectiveness of law enforcement incentives has been greatly overstated.

1. Introduction

More than two decades have passed since Becker published his seminal work on the economics of crime (Becker 1968). Since then, a large empirical literature has developed around the estimation and testing of the economic model of crime. Almost all of the contributions to this literature have used aggregate data, usually at the state or national level. Ideally, the economic model of crime should be estimated with individual level data since the model purports to describe the behavior of individuals. However, the expense and difficulty of creating a random sample of the population large enough to include representative information about individual criminal activity has been, and continues to be, an obstacle to individual level analysis. The few exceptions in the literature that have used individual data are fundamentally recidivism studies.

In the absence of empirical work at the individual level, interest in tests of the economic model of crime with aggregate data continues (see Craig (1987), Avio (1988) and Trumbull (1989)). While estimation with aggregate data has been criticized, results from such estimation have influenced public policy. For example, the conclusion of Ehrlich (1975) that capital punishment has a strong deterrent effect found its way into the proceedings of

* We wish to thank Steve Craig, Tom Orsagh and three anonymous referees for their helpful comments. Support from the Regional Research Institute at WVU is gratefully acknowledged. Expert research assistance was provided by Sudha Subrahmanyam.

the Supreme Court during its series of decisions in the 1970s concerning the constitutionality of capital punishment (see Blumstein et al. (1978)).

The consensus of the empirical literature is that a strong deterrent effect of punishment (certainty and severity) exists. This consensus is reflected in most Law and Economics textbooks.

> "Estimates of the magnitude of the deterrent effect vary, but it appears that an increase in law enforcement activity that increases either the probability of punishment or the severity of punishment by 1 percent is on the average associated with a reduction in the number of offenses somewhere between 0.3 and 1.1 percent. Further empirical investigation is necessary in order to gain a more accurate estimate of the magnitude of this deterrent effect coefficient, *though the true value of the coefficient is probably closer to* 1 *than to* 0.3." (Hirsch (1988) p. 271, italics ours).

In this paper, we present empirical evidence that the ability of the criminal justice system to deter crime is much *weaker* than previous results indicate.

Our deterrent effects estimates are obtained from a new *panel* dataset in which the unit of observation is the county. Since our data are county level, we are able to achieve a relatively low level of aggregation. The availability of panel data allows us to control for unobservable county-specific characteristics that may be correlated with the criminal justice variables in the model. In general, failure to condition on these unobservables will result in inconsistent estimates of the coefficients of these variables. Previous empirical work using cross-section data neglect this type of "endogeneity." This is even true of studies that estimated simultaneous equations models. In these studies, researchers were focused on conventional sources of endogeneity (simultaneity), such as those arising from the dependency of the probability of arrest or the size of the police force on the crime rate.

We apply both single and simultaneous equations panel data estimators to the economic model of crime, thereby addressing both sources of endogeneity. This is the first contribution to the economics of crime literature to exploit panel data in this way.[1] The results of our empirical investigation indicate that unobserved county heterogeneity is statistically important in our sample. In every case where county effects are controlled for, we obtain estimated deterrent effects that are substantially *smaller* than those obtained when county heterogeneity is ignored.

2. Review of Previous Work

The results of some of the more prominent empirical contributions to the criminal deterrence literature using aggregate, cross-section data are summarized in table 1. For each study noted, table 1 indicates the estimation procedure, the crime on which the study was based, and the estimated elasticities of the probability of arrest (P_A), the probability of conviction (usually conditional on arrest) (P_C), the probability of imprisonment (usually conditional on conviction) (P_P), and the severity of punishment (S). About one-half of the reported regressions were estimated simply by ordinary least squares (OLS). The other half were estimated either by two or three stage least squares (2SLS or 3SLS), reflecting

Table 1   Summary of previous cross-section results

Study (Data)	Estimation Procedure	Crime Type	P_A	P_C	P_P	S
Ehrlich (1973)	OLS	All, 1960			-0.526^a	-0.585^a
(U.S. states)	2SLS				-0.991^a	-1.123^a
Sjoquist (1973)	OLS	Robbery, Burglary	-0.342^a			-0.212
(U.S. cities)		& Larceny				
Carr-Hill & Stern (1973)	2SLS	All, 1961	-0.66^a			-0.28^a
(U.K. police districts)		All, 1966	-0.59^a			-0.17^a
Orsagh (1973)	OLS	Felonies		-0.26^a		
(CA counties)	2SLS			-1.8^a		
Phillips &	OLS	Felonies	-0.622^a			-0.347^a
Votey (1975)	2SLS/3 eq		-0.610^a			-0.342^a
(CA counties)	2SLS/4 eq		-0.701^a			-0.376^a
Mathieson &	OLS	Robbery	-1.06^a			
Passell (1976)		Murder	-0.743^a			
(NYC precincts)	2SLS	Robbery	-2.95^a			
		Murder	-1.96^a			
Craig (1987)	3SLS	Felonies	-0.57^a			
(Baltimore police beats)						
Trumbull (1989)	OLS	All	-0.217^a	-0.451^a	-0.325^a	-0.149^a
(NC counties)						

[a]   Statistically significant at the 5% level.

attempts at modelling simultaneity between the criminal justice variables, particularly P_A, and the crime rate.[2]

The economic model of crime predicts that the estimated coefficients of P_A, P_C, P_P, and S will be negative since an increase in the probability or severity of punishment increases the expected cost, or decreases the expected utility, of crime. Furthermore, under certain assumptions the economic model of crime implies an ordering of deterrent effects (excluding S); the greatest impact on crime coming from P_A, followed by P_C and P_P. The estimated elasticities reported in table 1 are generally consistent with the predictions of the theoretical model. In all cases the estimated elasticities are negative, and where more than one criminal justice variable is included, the results satisfy *a priori* expectations. Finally, note that the estimated arrest elasticities tend to confirm Hirsch's assertion, with several exceeding one in absolute value.

A fundamental flaw in each of the studies is an inability to control for unobserved heterogeneity in the unit of observation. The use of 2SLS and 3SLS in these studies does not treat this problem. Neglected heterogeneity also may be correlated with the instrumental variables used to compute the 2SLS and 3SLS estimates. With panel data we can account for unobservable county characteristics by conditioning on county effects in estimation. As a result, we are able to treat both sources of "endogeneity," conventional simultaneity *and* neglected heterogeneity.

As an example of how the other source of "endogeneity" – correlation between the explanatory variables and omitted county attributes – might arise, consider two *identical* jurisdictions or counties, except that the police in jurisdiction 1 record half the crimes reported to them and the police in jurisdiction 2 record all crimes reported. Jurisdiction 1 will appear to have a lower crime rate and higher probability of arrest than jurisdiction 2. If this pattern of under-reporting is repeated in the sample, then the estimated deterrent effect of raising the probability of arrest will be overstated. Nagin (1978) and others have suggested that differences in the rate at which police record the crimes reported to them can result in an estimated deterrent effect that is simply an artifact of the (reported) data. By exploiting the longitudinal nature of our sample, we can capture jurisdictional differences in crime reporting without data on actual crimes.

3. Model and Alternative Estimators

The basic assumption of the economic model of crime is that expected utility maximizing individuals participate in the criminal sector in response to the benefits and costs of illegal activities (see Becker (1968), Ehrlich (1973), Block and Heineke (1975), and Schmidt and Witte (1984)). This suggests an individual's participation depends on the relative monetary return to illegal activities and the degree to which the criminal justice system is able to affect the probabilities of apprehension and punishment. Using panel data on the counties of North Carolina, we specify the following crime equation:

$$R_{it} = X'_{it}\beta + P'_{it}\gamma + \alpha_i + \epsilon_{it} \quad i = 1, \ldots, N; t = 1, \ldots, T \tag{1}$$

where R_{it} is the crime rate, X'_{it} contains variables which control for the relative return to legal opportunities, and P'_{it} contains a set of deterrent variables which proxy for P_A, P_C, P_P and S. The α_i are fixed effects which reflect unobservable county-specific characteristics that may be correlated with (X'_{it}, P'_{it}).[3] The ϵ_{it} are typical disturbance terms, assumed to be iid with a zero mean and constant variance σ^2_ϵ.[4]

Since we wish to contrast cross-section and panel data estimators for our model, we define the "between" and "within" transformations of (1):

$$R_i = X'_i\beta + P'_i\gamma + \alpha_i + \epsilon_i \tag{2}$$

and

$$\bar{R}_{it} = \bar{X}'_{it}\beta + \bar{P}'_{it}\gamma + \bar{\epsilon}_{it} \tag{3}$$

In the former, the data are expressed in county means (for example, $R_i = T^{-1}\sum_t R_{it}$), while in the latter the data are in deviations from means (so that $\bar{R}_{it} = R_{it} - R_i$). Note that (3) does not depend on the county effects.

Basing estimation on (2) leads to standard cross-section estimators which neglect unobserved county heterogeneity. Thus, if unobserved characteristics are correlated with (X'_{it}, P'_{it}), such procedures will produce inconsistent estimates. This is true for OLS and simultaneous equations estimators. The problem with simultaneous equations estimators like 2SLS is that the α_i also appear in the reduced form, rendering the instrument set invalid.

However, by using (3) as a basis for estimation, both sources of endogeneity may be addressed. First, if the only problem is correlation between (X'_{it}, P'_{it}) and unobserved heterogeneity, then consistent estimation is possible by simply performing least squares on (3). This produces the so-called within estimator, which can be viewed as an instrumental variables estimator with instruments (deviations from means) that are orthogonal to the effects by construction. Conventional simultaneity can be accounted for by using 2SLS to estimate (3), where all variables have been subjected to the within transformation (Cornwell, Schmidt and Wyhowski (1992)).

4. Empirical Results

Empirical measures of our crime rate and deterrent variables are constructed from several sources. The crime rate, R, is the ratio of FBI index crimes to county population, both taken from the FBI's Uniform Crime Reports, county level arrest and offense data. The probability of arrest, P_A, is proxied by the ratio of arrests to offenses, again from the arrest and offense files. We assume there is a direct correlation between this ratio and individuals' perceptions of the probability of arrest. Similar assumptions are made concerning individuals' perceptions of the probabilities of conviction and prison. We proxy these probabilities, P_C and P_P, by the ratio of convictions to arrests and proportion of total convictions resulting in prison sentences, respectively. The number of convictions was taken from the prison and probation files of the North Carolina Department of Correction. Finally, sanction severity, S, is measured by the average prison sentence length in days.

The variables in X are intended to control for the relative return to legal activities, as well as other observable county characteristics that may be correlated with the crime rate. Opportunities in the legal sector are captured by the average weekly wage in the county by industry. The industry categories for which we observe wages are: construction (*WCON*); transportation, utilities and communications (*WTUC*); wholesale and retail trade (*WTRD*); finance, insurance and real estate (*WFIR*); services (*WSER*); manufacturing (*WMFG*); and federal, state and local government (*WFED, WSTA* and *WLOC*). The wage data were provided by the North Carolina Employment Security Commission. Participation in the legal sector may differ across urban and rural environments. These differences are accounted for by a dummy variable (*URBAN*) for counties that are included in SMSAs and have populations over 50,000, as well as population density (*DENSITY*), which is county population divided by county land area, the latter obtained from Census data. Regional or cultural factors that may affect the crime rate are controlled for through dummies for western and central counties (*WEST* and *CENTRAL*). Since crime rates tend to vary with county demographic characteristics, we include the proportion of county population that is male and between the ages of 15 and 24 (*PERCENT YOUNG MALE*), along with the proportion that is minority or nonwhite (*PERCENT MINORITY*). Both of these variables were constructed from Census data.

The number of police per capita (*POLICE*) is included in the control vector X as a measure of a county's ability to detect crime. Previous empirical work suggests that the greater the number of police, the greater the number of reported crimes. As we explain below, this result may be due to a dependency of the size of the police force on the crime rate. We obtained our measure of *POLICE* from the FBI's police agency employee counts.

Table 2 reports summary statistics for the variables used in our empirical model. The results from estimation are presented in table 3. In each case, we adopt a log-linear specification so that our estimated coefficients are interpretable as elasticities. First, consider the "between" estimates, which are calculated by applying OLS to (2). Focusing on the coefficients of the variables in P_{it}, their estimates tend to corroborate previous empirical work that has concentrated on cross-section estimation of the economic model of crime with aggregate data. With the exception of the estimated coefficient of P_P, the elements of $\hat{\gamma}$ have the correct (negative) signs. However, only the estimated coefficients of P_A and P_C are statistically significant. The estimated arrest and conviction elasticities are, respectively, -0.65 and -0.53.

The between estimator is consistent only if (X'_{it}, P'_{it}) is orthogonal to both α_i and ε_{it}. The within estimator is a simple solution to the violation of the orthogonality condition that (X'_{it}, P'_{it}) is uncorrelated with unobserved heterogeneity. The second column of table 3 provides the within coefficient estimates.[5] Again, focusing on the estimated deterrent effects, the difference in the within and between estimates is striking. Conditioning on the county effects causes the (absolute value of the) estimated deterrent elasticities associated with P_A and P_C to *decrease* by approximately 45%. The estimated coefficient of P_P has the correct sign and is statistically significant. In addition, the estimated deterrent effects are ordered according to the prediction of restricted versions of the economic model of crime. Finally, the within estimate of the deterrent effect of S is small and statistically insignificant, possibly reflecting the fact that North Carolina has a policy of determinate

Table 2   Means and standard deviations ($N = 90$ and $T = 7$)

	Mean	*Standard Deviation*
CRIME RATE	0.0316	0.0181
P_A	0.309	0.171
P_C	0.689	1.690
P_P	0.426	0.087
S	8.955	2.658
POLICE	0.00192	0.00273
DENSITY	1.386	1.440
PERCENT YOUNG MALE	0.089	0.024
WCON	245.67	121.98
WTUC	406.10	266.51
WTRD	192.82	88.41
WFIR	272.06	55.78
WSER	224.67	104.87
WMFG	285.17	82.36
WFED	403.90	63.07
WSTA	296.91	53.43
WLOC	257.98	41.36
WEST	0.233	0.423
CENTRAL	0.378	0.485
URBAN	0.089	0.285
PERCENT MINORITY	0.257	0.169

Table 3 Results from estimation
(standard errors in parentheses)

	Between	Within	2SLS (fixed effects)	2SLS (no fixed effects)
CONSTANT	−2.097			−3.719
	(2.822)			(8.189)
P_A	−0.648	−0.355	−0.455	−0.507
	(0.088)	(0.032)	(0.618)	(0.251)
P_C	−0.528	−0.282	−0.336	−0.530
	(0.067)	(0.021)	(0.371)	(0.110)
P_P	0.297	−0.173	−0.196	0.200
	(0.231)	(0.032)	(0.200)	(0.343)
S	−0.236	−0.00245	−0.0298	−0.218
	(0.174)	(0.02612)	(0.0300)	(0.185)
POLICE	0.364	0.413	0.504	0.419
	(0.060)	(0.027)	(0.617)	(0.218)
DENSITY	0.168	0.414	0.291	0.226
	(0.077)	(0.283)	(0.785)	(0.103)
PERCENT	−0.0951	0.627	0.888	−0.145
YOUNG MALE	(0.1576)	(0.364)	(0.139)	(0.336)
WCON	0.195	−0.0378	−0.0358	0.329
	(0.210)	(0.0391)	(0.0467)	(0.279)
WTUC	−0.196	0.0455	0.0398	−0.197
	(0.170)	(0.0190)	(0.0282)	(0.197)
WTRD	0.129	−0.0205	−0.0196	0.0293
	(0.278)	(0.0405)	(0.0426)	(0.3240)
WFIR	0.113	−0.00390	−0.00700	0.0506
	(0.220)	(0.02806)	(0.03270)	(0.3224)
WSER	−0.106	0.00888	0.00600	−0.127
	(0.163)	(0.01913)	(0.02536)	(0.176)
WMFG	−0.0249	−0.360	−0.406	−0.0493
	(0.1339)	(0.112)	(0.217)	(0.1672)
WFED	0.156	−0.309	−0.273	0.170
	(0.287)	(0.176)	(0.296)	(0.327)
WSTA	−0.284	0.0529	−0.0129	−0.181
	(0.256)	(0.114)	(0.2599)	(0.300)
WLOC	0.0103	0.182	0.136	0.0237
	(0.4635)	(0.118)	(0.165)	(0.5187)
WEST	−0.229			−0.198
	(0.108)			(0.117)
CENTRAL	−0.164			−0.173
	(0.064)			(0.067)
URBAN	−0.0346			−0.0874
	(0.1324)			(0.1508)
PERCENT	0.148			0.174
MINORITY	(0.049)			(0.057)
s.e.	0.216	0.137	0.141	0.224

sentencing. An alternative interpretation is that increasing the severity of punishment is not a very effective means of deterring crime.

Given the dramatic differences in our within and between estimates, it is not surprising that the null hypothesis of no correlation between (X'_{it}, P'_{it}) is soundly rejected. A Wu-Hausman test of this null can be constructed around the within/between contrast. The value of the test-statistic, which is asymptotically distributed as χ^2_{16}, is 97.31. We conclude that heterogeneity is statistically important in our sample and reject estimators that do not condition on county effects.

Controlling for county effects in estimation addresses only one source of endogeneity. Conventional simultaneity may exist between R, P_A and $POLICE$. For example, while the standard Becker model predicts that the crime rate will fall as the probability of arrest rises, counties experiencing rising crime rates, holding police resources constant, would see probabilities of arrest fall. But, increases in crime may motivate a county to increase policing resources which, in turn, would increase the probability of arrest. Thus, we also allow for the possibility that P_A and $POLICE$ may be correlated with ε.

To address simultaneity, as well as unobserved heterogeneity, we apply 2SLS to (3), the within-transformed model. Because both P_A and $POLICE$ are treated as endogenous, identification requires at least two instruments. These instruments must be *exogenous* variables that are excluded from the crime equation, where exogenous means *uncorrelated with ε and the effects*. Hence, the instruments also will be expressed in terms of *deviations from means*. We use as instruments a mix of different offense types and per capita tax revenue. Offense mix is defined as the ratio of crimes involving "face-to-face" contact (such as robbery, assault and rape) to those that do not.[6]

The rationale for offense mix is as follows. Since arrest is facilitated by positive identification of the offender, P_A should be higher in counties with a higher relative incidence of "face-to-face" offenses. However, it is unlikely that the offense mix has much effect on the overall crime rate. Our use of per capita tax revenue is based on the argument that counties with residents who have greater preferences for law enforcement will express their preferences by voting for higher taxes to fund larger police forces. Such counties would have larger police forces for reasons not directly related to the crime rate. Our sample provides little evidence to reject our instrument set. When offense mix and per capita total revenues are included in (3), they do not add to the predictive power of the model. An F-test of the null hypothesis that their joint effect is zero leads to a test-statistic with a value of just 0.053.

The fixed effects 2SLS estimates are reported in the third column of table 3. Treating both sources of endogeneity yields estimated deterrent effects that are no longer significant, although the point estimates are closer to the within than the between estimates. By comparison, high (especially manufacturing) wages appear to be very effective in deterring crime. In both fixed effects 2SLS and within regressions, the estimated coefficient of $WMFG$ is statistically significant and at least as large in absolute value as any of the deterrent variables' coefficient estimates. The other variable revealed to influence the crime rate statistically significantly is $PERCENT\ YOUNG\ MALE$, whose estimated coefficient is 0.888. The large, positive effect of $PERCENT\ YOUNG\ MALE$ is consistent with the fact that young males commit most of the crime. Interestingly, the effects of $WMFG$ and $PERCENT\ YOUNG\ MALE$ are *not* statistically significant in regressions that do not account for unobserved heterogeneity.

One interpretation of our fixed effects 2SLS estimates is that the efficacy of labor market solutions to the problem of crime exceeds that of traditional criminal justice strategies (along the lines of Myers (1983)). However, a Wu-Hausman test of the contrast between the within and fixed effects 2SLS estimates cannot reject the null hypothesis that P_A and *POLICE* are uncorrelated with ε.[7] Therefore, on efficiency grounds we prefer the within estimates, and conclude that both labor market and law enforcement incentives matter (consistent with Grogger (1991)).

Although estimators that ignore unobserved heterogeneity are inconsistent, it is instructive to contrast our fixed effects 2SLS estimates with those obtained from applying 2SLS to (2). The latter are presented in the last column of table 3, and are directly analogous to the 2SLS and 3SLS estimates listed in table 1. With the exception of P_A, the estimated deterrent effects are very similar to those produced by the between estimator. However, the difference in the between and conventional 2SLS estimates of the P_A coefficient may have little to do with simultaneity. Since the *county means* of the instruments are used in the cross-section application of 2SLS, they may be capturing some of the dependence of P_A on the effects. As the within results demonstrate clearly, controlling for heterogeneity in estimation serves to reduce substantially the estimated deterrent effect of P_A. In any case, the P_A coefficient estimate is still greater than 0.50 in absolute value. We conclude that the statistical consequences of neglecting unobserved heterogeneity in our sample are serious whether single or simultaneous equations estimators are used.

5. Conclusions

Previous attempts at estimating the economic model of crime with aggregate data relied heavily on standard cross-section econometric techniques. We show that the results of these attempts are suspect since standard estimation procedures cannot control for unobserved heterogeneity. This is even true of studies that estimated simultaneous equations models to account for dependencies between the probability of arrest and the size of the police force and the crime rate.

Using a new panel dataset of North Carolina counties, we exploit both single and simultaneous equations panel data estimators to address both sources of endogeneity: unobserved heterogeneity and conventional simultaneity. In general, our results lead us to conclude that both labor market and criminal justice strategies are important in deterring crime, but that the effectiveness of law enforcement incentives has been greatly overstated. Specifically, we find the deterrent effects of arrest and conviction probabilities to be much smaller than those obtained from cross-section estimation. Neglecting county heterogeneity biases upward deterrent effects estimates. Given the statistical consequences of unobserved heterogeneity, future estimation of the economic model of crime with aggregate data should no longer disregard this important source of specification error.

Notes

1 Wolpin (1980) and Craig and Heikkila (1989) also used panel data, but not for the purpose of determining the statistical consequences of ignoring unobserved heterogeneity.

2   Not represented in table 1 are empirical studies using individual level data. While these studies typically are based on samples of prison releases, they avoid problems emanating from the endogeneity of law enforcement. Good examples of this individual level work are Witte (1980), Myers (1983) and Grogger (1991). Witte found evidence of criminal justice deterrent effects, but little evidence of labor market effects, while Myers' results support the opposite conclusion; Grogger found evidence of both.

3   In estimation, we also include time effects to capture variations in the crime rate common to all counties. For convenience, we omit them from the formal presentation of our model.

4   Following Bhargava, Franzini and Narendranathan (1982), we tested for serial correlation in the ϵ_{it}s. We could not reject the null hypothesis of no serial correlation.

5   Since the region and urban dummies and percentage minority variable do not vary over time in our sample, they are eliminated by the within transformation.

6   Offense mix was suggested by an anonymous referee. Our use of per capita tax revenue also is based on this referee's comments.

7   The value of the test-statistic, which is asymptotically distributed as χ_2^2, is 0.031.

References

Avio, Kenneth L. (1988) "Measurement Errors and Capital Punishment," *Applied Economics*, 20, September, 1253–62.

Becker, Gary S. (1968) "Crime and Punishment: An Economic Approach," *Journal of Political Economy*, 76, (March/April), 169–217.

Bhargava, A. L. Franzini, and W. Narendranathan (1982) "Serial Correlation and the Fixed Effects Model," *Review of Economic Studies*, 49, 533–49.

Block, Michael K., and John M. Heineke (1975) "A Labor Theoretic Analysis of the Criminal Choice," *American Economic Review*, 65, June, 314–25.

Blumstein, Alfred, et al., (1978) "Report of the Panel," in Alfred Blumstein, Jacqueline Cohen, and Daniel Nagin (eds.), *Deterrence and Incapacitation: Estimating the Effects of Criminal Sanctions on Crime Rates*, Washington, D.C.: National Academy of Sciences.

Carr-Hill, R. A. and N. A. Stern (1973) "An Econometric Model of the Supply and Control of Recorded Offenses in England and Wales," *Journal of Public Economics*, November, 2, 289–318.

Cornwell, C. M., P. Schmidt and D. Wyhowski (1992) "Simultaneous Equations and Panel Data," *Journal of Econometrics*, 51, 151–181.

Craig, Steven G. (1987) "The Deterrent Impact of Police: An Examination of a Locally Provided Public Service," *Journal of Urban Economics*, 21, May, 298–311.

Craig, Steven G., and Eric J. Heikkila (1989) "Urban Safety in Vancouver: Allocation and Production of a Congestible Public Good," *Canadian Journal of Economics* 22, November, 869–84.

Ehrlich, Isaac (1973) "Participation in Illegitimate Activities: A Theoretical and Empirical Investigation," *Journal of Political Economy*, 81, May and June, 1973, 521–67.

—— (1975) "The Deterrent Effect of Capital Punishment: A Question of Life or Death," *American Economic Review*, 65, June, 397–417.

Grogger, J. (1991) "Certainty, vs. Severity of Punishment," *Economic Inquiry*, 29, April, 297–309.

Hirsch, Werner Z. (1988) *Law and Economics*, 2nd edn. San Diego, CA: Academic Press.

Mathieson, Donald, and Peter Passell (1976) "Homicide and Robbery in New York City: An Economic Model," *Journal of Legal Studies*, 5, January, 83–98.

Myers, S. B. (1983) "Estimating the Economic Model of Crime: Employment versus Punishment Effects," *Quarterly Journal of Economics*, February, 1983, 157–166.

Nagin, Daniel (1978) "General Deterrence: A Review of the Empirical Evidence," in Alfred Blumstein, Jacqueline Cohen, and Daniel Nagin (eds), *Deterrence and Incapacitation: Estimating the Effects of Criminal Sanctions on Crime*, Washington, D.C.: National Academy of Science.

Orsagh, Thomas (1973) "Crime, Sanctions, and Scientific Explanation," *Journal of Criminal Law and Criminology*, 64, September, 1973, 354–61.

Phillips, Llad, and Harold L. Votey, (1975) "Crime Control in California," *Journal of Legal Studies*, 4, June, 327–49.

Schmidt, Peter, and Ann D. Witte (1984) *An Economic Analysis of Crime and Justice: Theory, Methods, and Applications.* New York: Academic Press.

Sjoquist, David L. (1973) "Property Crimes and Economic Behavior: Some Empirical Results," *American Economic Review*, 63, June, 1973, 439–46.

Trumbull, William N. (1989) "Estimations of The Economic Model of Crime Using Aggregate and Individual Level Data," *Southern Economic Journal*, 56, October, 1983, 423–39.

Witte, Ann D. (1980) "Estimating the Economic Model of Crime with Individual Data," *Quarterly Journal of Economics*, 94, February, 1980, 57–84.

Wolpin, Kenneth I. (1980) "A Time Series-Cross Section Analysis of International Variation in Crime and Punishment," this Review, 62, August, 1980, 417–23.

Further Reading Samples

Opening Paragraphs of *Why Do So Many Young American Men Commit Crimes and What Might We Do About It?*

RICHARD B. FREEMAN

Source: *Journal of Economic Perspectives*, 10(1), Winter 1996, 25–42. Reprinted by permission of American Economic Association.

In the past two decades or so, more and more American men, particularly the young, the less educated and blacks, have been involved in crime, despite an increased risk of imprisonment. From the mid-1970s to the mid-1990s, the United States roughly tripled the number of men in prison or jail, so that by 1993 one man was incarcerated for every 50 men in the workforce. Incapacitation of so many criminals should have greatly reduced the crime rate: if the worst offenders are in prison, they can't mug, rob or otherwise commit offenses against the citizenry. But no such drastic reduction in crime occurred. The number of crimes reported to the police roughly stabilized while the rate of victimizations (which includes crimes not reported to the police) dropped far less rapidly than could reasonably be expected. Noninstitutionalized men evidently "replaced" incarcerated criminals in committing crimes.

Why? What induces young American men, particularly less educated and black men, to engage in crime in large numbers despite the risk of imprisonment? Is the rising rate of criminal involvement related to the collapse in the job market for the less skilled? Is "locking them up" the only efficacious way to fight crime?

In this essay I examine these questions. I show that participation in crime and involvement with the criminal justice system has reached such levels as to become part of normal economic life for many young men. I present evidence that labor market incentives influence the level of crime and argue that the depressed labor market for less skilled men in the 1980s and 1990s has contributed to the rise in criminal activity by less skilled men. Given the high costs of crime and imprisonment, even marginally effective crime prevention policies can be socially desirable.

Abstract from *The Spatial Concentration of Crime*

SCOTT FREEMAN, JEFFREY GROGGER, AND JON SONSTELIE

Source: *Journal of Urban Economics*, 40, 1996, 216–31. © 1996 Academic Press, Inc. All rights of reproduction in any form reserved.

This paper presents a model explaining the spatial concentration of crime. The model features two neighborhoods identical in preferences, abilities, and environment. We find, however, that in equilibrium crime concentrates in one neighborhood. In a dynamic version of the model we also show that initial conditions may determine the steady-state crime rate. The key assumption is that a criminal's chance of capture is a decreasing function of the number of other criminals operating in the area.

Abstract from *Arrests, Persistent Youth Joblessness, and Black/White Employment Differentials*

JEFF GROGGER
Source: Review of Economics and Statistics, 74, 100.

Economists have long been concerned with the labor market problems of young men. Recently, research has indicated that one-fourth to one-half of all men are active in crime at some point during their youth. Furthermore, joblessness and criminal activity vary similarly by age and race. I analyze two data sets containing arrest and employment information to assess whether criminal activities may underlie persistent joblessness and black/white employment differentials among young men. Two different approaches are taken to control for individual heterogeneity. Arrests generate some persistence in non-employment. Moreover, arrests account for nearly two-thirds of the black/white employment differential in a sample of arrestees, and nearly one-third of the difference in a more general sample.

Discussion Questions

1   Anderson describes the *back-end/front-end* approaches to criminal justice activity. What is he referring to? Based upon Witte's survey and the empirical work of Cornwell and Trumbull, describe some of the major back-end and front-end criminal justice activity undertaken in the United States? Is there any proof of which approach is more effective at reducing urban crime?

2   The basic assumption of the economic model of crime is that expected utility maximizing individuals weigh the benefits and costs of criminal activity when deciding to participate in it. The Anderson and Lazaroff/Blair newspaper articles report on different factors that have been put forth to explain the reduction in crime rates in the USA. Describe what these factors are. How do they fit into the economist's view of individual decision-makers deciding to pursue illegal activity or not?

3   As described in Witte, what are the inextricable links between drugs and crime in urban areas? Realizing these, what does she recommend as policy options? Can you think of others?

4   Does Witte believe that local, state, or federal government policies exert a greater influence on crime prevention and reduction in urban areas? Why?

5   In Table 1, Cornwell and Trumbull report the influence found in previous regression studies of particular explanatory variables on crime rates. Compare these results to what they find. How are they different? How are they similar? What is the reason that Cornwell and Trumbull believe that their findings are more accurate?

PART VIII

Urban Transportation

Economists' dreams can be politicians' nightmares, and 'congestion pricing' is no exception. Charging people for what has been free is no more popular in the United States than it is in Russia.

Kenneth A. Small

Or, Why Motorists Always Outsmart Planners, Economists, and Traffic Engineers: The Unbridgeable Gap

THE ECONOMIST

Source: The Economist, 5.9.98. © The Economist Newspaper Ltd. All rights reserved.

The blue waters of the Bosporus, crowded with oil tankers moving between the Mediterranean and the Black Sea, and with ferry boats darting back and forth, no longer separate Asia and Europe the way they used to. Now the six-lane Ataturk Bridge and the eight-lane Fatih Sultan Muhammed Bridge, a few miles to the north, carry a quarter of a million vehicles a day across the narrow waterway. Both often have long queues. Turkey's highway agency says the only way to untangle the traffic is to build a third bridge, midway between the two. But will the multi-billion-dollar project make traffic move faster, or will it simply make for more traffic? The answer requires some familiarity with the economics and behavioural science of motoring – and a great deal of guesswork.

Traffic experts typically view congestion as an elementary problem in economics: a case of incomplete markets and mispriced resources. To think about it in this way, imagine you are zipping along an open road, the sort of place where you can put your foot down and move as fast as the engine – or the law – will allow. From the slip road just ahead, a Ford Fiesta enters the motorway. It disturbs your idyll, your illusion of having the road entirely to yourself, but it does not force you to lower your speed. Your travel time does not increase and the car's presence has no economic impact on you. But as other vehicles start to join, your strategy of shifting lanes to stay clear of the merging traffic eventually reaches its limits. As a white Fiat Uno enters the road ahead of you, you lightly tap your brakes. Almost instantly, brake lights blink for 500 metres behind you. On a road with hitherto free-flowing traffic, the additional presence of that one white Fiat has created congestion.

This is what economists call a negative externality, an action by one individual that imposes costs on others. Although each motorist will weigh only his own personal costs, his decision to drive may well lead to higher costs, in both time and out-of-pocket expenditure, for everyone else on the road. In that sense, the car whose arrival occasioned all that braking is analogous to a factory that spews smoke into the air or a sheep farmer whose flock squeezes under the fence to eat a neighbour's grass. Quantifying the consequences of such externalities is notoriously difficult. In a world with many polluters, how much of a town's lung disease and peeling paint can reliably be traced to the smokestack of a particular plant? And if the plant's owners were to spend $10m to reduce harmful emissions by 20%, to what extent would those problems be alleviated? Measuring the cost of congested traffic poses the same sorts of problems, only more so.

Some of the cost estimates are huge. In 1990, Japan's international co-operation agency calculated that Bangkok loses as much as one-third of its potential output because of overcrowded roads. In 1994, two economists, Richard Arnott and Kenneth Small, put the annual cost of driving delays in the United States at $48 billion, or about 0.7% of GDP. The Texas Transportation Institute says the delay experienced by the average urban driver in America rose from 19 hours in 1982 to 34 hours in 1994; reckoning $11.50 for each lost hour, including the cost of wasted fuel and drivers' own estimates of the value of their time, the institute worked out the average cost per driver at about $400 nationwide and roughly $1,000 in Los Angeles. The European Union's transport directorate, in a 1995 green paper, put the cost of congestion in Europe at 2% of GDP. Lex, a car-leasing firm, says congestion wastes 1.5 billion hours of British motorists' time a year, costing the economy £10 billion ($16.5 billion).

Pass the Salt

These alarming figures need to be taken with a large pinch of salt, for several reasons. First, many of them assume an ideal state of traffic-free roads. There is no obvious reason to think, as the Texas Transportation Institute does, that society loses out when freeway traffic in Los Angeles averages only 38 miles per hour at peak periods instead of 55mph at other times. Roads that are always uncongested would be economically wasteful because they would be seriously underused for most of the day. Research in the Netherlands suggests that a motorway is being used optimally when, averaged over the course of a year, 2% of each day's traffic encounters a queue. The EU's estimate that 2% of GDP is lost to congestion thus "lacks a clear empirical and methodological foundation," Piet Bovy, a Dutch engineering professor, and Ilan Salomon, an Israeli geographer, told European transport ministers last December. The two experts reckon that in the Netherlands, Europe's most congested country, the true annual cost is closer to 0.25% of GDP.

Second, none of the estimates of the costs of congestion takes any account of the social benefits of being able to drive in the first place. If the motorways did not exist, many trips that are now routine would never be undertaken. Yet those trips, even with congestion, represent a benefit to society by, for example, allowing employers to draw from a larger labour force and permitting shoppers a wider choice of stores. Ignoring that benefit skews the estimate of congestion costs upwards.

Third, it is odd to argue that all drivers lose from congestion when many of them choose quite voluntarily to bear it. Someone who decides to live on a farm in eastern Pennsylvania while working 100km (62 miles) away in New Jersey, or who has a job in London but moves to Oxfordshire to let the kids enjoy village life, knows from the start that traffic delays are part of the deal. If he then incurs them, why should the time he spends in traffic jams be counted as part of society's loss?

Congestion undoubtedly does have economic costs. If unpredictable traffic forces factories to keep extra components on hand in case deliveries run late, capital is being wasted. If clogged delivery routes mean that consumers pay higher prices for groceries or that working time is unproductive, that too represents a genuine economic loss. Businesses would willingly pay a price, and often a steep one, in order to avoid the externalised costs of too much traffic, but generally there is no way for them to do so. In that sense, the transport market can truly be said to have failed. But this failure is mostly of fairly minor economic importance.

There is one other factor that sharply distinguishes traffic congestion from many other activities that cause negative externalities. Its root cause is human behaviour, and if there is one thing that can safely be said about human behaviour when driving, it is that it is impossible to understand or to predict.

See a Psychologist

Economists and traffic planners have spent many hours and sacrificed many trees to try to understand what motivates people to drive rather than walk or take the bus, and what motivates them to choose one route over another. The result of all that effort is most unimpressive. "The system is too chaotic to understand at more than a macro level," says Tim Lomax of the Texas Transportation Institute.

To see why this is so, suppose that an individual's travel decisions are determined by only two factors, tolls and the expenditure of time, and assume that he values his time geometrically at, say, $1 times the square of hours of travel time (a mathematical way of saying that short delays are unimportant but long ones matter a lot). Travelling between two towns he would favour route 1, with a $4 toll and a one-hour driving time (total cost $5), over route 2, with a $2 toll and a two-hour driving time (total cost $6). But suppose route 1 were to grow more congested. Once the driving time exceeds 1 hour 25 minutes, the driver would switch to route 2. But if he and other road-switchers clogged route 2 enough to slow the drive by just a few minutes, route 1 would again be more attractive and he would switch back.

If this seems clear, keep in mind that each individual's precise preferences cannot be known in advance. How he values his own time will become clear only from observing his real-world behaviour. Even then an element of uncertainty remains, because the driver must make a new guess each day as to which route is likely to take up less of his time. Change the traffic situation, and the driver will change his behaviour.

This leads to a series of paradoxes that bedevil transport planners. Measures meant to reduce congestion may fail to do so, because if a given route becomes faster it will quickly attract drivers who previously used other routes, drove at other times or used public transport. Building new roads may cause people to undertake trips they would otherwise not have attempted, creating congestion anew: when Phil Goodwin, an economist at London University, looked at 12 British projects meant to unclog congested highways, he found that total traffic volumes, counting old and new roads together, far exceeded the previous volumes. Subsidising a new rail scheme may draw commuters from buses, leading to a reduced level of bus service and thus causing bus passengers whose needs are not served by the rail system to use their own cars.

There is yet another paradoxical possibility, intensely controversial among transport experts, known as the law of the constant travel-time budget. This holds that individuals seek not to minimise their travel time – the sort of behaviour economists would normally expect – but rather to hold their travel time at a level they deem acceptable. Widen the motorway so that their half-hour commute becomes a 20-minute trip, and they will move further away from their workplace. Although this "law" clearly does not apply across the board, there is something in it. Both in America and in Europe, average daily travel distances have been lengthening while average commuting times have stayed much the same.

All of these paradoxes loom in the background as Turkey debates a new Bosporus crossing. The basic facts are not disputed. Whereas 35% of Istanbul's people live on the Asian side of the waterway, only 25% of the city's jobs are there. The big new office towers and shopping centres are almost all on the European side, far away from the ferry landings and the new underground line still under construction. Car ownership, now 100 per 1,000 people, is expected to double over the next ten years. And Istanbul's Asian shore is home to a disproportionately large share of the city's rapidly growing middle class, people who can afford their own cars and would not dream of spending hours standing in a slow, crowded bus.

Kazin Apaydin, an official of the highways directorate, looks at the Bosporus and sees the Seine. "Two bridges are not enough," he insists. "In Paris there are a lot of bridges. In Budapest there are a lot of bridges. Across the Thames, you have a lot of bridges. This is necessary." And where will the cars go once they have crossed the new bridge? "This problem is the responsibility of the municipality," says Mr Apaydin. "They must solve it."

Mustafa Ilicali, the city's chief planner, does not favour Mr Apaydin's bridge; he wants a railway tunnel to join lines that now terminate on either side of the strait. But more trains would not get people to destinations such as Akmerkey, a big shopping-and-office complex a dozen miles north of the Topkapi Palace. An expanded underground system might help, but building it will take decades; the line now under construction does not even go to the Asian side of the Bosporus. Mete Orer, a transport engineer who works near Akmerkey, says that the cheapest way to reduce delays on the city's streets would be to tow away illegally parked cars. But that might persuade even more middle-class suburban-ites to drive into the city. What about raising tolls on the bridges, now 250,000 liras ($1) per round trip? Higher tolls, traffic experts concur, would have little effect because, away from the waterfront, public transport between Istanbul's two halves is so poor that middle-class workers have no real alternative to using their cars.

So is ever more jammed-up traffic an unalterable reality of modern urban life? Opti-mists insist that it need not be. The right combination of public transport, high technology and economic policies, they say, can solve the problem.

CHAPTER THIRTY-THREE

You Ride, I'll Pay: Social Benefits and Transit Subsidies

JANET ROTHENBURG PACK

Source: The Brookings Review, Summer 1997. Brookings Institution Press, Washington DC, 1998.

The public subsidies underwriting the nation's mass transit bus and rail systems are enormous. In 1989 federal, state, and local governments contributed $7.1 billion to transit operating costs. Capital subsidies brought the total to more than $10 billion. For every dollar transit riders paid in fares, taxpayers paid two dollars in subsidy.

Not unexpectedly, during a decade of huge federal deficits, tax revolts in the states, and increased interest in privatization and public efficiency, the transit subsidies have been widely attacked. In 1985 President Reagan advised a group of Miami, Florida, county officials that they could have saved money by buying a limousine for each of Miami's transit users instead of building their new system. Tony Snow, in a 1986 article entitled "The Great Train Robbery" in *Policy Review*, estimated that Miami "could have purchased each passenger a $45,000 condomininium for the cost of building the system – and would have been able to throw in a subcompact car with the first year's operating losses." In the case of the Washington, D.C., Metrorail system, Snow suggested that the city could have bought "a BMW for each of its daily passengers." (No one has addressed the question of whether it would be better to buy a limousine, a subcompact, or a BMW.)

The critical issue is whether there is any justification for the subsidies. The argument that transit systems should not run at a deficit assumes that riders are the sole beneficiaries and should be made to cover full marginal costs through their fares. As noted by Patrick G. Marshall in a 1988 report for Congressional Quarterly, "The key to achieving a more efficient transportation system, say many transportation experts, is to make sure that each mode carries its own weight, with users fully funding the infrastructure, and let the market decide which are the most efficient modes for given purposes."

But consider the implications of closing down the transit systems. Immediately more automobiles will take to the roads. Traffic accidents will increase, congestion will worsen, air quality will deteriorate, and more land will be gobbled up by parking garages. According to the Urban Institute, in 1988 some 14.8 million traffic accidents, involving 47,000 deaths and five million injuries, cost the nation $334 billion. If public transit systems helped avoid accidents equal to 1 percent of that total, the nation saved about $3.3 billion, nearly half the total public operating subsidy in 1989. And in his 1988 report,

Marshall, quoting Robert A. Poole, Jr., of the Reason Foundation, noted that the time and gasoline wasted in Los Angeles County traffic jams each year could be valued conservatively at half a billion dollars. Even if public transit carries only a fraction of rush hour commuters – in the Philadelphia metropolitan area, for example, about 20 percent of the total, but about 70 percent of those traveling to jobs downtown – congestion and congestion costs would be substantially greater if transit riders got back into their cars.

It is too often forgotten that transit riders are not the sole beneficiaries of mass transit. Society as a whole benefits as well. The question is how the benefits and the subsidies measure up. With public budgets under increasing scrutiny, urban infrastructure aging, and demands for funding of social programs growing more pressing, the billions of dollars spent to subsidize public transportation will surely be a target for cutbacks. If the social benefits derived from public transportation are demonstrably smaller than the subsidy, it may be time to reallocate resources away from transit subsidies. If the social benefits actually outweigh the subsidies, a case can be made to defend the subsidies. (This is not to argue that the existing level of subsidy is warranted since it is also true that subsidies may promote inefficiency. With improved efficiency, the same level of benefits could be achieved with lower subsidies.)

The Need for Cost–Benefit Analysis

Although much lip service is paid to the need for cost–benefit analysis of public programs, few such studies exist for mass transit. In their absence, proponents can argue that programs are justified by the many obvious social benefits they generate, and opponents can simply assert that the huge expenditures proposed could not possibly be outweighed by the social benefits.

In what follows I sketch out a simple cost–benefit analysis of a single mass transit system. My aim is limited. I do not address questions about whether the billions spent on mass transit subsidies would be better spent on road repair or highway expansion – which are themselves, of course, highly subsidized by all levels of government. Nor do I consider whether air quality and congestion could be more effectively reduced by other means. Radical policy shifts to limit automobile use – a dollar-a-gallon gas tax, a charge for driving in congested or polluted areas, downtown parking restrictions, parking taxes – have been regularly proposed and rejected for decades. What is certain is that the costs of existing transit systems will annually far exceed their revenues. Each year subsidies will be needed and will be the subject of heated debate. Estimates of social benefits can help resolve arguments about whether and how much subsidy is appropriate – particularly if other major public expenditures are similarly evaluated.

My focus is on the commuter rail operations of one of the nation's largest public transport agencies, SEPTA, the Southeastern Pennsylvania Transportation Authority. The SEPTA system faces problems similar to those facing systems in older urban areas – MBTA in Boston, Metro-north in New York, New Jersey Transit. In 1989 the SEPTA farebox covered only 37 percent of costs – roughly the same portion as other systems nationwide – and operating subsidies were nearly $100 million a year.

Rail systems in general, and in particular the commuter rail systems serving low-density areas, have the highest – and most heavily attacked – subsidy rates of all mass transit. It is here that the potential for wasteful subsidies is greatest and that the need to value benefits is particularly important.

Measuring Social Benefits

Five benefits are clearly attributable to the commuter rail system. First, when traffic is diverted to commuter rail from automobiles, accidents decrease. (The incidence of transit accidents themselves is far less predictable than highway accidents. Serious accidents, however, are infrequent and idiosyncratic. In 1989, for example, there were no fatal accidents on SEPTA commuter rail and a total of only 46 collision-related injuries.)

Second, reduced road congestion shortens automobile commuting time, a benefit reflected in the familiar drop-off in house values as commuting distances increase from the city center. Third, downtown noise and pollution decrease. Fourth, congestion on alternate transit facilities decreases. And, finally, the welfare of the commuter rail riders increases.

Many transportation analysts believe that the benefit to commuter rail riders in excess of the fares they pay – known as "consumer surplus" – outweighs the losses of the transit system. In the case of SEPTA, this turns out not to be true. Social benefits would not exceed subsidies were it not for the additional benefits to the general public.

Putting a dollar value on these social benefits requires calculating how much beneficiaries are willing to pay for the indirect benefit received. Table 1 shows, in 1989 dollar terms, the estimated value of the five major social benefits from SEPTA for the years 1981, 1982, and 1989. (The two values given for each benefit each year reflect alternative assumptions about underlying magnitudes or alternative estimating procedures.) In 1989 social benefits exceeded the subsidy by $39–75 million; in 1981, by $11–31 million; in 1982, by $20–34 million. Even the more conservative assumptions yield positive gains for society despite the huge subsidy. In the early 1980s, about two-thirds of the benefits not covered by fares accrued to the general public and only one-third was consumer surplus for the rail riders; in 1989 the two were about equally divided.

The increase in the estimated benefits from the early 1980s to 1989 is largely attributable to the substantial gain in the value of access to the commuter rail line as reflected in housing prices (line 5 of the table). The oil price shocks of the 1970s increased rail ridership, as did the growth of the downtown in the 1980s.

Another important influence on the net social benefits was SEPTA's cost-control efforts. During 1981 and 1982 Conrail (reluctantly) operated the Philadelphia commuter rail system. In 1983 SEPTA assumed full responsibility for its commuter rail services. Generous federal subsidy guarantees had given Conrail little incentive to reduce costs. After SEPTA took over, incentives to control costs increased substantially: the federal contribution to subsidies declined from nearly 50 percent to about 10 percent. Between 1981 and 1989 SEPTA's real costs fell by 5 percent. As a result, although real revenues fell, the required subsidy grew only 16 percent, and net benefits from the system increased two-to threefold.

Table 1 Estimated Social Benefits of Philadelphia's Commuter Rail System[1]
(millions of 1989 dollars)

	1981		1982		1989	
	LOW	*HIGH*	*LOW*	*HIGH*	*LOW*	*HIGH*
1. **DECREASED ACCIDENTS**[2]						
Fatal	2.4	5.8	2.4	4.5	2.4	5.4
Nonfatal	4.8	11.6	4.8	9.0	4.8	10.8
2. **DECREASED CAR AND TRUCK COMMUTING TIME**[3]	29.0	32.5	26.6	26.6	34.0	49.0
3. **DECREASED CONGESTION AND POLLUTION**[4]	3.4	3.4	2.7	2.7	3.0	6.0
4. **WELFARE GAINS FOR TRANSIT RIDERS**[5]	25.0	32.0	19.0	27.0	21.0	30.0
5. **WELFARE GAINS FOR COMMUTER RAIL RIDERS**[6]	30.0	30.0	31.0	31.0	72.5	72.5
TOTAL SOCIAL BENEFIT	95.6	115.3	86.5	100.8	137.7	169.8
SUBSIDY	84.3		66.3		98.9	
NET BENEFITS	11.3	31.0	20.2	34.5	38.8	74.8

[1] Behind the calculations are important assumptions about how many commuter rail riders would have driven or been passengers in automobiles; how many would have ridden other forms of public transit and how many existing highway and public transit users would have been affected by increased congestion and delay as a result; and average distances traveled and travel times.

[2] Calculated based on road fatalities of 1–1.5 people per 100 million miles traveled; on the Urban Institute's detailed May 1991 study of the costs of fatal highway crashes; and on the ratio of the costs of nonfatal to fatal highway crashes as estimated by the Urban Institute.

[3] The decrease in commuting time for all highway commuters on routes parallel to commuter rail lines is assumed to be proportional to the potential increase in traffic and is valued, following Federal Highway Administration estimates, at $7 an hour. As an alternative I have used annualized values of estimates of the increase in house prices due to reduced highway commuting times in the Philadelphia area (Richard Voith, study for the Federal Reserve Bank of Philadelphia, November 1991). The value of lost time for heavy trucks is based on calculations made in a June 1991 Urban Institute study by William A. Hyman.

[4] The social benefits of the additional congestion and air and noise pollution avoided are assumed to be $1 to $2 per vehicle each day.

[5] The average increase in travel time on the other forms of public transit most likely to have been used by commuter rail riders is assumed to be proportional to the average change in ridership on the relevant routes. The time saved is valued at $7 an hour (23–35 cents per passenger trip). I assume a willingness to pay 10 cents a day for less crowding.

[6] Estimates of the capitalization into house values of accessibility to the regional rail system have been converted to figures reflecting the willingness of households to pay premiums for houses in census tracts with commuter rail stations (Richard Voith, *American Real Estate and Urban Economics Association Journal*, March 1991).

Tough Decisions

In trying to make sense of the highly charged ritual attacks on public subsidies, the analytic challenge is to identify and value the social benefits. The practical issue facing public decisionmakers is that social benefits are difficult to explain and subsidies are unpopular.

Those who run and finance the more than 500 mass transit systems in the United States repeatedly face these issues. Should public transit be expanded or cut back? Are the current subsidies too large or too small? Would the community be better off if more riders were enticed to ride the trains? And the ever-present question: why don't fares cover costs, no matter how many times they are raised?

In the case of Philadelphia, it is clear that commuter rail, operating at its current level, generates benefits substantially greater than its costs. If public officials decided to phase out commuter rail in the Philadelphia region, the community would be far worse off, unless some better means to achieve the social benefits were found.

Capturing the Value of Social Benefits

The problem for public policy is that although social benefits are real, they are not translated into transit revenues. No doubt the social benefits of transit systems are reflected in the willingness of homeowners to pay higher prices for houses near train stations and in the development of property in the vicinity of new transit facilities. But these benefits are realized by landowners and developers, not by the transit authority.

If transit authorities could capture this property value enhancement, the required subsidies would be much lower. It is virtually impossible for older systems to capture the value they generate. Development has already taken place, and the original landowners and developers have already reaped the gains. But new systems can use a variety of measures – joint development ventures between the transit agency and private firms, value-capture taxation on new development, and tax-increment financing, to name just a few.

John Landis, Robert Cervero, and Peter Hall, of the University of California, Berkeley, have identified 114 transit joint development projects in some 25 American cities as of October 1990. The projects have not yet resulted in much income to the transit authorities, "either through capital contributions or through yearly lease payments," say Landis and his colleagues, but experiences vary.

Since 1984 New York's MTA system has financed an estimated 3–5 percent of its capital expenditures through joint development projects. Washington's Metrorail, one of the most innovative and active joint-developers, has financed less than 1 percent of its capital expenditures since 1979 in this way – although the period has seen major capital expansion. Washington's "Metro" receives $1.6 million a year in lease fees from Bethesda Metro Center, as well as smaller sums from a host of other projects at Metro stations. Nonetheless, "such payments have never amounted to more than 0.7 percent of annual operating expenses," say Landis and his colleagues. They identify only six systems that pursued joint developments yielding such annual payments.

They suggest that transit operators may just be beginning to move "up the learning curve" in these matters. In the past transit authorities have neither pursued value-capturing projects with sufficient entrepreneurial vigor nor extracted sufficient revenues from them. If Landis is right, we will see more such projects, and transit officials will make better deals in the future.

If public authorities could make all beneficiaries pay fully for the benefits they receive from the existence of the transit system, the problem of subsidies would disappear, at least where social benefits exceed costs. If SEPTA could tax the substantial benefits it provides in the form of increased land value that now accrues to the landowners, the subsidy picture would look far different, and the decibel level of public discussion would diminish considerably. With only limited value-capture possible, efforts to contain subsidies will have to continue to concentrate on reducing inefficiency.

Worth Every Penny

If the repeated and rancorous battles over transit subsidies succeed in seriously diminishing transit service, the loss may extend beyond those who rely on commuter rail. In Philadelphia, at least, and perhaps in New York and Boston and other cities as well, the general public gets more than its subsidy's worth from the fact that others ride the commuter trains.

CHAPTER THIRTY-FOUR

Urban Traffic Congestion: A New Approach to the Gordian Knot

KENNETH A. SMALL

Source: *The Brookings Review*, Spring 1993, 6–11. Brookings Institution Press, Washington DC, 1998.

As traffic policy in the United States has lurched from the contentious highway building of the 1960s to the ineffectual travel-demand management of more recent years, congestion in the nation's cities has worsened steadily. In his recent book, *Stuck in Traffic*, Brookings' urban policy expert Anthony Downs threw up his hands and advised motorists, only partly tongue-in-cheek, "to learn to enjoy congestion."

It is hard to imagine frazzled American drivers taking that advice. And in fact they may not need to. The time may soon be ripe for a radically new approach to the problem of urban congestion.

Dreams and Nightmares

Economists have long recognized that congestion can be dealt with simply and efficiently by charging motorists a very high premium for using the most popular roads during peak hours. But economists' dreams can be politicians' nightmares, and "congestion pricing" is no exception. Charging people for what has been free is no more popular in the United States than it is in Russia. And the efficiency rationale for making motorists pay steep fees to commute to and from work in Los Angeles is no more self-evident than that for raising the price of sugar in St. Petersburg.

Still, interest in congestion pricing is growing and has reached far beyond academia. A surge of conference activity has brought it to the fore among transportation planners and even some politicians. Important interest groups, ranging from business organizations, such as the Bay Area Economic Forum, to environmental groups, such as the Environmental Defense Fund, are now open advocates. European policy analysts are infatuated, with Britain embarking on a third and massive study of how congestion pricing would work in London. In the past eight years, politicians nearly (but not quite) signed off on trials in Hong Kong, Norway, Sweden, the Netherlands, and Cambridge, England. The government of Chile is seriously considering it.

A few systems have even been implemented. Singapore has had a citywide system since 1975. In April of last year France began applying congestion pricing to Sunday traffic on the A1 motorway into Paris. California is planning congestion pricing on at least two of the four privately built highways recently contracted for by the state.

Why the sudden burst of interest? Several developments have combined to give currency to the unthinkable. For one thing, the failure of all other congestion policies gives new allure to drastic options. In addition, technology has made long waits at toll booths obsolete. From here on out toll collection can be nonintrusive and easy for the traveler. And finally, the potential of congestion pricing as a prodigious source of much-needed new revenue is being recognized by local, state, and federal officials alike.

Failures of the Past

Congestion, obviously, is a matter of too few roads carrying too many cars and trucks. Most suggested remedies attempt to rectify the imbalance either by increasing the supply of roads or by reducing the number of vehicles. Among the former remedies are constructing or widening highways, improving signal timing, and (more futuristically) using electronic sensors to allow closer vehicle spacing. All require large public outlays. Strategies to reduce demand include parking controls, ridesharing, mass transit, employer-based commuting requirements, staggered work hours, telecommuting, and measures to encourage workers to live closer to their jobs. These policies are costly too – not in terms of public spending, but in terms of changing people's behavior. High-occupancy-vehicle lanes are a combination of supply- and demand-side policies: they usually put new capacity in place and at the same time promote carpooling.

But these steps relieve congestion only temporarily. Once traffic begins to thin out a bit, heretofore respectable folks who have eschewed antisocial activities like driving to work alone find reasons to join the immoral majority. All sorts of people in changed circumstances – new workers, people who just moved, young professionals with new families – find, in greater numbers than before, that solo driving during peak hours is just what they need to juggle their busy lives. Evidence for this abounds in before-and-after studies of travel choices when lanes are added, bridges opened or closed, transit lines installed.

Every large congested city in this country harbors a reservoir of potential peak-period drivers, a sort of reserve army of the unfulfilled, more prosaically known as *latent demand*. Congestion itself deters them from traveling when and where they would prefer – namely, on busy streets and highways during peak hours. As soon as additional road space appears because of a policy "success," it is taken by someone who was once part of that latent demand.

Conventional congestion policy fulfills the desires of latent demanders for more convenient travel – a genuine and important benefit. But it does not eliminate congestion or even reduce it much for any length of time.

The Role of Congestion Pricing

Congestion pricing would break this cycle by using money – instead of congestion delay – to ration scarce capacity. This approach is more efficient because time spent in congestion delay is lost forever, so is a real drain on national resources. By contrast, tolls paid by travelers can be spent on something useful or just substituted for some other revenue source; the only net costs are those of collecting the tolls – and with today's technology, they are minimal.

Congestion pricing is also a demand-side policy, but it differs from others by addressing its incentives to *all* highway users, not just a fraction of them. For example, parking controls discourage trips ending in the area but not through trips. Employer-based ride-sharing programs target commuters, but not people traveling to school, shopping, or social activities. Unlike most demand-side policies, congestion pricing will promote a wide variety of alternatives to peak-hour driving, leaving the traveler to decide which is best. Of course, alert suppliers should be permitted to add or expand services where called for so that the number of alternatives actually available is as large as possible.

Two characteristics are essential to congestion pricing. First, tolls must vary widely by time of day, so that only peak travel is discouraged. Second, the peak price must be high enough to make serious inroads into peak demand and thus reduce congestion measurably. It is these traits that make congestion pricing a policy narrowly targeted at reducing congestion, which in turn makes it more likely to succeed.

Congestion pricing is one of a broader array of policies, known as *road pricing*, that use fees to influence travel behavior. Road pricing, which also includes conventional toll roads, fuel taxes, parking fees, and other financial incentives to reduce road use, may be aimed at a number of goals, such as infrastructure finance, environmental protection, historic preservation, and neighborhood revitalization. It is important to keep these goals distinct. Although congestion pricing can have beneficial effects on these other goals, and, conversely, other forms of road pricing can reduce congestion slightly, no single policy can be expected to succeed on all fronts. A combination is in order to accomplish that.

The Infrastructure Connection

In its 1991 federal highway reauthorization bill, Congress agreed to spend $150 million for up to five congestion-pricing demonstration projects. (Proposals for 16 cities have now been received.) The bill was passed by a Democratic Congress and crafted in considerable part by a Democratic senator, Daniel Patrick Moynihan. Still, there is no doubt that the market orientation of the Republican administrations of the 1980s was important to the emergence of policies such as congestion pricing. Can the idea, whose most direct political appeal is to high-income people who greatly value their time, survive a more liberal administration?

Current politics suggests an intriguing answer. Congestion pricing could provide President Clinton just the key he needs to keep his pledge of costly infrastructure improvements. How? By pointing the way to increasing the efficiency of U.S. infrastructure investment.

For example, a large American city, facing growing congestion in its suburbs, proposes building a new freeway. Engineers calculate that eight lanes are needed to cope with immediate demand and foreseeable traffic growth. But a road that large is costly, consumes valuable land, and has adverse effects on the environment and on the quality of residential life – and thus poses problems for local and federal sponsors alike.

Suppose, however, that the federal government conditions its financial assistance on the requirement that the new road be paid for in part by "peak-hour user fees" that will discourage some traffic and spread the rest more evenly over the day. Under those conditions, the highway needs only six lanes. Such a requiremnt for federal cost sharing, then, has double merit: it reduces capital requirements as well as adverse environmental and land-use impacts. These are just the ingredients that could make possible a political compromise while conserving federal and local financial resources.

It may be objected that the smaller road would not relieve as much congestion on parallel routes as would the originally planned eight-lane road. True. But it might still relieve enough to form a satisfactory compromise, and it might also provide funds to improve the parallel routes. And we can go one step further. Suppose congestion pricing is instituted on those routes too – admittedly a much greater political challenge. Such a move would not only bring in more money for other infrastructure improvements such as bridge replace-ments or new transit systems, but would also reduce the pressure on those older roads and thereby postpone the time when they might need to be widened or repaired. Congestion would be relieved, investment requirements reduced, and financial resources increased.

Looked at this way, congestion pricing exemplifies a broader argument about infra-structure policy. The infrastructure question should not be framed simply as "how much should we spend?" but as "how can we improve the efficiency of that investment so we can afford it?" Better design of user fees for a host of infrastructure components, ranging from airport runways to water reservoirs, can make limited federal, state, and local dollars go further in shoring up our infrastructure.

High-Tech Toll Collection

In the long run technology will drive policy and make some form of congestion pricing almost a certainty. Electronic road pricing has been thoroughly tested in Hong Kong and is now used on many toll roads in the United States and elsewhere. Its widespread adoption for prosaic toll collection is already guaranteed. For example, toll authorities in New York, New Jersey, and Pennsylvania have agreed to develop common technology for optional electronic toll collection, which will result in millions of cars being equipped with devices that simplify toll payments – either through monthly bills or by deductions from prepaid magnetic cards (similar to modern transit fare cards).

From there, it is an easy technical step to collect tolls that are differentiated by time of day. In Oslo, Norway, for example, collection stations for a toll ring around the inner city, which opened in 1990, were designed with this capability in mind for possible future use. Closer to home, a road pricing system now in place at Los Angeles Airport for service vehicles could easily be adapted to incorporate differentials between peak and off-peak traffic.

Inevitably the potential of time-varying tolls to increase revenues and reduce infra-structure requirements will lead to experimentation. Suppose a toll road is proposed parallel to a congested free road, but construction financing is questionable. With a constant all-day toll rate, setting the rate too high could cause most off-peak traffic to use the parallel free road, making it impossible to raise enough revenue. But if the toll can be differentiated by time of day, the rate during peak hours can be adjusted to limit traffic just enough to maintain a time advantage over the congested free roads while still bringing in plenty of revenue. And off-peak tolls can be kept low enough to maintain patronage and bring in some supplementary revenue.

Where and when such experiments take place will no doubt depend on idiosyncratic political factors. But once people get used to time-differentiated tolls and realize that they promote a smoothly flowing road system, congestion pricing will spread – not everywhere, and certainly not in the ideal form economists propose, but enough to begin to change the nature of urban transportation.

Beginning to Look Ahead

What would happen if congestion pricing were to become truly widespread? The most immediate and important change would, of course, be less congestion. Both in Singapore and outside Paris congestion pricing has flattened severe peaks in travel volumes. If pricing were widespread, the resulting time savings, valued at tens of millions of dollars a year in any large city, would provide important economic advantages. (Depending on how fees are set, there may be some offsetting increases in congestion just outside the peak periods or the geographical area in which the higher fees apply.)

People's broader responses to the targeted fees are more difficult to predict. The value of property whose accessibility is improved would increase at the expense of property that becomes more costly to reach. Relative wages for jobs with changed access would also shift, offsetting some of the immediate financial effects of the fees themselves. As people shifted to other travel arrangements, the nature of transportation services themselves would change. Carpools would be easier to arrange because more people would be trying to form them. Transit systems would be used more widely, requiring increased service that should make transit more convenient. Less congested city streets would increase both labor productivity and service quality for buses or streetcars.

As people weighed commuting time and costs in making their housing choices, they would find the balance shifting further toward short commutes, at least in areas where congestion charges apply. The ultimate result could be greater residential centralization or greater job decentralization, both of which are goals now pursued through cumbersome land-use controls. A change that could take place more quickly is a drop in the large amount of "cross-hauling" in American cities. Congestion pricing would give people who are moving anyway (because of a job or family change, for example) more reason to shorten commutes, thus reducing the number of people who live considerably farther away from their jobs than the availability of suitable housing requires.

Reducing peak-hour congestion would tend to improve air pollution both by reducing total daily traffic on existing highways and by eliminating the higher emissions rates that characterize congestion. Off-peak travel, however, would probably increase and thus offset some of those gains. As noted, congestion pricing is not the most direct way to address air pollution and should not be judged primarily by its environmental benefits.

Like any price change, congestion pricing could have significant effects on the distribution of real incomes. Although the complexity of shifts in labor, housing, and land markets makes these effects hard to predict, the direct effects would hit relatively hardest at low-income people. Not only does road use rise less than proportionally with income, but also time savings are less valuable to low-income than to high-income drivers. That inequity is a significant political barrier to enactment of congestion pricing and must be addressed in designing a policy.

The full distributional effect of congestion pricing, of course, depends on who benefits from the revenues collected by the tolls. If revenues were spent entirely on improving inner cities, the net result would surely be progressive; if spent mainly on services for affluent suburbs, it would be regressive. A plan for using the revenues, then, is an integral and critical component of any congestion-pricing proposal.

Uses of Revenues

Any such plan must be carefully molded if it is to appeal to voters. Surveys and elections from London and California have demonstrated people's willingness to consider taxes or fees as part of an explicit package that includes strongly desired revenue uses.

To illustrate the possibilities, I have outlined a plan to use the revenue from a hypothetical congestion-pricing program for greater Los Angeles that was proposed by the Environmental Defence Fund (EDF) and the Regional Institute of Southern California. Its aim is twofold: to offset the direct adverse effects of the fee payments themselves and to appeal to some key political interest groups.

The EDF proposal is based on a fee structure in which average peak-period fees of 15 cents per vehicle-mile apply to roughly a quarter of the region's traffic. Annual revenues, less collection costs, would be nearly $3 billion. It is the astounding size of this figure that creates the opportunity to provide significant offsets to the sharp pinch that people paying the fees would feel. For a typical commuter traveling 10 miles each way on congested roads, that pinch would be about $66 a month – offset, of course, by the time savings.

Revenue would go into three roughly equal packages, summarized in table 1. The first would put money directly back in the hands of frequent users of the transportation system. The second would reduce general taxes now used for transportation. The third would improve transportation services. Thus, all revenue would go to support transportation, either substituting for or supplementing current sources. My proposal leans heavily toward substitution – for two reasons. First, lower peak-period demand would reduce infrastructure needs, so increasing spending by anything like the full amount of the toll collections is likely to be wasteful – better to give some of it back through other means. Second, many citizens will view the new fees as taxes, so may support congestion pricing only if other taxes are reduced. In addition, with revenue of this size at stake, it is crucial to minimize opportunities for powerful groups to appropriate it for uses that do not enhance people's welfare.

The first revenue package, reimbursements to travelers, would include a commuting allowance of $10 a month, channeled through employers to every worker in the region, and a five-cents-a-gallon cut in fuel taxes. Both would return some congestion-fee revenues to road users – thus easing their unhappiness with the increased cost of getting to work – without undermining the incentive to curtail solo driving on congested routes. Lowering the fuel tax would emphasize that congestion fees are being substituted for other taxes as a method of highway finance. It would also reduce a regressive tax.

The general tax-reduction package would feature cuts in the sales tax and in the property tax. A dedicated sales-tax surcharge (1 percentage point in Los Angeles County, half a point

Table 1   A package of revenue uses for the Los Angeles region

	MILLIONS OF 1990 DOLLARS *ANNUAL AMOUNT*
REIMBURSEMENTS TO TRAVELERS	
Employee commuting allowance ($10 a month)	$ 695
Fuel tax reduction (5¢ a gallon)	350
GENERAL TAX REDUCTIONS	
Sales tax reduction (1/2 of transportation surcharge)	525
Property tax rebate (eliminate local highway subsidy)	465
NEW TRANSPORTATION SERVICES	
Highway improvements	315
Transit improvements	310
Services in business centers	320
TOTAL (NET REVENUE)	$ 2,980
COLLECTION COSTS	140
TOTAL (GROSS REVENUE)	$3,120

Source: Author's estimates based on data from the U.S. Federal Highway Administration, California Department of Transportation, and California State Board of Equalization. For details see Kenneth A. Small, "Using the Revenues from Congestion Pricing," *Transportation* (1992), 19, 359–81.

in most of the rest of the region) now goes to finance regional transportation. Cutting that surcharge in half would lower another regressive tax. It would also emphasize the link between the congestion charges and transportation funding. So would a property tax rebate, which would allow taxpayers to keep the portion of local taxes now spent on highways.

The transportation services package would help the region work off its backlog of unfunded highway projects, improve mass transit service, and target some specific transportation-related services – street improvements, lighting, pedestrian amenities, transit shelters, and so forth – to business centers that are heavily affected by the fees. These targeted services would help offset any tendency for businesses to leave those centers for less heavily priced areas, and thereby prevent the pricing scheme from promoting job loss or urban decay.

Taken together, these programs would provide benefits to a wide cross-section of urban residents and business owners, but would be targeted especially at groups most likely to be hurt by the new fee structure. They would enable most people to benefit from the policy package as a whole and make real progress in solving the region's urban transportation problems.

The Next Steps

What is the role of congestion pricing in our future? Coupled with intelligent and understandable programs for using the revenues, congestion pricing shows great promise as part of a comprehensive strategy toward urban transportation. Alone among proposed policies, it can bring about dramatic reductions in the severity of congestion while leaving individuals flexibility as to how to respond to its incentives. It also raises money instead of spending it, creating the opportunity to ease fiscal constraints on federal, state, and local governments while providing large and tangible benefits.

This is an ambitious, long-term agenda. For the more immediate future, Congress and the Clinton administration can proceed with three steps. First, they can pursue aggressively the demonstration projects already authorized by Congress, working with local and state authorities to design good projects and helping overcome obstacles. Second, they can expand the demonstration program to accommodate additional projects. Third, they can develop an infrastructure policy that stretches the utility of federal spending by requiring states to demonstrate that each infrastructure element will be used efficiently. If the latter requirement is correctly defined and enforced, pricing will be the only option in many cases. These measures will make a start. If I am right, momentum will carry the day.

CHAPTER THIRTY-FIVE

Infrastructure Services and the Productivity of Public Capital: The Case of Streets and Highways

Marlon G. Boarnet

Source: National Tax Journal, 50(1), 1997, 39–57.

This paper examines the link between highway congestion, labor productivity, and output in a sample of California counties for the years 1977 through 1988. A county production function is modified to include both the value of each county's street and highway capital stock and a measure of the congestion on each county's highway network. This allows a comparison of two distinct policies – expanding the street and highway stock versus reducing congestion on the existing stock. The evidence suggests that congestion reduction is productive. The effects of expanding the street and highway stock are more suspect. Overall, the results provide evidence that using existing street and highway infrastructure more efficiently can produce economic benefits.

Introduction

There is now a large literature on the link between public capital and private sector economic productivity. In almost all the research on that topic, public capital is measured as the dollar value of the infrastructure stock. Yet if infrastructure is productive, it is because of the services it provides. The services provided by infrastructure are determined not only by the stock of public capital, but also by a host of factors including how efficiently that capital is used.

I am grateful to Eugene Kim, Nicholas Compin, and Inha Yoon for outstanding research assistance and to Jim Benbrook of the California Department of Transportation for supplying capacity adequacy data for California highways. I also thank Peter Gordon, James R. Hines, Jr., Keith Ihlanfeldt, Kenneth Small, Clifford Winston, and two anonymous referees for comments on earlier drafts, and Douglas Holtz-Eakin and Alicia Munnell for providing private capital stock data for California. This research was supported by the U.S. and California Departments of Transportation with a grant administered through the University of California Transportation Center.

While many authors have recognized the importance of efficiently using existing infrastructure (e.g., Holtz-Eakin, 1993b; Winston, 1990), recent empirical work on this topic has rarely measured anything other than the stock of public capital. The result is an empirical literature that implicitly (and at times explicitly) focuses attention on the size of the infrastructure stock. This is troubling both because a focus on the stock risks mis-specifying the empirical analysis and because recent studies cannot directly evaluate policies that increase the efficiency of existing public capital. This study begins to bridge both gaps by examining how the services provided by one type of public capital, street and highway infrastructure, are related to measures of economic output and productivity.

Public Capital Inputs and Service Flow Outputs

Bradford, Malt, and Oates (1969) noted that public goods are characterized both by inputs and by service flow outputs. In the case of infrastructure, the dollar value of the stock represents an input. Those inputs are productive to the extent that they produce some useful service flow output (U.S. Department of Transportation, 1992; Kessides, 1993). Formally, infrastructure services are the output of a production function that has dis-counted investment flows as inputs, as shown below.

$$S_T = f\left(\sum_{t=1}^{T}(1-\delta)^{T-t}G_t, Z_T\right) \tag{1}$$

where

S_T = services produced by public capital in time period T;
G_t = public capital investment in time period t;
δ = discount rate that measures the depreciation of G_t; and
Z_T = vector of other variables that affect infrastructure service flows.

The vector **z** includes factors such as congestion, how efficiently the stock is used, the suitability of the stock design (or technology) to the problem at hand, and anything else that could affect service flows from a given discounted public capital investment.

Of course, the framework in equation 1 applies equally well to service flows from private capital. Yet while market forces might lead to optimal investments in capital which yield strictly private returns, the same cannot be expected for public capital. To the extent that infrastructure is a public good, governments must make decisions about the optimal levels of the public capital stock. It is thus vitally important to have information on the service flows provided by a given stock of public infrastructure and to understand how those service flows are linked to private sector economic performance.

Most recent studies of public capital and productivity have measured infrastructure as the present value of the stock, using a perpetual inventory method that is compatible with the discounted investment flow that is the first argument on the right-hand side of equation 1. See, e.g., Aschauer (1989), Duffy-Deno and Eberts (1991), Garcia-Mila and McGuire (1992), Holtz-Eakin (1994), Kelejian and Robinson (1994), Munnell (1990a, 1990b), and the reviews in Gramlich (1994) and Munnell (1992). Yet as the formulation in equation 1 makes clear, the services provided by public capital are potentially mis-measured by looking at only the value of the stock. More importantly, many infrastructure policy recommendations involve using the existing stock more efficiently, a point that is missed when the value of the stock is the only variable that measures public capital services.

This mismatch between research and policy is not a minor issue. Consider the case of street and highway infrastructure, which constitutes one-third of all the public capital stock in the United States (Gramlich, 1994). The congestion pricing literature has argued for years that unpriced highways are an inefficient use of the transportation infrastructure stock. See, e.g., Keeler and Small (1977), Mohring and Harwitz (1962), Small (1983), Small, Winston, and Evans (1989), and Vickrey (1963). As such, one policy for increasing the service flow from congested highways is to price the existing stock more efficiently, rather than to build more stock (Gramlich, 1994; Winston, 1990).

This research looks at the specific case of street and highway capital. Based on equation 1, both the street and highway capital stock and a measure of how efficiently that stock moves traffic are included in an aggregate production function. The efficiency variable is the inverse of a congestion measure, and the resulting production function is[1]

$$Q = f(L, K, H, A) \tag{2}$$

where

Q = output;
L = labor inputs;
K = private capital stock inputs;
H = street and highway stock inputs; and
A = inverse congestion measure that will be defined more formally later.

Note that a production function such as equation 2 gives comparisons of the output effects of two distinct infrastructure policies – expanding the street and highway stock and reducing congestion on the existing stock. By examining the effects of highway congestion, while holding street and highway capital constant, this paper provides insights into policies such as congestion pricing, which can use the existing road infrastructure more efficiently.

The remainder of the paper proceeds in four parts. The next section describes the data used for an empirical test of the hypothesis that highway congestion affects economic output. This includes a description of a congestion measure that is based on highway capacity adequacy data that were obtained from the California Department of Transportation for the years 1977 through 1988. After that, the empirical specification and results are discussed. The last section contains concluding remarks.

Data and Study Area

Data are available on gross output, employment, private capital stock, street and highway capital stock, and highway network congestion in all 58 California counties for the years 1977 through 1988.[2] The sources for the output, labor, private capital, and street and highway capital data, and the methods used to construct the private capital stock variable, are described in Boarnet (1995b). Because the output, labor, and private capital data are constructed similarly to the measures used in state and national studies (e.g., Aschauer, 1989; Garcia-Mila and McGuire, 1992; Holtz-Eakin, 1994; Munnell, 1990a, 1990b), the focus here is on describing the street and highway stock and highway congestion variables.

Street and highway capital stock is constructed using a perpetual inventory method based on annual highway and street expenditures in each county, starting in 1957. The base year street and highway capital stock is estimated by apportioning Bureau of Economic Analysis stock estimates for 1957 to California counties based on each county's proportion of total street and highway miles in that year. While this technique might induce some error in the 1957 stock measurement, by 1977 (the first year used in the empirical analysis), the perpetual inventory measure is dominated by annual spending flows, which are based on actual street and highway spending data for California counties. See Boarnet (1995b) for a description of the data sources. Following the results obtained by Holtz-Eakin (1993a), a depreciation rate of 4.1 percent was used to discount annual street and highway investment flows. This is similar to other depreciation rates commonly used for nonresidential capital (Holtz-Eakin, 1993a).

The congestion variable is motivated by the framework in equation 1. Equation 1 emphasizes that policymakers can increase the service flow from streets and highways either by increasing the street and highway stock or by using the existing stock in ways that facilitate more efficient travel. One measure of the ability of streets and highways to facilitate travel is congestion. For this research, we need to measure congestion throughout the entire highway network in a county. While such county-wide congestion measures do not exist, one can be constructed from available data from the California Department of Transportation (Caltrans).

Caltrans keeps annual records on highway capacity adequacy at every mile marker in the state highway system. The state highway system includes all interstate, federal, and state highways, and the records on capacity adequacy are available annually from 1977 through 1988 (California Department of Transportation, 1977–88). A mile marker is simply a designated location on a highway, and markers do not necessarily appear every mile.[3]

For any mile marker, capacity adequacy is the ratio of the highway's rated capacity divided by a measure of peak hour travel flow, multiplied by 100.[4] Thus, the capacity adequacy (CA) variable is the inverse of a congestion (or volume/capacity) measure. Locations with a CA greater than 100 could carry more traffic at peak hour (i.e., they are not congested). Locations with a CA of less than 100 are carrying more than their rated capacity at peak hour (i.e., they are congested).

Since the CA variable measures the inverse of congestion at a particular point on the highway network, CA needs to be aggregated to the county level. That aggregation was done in two steps. First, for each county, CA was summed for each highway. The sum is weighted by average daily travel (ADT) at a mile marker. The result is a congestion measure for a highway segment, as shown below.

$$HWYCA_{j,k} = \sum_{i=1}^{N} \frac{ADT_{i,j,k}}{TOTADT_{j,k}} CA_{i,j,k} \tag{3}$$

where

> $HWYCA_{j,k}$ = congestion measure for highway j in county k;
> $CA_{i,j,k} = CA$ at marker i on highway j in county k;
> $ADT_{i,j,k}$ = average daily travel at marker i on highway j in county k;
> N = number of mile markers on highway j in county k; and

$$TOTADT_{j,k} = \sum_{i=1}^{N} ADT_{i,j,k} \tag{4}$$

such that $TOTADT_{j,k}$ = sum of the ADT at each marker i on the segment of highway j that is in county k.

Once $HWYCA_{j,k}$ is calculated for each highway segment in a county, those segment variables are summed into a county measure. Again, the sum is weighted by ADT, as shown below.

$$ACCESS_k = \sum_{j=1}^{M} \frac{TOTADT_{j,k}}{CNTYADT_k} HWYCA_{j,k} \tag{5}$$

where

> $ACCESS_k$ = congestion measure for county k;
> M = number of highways in county k;

and

$$CNTYADT_k = \sum_{j=1}^{M} TOTADT_{j,k} \tag{6}$$

such that $CNTYADT_k$ = sum of highway segment $TOTADT$'s for county k.

The result, $ACCESS$, is a weighted average of CA within the county.[5] Like CA, $ACCESS$ is an inverse congestion measure. Larger values of $ACCESS$ imply less congestion and, hence, easier travel (or access) to locations throughout the network.

In 1988, $ACCESS$ ranged from 57 in Alameda County (in the San Francisco Bay Area) to 377 in sparsely populated Modoc County. The more urbanized counties (e.g., Alameda, Los Angeles, Orange, San Diego, and San Francisco) have lower values of $ACCESS$, reflecting higher peak hour congestion in those counties. Furthermore, most urban counties, including the five examples cited in the previous sentence, have values of *ACCESS* less than 100 in 1988, suggesting that, on average, their highway networks were congested in that year.

Time-series graphs of *ACCESS* (available upon request) show that *ACCESS* typically follows the business cycle. In recessions (e.g., 1982 and 1983), *ACCESS* often improves, presumably due to less peak hour work-based travel. In expansions (e.g., 1984 and 1985), *ACCESS* typically drops.

One obvious implication is that *ACCESS* is endogenous to the local economy, both in the time-series (or business cycle) sense and to the extent that the more urbanized (and more prosperous) counties have lower *ACCESS*. For that reason, *ACCESS* was instrumented in the regression results reported below. Before that is discussed further, consider a regression model of county production, based on equation 2, that includes *ACCESS* as the congestion measure.

Empirical Model

There are three potential problems with estimating a regression based on equation 2. First, *ACCESS* is likely endogenous, for the reasons discussed above. Second, there are potential problems with unit roots and thus spurious correlations between the dependent and independent variables. See, e.g., Jorgenson (1991) and Tatom (1991) for a discussion of this problem in the context of regressions on U.S. time-series data. Third, a regression based on equation 2 must incorporate assumptions about how *ACCESS* and *H* enter into the production function. Consider first this last issue.

Functional form

Because *ACCESS* and *H* are external to individual firms, they are modeled as arguments of a shift factor, as shown below.[6]

$$Q_{c,t} = g(ACCESS_{c,t}, H_{c,t}) f(L_{c,t}, K_{c,t}) \tag{7}$$

where

> $g(.)$ = shift factor;
> $ACCESS$ = inverse congestion measure defined above;
> Q, L, K, and H = values previously defined;
> c indexes counties; and
> t indexes years.

The unknown functional form of the shift factor is approximated by a second-order translog expansion. See, e.g., Deaton and Muellbauer (1980) for a discussion of translog functional forms. The use of a second-order translog expansion has two advantages. First, the translog expansion includes an interaction term for log ($ACCESS$) and log(H). Since increases in the street and highway stock should have the largest productive effect in the most congested counties, a test for an interaction between $ACCESS$ and H should be part of the regression specification. Second, the translog expansion allows the effect of $ACCESS$ to be nonlinear. This is required by the way that the $ACCESS$ variable was constructed. Values of $ACCESS$ that are less than 100 correspond to a highway network that is, on average, congested, and values of $ACCESS$ over 100 imply, on average, that the county network is uncongested. Since reducing congestion on already uncongested networks should have no productive effect, the effect of increasing $ACCESS$ should be nonlinear, with a kink or turning point at values near 100.

Taking a second-order translog expansion of $g(.)$ in equation 7, assuming that $f(.)$ is Cobb–Douglas, and including year dummy variables gives

$$
\begin{aligned}
\log(Q_{c,t}) = {} & \alpha_0 + \alpha_1 \log(ACCESS_{c,t}) + \alpha_2 \log(ACCESS)_{c,t}^2 \\
& + \alpha_3 \log(ACCESS_{c,t}) * \log(H_{c,t}) + \alpha_4 \log(H_{c,t}) + \alpha_5 \log(H_{c,t})^2 \\
& + \alpha_6 \log(L_{c,t}) + \alpha_7 \log(K_{c,t}) + \sum_{i=0}^{10} \alpha_{8+i} YEAR_{1978+i} + \varepsilon_{c,t}
\end{aligned}
\tag{8}
$$

where

$YEAR_{1978}$ = one for 1978, zero otherwise (similarly for $YEAR_{1978+i}$ variables); and
ε = regression error term.

Endogenous $ACCESS$

Since $ACCESS$ is likely endogenous, it must be instrumented. This requires some consideration of the determinants of $ACCESS$ or, equivalently, the determinants of highway congestion. The equation below postulates that $ACCESS$ is a function of county output, street and highway capital, highway network design, and demographic characteristics.[7]

$$
ACCESS = f(Q, H, NET, Demo)
\tag{9}
$$

where

NET = vector of road and highway characteristics that affect congestion; and
$DEMO$ = vector of county demographic characteristics that affect congestion.

Because Q and H are included in equation 8, valid instruments must be chosen from variables that measures road network and demographic characteristics that are correlated

with driving patterns, and thus congestion, but that are exogenous to county output. Data were available on four such possible instruments, defined below.[8]
Road Network Characteristics:

> *HWY_RATIO*: The ratio of state highway miles divided by total road miles in a county.
> *FATACC_PROP*: The proportion of all accidents in a county that cause at least one fatality.

Demographic Characteristics:

> *VEHCAP*: The number of vehicles per capita in a county.
> *DRIVECAP*: The number of licensed drivers per capita in a county.

While it is possible to describe the characteristics needed for each of these four variables to be exogenous to county output, diagnostic tests suggested that only two of the four possible instruments should be used in the empirical work that follows. For brevity, justifications are given below only for the two instruments that were used in the analysis that follows.

FATACC_PROP: The proportion of accidents that result in fatalities is affected by local road conditions, driving habits, and highway network design. All of these characteristics should be exogenous to the economic fluctuations in the data used here. To the extent that fatal accidents are influenced by road network conditions, *FATACC_PROP* can proxy for geographic characteristics and highway design decisions that affect the flow of traffic, and thus congestion, but that are exogenous to output. Intuitively, highway networks with higher travel speeds typically have both less congestion and a higher proportion of fatal accidents.

VEHCAP: Counties with more vehicles per capita might have more driving and thus more congestion. Conversely, counties with high congestion (i.e., low *ACCESS*) might be undesirable places to drive, and residents might own fewer cars. The data suggest that the latter effect dominates, at least in the bivariate relationship in the California data used here. The correlation between log (*ACCESS*) and log (*VEHCAP*) is 0.19. While auto purchases fluctuate with the health of the economy, in many (if not most) instances, a newly purchased vehicles replaces an existing one. Since *VEHCAP* is not a measure of auto purchases, but rather a measure of the number of vehicles held per person, it might proxy for characteristics of a county that are linked to driving patterns and the propensity to drive but that are exogenous to local economic fluctuations.[9]

DRIVECAP was not used as an instrument because it is only weakly correlated with *ACCESS*. (The bivariate correlation coefficient for the log of *ACCESS* and the log of *DRIVECAP* is −0.05.) For the other three variables, diagnostic tests suggested that *HWY_RATIO* might be correlated with output. Specifically, two tests were used to get insight into the validity of the assumption that each instrument is exogenous to output.

First, the vector-autoregression techniques described in Holtz-Eakin, Newey, and Rosen (1988) were used to test both the hypothesis that each instrument does not cause county output and the converse hypothesis that output does not cause each instrument.[10] For *FATACC_PROP*, *VEHCAP*, and *HWY_RATIO*, no evidence of simple bivariate causation in either direction was detected (test results are available upon request). Second, to test for more complicated causal relationships, each of the three potential instruments was added to a log-linear production function for county output, which included labor, private capital, street and highway capital, and year and county dummy variables. *FATACC_PROP* and *VEHCAP* were both statistically insignificant in those regressions (at larger than the 25 percent level), but *HWY_RATIO* was significantly different from zero (at the one percent level). Because this suggests some link between *HWY_RATIO* and county output, only *FATACC_PROP* and *VEHCAP* were used as instruments.[11] Because the endogenous variable, log (*ACCESS*), enters equation 8 nonlinearly, the nonlinear two-stage least-squares (NL2SLS) techniques described in Bowden and Turkington (1984) were used.[12] First, the log of *ACCESS* was regressed on the set of exogenous and predetermined variables and the instruments. A first-stage regression for the specification shown in equation 8 is thus

$$\log(ACCESS) = \alpha_0 + \alpha_1\log(L) + \alpha_2\log(K) + \alpha_3\log(H)$$
$$+ \alpha_4\log(H)^2 + \alpha_5\log(FATACC\_PROP) + \alpha_6\log(VEHCAP) + \varepsilon \tag{10}$$

The predicted value of log(*ACCESS*) from the regression in equation 10, call it log (*ACCESS*)-∧, was used as an instrument for log(*ACCESS*) in equation 8. Similarly, the square of the predicted value of log(*ACCESS*), called log(*ACCESS*)-∧², was used as an instrument for log(*ACCESS*)², and log(*ACCESS*)-∧*log(*H*) instrumented log(*ACCESS*)*log(*H*). Bowden and Turkington (1984) note that the instruments themselves can be used in addition to the predicted values of the endogenous variable to get greater efficiency. Given that, the instruments for equation 8 are log(*ACCESS*)-∧, log(*ACCESS*)-∧², log(*ACCESS*)-∧* log(*H*), log(*FATACC_PROP*), and log (*VEHCAP*).[13] Given those instruments, standard two-stage least-squares procedures can be used for the endogenous variables, log(*ACCESS*), log(*ACCESS*)², and log(*ACCESS*)*log(*H*), in equation 8.

Unit roots

The last potential econometric problem is unit roots in the time series. Variables have unit roots if their time series have stochastic trends. Intuitively, variables have stochastic trends if they trend upward over time, and if the trend contains a random component. See Stock and Watson (1988) for a formal definition of this concept. Much evidence suggests that many macroeconomic variables, output included, have unit roots (Stock and Watson, 1988).

In a regression analysis, if the dependent variable and one or more independent variables have unit roots, standard least-squares techniques risk estimating a spurious relationship or estimating the parameters of a cointegrating vector, which requires non-standard asymptotic theory for hypothesis tests. Given these difficulties, diagnostic tests proceed in two steps. First, each variable is tested for a unit root. If both the dependent variable and one or more of the independent variables have a unit root, all the variables are tested for cointegration (Stock and Watson, 1988; MacNair et al., 1995).

Augmented Dickey–Fuller (ADF) tests suggested that the hypothesis of a unit root could not be rejected for any of the variables in equation 8 except $\log(ACCESS)*\log(H)$. A cointegration test further suggested that the levels of the variables in equation 8 are cointegrated. Complete test results are available upon request.[14]

This implies that there is a long-run relationship between the variables, but standard asymptotic significance tests will be misleading (Davidson and MacKinnon, 1993). One of the most common ways to deal with this problem is to difference the variables, which often eliminates the unit roots in the time series. Yet estimating equation 8 in first differences identifies the parameters based on year-to-year fluctuations in the variables. Other authors have noted that this is undesirable in studies of public infrastructure, because it obscures the long-run relationship between the variables (Garcia-Mila and McGuire, 1992; Munnell, 1992). An alternative approach is to transform the specification in equation 8 in ways that eliminate the unit roots while preserving information on the long-run relationship between the variables. Two such transformations are used here.

The first assumes that there are constant returns to scale (CRTS) in the private inputs in equation 7. It is then appropriate to divide both sides of the equation by L, which gives

$$\log \frac{Q}{L} = g(ACCESS, H) f\left(\frac{K}{L}\right). \tag{11}$$

A second-order translog expansion of $g(\cdot)$, with year dummy variables and a Cobb–Douglas specification for $f(\cdot)$, gives[15]

$$
\begin{aligned}
\log\left(\frac{Q_{c,t}}{L_{c,t}}\right) = {}& \alpha_0 + \alpha_1 \log(ACCESS_{c,t}) \\
& + \alpha_2 \log(ACCESS_{c,t})^2 + \alpha_3 \log(ACCESS_{c,t}) \\
& * \log(H_{c,t}) + \alpha_4 \log(H_{c,t}) + \alpha_5 \log(H_{c,t})^2 \\
& + \alpha_6 \log\left(\frac{K_{c,t}}{L_{c,t}}\right) + \sum_{i=0}^{10} \alpha_{7+i} YEAR_{1978+i} \\
& + \varepsilon_{c,t}
\end{aligned}
\tag{12}
$$

The second transformation, suggested by Holtz-Eakin and Schwartz (1995), is to difference the variables in equation 8 over several years. This identifies the parameters based on changes rather than levels but preserves information on long-run relationships. A regression based on what Holtz-Eakin and Schwartz (1995) call "long differences" has the added advantages of requiring no assumption about returns to scale and allowing for fixed county effects. Other authors (e.g, Evans and Karras, 1994; Holtz-Eakin, 1994; Garcia-Mila, McGuire, and Porter, 1996) have noted that fixed effects are appropriate in similar work that uses state data.

Before presenting the regression results, I should emphasize that the unit root and cointegration tests used here have limited power in short time series (Campbell and Perron, 1991; Davidson and MacKinnon, 1993). Given the sometimes unreliable small sample properties of those tests (which are based on the length of the time series), the variables in equation 8 might not have unit roots even though the ADF tests could not reject that null hypothesis. The approach taken here, which proceeds as if the series have unit roots and are cointegrated, is the cautious one. Even if the transformations described above are not required, they will still yield consistent estimates of the parameters in equations 7 and 8 and the standard errors of those parameters.

Results

The regression in equation 12 was estimated using the NL2SLS techniques from Bowden and Turkington (1984). The regression for log($ACCESS$) was adapted to match the specification in equation 12, such that log($ACCESS$) was regressed on log(K/L), log(H), log(H)^2, log($FATACC\_PROP$), and log($VEHCAP$). The results from that first-stage regression are shown in Table 1. The results of estimating equation 12 are shown in column A of Table 2.[16]

Note that log($ACCESS$), log($ACCESS$)^2, and log($ACCESS$)*log(H) are all statistically significant in column A of Table 2. As expected, the effect of $ACCESS$ is quadratic. Evaluating the slope at sample means, the effect of increasing $ACCESS$ is positive for values less than 105 and negative for larger values.

The negative log($ACCESS$)*log(H) interaction term suggests that congestion reduction and street and highway building are substitute policy instruments. The effect of increasing the street and highway stock is larger, *ceteris paribus*, for counties with lower $ACCESS$ (i.e., more congested counties).

Table 1   First-stage regression results for equation 12 (dependent variable = LOG($ACCESS$))

Independent Variable	
Log(K/L)	0.19
	(0.03)
Log(H)	−1.03
	(0.24)
Log(H)^2	0.02
	(0.006)
Log($FATACC\_PROP$)	0.40
	(0.03)
Log($VEHCAP$)	−0.25
	(0.06)
Constant	14.90
	(2.45)
R^2	0.51
R^2_{adj}	0.50

Standard errors are in parentheses.
All coefficients are statistically significant at the 0.01 level.

Table 2 Regression results

Independent Variable	Column A CRIS Dependent Variable = Log(Q/L)	Column B Ten-year Differences Dependent Variable = Log(Q)	Column C Ten-year Differences Dependent Variable = Log (Q)	Column D Long Differences Dependent Variable = Log(Q)
Log(ACCESS)	14.38***	11.45	2.74**	3.14**
	(4.92)	(7.87)	(1.34)	(1.56)
Log(ACCESS)^2	−0.89***	−0.65*	−0.31*	−0.20**
	(0.26)	(0.36)	(0.17)	(0.08)
Log(ACCESS)*Log(H)	−0.31**	−0.25	–	−0.05
	(0.13)	(0.22)		(0.06)
Log(H)	3.70***	4.34	0.26*	2.90
	(1.30)	(5.26)	(0.15)	(2.70)
Log(H)^2	−0.06***	−0.07	–	−0.06
	(0.02)	(0.12)		(0.07)
Log(K/L)	0.64***	–	–	–
	(0.04)	–		
Log(L)	–	0.69***	0.67***	0.56***
		(0.11)	(0.08)	(0.08)
Log(K)	–	0.33***	0.25***	0.22***
		(0.12)	(0.07)	(0.05)
R^2	0.13	0.26	0.58	0.89
R^2_{adj}	0.11	0.21	0.56	0.89
N	694	116	116	347

* Statistically significant at the 0.10 level. ** Statistically significant at the 0.05 level.
*** Statistically significant at the 0.01 level.

Standard errors are in parentheses. Coefficients on year dummy variables are not shown.

All regressions are estimated with a nonlinear, two-stage least-squares technique. All terms
that contain log (ACCESS) are instrumented. Details are provided in the text. Column
D uses a generalized least squares connection for the error term, as described in the
text.

The coefficient on private capital, $\log(K/L)$, is significantly positive. The coefficients
on $\log(H)$ and $\log(H)^2$ are statistically significant, suggesting that returns to street and
highway capital follow a quadratic effect.

Columns B through D of Table 2 show the results of estimating equation 8, which
relaxes the assumption of constant returns. The estimates in columns B through D are all
from long difference specifications, in which the differences are taken over several years.[17]
In column B, equation 8 is re-expressed as ten-year differences.[18] Given the short time
span of the data, only 2 ten-year differences can be formed – the difference between 1977
and 1987 and the difference between 1978 and 1988.

Those 2 ten-year differences are pooled, and the regression results are shown in column B of Table 2. Note that, in column B, only the private inputs are significant at the five percent level. The coefficient on $\log(ACCESS)^2$ is significant at the ten percent level. The interaction term is not significant, giving no evidence of the trade-off between congestion reduction and street and highway infrastructure that was suggested by column A.

Given that both higher-order terms, $\log(ACCESS)*\log(H)$ and $\log(H)^2$, were insignificant in column B, they were dropped from the ten-year differences specification, and the results are shown in column C. Note that column C retains a quadratic specification for $\log(ACCESS)$, both because theory suggests that the effect of $ACCESS$ is nonlinear and because the $\log(ACCESS)^2$ term was significant at the ten percent level in column B.

While the coefficients on the private inputs, $\log(L)$ and $\log(K)$, are similar to the estimates in column B, column C shows that the coefficient on $\log(ACCESS)$ is significantly positive at the five percent level and the coefficient on $\log(ACCESS)^2$ is significantly negative at the ten percent level. The magnitudes of the coefficients suggest that the effect of increasing $ACCESS$ is positive for values of $ACCESS$ less than 83. The coefficient on $\log(H)$ is significant at only the ten percent level in column C.

One disadvantage of the ten-year differences specification is that the regressions in columns B and C are fitted on only 116 observations. Holtz-Eakin and Schwartz (1995) suggested an alternative form of long differences, which takes advantage of more of the available data.

Holtz-Eakin and Schwartz (1995) suggested forming differences from the base year values (in 1977) to values several years later. This involves taking the difference between 1988 and 1977 values, 1987 values minus 1977 values, and so on. Following Holtz-Eakin and Schwartz (1995), long differences are taken for all intervals that are at least six years from the base year (i.e., for 1983 and later years), and the resulting differences are pooled. This gives a regression with 348 observations. For a more detailed discussion of this technique, see Holtz-Eakin and Schwartz (1995).

Like the ten-year differences, this allows for county-specific fixed effects while using information on the long-run variation in the variables. Holtz-Eakin and Schwartz (1995) note that pooling long differences that are formed from a common base year induces serial correlation. Using the information on the covariance structure of the error terms given in Holtz-Eakin and Schwartz (1995), generalized least-squares estimates were used to obtain consistent estimates of the coefficients and standard errors. The results are shown in column D of Table 2.

As before, the coefficients on $\log(L)$ and $\log(K)$ are significantly positive. $\log(ACCESS)$ has the predicted quadratic effect, and the coefficients on $\log(ACCESS)$ and $\log(ACCESS)^2$ are both significant at the five percent level. The interaction term, $\log(ACCESS)*\log(H)$, is insignificant, again giving no evidence that congestion reduction and street and highway stock increases are substitute policies. Neither $\log(H)$ nor $\log(H)^2$ is significant.

The estimates in column D are preferred for several reasons. The specification in column D requires no assumption of constant returns, incorporates fixed county effects, exploits long-run variation in the data, and uses more of the available data than the ten-year differences in columns B and C. Overall, $ACCESS$ has the expected quadratic form in three of the four specifications reported in Table 2, including the preferred specification in column D.[19] Street and highway capital (H) is only statistically significant at the five percent level in column A, and the interaction term for *ACCESS* and H is also only significant in column A. This provides somewhat strong evidence that congestion reduction can affect county output but weaker evidence that street and highway capital stock increases are productive.

A final question concerns how congestion reduction can be productive if the street and highway capital stock is not productive. One explanation is that marginal changes in the street and highway capital stock do not have output or productivity effects. This is consistent with the results of recent state panel studies (e.g., Evans and Karras, 1994; Garcia-Mila, McGuire, and Porter, 1996; Holtz-Eakin, 1994; Kelejian and Robinson, 1994; Krol, 1995). If roads are not productive at the margin, it is sensible that the returns to congestion are realized as enhanced returns to private inputs, which is consistent with the inclusion of *ACCESS* in the shift factor. Possibly because congestion reduction frees more time for private production, the economic benefits are largely realized as increased returns from private inputs, rather than as returns from the street and highway stock.

The specifications in Table 2 can be evaluated using sample data to get elasticities. Table 3 lists the estimated *ACCESS* elasticity obtained by using 1988 data. Counties are listed in ascending order based on their 1988 value of *ACCESS*. In other words, counties are listed from the most to the least congested in Table 3. The four columns in Table 3 correspond, respectively, to columns A through D of Table 2.[20]

Note that the magnitude of the *ACCESS* elasticity is larger for the more congested counties and is often negative for uncongested counties. One interpretation is that the negative elasticities reflect the inefficiency of reducing traffic on already uncongested roadways.[21]

Also note that all four specifications give positive *ACCESS* elasticities for the 12 most congested counties. Yet the more rural counties (e.g., Toulumne and Calaveras) often have larger *ACCESS* elasticities than similarly congested urban counties (e.g., San Francisco and Orange). This is due to the negative log(*ACCESS*)*log(H) term in columns A, B, and D of Table 2. Given the mixed evidence on the statistical significance of this interaction term, one might wish to consider the effect of omitting log(*ACCESS*)*log(H) when calculating elasticities. Column C shows the effect of omitting log(*ACCESS*)*log(H) from the ten-year differences specification. For column D, log(*ACCESS*)*log(H) has such a small magnitude that recalculating the elasticities without that term gives little change. The trend toward larger elasticities for rural counties, while present in column D, is less pronounced than in columns A and B.

Conclusions

While the regression results in Table 2 show some important differences across the four specifications, congestion levels are a statistically significant predictor of output in three of the four regressions, including the preferred specification in column D. This suggests that transportation policies should focus at least as much on reducing congestion as on building more street and highway capital. The elasticities in Table 3 further suggest that congestion reduction policies should focus on those places that are most congested.

Table 3 Elasticities, by county

County	Column A	Column B	Column C	Column D
Alameda	0.48	0.79	0.23	0.44
Santa Cruz	1.07	1.27	0.21	0.53
Marin	0.92	1.15	0.20	0.51
Santa Clara	0.34	0.68	0.19	0.41
Sonoma	0.78	1.04	0.19	0.48
Contra Costa	0.53	0.84	0.19	0.44
Toulumne	1.11	1.32	0.14	0.53
San Francisco	0.48	0.81	0.13	0.42
El Dorado	0.75	1.03	0.11	0.46
Calaveras	1.00	1.25	0.05	0.49
Placer	0.50	0.85	0.05	0.41
San Mateo	0.16	0.57	0.04	0.35
Orange	−0.19	0.29	0.03	0.30
Napa	0.63	0.95	0.02	0.43
Nevada	0.59	0.92	0.02	0.42
Los Angeles	−0.74	−0.14	−0.004	0.20
Solano	0.33	0.72	−0.004	0.37
Sacramento	−0.03	0.43	−0.02	0.31
Santa Barbara	0.17	0.59	−0.03	0.34
Monterey	−0.02	0.46	−0.09	0.30
San Diego	−0.56	0.02	−0.09	0.22
Mendocino	0.02	0.49	−0.10	0.31
Riverside	−0.38	0.17	−0.11	0.24
Amador	0.49	0.87	−0.11	0.38
Ventura	−0.29	0.24	−0.13	0.25
San Bernardino	−0.49	0.09	−0.15	0.22
Fresno	−0.35	0.20	−0.15	0.24
San Joaquin	−0.31	0.23	−0.15	0.24
Madera	0.19	0.64	−0.16	0.32
Stanislaus	−0.12	0.39	−0.16	0.27
Yuba	0.26	0.70	−0.17	0.33
Sutter	0.02	0.52	−0.022	0.28
San Luis Obispo	−0.30	0.26	−0.23	0.23
Shasta	−0.31	0.26	−0.23	0.23
San Benito	0.24	0.70	−0.23	0.32
Trinity	0.03	0.53	−0.23	0.28
Merced	−0.22	0.33	−0.24	0.24
Yolo	−0.35	0.22	−0.25	0.22
Colusa	0.002	0.51	−0.26	0.27
Butte	−0.35	0.23	−0.28	0.21
Kern	−0.77	−0.11	−0.29	0.14
Del Norte	−0.29	0.29	−0.33	0.22
Tehama	−0.34	0.25	−0.33	0.21
Tulare	−0.63	0.02	−0.34	0.16
Humboldt	−0.28	0.30	−0.37	0.21
Plumas	−0.34	0.26	−0.37	0.20

Table 3 (*Cont.*)

County	Column A	Column B	Column C	Column D
Lake	0.30	0.29	0.37	0.21
Glenn	−0.32	0.28	−0.38	0.20
Siskiyou	−0.85	−0.14	−0.43	0.11
Sierra	−0.37	0.25	−0.44	0.18
Mariposa	−0.34	0.27	−0.44	0.19
Kings	−0.70	−0.01	−0.46	0.13
Mono	−0.73	−0.04	−0.47	0.12
Inyo	−0.66	0.02	−0.48	0.13
Lassen	−0.72	−0.02	−0.50	0.12
Alpine	−0.38	0.26	−0.52	0.17
Imperial	−1.23	−0.41	−0.58	0.02
Modoc	−1.85	−0.83	−0.94	−0.15

Counties listed in ascending order by 1988 value of *ACCESS* (i.e., from most congested to least congested). Columns A, B, C, and D are from the coefficient estimates in columns A, B, C, and D, respectively, in Table 2.

Given this conclusion, policy design becomes less direct than some might have previously thought. While the stock of public capital is a policy instrument that can be directly manipulated, congestion reduction requires some consideration of *how* to reduce congestion. Fortunately, there is a large literature that has studied ways to reduce traffic congestion (e.g., Downs, 1992; Small, Winston, and Evans, 1989). While the conclusions are too broad to summarize here, one consensus is that a theoretically promising solution to traffic congestion is road pricing. This research reinforces the importance of pricing highway infrastructure to reduce congestion and supports those (e.g., Holtz-Eakin, 1993b, Winston, 1990) who have claimed that efficient pricing is at least as important a policy tool as expanding the public capital stock.

More generally, this work emphasizes that studies of public capital should focus more on the service flow delivered by infrastructure. Future research should examine more closely how to measure service flows from different types of infrastructure and then link those measurements to the study of private sector economic performance.

Along those lines, future work should be more disaggregate. Measuring service flows requires detailed data often not available at the state or national level. Furthermore, the elasticities in Table 3 show considerable variation in the effect of congestion reduction in different counties. This suggests that the productive effects of infrastructure policy will vary depending on the local context. As other authors have suggested, this is both an important element of policy design (e.g., Holtz-Eakin, 1993b) and a point to consider in future research (e.g., Gramlich, 1994).

Overall, the evidence presented here supports those who argue that service flows are at least as important as capital stocks for public infrastructure policy. In the case of highway policy, the idea that congestion can be managed by pricing is well established in academia. This research reinforces that point and suggests that, in many cases, economic benefits from streets and highways can best be realized by using the existing stock more efficiently.

Notes

1   The aggregate production function in equation 2 has an obvious simultaneity problem. Traffic congestion, especially peak hour congestion, is likely endogenous to the economy. The congestion measure developed later in this paper is modeled as an endogenous variable and is instrumented in the empirical work that follows.

2   Congestion data are only available for the highway network, while the public capital stock variable combines streets and highways. This is not likely to be a serious problem. One would expect highway congestion to be closely related to congestion on the total street and highway network. If so, a highway congestion measure gives direct information on congestion on the highway network and can proxy for conditions on the street network in the same county.

3   The number of mile markers on the state highway system ranges from 3108 in 1977 to 3,793 in 1988. In 1988, Los Angeles County had the most mile markers (275) and Alpine County had the fewest (13). In general, highways in urban areas have more markers at closer distance intervals than do highways in rural areas.

4   The peak hour traffic flow reported by Caltrans is the flow during the $30th$ highest volume hour during the year for rural mile markers. For urban mile markers, peak hour flow is the volume during the $200th$ highest volume hour for each year. The measure of capacity adequacy that Caltrans reports thus excludes peak hours that are extreme outliers. See California Department of Transportation (1977–88) for more information on how capacity adequacy is measured.

5   Note that $ACCESS$ is similar to the measures of volume to capacity and levels of service, which are described in Meyer (1994), yet $ACCESS$ has two advantages when compared to those measures. First, $ACCESS$ can be collected for an entire state for several years, while most other congestion measures are unique to metropolitan areas. Second, $ACCESS$ measures differences in congestion levels on already congested networks, while many other measures are truncated once a highway or location congests. For a more detailed discussion of congestion measures used in previous research, see Meyer (1994). For a discussion of the choice of weights used in aggregating CA, see Boarnet (1995a).

6   Including H in a shift factor differs from recent work (e.g., Evans and Karras, 1994; Garcia-Mila, McGuire, and Porter, 1996; Holtz-Eakin, 1994). Those studies modeled H as an input in the production function. Note that, if H is more properly an input in $f(.)$, the higher-order terms in $g(.)$ in equation 8, i.e., $\log(H)^2$ and $\log(ACCESS)*\log(H)$, will be statistically insignificant. All models with insignificant higher-order terms were re-estimated with only the theoretically required $\log(ACCESS)^2$ term and the linear terms. With the exception of the specification reported in column C of Table 2, the sign and significance pattern is not changed by dropping insignificant $\log(ACCESS)*\log(H)$ and $\log(H)^2$ terms.

7   One might also include employment or population density in an equation for $ACCESS$. Yet neither is a valid instrument, since employment is in the production function in equation 8 and population density was added to the production function as a robustness test. Equation 9 is largely intended to focus attention on variables that are determinants of $ACCESS$ but that are excluded from the production function, and thus might be valid instruments.

8   Data on state and total road miles are from the California Statistical Abstract (various years), printed by the California Department of Finance, Sacramento, CA. Fatal and total accident data are from the Department of the California Highway Patrol, Support Services Section. Data on registered vehicles and licensed drivers are from the California Department of Motor Vehicles, Forecasting and MIS Unit.

9   The claim is not that driving behavior is exogenous to the economy. One could easily imagine that commuting behavior is affected by the business cycle, since persons who lose their jobs no

longer commute. Yet if those persons keep their cars, which is likely, then *VEHCAP* will be unaffected by short-run economic fluctuations.

10 "Cause" is used in the sense of Granger (1969). The vector-autoregression test regresses changes in one variable, e.g., county output, on lagged changes in the dependent variable (output) and lagged changes in one of the potential instruments. The hypothesis that the instrument does not cause output is accepted if one cannot reject the hypothesis that the coefficients on the lagged changes in the instrument are zero. This does not strictly rule out causality, but it is evidence against a simple bivariate causal relation. See Holtz-Eakin, Newey, and Rosen (1988) for a discussion.

11 Note that the tests described above are not tests of overidentifying restrictions. Most tests of overidentifying restrictions have been used in linear cases, rather than in the case of a nonlinear endogenous variable, as appears in equation 8. Readers are cautioned that the tests used above do not definitively establish the appropriateness of using *FATACC_PROP* and *VEHCAP* as instruments. The argument here is that *FATACC_PROP* and *VEHCAP* are preferred over the other two available instruments, and that there are sound *a priori* reasons to believe that *FATACC_PROP* and *VEHCAP* are valid instruments, and that the tests used above do not give any reason to doubt the appropriateness of those two instruments.

12 NL2SLS is used, despite the fact that the model is linear in the parameters, because the nonlinearity in the endogenous variable can influence the desirability of different instrumental variable approaches. Briefly stated, the instrumental variables should proxy for the nonlinearity in the endogenous variable, and this typically requires either higher-order terms in the instruments, higher-order terms in predicted values of the endogenous variables, or both. See Bowden and Turkington (1984) for a discussion.

13 Fisher (1966) notes that it is possible, in some instances, to identify equations that are nonlinear in the endogenous variables with as few as one instrument per endogenous variable. Intuitively, this can occur because squares, cross-products, and higher-order terms for either the instruments or the predicted values of endogenous variables can themselves be valid instruments. The models in equations 8 and 12 have one endogenous variable, log(*ACCESS*), which appears in three terms. There are two excluded instruments for equations 8 and 12 – log(*FATACC_PROP*) and log(*VEHCAP*). Applying the formal criterion for identification described in Fisher (1966) shows that equations 8 and 12 are identified with two excluded instruments.

14 The ADF test used is the procedure with a constant and a linear time trend, described in Davidson and MacKinnon (1993). The cointegration test is based on a unit root test on the residuals obtained by estimating equation 8 without the year dummy variables. See Davidson and MacKinnon (1993) for a description. Modified *t*-tables must be used for both the unit root and cointegration tests. See Davidson and MacKinnon (1993), for the appropriate five percent critical values for the unit root and cointegration tests.

15 An ADF test suggests that this transformation eliminates the unit root in the dependent variable, log(*Q/L*). The relevant *t*-statistic is -3.728, and the five percent critical value for rejecting the null hypothesis that log(*Q/L*) has a unit root is -3.41.

16 Fixed effects were not used for equation 12, because that technique identifies the parameters based on short-run, year-to-year fluctuations and thus is open to the criticisms given by Garcia-Mila and McGuire (1992) and Munnell (1992). For comparison, the specification in equation 8 is estimated using fixed effects.

17 In columns B through D of Table 2, the first-stage regression for log(*ACCESS*) reflects the variables that are in the regression. The log of *ACCESS* is regressed on log(*L*), log(*K*), log(*H*), log(*H*)^2, log(*FATAC_PROP*), and log(*VEHCAP*). Long differences of the predicted value of log(*ACCESS*) are then used as instruments, following the procedure described in the previous section. In addition to long differences of log(*ACCESS*)-∧, log(*ACCESS*)-∧^{2}, and log(*ACCESS*)-∧*log(*H*), the levels (not differences) of log(*FATACC_PROP*) and

log($VEHCAP$) were also used as instruments, again following the discussion in the previous section. Note that using levels of those two instruments will not cause unit root problems, since ADF tests reject the hypothesis (at better than the one percent level) that either log($FATACC\_PROP$) or log($VEHCAP$) has a unit root.

18   Research on lagged adjustment models of urban economies gives justification for using ten-year differences. Carlino and Mills (1987) estimated a lagged adjustment model of population and employment growth in counties. They found that, for both county population and county employment, approximately 15 percent of the gap between actual and equilibrium values was closed in ten years. Grubb (1982) and Luce (1994) estimated similar models for cities. They found adjustment speeds that implied that the cities in their samples closed between 30 and 100 percent of the gap between actual and equilibrium values in ten years. These results suggest that ten years is a sufficient time period to capture a reasonable amount of long-run change.

19   To be certain that $ACCESS$ was not proxying for the effect of population density in Table 2, regressions were run that included population density in the shift factor in equation 7. The $g(.)$ term was modeled as a second-order translog expansion of three arguments – $ACCESS$, H, and population density. The sign and significance pattern in Table 2 was largely unchanged when population density was added as an argument of $g(.)$. The only changes were that the log($ACCESS$)* log(H) term becomes insignificant in column A when population density is added to the shift factor, and log($ACCESS$) is not significant in column C when population density is added to the shift factor.

20   Note that column A gives the elasticity of labor productivity with respect to $ACCESS$, while the other three columns in Table 3 show the elasticity of output with respect to $ACCESS$.

21   If maintenance costs and externalities are ignored, travel on uncongested roads is nonrival. Thus, if the focus is limited to congestion reduction, eliminating traffic from uncongested roads is inefficient. This is similar to the insight that one gets from viewing congestion tolls as a peak-load pricing problem. In that case, tolls for traffic should only be charged when traffic is congested. See, e.g., Small, Winston, and Evans (1989).

References

Aschauer, David Alan (1989) "Is Public Expenditure Productive?" *Journal of Monetary Economics*, 23(2), March, 177–200.

Boarnet, Marlon G. (1995a) "The Economic Effects of Highway Congestion." University of California Transportation Center Working Paper No. 292. Berkeley: University of California Transportation Center.

Boarnet, Marlon G. (1995b) "Transportation Infrastructure, Economic Productivity, and Geographic Scale: Aggregate Growth Versus Spatial Redistribution." University of California Transportation Center Working Paper No. 255. Berkeley: University of California Transportation Center.

Bowden, Roger J., and Darrell A. Turkington (1984) *Instrumental Variables*. Cambridge: Cambridge University Press.

Bradford, David F., R. A. Malt, and Wallace E. Oates. (1969) "The Rising Cost of Local Public Services: Some Evidence and Reflections." *National Tax Journal*, 22(2), June, 185–202.

California Department of Transportation (1977–88) *Route Segment Report*. Sacramento: California Department of Transportation.

Campbell, John Y., and Pierre Perron (1991) "Pitfalls and Opportunities: What Macroeconomists Should Know about Unit Roots." In *NBER Macroeconomics Annual 1991*, edited by Olivier Blanchard and Stanley Fischer. Boston: MIT Press.

Carlino, Gerald A., and Edwin S. Mills (1987) "The Determinants of County Growth." *Journal of Regional Science*, 27, 39–54.

Davidson, Russell, and James G. MacKinnon (1993) *Estimation and Inference in Econometrics.* Oxford: Oxford University Press.

Deaton, Angus, and John Muellbauer (1980) *Economics and Consumer Behavior.* Cambridge: Cambridge University Press.

Downs, Anthony. (1992) *Stuck in Traffic: Coping with Peak-Hour Traffic Congestion.* Washington, D.C.: The Brookings Institution.

Duffy-Deno, Kevin T., and Randall W. Eberts (1991) "Public Infrastructure and Regional Economic Development: A Simultaneous Equations Approach." *Journal of Urban Economics,* 30(3), November, 329–43.

Evans, Paul, and Georgios Karras (1994) "Are Government Activities Productive? Evidence from a Panel of U.S. States." *Review of Economics and Statistics,* 76(1), February, 1–11.

Fisher, Franklin M. (1966) *The Identification Problem in Econometrics.* New York: McGraw-Hill Book Company.

Garcia-Mila, Teresa, and Therese J. McGuire (1992) "The Contribution of Publicly Provided Inputs to States' Economies." *Regional Science and Urban Economics,* 22(2), June, 229–41.

Garcia-Mila, Teresa, Therese J. McGuire, and Robert H. Porter (1996) "The Effect of Public Capital in State-Level Production Functions Reconsidered." *Review of Economics and Statistics,* 78(1), February, 177–80.

Gramlich, Edward M. (1994) "Infrastructure Investment: A Review Essay." *Journal of Economic Literature,* 32(3), September, 1176–96.

Granger, Clive W. J. (1969) "Investigating Causal Relationships by Econometric Models and Cross-Spectral Methods." *Econometrica,* 37(3), July, 424–38.

Grubb, W. Norton (1982) "The Dynamic Implications of the Tiebout Model: The Changing Composition of Boston Communities, 1960–1970." *Public Finance Quarterly,* 10(1), January, 17–38.

Holtz-Eakin, Douglas (1993a) "State-Specific Estimates of State and Local Government Capital." *Regional Science and Urban Economics,* 23(2), April, 185–209.

Holtz-Eakin, Douglas (1993b) "Why a Federal Plan Isn't Needed." *Spectrum – The Journal of State Government,* 66(4), Fall, 35–44.

Holtz-Eakin, Douglas (1994) "Public-Sector Capital and the Productivity Puzzle." *Review of Economics and Statistics,* 76(1), February, 12–21.

Holtz-Eakin, Douglas, Whitney Newey, and Harvey Rosen (1988) "Estimating Vector Auto-regressions with Panel Data." *Econometrica* 56(6), November, 1371–95.

Holtz-Eakin, Douglas, and Amy Ellen Schwartz (1995) "Spatial Productivity Spillovers from Public Infrastructure: Evidence from State Highways." *International Tax and Public Finance,* 2(3), November, 459–68.

Jorgenson, Dale W. (1991) "Fragile Statistical Foundations: The Macroeconomics of Public Infrastructure Investment." Conference Paper. Washington, D.C.: American Enterprise Institute February.

Keeler, Theodore E., and Kenneth A. Small (1977) "Optimal Peak Load Pricing, Investment, and Service Levels on Urban Expressways." *Journal of Political Economy,* 85(1), February, 1–25.

Kelejian, Harry H., and Dennis P. Robinson (1994) *Infrastructure Productivity: A Razor's Edge.* University of Maryland working paper. College Park: University of Maryland.

Kessides, Christine (1993) *The Contributions of Infrastructure to Economic Development: A Review of Experience and Policy Implications.* World Bank discussion paper. Washington, D.C.: The World Bank.

Krol, Robert (1995) "Public Infrastructure and State Economic Development." *Economic Development Quarterly,* 9(4), November, 331–8.

Luce, Thomas F., Jr. (1994) "Local Taxes, Public Services, and the Intrametropolitan Location of Firms and Households." *Public Finance Quarterly,* 22(2), April, 139–67.

MacNair, Elizabeth S., James C. Murdoch, Chung-Ron Pi, and Todd Sandler (1995) "Growth and Defense: Pooled Estimates for the NATO Alliance, 1951–1988." *Southern Economic Journal*, 61(3) January, 846–60.

Meyer, Michael D. (1994) "Alternative Methods for Measuring Congestion Levels." In *Curbing Gridlock: Peak-Period Fees to Relieve Traffic Congestion*, Volume 2. National Research Council Special Report 242. Washington, D.C: National Academy Press.

Mohring, Herbert, and Mitchell Harwitz (1962) *Highway Benefits: An Analytical Framework*. Evanston, IL: Northwestern University Press.

Munnell, Alicia H. (1990a) "How Does Infrastructure Affect Regional Economic Performance?" In *Is There a Shortfall in Public Capital Investment?* Boston: Federal Reserve Bank of Boston.

Munnell, Alicia H. (1990b) "Why Has Productivity Growth Declined? Productivity and Public Investment." *New England Economic Review*, January–February, 3–22.

Munell, Alicia H. (1992) "Policy Watch: Infrastructure Investment and Economic Growth." *Journal of Economic Perspectives*, 6(4), Fall, 189–98.

Small, Kenneth A. (1983) "The Incidence of Congestion Tolls on Urban Highways." *Journal of Urban Economics*, 13(1) January, 90–111.

Small, Kenneth A., Clifford Winston, and Carol A. Evans (1989) *Road Work: A New Highway Pricing and Investment Policy*. Washington, D.C.: The Brookings Institution.

Stock, James H., and Mark W. Watson (1988) "Variable Trends in Economic Time Series." *Journal of Economic Perspectives*, 2(3), Summer, 147–74.

Tatom, John A. (1991) "Public Capital and Private Sector Performance." *Federal Reserve Bank of St. Louis Review*, 73(3), May–June, 3–15.

U.S. Department of Transportation (1992) *Assessing the Relationship Between Transportation Infrastructure and Productivity*. Policy Discussion Series No. 4. Washington, D.C.: U.S. Department of Transportation.

Vickrey, William S. (1963) "Pricing in Urban and Suburban Transport." *American Economic Review*, 53(2), May, 452–65.

Winston, Clifford M. (1990) "How Efficient Is Current Infrastructure Spending and Pricing?" In *Is There a Shortfall in Public Capital Investment?* Boston: Federal Reserve Bank of Boston.

Further Reading Samples

Abstract from *Is Public Infrastructure Productive? A Metropolitan Perspective Using New Capital Stock Estimates*

JOHN B. CRIHFELD AND MARTIN P.H. PANGGABEAN

Source: Regional Science and Urban Economics, 25, 607–30. © 1995 Elsevier Science. Reprinted with permission from Elsevier Science.

This paper studies the productivity of public investment within the context of a neoclassical growth model. We use recently developed estimates of public infrastructure from Crihfield–Panggabean, Holtz-Eakin, Munnell, and the National Cooperative Highway Research Program (NCHRP) to calculate public and private-sector investment rates. These infrastructure measures are combined with disaggregated data for the states and 282 metropolitan areas in order to estimate the growth model. The estimations show that public infrastructure, however measured, has at most a modest effect on factor markets, and an even smaller impact on growth in per-capita income. Public infrastructure surely plays an important role in metropolitan economies. However, its marginal contribution is no more than, and may be less than, other forms of investment.

Abstract from *Is the Journey To Work Explained by Urban Structure?*

GENEVIEVE GIULIANO AND KENNETH A. SMALL

Source: Urban Studies, 30(9), 1993, 1485–1500. Taylor & Francis Ltd.

Basic to several key issues in current urban economic theory and public policy is a presumption that local imbalances between employment and residential sites strongly influence people's commuting patterns. We examine this presumption by finding the commuting pattern for the Los Angeles region in 1980 which would minimise average commuting time or distance, given the actual spatial distributions of job and housing locations. We find that the amount of commuting required by these distributions is far less than actual commuting, and that variations in required commuting across job locations only weakly explain variations in actual commuting. We conclude that other factors must be more important to location decisions than commuting cost, and that policies aimed at changing the jobs–housing balance will have only a minor effect on commuting.

Opening paragraph from *'Wasteful' Commuting: A Resolution*

KENNETH A. SMALL AND SHUNFENG SONG

Source: *Journal of Political Economy*, 100(4). © 1992 The University of Chicago Press.

A debate over the empirical underpinnings of urban economic models is emerging under the unlikely rubric of "wasteful commuting." Hamilton (1982) shows that a commonly used monocentric model, in which employment and population densities decline exponentially from a center, greatly underpredicts actual commuting distances in typical U.S. and Japanese metropolitan areas. He concludes that the monocentric model is fundamentally flawed. This conclusion is challenged by White (1988b), who examines the cost-minimizing assignment of households to residential locations, taking density patterns as they are and measuring cost by travel time. White finds that for a sample of U.S. metropolitan areas, only 11 percent of actual commuting cost is in excess of the cost-minimizing amount, rather than the 87 percent found by Hamilton. Hamilton (1989) and Cropper and Gordon (1991), using variations of White's technique, obtain results intermediate between these extremes.

References

Cropper, Maureen L. and Patrice L. Gordan (1991) "Is there a Consensus Among Economists in 1990s?" *American Economic Review*, 82(2), May, 203–9.
Hamilton, Bruce W. (1982) "Wasteful Commuting, "*Journal of Political Economy*, 90, 1035–53.
Hamilton, Bruce W. (1989) "Wasteful Commuting, Again, "*Journal of Political Economy*, 97, December, 1497–504.
White, Michelle J. (1988) "Location Choice and Commuting Behaviour in Cities with Decentralized Employment," *Journal of Urban Economics*, 24, September, 129–52.

Abstract from *Fares, Service Levels, and Demographics: What Determines Commuter Rail Ridership in the Long Run?*

RICHARD A. VOITH

Source: *Journal of Urban Economics*, 41, 176–97. © 1997 Academic Press. All rights of reproduction in any form reserved.

Using panel data covering a 13-year period, this paper examines the roles of transportation policy and demographic changes in determining rail ridership. The paper presents a model which allows identification of long-run responses of ridership to changes in prices and service independently of exogenous shocks to ridership caused by demographic factors. Long-run price and service elasticities are estimated to be almost twice as large as short-run elasticities. After controlling for transportation prices and service levels, demographic variables contribute little to explaining residual differences in ridership. To the extent that demographic changes are driven by transportation variables, these effects are captured in the estimated long-run elasticities.

Discussion Questions

1   With a critical eye, go back and review the three reasons given in *The Economist* article as to why cost estimates of traffic congestion need to be "taken with a pinch of salt." First, do these studies assume an ideal state of traffic-free roads or do they look at optimal use (based on level of congestion) given the highway stock available? Second, is it true that none of the cost estimates take account of the social benefits of driving? Should they? Third, is it reasonable to say that it is odd to argue that all drivers lose from congestion even if they choose to drive?

2   *The Economist* article describes how some transportation experts believe in the law of the constant travel-time budget. Describe what this is? Does it violate the usual economic thinking on the decision of how much to pursue an activity? Does the traditional economic way of thinking about a housing location relative to school or work, or the constant travel-time model, better fit your own decision on where to live? (If you made your own decision of where to live relative to school and/or work you can answer this question directly. If you did not, ask it of someone who did.)

3   How does the concept of *latent demand* fit into efforts to reduce traffic congestion? How would an appropriately crafted system of *congestion prices* reduce the offsetting effect of latent demand?

4   Develop a proposal to put in place a system of congestion pricing in your metropolitan area. In this proposal, sell it to people or policymakers based upon economic arguments. As Small suggests, also describe in your proposal how the revenue from congestion fees will be spent. Write up this proposal in a few paragraphs that are accessible to a layperson and distribute your write-up to ten people you know. After they have read it, ask if they would vote for such a proposal. If no, record their reasons for opposing it.

5   As described by Pack, what is wrong with the popular argument that you could save government money by buying each transit rider a limousine, condominium, or a BMW instead of subsidizing the transit service?

6   Describe the techniques that Pack used to come up with the benefits and costs of the Philadelphia commuter rail system that are given in her article's Table 1. Do you agree with all her values? What is the purpose of placing a low and high estimate in the table?

7   Boarnet points out that previous regression analyses in this area concentrated on the influence that the stock of street and highway infrastructure has on private sector productivity. What is the problem with this? Besides street and highway capital stock, Boarnet also uses a congestion measure. How did he develop the stock of infrastructure and congestion of infrastructure measures that are used in his regression analysis? Interpret the meaning of the regression coefficients for these variables as they are recorded in Boarnet's Table 2.

PART IX
Local Government

Suburban government seems to be more representative and accountable to its citizenry.
Urban government, however, imposes one oppressive fee after another, from a tax on
garbage to metered parking.

Debra Meyers

CHAPTER THIRTY-SIX

Why I Love the Suburbs

Debra Meyers

Source: *Buffalo News*, 3.8.97. © 1999 Dow Jones & Company, Inc. All rights reserved.

In my capacity as a third-generation suburbanite, and as someone who is continuing the tradition by raising my family in the "burbs," I was asked recently, "Why do you choose this bland, colorless, culturally bankrupt, thoroughly banal lifestyle?" To this urban dweller I responded by smiling softly, shaking my head gently from side to side and saying: "Living in the suburban world goes beyond choice. It is a matter of selection."

You see, we who sleep with our unbarred windows open and doors unlocked are among the humans of our species lucky enough to live where the evolution of communities has produced a higher-quality, more workable design than the old one, the traditional city. We who have neighborhood schools with the highest academic ratings – be they public, parochial or private – lead the way to the next level of development for human living styles – because we understand that basic to a suburban existence is the pursuit of civilized behavior.

We expect this from our politicians and the policies they set forth; from our police force, in their dealings with civilians and pursuit of criminals; from our school systems, in teaching children reading, writing, math, science and citizenship; from our neighbors, in their desire for a community that is a safe, healthy and happy; from our children, in treating themselves and others with respect; and from ourselves, in our treatment of people and in striving to make our actions examples of good behavior for the next generation.

If we are homogenized, as many city people like to call us, it is in our collective expectation of a higher quality of life and not in the racial, ethnic and cultural diversity of our neighborhoods. In the suburbs, homes are filled with people of all shades of skin, from all regions of the world – longtime citizens, new Americans and those who are just visiting. We hear the heartfelt voices of prayer from all churches and synagogues, be they organized, agnostic or atheistic. Our children play together, we dine together and we help each other when the need arises. For example, when I came home from the hospital this winter with my new baby, each night for a week my neighbors brought a home-cooked dinner to my family of six.

In the suburbs, if we are "armed," it is to protect ourselves against threats posed by the deer and mosquitoes, not humans. As to the charge that the suburbs are "ever so boring" because they are filled with office complexes, shopping malls and grocery stores I answer,

"Hallelujah!" These conveniences provide my husband with a short commute to work, without a parking charge, allowing him to spend more time and money with his family. And I don't have to worry about him getting mugged as he walks from the car to his building.

As a mother of four, I like "one-stop" shopping with free parking, especially when the weather is bad. And having several grocery stores only minutes away from my house means I can spend much less energy on the tedious chores of the day and more time with the activities that make life rich, like playing peek-a-boo with my baby, making sand castles with my toddler, reading a book with my 7-year-old or playing tennis with the 10-year-old. It is simply one more component in the pursuit of civilized living.

Are the suburbs a perfect place? Of course not. We have our share of people poor in character, government officials making bad decisions and felonious acts of crime. But the majority of us come together in peaceful discourse and work to repair the damage that sometimes occurs, ever mindful that our reason for living here is to make our quality of life better.

Oh sure, the city can be a fun place to visit. It has great boutiques, theaters, restaurants, art galleries, museums, a philharmonic, ethnic and art festivals, and sports arenas. However, with the exception of legitimate stage productions, a stupendous sushi bar, the opportunity to view major works of art, and being accosted by panhandlers, these attractions are not unparalleled in the suburbs. In fact, some wonderful things, like Starbuck's coffee, can only be found in the suburbs.

Suburban government seems to be more representative and accountable to its citizenry. Urban government, however, imposes one oppressive fee after another, from a tax on garbage to metered parking. And to add to the aggravation, the city never seems able to efficiently remove snow from its streets. Buffalo politicians pick away at the spirit of the good, hard-working and stalwart people of the city. They make life a constant struggle so that civility in city living becomes unreachable.

The color in our lives out here in suburbia comes from the sounds of cardinals singing, ducks quacking and tree frogs barking, not sirens blaring, traffic humming and horns blowing.

It is acquired as great blue herons dive for fish while we canoe in our creeks, by listening to our children rehearse with the summer band program taught by our school's music teachers and with the scent of fresh strawberries as we bend to pick them from our fields.

To be raised and live in the suburbs means being given the best chance of achieving a life filled with meaning and prosperity of the soul. I give thanks daily for the blessings that living here provides my family and me.

It's rather like being an American: Yes, there are other countries that are nice, but none greater than this.

DEBRA MEYERS lives in East Amherst, a suburb of Buffalo, NY. She spends a lot of time under the shade of tall trees in her sprawling suburban yard.

CHAPTER THIRTY-SEVEN

Metropolitan Fiscal Disparities

Roy Bahl

Source: Cityscape: A Journal of Policy Development and Research, 1994, 1.

In 1990 central-city residents had a median income equivalent to about 74 percent of that earned by suburban residents. The central cities have become home to a disproportionate share of social problems: Their infrastructure is arguably in poorer condition, their unemployment rates higher, and their governments more impoverished than those of the suburbs. The evidence suggests that these conditions have remained the same or worsened over the past 20 years. Urban areas are not all the same, and suburbs are not all wealthy, but it would not be at all misleading to say that America's poor places have become poorer over the past two decades.

This article reviews the evidence on the chronic problem of fiscal disparities among city and suburban governments in metropolitan areas. There is a nexus between the fiscal disparities problem and the spatial mismatch problem – the suburbanization of jobs and housing discrimination have led to a surplus of workers relative to jobs in inner-city neighborhoods. One of these problems argues that there are market and discrimination constraints on the ability of the central-city population to realize its full potential in the job market, and that these constraints exacerbate the social problems that plague the city. The other argues that there are market and government policy constraints that limit the ability of urban governments to deliver adequate services at reasonable, competitive tax rates. There are no equilibrating forces in place that would reverse either disparity, and the policy options open to redress the imbalances are very limited.

Fiscal Stress and Fiscal Disparities

City-suburb fiscal disparities are a policy concern that dates back to the 1960s. Campbell and Sacks, writing about metropolitan fiscal disparities in 1967, said (p. 179):

> Of particular importance ... is the impact on service needs caused by the "sorting out" of population that is taking place within metropolitan areas. The resulting pattern of different kinds of service needs in central cities and their outside areas becomes one of the most crucial metropolitan aspects of the service issue. Of most concern currently is the adequacy of those services for the poor who reside in increasing numbers in central cities.

There was some optimism about policy solutions to this problem 25 years ago, and no shortage of suggested government actions: Federal and State assumption of responsibility for the local government functions that aided the poor, increasing amounts of equalizing State aid, regional tax base sharing, and various forms of metropolitan government.

Observers felt that the Federal Government, the State governments, or even the courts would step in and redress the situation sooner or later.

But that never happened. Twenty-five years after the Campbell and Sacks book was published, a National League of Cities report (Ledebur and Barnes, 1992, p. 4) concluded that:

> Major demographic shifts are also causing increased disparities between cities and suburbs. More than 5.5 million more people lived in poverty at the end of the decade of the 1980s than 10 years previously. Over this period, poverty became increasingly concentrated in the nation's central cities. These trends result in systematic differentials among localities in income, wealth and poverty. These differences create fiscal stress in many central cities. Changes in the intergovernmental system are compounding these disparities and increasing the fiscal squeeze on cities as they attempt to respond to these problems.

This state of affairs should cause those who help frame national urban policy to raise three questions: have the city fiscal condition and city-suburb fiscal disparities changed so little since the 1960s; how have Federal, State, and local government policies affected this situation; and what prospects may the future hold for redressing this imbalance?

The concept of disparities

What is fiscal disparity, and can we distinguish the "disparities problem" from the more general fiscal problems facing local governments in metropolitan areas? Suppose metropolitan areas are each fragmented into n local governments and, for simplicity, assume that neither tax exporting nor suburban exploitation occur and that none of the jurisdictions overlap.[1] In this case, one might define a resource-requirements gap, d_{ij}, for the *ith* jurisdiction in the *jth* metropolitan area as

$$d_{ij} = R_{ij} + F_{ij} + S_{ij} - N_{ij}$$

where: $R_{ij} = $ revenues raised from own sources, from a uniform tax effort, by the *ith* jurisdiction in the *jth* metropolitan area,
$F_{ij} = $ Federal aid,
$S_{ij} = $ State aid,
$N_{ij} = $ expenditures required to produce a "standard" package of local public services,
and all values are expressed in per capita terms.

Variations across metropolitan areas in d_{ij} for central cities mark the relative fiscal problems of urban areas, whereas variations in d_{ij} across local governments within a metropolitan area point to the fiscal disparities problem. This needs–resources gap is a far cry from the ratio of observed expenditures, taxes, or aid between central cities and suburbs that most studies have used as a measure of disparities.

A resource-requirement gap is more easily conceptualized than measured, because local government tax effort has never been satisfactorily estimated, and the notion of a "standard package" of public services raises the difficult problem of measuring government output. A few studies have attempted to estimate something like this resources-requirements gap. Bradbury et al. (1984) proposed a definition that suggests "fiscal disparities exist when local governments must levy different tax rates to provide the same level of public service" (p. 151). Thus fiscal disparities exist if there are differences between jurisdictions in the cost of providing a given level of services, and this cost is largely due to "environmental factors" outside the control of the local government. The strength of this approach is that it is truer to the idea of measuring differences in the balance between resources and needs. Its weakness is that it requires estimation of the cost of providing a standard package of services although the correct cost determinants have not been identified and consumer preferences not adequately taken into account.[2]

Perhaps for these reasons, most studies have started by examining ex post fiscal disparities – in per capita expenditures, taxes, and aid. There has been no attempt to adjust the initial baseline measure of disparities for differences in need, tax effort, or preference for public versus private goods. The raw disparities in per capita expenditures, taxes, and aid are acknowledged to be due to some combination of choice, environmental factors, resource endowment, and so on. Most of these studies have then turned to an explanation of the city-suburb differences, usually in terms of needs, resources, and environmental differences. Campbell and Sacks (1967), Sacks and Callahan (1973), Advisory Commission on Intergovernmental Relations (1984), and Bahl, Martinez-Vazquez, and Sjoquist (1992) are all in this tradition.

Financial condition and fiscal disparties

The 1970s were a time of great concern about the fiscal and economic problems of cities. New York and several other cities teetered on the edge of bankruptcy; city–suburb fiscal disparities were pronounced and attracted much attention from the courts and the Federal Government; and there was policy action. Direct Federal grants to cities in the form of Comprehensive Employment and Training Act (CETA), Antirecession Fiscal Assistance (ARFA), and Local Public Works were substantial, General Revenue Sharing had a passthrough provision, and there was a push for equity in school financing.

The 1980s brought new economic growth to the country, a new view of cities, and a new set of priorities for city officials. As the economy improved at the end of the 1970s and grew in the 1980s, most policymakers seemed willing to accept the "rising tide" argument – the absence of evidence notwithstanding. The Federal Government decreased its direct support of cities, the courts pulled back on the school financing issue, and city governments became more focused on financial solvency than on economic viability.

In fact, there were few rumors of imminent default in the 1980s, and many cities were applauded for their remarkable recoveries. A survey of 67 percent of U.S. urban counties showed that the great majority perceived that their financial condition had improved in 1988–89 as compared to the situation 5 years earlier (Downing, 1991). New York City, the prototype of a troubled city in the 1970s, went from "basket case" to success story, even running enough of a surplus by the end of the decade to prepay expenditure for certain local services.

However, all U.S. cities did not fare equally well during this decade. Comparative analyses in the 1970s and 1980s identified a number of Eastern and Midwestern cities as fiscally "distressed." Though these studies were subjective to some extent, they usually came to similar conclusions about the cities in trouble. In the most recent analysis of this type, Ladd and Yinger (1989) analyzed the fiscal and economic performance of large cities through 1986. They concluded that the average improvement in city fiscal health in the 1980s was modest and that the average city was in worse fiscal shape in 1986 than it had been in 1972, with cities in the Northeast and Midwest again heading the list.

One can conclude from this analysis that cities tightened their belts in the 1980s, and that many of them entered the recession in the early 1990s in reasonably good shape compared with earlier decades (Bahl, Martinez-Vazquez, and Sjoquist, 1992). In order to do this, however, some cities may have shifted their resources to protect fund balances and to service debt (Dorsey, 1990). In the course of this fiscal belt tightening, they may have weakened their long-run potential for development, hence Ladd and Yinger's observation about their continued distress.

Cities in the 1990s

As the decade ended, another recession began, revealing many cities as still having fundamental fiscal problems. While there was much variation in the performance of cities in the first part of this decade, some suffered far more than others and have not shown signs of easy recovery. Pagano found a gap of more than 5 percent between expenditure and revenue growth for a sample of 525 cities in 1991, suggesting a widespread drawing on accumulated balances. Other evidence included the aggregate National Income Accounts surplus for the entire local government sector becoming negative and the National Association of Counties reporting that 4 of every 10 populous counties in the Nation faced budgetary shortfalls in 1991. In many cases "service cutbacks" has become a watchword, and the newer issues of AIDS, homelessness, and drug abuse have not received adequate attention. In a few cases, a city's financial condition has approached bankruptcy.

Dearborn (1992) studied the financial conditions of 30 large cities and found substantial deterioration as a result of the 1991 recession. He noted (p. 31) that:

> 1991 saw a sharp reversal of fiscal fortunes of cities. Imbalances became more pervasive and much larger, thereby diminishing reserves, and revenues stopped growing at rates sufficient to maintain basic services. ... Historically, such patterns have signaled impending financial emergencies.

Dearborn's view is that some cities, such as Detroit and East St. Louis, have run out of financial options and cannot escape their budget crises. Other cities, such as Cleveland, St. Louis, and New Orleans, have very few options for dealing with chronic fiscal problems. In general, the picture he paints is one of cities coping with recession by drawing on accumulated balances, some finding one-time adjustments, while others muddle through with little hope of fundamental improvement. It would be an overstatement to say that all large cities are coming out of the 1991–92 downturn fiscally sound.

A National League of Cities survey (Pagano, 1993) supports Dearborn's conclusions. Its findings may be summarized as follows:

- City fiscal conditions will not improve in 1993, compared with the 1990–92 period. Expenditure growth will exceed revenue growth by a factor of 2.5, and expenditures will grow at less than the rate of inflation; ending balances will drop by nearly 10 percent; and two-thirds of cities reported that they are less able to meet their needs in 1993 than they were in 1992.
- General fund balances appear to be lower in Northeastern cities, central cities, and cities with populations over 300,000.
- More than 70 percent of all cities report that they increased taxes and charges during 1992 and early 1993. Nearly 40 percent of large cities (17 percent of all cities) claimed to have cut services. About 38 percent froze hiring, and 40 percent actually cut employment.

There was also some good news in the League's survey, highlighting the great variation in the financial condition of American cities. Three of every four cities expected positive fund balances at the end of 1993, and two in five identified areas in which productivity improvements have been made. Still, even discounting for the expected bent towards a crisis reply to such a survey, the picture appears to be one of a slow financial recovery for many cities.

Fiscal disparities

The most recent measurement and analysis of metropolitan fiscal disparities was carried out by Bahl, Martinez-Vazquez, and Sjoquist (1992), who analyzed 1987 data for a sample of 35 large metropolitan statistical areas (MSAs).[3] The results show that the average per capita expenditure disparity between city and suburb in 1987 was 1.51, that is, cities spent $1.51 per capita for every $1.00 spent by suburban governments (Table 1). This disparity was due to the much higher level of noneducation expenditures made by central cities, presumably because of the service "overburden" they faced. Suburban governments, by contrast, maintained an advantage in per capita spending for education. This pattern is not markedly different from that of earlier years. If anything central-city budgets have become even more weighted toward noneducation responsibilities, and there is no evidence that education spending disparities have narrowed in the past decade.

On the financing side, the per capita level of taxes remains about 25 percent higher in cities than in suburbs. However, when this level of taxation is adjusted by family income, the results suggest that the overall level of tax effort is 44 percent higher in central cities than in suburbs. The pattern over the past decade has shown a declining per capita tax revenue advantage for the central city relative to the suburbs, but a growing disparity in tax burden in favor of the suburbs. This situation may be interpreted as a consequence of the slower growth in income in the central city and the pressures on the expenditure budget brought by the increasing concentration of needy families in the central city.[4]

Table 1   Average values of fiscal disparities for a common sample of MSAs

Year	Fiscal disparities[a]				
	1957	1970	1977	1981	1987
Per capita expenditures					
Total	1.32	1.39	1.47	1.40	1.51
Education	0.77	0.86	0.95	0.90	0.91
Noneducation	2.07	2.13	2.04	1.87	2.17
Per capita taxes	1.59	1.42	1.32	1.31	1.25
Taxes as a percent of income[b]	1.54	1.53	1.31	1.18	1.44
Per capita Federal and State aid – total	0.99	1.36	1.69	1.64	1.53
Taxes as a percent of State and Federal aid – Disparity central city/outside central city	1.76	1.20	0.89	0.89	0.91

Notes:
a   All variables are measured as the ratio of central city (CC) to outside central city (OCC).
b   An index number computed as the CC/OCC ratio of the following: per capita taxes divided by average family income.

To what extent has the Federal and State aid system been structured to reduce these disparities, or at least to relieve some of the fiscal disadvantages of central cities? In 1977, central cities received $1.69 in State and Federal aid for every $1 received by suburban governments. By 1987, the amount had fallen to $1.53, due to the phasing out of large Federal urban aid programs and to State governments not stepping in to offset the loss.

This description of city and suburban fiscal disparities applies to all regions, although there is some variation in the extent of the disparity. By comparison with the other regions, the Northeastern and Midwestern MSAs spend more than their suburbs for noneducation services and less for education. Their cities receive much more aid relative to their suburbs than do those of the South and West, and have lower per capita taxes relative to their suburbs. The pattern among Southern and Western MSAs seems to be one of less disparity, less Federal and State aid equalization, and higher relative levels of city taxation.

Nathan (1992, chapter 2) reached a similar conclusion about the deteriorating condition of cities relative to their suburbs. His index of hardship – based on unemployment, educational attainment, income level, crowded housing, and poverty – shows that there was continued deterioration in the most distressed cities.

The Role of Policy: 1980s and 1990s

When the financial problems of cities and metropolitan fiscal disparities held the attention of policy makers in the 1970s and early 1980s, there were hopes for reform. In contrast to the present condition of some cities, characterized by Dearborn (1992) as "out of options," there seemed to be an optimism about feasible solutions to the problems. Most of these options centered around ways to spread the wealth: by capturing the suburban tax base to finance urban functions, by receiving a greater share of the State and Federal government budgets to support urban functions, or by reassigning important functions (especially redistributive functions) to the State or Federal government. However, few of the reforms have materialized, leaving economists to speculate as to whether they are still options for U.S. cities.

Federal aid

One possible way to resolve the fiscal problems of cities and redress disparities in fiscal capacity would be to increase the flow of Federal aid to cities and target the most distressed areas. In fact, this happened for a time with CETA, ARFA, Local Public Works, and General Revenue Sharing, using mandated passthroughs. In 1980, Federal aid to cities accounted for 14.4 percent of Federal expenditures, 26 percent of State and local government revenues, and 3 percent of the gross national product (GNP).

But the large, targeted programs were eventually dropped, and the aggregate flow of Federal aid to State and local governments slowed markedly throughout much of the 1980s. By 1991, Federal aid accounted for less than 2.7 percent of GNP, 20 percent of total State and local government revenues, and 11.5 percent of Federal Government expenditures. The decline in the percentage of Federal expenditures most clearly makes the case that State and local governments have become much less of a Federal priority now than in the pre-1980 period. The result of these declines is that the real per capita amount of Federal aid to State and local governments is about the same in 1993 as it was in 1972.

The targeting of Federal assistance has also changed. There has been no clamor for a return to the urban aid programs of the mid- and late-1970s. In fact, direct Federal aid to local governments has slowed more than Federal aid to State governments since the 1980s. The share of total Federal aid going to local governments has declined from a high of 28 percent in 1978 to about 12 percent in 1991. Federal aid to cities was $63 per capita in 1980 but only $30 per capita in 1993 (Pagano, 1993).

Federal assistance to support infrastructure financing has also been reduced. Mann and Bell (1993) point out that nominal Federal funding of infrastructure grants remained virtually unchanged during much of the 1980s, but the purchasing power of these grants declined by 29 percent.

Another aspect of Federal assistance is the increased costs imposed by the Federal Government on State and local governments. Certainly the tax reform of 1986 increased the "price" of State and local government taxes by disallowing the deductibility of sales taxes and reducing the marignal income tax rate, thereby eroding the value of deductibility. To date, most empirical research points to a small effect for these changes (Courant and Rubinfeld, 1987), but there is some debate about the correctness of this conclusion. Moreover, a proliferation of mandates also increased the costs of local government finances.

State assistance

Because State governments rely on the most elastic and productive tax bases – those of income and sales – they can generate funds to relieve the fiscal problems of cities. This can be done in two ways: by direct assumption of responsibility for government functions that weigh heavily in urban budgets and by an increased flow of equalizing State aid. State legislatures may also assist cities by authorizing increased taxing powers, making boundary changes possible, and instituting regional taxing districts.

The last two decades have seen an increased role for State governments in the Federal system. The State government share of total State and local government spending rose from 37 percent in 1970 to 40 percent in 1990, and the State government share of taxes rose from 55 percent to 60 percent over this period. However, even though State government budgets increased in the 1980s, grants to local governments declined as a share of total State government expenditures (Table 2), although as a share of total personal income they remained the same. Gold and Ritchie (1993) showed that if welfare and education grants are excluded, State aid to local governments has grown at a slower rate during each successive year in the 1990s. There is also some evidence of reduced targeting. City–suburb fiscal disparities have not been reduced by a greater allocation of State aid to central cities. Bahl, Martinez-Vazquez, and Sjoquist found that the city–suburb ratio of per capita Federal and State aid declined from 1.64 in 1981 to 1.53 in 1987 (Table 1).[5]

Why have State governments not come to the rescue of local governments? A number of reasons might be cited. First, the era since California's Proposition 13[6] has been a time of slow growth in State government taxes – a factor often attributed to the antigovernment bias of voters. The effective rate of total State and local government taxes in 1991 was 10.9 percent, compared with 10.4 percent in 1970. When coupled with reductions in Federal aid and new mandates, States felt that they did not have enough money to fund all activities, and local governments apparently had a low priority. Instead of stepping in to assist local governments, States borrowed a page from John Shannon's "Fend for Yourself Federalism" (see Shannon, 1991) and passed the reductions along to their constituent local governments.

Second, the recession's impact on State budgets was substantial. The resulting revenue shortfalls – particularly those in medical assistance expenditures – forced States to near-record levels of discretionary rate increases in 1991 and 1992 (MacKey, 1992, p. 4). Gold (1992) points out that Medicaid grew rapidly as a component of State budgets because of (a) health cost inflation, (b) increased participation due to mandates, and (c) increased participation due to the recession and the AIDS virus. Not surprisingly, States sought to cut their expenditures by passing the costs on to their local governments.[7]

Table 2 State government grants to local governments

	Real per capita amount[a]	As a percent of total State government expenditures	As a percent of total personal income
1980	$441	36.7 percent	3.7 percent
1985	466	34.7	3.6
1990	536	34.4	3.7

[a] Deflated using the consumer price index, 1982–84 = 100.
Sources: U.S. Department of Commerce, Bureau of the Census, Government Finances, various years; U.S. Department of Commerce, Bureau of the Census, Survey of Current Business, various years.

Third, with a changing mix of population, the dominance of suburban representation in State legislatures became even stronger. The new mix should lead one to expect greater protection of the fiscal position of suburban residents through such measures as less targeting of State aid, resistance to authorizing legislation for various forms of metropolitan governance, and regional taxing measures. Fourth, there may be an anti-city bias in some legislation, and sometimes a notion that cities have brought many of their problems on themselves. Even the bailouts of troubled local governments are more likely to take the form of State control than that of State subsidies. A recent NCSL survey (1993) found that 13 States have general statutes to meet local fiscal emergencies, and 6 others passed special acts to bail out local governments during the preceding 3 years. The survey concludes, however, that the most common form of help available to local governments is State technical assistance. Many States provide for the setting up of financial control boards, and four States – Illinois, Michigan, Ohio, and Tennessee – require that such boards be established as a condition of receiving other emergency assistance.

The results of State government fiscal restraint were predictable, and local governments responded by increasing taxes. In fact, local taxes have increased faster than State taxes over most of the past decade. Gold (1993) reports that from 1985 to 1991, local taxes increased by 60 percent and State taxes by only 44 percent – a pattern that holds for 39 of the 50 States. Remarkably, there has been a revival of the property tax in recent years after a long period of decline. The property tax accounted for 18.3 percent of total State and local government taxes in 1990 in comparison with 17.4 percent in 1985.

Metropolitan government

The expansion of city boundaries to include the wealthier suburbs has always been seen as one solution to the urban fiscal problem. At one time, such a move would have eliminated intergovernmental fiscal disparities and increased the financial capacity of the central cities, but very little consolidation of metropolitan governance occurred in the 1980s. Aside from Jacksonville, Nashville, and Indianapolis, relatively little has happened in the bigger metropolitan areas. Some of the largest cities, such as St. Louis, New York, and Philadelphia, also hold county status but even in those cases few of the wealthier suburbs have been captured in the central county tax base.

Why so little consolidation? The reasons are clear. The more affluent suburban residents are loathe to take on the severe problems confronting cities and are convinced that they can escape these problems through physical separation. Moreover, black leadership in the cities is unwilling to give up its political gains, as metropolitan government would surely require. In short, there is no constituency for metropolitan government, nor is there a good, salable rationale. Metropolitan government and consolidation have usually been sold as methods of increasing technical efficiency in the delivery of public services, that is, as cost-cutting measures. It seems intuitively correct that fragmentation of government leads to duplication of services and diseconomies of scale, but there is little evidence that consolidation captures economies of scale. It is more likely that the chief gain from area wide governance would be equity, that is, the provision of better services to lower income communities. Moreover, the strong sentiment for home rule always weighs heavily against regional governance.

Regional tax base sharing

Cities could strengthen their positions dramatically by taxing the entire region rather than just their own base, and there are a number of ways that this might be done. Commuters could be taxed explicitly or indirectly through local sales and payroll taxes, or tax bases could be shared between cities and suburbs.

One justification for commuter or regional taxes is the so-called exploitation hypothesis. The argument supporting this hypothesis is that central cities are overburdened by the service demands placed on them by suburban residents and are not fully compensated by suburban commuters or by businesses that depend on suburbanites. But research has not clearly shown that such exploitation does exist, and the competitive position of the central city is fragile enough to dissuade local politicians from pushing too far with such taxes.

The Minneapolis/St. Paul property tax base sharing scheme is an example that has been spotlighted perhaps as much as any local tax scheme, but it has not been imitated to any significant extent. Many cities enacted sales and payroll taxes and commuter taxes that served them reasonably well in the 1980s but as Dearborn points out, these taxes made several of the cities susceptible to the recession, and revenues fell precipitously. Moreover, such taxes could make the city less competitive for the economic development it so badly needs. Detroit is a good case in point. Dearborn (1992, p. 3) reports that:

> The city's wage tax revenues declined in 1990 and 1991; the total revenue received in 1991 was less than the amount received in 1987. In the past, rate increases have helped increase revenues, but the city is reluctant to increase the wage tax rate beyond its current 3 percent for fear of accelerating the decline in the number of filers. In recent years, this decline in filers has, in effect, offset growth in the tax base from wage increases.

THE PROPERTY TAX. During the 1980s, many analysts felt that reliance on the property tax was a major problem facing central cities and a major underlying cause of fiscal disparities. Cities were declining, and the decline was reflected in property values. A substantial part of the cities' economic growth was related to nonprofit activities, and much of the property in central cities was not taxed. There was also a hesitancy to revalue or raise tax rates because of the fragile economic setting in most cities. The result was that city finances became tied to a slow-growing tax base.

Some thought that time would heal this problem, because the property tax was inherently unpopular, sales and income taxes were more elastic an would increasingly dominate the revenue structure, and the future held an increasing fiscal role for State governments. There has, in fact, been a revival of the property tax, and local governments have become increasingly reliant on it in recent years.

The increased dependence on property taxes raises some especially worrisome problems for cities because declining property values will eventually erode the tax base. Peterson and Edwards (1993) showed that the drops can be substantial once assessment lags are eliminated. Their case study of Loudoun County, Virginia, where assessment lags are short, showed that declining commercial-industrial property values led to a 15-percent decline in assessed value between 1990 and 1992, forcing the local government to increase the tax rate significantly and cut expenditures.

GENTRIFICATION. Planners and other optimists in the late 1970s saw a rebirth of cities as centers of residential, commercial, and cultural activity. This rebirth was supposed to bring a larger tax base to cities and an influx of citizens who impose low public service costs relative to the taxes they pay. However, gentrification never occurred on a scale that could have offset the declines elsewhere in the city, and much of the new construction was not taxed.

SCHOOL FINANCE. Many believed that a major part of the solution to the disparities issue rested with the courts and the school finance cases. The basis of the argument was that, since per-student property values varied widely across school districts, property-tax financing of public schools did not provide access to education of equal quality for all students. To make matters worse, there were States in which State school aid per student was greater for suburban than for central-city districts, but the court actions that would have redressed these imbalances flagged during the 1980s.

Clearly, central cities are at a disadvantage because of the present methods of school finance. Bahl, Martinez-Vazquez, and Sjoquist (1992) showed that expenditures in central-city school districts are about 90 percent of those made in suburban school districts and have remained at that level since the early 1980s (see Table 1). Why does such a disparity exist? A long-held hypothesis points to municipal overburden; that is, because cities have so many other functions to deal with, the amount left over for education is too small. The data in Table 1 seem to support this argument. Central cities spent 1.5 times more per capita on noneducation functions than did suburban governments in 1987, and the gap widened over the preceding decade. The results of a linear regression analysis to explain the variation in per capita education expenditure disparities between cities and suburbs show that disparity is smaller if (a) the average family income level in the suburbs is greater, and (b) the per capita level of Federal and State aid coming to the city is greater.

Conclusions

When policy analysts discuss distressed urban areas, they usually mean the central cities in the Nation's largest metropolitan areas. If one takes this to mean the central cities of the 60 largest MSAs, then only about 20 percent of the national population is involved. But the problem is one of national dimensions. The well-being of these cities is linked to the economic viability of the most important part of urban America, and these cities are home to a disproportionately large share of America's urban poor. The well-being of these cities is a national issue.

Neither the financial conditions of the most distressed cities nor the fiscal disparity between cities and suburbs improved during the last decade. If anything the situation worsened, because these urban areas missed out on the economic gains of the 1980s. Tax burdens remained higher in the central cities, and per capita expenditures for education were lower. Those cities on the "distressed lists" in the 1970s remain there in the 1990s, and in some cases they appear to be out of options.

Policy at the Federal and State levels has failed the central cities. The Federal Government has pulled back its assistance to local governments, States have not stepped in to fill the gap, and local governments have resorted more heavily to property taxes to make up for the shortfalls. For political and economic reasons, various forms of metropolitan governance have not caught on, nor has a meaningful program of regional tax-base sharing.

There are no automatic forces that will create a new equilibrium, free of disparities. The economic base of central cities has not been revitalized, as some thought it would be. Manufacturing and service jobs alike find the suburbs appealing, and the vision of bargain prices in housing attracting the middle class back to the city never materialized. Suburban governments have not come to regard their vested interest in central cities in a way that would cause them to vote for regional taxes or consolidation. In the absence of a concrete government policy, the fiscal disparities and the weakened financial condition of the distressed cities will likely continue.

The policy options available to deal with the urban fiscal issue are limited. Given the fiscal condition of the Federal Government and the paucity of new urban initiatives, large amounts of new, targeted Federal aid would not appear to be a likely alternative. Instead, responsibility is apt to be shifted to the States in four areas: initiatives to promote regional taxation, increases in targeted assistance to local governments, facilitation of regional governance solutions, and direct assumption of responsibility for certain social services. All of these areas will require increased revenue mobilization by State governments.

Notes

1 The model is discussed in Bahl, 1970.
2 For a good discussion of the conceptual problems involved in measuring disparities, see Oakland, 1993.
3 The 35 cities were included in the set of 37 cities used in the earlier ACIR (1984) study of fiscal disparities. A common definition of the MSA has been used. Two cities (Paterson, New Jersey, and San Bernardino, California) are omitted because of missing data.
4 Of course, if the central city can export a greater share of its taxes than can the suburban governments, this ratio overstates the relative disadvantage of the central city.
5 State and Federal aid were not separated in this article, so it is not possible to determine how much of the reduction is due to each component.
6 California's Proposition 13 (1978) rolled back property taxes and significantly limited property tax growth.
7 Gold and Ritchie (1993) report that 14 States cut aid to local governments in 1992, while 10 increased aid.

References

ACIR (Advisory Commission on Intergovernmental Relations) (1984). *Fiscal Disparities: Central Cities and Suburbs, 1981*. Washington, D.C.: U.S. GPO.

Bahl, Roy, Jorge Martinez-Vazquez and David L. Sjoquist (1992). "Central City–Suburban Fiscal Disparities," *Public Finance Quarterly*, 20(4), October, 420–32.

Bahl, Roy (1970). "Public Policy and the Urban Fiscal Problem: Piecemeal vs. Aggregate Solutions," *Land Economics*, XLXI(1), February.

Bartik, Timothy J. (1991). *Who Benefits From State and Local Development Policies?* Kalamazoo, MI: W.E. Upjohn Institute for Employment Research.

Bradbury, Katharine L., Helen F. Ladd, Mark Pernault, Andrew Reschovsky, and John
   Yinger (1984). "State Aid to Offset Disparities Across Communities," *National Tax Journal*, 37,
   June, 151–70.
Campbell, Alan K., and Seymour Sacks (1967). *Metropolitan America: Fiscal Patterns and
   Government Systems*. New York: The Free Press.
Courant, Paul, and Edward M. Gramlich (1990). "The Impact of the Tax Reform Act of 1986
   on State and Local Fiscal Behavior," in *Do Taxes Matter*, edited by Joel Slemrod. Cambridge:
   MIT Press.
Courant, Paul, and Daniel S. Rubinfeld (1987). "Tax Reform: Implications for the State-Local
   Public Sector," *Journal of Economic Perspectives*, Summer, 87–100.
Dearborn, Phillip. (1992). "City Finances in the 1990s," prepared for The Urban Institute.
Dorsey, Thomas A. (1990). "Fiscal Stress: The Credit Market View," in the 1989 *Proceedings of
   the National Tax Association-Tax Institute of America*. Columbus, Ohio: NTA-TIA, 85–9.
Downing, R.G. (1991). "Urban County Fiscal Stress: A Survey of Public Officials' Perceptions and
   Government Experiences," *Urban Affairs Quarterly*, 27(2), December, 323–31.
Gold, Steven. (1993). "Local Taxes Outspace State Taxes," State Fiscal Brief, Center for the
   Study of the States.
——— . (1992). "The Federal Role in State Fiscal Stress," *PUBLIUS: The Journal of Federalism*,
   22(3), Summer, 33–49.
Gold, Steven, and Sarah Ritchie (1993). "State Policies Affecting Cities and Counties in 1992,"
   Public Budgeting & Finance, 13(1), Spring, 33–46.
Ladd, Helen, and John Yinger (1989). *America's Ailing Cities: Fiscal Health and the Design of
   Urban Policy*. Baltimore: Johns Hopkins University Press.
Ledebur, Larry, and William Barnes (1992). "Metropolitan Disparities and Economic Growth,"
   paper prepared for the National League of Cities.
MacKey, Scott R. (1992). "State and Local Tax Levels: Fiscal Year 1991," Legislative finance
   paper no. 80. Washington, D.C.: National Conference of State Legislatures, February.
Mann, Joyce Y., and Michael E. Bell (1993). "Federal Infrastructure Grants-in-Aid: An Ad Hoc
   Infrastructure Strategy," *Public Budgeting &* Finance, 13(3), Fall, 9–22.
Nathan, Richard P. (1992). *A New Agenda for Cities*. Columbus: Ohio Municipal League Educa-
   tional and Research Fund.
Oakland, William H. (1993). "Recognizing and Correcting for Fiscal Disparities: A Critical
   Analysis," paper presented at the Joint National Conference of State Legislatures – National
   Tax Association Conference on "The Challenge of Fiscal Equalization of State and Local
   Finance," held in Denver, Colorado, January 7, 1993.
Pagano, Michael (1993). "City Fiscal Conditions in 1993," paper prepared for the National League
   of Cities.
Peterson, George E. (1986). "Urban Policy and the Cyclical Behavior of the Cities," in *Reagan and
   the Cities*, edited by George E. Peterson and Carol Lewis, Washington, D.C.: The Urban
   Institute, 11–36.
Peterson, John, and Kimberly Edwards (1993). "The Impact of Declining Property Values on
   Local Government Finances," Urban Land Institute working paper series 626.
Sacks, Seymour, and John Callahan (1973). "Central City–Suburban Fiscal Disparity," in *City
   Financial Emergencies: The Intergovernmental Dimension*, by the Advisory Commission on Inter-
   governmental Relations. Washington, D.C.: U.S. GPO.
Shannon, John (1991). "Federalism's 'Invisible Regulator' – Interjurisdictional Competition," in
   Competition Among States and Local Governments, by The Urban Institute. Washington, D.C.: The
   Urban Institute, 117–25.

CHAPTER THIRTY-EIGHT

Economic Influences on the Structure of Local Government in U.S. Metropolitan Areas

Ronald C. Fisher and Robert W. Wassmer*

Source: Journal of Urban Economics, 43, 444–71. © 1998 Academic Press.

There is a large degree of variation in the number of general-purpose local governments and school districts, per square mile and per person, among United States' metropolitan areas. Using data from 1982, this paper provides an empirical test of whether economic factors (especially variation in demand for local government services) partly account for these differences. The empirical findings show that after controlling for political, historic, and institutional factors, variations in the characteristics that affect demand for local government services do influence the number of local governments. This result is consistent with the hypothesis first put forth by Tiebout.

1. Introduction

Local governments in the United States and many other nations play a substantial role in providing and financing public services. In terms of participation and the perception of derived benefits, individuals also relate most directly to their local governments.[1] Yet the structure of government used to provide local public services varies widely. Since the seminal work of Tiebout [25], economists have theorized that economic factors play an important role in determining the observed variation in local government structure. Considering the theories that exist about local government structure, there has been very little empirical examination of what determines the structure of localities in an area.

* The authors presented an earlier version of this paper at a session sponsored by the American Real Estate and Urban Economics Association at the A.S.S.A. Meetings. Wassmer acknowledges financial support from Wayne State University's Summer Research and CULMA Grants. Priya Rajagopalan provided able data assistance. We appreciate the many helpful comments from Jan Brueckner, William Fischel, Phil Grossman, Jeffrey Wooldridge, and several anonymous referees.

Differences in the number and size of local governments among major U.S. metropolitan areas are striking. Among the 168 U.S. Standard Metropolitan Statistical Areas (SMSAs) with a 1980 population of at least 200,000, the average municipal population varied between approximately 2,300 and 316,000 in 1982, with a median of about 19,000 and a coefficient of variation of 1.23.[2] Similarly, the median municipal area (in square miles) within these large metropolitan areas was about 60, with a range between 4 and nearly 2,300 square miles, and a coefficient of variation of 2.08.[3] Substantial variation also existed in the average population and size of school districts in these 168 large SMSAs.

Across municipalities in a metropolitan area, and even between U.S. metropolitan areas, a sizable variation in economic characteristics also exists. The 1980 average coefficient of variation of municipal per capita income within a large SMSA is 0.96. This average coefficient of variation ranges from 0.74 to 1.33, with a standard deviation of 0.11. That there is income variation within a metropolitan area is not surprising. What is noteworthy is that there is nearly twice as much municipal per capita income variation within the most heterogeneous metropolitan area as compared to the least.

Has the local government structure observed in a metropolitan area been influenced by the variation in economic characteristics among residents in the area? The expectation, rooted in the theory of Tiebout, is that greater variation in the economic characteristics of residents results in greater variation in the quantity, quality, and mix of services demanded from local governments.

In addition to an understanding of how local government structure arises, this issue is important for at least two other reasons. First, a confirmation of the proposed positive relationship between the variation in the demands for local government services and the number of local governments is essential to Tiebout's [25] notion that residential mobility and choice can lead to an efficient level of government service. Second, the Leviathan theory has proposed that if the number of governments is small, then budget-maximizing bureaucrats can use their monopoly power to expand the size of the public sector beyond what is publicly desirable. Empirical tests of this theory have assumed that the number of governments is exogenous to economic factors that influence the size of the public sector. This research offers a direct challenge to this assumption.[4]

Although there is substantial work on suburbanization as flight from a central city (see Mieszkowski and Mills, [17]), our concern is the overall structure of localities surrounding the central city. Nelson [19] has provided one examination of this issue. He looks at the relationship between variations in the social and economic characteristics of residents in a metropolitan area and the average size of localities within it for the 296 largest SMSAs in the United States in 1982. Nelson finds that increasing variation in age and income increases the number of localities, although his age result is insignificant if he includes a measure of racial variation. In this journal, Martinez-Vazquez et al. [16] have more recently used panel data from the 48 contiguous United States and all U.S. metropolitan areas and find significant nonlinear effects of income, age, and racial variation on the number of school districts in a state. They also find that as age and racial variation increase, the number of school districts in a metropolitan area first increases and then decreases. Martinez-Vazquez et al. find no such relationship between age, racial, and income variation and the number of special districts in a state. They use these findings to support their hypothesis that racial heterogeneity reflects the influence of taste for association, rather than heterogeneous demand for public goods. Martinez-Vazquez et al.

do not apply their estimation technique to municipalities. Nelson reports only linear relationships between variation in characteristics and local government size, whereas Martinez-Vazquez et al. find nonlinear effects.[5]

Our purpose is to expand the evidence concerning the degree that economic factors influence the number of local governments in major U.S. metropolitan areas. We focus on the process of variation in the social and economic characteristics of residents influencing the demand for local government services and hence the structure of local governments that deliver them. To do this properly, we must control for the political, historical, and institutional factors that are at work as well. Consistent findings between our study and previous studies would provide a body of preliminary evidence in support of the theory that has taken a central place in local public finance. A time series analysis, yet to be done, would show whether an increasing variation in demand characteristics leads to an increasing number of governments, and if so, how quickly.[6]

In the next section we present a brief discussion of Tiebout's model, extensions of it, and our proposed empirical test. Data issues related to the empirical test are discussed in Section 3. The results of the test are in Section 4. Section 5 contains a brief summary and some implications of our study.

2. Tiebout's Model, Extensions, and the Proposed Empirical Test

Since the initial work of Tiebout [25], economists have widely adopted the idea that a system of small local governments, competing with each other to attract residents, can result in the efficient provision of local public goods. This view requires that the number of local governments be sufficient to satisfy the diversity of residential preferences present in the area. This suggests the testable hypothesis that there should be more (or smaller) local governments in a given metropolitan area the greater the variation in preferences for local public services. The appropriate empirical test of this hypothesis requires a few additional considerations.

Oates [20] used Tiebout's model to further consider the tradeoffs involved in determining the optimal size for a local government. The cost of increasing the size of local jurisdictions, such that they no longer satisfy all individual preferences for local public services, must be weighed against the benefits of a reduction in the average cost of services due to scale economies and a reduction in jurisdictional spillovers.[7] Given the similar sets of services provided by most general-purpose localities, the nature of scale economies is not likely to vary between metropolitan areas. However, localities may achieve scale economies by contracting with other governments or with private firms for services. If state regulations restrict or encourage the opportunities for such contracting, then the ability to achieve scale economies could vary by region.[8]

The issue of interjurisdictional externalities is more problematic to the development of our hypothesis test. It is not feasible, given the known data, to directly measure the existence or magnitude of spillovers. An alternative is to proxy for the welfare loss from uncorrected spillovers by controlling for the factors that could cause them to vary between metropolitan areas: greater interjurisdictional mobility (due to more commuting or lower transportation costs), physical or geographic differences in the metropolitan areas themselves, less extensive use of state grants to offset spillovers, differences in the level of income variation (reflecting different marginal values of public service), etc.

In addition, in a fully functioning Tiebout world, individuals must know about local fiscal differences, be substantially mobile between localities in the area, and in any locality have reasonable access to work locations. Square miles simply reflects many of the differences among metropolitan regions with regard to these characteristics. But for any given area, the availability of residential locations that provide access to work depends on the transportation network and the cost to use it.

The large body of research on the history and process of suburbanization is also relevant. Jackson [11], an urban historian, argues that suburbanization was primarily a reaction to racial concerns and economic developments. In assessing these forces, he argues [11, p. 290] that "Economic causes have been even more important than skin color in the suburbanization of the U.S." Similarly, Mieszkowski and Mills [17, p. 144] conclude that "MSA size, income levels and distribution, transportation evolution and housing demand are important in understanding MSA structure" and that other important factors include "central-city racial mix and suburban land use controls."[9]

Historical development, political forces, state procedures for creating new governments, geographical constraints, and other institutional factors also influence the number of local governments in a metropolitan area.[10] Despite factors that favor change, a metropolitan area may be unable to alter the set pattern of earlier development. The political and institutional costs of changing boundaries or creating new governments should be particularly important. Indeed, the substantial research on local government adjustment through annexation, incorporation, and consolidation suggests that boundary changes are more common than thought. Trueblood and Honadle [26] report more than 75,000 annexations between 1980 and 1984, which involved nearly 2.6 million people and 8,700 square miles. Abrahamson and Hardt [1] find that nearly one-third of the incorporated places in the United States engage in some form of annexation each year. Rigos and Spindler [23] report 249 newly incorporated cities between 1980 and 1986, or a growth of about 1.5%.[11] Yet the real issue is whether residents affect this institutional setting and thereby determine their local government structure. In this regard, Weiher [30, p. 181] concludes that "studies do little to refute the argument that boundary formation is pretty much a matter of citizen discretion in the United States."

To empirically test the premise that the greater the variation in the demand for local services in a metropolitan area (*ceteris paribus*), the greater the number of jurisdictions, we must control for the considerations just described. Our empirical model is:

$$G_i^k = G[(\text{size characteristics})_i,$$
$$(\text{political and institutional characteristics})_i,$$
$$(\text{economic characteristics})_i,$$
$$(\text{variation in citizen demands for government services})_i,$$
$$(\text{regional characteristics})_i], \tag{1}$$

where G_i^k is the number of governments of type k in metropolitan area i.

3. Data Issues

The foremost data issue is which local governments to include when measuring the number of them in a metropolitan area. One possibility is to make an area-by-area determination of the localities with specific responsibilities.[12] Nevertheless, any decision about which responsibilities to focus on and the interpretation of various local laws is quite arbitrary and could influence the results, as well as ignore fine institutional differences. Our approach is to focus on two broad sets of localities: (1) the sum of municipalities and townships in a metropolitan area and (2) the number of school districts in the area.[13] Observations for these two dependent variables are drawn from 1982. The U.S. Census counts as school districts only those that are "fiscally and administratively independent" of other subnational governments. We have added dependent school systems, or those that are administrative agencies of other governments to the Census measure of school districts.[14]

With regard to counties, we view them as an overlapping form of government that assists in the coordination of local government activity among contained municipalities or school districts.[15] The greater the number of counties in a metropolitan area, holding all else constant, the less may be the concern about spatial externalities, and more local governments can form.[16] The same expected positive relationship between county and local government number could also occur if more counties designate a historical preference for greater government.

We assume that the structure of local government in a metropolitan area does not influence the variation in citizen demand characteristics observed in a metropolitan area. This assumption rests upon the belief that intermetropolitan migration is not primarily based on an individual's search for their ideal structure of local government. Concerning the variation in citizen demands for local government services, an individual maximizes a utility function involving private consumption and public services, subject to a personal budget constraint and the local government's budget constraint. The well-established demand function for public service, for each individual in a metropolitan area, resulting from this procedure is

$$E_{i,j} = E(Y_j, t_j, g_i, Z_j) \qquad (2)$$

where $E_{i,j}$ is the individual's (i's) desired quantity of public service in community i, Y_j is the individual's income, t_j is the individual's local tax price, g_i represents lump-sum grants to the individual's government, and Z_j is a vector of characteristics that influence taste.

Because the actual variation in desired levels of public service in different metropolitan areas is unobservable, we use the variation in the demand parameters to reflect the expected variation in demand. In this study we have chosen to focus on the influence of variation in income, the variation in age, and the variation in race to represent the taste vector Z. This choice is based on variables regularly collected for metropolitan areas by the U.S. Census and most often included in previous studies of demand for local government service. Unfortunately, we do not have data for variation in individual tax prices or grants.

If the individual's demand for local government services takes the following simple linear form:

$$E_j = a + b_1 Y_j + b_2 \text{AGE}_j + b_3 \text{RACE}_j \tag{3}$$

and Y, AGE, and RACE are not fully independent, the variation in desired government service is,

$$\begin{aligned} \text{Var}(E_j) = {}& b_1^2 \text{Var}(Y_j) + b_2^2 \text{Var}(\text{AGE}_j) + b_3^2 \text{Var}(\text{RACE}_j) \\ & + 2b_1 b_2 \text{Cov}(Y_{ji}\text{AGE}_j) + \cdots \end{aligned} \tag{4}$$

Because variance is obviously dependent on magnitudes, the coefficient of variation reflects the relative degree of variation within metropolitan areas. We believe it is the relative variation in demand in each metropolitan area that influences the degree of decentralization. Equation (4) shows that it is important to consider the covariance among demand characteristics.[17] The combined effect of the variance of two demand variables moving together may exert an effect separate from each demand variable itself.

Two measurement issues arise because of the nature of the available data. The census records income and age distribution data for metropolitan areas as the number of individuals in different ranges of the distribution. The standard calculation applied to frequency distributions yields the standard deviations and coefficients of variation for income and age.[18] Regarding variation in race, the Census reports only the numbers of people that fall into designated categories of race. We measure the variation in race in a metropolitan area across the eight categories recorded by the census with a Leick [13] index.[19] Leick derived this index to account for the degree of consensus on a multicategory survey question. His index is configured to range between 0 and 1, with 1 representing the greatest dispersion.[20] Greater Leick dispersion across racial categories indicates a less of a concentration of metropolitan residents in a limited number of categories. If persons in a type of racial category exhibit a unique demand for local government services, then less of a concentration in a few categories (measured as a higher Leick index) indicates greater variation in the demand for government-provided services.

The number of local governments in a region may differ based on the level of demand for government services as well as the variance in demand. To capture this potential influence, we include SMSA median income, median age, and the share of the housing stock that is owner-occupied as independent variables. As suggested by Mieszkowski/ Mills and Jackson, including median income effectively tests whether government decentralization (the number of jurisdictions) itself is a normal good. Following the prediction from the traditional urban model, a high median income in a metropolitan area could also indicate a greater tendency for decentralization. The influences of age and owner-occupied housing are less clear, although the housing stock measure may reflect both mobility within the metropolitan area and attachment to or permanence in that region.

Other variables capture economic conditions directly related to Tiebout's theory. A decentralized local government structure contributes to efficiency only if residents are mobile and are not restricted in employment choice by job location. To measure mobility, we include for each SMSA the share of central city employment held by central city residents and the miles of state highway per square mile in each state. Compared to the dependent variables that are taken from 1982, these are both measured as lagged 1950 values.[21] If the share of central city jobs held by residents is low, then jobs tie many suburban residents to the central city and presumably limit their choice of suburban residential locations.

Size characteristics of the metropolitan area include scale economies, land availability and costs, and transaction costs. Given an optimal population and area to minimize costs in the production of local government services, the number of governments should rise as the SMSA's population and area increase (assuming that the optimal size is smaller than the SMSA's size). Because of increased administration and compliance costs or more costly coordination, diseconomies can also arise from more localities for a given population or area. The metropolitan area's square miles and population, and the square of these variables (to allow for any diseconomies), capture these influences. To further capture land availability, we include the SMSA's land area as a fraction of state land area. The greater this is, the less available land there is in the state and the more entities wishing to be in the state will have to pay for the right. This will likely slow the suburbanization of a metropolitan area and may have an effect on the number of local governments in it.

As Jackson [11] stresses, the period and historic setting in which a metropolitan area and its central city developed also influence the area's local governance structure. We expect political inertia to be less of a problem for newer metro areas. To denote a newer metropolitan area, we include a dummy variable equal to 1 if the central city incorporated after 1950.

The relative importance of the central city in different metropolitan areas can be a major factor influencing the size distribution of local governments. Rather than excluding central cities from our analysis (the technique adopted by Fischel [7]), we include all localities in each metropolitan area and correct for central city dominance by including its area as an independent variable.[22] A central city bordered by a body of water impassable by auto or by a national boundary has relatively less land surrounding it in which suburbs can form and therefore (*ceteris paribus*) may have fewer local governments. We include a dichotomous variable equal to 1 if the central city faces this geographic constraint. A number of urban specialists have suggested that suburbanization or flight from central cities was driven by a desire to avoid redistribution as much as by a desire for racial or government service homogeneity. We measure the potential demand for direct redistribution or redistributive services by the 1950 ratio of central city median income to the median income of residents in the entire SMSA.

Several variables represent the political and institutional circumstances in the metropolitan area or state. The vertical structure of government in each state is captured by four variables: the shares of total state and local expenditure separately represented by state intergovernmental transfers, county expenditures, and special district expenditures; and the number of counties in each metropolitan area. One might argue that the vertical structure of state and local government is itself endogenous. By region within a state, intergovernmental aid is often given differentially, the number and size of special districts can vary, and counties take on responsibilities beyond those mandated by state law (perhaps through intergovernmental contracting). We correct for the potential simultaneity of the relative roles of other government levels by using lagged values taken from 1957.

If economic factors are to influence local government structure, then institutions must allow the number of governments to change. Annexation is the primary means by which existing cities grow. Incorporation is the method that yields new cities. Rigos and Spindler [23] have used regression analysis to explain differences in local incorporation activity across states. Controlling for other factors, they found that easy annexation laws are a major determinant of incorporation (presumably defensive), while the ease of laws regarding incorporation itself had no significant influence on incorporation activity. Considering this finding and other observations, Rigos and Spindler [23, p. 80] conclude that "Easy annexation laws trigger incorporations even when incorporation laws are difficult."

To capture the substantial differences among states in the rules and procedures governing incorporation and annexation, we divide the states into four groups reflecting the difficulty of annexation (see ACIR [28]). The most liberal rules allow a city to annex territory only if the city council approves, or only if the residents of the area approve the annexation. The two more restrictive categories allow annexation only if both areas approve or prohibit annexation altogether. Even given the findings of Rigos and Spindler [23], liberal annexation laws in a state could still result in a smaller number of local governments than otherwise through larger governments annexing smaller ones and making it easier for smaller local governments to combine. Therefore the influence of these laws is unpredictable. A Hausman specification error test for endogeneity was consistent with the state annexation measures being exogenous to the factors influencing the number of localities. Whatever the annexation rules, there is some evidence (see Dye [6]) that city manager forms of local government are more likely to engage in annexation. We therefore include a dummy variable to represent a nonmayoral form of government in the metropolitan area's central city.

Seven states require school districts to be coterminous with counties. This restriction affects the number of school districts (given predetermined and fixed counties) and may influence other local governments as well in an attempt to minimize overlapping and conflicting boundaries. We include a dummy variable for these states, and that variable is exogenous according to the earlier described Hausman specification error test.

Finally, there is no clear theoretical expectation regarding the most appropriate functional form for the regressions, although a nonlinear relationship seems reasonable if marginal costs rise and marginal benefits decline, as is often assumed. Martinez-Vazquez et al. [16] also find nonlinear effects. We use a simple ordinary least-squares specification, with the number of governments related to the independent variables and their quadratic forms, where supported by the data.[23] A heteroskedasticity-consistent covariance matrix corrected the heteroskedasticity present. We capture regional differences, unaccounted for by the other explanatory variables, by including dummy variables for eight of the nine Census Regions.

4. Results

Table 1 contains the regression results for the number of municipalities and townships in the 167 largest U.S. metropolitan areas in 1982. Table 2 contains the results for school districts in the 165 largest metropolitan areas.[24] The first regression reported in each table

Table 1 Regression results with 1982 municipalities and townships as dependent variable

Right-side variable	Regression 1 coefficient (standard error)	Regression 2 coefficient (standard error)
Constant	44.376	−710.05***
	(39.350)	(247.80)
1980 SMSA population	0.481E−4***	0.514E−4***
	(0.095E−4)	(0.100E−4)
1980 SMSA population squared	−0.291E−11**	−0.287E−11**
	(0.124E−11)	(0.120E−11)
1980 SMSA area	0.012***	0.010***
	(0.003)	(0.002)
1980 SMSA area squared	−0.447E−6***	−0.401E−6***
	(0.094E−6)	(0.756E−7)
1980 SMSA area relative to state area	−0.024***	−0.021***
	(0.005)	(0.005)
1980 central city area	−0.086***	−0.078***
	(0.030)	(0.026)
National or water boundary dummy	−8.799*	−8.030
	(5.152)	(5.528)
1957 state's spec. dist. exp. relative to all state and local expenditure	−1.409	−2.056
	(1.983)	(1.696)
1957 state's county exp. relative to all state and local expenditure	−1.582***	−1.194*
	(0.599)	(0.613)
1957 state's intergov. exp. relative to all state and local expenditure	−0.486	−0.405
	(0.784)	(0.763)
1980 number of counties	6.959**	6.907***
	(2.900)	(2.590)
Annexation only if both approve dummy	−36.58***	−28.037**
	(11.20)	(12.340)
Annexation allowed if one approves dummy	−36.12***	−30.341***
	(12.42)	(11.850)
Annexation allowed if city council approves dummy	−28.05**	−26.496*
	(16.65)	(15.600)
1950 central city nonmayoral government dummy	5.570	6.377
	(4.381)	(4.435)
Central city incorporated after 1950 dummy	13.284*	20.395***
	(7.829)	(7.782)
1982 required county and school district same dummy	−9.345	−8.424
	(7.548)	(7.665)
1950 central city residential share of employment	−0.100	−0.195**
	(0.093)	(0.094)
1950 central city median income relative to SMSA's	−0.104**	−0.130***
	(0.046)	(0.046)

Table 1   *(Cont.)*

Right-side variable	Regression 1 coefficient (standard error)	Regression 2 coefficient (standard error)
1950 state highway miles per state square mile	2.475 (8.564)	−2.000 (7.983)
1980 SMSA median income	−2.069E−3 (1.316E−3)	−0.140E−2 (0.210E−2)
1980 SMSA median age	−0.258 −0.793	5.900*** (1.963)
1980 owner-occupied housing share	0.527* (0.327)	−0.070 (0.288)
1980 coefficient of income variation		5.886** (2.119)
1980 coefficient of income variation squared		−0.033** (0.014)
1980 coefficient of age variation		4.567*** (1.276)
1980 racial variation index		−89.728*** (29.720)
1980 age and income covariance proxy		9.866** (4.754)
1980 age and race covariance proxy		−3.040 (4.144)
1980 income and race covariance proxy		4.141 (3.724)
R-squared	0.804	0.833
Adjusted *R*-squared	0.759	0.783

Note: Heteroskedasticity-corrected standard errors, regional dummies included but not reported, 167 observations.
F-Statistic for the joint statistical significance of variation in demand variables = 3.26 (1% critical value = 2.79).
*** Two-tailed statistical significance at greater than 99% confidence, **95–98% confidence, *90–94% confidence.

includes variables that reflect institutional and other physical differences, while the second regression adds measures of variation in demand for government services.

4.1 Variation in consumer preferences

The results reported in the latter two regressions in Tables 1 and 2 provide persuasive evidence that the number of local governments in a metropolitan area partly reflects the variation in consumer preferences for local government services. For both general local governments and school districts, the set of demand-variance variables are statistically significant as a group.[25]

Of special interest are the results concerning metropolitan-wide variation in per capita income. As Tiebout's notion suggests, increasing income variation initially yields more

Table 2 Regression results with 1982 school districts as dependent variable

Right-side variable	Regression 1 coefficient (standard error)	Regression 2 coefficient (standard error)
Constant	−8.025	−623.78***
	(26.570)	(180.10)
1980 SMSA population	0.248E−4***	0.210E−4***
	(0.057E−4)	(0.055E−4)
1980 SMSA population squared	−0.367E−12	−0.147E−12
	(0.870E−12)	(0.784E−12)
1980 SMSA area	0.464E−2**	0.360E−2**
	(0.194E−2)	(0.182E−2)
1980 SMSA area squared	−0.141E−6**	−0.111E−6**
	(0.066E−6)	(0.061E−6)
1980 SMSA area relative to state area	−0.016***	−0.014***
	(0.003)	(0.003)
1980 central city area	−0.034	−0.037
	(0.026)	(0.024)
National or water boundary dummy	−2.755	−0.015
	(2.937)	(3.199)
1957 state's spec. dist. exp. relative to all state and local expenditure	1.518	0.800
	(1.739)	(1.423)
1957 state's county exp. relative to all state and local expenditure	−0.550**	−0.493*
	(0.267)	(0.286)
1957 state's intergov. exp. relative to all state and local expenditure	−0.633	−0.460
	(0.517)	(0.493)
1980 number of counties	1.829	2.628*
	(1.587)	(1.475)
Annexation only if both approve dummy	4.075	9.961**
	(5.973)	(5.431)
Annexation allowed if one approves dummy	−2.469	0.944
	(8.328)	(6.244)
Annexation allowed if city council approves dummy	−0.094	3.778
	(8.766)	(7.214)
1950 central city nonmayoral government dummy	7.856**	8.125***
	(3.132)	(3.169)
Central city incorporated after 1950 dummy	−3.332	1.049
	(4.168)	(4.189)
1982 required county and school district same dummy	−10.638***	−9.334**
	(3.929)	(4.059)
1950 central city residential share of employment	−0.045	−0.119*
	(0.060)	(0.066)
1950 central city median income relative to SMSA's	−0.093**	−0.103***
	(0.033)	(0.031)

Table 2 *(Cont.)*

Right-side variable	Regression 1 coefficient (standard error)	Regression 2 coefficient (standard error)
1950 state highway miles per state square mile	2.034 (3.972)	−0.665 (3.829)
1980 SMSA median income	4.01E−4 (9.76E−4)	0.141E−2 (0.124E−2)
1980 SMSA median age	0.011 (0.567)	3.673*** (1.350)
1980 owner-occupied housing share	0.542** (0.261)	0.360 (0.280)
1980 coefficient of income variation		6.198*** (1.980)
1980 coefficient of income variation squared		−0.032*** (0.010)
1980 coefficient of age variation		2.501*** (0.923)
1980 racial variation index		4.310 (17.580)
1980 age and income covariance proxy		8.040** (3.460)
1980 age and race covariance proxy		1.432 (2.220)
1980 income and race covariance proxy		5.800* (2.875)
R-squared	0.751	0.786
Adjusted *R*-squared	0.693	0.722

Note: Heteroskedasticity-corrected standard errors, regional dummies included but not reported, 165 observations.

F-Statistic for the joint statistical significance of variation in demand variables = 3.04 (1% critical value = 2.79).

*** Two-tailed statistical significance at greater than 99% confidence, **95–98% confidence, *90–94% confidence.

(smaller) local governments and school districts. But at some point the negative nonlinear effect can dominate and cause the number of governments and school districts to decline. Setting all independent variables to their average level and allowing income variation to change between the range of observable values (between 74 and 133), the number of municipalities and townships peaks near 46.6, with an income covariance of 89.2. The sample mean is 52.8 for municipalities and townships in our sample and 96.3 for income covariance. If all of the independent variables are set to their average level and income variation is allowed to vary among the range of observable values, the number of school districts peaks at 29.0 and an income covariance of 96.8. The sample mean for school districts in our sample is 27.0 and 96.3 for income covariance. So for the average municipality or township in the sample, the nonlinear negative effect does dominate.

While for the average school district in the sample, the nonlinear effect does not dominate. The level of median income in the SMSA exerts no significant effect on the number of municipalities or school districts.

Interpreting the results of income variation alone is difficult because we do not have data on variation in tax prices. As noted by Bergstrom and Goodman [4], the relationship between income and desired government spending is uncertain if higher income results in higher tax prices. Suppose that individuals with both low and high incomes desire higher levels of government service than those with middle incomes. This pattern could arise as a result of higher-income individuals demanding higher levels of service because local government goods are normal (the income effect dominating any price effect), while lower-income individuals also demand higher levels of service because of very low tax prices (sometimes these are even perceived as zero).[26] If all of these individuals live in one community, than clearly the lower- and higher-income groups can form a coalition to achieve higher levels of service than desired by the median-income voter. If the number of governments in an area is variable and these individuals can select their communities (or even create new ones), then more income variation does not necessarily lead to more variation in desired government spending and require more local governments. If income variation increases because of an increase in the relative number of both high- and low-income residents, then fewer governments are required, as both desire the same level of spending.[27] For this reason, the nonlinear result for general local government is not surprising.

Variation in the age distribution of individuals in a metropolitan area affects the number of general local governments in the expected positive manner.[28] This confirms Nelson's [19] earlier finding, although Nelson's age result is insignificant when he includes a measure of racial composition. Martinez-Vazquez et al. [16] also report significant positive effects of both age and racial variation on the number of school districts at the metropolitan and state levels. They also found that income variation influences the number of schools at the state but not the metropolitan level. However, neither of these other studies accounts for the median level of age and income in a metropolitan area.

The average age in a metropolitan area exerts an independent influence on the demand for government services. This influence likely comes from a concentration of residents at either end of the age distribution. Children and retired citizens have clear and distinct demands for local government services. In that spirit, some might suggest that government services and structure determine the age structure of the population, but a Hausman specification error test for exogeneity supported the assumption that the age structure of the population is exogenous to the forces influencing the number of governments.

The reason why greater dispersion (measured by a higher Leick index) across racial categories in a metropolitan area negatively affects the number of general purpose local governments is not clear. There is little previous understanding of what race suggests for the demand for government services. Martinez-Vazquez et al. [16] argue that a greater dispersion of metropolitan residents across racial categories will result in more local governments because of discrimination and a "taste for association" by race. But as many studies of voting on public budgets have found differences among racial groups, race might also act as a taste proxy and separately influence the demand for government services. In our minds, the reason for the significant effect of race dispersion remains unresolved. It may be based in a desire for different races to live in different communities, or alternatively, different races (or cultures) may exhibit different desires for local government services.

The age and income covariance proxy exerts a positive influence on the number of municipalities and townships, and the number of school districts in a metropolitan region. In addition, the income and race covariance proxy exerts a positive influence on the number of school districts.[29] If within a metropolitan area the measures of variance for these taste proxies are the same number of positive standard deviations from the mean observed across all metropolitan areas, then there is a tendency for a larger number of local governments. The combined influence of similar variation in two demand proxies exerts a distinct positive effect. Once the variation in demand for government services is accounted for, differences in housing type (owner-occupied versus rental) show no influence on the number of localities.

One way to assess the marginal influence of variation in demand for government services on the number of local municipal and township governments is to run a regression-based simulation. We use the means of all the variables included in regression 1, plus the covariance proxies, with the coefficients in regression 2 to simulate the effects of changes in variation in demand.[30] The values for income variation, income variation squared, age variation, and racial variation are calculated as a negative or positive increment of standard deviations from all of their means. These increments run from two standard deviations below the mean to two standard deviations above the mean. The result is the fitted number of municipalities and townships for a hypothetical average metropolitan area that has different degrees of variation in consumer demand for local governments. With little variation in income, age, and race (all variation measures at two standard deviation measures below their means), the hypothetical average SMSA has only about five local jurisdictions. With much variation in income, age, and race (all variation measures at two standard deviations above their means), the hypothetical average SMSA has about 101 jurisdictions. The range of 5 to 101 general purpose local governments that is generated through this exercise encompasses all but 34 (20.4%) of the actual observations of the number of local governments in the 167 SMSAs.

An analogous simulation results in the predicted number of school districts in the hypothetical average SMSA. With little variation in income, age, and race (all variation measures at two standard deviations below their means), the hypothetical average SMSA has only about one school district. With substantial variation in income, age, and race (all variation measures at two standard deviations above their means), the hypothetical average SMSA has about 54 school districts. There are more school districts than predicted by this simulation in only 11 of the 165 large metropolitan areas in the sample.

These simulations show that changes in the variation in consumers' demands for local government service alone can generate nearly the degree of variation actually observed in the number of general local governments and school districts in large U.S. metropolitan areas in 1982. Local government structure is neither fixed nor determined solely by institutional factors, but appears to respond to residents' economic demands for services provided by those local governments.

4.2 Institutional and physical influences

As expected, the number of governments in a metropolitan area relates positively to both population and area, although the influence of both increases at a declining rate (except for the influence of population on school districts). An increase of 100,000 in population for the average metropolitan area in our sample leads to about seven more general governments and two school districts. One hundred square miles added to the average metropolitan area implies one additional local general government and about another third of a school district. Although the marginal effect of increasing population and area diminishes, diseconomies do not dominate, except for large sizes that are well out of the range of values observed for the average metropolitan area.[31]

The larger the metropolitan area relative to the state, the fewer the number of municipalities and school districts. This finding is consistent with the idea that a relatively smaller supply of undeveloped land outside the SMSA, and hence higher land prices, restricts expansion and the creation of new localities. Not surprisingly, a larger central city results in fewer municipalities.

Legal and physical barriers to the creation of local governments also offer reasons for differences in the number of jurisdictions. If annexation occurs either by vote of both jurisdictions, or by vote of one jurisdiction, or with only legislative approval of the annexing city, then there are 26–30 fewer general-purpose governments than if annexation of any form is prohibited. However, because of the magnitude of the coefficient's standard errors, there is no statistically significant difference in the number of these governments based on different annexation procedures alone. Apparently the details of how annexation may proceed are less important than the option for annexation itself. For school districts, if a state allows annexation by requiring approval from both effected entities (rather than no annexation), then there are approximately 10 more school districts.

If the regression specification accounts for demand variance, the influence of the geographical constraint on the number of general local governments just loses its statistical significance. This offers only limited support of the hypothesis that a body of water or national boundary restricts the supply of land (area) to a metropolitan region and thus reduces the number of local governments. Although a region theoretically could increase the supply of land by growing in a different direction, constraints of distance may limit this alternative.[32]

Metropolitan areas whose central city incorporated after 1950 have approximately 20 more (smaller) general local governments than areas whose central cities incorporated before 1950. To the contrary, the age of the central city (SMSA) has no effect on the number of school districts in the metropolitan area. It appears that on average, an earlier socioeconomic environment called for fewer municipal and township governments than more recent conditions warrant. In older metropolitan areas it is difficult to create these new communities, because an existing local government structure is in place. Since the national trend over the past 30 years has been a reduction in the number of school districts through consolidation, this barrier is inconsequential to the desired structure of school governance.

Vertical centralization in the federal fiscal system is a complement to horizontal centralization within metropolitan areas. A larger fiscal role for counties exerts a negative effect on the number of municipalities and school districts. Apparently the forces that lead to greater fiscal responsibility for counties also contribute to having fewer and larger municipalities. On the other hand, an increase in the number of county governments in a metropolitan area (holding their fiscal responsibility constant) results in greater municipalities and school districts. As counties contain municipalities, townships, and school districts, and city–county consolidations are quite rare, it is not surprising that the existing county structure influences the number of subcounty governments. These findings support the earlier notion that the number of overlapping counties mitigates concerns about local spatial externalities and offers evidence of a historical preference for greater local governance.

Economic characteristics of the SMSA, and especially those of the central city relative to the metropolitan area, are also relevant to local decentralization. The lower the historical ratio of the central city's median income to the rest of the SMSA's median income, the greater the number of general-purpose governments and school districts observed. It appears that small Tiebout-like suburban localities allow residents to avoid redistribution to a poorer central city. The share of central-city employment held by central-city residents in 1950 exerts a negative effect on the number of both types of governments. This is contrary to our expectations and suggests that this employment share, even lagged to 1950, is not a good measure of worker mobility. An explanation may be that work location follows residential choice. Highway miles per square mile of area is not statistically significant in any of our regressions. Rather than transportation cost not being important, this suggests that our measure is not the best proxy for transportation cost.

A statewide requirement that counties and school districts be the same yielded about nine fewer school districts in the average metropolitan area. A nonmayoral form of government in the central city in 1950 is positively correlated with a greater number of school districts in 1982.

4.3 Regional differences

The regressions also included dichotomous variables for eight of the nine census regions (Pacific being the excluded region). Table 3 contains the regional coefficients and the average number of local governments of each type for each region. For general governments, there tends to be relatively more (smaller) local governments in metropolitan areas in the West North Central, East North Central, and Mid-Atlantic states. Conversely, there are fewer (bigger) local governments than one would expect, based on their specific characteristics, in the Mountain states. It is not surprising that the most decentralized and fragmented local government structure, after adjusting for differences in characteristics, is in the North Central and Mid-Atlantic regions. These regions have a relatively high number of localities compared to the simple average. The Mountain finding is likely due to the geologic constraints in this region of the country.

For school districts, the regional coefficients are significant (and negative) in both regressions for the Mountain, South Atlantic, and New England states. Relative to the Pacific region, states in these three regions have substantially fewer school districts than expected, based on their measured characteristics.

Table 3 Regional dummy coefficients, standard errors, and regional averages for appropriate number of municipalities and townships or school districts

Regional dummy variable	1982 municipalities and townships regression 1	1982 municipalities and townships regression 2	1982 school districts regression 3	1982 school districts regression 4
Mountain	−42.655*** (16.130) [19.25]	−33.202** (15.570) [19.25]	−30.724*** (9.190) [15.75]	−23.204*** (9.635) [15.75]
West North Central	38.835* (20.080) [93.40]	42.247** (19.020) [93.40]	−4.368 (8.147) [37.10]	−1.847 (8.523) [37.10]
West South Central	−3.9777 (11.950) [38.88]	−0.247 (13.920) [38.88]	−9.290 (9.894) [25.13]	−4.861 (11.190) [25.13]
East North Central	57.612*** (17.760) [87.80]	55.811*** (17.840) [87.80]	3.404 (13.100) [38.50]	9.307 (12.680) [38.50]
East South Central	8.691 (13.600) [29.59]	12.327 (15.140) [29.59]	−18.684* (10.790) [6.94]	−11.585 (11.710) [6.94]
South Atlantic	−1.779 (11.790) [21.91]	5.352 (12.640) [21.91]	−19.439* (8.516) [5.36]	−14.371** (8.467) [5.36]
Mid-Atlantic	40.568*** (13.150) [93.04]	38.907*** (13.960) [93.04]	1.222 (8.105) [43.56]	4.176 (7.675) [43.56]
New England	2.369 (17.280) [83.33]	−0.271 (18.040) [83.33]	−28.988* (15.460) [18.33]	−25.946** (17.210) [18.33]
F-Statistic for joint significance	5.05*** (1% critical value = 2.47)	4.25*** (1% critical value = 2.47)	2.57*** (1% critical value = 2.47)	2.33** (1% critical value = 2.47)

Note: Pacific is the excluded category.
*** Two-tailed statistical significance at more than 99% confidence.
** 95–98% confidence, *90–94% confidence.

5. Summary and Implications

Particularly since the pioneering work of Tiebout [25] and Oates [20] there has been substantial interest in whether individual mobility and residential choice among a set of localities could lead to efficient levels of local government service. A substantial body of theoretical research implies that if there is some form of effective fiscal zoning or capitalization, and if the number of communities is variable, then the Tiebout process can generate efficiency in the local government provision of services. Moreover, as argued by Mieszkowski and Zodrow [18] and Oates and Schwab [21], if efficiency is achieved and the number of communities is variable, then the property tax used to finance local services becomes a benefit tax and creates no distortion in the housing market. For such a result the possibility of changing the number or size of local communities is crucial. Indeed, much of the difference in the positions of various scholars regarding the Tiebout process and the possibility of efficiency depends on whether they believe that the number of communities in a metropolitan area is rigid or variable.[33]

Although some studies have reported on changes in the number of localities, this paper shows directly that the large observed differences in the number of local governments in U.S. metropolitan areas is due in part to residential variation in the demand for government service. Our results are consistent with the idea that there will be more (smaller) local governments when the differences among citizens with regard to desired government services expand. These results are also compatible with those of Gramlich and Rubinfeld [9], who find a high degree of grouping by public spending demand in urban communities. If the variance in public sector demands among individuals within urban communities is to be low, then the number of such communities must be greater in metropolitan areas where there is greater variation in public service demands. This is precisely what our results indicate.

Data Appendix

The calculation of a covariance measure between data reported as the number in quantitative ranges or qualitative categories creates a problem. The data only show the percentage of individuals in each metropolitan area in various categories of demand characteristics. Because we have data about the overall distribution of each characteristic, rather than actual individual data, covariances cannot be calculated. Thus we proxy for covariance in a way that captures in part the degree to which demand variables move together in the region.

For all possible two-pair combinations of demand variables, we calculate the number of standard deviations that the mean for a metropolitan area's demand variable is away from the mean for that demand variable for all SMSAs in the sample. For example, if two demand variables in a metropolitan area are both the same numbers of standard deviations above or below the mean for all metropolitan areas in the sample, then the two demand variables are considered to move together.

The procedure for deriving this correlation proxy involves first calculating the average and standard deviation of the coefficients of variation. Next (shown only for age) we derive the following for each variable, for each of the 167 SMSAs denoted by i:

$$R_i = \frac{AGECV_i - AGECV_{average}}{AGECV_{standard\ deviation}},$$

where the value of R_i is then rounded to the nearest whole number.

Table 4 Data description

Variable name	Expected effect	167 city sample mean (for population greater than 1,000,000)	Source
Dependent			
1982 municipalities and townships	—	52.8 (105.3)	1982 Census of Governments
1982 school districts	—	27.0 (61.4)	1982 Census of Governments
Size characteristics			
1980 SMSA population	Positive	893,670 (2,457,700)	1980 U.S. Decennial Census
1980 SMSA population squared	Negative	$0.231E + 13$ $(0.939E + 13)$	1980 U.S. Decennial Census
1980 SMSA area	Positive	2,374.4 (3,790.1)	1980 U.S. Decennial Census
1980 SMSA area squared	Negative	125,040 (327,210)	1980 U.S. Decennial Census
1980 SMSA area relative to state area	Uncertain	5.1 (6.0)	1980 U.S. Decennial Census
1980 central city area	Negative	84.8 (153.9)	1980 U.S. Decennial Census
National or water boundary dummy	Negative	0.31 (0.50)	Atlas
Political and institutional characteristics			
1957 state's spec. dist. exp. relative to all S & L expend.	Negative	2.95 (3.45)	1957 Census of Governments
1957 state's county exp. relative to all S & L expend.	Negative	10.82 (11.19)	1957 Census of Governments
1957 state's intergov. exp. relative to all S & L expend.	Uncertain	13.42 (13.26)	1957 Census of Governments
1980 number of counties	Positive	2.82 (4.45)	1982 Census of Governments
No annexation allowed dummy (excluded)	—	0.12 (0.09)	State/Local Roles in Fed. Sys. A.C.I.R., 1982
Annexation only if both approve dummy	Uncertain	0.26 (0.18)	State/Local Roles in Fed. Sys. A.C.I.R., 1982
Annexation allowed if one approves dummy	Uncertain	0.43 (0.55)	State/Local Roles in Fed. Sys. A.C.I.R., 1982
Annexation allowed if city council approves dummy	Uncertain	0.19 (0.18)	State/Local Roles in Fed. Sys. A.C.I.R., 1982
1950 central city nonmayoral government dummy	Negative	0.55 (0.37)	1953 Municipal Yearbook
Central city incorporated after 1950 dummy	Uncertain	0.07 (0.03)	Webster's Geographical Dict.
1982 required county and school district same dummy	Negative	0.14 (0.13)	1982 Census of Governments
Economic characteristics			
1950 central city residential share of employment	Positive	51.2 (49.2)	1953 Municipal Yearbook

Table 4 *(Cont.)*

Variable name	Expected effect	167 city sample mean (for population greater than 1,000,000)	Source
1950 central city median income relative to SMSAs	Positive	72.5 (80.7)	1953 Municipal Yearbook
1950 state highway miles per state square mile	Positive	1.01 (0.99)	1953 Statistical Abstract of U.S.
1980 SMSA median income	Uncertain	17,376 (18,718)	1980 U.S. Decennial Census
1980 SMSA median age	Uncertain	29.9 (30.6)	1980 U.S. Decennial Census
1980 owner-occupied housing share	Uncertain	60.4 (56.9)	1980 U.S. Decennial Census
Variation in demand for government services			
1980 coefficient of income variation	Positive	96.3 (97.0)	1980 U.S. Decennial Census
1980 coefficient of income variation squared	Negative	9,9391.7 (9,515.3)	1980 U.S. Decennial Census
1980 coefficient of age variation	Positive	73.0 (70.8)	1980 U.S. Decennial Census
1980 Leick racial variation index	Uncertain	0.099 (0.127)	1980 U.S. Decennial Census
1980 age and income covariance proxy	Uncertain	0.209 (0.386)	1980 U.S. Decennial Census
1980 age and race covariance proxy	Uncertain	0.158 (0.250)	1980 U.S. Decennial Census
1980 income and race covariance proxy	Uncertain	0.248 (0.184)	1980 U.S. Decennial Census
Regional dummies			
Pacific (excluded)	–	0.138 (0.237)	1980 U.S. Census Definitions
Mountain	Uncertain	0.047 (0.053)	1980 U.S. Census Definitions
West north central	Uncertain	0.059 (0.105)	1980 U.S. Census Definitions
West south central	Uncertain	0.096 (0.079)	1980 U.S. Census Definitions
East north central	Uncertain	0.180 (0.184)	1980 U.S. Census Definitions
East south central	Uncertain	0.102 (0.026)	1980 U.S. Census Definitions
South Atlantic	Uncertain	0.198 (0.132)	1980 U.S. Census Definitions
Mid-Atlantic	Uncertain	0.162 (0.158)	1980 U.S. Census Definitions
New England	Uncertain	0.018 (0.026)	1980 U.S. Census Definitions

To derive the covariance proxy for two demand variables, such as age and income, compare the values calculated from the above equation. If values rounded to the nearest whole number are both the same, the correlation measure equals 1. If one value is negative and the other is its absolute value, then the variable equals -1. Other possible values are 0.66 (3 and 2), 0.50 (2 and 1), 0.33 (3 and 1), and 0 if one value is 0 and the other is any other possibility. We calculate these covariance proxy measures for all possible combinations of the demand variables. This proxy of covariance is not continuous and only takes on the absolute values of 0, 0.33, 0.50, 0.66, and 1 that fall between -1 and 1.[34]

Notes

1 In the 1991 version of the continuing ACIR [27] survey on public attitudes, 31% of the respondents (more than for any other level of government) identified local government as giving them the most for their money.

2 Local government values are from 1982, because this was the most recent year that corresponded to available decennial census data when we began this research.

3 This variation exists within states as well as between them. Among the seven largest California SMSAs, average municipal and township government population varied in 1982 from 44,000 to 116,000, while average area ranged from 31 to 780 square miles. Similarly, the sizes of local governments are quite different in the Dallas, Houston, and San Antonio metropolitan areas.

4 Auerbach [2, p. 105] has expressed the same concern when he commented on research by Zax [32]. "For simultaneity bias to be avoided, it is necessary that the variations in government structure be independent of the population characteristics. Generally, however, one might expect that counties inhabited by people with a strong taste for public goods might find it sensible to establish more governments per capita to supply these goods."

5 Kenny and Schmidt [12] have also produced a working paper that explains the decline in the number of U.S. school districts in part in terms of the decline in income heterogeneity.

6 A problem in carrying out the time-series analysis is that the 1980 census was the first to report city data on age and income variation in a widely available computer readable form. We have developed a panel for 1980 and 1990 and are conducting some analysis; but the length of this available period may be too short to observe a change from one equilibrium government structure to another.

7 See Oates [20, pp. 38–44], and Fisher [8, pp. 129–133].

8 Nelson [19] reports no relationship between the number of localities and state laws allowing intergovernmental contracting. This finding is perhaps due to low population levels at which all scale economies are exhausted or because Nelson's measure of contracting opportunity is not precise.

9 The issues of race and public service choice often operate together. Jackson [11, p. 285] notes that: "High quality municipal services, and especially well-funded public schools that offered racial homogeneity and harmony, attracted still more high-status residents, which in turn made suburbs even wealthier and more attractive."

10 Some economists take a similar institutional position. For an example see Wagner [29].

11 Rigos and Spindler [23] suggest that annexation and consolidation are substitutes (perhaps explaining why most consolidations fail) and that permissive annexation rules stimulate greater incorporation – what they denote as "defensive incorporation." Among other results, annexations are more common when there are not substantial racial or wealth differences between the central city and suburbs, and new incorporation is more likely if the state government takes a relatively more dominant fiscal role.

12 This is the approach taken by Fischel [7], who groups counties and townships with municipalities if the first two have zoning authority. A referee has appropriately suggested that an ideal approach would be to tally the number of territories in a metropolitan area in which residents receive the same services from the same array of local government entities (municipalities, school districts, special districts, and counties). Although an excellent idea, this information is nowhere gathered, and the task of doing it for 167 metropolitan areas would be daunting. We have chosen instead to measure separately the number of municipalities and townships, and school districts, and use explanatory variables to control for concerns regarding our less than precise choice of dependent variables. To limit the scope of this paper, we do not consider special districts.

13 Although the U.S. Census Bureau distinguishes municipalities from townships (with municipalities requiring a minimum population density), in actuality all municipalities and townships serve a similar function in the U.S. federal system.

14 It would not be appropriate to combine dependent and independent schools into one measure if we employed the suggested territorial approach to government structure. We do it here because either type of school district offers a distinct choice of education provision for residents. Dependent school districts are the rule in Alaska, Hawaii, Maryland, North Carolina, Virginia, and the District of Columbia, and exist occasionally in 11 other states. Municipalities and townships in Massachusetts usually have independent school systems unless they have consolidated with localities. Because the first volume of the 1982 Census of Governments offers no details on consolidation in Massachusetts, we dropped the two metropolitan areas in Massachusetts from the school district sample.

15 For this reason we do not count New England townships as counties. We include a New England dummy to account for any differences in local government due to an absence of overlapping county government structure.

16 A possible variable to consider is a dummy if the area had a form of metropolitan-wide government. To avoid the likely problem of endogeneity, we chose not to.

17 Because of the characteristics of the Census data used, a standard measure of covariance cannot be calculated. We use a form of correlation coefficient to proxy for covariance. (The Data Appendix offers a discussion of the method used to calculate this proxy.)

18 See [15, pp. 53–58] for a description of this standard technique.

19 The eight categories used by the Census are White, Black, American Indian, Eskimo, Aleutian, Asian, Pacific Islander, and Other.

20 Martinez et al. also use the Leick Index to measure categorical variation in race across an area, although they choose to condense the eight Census categories into three: White, Black, and All Other. As explained in Rhoades [22], we do not use the Herfindahl–Hirschman Index because it places greater weight on categories with large percentages.

21 To measure an explanatory variable for an SMSA that overlaps more than one state, we chose to weight the calculation based on the percentage of the population in each state in 1980.

22 A Hausman specification error test is consistent with central-city area being exogenous in our regressions. A full description of this test is in Maddala [14, pp. 435–439]. Briefly, the test involves regressing each of the right-side variables expected to be endogenous against all exogenous variables to derive fitted values. The fitted values for all suspected endogenous variables are then placed in the original regression and the hypothesis that the regression coefficients on these fitted values are jointly equal to zero is tested with the F statistic. By not rejecting this hypothesis, one can safely assume that the tested variables are exogenous.

23 We explored other possible formulations, including linear and linear in the logs, but these were not consistent with the data or expectations.

24 The school district sample is smaller because there was no information on consolidation for the two Massachusetts metropolitan areas. We also delete Honolulu from the municipal/township and school district samples because lagged state data for 1950 are not available.

25 The appropriate F-test at a 99 percent confidence level offers the reason to reject the null hypothesis that all of the coefficients on all demand variables equal zero.

26 Brown and Saks [5], Beck [3], and others have reported such a U-shaped relationship between desired spending on local schools and income. Their approach was to suggest that estimates of demand for government services should include the variance of income as well as its level as independent variables. We have gone a step further and suggest that the variance of income should affect the number of governments, not just the choice of service level in each.

27 To put it differently, our estimation allows for differences in demand curves for government service, but not differences in quantity demanded because tax prices are not included separately in the model.

28 We also tested for the nonlinear influence of age and racial variation on local government structure, but unlike for income, the nonlinear terms were never statistically significant.

29 Recall that unlike Martinez-Vazquez et al. [16], who found a significant positive but declining relationship between Leick racial variation and number of school districts, we find an insignificant positive relationship. But they did not control for the movement of income and race together as we have. It appears that both greater racial and income variation is necessary for the creation of more school districts in a large U.S. metropolitan area.

30 Given the way that covariance is measured between age and income, covariance does not necessarily have to change when the variance in age and income changes. Hence in this simulation we keep the covariance measures constant at their average values.

31 The negative effect does not dominate for general governments for an SMSA population of less than about 9 million and an area of less than almost 12,500 square miles. For school districts the appropriate value is an area of 1.6 million square miles.

32 Louis Rose [24] has reported similar effects on the price of land in urban areas.

33 For instance, compare Henderson [10] to Yinger [31].

34 As suggested by a referee, an alternative is to use a set of dummy variables to represent eight of the nine possible values $(-1, -0.66, -0.50, -0.33, 0, 0.33, 0.50, 0.66,$ and $1)$ that our covariance proxy can take on. This results in a total of 24 dummy variables being added to the regression. We tried this and found that perfect collinearity produced a failure to calculate any of the regression coefficients. We then dropped all but one of the dummy variables that took on the same values. This resulted in little change in the magnitude or significance of the noncovariance coefficients, but all of the coefficients on dummy variable covariance measures were statistically insignificant (likely because of multicollinearity). Considering these results, we decided to use the covariance measure described here.

References

1 **Abrahamson, M. and Hardt, M.** (1990) "Municipal Annexations within Major Metropolitan Areas, United States: 1980–1986," *Sociology and Social Research*, 75, 49–51.

2 **Auerbach, A. J.** (1988) Comment, in "Fiscal Federalism: Quantitative Studies" (H. Rosen, ed.), 105–106, Chicago: University of Chicago Press.

3 **Beck, J. H.** (1984) Nonmonotonic Demand for Municipal Services, *National Tax Journal*, 37, 55–68.

4 **Bergstrom, T. C. and Goodman, R. P.** (1973) "Private Demand for Public Goods," *American Economic Review*, 63, 280–96.

5 **Brown, B. W. and Saks, D. H.** (1983) "Spending for Local Public Education: Income Distribution and the Aggregation of Private Demands," *Public Finance Quarterly*, 11, 21–45.

6 Dye, T. (1964) "Urban Political Integration: Conditions Associated with Annexation in American cities," *Midwest Journal of Political Science*, 8, 430–46.

7 Fischel, W. A. (1981) "Is Local Government Structure in Large Urbanized Areas Monopolistic or Competitive?" *National Tax Journal*, 34, 95–104.

8 Fisher, R. C. (1996) *State and Local Public Finance*, 2nd edn. Irwin, Glenview, IL.

9 Gramlich, E. M. and Rubinfeld, D. L. (1982) "Micro Estimates of Public Spending Demand Functions and Tests of the Tiebout and Median-voter Hypotheses," *Journal of Political Economy*, 90, 536–60.

10 Henderson, J. V. (1985) "The Tiebout model: Bring Back the Entrepreneurs," *Journal of Political Economy*, 93, 248–64.

11 Jackson, K. T. (1985) *Crabgrass Frontier*. New York: Oxford University Press.

12 Kenny, L. and Schmidt, A. (1991) *The decline in the number of school districts in the U.S.: 1950–1980*, working paper, University of Florida.

13 Leick, R. (1966) "A measure of ordinal consensus," *Pacific Sociological Review*, 9, 85–90.

14 Maddala, G. S. (1988) *Introduction to Econometrics*. New York: Macmillan Publishing.

15 Mansfield, E. (1991) *Statistics for Business and Economics*. New York: Norton and Company.

16 Martinez-Vazquez, J. Rider, M. and Walker, M. B. (1997) "Race and the Structure of Local Government," *Journal of Urban Economics*, 41, 281–300.

17 Mieszkowski, P. and Mills, E. S. (1993) "The Causes of Metropolitan Suburbanization," *Journal of Economic Perspectives*, 7, 135–47.

18 Mieszkowski, P. and Zodrow, G. (1989) "Taxation and the Tiebout Model," *Journal of Economic Literature*, 1098–146.

19 Nelson, M. A. (1990) "Decentralization of the Subnational Public Sector: An Empirical Analysis of the Determinants of Local Government Structure in Metropolitan Areas of the U.S.," *Southern Economic Journal*, 57, 443–57.

20 Oates, W. E. (1972) *Fiscal Federalism*. New York: Harcourt Brace Jovanovich.

21 Oates, W. E. and Schwab, R. M. (1988) "Economic Competition among Jurisdictions: Efficiency Enhancing or Distortion Inducing?" *Journal of Public Economics*, 35, 333–54.

22 Rhoades, S. A. (1993) "The Herfindahl–Hirschman Index," *Federal Reserve Bulletin*, 79, 188–9.

23 Rigos, P. H. and Spindler, C. J. (1991) "Municipal Incorporation and State Statutes: A State-level Analysis," *State and Local Government Review*, 76–81.

24 Rose, L. A. (1989) "Urban Land Supply: Natural and Contrived Restrictions," *Journal of Urban Economics*, 25, 325–45.

25 Tiebout, C. M. (1956) "The Pure Theory of Local Expenditures," *Journal of Political Economy*, 416–24.

26 Trueblood, M. A. and Honadle, B. W. (1994) *An Overview of Factors Affecting the Size of Local Government*, staff paper P94–7, Department of Agricultural and Applied Economics, University of Minnesota.

27 U.S. Advisory Commission on Intergovernmental Relations (1991) *Changing Public Attitudes on Governments and Taxes*, Report S-20, Washington, DC.

28 U.S. Advisory Commission on Intergovernmental Relations (1982) *State and Local Roles in the Federal System*, Report A-88, Washington, DC.

29 Wagner, R. E. (1976) "Institutional Constraints and Local Community Formation," *American Economic Review*, 66, 110–15.

30 Weiher, G. R. (1991) *The Fractured Metropolis*. Albany, NY: State University of New York Press.

31 Yinger, J. (1982) "Capitalization and the Theory of Local Public Finance," *Journal of Political Economy*, 90, 917–43.

32 Zax, J. S. (1988) "The Effects of Jurisdiction Types and Numbers on Local Public Finance," in *Fiscal Federalism: Quantitative Studies* (H. Rosen, ed.), 79–103, Chicago: University of Chicago Press.

Further Reading Samples

Abstract from *Are Municipalities Tieboutian Clubs?*

ERIC J. HEIKKILA

Source: Regional Science and Urban Economics, 26, 1996, 203–26. © 1996 Elsevier Science. Reprinted with permission from Elsevier Science.

This paper seeks empirical confirmation of the hypothesis that municipalities are Tieboutian clubs. Using data from the 1990 Census for Los Angeles County, the work proceeds in three stages. First, factor analysis identifies the basis vectors to describe census tracts. Secondly, an analysis of variance for each factor shows that municipal boundaries reinforce club distinctions along four dimensions: urban scale, ethnicity, household type, and economic class. Finally, using cluster analysis we conclude that the structure of clubs here is highly fragmented. We conclude that municipalities are indeed Tieboutian clubs, although there may be further spatial clustering at a higher level of aggregation.

Abstract from *Fiscal Impacts of Local Population Growth: A Conceptual and Empirical Analysis*

HELEN F. LADD

Source: Regional Science and Urban Economics, 24(6), 661–86. © 1994 Elsevier Science. Reprinted with permission from Elsevier Science.

This paper examine the legitimacy of concerns of local residents about the adverse fiscal impacts of population growth. The conceptual discussion shows that economic theory provides no clear prediction of the impact of population growth on per capital spending. Based on a national data set of large counties, simple descriprive analysis indicates that greater population growth is associated with higher per capita current spending and interest outlays. More detailed analysis both of 1978–85 changes and of 1985 levels of current spending indicates that higher growth-related per capita spending primarily reflects the combined effects of greater density and increased local spending shares. In sum, established residents in fast-growing areas may experience declines in service quality as well as rising local tax burdens.

Discussion Questions

1 If in the suburbs of a metropolitan area there are many jurisdictions to choose to live in, and only one central city, is it any surprise that the characteristics of people who live in the suburbs are more homogeneous than those who live in the central city are? Is homogeneity of citizens in a community bad or good from an economic and political efficiency standpoint? What about from an equity standpoint?

2 How does Bahl define a fiscal disparity between two jurisdictions in a metropolitan area? Could this be measured with real-world data? What problems would have to be overcome? How were the results recorded in Bahl's Table 1 produced?

3 Even though Bahl makes a strong argument for why state government should intervene to equalize fiscal disparities in a metropolitan area there has been little activity on this front. What are the reasons given for why this may be the case? Can these reasons be overcome?

4 In Fisher and Wassmer's empirical analysis of the number of municipalities and school districts in a metropolitan area they include both income variation and income variation squared as explanatory variables. What is the theoretical reason for this? Describe and interpret the influence of a one-unit increase in income variation on municipalities and school districts. How is racial variation measured? How would you interpret the finding that a one-unit increase in racial variation exerts a significant negative influence on municipalities?

Appendix: Academic Journals in Applied and Policy Orientated Urban Economics

Note that all information contained below was current as of April 1999. Currency beyond this date is not guaranteed. The description of each journal is taken directly from the web page.

Annals of Regional Science

DESCRIPTION: This journal is a quarterly in the interdisciplinary field of regional and urban studies. Its purpose is to promote high quality scholarship on the important theoretical and empirical issues in regional science. The journal publishers papers which make a new or substantial contribution to the body of knowledge in which the spatial dimension plays a fundamental role, such as regional economics, resource management, location theory, urban and regional planning, transportation and communication, human geography, population distribution and environmental quality.

WEB ADDRESS: *http://link.springer-ny.com/link/service/journals/00168/index.htm*

CONTENTS SEARCHABLE ON WEB: yes
ABSTRACT AVAILABLE FROM WEB: yes
RECENT TABLES OF CONTENTS ON WEB: no

Cityscape: A Journal of Policy Development and Research

DESCRIPTION: *Cityscape: A Journal of Policy Development and Research* strives to share HUD-funded and other research on housing and urban policy issues with scholars, government officials, and others involved in setting policy and determining the direction of future research. *Cityscape* focuses on innovative ideas, policies, and programs that show promise in revitalizing cities and regions, renewing their infrastructure, and creating economic opportunities. A typical issue consists of articles that examine various aspects of a theme of particular interest to our audience. The *Notes* section highlights HUD research-in-progress on current policy and program issues.

WEB ADDRESS: *http://www.huduser.org/periodicals/cityscape.html*

CONTENTS SEARCHABLE ON WEB: no
ABSTRACT AVAILABLE FROM WEB: yes
RECENT TABLES OF CONTENTS ON WEB: yes

Economic Development Quarterly

DESCRIPTION: Economic development – jobs, income and community prosperity – is a continuing challenge to modern society. To meet this challenge, economic developers must use imagination and common sense, coupled with the tools of public and private finance, politics, planning, micro- and macroeconomics, engineering, and real estate. In short, the art of economic development must be supported by the science of research. And only one journal – *Economic Development Quarterly* – effectively bridges the gap between academics and practitioners while linking the various economic development communities

WEB ADDRESS: *http://www.sagepub.co.uk/journals/usdetails/j0014.html*

CONTENTS SEARCHABLE ON WEB: no
ABSTRACT AVAILABLE FROM WEB: no
RECENT TABLES OF CONTENTS ON WEB: no

Environmental and Planning A

DESCRIPTION: *Environment and Planning A* is an interdisciplinary journal of urban and regional research. It is the only journal in the field that, because of its size and frequency, can provide the breadth of coverage that allows it to maintain its core interests while simultaneously developing new fields of research as they emerge. The journal is concerned with the fate of cities and regions. The urgency of the problems that have to be faced is clear: rapid economic skills; economic, social, and cultural exclusion; strains on transport; and environmental damage are just some of the problems that now plague cities and regions all around the world. Confronting these problems involves the mobilization of many disciplines – geography, economics, environmental science, political science, demography, engineering, and regional science, for example – and many different strategies of work – quantitative and qualitative, economic and cultural, theoretical and applied.

WEB ADDRESS: *http://www.pion.co.uk/ep/index.html*

CONTENTS SEARCHABLE ON WEB: yes
ABSTRACT AVAILABLE FROM WEB: yes
RECENT TABLES OF CONTENTS ON WEB: yes

Growth and Change

DESCRIPTION: For over twenty-six years, *Growth and Change* has provided a broadly based forum for scholarly research on regional and urban policymaking and its empirical foundations. It is interdisciplinary in scope and seeks both theoretical and empirical investigations dealing with facets of regional and urban economic development in both domestic and international contexts. The bulk of the journal is devoted to original contributions that extend knowledge of theory and policy and connect to existing literature.

WEB ADDRESS: *http://gatton.gws.uky.edu/cber/grocha.htm*

CONTENTS SEARCHABLE ON WEB: no
ABSTRACT AVAILABLE FROM WEB: no
RECENT TABLES OF CONTENTS ON WEB: yes

Housing Policy Debate

DESCRIPTION: The Fannie Mae Foundation conducts and sponsors policy analysis and empirical and theoretical research that makes significant contributions to the state of knowledge on housing policy, housing finance, and community development issues related to the Foundation's focus areas. This research is intended to stimulate thoughtful and insightful discussion on a broad range of housing and community development topics, including barriers to decent and affordable housing production, government housing policies, financial models, housing markets, housing demand and need, and other topics related to the provision of housing and the creation of healthy communities. The Foundation publishes two peer-reviewed journals, *Housing Policy Debate* and *Journal of Housing Research*, and other special publications.

WEB ADDRESS: *http://www.fanniemaefoundation.org/research/index.htm*

CONTENTS SEARCHABLE ON WEB: no
ABSTRACT AVAILABLE FROM WEB: yes
RECENT TABLES OF CONTENTS ON WEB: yes

Journal of Housing Economics

DESCRIPTION: The *Journal of Housing Economics* provides a focal point for the publication of economic research related to housing and encourages papers that bring to bear careful analytical technique on important housing-related questions. The journal covers the broad spectrum of topics and approaches that constitute housing economics, including analysis of important public policy issues.

WEB ADDRESS: *http://www.europe.apnet.com/www/journal/he.htm*
CONTENTS SEARCHABLE ON WEB: yes
ABSTRACT AVAILABLE FROM WEB: yes
RECENT TABLES OF CONTENTS ON WEB: yes

Journal of Regional Science

DESCRIPTION: This prestigious journal publishes original articles at the cutting edge of regional science. Combining theoretical, methodological, and empirical research with a consistent editorial focus, the *Journal of Regional Science* is one of the most highly cited journals in the field, bringing to regional and urban analysis the most useful techniques from other disciplines.

WEB ADDRESS: *http://www.blackwellpublishers.co.uk/asp/journal.asp?ref=0022-4146*

CONTENTS SEARCHABLE ON WEB: no
ABSTRACT AVAILABLE FROM WEB: no
RECENT TABLES OF CONTENTS ON WEB: yes

Journal of Urban Economics

DESCRIPTION: The *Journal of Urban Economics* is the leading journal for articles that illustrate empirical, theoretical, positive, and normative approaches to urban economics. The journal also features brief notes that contain new information, provide commentary on published work, and make new theoretical suggestions about theory.

WEB ADDRESS: *http://www.academicpress.com/jue*

CONTENTS SEARCHABLE ON WEB: yes
ABSTRACT AVAILABLE FROM WEB: yes
RECENT TABLES OF CONTENTS ON WEB: yes

Land Economics

DESCRIPTION: *Land Economics* is celebrating its 75th year of publication in 1999 and is the oldest American journal dedicated to the study of land use, natural resources, public utilities, housing, and urban land issues. Established in 1925 by the renowned economist and founder of the American Economic Association, Richard T. Ely at the University of Wisconsin, *Land Economics* has consistently published innovative, conceptual, and empirical research of direct relevance to economists. Each issue brings the latest results in international applied research on such topics as transportation, energy, urban and rural land use, housing, environmental quality, public utilities, and natural resources.

WEB ADDRESS: *http:// www.press.uchicago.edu/ cgi-bin/ hfs.cgi/ 66/ wisconsin/ le.ctl*

CONTENTS SEARCHABLE ON WEB: no
ABSTRACT AVAILABLE FROM WEB: no
RECENT TABLES OF CONTENTS ON WEB: no

Regional Science and Urban Economics

DESCRIPTION: *Regional Science and Urban Economics* exists to facilitate and encourage high quality scholarship on important theoretical and empirical issues in urban and regional research. Given a rapidly changing field, the Journal's emphasis is on microeconomic analyses of spatial phenomena. The Journal solicits original research contributions in spatial economics, economic geography, and related disciplines. The editors encourage the submission of theoretical and empirical contributions related to market organization in space, housing and labor markets, transportation, and local public economies.

WEB ADDRESS: *http://www.elsevier.com/ inca/ homepage/ sae/ econbase/ regec/*

CONTENTS SEARCHABLE ON WEB: yes
ABSTRACT AVAILABLE FROM WEB: yes
RECENT TABLES OF CONTENTS ON WEB: yes

Regional Studies

DESCRIPTION: *Regional Studies* has developed an international reputation for the publication of original research and reviews on urban and regional development. The journal is of special interest to economists, geographers, sociologists, planners and policy-makers for its cross-disciplinary approach to topics such as industrial, retail and office location, labor markets, housing, migration, recreation, transport, communications and the evaluation of public policy. *Regional Studies* aims to be truly international in appeal.

WEB ADDRESS: *http://www.carfax.co.uk/ res-ad.htm*

CONTENTS SEARCHABLE ON WEB: no
ABSTRACT AVAILABLE FROM WEB: no
RECENT TABLES OF CONTENTS ON WEB: yes

Urban Studies

DESCRIPTION: *Urban Studies* was established in 1964 to provide an international forum for the discussion of issues arising in the field of urban and regional planning. Regular contributions are drawn from the fields of economics, planning, political science, demography, statistics, geography, sociology and public administration. The Journal also publishes the occasional 'state of the art' article, consisting of an analytical review of the major strands of contemporary thinking in a given topic area, supported by an extended bibliography of the topic. *Urban Studies* thus deals with every kind of urban and regional problem that can be tackled by the social sciences or other related modes of systematic analysis. This includes problems ranging from optimal city size, local and regional economies and transport patterns to urban housing, employment, race, politics and crime. Although most articles deal with problems located in the advanced industrial societies of Europe and the Americas, increasing numbers of articles dealing with similar issues in Asia, the Third World and Eastern Europe are appearing in every issue.

WEB ADDRESS: *http://www.carfax.co.uk/urs-ad.htm*

CONTENTS SEARCHABLE ON WEB: no
ABSTRACT AVAILABLE FROM WEB: no
RECENT TABLES OF CONTENTS ON WEB: yes

Index